The **Rough G**

D0331873

Romania

written and researched by

Tim Burford and Norm Longley

ROUGH GUIDES

NEW YORK · LONDON · DELHI

www.roughguides.com

Contents

The great outdoors
colour section
following p.408

**Romania's religious
architecture** colour
section following p.248

◄◄ Gura Apei Lake, Retezat mountains, Transylvania ◄ Local transport, Maramureş

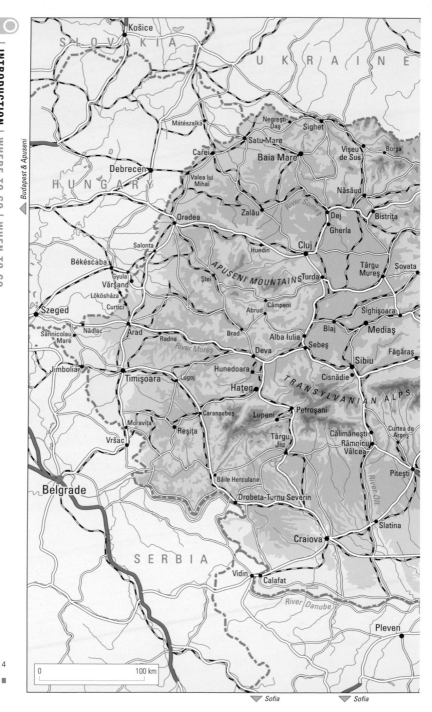

SLOVAKIA

Košice

UKRAINE

Mátészalka

Negreşti-Oaş Sighet

Satu-Mare

Carei

Baia Mare

Vişeu de Sus Borşa

Debrecen

Valea lui Mihai

HUNGARY

Năsăud

River Someş

Oradea

Zalău

Dej Bistriţa

Gherla

Salonta

Huedin

Cluj

Békéscsaba

APUSENI MOUNTAINS Turda

Târgu Mureş Sovata

Gyula

Vărşand

Ştei

Lökösháza

Curtici

Abrud Câmpeni

Sighişoara

Szeged

Sânnicolau Mare Nădlac

Arad

Radna

Brad

Alba Iulia

Blaj Mediaş

River Mureş

Deva

Sebeş

Sibiu Făgăraş

Jimbolia

Hunedoara

Cisnădie

Timişoara Lugoj

Haţeg

TRANSYLVANIAN ALPS

Moraviţa

Caransebeş

Lupeni Petroşani

Vršac

Reşiţa

Târgu Jiu

Călimăneşti Curtea de Argeş

Rămnicu Vâlcea

Piteşti

River Olt

Băile Herculane

Belgrade

Drobeta-Turnu Severin

Slatina

Craiova

SERBIA

Vidin Calafat

River Danube

Pleven

0 100 km

Sofia Sofia

4

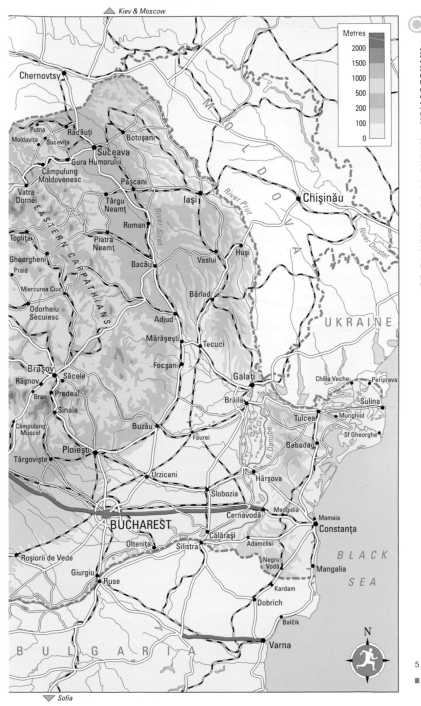

Kiev & Moscow

Chernovtsy

Putna
Moldovița   Rădăuți   Botoșani
         Sucevița   Suceava
              Gura Humorului
   Câmpulung   Pașcani
   Moldovenesc
Vatra
Dornei   Târgu   Iași
               Neamț
            Roman
Topliţa   Piatra
           Neamț   Vaslui   Huși
Gheorgheni   Bacău
   Praid
                          Bârlad
Miercurea Ciuc
   Odorheiu   Adjud
   Secuiesc
                     Mărășești   Tecuci
                       Focșani
Brașov   Galați
Râșnov   Săcele   Chilia Veche   Periprava
   Bran   Predeal   Brăila   Sulina
         Sinaia   Tulcea   Murighiol
Câmpulung   Buzău   Sf Gheorghe
Muscel   Făurei   Babadag
   Ploiești
Târgoviște   Urziceni   Hârșova
                            Slobozia
                              Cernavodă   Medgidia
      BUCHAREST   Mamaia
              Oltenița   Călărași   Constanța
Roșiorii de Vede   Silistra   Adamclisi
   Giurgiu   Negru
              Ruse   Vodă   Mangalia
                              Kardam
                         Dobrich
                              Balčik
B U L G A R I A   Varna

MOLDOVA

River Prut

Chișinău

River Dnister

UKRAINE

River Siret

EASTERN CARPATHIANS

R. Danube

BLACK
SEA

Metres
2000
1500
1000
500
200
100
0

N

Sofia

Introduction to
Romania

Travel in Romania is as rewarding as it is challenging. The country's fantastic mountain scenery and great diversity of wildlife, its cultures and people, and a way of life that at times seems little changed since the Middle Ages, leave few who visit unaffected. Rather than expecting an easy ride, try to accept whatever happens as an adventure – encounters with Gypsies, wild bears and tricky officials are likely to be far more interesting than anything purveyed by the tourist board.

As fascinating as the major towns and cities are – such as the capital, Bucharest, Braşov, Cluj, Timişoara and, most enchantingly, Sighişoara – Romania's charm essentially lies in the remoter, less visited regions. Almost any exploration of the **villages** of rural Romania will be rewarding, with sights as diverse as the log houses in Oltenia, Delta villages built of reeds, and the magnificent wooden churches, with their sky-scraping Gothic steeples, of Maramureş, not to mention the country's abundance of more traditional churches, which reflect a history of competing communities and faiths. Romanians trace their **ancestry** back to the Romans, and have a noticeable Latin character – warm, spontaneous, anarchic, and appreciative of style and life's pleasures. In addition to ethnic Romanians, one and a half million Magyars pursue a traditional lifestyle long since vanished in Hungary, while dwindling numbers of Transylvanian Germans (Saxons) reside around the fortified towns and churches their ancestors built in the Middle Ages to guard the mountain passes. Along the coast, in the Delta and in the Banat, there's a rich mixture of Russians, Ukrainians, Serbs, Slovaks, Bulgars, Gypsies, Turks and Tatars.

In many ways, Romania is only just emerging from the shadow of the regime of the dictator **Nicolae Ceauşescu** who, during more than two decades of rule, drove the country to the brink of bankruptcy. Today,

Fact file

• Occupying an **area** of some 237,000 square kilometres, and with a **population** of around 23 million, Romania is one of central-eastern Europe's largest nations. Its capital, Bucharest, lies in the far south of the country on the plains of Wallachia, located between the Danube and the mountainous region of Transylvania to the north. The high-est peak is Moldoveanu (2544m), in the Carpathian mountains.

• The constitution sets in place a **parliamentary system of government**, elected every four years, with the prime minister at its head – the president is head of state.

• **Tourism** is one of the fastest-growing sectors of the Romanian econo-my, with mountain, coast-al and health spa resorts absorbing the bulk of the country's tourist traffic. Romania's most impor-tant **exports** are textiles and footwear, metal products, and machinery and equipment, and its main trading partners are Italy and Germany.

• Romania's most famous **historical figure** is Vlad Țepeș (*c.*1431–76), also known as Vlad the Impaler and, more familiarly, as Dracula.

although Romania remains one of Europe's poorer cousins, its admission into NATO in 2004 and then, more importantly, the **European Union** in 2007, has finally cemented its place in the wider interna-tional community.

Where to go

The first point of arrival for many visitors to Romania is the capital, **Bucharest**. While far from alluring – its wide nineteenth-century Parisian-style boulevards are choked with traffic, once-grand fin-de-siècle buildings are crumbling and the suburbs are dominated by grim apartment blocks – it remains the centre of the country's commercial and cultural life.

▼ Bârsana monastery, Maramureş

From the capital, most visitors make a beeline for the province of **Transylvania** to the north, setting for the country's most thrilling scenery and home to its finest cities: the gateway to Transylvania is **Braşov**, whose medieval old town is a good introduction to the Saxon architecture of the region, which reaches its peak in the fortified town of **Sibiu** and the jagged skyline

of **Sighişoara**, Romania's most atmospherically sited town and the birthplace of Vlad the Impaler (Dracula). Further north and west, the great Magyar cities of **Târgu Mureş**, **Cluj** and **Oradea** have retained a wealth of medieval churches and streets, as well as impressive Baroque and Secession edifices. To the southwest of the country, near the border with Serbia, is **Timişoara**, source of the 1989 Revolution and a fine place to spend a day or two.

The best of Romania, though, is its countryside, and in particular the wonderful mountain scenery. The wild **Carpathians**, forming the frontier between Transylvania and, to the east and south, Moldavia and Wallachia, shelter bears, stags, chamois and eagles; while the Bucegi, Făgăraş and Retezat ranges and the Padiş plateau offer some of the most undisturbed and spectacular hiking opportunities in Europe. In contrast to the crowded **Black Sea beaches** along Romania's east coast, the waterlogged **Danube Delta** is a place set apart from the rest of the country, where life has hardly

Spas

Romania boasts one third of all Europe's mineral springs, and around 160 **spa resorts** (*băile*), many of which were made fashionable by the Habsburgs during the nineteenth century. **Spa holidays** are tremendously popular, the theory being that you stay in a resort for about eighteen days, following a prescribed course of treatment, and ideally return regularly over the next few years. However, if you can get cheap accommodation, a spa can also make a good base for a one-off holiday. In any case, it's worth bearing in mind that even the smallest spas have campsites and restaurants.

The basic treatment naturally involves drinking the **waters**, which come in an amazing

▲ Thermal pool at Băile Felix

variety: alkaline, chlorinated, carbogaseous, and sodium-, iodine-, magnesium-, sulphate- or iron-bearing. In addition, you can bathe in hot springs or sapropelic muds, breathe in foul fumes at mofettes, or indulge in a new generation of complementary **therapies** such as ultrasound and aerosol treatment, ultraviolet light baths, acupuncture and electrotherapy.

The spas all have their own areas of specialization: Sovata is the best place for **gynaecological problems**; Covasna, Vatra Dornei and Buziaş deal with **cardiovascular complaints**; Călimăneşti-Căciulata, Slănic Moldova, Sângeorz-Băi and Băile Olăneşti with **digestion**; and others (notably Băile Herculane and Băile Felix) with a range of **locomotive and rheumatic ailments**. Mountain resorts such as Sinaia, Băile Tuşnad and Moneasa treat **nervous complaints** with fresh air, which has an ideal balance of ozone and ions.

changed for centuries and where boats are the only way to reach many of the settlements. During spring and autumn, especially, hundreds of species of birds from all over the Old World migrate through this area or come to breed. Whilst not quite as remote, the northern region of **Maramureş**, bordering the Ukraine, retains an almost medieval-like feel, its villages renowned for their fabulous wooden churches. Close by, sprinkled amidst the soft, rolling hills of **Bucovina**, are the wonderful painted monasteries, whose specimens of religious art are among some of the most outstanding in Europe.

When to go

The **climate** is pretty crucial in deciding where and when to go to Romania. **Winters** can be fairly brutal – snow blankets much of the country, temperatures of minus fifteen to twenty degrees are not uncommon, and a strong, icy wind (the *crivaţ*) sweeps down from Russia. Conditions improve with **spring**, bringing rain and wildflowers to the mountains and the softest of blue skies over Bucharest, and prompting the great migration of birds through the Delta. By May, the lowlands are warming up and you might well find strong sunshine on the coast before the season starts in July. Although by far the hottest time of the year, **summer**

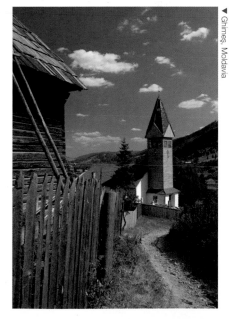

Ghimeş, Moldavia

11

or early autumn is the perfect time to investigate Transylvania's festivals and hiking trails (though brief but violent thunderstorms are common in the Carpathians during this period), and to see the Painted Monasteries of Bucovina, while flocks of birds again pass through the Delta towards the **end of autumn**.

Average monthly temperature

	Jan	Feb	Mar	Apr	May	Jun	Jul	Aug	Sep	Oct	Nov	Dec
Braşov (The mountains)												
(°C)	1	1	6	11	16	19	21	21	18	13	7	2
(°F)	34	34	42	52	61	66	69	69	65	55	45	36
Bucharest												
(°C)	-3	-1	4	11	17	21	23	22	18	12	5	1
(°F)	26	31	40	52	62	69	71	70	65	53	41	34
Constanţa (The coast)												
(°C)	-1	1	3	13	19	24	26	26	22	17	11	6
(°F)	31	34	39	55	66	75	79	79	70	62	52	43
Timişoara (The Banat)												
(°C)	-2	1	5	11	16	20	20	18	18	12	6	1
(°F)	28	34	41	52	61	67	67	65	65	53	43	34

things not to miss

It's not possible to see everything Romania has to offer in one trip – and we don't suggest you try. What follows is a selective and subjective taste of the country's highlights: outstanding architecture, natural wonders, spectacular hikes and unforgettable festivals. They're arranged in five colour-coded categories, so you can browse through to find the very best things to see, do, buy and experience. All highlights have a page reference to take you straight into the guide, where you can find out more.

01 Braşov Page **157** • Shadowed by mountains and containing a fine Baroque centre, Braşov is one of Transylvania's most appealing cities.

02 Bear and wolf tracking
Page **170** • This excellent ecotourism project offers a rare chance to get close to Romania's most feared and revered creatures.

03 Peleş Castle, Sinaia
Page **152** • Once a refuge for Ceauşescu and visiting dignitaries, Peleş remains the country's most opulent palace.

05 Village homestays
Page **37** • Wonderful rural retreats offering cheap, friendly and relaxing accommodation and great home-cooked food.

04 Karst formations
Page **249** • Romania's impressive karst landscape offers fantastic subterranean wonders, including Cetăţile Ponorului in the Apuseni mountains.

06 **Fãgãraş mountains** Page **171** • The spectacular peaks of the Fãgãraş are among the highest in Romania, providing access to some of the Carpathians' most rewarding hikes.

07 **Timişoara** Page **374** • The crucible of the 1989 revolution, Timişoara is one of Romania's most vibrant and engaging cities.

08 Sighişoara Page **177** • A brooding skyline of ramparts, towers and spires marks Sighişoara out as Transylvania's most atmospheric medieval town.

09 Black Sea Page **407** • Strewn with brash resorts, the Black Sea coast offers opportunities aplenty for swimming, sailing or windsurfing.

11 Bucovina hills Page **302** • Cloaked in beech, fir and pine, the gorgeous, rolling Bucovina hills are a walker's paradise.

10 Dracula Page **113** • The tomb at Snagov, old castle ruins at Poienari, the Princely Court at Târgovişte and the birthplace in Sighişoara – the Dracula legend is alive and kicking.

12 Painted monasteries See *Romania's religious architecture* colour section •
Nestled behind huge walls, the monasteries of southern Bucovina and Moldavia are
renowned for their magnificent exterior frescoes.

13 Vişeu de Sus train ride Page **352** • Jump aboard the early-morning logging
train for a slow, meandering ride up the picturesque Vaser valley.

14 **Hiking in the Carpathians** Page **148** • One of Europe's most stunning and least spoilt mountain ranges, the Carpathians are a first-class hiking region.

16 **Constantin Brâncuşi** Page **127** • Romania's greatest sculptor has bequeathed an impressive legacy of striking, yet simple, works of art, such as the *Endless Column* in Târgu Jiu.

15 **Pageant of the Juni** Page **163** • Dancing, costumes and brass regiments constitute Braşov's liveliest event.

17 Bucharest Page **56** • Romania's noisy, chaotic capital boasts a number of terrific museums, some surprisingly appealing architecture, and the country's most vigorous nightlife.

18 Sheep's cheese Page **184** • Fresh from the highland pastures, a sample of tasty sheep's cheese is a must.

19 Measurement of the Milk Festival Page **252** • Enjoyable and unusual spectacle in which shepherds vie to see who has the most productive animals.

20 Fortified churches Pages **183** & **175** • Scattered among the lush green hills of southern Tranyslvania are dozens of marvellous fortified Saxon churches, such as those at Mălâncrav and Viscri.

21 Skiing Page **166** • Hit the slopes in Poiana Braşov, Romania's premier ski resort.

23 Girl Fair of Muntele Găina
Page 248 • Taking place atop Mount Găina, this feverish spectacle of music, song and dance is one of the most anticipated festivals on the Romanian calendar.

22 Bicaz gorges
Page 280 • Take a drive through the majestic Bicaz gorges, bisected by sheer, three-hundred-metre-high limestone cliffs.

24 Merry Cemetery, Sapânţa
Page 344 • True to its name, the Merry Cemetery is a riot of beautifully carved and brightly coloured headstones.

25 **Folk and Gypsy music** Page **459** • Don't miss the chance to experience the wild, irrepressible sounds of Romanian folk and Gypsy music.

26 **Wooden churches of Maramureş** See *Romania's religious architecture colour section* • The villages of this remote northern region are dominated by marvellous wooden churches, characterized by their magnificent spires.

23

27 **Ţuică** Page **41** • A typically powerful Balkan brandy, Romania's national drink should be tried at least once.

28 **Danube Delta** Page **390** • Bordering the Ukraine, this remote and beautiful landscape has an abundant array of wildlife, and offers some of the finest birdwatching in Europe.

29 **Spas** Page **382** • Wallow in temperatures of 30°C at one of the country's many spa resorts, such as elegant Băile Herculane with its faded grandeur.

30 **Sibiu** Page **186** • Beautiful squares and architecture, terrific museums and some fabulous festivals make the once great Saxon town of Sibiu one of Romania's most alluring destinations.

Basics

Basics

Getting there

The easiest way to reach Romania is to fly, with several airlines now travelling direct from airports in the UK. There is also one direct flight from the United States, but presently no direct flights from Canada or Australasia. Travelling overland from Britain is a long haul, and you'll save little, if anything, by taking the train, although with a rail pass you can take in Romania as part of a wider trip. Driving there will involve a journey of some 2000km; an absorbing trip but one best covered slowly.

Airfares are highest from June to August, and drop during the "shoulder" seasons – March to May and September to October. The best prices are found during the low season, from November to February (excluding Christmas and New Year when fares are hiked up and seats are at a premium).

The **cheapest flights** from the UK and Europe are usually with no-frills budget and charter airlines, especially if you're prepared to book weeks in advance or take a chance on a last-minute bargain. Budget airline tickets are sold direct (by phone or online) on a one-way basis; the price of your outward and return leg may differ significantly. Don't forget to reckon in the cost of **airport taxes**, which can be more expensive than the flight itself, and things like in-flight meals and luggage allowances, which tend to cost extra. Cheap flights also tend to have fixed dates, and are non-changeable and non-refundable.

Flights from the UK and Ireland

Flying from the UK to Romania takes approximately three hours. British Airways and TAROM (the Romanian national carrier) both have daily direct **scheduled flights from London Heathrow to Bucharest Henri Coanda airport** – expect to pay around £140 return low season, £180–200 high season. As for **budget carriers**, easyJet operates from London Gatwick to Bucharest Baneasa, while WizzAir flies from London Luton to Cluj (in Transylvania), and from Liverpool to Baneasa. Tickets cost as little as £50–60 return, though you need to book well in advance to secure these prices.

Another possibility is to fly to one of the **neighbouring countries** and continue your journey overland. EasyJet, Ryanair and WizzAir fly from the UK to Budapest, in Hungary, from where there are good, cheap, onward connections by bus or train to Romania. EasyJet also fly from London to Sofia, in Bulgaria.

Indirect flights with other airlines, such as Austrian Airlines, Air France and Lufthansa, are also worth looking into – they do take longer and connections times are often very tight, but they can be competitive in price, with tickets from around £150.

There are no direct scheduled flights from **Dublin** or **Belfast**, so you'll have to take a flight to London and an onward connection.

Flights from the US and Canada

The only direct **flight from the US** to Romania is from New York to Bucharest with Delta Airlines, with a return fare from around US$1200 in high season, US$700 low season. There are **no direct flights from Canada**, so you'll have to use one of the bigger European airlines to fly you into their home hub, from where you can continue the journey – expect to pay around US$750/Can$1300 low season and US$1100/Can$1600 high season. An alternative is to fly into Budapest, in Hungary, from where there are good onward bus and train connections into Romania. Malev, the Hungarian carrier, flies direct from both New York's JFK and Chicago to Budapest, with fares from around US$650 low season and US$800 high season, and they also schedule direct flights from Toronto, with fares from around Can$900 low season and Can$1100 high season.

Fly less – stay longer! Travel and climate change

Climate change is the single biggest issue facing our planet. It is caused by a build-up in the atmosphere of carbon dioxide and other greenhouse gases, which are emitted by many sources – including planes. Already, flights account for around 3–4 percent of human-induced global warming: that figure may sound small, but it is rising year on year and threatens to counteract the progress made by reducing greenhouse emissions in other areas.

Rough Guides regard travel, overall, as a global benefit, and feel strongly that the advantages to developing economies are important, as are the opportunities for greater contact and awareness among peoples. But we all have a responsibility to limit our personal "carbon footprint". That means giving thought to how often we fly and what we can do to redress the harm that our trips create.

Flying and climate change

Pretty much every form of motorized travel generates CO_2, but planes are particularly bad offenders, releasing large volumes of greenhouse gases at altitudes where their impact is far more harmful. Flying also allows us to travel much further than we would contemplate doing by road or rail, so the emissions attributable to each passenger become truly shocking. For example, one person taking a return flight between Europe and California produces the equivalent impact of 2.5 tonnes of CO_2 – similar to the yearly output of the average UK car.

Less harmful planes may evolve but it will be decades before they replace the current fleet – which could be too late for avoiding climate chaos. In the meantime, there are limited options for concerned travellers: to reduce the amount we travel by air (take fewer trips, stay longer!), to avoid night flights (when plane contrails trap heat from Earth but can't reflect sunlight back to space), and to make the trips we do take "climate neutral" via a carbon offset scheme.

Carbon offset schemes

Offset schemes run by **climatecare.org, carbonneutral.com** and others allow you to "neutralize" the greenhouse gases that you are responsible for releasing. Their websites have simple calculators that let you work out the impact of any flight. Once that's done, you can pay to fund projects that will reduce future carbon emissions by an equivalent amount (such as the distribution of low-energy light bulbs and cooking stoves in developing countries). Please take the time to visit our website and make your trip climate neutral.

www.roughguides.com/climatechange

Flights from Australia and New Zealand

There are **no direct flights from either Australia or New Zealand** to Romania, so you'll have to change airlines, either in Asia or Europe, although the best option is to fly to a Western European gateway city and get a connecting flight from there. A standard return fare from eastern **Australia** to Bucharest, via London, with Qantas, is around AU$2200 low season and AU$2700 high season. Most flights typically require a stop in London, Paris or Frankfurt, continuing onwards from there. The same routings apply for flights from **New Zealand**, with a standard return fare from around N$2400 low season and NZ$3000 high season.

Flights from South Africa

There are no direct **flights** from South Africa to Romania, so you'll have to change airlines at one of the main European gateways. A standard return fare from Johannesburg to Bucharest, via Frankfurt or Vienna (with South African Airways or a leading European airline), is around ZAR9500 low season and ZAR11,500 high season.

By train from the UK

Travelling **by train** is likely to be considerably more expensive than flying, and the shortest journey takes about 36 hours. However, it can be a leisurely way of getting to the country if you plan to stop off in other parts of Europe along the way.

A standard second-class **return ticket**, incorporating Eurostar, will cost around £350. Eurostar trains depart more or less hourly (roughly 6am–7.30pm) from London St. Pancras through the Channel Tunnel to Paris Gare du Nord (2hr 15min). Arriving in Paris, you take a train to either Munich or Vienna and change there for the next leg to Budapest. In Budapest, you need to change again for the last leg to Bucharest. Tickets are usually valid for two to three months and allow for unlimited stopovers.

You can get through-ticketing from stations around Britain from Eurostar, many travel agents and main-line stations. Inter-Rail, Eurail, Britrail and Eurodomino passes give discounts on Eurostar trains; for details of **rail passes**, see "Getting around", p.34.

By car from the UK

Driving to Romania, a distance of 2000km from London, can be a pleasant proposition. However, it's really only worth considering if you are planning to travel around Romania extensively or want to make various stopovers en route.

Once across the channel (see p.30), the best **route** (around thirty hours at a leisurely pace with plenty of stops) is through France, Germany, Austria and Hungary, passing Frankfurt, Nuremberg, Regensburg, Linz, Vienna and Budapest, and then taking the E60 down to the Borş frontier crossing near Oradea or the E75/E68 to Nădlac near Arad. Detailed printouts of the route can be obtained from the websites of the AA (@www .theaa.com), or RAC (@www.rac.co.uk). See p.34 for details of driving within Romania.

By bus from the UK

The **bus journey** from **London to Bucharest** is a stamina-sapping 49 hours, with one change in Cologne; the bus also stops in Arad, Timişoara, Deva, Sibiu, Braşov and Ploieşti before reaching Bucharest – the same service then continues to Constanţa. A standard return fare costs around £180 (valid for six months), though look out for promotional fares.

Package tours

There is no shortage of operators in the UK offering **package and specialist-interest tours** to Romania – from the standard ski and coastal resort holidays to more specialized cultural, hiking and wildlife and conservation trips. For fanatics, there are even Dracula-themed tours. In Romania, there are several more agencies offering ready-made and tailor-made tours – these are detailed in the relevant parts of the guide.

Airlines, agents and operators

Online booking

@ www.airfaresflights.com.au (in Australia)
@ www.cheapflights.co.uk (in UK)
@ www.cheapflights.ie (in Ireland)
@ www.cheapflights.com (in US)
@ www.cheapflights.ca (in Canada)
@ www.cheapo.com (in UK)
@ www.expedia.co.uk (in UK)
@ www.expedia.com (in US)
@ www.expedia.ca (in Canada)
@ www.lastminute.com (in UK)
@ www.opodo.co.uk (in UK)
@ www.orbitz.com (in US)
@ www.travelocity.co.uk (in UK)
@ www.travelocity.com (in US)
@ www.travelocity.ca (in Canada)
@ www.zuji.com.au (in Australia)
@ www.zuji.co.nz (in New Zealand)

Airlines

Air Canada US and Canada ☎1-888/247-2262, UK ☎0871/220-1111, Ireland ☎01/679-3958, Australia ☎1300/65576, New Zealand ☎0508/747-767; @ www.aircanada.com.
Air France UK ☎0870/142-4343, US ☎1-800/237-2747, Canada ☎1-800/667-2747, Australia ☎1300/390-190; @www.airfrance.com.
Air New Zealand New Zealand ☎0800/737-000, UK ☎0800/028-4149, Ireland ☎1800/551-447, US ☎1-800/262-1234, Canada ☎1-800/663-5494; @www.airnewzealand.com.
Austrian Airlines UK ☎0870/124-2625, Ireland ☎1800/509, US and Canada ☎1-800/843-0002, Australia ☎1800/642-438 or 612/9200-4800; @www.aua.com.
British Airways UK ☎0870/850-9850, Ireland ☎1890/626-747, US and Canada ☎1-800/AIRWAYS, Australia ☎1300/767-177, New Zealand ☎09/966-9777; @www.ba.com.

Delta US and Canada ☎ 1-800/221-1212,
UK ☎ 0845/600-0950, Ireland ☎ 1850/882-031
or 01/407-3165, Australia ☎ 1300/302-849,
New Zealand ☎ 09/379-3370; ⓦ www.delta.com.
easyJet UK ☎ 0871/750-0100; ⓦ www
.easyjet.com.
KLM (Royal Dutch Airlines) UK ☎ 0870/507-
4074, Australia ☎ 1300/303-747, New Zealand
☎ 09/309-1782; ⓦ www.klm.com.
Lufthansa US ☎ 1-800/645-3880, Canada
☎ 1-800/563-5954, UK ☎ 0870/837-7747,
Republic of Ireland ☎ 01/844-5544, Australia
☎ 1300/655-727, New Zealand ☎ 09/303-1529;
ⓦ www.lufthansa.com.
Malev Hungarian Airlines UK ☎ 0870/909-0577,
Ireland ☎ 0818/555-577, US ☎ 1-800/223-6884,
Canada ☎ 1-866/3797-313, Australia ☎ 612/9767-
4315; ⓦ www.malev.hu.
Qantas Airways Australia ☎ 13-13-13, New
Zealand ☎ 0800/808-767 or 09/357-8900, UK
☎ 0845/774-7767, Ireland ☎ 01/407-3278, US and
Canada ☎ 1-800/227-4500; ⓦ www.qantas.com.
Ryanair UK ☎ 0871/246-0000, Ireland ☎ 0818/30-
30-30; ⓦ www.ryanair.com.
South African Airways SA ☎ 11/978-1111,
US and Canada ☎ 1-800/722-9675, UK
☎ 0870/747-1111, Australia ☎ 1800/221 699,
New Zealand ☎ 09/977 2237; ⓦ www.flysaa.com.
TAROM UK ☎ 020/7224-3693, ⓦ www.tarom.ro.
WizzAir Poland ☎ 4822/500-9499; ⓦ www
.wizzair.com.

Rail contacts

CIT Rail US ☎ 1-800/CIT-TOUR. Eurail passes.
CIT World Travel Australia ☎ 02/9267-1255
or 03/9650-5510, ⓦ www.cittravel.com.au. Eurail
passes.
DER Travel US ☎ 1-888/283-2424, ⓦ www
.dertravel.com/rail. Eurail and country passes.
Europrail International Canada ☎ 1-888/667-
9734, ⓦ www.europrail.net. Eurail and country passes.
Eurostar UK ☎ 0870/160 6600, ⓦ www
.eurostar.com.
Rail Europe UK ☎ 0870/584-8848, ⓦ www
.raileurope.co.uk; US ☎ 1-877/257-2887, Canada
☎ 1-800/361-RAIL, ⓦ www.raileurope.com/us.
Discounted rail fares for under-26s on a variety of
European routes; also agents for Inter-Rail, Eurostar,
Eurodomino and the North American Eurail Pass.
Rail Plus Australia ☎ 1300/555-003 or 03/9642-
8644, ⓦ www.railplus.com.au; NZ ☎ 09/377-5415,
ⓦ www.railplus.co.nz. Eurail passes.
ScanTours US ☎ 1-800/223-7226 or 310/636-
4656, ⓦ www.scantours.com. Eurail and European
country passes.
STA Travel UK ☎ 0871/230-0040, ⓦ www
.statravel.co.uk; US ☎ 1-800/781-4040,
ⓦ www.statravel.com; Australia ☎ 134-782,
ⓦ www.statravel.com.au; New Zealand
☎ 0800/474-400, ⓦ www.statravel.co.nz; South
Africa ☎ 0861/781-781, ⓦ www.statravel.co.za.
Rail passes and discounts for under-26s.
Trailfinders UK ☎ 0845/058-5858, Ireland
☎ 01/677-7888, Australia ☎ 1300/780-212,
ⓦ www.trailfinders.com. All-Europe passes.

Ferry contacts

Brittany Ferries UK ☎ 0870/366-5333, Ireland
☎ 021/4277-801; ⓦ www.brittanyferries.co.uk.
DFDS Seaways UK ☎ 0870/252-0524,
ⓦ www.dfdsseaways.co.uk.
Hoverspeed UK ☎ 0870/240-8070,
ⓦ www.hoverspeed.co.uk.
Irish Ferries UK ☎ 0870/517-1717, Ireland
☎ 0818/300-400, ⓦ www.irishferries.com.
Norfolkline UK ☎ 0870/0600-4321,
ⓦ www.norfolkline.com.
P&O Ferries UK ☎ 0870/598-0333,
ⓦ www.poferries.com.
SeaFrance UK ☎ 0870/443-1653,
ⓦ www.seafrance.com.
SpeedFerries UK ☎ 0871/222-7456,
ⓦ www.speedferries.com.
Stena Line UK ☎ 0870/570-7070, Northern Ireland
☎ 0870/520-4204, Republic of Ireland ☎ 1/204-
7777, ⓦ www.stenaline.co.uk.

Superfast Ferries UK ☎0870/234-0870, Ⓦ www.superfast.com.
Transmanche UK ☎0800/917-1201, Ⓦ www.transmancheferries.com.

Bus contacts

Eurolines UK ☎0870/514-3219, Ⓦ www.eurolines.co.uk; Ireland ☎01/836-6111, Ⓦ www.eurolines.ie.
STA Travel see opposite.
Trailfinders see opposite.

Agents and operators

ebookers UK ☎0800/082-3000, Ⓦ www.ebookers.com; Ireland ☎01/488-3507, Ⓦ www.ebookers.ie. Low fares on an extensive selection of scheduled flights and package deals.
North South Travel UK ☎01245/608-291, Ⓦ www.northsouthtravel.co.uk. Friendly, competitive travel agency, offering discounted fares worldwide. Profits are used to support projects in the developing world, especially the promotion of sustainable tourism.
Trailfinders see opposite. One of the best-informed and most efficient agents for independent travellers.
STA Travel see opposite. Worldwide specialists in independent travel; also student IDs, travel insurance, car rental, rail passes and more. Good discounts for students and under-26s.

Specialist operators in the UK

Ancient World Tours ☎020/7917-9494, Ⓦ www.ancient.co.uk. Archeological tours taking in sites such as Histria, Adamclisi, and Sarmizegutsa, as well as the Saxon churches and painted monasteries.
Avian Adventures ☎01384/372-013, Ⓦ www.avianadventures.co.uk. Birding in the Danube Delta.
Balkan Holidays ☎0845/130-1114, Ⓦ www.balkanholidays.co.uk. Two-country holidays on the Romanian and Bulgarian Black Sea Coast, and ski packages in Poiana Braşov.
Birdfinders ☎01258/839-066, Ⓦ www.birdfinders.co.uk. Birdwatching in the Danube Delta and Carpathian mountains.
Equine Adventures ☎0845/130-6981, Ⓦ www.equineadventures.co.uk. Horse-riding and carriage-driving in Transylvania.
Exodus ☎020/8675-5550, Ⓦ www.exodus.co.uk. Hiking and conservation tours – including wolf tracking – in the Carpathians – with accommodation in local guesthouses. In Ireland, contact Worldwide Adventures ☎01/679-5700.
Explore Worldwide ☎01252/760-000, Ⓦ www.explore.co.uk. Guided tours (with some hiking) of

the Maramureş villages, the painted monasteries of Bucovina, and the Danube Delta.
High Places ☎0114/275-7500, Ⓦ www.highplaces.co.uk. Hikes – moderate to difficult – in several mountain ranges in the Carpathians.
Inghams ☎020/8780-4433, Ⓦ www.inghams.co.uk. Ski packages in Poiana Braşov.
Limosa Holidays ☎01263/578-143, Ⓦ www.limosaholidays.co.uk. Nature trips in the Danube Delta and along the Black Sea coast, and a two-country (with Hungary) Birds and Bears trip.
Martin Randall Travel ☎020/8742-3355, Ⓦ www.martinrandall.com. Summer tour of Bucovina's painted monasteries, with accommodation in comfortable three- and four-star hotels.
Naturetrek ☎01962/733-051, Ⓦ www.naturetrek.co.uk. Wildlife tour – flora and fauna – in the Carpathians in May and Aug.
Ride World Wide ☎01837/82544, Ⓦ www.rideworldwide.co.uk. Riding holidays in the Carpathians between April and Oct; four to six hours' riding daily and accommodation in local guesthouses.
Romania Travel Centre ☎01892/516-901, Ⓦ www.romaniatravelcentre.com. Romania specialists offering a comprehensive programme including Bucharest city breaks, coastal, ski and spa holidays, eco-tours and biking trips. Flights and tailor-made accommodation deals too.
Transylvan ☎020/8568-4499, Ⓦ www.transylvan.co.uk. Treasures of Transylvania, Best of Romania, Bucharest city tours and tailor-made trips.

Transylvania Uncovered ☎01482/350-216, ⓦwww
.beyondtheforest.com. Comprehensive Romania
specialists offering package and special interest tours
(wilderness, wine and culture, riding, spas, Dracula),
flights, accommodation, car hire and rail tickets.
Travelling Naturalist ☎01305/267-994, ⓦwww
.naturalist.co.uk. Birdwatching trips to the Danube
Delta/Transylvania in May and Sept.
Vamos Travel ☎0870/762-4017, ⓦwww
.vamostravel.com. Various offerings including the
painted monasteries, Bucharest city breaks (plus stag
weekends and opera and ballet), and Dracula tours.

ⓦwww.dreamtourist.com. Tours of the castles and
palaces of Transylvania and the Bucovina monasteries,
as well as Dracula tours.
Elderhostel ☎1-877/426-8056, ⓦwww
.elderhostel.org. Multi-country tours and cruises.
Quest Tours and Adventures ☎1-800/621-
8687, ⓦwww.romtour.com. Wide range of tours and
fully customized packages, including Jewish Heritage
and Dracula tours, as well as Bucharest city packages.
Wilderness ☎1-800/368-2794, ⓦwww
.wildernesstravel.com. Hiking expeditions throughout
the Carpathians.

Specialist operators in the US and Canada

Adventure Center ☎1-800/228-8747 or 510/654-
1879, ⓦwww.adventurecenter.com. Trekking and
conservation and wildlife tours in the Carpathians,
and village folklore and Danube Delta tour.
Adventures Abroad ☎1-800/665-3998, ⓦwww
.adventures-abroad.com. Countrywide tour, including
Transylvania and the painted monasteries, as well as
multi-country tours (Romania/Hungary/Bulgaria/
Ukraine and so on).
Contiki Tours ☎1-888/CONTIKI, ⓦwww.contiki
.com. 18- to 35-year-olds-only tour operator.
Extensive European tours, some of which
incorporate Romania.
Dream Tours International ☎818/956-8397,

Specialist operators in Australia and New Zealand

Adventure World Australia ☎02/8913-0755,
ⓦwww.adventureworld.com.au; New Zealand
☎09/524-5118, ⓦwww.adventureworld.co.nz.
Agents for Explore's escorted tours through the
Maramureş and Danube Delta regions.
Eastern Eurotours Australia ☎1800/242-353 or
07/5526-2855, ⓦwww.easterneurotours.com.au.
Transylvanian ski and snowboarding holidays, painted
monasteries tours and Dracula tours.
High Places New Zealand ☎03/540-3208, ⓦwww
.highplaces.co.nz. Hikes – moderate to difficult – in
several mountain ranges in the Carpathians.

Getting around

Most Romanian towns are easily reached by train, and although it is not the
fastest or cleanest system in the world, it is remarkably cheap and reliable. In the
absence of a coordinated bus network, maxitaxis (minibuses) are everywhere,
linking many of the larger centres and often providing a more direct and frequent
mode of transport than trains. Driving is another attractive proposition, enabling
you to visit anywhere you please, and in your own time.

By rail

The **SNCFR** (*Societatea Naţională a Căilor
Ferate Române*, generally known as the
CFR, or ChéFéRé) network covers most of
the country. Tickets are incredibly cheap –
a one-hundred-kilometre trip (second class)
is around €3–8 – though this is offset by the
habitually derelict carriages, bizarre timetable

and sweltering/freezing conditions. Often
crowded, trains frequently lack light and
water, making long journeys somewhat
purgatorial. Those who use the trains
regularly, however, often end up very much
in sympathy with their rough-and-ready spirit
and the generally excellent timekeeping.
Moreover, many routes are wonderfully
scenic, particularly in Transylvania.

There are several types of train: **Intercity** ("IC") and **Rapid** ("R") services, halting only at major towns, are the most comfortable and expensive types of train, while **Accelerats** ("A") are only slightly slower, with more frequent stops, and are the standard means of inter-urban travel. The painfully slow **Personal** ("P") trains should be avoided as a rule, unless you're heading for some tiny destination. **EuroCity** ("EC") and **EuroNight** ("EN") trains have final destinations abroad.

Trains generally conform to the **timetables** (*orar trenurilor*) displayed in stations and CFR offices; arrivals are often on a white board, departures on a yellow one. For key terms, see p.487. Watch out for services that run only during certain months (*circulă numai,* eg *Óntre 9.V şi 8.IX* – May 9 and Sept 8), or only on particular days (1 represents Mon, 2 represents Tues and so on; *nu circula Sâmbata şi Duminica* means the service doesn't run on Sat or Sun). If you're planning to travel a lot by train, try to get hold of the notoriously elusive national **CFR timetable**, the *Mersul Trenurilor*, issued each December. Otherwise, you could check out the web version, ⓦwww.cfr.ro. In any case, you should always check at the station. Details of main **routes** are given in the text, and summarized at the end of each chapter.

Left luggage offices (*bagaje de mănă*) exist in most train stations, where you'll usually have to pay around €1; there may also be lockers, but it's best to avoid these, as the locks have a tendency to jam.

Tickets

Fares (calculated by distance travelled) are extremely low; for example, a journey of 100km on an Intercity service will cost around €9 second class, and around €12 first class (around €8/10 on a Rapid, and €3/5 on a Personal), which makes travelling first class a bargain. Supplements are required on Intercity and Rapid services, costing around €5 and €3 respectively for a 100km journey. Advance **bookings** for fast services are recommended, and on most such trains you're required to have a **seat reservation**, although if you board at a relatively minor stop you may have to take pot luck. In most stations, **tickets** are now computerized, with all information on one piece of paper. In smaller places, however, your ticket (*bilet*) will usually be accompanied by a second piece of card, indicating the service (*nr. trenului*), your carriage (*vagon*) and reserved seat (*loc*). Return tickets (*bilet dus íntors*) are rarely issued except for international services. Many long-distance overnight trains have **sleeping cars** (*vagon de dormit*) and couchettes (*cuşete*), for which a surcharge of around €10–15 and €6–10 (depending upon how many berths there are) respectively is levied.

With the exception of Personal trains, **tickets** are sold at stations only an hour before departure time, and usually at specific windows for each train; these are not always clearly marked, so buying a ticket can lead to a bit of a scrum. Far easier (though costing a little extra) is to book tickets a day ahead – or seven days for services to the coast during summer – at the local **Agenţia CFR**. Addresses of offices are given in the guide, and in the CFR timetable. Should you fall victim to double-booking, ticket collectors are notoriously corrupt and a small

Useful train publications

The red-covered *Thomas Cook European Timetables* details schedules of the main Romanian **train** services, as well as timings of **ferry** routes and **rail-connecting bus services**. It's updated and issued every month; main changes are in the June edition (published mid- to end May), which has details of the summer European schedules, and the October one (published mid- to end Sept), which includes winter schedules; some have advance summer/winter timings also. The book can be bought online (for a ten percent discount) at ⓦwww.thomascookpublishing.com or from branches of Thomas Cook (see ⓦwww.thomascook.co.uk for your nearest branch), and costs £10.50. Their useful *Rail Map of Europe* can also be purchased online for 25 percent off the normal retail price of £7.95.

tip can work wonders. Indeed, some people never buy tickets, simply paying off the conductor instead.

Rail passes

There are a number of **rail passes** available for travelling in Romania. **Inter-Rail passes** (ⓦ www.interrail.net) are only available to European residents (or if you've been resident in a European country for at least six months), and you will be asked to provide proof of residency before being allowed to buy one. They come in over-26 and (cheaper) under-26 versions, and cover 31 countries.

The old zonal passes have been replaced with a **global pass**, covering all 31 countries (one month continuous €599 for over-26s/€399 for under-26s; 22 days continuous €469/309; 10 days in 22 €359/239; 5 days in 10 €249/159), and **one-country passes**. For Romania this costs: 8 days in one month €139 over-26s/€90 under-26s; 6 days in one month €119/77; 4 days in one month €89/58; 3 days in one month €69/45.

Inter-Rail passes do not include travel between Britain and the continent, although holders are eligible for discounts on rail travel in Britain and Northern Ireland and cross-Channel ferries, as well as reduced rates on the London–Paris Eurostar service.

Non-European residents qualify for the **Eurail pass** (ⓦ www.eurail.com), which must be bought before arrival in Europe (or from RailEurope in London). The pass allows unlimited travel in eighteen European countries and is available in increments from 15 days to three months. There is also a **Romania pass**, which allows for five days (€127 for over-26s/€101 for under 26s) or ten days (€221/177) first-class travel over a two-month period.

By bus or maxitaxi

Romania's **bus network** consists of a confusing and poorly coordinated array of private companies, and is really only useful if you're planning to visit some local village not served by train. In the countryside, knowing when and where to wait for the bus is a local art form, and on Sundays many regions have no local buses at all.

An increasingly popular mode of road transport are **minibuses**, or **maxitaxis**. The advantage they have over trains is the frequency and speed with which they can get you to your chosen destination. That said, passengers are usually crammed aboard with scant regard for comfort, and there's generally very little luggage space available. Moreover, the speed and reckless-ness with which many drivers go about getting to their destination leaves a lot to be desired. Prices are slightly higher than trains – expect to pay around €3.50 from Bucharest to Piteşti (100km), or €6 from Bucharest to Braşov (250km). Maxitaxis often begin and end their journeys from the local bus or train station. Main bus and maxitaxi routes are listed in the "Travel Details" section at the end of each chapter in this Guide.

All towns have **local bus services**, and in the main cities you'll also find **trams** (tramvai) and **trolley buses** (troleibuz). Tickets are normally sold in pairs (around €0.30) from street kiosks. Validate them yourself aboard the vehicle, but be prepared to fight your way to the machine through the crush.

By car or motorbike

Driving in Romania is, on the whole, an attractive proposition. Outside the major towns and cities, you'll find the roads relatively traffic-free, and many routes, particularly through Transylvania, are wonderfully scenic. The **main roads** (Drum Naţional or DN) are, generally speaking, in good condition. The quality of the **county roads** (Drum Judeţean), however, is variable, while many of the local roads are disinte-grating – potholes are a particularly nasty hazard. It is also a big country, and long distances are best covered at a steady pace, especially if driving in the more mountainous regions where greater powers of concentration are required.

More generally, Romanian **driving habits** often leave much to be desired, and a parti-cular danger is overtaking at absurdly risky moments. In rural areas, the danger isn't so much other motorized traffic as the risk of hitting horses and carts, drunks on bicycles and various animals that have yet to accept the impact of the motor age – squashed

Driving rules and regulations

The most important **rules** are to **drive on the right** and overtake on the left side, and for traffic on a roundabout to give way to traffic entering from the left. **Seat belts** are required outside towns. **Speed limits** for cars are 50kph in built-up areas, 90kph on the open road, and 120kph on the motorway. **Drinking** and driving is absolutely prohibited and severely punished. It is also forbidden to use a hand-held **mobile phone** while driving.

Police (*poliţia*) are empowered to levy on-the-spot **fines** for road traffic offences, but they cannot collect them; instead you'll be issued with a ticket (typically €40–80); if you settle up within 48 hours – at one of the CEC savings banks found in most towns – then you'll only have to pay half the fine.

If you have an **accident**, you're legally obliged to await the arrival of the police. You can get **technical assistance** and motoring information from **ACR** (Romanian Automobile Club), whose main Bucharest offices are at Str. Tache Ionescu 27 (☏021/315 5510) and Şos. Colentina 1 (☏021/635 4140). In the event of a **breakdown**, call ACR's 24-hour **breakdown service** on ☏222 2222, whereupon an English-speaking operator will direct you to the nearest point of assistance.

dogs lying on the side of the road are an all too common sight. For these reasons, it's best to **avoid driving after dark** wherever possible. The usual precautions apply when it comes to the potential for **theft**: never leave valuables inside the car and always lock it, even if you're just popping into a shop for five minutes.

Romania makes a fine country for **motorcycling**, though the speed limit for **motorbikes** is ludicrously low: 40kph in built-up areas and only 50kph (30mph) on the open road. Helmets are compulsory and you should bring vital spares, as well as a tool kit.

Petrol stations (*benzarie*) can be found almost everywhere, even in the most rural backwaters – the best and most common are those run by the Romanian-run PETROM, OMV (Austrian), MOL (Hungarian) and Shell, many of which have good refreshment and toilet facilities; you should avoid the small, private stations, where fuel may be dirty or diluted. Most cars just use regular *benzină*, but super and lead-free petrol (*fără plomb*) and diesel (*motorina*) are widely available – expect to pay around €0.70 per litre of unleaded. Credit cards are accepted at most stations. While most service stations operate from around 7am to 8 or 9pm, quite a few are open around the clock, usually located on the outskirts of larger towns and cities.

Car rental

Renting a car is simple enough, provided you are 21 or older, and hold a valid national driving licence. You can order a car through rental agencies in your home country (see below), which sometimes works out cheaper, particularly if you book online. Most of the major companies have branches in Bucharest (and Henri Coanda airport) and the other major cities. **Costs** are not especially cheap; expect to pay around €45–55 for a day's hire (unlimited mileage), the rate decreasing slightly the longer the hire period. You may find that **local companies**, such as Pan Travel (see p.242), offer better deals. Credit cards are usually required for a deposit.

Car rental agencies

Avis UK ☏0870/606-0100, ⊛www.avis.co.uk; Northern Ireland ☏028/9024-0404, Republic of Ireland ☏021/428-1111, ⊛www.avis.ie; US ☏1-800/230-4898, Canada ☏1-800/272-5871, ⊛www.avis.com; Australia ☏13/6333 or ☏02/9353-9000, ⊛www.avis.com.au; NZ ☏09/526-2847 or 0800/655 111, ⊛www.avis.co.nz.
Budget UK ☏0800/973-159, ⊛www.budget .co.uk; Ireland ☏09/0662-7711, ⊛www.budget .ie; US ☏1-800/527-0700, Canada ☏1-800/472-3325, ⊛www.budget.com; Australia ☏1300/362-848, ⊛www.budget.com.au; NZ ☏09/976-2222 or 0800/652-227, ⊛www.budget.co.nz.

Cosmo Thrifty Northern Ireland ⓣ 028/9445-2565, ⓦ www.thrifty.co.uk.

Dollar US ⓣ 1-800/800-3665, ⓦ www.dollar.com.

Europcar UK ⓣ 0870/607-5000, ⓦ www.europcar.co.uk; Northern Ireland ⓣ 028/9442-3444, Republic of Ireland ⓣ 01/614-2888, ⓦ www.europcar.ie; US & Canada ⓣ 1-877/940-6900, ⓦ www.europcar.com; Australia ⓣ 1300/131-390, ⓦ www.deltaeuropcar.com.au.

Hertz UK ⓣ 0870/844-8844, ⓦ www.hertz.co.uk; Ireland ⓣ 01/676 7476, ⓦ www.hertz.ie; US ⓣ 1-800/654-3001, Canada ⓣ 1-800/263-0600, ⓦ www.hertz.com; Australia ⓣ 03/9698-2555, ⓦ www.hertz.com.au; NZ ⓣ 0800/654-321, ⓦ www.hertz.co.nz.

Holiday Autos UK ⓣ 0870/400-0099, ⓦ www.holidayautos.co.uk; Ireland ⓣ 01/872-9366, ⓦ www.holidayautos.ie; Australia ⓣ 1330/554-432, ⓦ www.holidayautos.com.au; NZ ⓣ 0800/144-040, ⓦ www.holidayautos.co.nz.

National UK ⓣ 0870/536-5365, ⓦ www.nationalcar.co.uk; US ⓣ 1-800/962-7070, ⓦ www.nationalcar.com; Australia ⓣ 13/1045, ⓦ www.nationalcar.com.au; NZ ⓣ 0800/800-115 or 03/366-5574, ⓦ www.nationalcar.co.nz.

SIXT Republic of Ireland ⓣ 1850/206-088, ⓦ www.irishcarrentals.ie.

Suncars UK ⓣ 0870/500-5566, ⓦ www.suncars.com.

Thrifty UK ⓣ 01494/751-600, ⓦ www.thrifty.co.uk; Republic of Ireland ⓣ 1800/515-800, ⓦ www.thrifty.ie; US and Canada ⓣ 1-800/847-4389, ⓦ www.thrifty.com; Australia ⓣ 1300/367-227, ⓦ www.thrifty.com.au; NZ ⓣ 09/309-0111, ⓦ www.thrifty.co.nz.

Cycling

Given the mountainous terrain and the poor state of many of the country roads, you'll need to be fit and self-reliant to **cycle** around Romania. Cycle shops are few and far between, although most village mechanics can manage basic repairs. Carry a spare tyre and a few spokes, and check carrier nuts regularly, as the potholes and corrugations will rapidly shake them loose. A touring bike is better than a mountain bike unless you want to go off-road; with the immense network of forestry roads (*Drum Forestiere*) and free access to the hills, genuine mountain biking is wonderful here. If you do bring your own bike, avoid cycling in **Bucharest**, where the roads are so hazardous that few people ever cycle there and drivers will have little idea how of to avoid you. Carrying your bike by train is easiest on Personal services, where you can simply put it in the carriage, though you should stay with it at all times and probably have to tip the conductor; on Accelerats, it'll have to be carried in the baggage van (this should be indicated on the timetable) and a good tip is necessary to ensure that it's properly guarded.

Hitchhiking

Hitchhiking (*autostop* or *occasie*) is an integral part of the Romanian transport system to supplement patchy or nonexistent services on backroads – it's even common (although illegal) on the autostrada. It's accepted practice to pay (a very small amount) for lifts; although this is often waived for foreigners, make sure you've got some small change to hand if you think it would be good to give the driver some money. Hitchhiking, however, is a risky business in any country, and if you decide to travel this way, take all sensible precautions. It goes without saying that women should never hitch alone, nor is hitching at night advisable.

By plane

Romania has a well-integrated **plane network**, serving most of the larger cities. **TAROM**'s domestic **services** depart most days from Bucharest's Henri Coanda airport to Bacau, Baia Mare, Cluj, Constanţa, Iaşi, Oradea, Satu Mare, Sibiu, Suceava, Timişoara and Târgu Mureş. In addition, **Carpatair** (ⓦ www.carpatair.ro) operates flights from Timişoara to Bacau, Bucharest, Cluj, Constanţa, Craiova, Iaşi, Oradea, Satu Mare, Sibiu and Suceava. A single **fare** for any destination within the country is typically around €40–60; bookings should be made at least 36 hours in advance.

Accommodation

You should have little trouble finding a bed in Romania, whatever the season. Hotels run the full gamut from plush, top-end establishments, to flea-pit dives with an intermittent water supply. There are now also a good number of youth hostels, in addition to a good spread of private rooms and village homestays, the last of which typically offer wonderfully peaceful retreats.

In summer, it's safer, though only really essential on the coast, to make advance hotel **reservations**. If you're keen to save money on accommodation and you're travelling around a lot, you can use the **trains** to your advantage. On the long overnight journeys by Rapid or Accelerat train, it only costs a little more to book a comfortable sleeping car or couchette.

Hotels

Hotels use the traditional five-star **grading system** for classification, although in many cases this often gives only the vaguest idea of **prices**, which can fluctuate wildly according to the locality and season. Outside Bucharest and the coast, the average three-star hotel can cost anything between €35 and €56 for a double room. Moreover, the ratings are not always indicative of the quality of a place, particularly at the lower end of the scale, where standards can, and do, vary tremendously. The plushest four- and five-star hotels (mostly confined to Bucharest, the coast and the major cities) offer all the luxuries one would expect of such establishments, while three-star hotels can be unpredictable in terms of both quality and cost; you should, however, expect a reasonable standard of comfort, as well as private bathroom and TV, in most.

In some of the most basic places you may find that **hot water** is only available for a few hours a day (*cu program*), so check before deciding to take a room. It's not unusual, either, to find some hotels in smaller towns doubling up as the local nightclub.

There are a growing number of **pensions**, too, many of which offer much better value than hotels of a similar price. **Motels** often have similar facilities and prices to the mid-range hotels, but since they're situated along main highways or beyond urban ring roads, are not much use unless you have your own transport. You may also come across **sport hotels** (an old East European institution), which were traditionally intended for visiting teams and school groups, but which now admit tourists too. Although often very basic, they invariably offer a clean and cheap place to bed down for the night.

Village homestays and private rooms

Village homestays (*agroturism*) – rural farmhouse-style accommodation – offer visitors the opportunity to spend some time with a Romanian family (not all of whom will speak English) in often lovely surrounds. The downside is that many places are in fairly remote locations, and are therefore difficult to

Accommodation price codes

Hotels listed in this guide have been coded according to the scale below. Prices given are for the cheapest **double room** available during peak season. Though you will generally pay for your room in leu, the codes are expressed in euros as the Romanian leu is still a relatively unstable currency.

❶ Under €15
❷ €16–25
❸ €26–35

❹ €36–45
❺ €46–55
❻ €56–70

❼ €71–85
❽ €86–100
❾ Over €101

reach without your own transport. Homestays are **graded** according to a **daisy classification system**; four or five daisies (of which there are few) denotes a house with large, well-furnished rooms with private bathroom or shower/toilet, while one or two daisies represents a more basic place offering shared shower and toilet facilities. Expect to pay between €10–15 per person per night depending upon the category; many places also offer breakfast (around €3) and dinner (€5–7) upon request. The excellent website ⓦwww.ruralturism.ro lists a number of homestays throughout the country.

In addition to the schemes listed here, you should also look out for signs reading *cazare la particular* or *camere de inchiriat* (**private rooms**) in traditional resorts and more touristed areas. In the countryside, where there is a strong custom of hospitality, people may take you in and refuse payment, but you should offer something anyway, or come armed with a few packets of coffee, which make welcome presents.

The official nationwide body for homestays is **ANTREC** (the National Association of Rural, Ecological and Cultural Tourism) B-dul. Maraşti 59, Bucharest (☎021/222 8001, ⓦwww.antrec.ro). The other two options are based outside Romania: the offices of **OVR** (Opération Villages Roumains) are in Charleroi, Belgium ☎+32/071/284082, ⓔovr@win.be), but bookings can be made in Romania through PanTravel, Str. Grozăvescu 13, 3400 Cluj (☎0264/420 516, ⓔoffice@pantravel.ro); while the Amsterdam-based **ECEAT** (the European Centre for Eco-Agro Tourism; ☎+31/20/668 1030, ⓦwww .eceat.org), with a less structured network in Alba, Mureş, Harğhita and Bucovina counties, is coordinated by the Focus Eco-Center in Târgu Mureş (OP 6, PO Box 620, Str. Crinului 22; ☎0265/262 170, ⓔinfo @focuseco.ro). In addition, there's a network of **Gästehäuser** in the Saxon villages; although these aren't homestays, they still provide village accommodation, coordinated by Kilian Dörr, Evangelisches Pfarrhaus, Piaţa Huet 1, 2400 Sibiu (☎&ⓕ0269/211 203) and Hugo Schneider, Str. Gh. Doja 23, Mediaş (☎0269/828 605). A guidebook to the Gästehäuser is available in English from The Mihai Eminescu Trust, 63 Hillgate Place,

London W8 7SS, UK (☎020/7792-9998, ⓦwww.mihaieminescutrust.org).

Hostels

Romania has a rapidly expanding network of **youth hostels** (ⓦwww.hi-hostels-romania .ro), with around half a dozen in Bucharest, as well as excellent options in Braşov, Cluj, Sibiu and Sighişoara and even in smaller towns such as Deva and Miercurea Ciuc. Expect to pay around €10–15 for a dorm bed, €18–20 for a bed in a double room, and €25 for a single-bed room – breakfast is usually extra.

While **student accommodation** is largely in short supply, you may find the odd student residence willing to let out a bed, though these are largely available only in July and August – however, these are unlikely to be advertised, so ask for details at the local tourist office or town agency.

Cabanas

In the countryside, particularly in the mountainous areas favoured by hikers, there are well over a hundred **cabanas** or hikers' huts, ranging from chic alpine villas with dozens of bedrooms to fairly primitive chalets with bunk beds and cold running water. The hikers' cabanas are generally friendly and serve as useful places to pick up information about trails and the weather. Some (mainly in the Bucegi range) can be easily reached by cable car, while others are situated on roads just a few kilometres from towns; however, the majority are fairly isolated and accessible only by mountain tracks or footpaths. The location of the cabanas is shown rather vaguely on an ONT map, *Cabane Turistice*, but more precisely on hiking maps. Cabanas are supposed not to turn hikers away, but in the Făgăraş mountains, in particular, it might be wise to **book in advance**, by phone or through a local agency. Beds in remoter areas cost about €3–4, a little more for a private room or in one of the more comfortable cabanas.

Camping

Romania has well over a hundred **campsites**, situated all over the country. You'll generally pay about €3 per person per night, though an ISIC student card may secure a thirty- to fifty-percent reduction. Second-class campsites are rudimentary, usually with filthy toilets, but first-class sites often have **cabins** or bungalows (*căsuțe*) for rent (about €5 for a two-bed cabin), hot showers and even a restaurant. Bear in mind that water shortages hit campsites especially hard, and that along the coast overcrowding is a major drawback.

In the mountains, though certain areas may be designated as a camping area (*loc de campare*), these are few and far between. However, providing you don't light fires in forests, leave litter or damage nature reserves, officialdom turns a blind eye to tourists **camping wild**, or, at the worst, may simply tell you to move along.

If you're planning to do a lot of camping, an **international camping carnet** is a good investment. The carnet gives discounts at member sites and serves as useful identification. Many campsites will take it as an alternative to depositing your passport during your stay, and it covers you for third-party insurance when camping.

In the **UK and Ireland**, the carnet costs £4.50/€10, and is available to members of the AA or the RAC (see p.29), or the **Camping and Caravanning Club** (☎024/7669-4995, ⓦwww.campingandcaravanningclub.co.uk) the **CTC** (☎0870/873-0061, ⓦwww.ctc.org.uk), or the **Carefree Travel Service** (☎024/7642-2024), which provides the carnet free if you take out insurance with them.

In the **US and Canada**, the carnet is available for US$10 from home motoring organizations, or from **Family Campers and FCRVers** (FCRV; ☎1-800/245-9755 or ☎716/668-6242, ⓦwww.fcrv.org).

Food and drink

Romanian cuisine tends to be filling and wholesome rather than particularly tasty or imaginative. That said, the range and quality of restaurants is steadily improving, particularly in Bucharest, where it's now possible to enjoy some superb cooking from a number of different countries. As a rule, you should be able to get a decent two-course meal, with a glass of wine or beer, for between €8.50–12 (or around half that for a more basic meal). For a glossary of food and drink terms, see p.492.

Breakfasts, snacks and sandwiches

If you're staying in a hotel, **breakfast** typically consists of a light meal of bread rolls and butter (sometimes known as *ceai complet*), to which an omelette, salty cheese or long, unappealing-looking skinless sausages can be added. This is washed down with an overly strong coffee or a cup of tea.

For **snacks**, known as *gustări* (also the Romanian word for hors d'oeuvres), look out for flaky pastries (*pateuri*) filled with cheese or meat, often dispensed through hatches in the walls of bakeries; brioche, a Moldavian speciality; sandwiches (*sandvici*); a variety of spicy grilled sausages and meatballs, normally sold by street vendors and in beer gardens; and small pizzas topped with cheese, salami and ketchup. Note that a "snack bar" serves only drinks. Ice cream, however, is sold on the streets almost all year round.

Main meals and desserts

Wherever you eat, it's best to go **upmarket** if you can, since the choice of dishes in cheaper **restaurants** – which tend to be thinly disguised beer halls – is limited to cutlet (*cotlet*) and chips. At least the grisly self-service **Autoservire canteens** that Ceauşescu intended to make the mainstay of Romanian catering have largely vanished; unfortunately, they've been replaced for the most part by burger bars. **Lacto-Vegetarian restaurants** are also vanishing; although not particularly vegetarian, where they still exist they offer affordable food in reasonably congenial surroundings. Whatever you settle on, always enquire *Care feluri le serviţi astazi, ve rog?* ("What do you have today?") or *Ce Óhmi recomandaţi?* ("What do you recommend?") before studying the menu too seriously, for sometimes the only thing going is the **set menu** (*un meniu fix*), usually dominated by pork.

Inevitably, standards of **service** vary depending upon the type of establishment you are dining in, but generally speaking, don't expect anything but the most perfunctory of service from staff who may or may not speak English. Increasingly, a number of restaurants have a **no-smoking** section, although this remains the exception rather than the rule.

Regional cuisines

At smarter restaurants, there's a fair chance of finding **authentic Romanian dishes**, which can be delicious. The best known is *sarmale* – cabbage leaves stuffed with rice, meat and herbs, usually served (or sometimes baked) with sour cream and horseradish; they are sometimes also made with vine leaves (*sărmăluţe in foi de viţă*) or, in Maramureş, with corn (*sarmale cu pasat*). *Mămăligă*, maize mush or polenta, often served with sour cream, is authentic country fare. Stews (*tocane*) and other dishes often feature a combination of meat and dairy products. *Muşchi ciobanesc* (shepherd's sirloin) is pork stuffed with ham, covered in cheese and served with mayonnaise, cucumber and herbs; while *muşchi poiana* (meadow sirloin) is beef stuffed with mushrooms, bacon, pepper and paprika, served in a vegetable purée and tomato sauce.

Keep an eye out for **regional specialities** (*specialităţile regiunii*). Moldavian cooking is reputedly the best in Romania, featuring rissoles (*pârjoale*), and more elaborate dishes such as *rasol moldovenesc cu hrean* (boiled

pork, chicken or beef, with a sour cream and horseradish sauce), *tochitură moldovenească* (a pork stew, with cheese, *mămăligă*, and a fried egg on top), *rulade de pui* (chicken roulade) and *pui Câmpulungean* (chicken stuffed with smoked bacon, sausage, garlic and vegetables). Because of Romania's Turkish past, you may come across moussaka and varieties of pilaf, while the German and Hungarian minorities have contributed such dishes as smoked pork with sauerkraut and Transylvanian hotpot.

Cakes and desserts are sticky and very sweet. Romanians enjoy pancakes and pies with various fillings, as well as Turkish-influenced baclava and *savarină* (crisp pastry soaked in syrup and filled with whipped cream).

Vegetarian food

The situation for vegetarians has improved in recent years, although in a country where voluntarily doing without meat is usually beyond comprehension, there remains a paucity of imagination. You can try requesting something *fără carne, vă rog* ("without meat, please"), or check *este cu carne?* ("does it contain meat?"), but you're unlikely to get very far. It's worth asking for *ghiveci* (mixed stewed veg); *ardei umpluţi* (stuffed peppers); *ouă umpluţe picante* or *ouă umpluţe cu ciuperci* (eggs with a spicy filling or mushroom stuffing); *ouă romăneşti* (poached eggs); or vegetables and salads (see p.492). However, in practice, you're likely to end up with omelette, *mămăligă* (maize mush or polenta) or *caşcaval pané* (cheese fried in breadcrumbs).

Drink

Cafés called *cofetărie* serve coffee, soft drinks, cakes, ice cream and beer. Romanians usually take their coffee black and sweet in the Turkish fashion; ask for *cafea cu lapte* if you prefer it with milk, or *fără zahăr* without sugar. The instant varieties are called Ness. **Bars**, meanwhile, are generally men-only places and range from dark rough-and-ready dives to places with a rather chintzy ice-cream-parlour atmosphere. They're all usually open well into the small hours, except in smaller towns. A *crama* is a wine cellar, while a *gradina de vară* is a terrace or garden, usually offering *mititei* (spicy sausages) as well as beer.

The **national drink** is *ţuică*, a tasty, powerful brandy usually made of plums, taken neat. In rural areas, homemade spirits can be fearsome stuff, often twice distilled (to over 50 percent strength, even when diluted) to yield *palincă*, much rougher than grape brandy (*rachiu* or *coniac*). All spirits are alarmingly cheap (and served in large measures, usually 10cl; ask for a *mic*, 5cl, if you want less), except for whisky, which retails for around €12 a bottle.

Most **beer** is European-style lager (*bere blondă*). Silva (from Reghin), Valea Prahova (from Azuga), Ciucaş (from Braşov), Ursus (from Cluj), Ciuc (from Miercurea Ciuc), Timişoreana (from Timişoara) and Haţeg are probably the best regional brews, while Bergenbier and Eggenburger are acceptable mass-produced brands; you will also occasionally find brown ale (*bere neagră* or *brună*). Beer is usually sold by the bottle, so a request for *o sticlă* will normally get you one of whatever's available; draught beer is known as *halbă*.

Romania's best **wines** – and they are good – are the white Grasa from Cotnari, near Iaşi; Tamaioasa, a luscious, late-harvested Moldavian dessert wine; Fetească Neagră, the blackberryish reds from Dealu Mare, east of Ploieşti; and the sweet dessert wines from Murfatlar (notably Merlot and Cabernet Sauvignon, and white Muscat Ottonel). They can be obtained in most restaurants, while some places may just offer you a choice of red or white. Sparkling (*spumos*) wines from Alba Iulia and Panciu (north of Focşani) are very acceptable. Wine is rarely sold by the glass, but it does no harm to ask – *Serviţi vin la pahar?*

Coca-Cola, Pepsi and Romanian mineral water are omnipresent; Romanian **soft drinks**, such as Cappy or Frutti Fresh, are good thirst-quenchers, but only severe dehydration justifies resorting to the indigenous *sirop*.

The media

Western newspapers are almost impossible to track down in Romania, though the classier hotels usually have a small kiosk selling same-day or previous day's editions, while you can read week-old newspapers (and monthly magazines) at the British, American, French and German libraries in Bucharest.

Most of Romania's **newspaper offices** are in the Casa Presei Libere, north of central Bucharest. There are supposedly some 1600 titles nationwide, many of them **local**, and very few of any real worth. There are plenty of private **radio stations**, but for news most listeners tune into foreign stations, especially the BBC World Service (ⓦ www.bbc.co.uk/worldservice), Radio Canada (ⓦ www.rcinet.ca) and Voice of America (ⓦ www.voa.gov). **Romanian television** offers the standard diet of news, soaps and gameshows, and is rarely turned off in many homes and bars. Once restricted to two hours a day, with half of that devoted to Ceauşescu's feats – ironically, it was TV that played a crucial role in his overthrow (see p.69) – these days there is no shortage of programming. Like many of the foreign-language programmes on Romanian TV, films at the **cinema** are shown in their original language with Romanian subtitles.

Newspapers and magazines

Nationalist papers have a total circulation of around a million, but the biggest sellers are the sensationalist **tabloid** *Tineretul Liber*

41

(Free Youth) and the most useful, *România Liberă* (Free Romania).

Most of the very few **English-language publications** that exist are found in Bucharest; *Nine O'Clock* (🌐www.nineoclock .ro), a reasonably informed, though not particularly well-written, daily news sheet available free in hotels, and *Bucharest Business Week* (🌐www.bbw.ro), a standard business weekly with the occasionally enlightening article, are useful. Of the **listings magazines**, *Bucharest In Your Pocket* (🌐www.inyourpocket.com) is by far the most informative and up-to-date, while *Bucharest* – *What, Where, When*, has local editions for Braşov, Cluj, Iaşi and Timişoara.

Television

The **state channel** TVR isn't too bad, offering a reasonable mix of independent news and documentaries on two channels (TVR1 and TVR2), while commercial channels such as ProTV and Antena 1 do the soap/quiz/sport thing to varying degrees of success. Many people also now have access to **cable TV**, offering the standard foreign channels – BBC World, CNN, MTV and so on. Any decent hotel should have TV with cable or satellite TV.

Festivals

Romanian festivals fall into four groups: those linked to the Orthodox religion, with its twelve Great Feasts and hosts of lesser festivals; those marking events such as birth, marriage and death; those marking stages in the agricultural cycle; and secular anniversaries.

While the last are public holidays, and never change their **dates**, other festivals are less predictable. The Orthodox Easter is a moveable feast and still reckoned according to the Julian calendar, rather than the Gregorian calendar that's used in the West and for secular purposes in Romania. Rural festivals take place on a particular day of a month, the actual date varying from year to year, and they can also be advanced or delayed depending on the progress of the crops. Check dates at the cultural office in the county prefecture. Festivals specific to particular places are listed at the appropriate point in the Guide; the following is an overview.

Winter festivals

Christmas (*Crăciun*) and **New Year** (*Revelion*) celebrations are spread over the period from December 24 to January 7, and preparations often begin as early as December 6 (St Nicholas' Day) while on December 20, pigs are slaughtered for the forthcoming feasts. Groups of youths and children meet to prepare the festival costumes and masks, and to rehearse the *colinde* – allegorical songs wishing good health and prosperity for the coming year that are sung outside each household on **Christmas Eve** (*Ajun*), when the faithful exchange pastries called *turte*.

In Moldavia and Bucovina, processions follow the *Capră*, a goat-costumed dancer whose mask has a moveable lower jaw which he clacks in time with the music (to represent the death pangs of the old year). The masked carnival on December 27 in the Maramureş town of Sighet has similar shamanistic origins.

On **New Year's Eve** in rural areas, groups of *plugăraşi* (ploughmen) pull a plough festooned with green leaves from house to house, cutting a symbolic furrow in each yard while a *doină* (an ancient song) calling for good health and fecundity is recited. In Transylvania this is accompanied by carolling, for example at Arpaş and Sercaia in Braşov county. In Tudora and the villages around Suceava, and in Maramureş, New Year's greetings are delivered by the *buhai*, a friction drum that imitates the bellowing of a bull when horse hair is drawn through a hole in the membrane. This accompanies the *pluguşor*, a mime play featuring people masked as goats, horses and bears.

Although the official holidays end on January 2, villagers may keep celebrating through to **Epiphany** (*Bobotează*) on the 6th, when water is blessed in church and taken home in bottles for medicinal purposes, and horse races are staged in areas like the Wallachian plain and Dobrogea. The Huţuls and Lipovani, who follow the Julian calendar, celebrate Christmas on January 6. The final festivity in January is **Three Hierarchs' Day** on the 30th, celebrated with great pomp in Iaşi's Three Hierarchs' Church, which is dedicated to the saintly trio.

A review of Gorj county's folk ensembles and miners' brass bands – the **Enchanted Water Springs** or *Izvoare fermecate* – is held on the third Sunday of **February** in Târgu Jiu, winter conditions permitting. March is the time of **Lent**, and though few Romanians are nowadays devout enough to observe the fast, some rural folk still bake twisted loaves (*colaci*) on March 9, **Forty Saints' Day**, and take them to the village church to be blessed and distributed as alms. On one weekend during the month (decided at fairly short notice) an early spring festival, the **Kiss Fair**, takes place at Hălmagiu, providing the opportunity for villagers from the Apuseni and Banat regions to socialize and trade crafts.

Spring festivals

With the onset of spring in **April** and **May**, agricultural work begins in earnest. Urbanization and collectivization have both affected the nature of **spring festivals**, so that Reşiţa's **Spring Parade** (*Alaiul primaverii*) features firefighters and engineers as well as folklore ensembles in its parade of floats (first week in April). Village festivals have tended to conglomerate, so that perhaps a dozen smallish fetes have been replaced by a single large event drawing participants and visitors from across the region – for example, the **Flowers of the Olt** (*Florile Oltului*) at Avrig on

the second Sunday of April, attended by dozens of communities around Sibiu, some of whom wear the traditional Saxon jewellery of velvet and paste. Similarly, the **Girl Fair** at Gurghiu, on the second Sunday in May, is an occasion for villagers from the Gurghiul, Beica and Mureş valleys to make merry. For pomp and crowds on a larger scale, the **Pageant of the Juni** (see p.163) is held in Braşov on the first Sunday of May.

Though its exact dates vary, the **Orthodox Easter** (*Paşte*), the holiest festival of the Christian year, also falls in April or May. From Palm Sunday (*Floriile*), through the **Week of Sufferings** (*Săptămâna patimilor*) – during which, it's believed, souls will ascend directly to heaven – the devout fast, clean their houses, and attend church services, culminating in the resurrection celebration at midnight on Easter Saturday. The cry *Hristos o-nviat* ("Christ has risen") and the reply *Adevărat c-o-nviat* ("Truly he has risen") resound through the candlelit churches, overflowing with worshippers. Hard-boiled eggs are hand-painted on **Maundy** ("Great") Thursday with red dyes obtained from onion skin, to be given to friends and relatives on Easter Sunday and kept by the family icons; it's said that the devil cannot win as long as people go on singing carols at Christmas and painting eggs at Easter. With the exception of **Pentecost** or **Whitsun** (*Rosalia*), fifty days after Easter Sunday, other Orthodox festivals are nowadays less widely observed.

In southern Romania, there's a traditional belief still held by a minority that groups of mimes and dancers could work magic, and to this end selected young men were initiated into the **ritual of Căluş**. On **Whit Sunday**, an odd-numbered group of these *Căluşari* began their ritual dance from house to house, accompanied by a flag-bearer and a masked *Mut* (a mute who traditionally wore a red phallus beneath his robe and muttered sexual invocations), thus ensuring that each household was blessed with children and a bountiful harvest, and, if need be, exorcizing anyone possessed by the spirits of departed friends and family. *Căluş* rites are still enacted in some Oltenian villages, and the *Căluşari* meet to celebrate their dancing and musical prowess at Whitsun, starting with a parade in Slatina and then two days of performances in Caracal. There's a similar festival, the **Festival of the Căluşari** (*Căluşarul Transilvanean*), in Deva during the second week of January, which doesn't have any particular magical significance, being nowhere near the heartland of *Căluş* culture, but is nevertheless impressive. The Roman Catholic Székely hold their **Whitsun pilgrimage** to Csíksomlyó (near Miercurea Ciuc) on a date set by the Gregorian calendar. Once common practice, the ritual garlanding of the plough is now rare, although the **Festival of the First Ploughman** or Tânjaua (first Sunday of May) at Hoteni, in Maramureş, is similar.

The age-old **pastoral rites and feasts** marking the sorting, milking and departure of the flocks to the hills are still widespread throughout Maramureş and the Apuseni mountains during late April or early May, depending on local tradition and climatic factors. The best-known **Measuring of the Milk** festivals (*Sâmbra oilor*) occur on the first or second Sunday of May, at the Huta pass into Oaş and on the ridge of Măgura Priei; lingering snows, however, can delay the smaller festivals until early July.

Summer and autumn festivals

The **Cherry Fair** at Brâncoveneşti on the first Sunday of June anticipates other harvest festivals later in the month, and the round of great **summer fairs** known as **Târg** or **Nedeias**. In the days before all-weather roads, these events provided the people of remote highland villages with an annual opportunity to arrange deals and marriages. On the second Sunday of June, folk from some thirty Banat settlements attend the **Nedeia of Tălcăłşele** at Avram Iancu; another village with the same name is the base for the famous **Girl Fair of Mount Găina** (see p.248), held on the Sunday before July 20. The highlanders of Oltenia gather for the similar **Polovragi Fair** on July 15 or 20.

Other summer festivals perpetuate Romania's old customs and folklore: the light-hearted **Buying Back of the Wives** at Hodac, near Târgu Mureş, and the funereal declamation of *boccas* during **The King of the Fir Trees** (see p.258) at Tiha Bârgăului in the heart of fictional Dracula country (on the

second and third Sundays of June). Various **"summer folk holidays"** occur between June 21 (**Midsummer Day**) and June 29 (**St Peter's Day**); **Drăgaica**, the pagan pre-harvest celebration in the fields on Midsummer Day, is only practised in a few districts of southern Wallachia. The most widespread, however, is the **feast of St John the Baptist** (*Sânziene*) on June 24, celebrated with bonfires and wreaths of yellow flowers that are thrown over the houses. The regional diversity of folk costumes and music can be appreciated at events like Şomcuta Mare's pastoral **The Oak Tree** (*Stejarul*), or the larger **Rarău Mountain festival** at Ilişeşti, held on the first and second Sundays of July respectively.

August is probably the best month for **music**, with four major festivals. During the first week of the month, the **Songs of the Olt** at Călimăneşti in Wallachia draws musicians and folklore ensembles from all over Oltenia. On the first Sunday, people from Maramureş, Transylvania and Moldavia meet for the great **Horă at the Prislop Pass** in their finest costumes; a week later, the **Festival of the Ceahlău Mountain** is held at Durău near the shores of Lake Bicaz. The music of panpipes and the bands of Gorj county characterize the **Tismana Garden festival** where you can also find a wide range of handicrafts. This is held on August 15, the **Feast of the Assumption** or Dormition of the Virgin Mary (known as **Great St Mary's**), when there are many church festivals and pilgrimages across the country, notably at Moisei in Maramureş and Nicula, north of Cluj. Fundata's **Nedeia of the Mountains**, on the last Sunday of August, is the traditional gathering for the highlanders of the Braşov, Argeş and Dâmboviţa regions.

Reaping preoccupies many villages during September, giving rise to **harvest festivals**, although the custom is gradually declining. The timing of these varies with the crop, and from year to year, but you can usually rely upon **At the Vintage** at Odobeşti in the eastern Carpathians being held on the last Sunday. On the second Saturday of September, the remaining Saxons gather for the **Sachsentreffen** at Biertan. Earlier in the month, on the first Sunday, you can hear the panpipers of the northwest perform the

Rhapsody of the Trişcaşi at Leşu, in Bistriţa-Năsăud county. Many of the musicians here are shepherds, who compete with each other at **The Vrancea Shepherd's Long Pipe**, a festival held at Odobeşti on the third Sunday of November. Finally, **December 1** is Romania's **national day**, celebrated above all in Alba Iulia, scene of the declaration of union between Transylvania and the rest of Romania.

Sports and outdoor activities

Romania's sporting pedigree is strong, thanks largely to the exploits of the tennis player Ilie Nastase and the legendary gymnast Nadia Comaneci, both of whom achieved significant success and fame during the 1970s. Sporting triumph in the 1980s and 1990s came on the football field, with notable achievements by both the country's leading club side, Steaua Bucharest, and the national team, led by the mercurial Gheorghe Hagi.

Football

In 1986 **Steaua Bucharest** became the first team from behind the Iron Curtain to lift the **European Cup** (the Champions' League), defeating Barcelona on penalties. Although Inter Milan allegedly offered to build a Fiat car plant in Romania in order to get their hands on Gheorghe Hagi, players were only able to move freely to West European clubs after 1990: by 1992, nine of the national team were playing abroad.

Romania progressed to the quarterfinals of the **1994 World Cup**, a tournament at which **Gheorghe Hagi** was arguably the best player. Dubbed the "Maradona of the Carpathians" – as much for his temperament as for his magical left foot – Hagi is a legend in Romania; born in Constanţa, he played for the local side before transferring to Steaua Bucharest on the orders of Ceauşescu's son Valentin, who effectively ran the team. After the revolution, he moved to Real Madrid for £1.8m, and after the 1994 World Cup to Barcelona, before flitting around a succession of lesser European clubs.

Romania's involvement in both the **1998 World Cup** and the **Euro 2000 Championships** ended at the second round stage, their defeat to Italy in the latter marking the end of Hagi's international career – ignominiously,

and somewhat predictably, with a sending off. After failing to qualify for both the 2002 and 2006 World Cups, and the 2004 European Championships, the team comfortably qualified for the **2008 European Championships**, with the help of a talented young team featuring the likes of Cristian Chivu, Adrian Mutu and Cosmin Contra.

The **domestic game** is dominated by the three big Bucharest clubs: **Steaua** (traditionally the army team), **Dinamo** (the police and Securitate), and **Rapid** (rail workers), who regularly carve up the championship between them. Although few other clubs in Romania have the financial muscle to put a stop to this hegemony, the big three have still to make an impression in European club competition, though this is hardly surprising when their best players are continually sold abroad. Every town has its stadium (*stadion*), and you should have no problem catching a game. **Matches** are usually played on Saturdays from August to May, with a break from November to February, and **tickets** for league games cost roughly €2–4.

Outdoor activities

The Romanian countryside lends itself perfectly to a multitude of **outdoor activities**, from hiking, skiing and cycling in the

45

Carpathians to birdwatching in the Danube Delta – activities which can be done either individually or as part of a group tour.

Although two-thirds of Romania is either plains or hills and plateaux, the country's geography is dominated by **mountains**, which almost enclose the "Carpathian redoubt" of Transylvania, and merge with lesser ranges bordering Moldavia and Maramureş. Throughout these areas, there are opportunities to pursue several outdoor activities – hiking, skiing, caving and even

shooting rapids. The **Danube Delta** is a totally different environment, unique for its topography – of which only one tenth is dry land – and as a wildlife habitat that attracts some three hundred species of bird during the spring and autumn migrations. A wide number of tours and trips are offered by a host of agencies in the UK (see p.31), and, to a lesser degree, in North America (see p.32) and Australasia (see p.32).

For more on all these activities, see the "The Great Outdoors" colour insert.

Travel essentials

Addresses

Written as Str. Eroilor 24, III/36 in the case of apartment buildings, ie Street (Strada) of Heroes, number 24, third floor, apartment 36. Some blocks have several entrances, in which case this is also given, eg *scara B*. Each district of Bucharest has a *sector* number, while in some towns each district (*cartier*) is named. In small villages, houses simply have a number and no street name. Streets, boulevards (*bulevardul*), avenues (*calea* or *Şoseaua*) and squares (*piaţa*) are commonly named after national heroes like Stephen the Great – Ştefan cel Mare – or Michael the Brave – Mihai Viteazul – or the date of an important event, such as December 1, 1918, when Transylvania was united with the Old Kingdom.

Children

From a practical point of view, **travelling with children** in Romania will present no obvious problems. Most of the better-quality hotels are well disposed to catering for kids, whilst most restaurants (at least those of a decent standard) should be able to provide highchairs for younger children and babies. Most car rental firms provide child or baby seats for a small extra charge.

Kids also qualify for various **reductions**, depending on their age. Rail transport is free

for under-5s, and half-price for under-10s. On TAROM flights, children under 2 pay only ten percent, and those up to the age of 12 receive a 33-percent discount. In big coastal resorts and at Poiana Braşov there are **kindergartens** for the benefit of holiday-makers. A few train stations have a specially heated room for mothers with babies (*camera mama şi copilul*). You'd be well advised to bring **supplies** of nappies (diapers) and baby food. Local milk is not to be trusted – bring enough with you. Mamaia and Poiana Braşov offer the best **entertainments** for kids, but most large towns have a puppet theatre (*Teatrul de Păpuşi*).

Costs

Generally, costs are **low** in Romania. As anywhere, your biggest expenditure is likely to be your hotel room, though there are some budget alternatives when it comes to accommodation (see p.37). **Eating out**, even in the better restaurants, remains very afford-able (see p.39) and public transport is extremely cheap (see p.32). **Car rental**, however, is on a par with most other European countries. Museum **admission** charges are extremely low, the typical fee being between €1–2. Note that some of the major attractions – such as the Palace of Parliament and Peles Castle – levy a fee (often twice the amount it costs to actually get in) for the use of cameras/camcorders. The more expensive hotels, flights, car rental and excursions are sometimes priced in **euros**, but must usually be paid for in **lei**.

Crime and personal safety

Romania remains generally **safe**, and it's unlikely that you'll have any problems; violent crime against tourists is almost nonexistent and petty crime rare, while a few common-sense precautions should minimize the risk of theft. The major thing to watch out for is **pickpockets**, in particular on public transport in Bucharest, where thieves are adept at relieving tourists of their belongings; wearing a (hidden) moneybelt is advisable. Take care on overnight trains, shutting the door of your sleeper compartment as securely as you can (there are no locks). Otherwise, be aware of the self-styled **tourist police** who prey on tourists on the streets of Bucharest (see p.61).

Since the revolution, the **police** (*politia*) have been reformed to a certain extent, and are generally regarded as honest if ineffectual – though they continue to attract Western disapproval by abusing the rights of Gypsies, homosexuals and other citizens. Unfortunately, the **Romanian Information Service** (the SRI, still generally known as the **Securitate**) is still on the scene, although an obsession with anti-socialist activities long ago changed to a commitment to keeping the ruling elite in power. Environmental and human rights activists may still be harassed, but the SRI doesn't normally concern themselves with tourists.

If your **passport** goes missing while in Bucharest, telephone your consulate immediately; anywhere else, contact the police. Thefts and other losses can be reported to the police who will issue the paperwork required for insurance claims back home, though only slowly and with painstaking bureaucratic thoroughness. To **call the police** dial ☏955.

Culture and etiquette

Although **tipping** is not obligatory, it is polite to round the bill up to a convenient figure in restaurants and when taking a taxi. In common with much of the Balkans, **smoking** is commonplace and many restaurants still allow smoking throughout. However, an increasing number do have no-smoking sections, and it's always worth asking to see if that's the case. On trains, smoking is allowed only in corridors or vestibules; buses are smoke-free.

In public places, **toilets** are generally awful; in larger train stations, you'll have to pay for regularly cleaned facilities. Elsewhere, a few clean private toilets are appearing. In any case, you should carry a supply of paper. "*Barbaţi*" means men and "*Femei*" means women.

Electricity

220 volts; a standard continental adaptor enables the use of 13 amp, square-pin plugs.

Entry requirements

Citizens of the EU, US, Canada, Australia and New Zealand can enter Romania with just a passport and may stay in the country for up to ninety days. Similarly, most other European citizens can enter the country without a visa, though can only stay for thirty days. However, **visa requirements** do change, so it's always advisable to check the current situation before leaving home.

If you require a **visa extension** once in Romania, you can go to any county (*judeţ*) police headquarters or the office at Str. Luigi Cazzavillan 11, Bucharest (Mon, Thurs & Fri 8.30am–1pm, Tues 8.30am–1pm & 5.30–7pm; ☏021/650 3050).

Gay and lesbian travellers

The communist regime was relentlessly **homophobic**. Sexual relations between consenting adults of the same sex were illegal; offenders were jailed or forced to submit to "voluntary treatment", including electric shocks, drugs or even castration, unless they agreed to become an informer for the Securitate, a bait for other victims. The Constantinescu government, however, committed to adhering to international norms such as the European Convention on Human Rights, finally repealed the law against homosexuality in July 2000, despite church opposition.

The majority of the population remains largely **unsympathetic** towards the gay and lesbian community, and there are very few manifestations of gay life, even in Bucharest. That said, the first **Gay Pride** was held in Bucharest in 2005 and is now an annual event, usually taking place in May or June. **Accept** (PO Box 34–56, Bucharest, ☎021/252 1637, ⓦwww.accept-romania .ro), is a Bucharest-based organization involved in the promotion of gay and lesbian activities in Romania, and they also offer counselling and HIV testing services.

Health

No **vaccinations** are required for Romania, although having hepatitis A, polio and typhoid boosters would be wise if you're planning to stay in remote areas where hygiene can sometimes be an issue. There's a **reciprocal health agreement** between Romania and western countries (including the UK, US, Canada, Australia and New Zealand), so emergency treatment (excluding drugs) is free.

Summers can be blisteringly hot, particularly along the coast, so make sure you take a high-factor **sun cream**, and very strong **insect repellent** if visiting the Danube Delta. Conversely, inclement weather in the **mountainous regions**, particularly at higher altitudes, can present potential dangers – take appropriate clothing, sufficient provisions and equipment, and keep an eye on the weather. **Tap water** is safe to drink practically everywhere, though bottled water (*apă minerala*) is widely available. **Diarrhoea**, though, can be a problem, and any contact with **stray dogs**, as there's a very slight risk of **rabies**.

In case of minor complaints, go to a **pharmacy** (*farmacie*), where the staff are usually well trained and have the authority to prescribe drugs, and – in the big towns at least – may understand English, French or German. Although pharmacies are typically open Monday to Saturday from 9am to 6pm, most towns should have at least one that's open 24 hours – failing that, dial the emergency number displayed in the pharmacy window.

In Bucharest, the British and American embassies can supply the address of an English-speaking **doctor or dentist**, and there's a special clinic for treating foreigners. In **emergencies**, dial ☎961 or ask someone to contact the local casualty (*stația de salvare*) or first aid (*prim ajutor*) station, which should have ambulances. Each county capital has a fairly well-equipped county **hospital** (*spital județean*), but **hospitals** and health centres (*policlinics*) in smaller towns can be poor.

Insurance

Even though EU health care privileges apply in Romania, you'd do well to take out an **insurance policy** before travelling to cover against theft, loss, and illness or injury. Before paying for a new policy, check whether you are already covered by your home insurance policy or private medical scheme. A typical travel insurance policy usually provides cover for the loss of baggage, tickets and – up to a certain limit – cash or cheques, as well as cancellation or curtailment of your journey. Most of them exclude dangerous sports unless an extra premium is paid: in Romania, this could mean, for example, skiing or trekking.

Rough Guides travel insurance

Rough Guides has teamed up with Columbus Direct to offer you **travel insurance** that can be tailored to suit your needs. Products include a low-cost **backpacker** option for long stays; a **short break** option for city getaways; a typical **holiday package** option; and others. There are also annual **multi-trip** policies for those who travel regularly. Different sports and activities (trekking, skiing, etc) can be usually be covered if required.

See our website (ⓦwww.roughguides.com/website/shop) for eligibility and purchasing options. Alternatively, UK residents should call ☎0870/033 9988; Australians should call ☎1300/669 999 and New Zealanders should call ☎0800/55 9911. All other nationalities should call ☎+44 870/890 2843.

Internet

Internet access is readily available in just about every town in Romania, although many places are full of kids playing games, while connections can be dreadfully slow. It is cheap, though, costing around €1 per hour or less.

The useful site ⓦ www.kropla.com gives details of how to plug your laptop in when abroad, as well as phone country codes around the world, and information about electrical systems in different countries.

Laundry

There are several **launderettes** in Bucharest, but elsewhere they can be almost impossible to find; it's usually a choice between washing clothes yourself or paying a hotel to do it.

Mail

Most **post offices** are open Monday to Friday from 7am to 8pm, and on Saturdays from 8am to noon; like the red-painted mail boxes, they are marked *Poştă*. **Stamps** (*timbru*) and prepaid envelopes (*plic*) can be bought here. Sending mail home from Romania costs around €0.70 to overseas destinations – and takes about five days to Britain, two weeks to North America and Australasia.

Letters can be sent **poste restante** to main post offices in Romania: make sure they're addressed Officiul Poştal *no. 1, poşte restante*, followed by the name of the town, and that the recipient's last name is underlined. To collect letters, you'll have to show your passport and pay a small fee. Important messages should be sent by postcard, as letters from abroad can go missing if they look as if they might contain dollars. American Express also offer their cheque/ cardholders a poste restante service at their office in Bucharest.

Maps

Nearly all the best **maps** of Romania are published outside the country, but they are available through most good map outlets, including a few shops in Romania itself. The country map published by the ADAC (the German motorists' association) is very detailed (at 1:500,000), as is the Szarvas/ Kárpátia/Top-O-Gráf atlas (including city

plans), which can be bought at Shell fuel stations in Romania (and through Stanfords bookstore in the UK). Other quality maps are produced by Falk (1:1,000,000), Cartographia (1:750,000), and Szarvas/Kárpátia/ Dimap (1:700,000), along with a Kümmerley & Frey map of Romania and Bulgaria (1:1,000,000), and The GeoCenter Euromap (1:800,000), which includes Moldova. Cartographia and Falk also publish good maps of **Bucharest**, while Top-O-Gráf/Freytag & Berndt produce maps of Transylvanian cities such as Cluj. DIMAP also publishes maps of most tourist areas.

The maps produced by the **national tourist offices** are fairly poor, though just about adequate for **motoring**, but the campsite and cabana maps are useful for hikers. There are also good **hiking maps** of the major mountain massifs, by Editura pentru Turism and Abeona in Bucharest and Editura Focul Viu in Cluj (available from bookstores as well as tourist offices). Hikers should also look out for the booklet *Invitaţie Ón Carpaţi*; the text is Romanian, but it contains detailed maps of the region's 24 main hiking areas, showing trail markings, huts, peaks, and so on (reproduced in *The Mountains of Romania* – see p.476). In **Bucharest**, the best place for maps is the Librăria Noi bookshop at B-dul. Bălcescu 18 (see p.95).

Money

Romania's unit of **currency** is the leu (abbreviation RON) – meaning "lion" (plural **lei**). Coins (*bani*) come in denominations of 1, 5, 10 and 50; and there are notes of 1, 5, 10, 50, 100 and 500 lei. The **exchange rate** is currently around L3.50 to €1, L5 to £1, and L2.50 to US$1 – for current rates, check the websites ⓦ www.xe.net/currency or ⓦ www .oanda.com/converter.

It is best to **change money** at one of the private exchange offices (*casa de schimb valuta*) found in most towns; in Bucharest and several other major cities, some are open 24 hours. Expect long queues when changing money in **banks** (*banca*) – which are generally open Monday to Friday between 9am and 3 or 4pm. As a rule, neither exchange offices nor banks charge commission. Make sure that you get rid of any unwanted lei before you leave the country, as it's unlikely you'll be able to change them once outside Romania.

If taking **cash**, a modest denomination of US dollar bills is advisable, though euros and pound sterling are also accepted in most places. **Cash machines** (*Bancomats*) are ubiquitous, even in the smallest towns, including many railway stations. **Credit cards** are accepted in most of the better hotels, restaurants and shops.

By far the most recognized **travellers' cheques** are American Express, either sterling or dollars. Although it may not be required in all instances, make sure you have your passport when changing travellers' cheques (or cash). Also note that, in some banks, you may have to show the receipt from the issuing bank, or another cheque to prove continuity of serial numbers.

Opening hours and public holidays

Opening hours in Romania are notoriously unreliable and weekends can be like the grave, with a surprising number of restaurants and cinemas closing mid-afternoon or not opening at all. **Shops** are generally open from 9 or 10am to 6 or 8pm on weekdays, with department stores (*magazin universal*) and some food stores opening from 8am to 8pm Monday to Saturday and from 8.30am to 1pm on Sunday. If you're trying to sort out flights, visas or car rental, be aware that most **offices** are closed by 4pm.

Museums (*muzeu*) are generally open Tuesday to Sunday from 9am to 5pm or 10am to 6pm, though some do also close on Tuesdays. For the opening hours of **post offices**, **banks** and **pharmacies**, see the relevant sections above.

Public holidays in Romania are on **January 1 and 2** (New Year); **May 1** (Labour Day); **December 1** (National Day) and **December 25 and 26** (Christmas). **Good Friday** and **Easter Monday** are not formal holidays, but women are usually given the days off to shop and cook.

Phones

Most **public phones** are orange **cardphones**, used both for internal and international calls. **Phone cards** (*cartelă telefonică*) currently cost €2 and €5; insert them with

the gold lozenge foremost and facing upwards, and after a few seconds you should get a sign indicating that you can start dialling; at the end, wait until the message *scoateţi cartela* indicates you can remove the card. Calls are most expensive from 7am to 7pm Monday to Friday and 7am to 3pm on Saturday, and cheapest from 11pm to 7am daily. All towns and many villages have a **Romtelecom office** (usually open weekdays 6.30am–10pm, sometimes seven days a week), where the staff will connect your call. You'll normally pay the three-minute minimum in advance, and the balance afterwards.

Calls to Britain **cost** about €1 a minute, and to North America and Australasia €2; from card phones, they cost a bit more, so the cards don't last long. In Bucharest, discounted international calls can also be made at NexCom, at Str. Academiei 35–37.

The main **mobile phone providers** in Romania are Connex, Cosmorom and Orange. All mobile numbers are designated by a phone code beginning with ☎07. Calling a mobile from within Romania, you must dial all the numbers; calling from abroad, you need to drop the "0". For further information about using your phone in Romania, check out ⊛www.telecomsadvice .org.uk/features/using_your_mobile_abroad.

In addition, ⊛www.kropla.com has a useful section on phone country codes around the world.

Time

Romania is two hours ahead of **GMT**, seven hours ahead of **Eastern Standard Time** and ten ahead of **Western Standard Time**: clocks go forward one hour for the summer at the same time as other European countries (from the last Sunday of March to the last Sunday of September).

Tourist information

Ensure that you pick up as much **information** as possible before you leave your own country, as getting hold of it in Romania is nigh on impossible. The **Romanian tourist board** has a site at ⊛www.romaniatourism .com – with a UK branch at 22 New Cavendish St, London W1G 8TT (☎020/7224 3692) and another at 355

Lexington Ave, 19th Floor, New York, NY 10017 (☏212/545 8484). Incredibly, **Bucharest** doesn't have a tourist office, though there are an increasing number in many towns; elsewhere, most places should have an agency (usually more concerned with selling package trips) where you might be able to extract some basic advice, and possibly a map.

Travellers with disabilities

Very little attention has been paid to the needs of people with disabilities in Romania, and there's no sign of any change in attitude. Getting around is a major problem, as public transport is often inaccessible and cars with hand controls are not available from the car rental companies. The only place where facilities for disabled people are likely to be anything like comprehensive are in some of the classier hotels. Perhaps the best solution is to book a stay in a spa, where there should be a degree of level access and some awareness of the needs of wheelchair users.

Make sure you carry a **prescription** for any drugs you need, including the generic name in case of emergency, and spares of any special clothing or equipment, as it's unlikely you'll find them in Romania.

Women travellers

It's rare for Romanian men to subject **female tourists** to **sexual harassment**. As independent women travellers are few and far between, they're likely to be accorded some respect but also viewed with amazement, particularly in rural areas. Romanians (both male and female) are highly tactile, so you may find yourself being prodded more than you care for. Most trouble is alcohol-fuelled, so it's best to avoid going alone to any but the classiest bars, especially on weekend evenings. Within earshot of other people, you should be able to scare away any local pest by shouting *lasaţi-ma in pace!* ("Leave me alone!") or calling for the *politia*.

Work

Opportunities for working in Romania are relatively few. The most traditional form of work abroad, **teaching English**, is one option. The British Council (🌐www.britishcouncil .org/work/job) recruits TEFL teachers and provides information about study opportunities and teacher development programmes in Romania. **International House** (🌐www .ihworld.com) also offers TEFL training and recruits for teaching positions. They have branches in Bucharest, at Str. Lanariei 93–95 (☏021/335 4490, 🌐www.ih.ro), and in Braşov, at Str. Lunga 8 (☏072/880 8619). The **TEFL** website (🌐www.tefl.com) is also worth a look.

You could also get involved in one of the country's **summer work camps** or **field research** projects. **Earthwatch Institute** (🌐www.earthwatch.org) is a long-established international charity with environmental projects and **archeological digs** in Romania. **Volunteers for Peace** (🌐www.vfp.org), meanwhile, is another non-profit organization offering summer work camps, including work in Romanian **orphanages**.

Guide

Guide

Bucharest

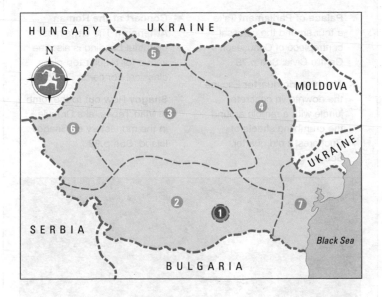

CHAPTER 1 # Highlights

✳ **National Art Museum** The country's biggest and best collection, the highlight of which is the spectacular Gallery of Romanian Medieval Art. See p.69

✳ **Museum of the Romanian Peasant** A superb display of traditional textiles, ceramics, carvings and replica buildings in the city's most enjoyable museum. See p.77

✳ **Palace of Parliament** Take a tour around the colossal centrepiece of Ceauşescu's Centru Civic. See p.78

✳ **The historic quarter** Escape the downtown concrete jungle with a ramble around the crumbling streets of Bucharest's old quarter. See p.82

✳ **Herăstrău Park** Combine a leisurely stroll through Bucharest's largest and greenest park with a cruise on the adjoining lake. See p.86

✳ **Village Museum** A varied assemblage of dwellings, churches, windmills and other structures from all over Romania, and the best place in the capital to buy craft souvenirs. See p.86

✳ **Concert at the Roman Atheneum** The city's most beautiful building is also the venue for regular top-class classical concerts. See p.93

✳ **Snagov** Row out to the tomb of Vlad Ţepeş, aka Dracula, in the monastery on Snagov Island. See p.99

▲ Cişmigiu Gardens

Bucharest

For many people, initial impressions of **BUCHAREST** (Bucureşti), a sprawling, dusty city of some two million people, are less than favourable. As Romania's centre of government and commerce and site of its main airport, most visitors to the country will find themselves passing through the city at some point, but its chaotic jumble of traffic-choked streets, ugly concrete apartment blocks and monumental but mostly unfinished communist developments are often enough to send most travellers scurrying off to the more obvious attractions further north. Yet it's a city that rewards patience, with a raft of terrific museums, first-rate restaurants and bars, and, behind the congested arteries, some superb architecture and abundant greenery.

The architecture of the old city, with its cosmopolitan air, was notoriously scarred by Ceauşescu's redevelopment project in the 1980s, which demolished an immense swathe of the historic centre – including many religious buildings and thousands of homes – and replaced it with a concrete jungle, named the **Centru Civic**. The centrepiece of this development was an enormous new palace for the communist leader, now known as the **Palace of Parliament**, which is Bucharest's premier tourist attraction. The palace aside, other sites that justify a visit to the city include the superbly renovated **National Art Museum**, housing a fine collection of Romanian medieval art, the **Village Museum**, an assemblage of vernacular buildings garnered from Romania's multifarious regions, and, best of all, the **Museum of the Romanian Peasant**, with its marvellous exhibits on peasant life and several superbly reconstructed buildings. There's plenty of greenery to explore, too – most obviously the **Cişmigiu Gardens** in the heart of the city, or the more expansive **Herăstrău Park**, with its large lake, to the north. Bucharest is also the only Romanian city that can boast of a clutch of international-class restaurants, as well as a bar and club scene that not only now rates among the best in the Balkans, but is also attracting a growing number of world-class DJs.

From Bucharest, there are excellent train and road connections to the rest of the country, but local bus and train services to the towns and villages in the immediate vicinity are often limited or tortuous. There are, however, some enjoyable visits to be had outside the capital, most notably the lake and monastery at **Snagov** (see p.99), the palace at **Mogoşoaia** (see p.100) and the village of **Clejani** (see p.101), known for its outstanding Gypsy music.

Some history

According to legend, Bucharest was founded by a shepherd called **Bucur**, who built a settlement in the Vlăsia forest. It was recorded as a nameless "citadel on the Dâmboviţa" in 1368, and named as Bucharest in an edict from the time of Vlad the Impaler (ruled 1456–76). Over the centuries, both

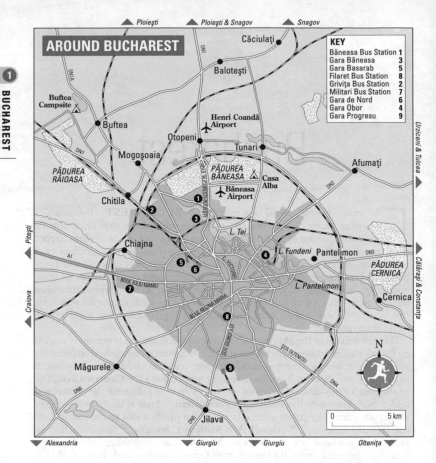

AROUND BUCHAREST

▲ Ploieşti   ▲ Ploieşti & Snagov   ▲ Snagov

Căciulaţi

Baloteşti

Buftea Campsite

Buftea

Henri Coandă Airport

Mogoşoaia

Otopeni

Tunari

Afumaţi

PĂDUREA RĂIOASA

PĂDUREA BĂNEASA   Casa Alba

Băneasa Airport

Chitila

L. Tei

Chiajna

L. Fundeni   Pantelimon

PĂDUREA CERNICA

BOUL IULIU MANIU

L. Pantelimon

Cernica

Măgurele

ŞOS OLTENIŢEI

N

Jilava

0   5 km

▼ Alexandria   ▼ Giurgiu   ▼ Giurgiu   Olteniţa ▼

KEY

Băneasa Bus Station	1
Gara Băneasa	3
Gara Basarab	5
Filaret Bus Station	8
Griviţa Bus Station	2
Militari Bus Station	7
Gara de Nord	6
Gara Obor	4
Gara Progresu	9

Târgovişte (see p.113) and Bucharest have served as the **Wallachian capital**, but the latter finally secured its claim in 1659 – its position at the convergence of the trading routes to Istanbul outweighing the defensive advantages of Târgovişte's location in the Carpathian foothills.

As the boyars (nobles) moved into the city they built **palaces** and **churches** on the main streets radiating from the centre; these streets were surfaced with timber baulks and known as "bridges" (*pod*). Despite earthquakes and periodic attacks by Turks, Tatars, Austrians and Russians over the course of its history, the city continued to grow and to modernize. New **boulevards** were driven through the existing street pattern in the 1890s, after the style of Haussmann's Paris, and they still form a ring road and the main north–south and east–west axes of the city today. Most of the major buildings, such as the **Romanian Atheneum** and the **Cercul Militar**, were designed by French or French-trained architects and built in the years immediately before World War I.

It was around this time that the city was dubbed the "Paris of the East", as much for its hectic and cosmopolitan social scene as for its architecture. The Romanian aristocracy was among the richest and most extravagant in Europe, but this lifestyle depended on the exploitation of the poor, and in Bucharest the two coexisted in what Ferdinand Lasalle described as "a savage hotchpotch", with beggars waiting outside the best restaurants, and appalling slums within a few steps of the elegant boulevards.

By 1918, the city's population had grown to 380,000 and roads such as Podul Mogoşoaiei, Podul de Pământ and Podul Calacilor were widened, paved and renamed as the Calea Victoriei, Calea Plevnei and Calea Rahovei respectively, in honour of the battles of the 1877–78 War of Independence from Turkey. After World War II, the city was ringed with ugly apartment buildings, first in areas such as "Red Griviţa", which the Allies had bombed flat (aiming for the rail yards), then expanding into the surrounding countryside.

A massive **earthquake** in 1977 reduced large parts of the city to rubble and left over 1500 people dead. While this prompted the construction of several major city projects, including a new metro system and an airport, it also provided Ceauşescu with the perfect excuse to implement his megalomaniac vision for the city. In 1984, and in order to create a new **Centru Civic**, Ceauşescu had most of the area south of the centre levelled, which entailed the demolition of thousands of homes, as well as churches, a monastery and a hospital. To this day, scores of unfinished projects litter the landscape and seem likely to scar the city for many years to come.

In December 1989, the city found itself at the centre of the most violent of the popular **revolutions** sweeping across Eastern Europe that year; nearly three hundred people were killed in the uprising. Ceauşescu's execution did not, however, mark a complete end to the violence, and the following summer similar scenes erupted when miners from the Jiu Valley were brought in to stamp out student protests against the government, which resulted in a further seventy deaths.

Whilst the post-communist era has brought back conspicuous consumption to the city, evidenced by the proliferation of luxury hotels, glossy shops full of designer clothes, and restaurants, bars and clubs, few Bucharestians can afford to indulge in them. This has particularly been the case in the last decade or so, and while there appears to have been little real tangible development, as capital of one of the two newest members of the EU, Bucharest's profile is certainly on the up, with tourist numbers slowly on the increase.

Arrival

While city transport, at least round the centre, is pretty good during the day, it's almost nonexistent at night, and street lighting throughout Bucharest leaves much to be desired. It is therefore best to avoid arriving late at night, unless you're willing to take a taxi to your hotel (for more on which, see p.63). Both of Bucharest's **airports** are on the main road north of the city and linked to the centre by express bus; the main **train station** is a little way out of the centre to the northwest, but is well connected to the downtown area by both bus and metro. There is no central bus station, but instead several smaller ones scattered around the city, all in the suburbs and mainly serving the local villages.

By air

Bucharest has two international airports, both located on the DN1 road north of the city: the main one, **Henri Coandă** (often still referred to as Otopeni), is 16km north of the centre. There are several exchange counters (with poor rates) and a cash machine here, as well as half a dozen car rental outlets (see Listings, p.96). The cheapest way to the city is by **express bus** #783 (5.30am–11.50pm

Mon–Fri every 15min, Sat & Sun every 30min; journey time 40–50min; €2, return ticket only), which departs for Piața Unirii, stopping at Băneasa Airport, Piața Presei Libere, Arcul de Triumf, Piața Victoriei, Piața Romană and Universității along the way. Buses leave from outside the domestic arrivals hall, one floor below international arrivals; buy your ticket from the booth by the stop.

Avoid all offers of a **taxi** from anyone within the terminal (you will almost certainly be ripped off), and head down to the exit where Fly Taxi – the only company licensed to operate from the airport – can transport you to the centre for around €8. Otherwise, you can call one of the reputable city companies (see p.63), who will charge you around half the price of Fly Taxi.

Băneasa Airport, 8km closer to the centre, is where the low-cost airlines and many internal flights land; from here you can also catch express bus #783, as well as buses #131 and #335 to Piața Romană, or bus #205 to the Gara de Nord.

By train

Virtually all international and domestic services terminate at the **Gara de Nord**, a much cleaner and less intimidating place than it used to be, thanks to a heavy security presence and a negligible entrance fee (payable if you don't possess a ticket). Outside, however, you may be accosted by any number of oddball characters, variously offering transport, accommodation or some other service – just ignore them and walk away. The station is also where many of the street kids congregate, though they are generally harmless and easily ignored. **Luggage** can be stored at the *bagaje de mână* (roughly €1.50; open 24hr) on the concourse opposite platforms 4 and 5. Local trains (mostly Personals, the very slow ones) terminate at the **Gara Basarab** (700m northwest of Gara de Nord or one metro stop towards 1 Mai), **Gara Obor**, northeast of the centre at the end of B-dul. Ferdinand I (trolley buses #69 and #85 to the town centre), and **Gara Progresu**, on the southern outskirts (bus #116). **Gara Băneasa**, north of Piața Presei Libere, is used mainly by a handful of summer trains to the coast.

It's a thirty-minute walk from the Gara de Nord to the city centre; head right along Calea Griviței to reach Calea Victoriei, the city's main north–south axis. Alternatively, you could take the metro (line M3) to Piața Victoriei, where you can change onto line M2 to reach Piața Universității, the nearest stop to the heart of the city, and Piața Unirii, in the Centru Civic. There are hordes of taxi drivers waiting to pounce as you leave the station, but be very careful only to use a reputable company (see p.63), which shouldn't cost more than a couple of euros. Buses and trams from the Gara de Nord run around the centre rather than straight through it.

By road

Driving in Bucharest is not recommended for those of a nervous disposition, but if you are arriving by road, beware of potholes, cyclists and horses and carts, to name just a few hazards. Approaching from Transylvania on the DN1 you'll pass both airports before reaching the Șoseaua Kiseleff, an avenue which leads directly to the centre. The approach from Giurgiu (the point of entry from Bulgaria) on the DN5 is uninspiring, with a long run through high-rise suburbs until B-dul. Dimitrie Cantemir finally reaches the Piața Unirii. Likewise, the A1 motorway from Pitești and the west brings you in through serried ranks of apartment blocks before reaching the Cotroceni Palace. The DN3 from the coast leads through the modern suburb of Pantelimon before reaching the older districts along B-dul. Carol I.

Bucharest doesn't possess a central **bus station**, which makes locating buses for specific destinations almost impossibly difficult. Instead, it has a smattering of stations on the edge of town which primarily serve the local villages: Filaret, on Piaţa Filaret (in Bucharest's first railway station, built in 1869), which sends buses south and southeast towards Giurgiu and Olteniţa; Băneasa, on B-dul. Ionescu de la Brad 1, serving Snagov, and Ploieşti to the north; Militari, B-dul. Păcii (Metro Păcii or bus #785), for points west; and Griviţa, Şos. Chitilei 221 (at the Mezeş terminal of tram #45), serving Târgovişte. Maxitaxis (for Braşov, Piteşti, Sibiu and other destinations) depart from a small bay opposite Gara de Nord, whilst there's another departure point at Str. Ritmului 35, to the northeast of town near Gara Obor.

Information and tours

Getting **information** in Bucharest is nigh on impossible, a situation not helped by the absence of a tourist office. Your best bet, therefore, is the highly informative and on-the-ball *Bucharest In Your Pocket*, available free from hotels and bookshops, and published bi-monthly. Otherwise, there is a stack of other, more straightforward business-orientated **listings magazines**, none of which particularly excels. The best **city map** of Bucharest is that published by Amco Press, which incorporates a separate public transport map, and Cartographia, which also covers some of the outlying areas, such as Mogoşoaia. *Nine O Clock*, the (poorly written) main English-language newspaper, is available free from major hotels and airline offices.

The best of the city's **sightseeing tours** is run by Jolly Tours (☎021/303 3796, ⊛www.jollytours.ro), located inside the lobby of the *Athénée Palace Hotel*; three- or four-hour themed trips (€25–40) include the services of a guide, transport and museum entrance fees – a minimum of two people is required and bookings should be made at least a few hours in advance. Longer

Bucharest hassles

While Bucharest is much safer than it used to be, there are a couple of hassles that it's as well to be aware of during your stay. If at some stage you're approached by anyone (usually two or three men) demanding to see your **passport**, don't be too alarmed. Ignore their demands and don't give them anything – simply saying that all your documents are at the hotel should be enough to put them off – and walk off confidently; these self-styled tourist police are nothing more than con men, and cowards at that. If they persist, insist that they accompany you to your hotel or the nearest police station, which should be enough to discourage them.

You should also be extremely vigilant where your **belongings** are concerned, in particular at the Gara de Nord, where bags can suddenly disappear, and on the buses, where a standard trick is to slit bags open, thus emptying some of the contents. Keep your bag close to your chest and eyes peeled.

Another fairly minor hassle is **stray dogs**. During Ceauşescu's systematization programme of the 1980s, many houses were bulldozed and owners had little choice but to kick their beloved canines out onto the street; this resulted in the little beasts multiplying like nobody's business, roaming the streets scavenging for food, and generally making a nuisance of themselves. If at any time you feel threatened, either walk on slowly and confidently or mime throwing a stone and they'll back off; do not run. While the chances of a nip on the ankles are slim, confrontations with these dogs can be unpleasant and intimidating.

tours, including excursions to other parts of the country, can be arranged upon request.

City transport

Public transport is a little chaotic, but has improved over recent years, and remains extremely cheap. Apart from some express buses on the main axes, most **bus** and **tram** routes avoid the central zone, though this is covered by the **metro system**. However, you may still find yourself walking a lot – no great hardship in this city of green, picturesque backwaters. Beyond the downtown thoroughfares, many roads are still so poor that buses and trams seem set to rattle themselves to pieces, and trolley buses frequently slip from the wires and stall.

Buses and trams

There is a flat fare of about €0.50 on **trolley buses** (*troleibuz*), **trams** (*tramvai*) and most **buses** (*autobuz*), all of which run from around 5am until 11.30pm. You need to buy tickets in advance from street kiosks (roughly Mon–Fri 6am–8/9pm, Sat 7am–7pm, Sun 7am–2.30pm) and punch them in one of the machines once aboard. Day passes cost €2 and weekly passes €5, both representing excellent value. It costs about double the standard fare to travel on the city's express buses, using tickets with a magnetic strip, also bought in advance from the kiosks (day and weekly passes not valid). In addition, private **minibuses (maxitaxis)** operate along the major arteries; these too charge about double the standard bus fare, the current rate being posted in the window. Ticket inspectors are ubiquitous, and travelling without a valid ticket will result in a fine of around €10.

The metro

Looking much older than its thirty-odd years, the Bucharest **metro** is not the most user-friendly system in the world – maps and signposting are somewhat confusing, lighting is poor and announcements are barely audible, but it is clean, cheap and safe. Trains run from 5.30am until 11.30pm, with magnetic tickets costing around €1 for two rides to €2.50 for ten. Running east–west, the M1 line (shown in red on maps) was built to serve the new working-class suburbs; the second line, the M2 (blue), runs north–south straight through the

Key bus and trolley-bus routes	
North–south	along B-duls Magheru and Bălcescu: #783 (express)
	along Calea Dorobanţilor: #131 and #301
East–west	(north of the centre)
	from Gara de Nord along B-dul. Dacia (via Piaţa Romană): #79 and #86
	along B-dul. Dacia: #133
	along B-duls Regina Elisabeta and Carol I (via the university): #66 (Metro Obor), #69 (Gara Obor).
	from Gara de Nord to Str. Baicului (Gara Obor): #85
East–west	(south of the centre)
	along Splaiul Independenţei and B-dul. Unirii: #104 (Opera–National Stadium), #123 (Gara de Nord–Vitan).
East	from Piaţa Rosetti: #63 (to Metro Obor).

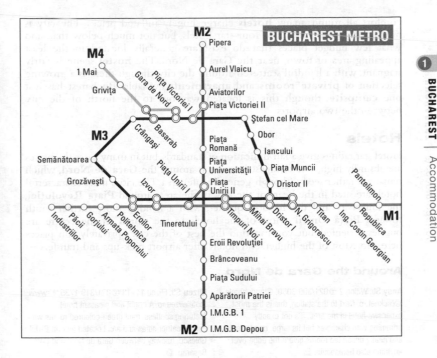

centre; and the third, M3 (yellow), does a complete loop to and from the Gara de Nord; the M4 (green) links Gara de Nord with 1 Mai in the northwest, although you'll have little reason to use this line.

Taxis

Bucharest's **taxi** drivers have a deserved reputation for harassing and ripping off foreigners, and though the situation is not nearly as bad as it once was, you should still be wary. Avoid any driver who approaches you at the airport or train station, and extra care should also be taken around Piaţa Universităţii and Piaţa Unirii. As a rule, trustworthy companies have their name and phone number plastered across the top or side of the taxi, while the fare (*Pornire* – starting price, and *Pret km* – price per km) should be displayed on the driver and passenger doors. Your safest bet is to stick to one of the following companies: Taxi Cobalescu (⊕021/9451), Cristaxi (⊕021/9461), Meridian (⊕021/9444) and Perozzi (⊕021/9631), each of which should have an operator who speaks English. The same can't be said for the majority of drivers, so have the address written down just in case. Prices are still remarkably cheap, and you should expect to pay around €0.30–0.50 per kilometre.

Accommodation

The range and quality of accommodation in Bucharest has improved markedly in recent years, and while this has meant higher standards of comfort all round, many **hotels** charge hugely inflated prices. The city is now awash with three- and four-star hotels, but not much below that, and what few budget places that do exist are generally located in the least appealing area of town, near the Gara de Nord. The **hostel** scene is fairly stagnant, with a handful scattered around the city, though there is a growing selection of **private rooms** and **apartments** available. Bucharest has just one **campsite**, though this is located way out to the north of the city between the two airports.

Hotels

Hotel star ratings give a fair indication of standards, but in many cases the prices are absurdly high. The cheapest location is around the **Gara de Nord**, which remains a rather seedy (though generally safe) area. The city's most characterful hotels are sited in the heart of the city, in the areas around **Piaţa Revoluţiei**, the university and the historic quarter, with a handful more further south towards **Piaţa Unirii**. Most of the hotels to the **north** of the centre are business-oriented, but you can find the best of the city's privately run places here, too. Most of the higher-end hotels offer airport pick-ups and transfers.

Around the Gara de Nord

Andy Str. Witing 2 ☎021/300 3050, ✉andyhotels @clicknet.ro. Next to the station, this is the most expensive hotel in the area; it's not exactly brimming with character, but its large, comfortable and neatly decorated rooms give it the edge over anything else hereabouts. ❼
Cameliei Str. Cameliei 37 ☎021/318 3726, ℻318 3730. Tucked away behind the market, this good little budget hotel offers decent rooms, though they are somewhat conservative and careworn. Breakfast is extra. ❹
Cerna B-dul. D. Golescu 29 ☎021/311 0535, ℻311 0721. Directly opposite the *Andy*, this is far from the friendliest place in town, but its rooms (with and without bathrooms) are respectable enough and it's reasonably cheap. ❹–❺

Elizeu Str. Elizeu 11–13 ☎021/319 1735, ☜www .hotelelizeu.ro. A bright and pleasant hotel, featuring spotless, mint green-coloured rooms with comfy leather sofas and a/c. Located just off B-dul. Golescu, midway between Gara de Nord and Gara Basarab. ❻
Ibis Calea Griviţei 143 ☎021/300 9100, ☜www .ibishotel.com. Injecting a dash of colour into this otherwise grim area, this is much like any other Ibis in the world: neat, clean and functional rooms with standard TV, mini-bar and a/c. ❼
Marna Str. Buzeşti 3 ☎021/310 7074, ☜www .hotelmarna.ro. One of the better options in this area, both for price and cleanliness. Singles and doubles, with and without bathrooms, at a range of prices, but with trams rattling by, it's fairly noisy. ❸–❹

Around Piaţa Romană and Piaţa Revoluţiei

Athénée Palace Hilton Str. Episcopiei 1–3, on the northern side of Piaţa Revoluţiei ☎021/303 3777, ☜www.hilton.com. Despite some stiff competition, this remains the city's most opulent and best-serviced hotel, with sumptuous rooms (doubles €330) and first-rate facilities, including sauna, gym and a gorgeous basement pool. It's the most famous hotel in Romania, with a long history of intrigue and espionage. ❾
Capitol Calea Victoriei 29 ☎021/315 8030, ☜www .hotelcapitol.ro. A fine nineteenth-century building, though the rooms are disappointing, as are the broom-cupboard sized bathrooms. There's little to distinguish between the two- and three-star rooms

(in terms of both quality and price), so you may as well opt for the former. Triples available too. ❽
Carpaţi Str. Matei Millo 16 ☎021/315 0140, ☜www.hotelcarpatibucuresti.ro. The best-value budget hotel in the downtown area, and a great central location to boot; numerous different rooms, including singles and doubles with and without bathrooms and TVs. Unusually welcoming staff, too. ❹–❺
Howard Johnson Plaza Calea Dorobanţilor 5–7 ☎021/201 5000, ☜www.hojoplaza.ro. Enormous glass tower rising above the surrounding concrete anonymity (plenty of which you can see from the vertiginous top floors). As comfy as the rooms are,

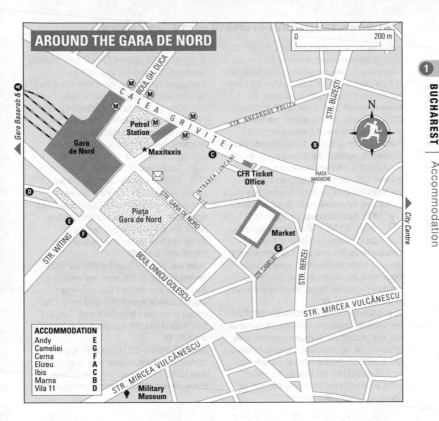

AROUND THE GARA DE NORD

0   200 m

Gara Basarab & **A**

C A L E A   G R I V I T E I

BDUL GH. DUCA

M M M M M

STR. GHEORGHE POLIZU

STR. BUZEȘTI

N

Petrol
Station M

Gara
de Nord

★ Maxitaxis

C

B

PIAȚA
MATACHE

CFR Ticket
Office

City Centre

D

Piața
Gara de Nord

STR. GARA DE NORD

INTRAREA LUNCANI

STR.

STR. CAMELI

E

F

STR. WȚING

BDUL DINICU GOLESCU

Market

G

STR. BERZEI

STR. MIRCEA VULCĂNESCU

ACCOMMODATION
Andy	E
Cameliei	G
Cerna	F
Elizeu	A
Ibis	C
Marna	B
Vila 11	D

STR. MIRCEA VULCĂNESCU

⚓ Military
Museum

---

there's nothing particularly exciting about them.
Doubles cost around €200. Also houses two
extremely classy restaurants. **9**

Lido B-dul. General Magheru 5–7 ☏ 021/314
4930, ⊛ www.lido.ro. Located on a busy downtown
thoroughfare, this stylish 1930s Art Deco hotel
offers large, bright rooms (doubles €240) furnished
in classical style. Sauna, gym, pool and Jacuzzi. **9**

Moxa Str. Mihail Moxa 37B ☏ 021/650
5555, ⊛ www.hotelmoxa.com. Very classy
boutique hotel just off Calea Victoriei with plush,
comfortable rooms (doubles €190) complete with
large plasma TV screens and Wi-Fi. Gym, sauna and
fitness suite and a delicious Swedish buffet
breakfast round things off superbly. **9**

Novotel Calea Victoriei 37B ☏ 021/312 5114,
⊛ www.novotel.com. Another glass behemoth,
this one distinguished by a faux Neoclassical
facade – a replica of the Old National Theatre

which stood here before being bombed during
World War II. The rooms (doubles €280), meanwhile,
are as plush as anything else in the city, while
there's a golf simulator and swimming pool for
active types. **9**

Opera Str. Ion Brezoianu 37 ☏ 021/312 4855,
⊛ www.hotelopera.ro. Lovely, albeit overpriced,
hotel in a super location next to the Cişmigiu
Gardens; the attractive, a/c and originally furnished
rooms (doubles €140) incorporate some thoughtful
touches, such as tea- and coffee-making facilities,
neat desk lamps, and pictures of old Bucharest on
the walls. **9**

Ramada Majestic Calea Victoriei 38–40
☏ 021/310 2720, ⊛ www.ramadamajestic.ro. A
magnificent building, though the rooms (doubles
€240) are surprisingly modest and really rather
dull given that it's one of the most expensive
places in town. **9**

Between Piaţa Universităţii and Piaţa Unirii

Horoscop B-dul. Dimitrie Cantemir 2 ☏021/335 4031, ✉office@horoscop-turism.ro. Modern and shiny place, if a little uninspiring, on the south side of Piaţa Unirii. Smallish but comfortable a/c rooms, and surprisingly quiet given the location. ❾

Intercontinental B-dul. N. Bălcescu 4 ☏021/310 2020, ⓦwww.intercontinental.com. This towering city landmark remains the businessmen's and journalists' hotel of choice – it was from where many watched the revolution unfold – and has all the class you'd expect of a five-star. Immaculate rooms (doubles €260), marble-tiled bathrooms and top-notch facilities, including sauna, gym and (very small) rooftop pool; the citywide views are unbeatable. ❾

🏃 **K&K Hotel Elisabeta** Str. Slănic 26 ☏021/311 8631, ⓦwww.kkhotels.com. Part of the hip Austrian-run chain of luxury boutique hotels, this is as cool as it gets; superbly designed rooms (doubles €160) – warm brown/beige tones, lots of smooth wood and soft armchairs – state-of-the-art amenities and service of the highest order. ❾

Hostel Miorita Str. Lipscani 12 ☏021/312 0361, ⓦwww.hostel-miorita.ro. Not really a hostel at all, this very pleasant and unassuming pension-style establishment has six homely a/c, en-suite rooms, and is terrifically located in this characterful old town street just off Calea Victoriei. Somewhat oddly, breakfast is payable for one half of those staying in a double. ❺

Marriott Grand Hotel Calea 13 Septembrie 90 ☏021/403 1000, ⓦwww.jwmarriott.ro. Originally conceived by Ceauşescu as a hotel for Communist Party hacks, this is now one of the most sumptuous establishments in town. Over 400 rooms (doubles €240) of unbridled luxury, each with a separate bath and shower; it also boasts a couple of high-class restaurants, a sports bar (see p.92) and a small shopping precinct. Bus #385. ❾

🏃 **Rembrandt** Str. Smărdan 11 ☏021/313 9315, ⓦwww.rembrandt.ro. This tall, narrow building conceals sixteen beautifully conceived rooms (doubles €120). Gorgeous wood furnishings – including the floor and panelling behind the bed – set the tone, along with sumptuous beds, etched glass windows and Tiffany-style lamps. ❾

Suter Inn Str. Aleea Suter 3 ☏021/337 3939, ⓦwww.suterinn.ro. This warm and welcoming guesthouse near the Carol Parc has elegant rooms furnished throughout in bold red and black colours (even down to the toilet seat). Tram #17 from Piaţa Unirii to Str. Xenofon, then up the steps and left. ❼

Tania Str. Şelari 5 ☏021/319 2758, ⓦwww.taniahotel.ro. Pleasant small hotel located in a quiet part of the old town, with stylish, sunny rooms, all with a/c and Internet. Good value. ❼

North of the centre

Casa Victor Str. Emanoil Porumbaru 44 ☏021/222 5723, ⓦwww.casavictor.ro. A pleasant private hotel with twenty tastefully decorated rooms in a quiet residential street just five minutes' walk from the Aviatorilor metro. ❼

Crowne Plaza Str. Poligrafiei 1 ☏021/224 0034, ⓦwww.bucharest.crowneplaza.com. Top-drawer hotel in the no-man's-land to the north beyond Piaţa Presei Libere. Superb facilities including pool, fitness suite, sauna and tennis courts. Double rooms around €200. Bus #331 from Piaţa Lahovari. ❾

Floreta de Aur Str. Aviator Popa Marin 2 ☏021/230 6496. Great-value place frequented in the main by athletic types using the adjoining sports facilities; big square rooms (singles, doubles and triples), each with fridge, phone and TV. Hidden away behind the swimming pool. ❺

Irisa Str. Banu Mantu 24 ☏021/223 4965, ⓦwww.irisa.ro. Fairly close to both the Gara de Nord and Piaţa Victoriei, this accomplished place holds enormous, immaculately furnished rooms (doubles €120) but, like so many hotels in the city, it's way overpriced. ❾

🏃 **Residence** Str. Clucerului 19 ☏021/223-1978, ⓦwww.residence.com.ro. Located in a pleasant, leafy street running parallel to Şos. Kiseleff (near the Arc de Triumf), this is one of Bucharest's best small hotels. Elegantly furnished with wrought-iron beds, desks and chairs, carved wooden cupboards, wall pictures and plants. Delightful. ❽

Sky Gate Calea Bucureştilor 283 ☏021/203 6500, ⓦwww.skygatehotel.ro. Typically sterile and very expensive airport hotel, almost exclusively geared towards business folk. Doubles around €170. Convenient if flying in late or stopping over for the night. ❾

Sofitel Piaţa Montreal 10 ☏021/318 3000, ⓦwww.sofitel.com. Catering largely to conference members from the Exhibition Centre nearby, this is the best of the top-end hotels in this rather anonymous part of the city. Doubles around €170; airport transfer included in the price. ❾

Triumf Şos. Kiseleff 12 ☎021/222 3172, ☎223 2411. A huge red-brick building in the indigenous neo-Brâncovenesc style, set in parkland (with tennis courts) just off this main boulevard. There's still a whiff of the state-owned about this place, manifest in the phenomenally dull rooms – singles and twins, all with showers – and antiquated bathrooms, but the location is lovely and there are few cheaper options in this part of town. ❼

Hostels

There is a handful of excellent small **hostels** in the city, all of which are open year-round. Booking ahead is advisable in the summer months. Pretty much all of these hostels offer a discount for stays of longer than a week. Note that none of these hostels has representatives at the train station.

Alex Villa Str. Avram Iancu 5 ☎021/313 3198. A quiet, simple hostel east of Universităţii, with a/c dorms sleeping between four and ten; free Internet access but laundry and breakfast are not included in the price. Take bus #85 from the station to the junction of B-dul. Carol I and Piaţa Protopopescu, from where it's a two-minute walk. Dorm beds for €10.

🏃 **Butterfly Villa** Str. Dumitru Zosima 82 ☎021/224 1918, ⓦwww.villa-butterfly .com. Small, cheerful and colourful hostel with cosy six-bed dorms. Bus #282 from Gara de Nord (on Calea Griviţei) to Piaţa Domenii (sixth stop), then cross the road, walk back 50m and it's on your right. Dorm beds for €10, including breakfast and laundry (all very neatly done by the staff).

Funky Chicken Str. General Berthelot 63 ☎021/312 1425, ☎funkychickenhostel@hotmail .com. Cracking central location just fifteen minutes' walk from Gara de Nord, near the Cişmigiu Gardens. This friendly, informal place has four-, six- and eight-bed dorms. Breakfast not included, but self-catering facilities are available. Cheapest of the bunch at €8 for a dorm bed.

Vila 11 Str. Institutul Medico Militar 11 ☎072/2495 900, ☎vila11bb@hotmail.com. Welcoming and quiet family-run B&B-style place in a peaceful back-street just five minutes' walk from the station. Four- and six-bed dorms as well as doubles with and without bathroom. Exit Gara de Nord by platform one, head north along B-dul. Golescu for 200m, turn left up Str. Vespasian, and it's your first left again. Dorm beds €12 per person, double rooms €28/40. Price includes a pancake breakfast.

🏃 **Villa Helga** Str. Mihai Eminescu 184 ☎021/212 0828, ⓦwww.rotravel.com /hotels/helga. The original Bucharest hostel has moved location but is all the better for it, especially with its lovely garden terrace. Homely and person-able, with clean and bright six- and eight-bed dorms and one double. Bus #79, #86 or #133 from Gara de Nord to Piaţa Gemini (along B-dul. Dacia) – from here cross the road and walk up Str. Vitorului and it's on your right. Dorm bed for €12 (€11 for IYHF members), which includes laundry, Internet and breakfast.

Private accommodation and homestays

In recent years, numerous agencies have emerged offering **private rooms** and **apartments**, and these generally represent good value. Two of the better ones are Relax Comfort Suites, at B-dul. Nicolae Balcescu 22 (☎021/311 0210, ⓦwww.relaxcomfort-suites.ro or ⓦwww.bucharest-accommodation.ro), and Professional Reality (☎021/232 4006, ⓦwww.accommodation.com.ro), both of which have centrally located rooms and apartments from around €40 per day. It's unlikely that you'll be approached at the Gara de Nord by locals offering a room, but do exercise caution if you decide to take up this option.

Camping

Bucharest's one **campsite**, the Casa Alba (open year-round; ☎021/230 5203, ⓦwww.casaalba.ro), is situated out towards Henri Coandă Airport in the Pădurea Băneasa woods at Aleea Privghetorilor 1–3. It's a large, well-guarded site with excellent facilities, including a wide range of cabins (❸–❹), some with showers, cooking amenities and postal services; there's also a snack bar on site, and a restaurant (the *Casa Alba*) nearby. To get there, take bus #301 from Piaţa Romană (or #783 if coming from Henri Coandă) and get off at the Băneasa restaurant stop, the fifth one after Băneasa Airport.

The City

The heart of the city is the **Piaţa Revolutiei**, site of the old Royal Palace and the scene of Ceauşescu's downfall. It lies halfway along Bucharest's historic north-south axis, the Calea Victoriei, which is still the main artery of city life. Buses heading north and south, however, use the scruffy boulevards east of Calea Victoriei; the main junction along them is the **Piaţa Universităţii**, scene of major events immediately after the 1989 revolution.

Many of the city's sights are within walking distance of these two squares. Just to the south lies the **historic centre**, a pleasant antidote to the noisy, modern surrounds, and which is currently in the throes of a major regeneration project. Beyond this, across the River Dâmboviţa, is the contrasting cityscape of Ceauşescu's compellingly monstrous **Centru Civic**, whose centrepiece, the extraordinary **Palace of Parliament**, is the city's main tourist attraction. Just west of the centre are the **Cişmigiu Gardens**, a tranquil space and a popular place for assignations.

For a taste of the old atmosphere of the city, you need to wander north and west of the gardens past the vine-covered facades, to suburbs where life retains a village-like slowness and intimacy. North from Piaţa Revoluţiei, beyond Piaţa Victoriei, lies Bucharest's best museum – the **Museum of the Romanian Peasant** – and further north still, along Şoseaua Kiseleff, is **Herăstrău Park**, the city's largest green space and location of the marvellous **Village Museum**.

Piaţa Revoluţiei and around

Piaţa Revoluţiei (Square of Revolution), a large, irregularly shaped square sliced down the middle by Calea Victoriei, was created in the 1930s to ensure

▲ Calea Victoriei

The fall of the Ceauşescus

Romania's revolution was the most dramatic of the popular revolts that convulsed Eastern Europe in 1989. On the morning of December 21, 1989, a staged demonstration – organized to show support for the **Ceauşescu** regime following days of rioting against it in Timişoara – backfired. Eight minutes into Ceauşescu's speech from the balcony of the Central Committee building, part of the eighty-thousand-strong crowd began chanting "Ti-mi-şoa-ra, Ti-mi-şoa-ra"; the leader's shock and fear were televised across Romania before transmissions ceased. From that moment, it was clear that the end of the Ceauşescu regime was inevitable. Though the square was cleared by nightfall, larger crowds poured back the next day, emboldened by news that the army was siding with the people in Timişoara and Bucharest. Strangely, the Ceauşescus remained inside the Central Committee building until midday, when they scrambled aboard a helicopter on the roof, beginning a flight that would end with their **execution** in a barracks in Târgovişte, on Christmas Day.

The revolution was tainted by having been stage-managed by the **National Salvation Front (FSN)** that took power in the name of the people. The FSN consisted of veteran communists, one of whom later let slip to a journalist that plans to oust the Ceauşescus had been laid months before. Among the oddities of the "official" version of events were Iliescu's speech on the Piaţa Revoluției at a time when "terrorist" snipers were causing mayhem in the square, and the battle for the Interior Ministry, during which both sides supposedly ceased firing after a mysterious phone call. Given the hundreds of genuine "martyrs of the revolution", the idea that it had been simply a ploy by Party bureaucrats to oust the Ceauşescus was shocking and potentially damaging to the new regime – so the secret police were ordered to mount an investigation, which duly concluded that while manipulation had occurred, the Russians, Americans and Hungarians were to blame.

a protective field of fire around the Royal Palace, in the event of revolution. While Romania's monarchy was overthrown by other means, the square fulfilled its destiny in 1989, when the Ceauşescus were forced to flee by crowds besieging Communist Party headquarters; two days of fighting left the buildings around the square burnt out or pockmarked with bullet holes – with the conspicuous exception of the Central Committee building, which was at the centre of the storm. Most of the edifices around the square have since been restored, giving Piaţa Revoluției a more purposeful air.

The Royal Palace and National Art Museum
The most imposing of the buildings surrounding the Piaţa Revoluției is the former **Royal Palace**, which occupies most of the western side of the square. When the original single-storey dwelling burnt down in 1927, the king, Carol II, decided to replace it with something far more impressive. The surrounding dwellings were razed in order to build a new palace, with discreet side entrances to facilitate visits by Carol's mistress, Magda Lupescu, and the shady financiers who formed the couple's clique. However, the resultant sprawling brownstone edifice has no real claim to elegance and the palace was spurned as a residence by Romania's postwar rulers, Ceauşescu preferring a villa in the northern suburbs pending the completion of his own palace in the Centru Civic.

Since 1950, the palace has housed the **National Art Museum** (Muzeul Naţional de Artă; Wed–Sun; May–Sept 11am–7pm; Oct–April 10am–6pm; €3) in the Kretzulescu (south) wing. During the fighting in December 1989, this building – along with the Central University Library (see p.73) – was the most seriously damaged of the city's cultural institutions, and over a thousand pieces

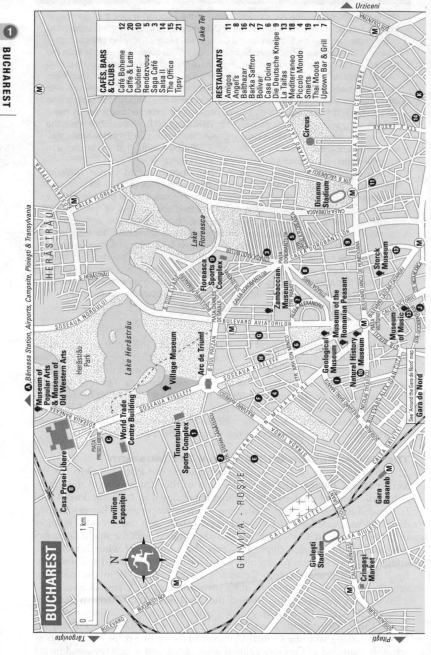

BUCHAREST

▲ Urziceni

Lake Tei

CAFÉS, BARS & CLUBS
Café Boheme 12
Caffe & Latte 20
Dubliner 10
Rendezvous 5
Saga Café 3
Salsa II 14
The Office 15
Tipsy 21

RESTAURANTS
Amigos 11
Angel's 8
Balthazar 16
Barka Saffron 2
Bolivar 17
Casa Doina 6
Die Deutsche Kneipe .. 9
La Taifas 13
Mediterraneo 18
Piccolo Mondo 4
Smarts 19
Thai Moods 1
Uptown Bar & Grill ... 7

Circus

Dinamo Stadium

Lake Floreasca

Floreasca Sports Complex

Zambaccian Museum

Storck Museum

Museum of Music

Geological Museum

Museum of the Romanian Peasant

Natural History Museum

Arc de Triumf

Village Museum

HERĂSTRĂU

Herăstrău Park

Lake Herăstrău

World Trade Centre Building

Tineretului Sports Complex

Museum of Popular Arts & Museum of Old Western Arts

Casa Presei Libere

Pavilion Expozitei

GRIVIŢA - ROŞIE

Giulesti Stadium

Cringasi Market

Gara Basarab

Gara de Nord

See 'Around the Gara de Nord' map

SOSEAUA KISELEFF

SOSEAUA NORDULUI

BULEVARD AVIATORILOR

CALEA FLOREASCA

CALEA DOROBANTILOR

CALEA GRIVIŢEI

CALEA GIULESTI

SOSEAUA STEFAN CEL MARE

0   1 km

N

▲ Bǎneasa Station, Airports, Campsite, Ploiesti & Transylvania

▲ Târgoviște

▲ Pitesti

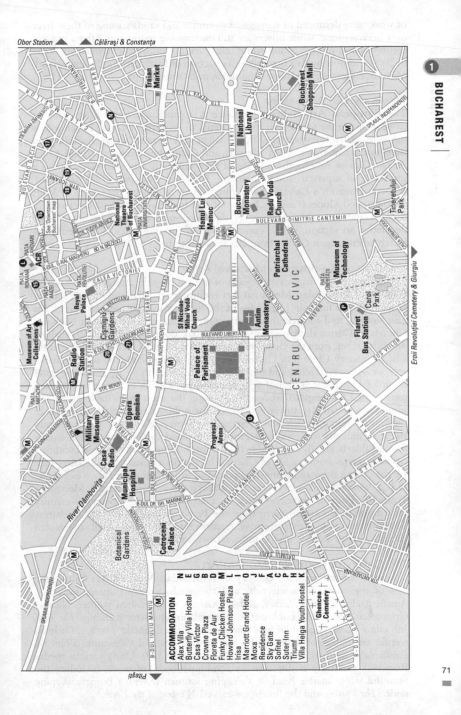

Obor Station ▲ ▲ Călărași & Constanța

Traian Market

Bucharest Shopping Mall

National Library

Bucur Monastery

Radu Vodă Church

BULEVARD DIMITRIE CANTEMIR

Hanul Lui Manuc

National Theatre of Bucharest

Patriarchal Cathedral

Museum of Technology

Tineretului Park

ACR

Royal Palace

St Nicolae Mihai Vodă Church

Antim Monastery

CIVIC

Carol Park

Filaret Bus Station

Museum of Art Collections

Radio Station

Cișmigiu Gardens

BULEVARD LIBERTĂȚII

Palace of Parliament

CENTRU

Military Museum

Opera Română

Casa Radio

Progresul Arena

Municipal Hospital

River Dâmbovița

Botanical Gardens

Cotroceni Palace

Ghencea Cemetery

ACCOMMODATION
Alex Villa N
Butterfly Villa Hostel E
Casa Victor G
Crowne Plaza B
Floreta de Aur D
Funky Chicken Hostel M
Howard Johnson Plaza L
Irisa I
Marriott Grand Hotel O
Moxa J
Residence F
Sky Gate A
Sofitel C
Suter Inn P
Triumf H
Villa Helga Youth Hostel K

Eroii Revoluției Cemetery & Giurgiu ▶

▲ Pitești

BUCHAREST

71

of work were destroyed or damaged by gunfire and vandals; some of these have now been repaired, while others are still undergoing restoration. After a massive reconstruction project taking some ten years, the museum reopened its doors in 2000, and now holds a marvellous collection of European and Romanian art. Moreover, there are excellent English captions throughout.

The European Art Gallery

The **European Art Gallery** (entrance A1) contains an impressive array of work spanning the fourteenth to the twentieth centuries. Divided by schools, it has particularly fine paintings from Italian and Spanish artists, including an exceptional *Crucifixion* by Da Messina, and Cano's beautifully mournful *Christ At The Column*. Among the line-up of predominantly lesser-known artists is a sprinkling of superstar names, including El Greco (*Adoration of the Shepherds*), Rubens (*Portrait of a Lady*), and a painting apiece by Sisley (*The Church in Moret in Winter*) and Monet (*Camille*). Look out, too, for Peter Brueghel's spectacularly detailed and gruesome *Massacre of the Innocents*. No less impressive is the decorative art section, which contains one of the museum's oldest items, the Reichsadlerhumpen Goblet from Bavaria, dating from 1596.

The Gallery of Romanian Medieval Art

Comprising works from every region of the country, the museum's exhaustive **Gallery of Romanian Medieval Art** is quite spectacular, and the one section to see if pushed for time. Highlights of the first few halls include a fresco of *The Last Supper*, a mid-fourteenth-century composition retrieved from St Nicholas' Church in Curtea de Argeş, and a carved oak door from 1453 with shallow figurative reliefs from the chapel of Snagov Monastery (which no longer exists). The Monastery Church in Curtea (see p.121) is represented by some remarkably well-preserved icons and fresco fragments, while there are also some quite beautiful Epitaphios, liturgical veils embroidered on silk or velvet which were usually used for religious processions. Among the most memorable pieces is a sumptuous gilded Kivotos (a vessel used for holding gifts) in the shape of an Orthodox church, which was presented to Horez Monastery by Constantin Brâncoveanu, and some exquisite, miniature wood-carved processional crosses from Moldavia, chiefly remarkable for the astonishing detail contained within – typically, scenes from the life of Christ. The standout items from the latter halls are the church door and iconostasis retrieved from Cotroceni Palace (see p.84), and a wood-carved iconostasis by Brâncoveanu from Arnota Monastery. Trumping both of these, however, is a six-metre-high, nineteenth-century carved walnut iconostasis taken from the Prince Şerban Church in Bucharest. The workmanship is extraordinary, featuring, in the finest detail, angels and cherubs, double-headed eagles, and warriors on horseback.

The Gallery of Romanian Modern Art

Up on the second floor, the **Gallery of Romanian Modern Art** features the best of the country's nineteenth- and twentieth-century painters, including Aman, Andreescu and Pallady, and Romania's most revered painter, Nicolae Grigorescu (see p.111). Look out for his brilliant character paintings *The Turk, Jew with a Goose, Gypsy Girl from Gherghani* and the dramatic *The Spy*. There's a terrific assemblage of sculpture, by Storck, Paciurea and Constantin Brâncuşi, Romania's one truly world-renowned artist (see p.128). Using various media, Brâncuşi's versatility is displayed in a sublime body of work, including the beautiful white marble head of a sleeping woman (*Sleep*), a bronze, weeping nude (*The Prayer*), and the limestone-carved *Wisdom of the Earth*.

Communist Party Headquarters

The southeastern corner of Piaţa Revoluţiei is dominated by the **former Communist Party Headquarters**, a Stalinist monolith that now houses government offices. The famous balcony where Ceauşescu delivered his last speech is surprisingly near ground level, and quite unmarked by bullet holes. Ironically, it was from the same spot, two decades earlier, that Ceauşescu had drawn cheers of approval for his denunciation of the Soviet invasion of Czechoslovakia, and made his vow that Romania would defend its own independence – casting himself as a "maverick communist" whom Western leaders could embrace. It was a delusion that persisted almost until the end; as Romanians point out, the honorary knighthood bestowed on Ceauşescu by Buckingham Palace in 1978 was only revoked after the revolution began. There are now two very contrasting memorials dedicated to those who died in the revolution: directly in front of the headquarters is a marble **memorial** with the inscription *Glorie Martirilor Nostri* ("Glory to our Martyrs"). Just across the way, and more controversially – as much for its brute ugliness than anything else – a nameless triangular column shoots upwards with what looks like a bird's nest sprouting from its upper reaches (it's known locally as the "Olive on a Stick"). Below, the semicircular wall is inscribed with the names of those who perished.

Piaţa Enescu and around

Piaţa Enescu sits just to the north of Piaţa Revoluţiei, and is notable for a couple of historically and culturally important buildings. Its northern side is filled by the **Athénée Palace Hilton Hotel**, which, since it was built in 1912, has been one of the most prestigious hotels in Bucharest. For decades the hotel was also a notorious hotbed of espionage, beginning in the 1930s when the liveried staff and almost all the characters who populated the lobby spied for the king's police chief, for the Gestapo or for British Intelligence. Symbolic of that fevered, corrupt era, Bucharest's elite would sometimes party here through the night while police were shooting strikers in the "Red" Griviţa district only a kilometre or so away. During the early 1950s the hotel was extensively refurbished as an "intelligence factory", with bugged rooms and tapped phones, to reinforce the reports of its informers and prostitutes.

To the east stands the **Romanian Athenaeum** (Ateneul Român), a magnificent Neoclassical structure built in 1888 almost entirely from funds generated from the city's citizens, after the original patrons ran out of money. Take a look inside at the rampantly *fin-de-siècle* dome decorated with lyres or, better still, try and catch a concert by the resident George Enescu Philharmonic Orchestra (see p.93). To the south is the **University Library**, totally gutted in December 1989 but now rebuilt. Glance upwards at the surrounding residential buildings, however, and you'll see that many of these are still quite heavily pockmarked with bullet holes. Just behind the library, at Str. Rosetti 8, is **Theodor Aman's House**, one of many "memorial houses" of notable artists dotted around the city. Aman (1831–91) trained in Paris before returning to be the first director of the Bucharest Art College. A somewhat academic painter, he was a leading member of the group of Francophile intellectuals (with fellow Romanians the painter Gheorghe Tattarescu and the sculptor Karl Storck) that dominated Bucharest's cultural life in the late nineteenth century. The house, finally undergoing major restorative work, was built in 1868 to Aman's own designs and decorated by himself and Storck. When it reopens (2009 at the earliest), expect to see a number of family portraits as well as some finely sculpted pieces, wooden chests and tables.

Southern Calea Victoriei

Originally built in the late seventeenth century as a wood-paved avenue named Podul Mogoşoaiei, **Calea Victoriei** ("Avenue of Victory") has been Bucharest's most fashionable street since wealthy boyars first built their residences along it. The arrival of the boyars encouraged Bucharest's most prestigious shops to open along the avenue and, after it was repaved and took its present name in 1918, strolling along the avenue became *de rigueur*, causing the writer Hector Bolitho to remark that "to drive down the Calea Victoriei between twelve and one o'clock will prove you a provincial or a stranger". Along the street were "huddles of low, open-fronted shops where Lyons silk and Shiraz carpets were piled in the half-darkness beside Siberian furs, English guns and Meissen porcelain", while lurking in the side streets were starving groups of unemployed, lupus-disfigured beggars and dispossessed peasants seeking justice in the capital's courts.

The avenue still displays marked contrasts: at its northern end near the Piaţa Victoriei, it seems verdant and sleepy with touches of Old-World elegance, while to the south it becomes an eclectic jumble of old apartment buildings, glass and steel facades, and shops selling cakes and Western couture – still the setting for a promenade around noon and in the early evening.

A short walk south along the avenue from Piaţa Revoluţiei, the **Creţulescu Church** (Biserica Creţulescu) fronts a tangle of streets which wend west towards Cişmigiu Gardens. The church – high and narrow with mock arches, bricks laid in saw-toothed patterns around the towers and elaborate carvings over the entrance – is built in the style created by Constantin Brâncoveanu, a seventeenth-century ruler of Wallachia who set out to forge a distinctive national genre of architecture (see p.131). It was paid for in 1720 by the boyar Iordache Creţulescu and his wife Safta, Brâncoveanu's daughter. Sadly, little remains of its frescoes by Tattarescu, or of the one on the porch, which features scenes from the apocalypse. Seriously damaged during the fighting in December 1989, the church exterior has now been restored, as has the Humanitas building next to it.

Further south, just beyond the currently defunct *Continental Hotel*, the **Pasajul Victoriei** ("Victory Passage") sneaks one block further east to Str. Academiei and the smoke-blackened **Enei Church**, built in 1702; the church is also known as the Dintr-o zi or "(Made) In One Day" church, as that's precisely how long it took to erect. Back on Calea Victoriei, the street continues down past several upmarket hotels to the noisy junction with B-dul. Regina Elisabeta, Bucharest's main east-west axis. Dominating the area is the Neoclassical **Cercul Militar** ("Army House"), which replaced the previous monastery church of Sărindar in 1912. It was originally built to cater to the social, cultural and educational needs of the Romanian army, and remains an important centre for military activity. Across B-dul. Regina Elisabeta, an alleyway just beyond *Pizza Hut* slips off to the courtyard of the picturesque **Doamnei Church** (Biserica Doamnei), built in 1683 under the orders of Princess Maria, wife of Prince Şerban Catacuzino. With renovation of the church almost complete, it's now possible to view the gloomy interior frescoes, while, architecturally, the most impressive aspect is the porch, featuring a thick-set stone portal and octagonal stone pillars, the first of their kind in Bucharest.

A short walk further down Calea Victoriei is Bucharest's **police headquarters**, now screened by a tall fence after it was stormed by a mob in 1990, an attack Iliescu used as his pretext for calling in the miners to smash the student opponents (see p.443). Directly opposite the headquarters, an inconspicuous portal leads into the **Pasajul Villacros** ("Villacros Passage"), whose glass roof and gracefully curved arcade of shops give an idea of why Bucharest once claimed to be the "Paris of the East", although its grandeur has faded badly over

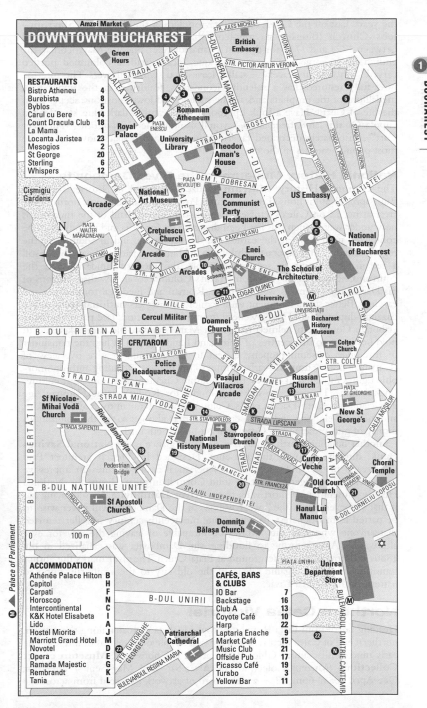

DOWNTOWN BUCHAREST

Amzei Market

Green Hours

British Embassy

RESTAURANTS
Bistro Atheneu	4
Burebista	8
Byblos	5
Carul cu Bere	14
Count Dracula Club	18
La Mama	1
Locanta Jaristea	23
Mesogios	2
St George	20
Sterling	6
Whispers	12

Royal Palace

Romanian Atheneum

PIAŢA ENESCU

University Library

Theodor Aman's House

STRADA C. A. ROSETTI

Cişmigiu Gardens

Arcade

National Art Museum

PIAŢA REVOLUŢIEI

Former Communist Party Headquarters

US Embassy

PIAŢA WALTER MĂRĂCINEANU

Creţulescu Church

STRADA CAMPINEANU

Enei Church

National Theatre of Bucharest

Arcade

Arcades

Subways

The School of Architecture

CAROL I

STRADA EDGAR QUINET

University

PIAŢA UNIVERSITĂŢII

Cercul Militar

Doamnei Church

B-DUL

Bucharest History Museum

B-DUL REGINA ELISABETA

CFR/TAROM

Coltea Church

STRADA EFORIE

Police Headquarters

STRADA LIPSCANI

Pasajul Villacros Arcade

Russian Church

PIAŢA SF GHEORGHE

Sf Nicolae-Mihai Vodă Church

STRADA MIHAI VODĂ

New St George's

River Dâmboviţa

STRADA SAPIENŢEI

STR. STAVROPOLEOS

National History Museum

Stavropoleos Church

STRADA LIPSCANI

Choral Temple

Pedestrian Bridge

STR. FRANCEZA

Curtea Veche

Old Court Church

B-DUL NAŢIUNILE UNITE

SPLAIUL INDEPENDENŢEI

STR. FRANCEZA

Hanul Lui Manuc

0   100 m

Sf Apostoli Church

Domniţa Bălaşa Church

B-DUL CORNELIU COPOSU

PIAŢA UNIRII

Unirea Department Store

B-DUL UNIRII

BULEVARDUL DIMITRIE CANTEMIR

ACCOMMODATION
Athénée Palace Hilton	B
Capitol	H
Carpati	F
Horoscop	N
Intercontinental	C
K&K Hotel Elisabeta	I
Lido	A
Hostel Miorita	J
Marriott Grand Hotel	M
Novotel	D
Opera	E
Ramada Majestic	G
Rembrandt	K
Tania	L

Patriarchal Cathedral

STR. GHEORGHE GEORGESCU

BULEVARDUL REGINA MARIA

CAFÉS, BARS & CLUBS
IO Bar	7
Backstage	16
Club A	13
Coyote Café	10
Harp	22
Laptaria Enache	9
Market Café	15
Music Club	21
Offside Pub	17
Picasso Café	19
Turabo	3
Yellow Bar	11

Palace of Parliament

the years. East off the Calea, on Str. Stavropoleos, is the diminutive **Stavropo-leos Church** (Biserica Stavropoleos) that gives the street its name. Built between 1724 and 1730 for the first Phanariot ruler, Nicolae Mavrocordat, the church has a gorgeous, almost arabesque, facade, with a columned portico carved with delicate tracery – stalks, leaves and stylized flowers. The interior, now fully restored, has a splendid iconostasis, featuring, in the upper part, medallions of the prophets and, in the middle and lower portions, scenes from the life of Christ. Have a look up, too, at the beautiful dark blue, star-flecked cupola. On this same street, at no. 3, you'll also find the *Carul cu Bere* ("The Beer Cart"), an ornately decorated tavern dating from 1875 that's now one of the most popular eateries in the city (see p.91).

National History Museum to the River Dambovita

The **National History Museum** (Muzeul National de Istorie; Tues–Sun 9am–5pm; €1.50) is housed in the former Post Office building, just north of the river at no. 12 on Calea Victoriei. A much-needed overhaul of the museum is now under way, though this has been dragging on for years and is unlikely to be completed until 2009 at the earliest. In the meantime, and in addition to the regular schedule of temporary exhibitions held in the capacious foyer, there's still a reasonable amount to see: for example, the modern lapidarium, in the courtyard, houses plaster casts from Trajan's Column covered with depictions of his Dacian campaigns, as well as Greek, Roman and medieval tombstones and carvings. Better still, a basement vault exhibits Romania's **national treasures**: a dazzling display of gold and jewellery, from prehistoric finds (see particularly the elaborate Coţofeneşti helmet) to Queen Marie's crown and the casket said to hold her heart, to the sceptres of Ferdinand I and Carol II. When the remainder of this huge museum reopens, expect to see a comprehensive overview of Romanian history from the earliest times to the present, including anthropomor-phic figures moulded in clay by the Neolithic Cucuteni and Hamangia cultures (including a "Thinker", possibly the model for Rodin's statue), Bronze Age Thracian tools, Geto-Dacian coins, Celtic weapons, Roman tools and glassware, and medieval clothing and manuscripts. You may also get to see the voluminous display of gifts presented to Ceauşescu on his sixtieth birthday.

Another building worth more than a passing glance is the **National Savings Bank**, directly opposite the museum. Designed by French architect Paul Gottereanu in the 1890s, its grimy Neoclassical facade features an impressive high arch linked together by two solid Corinthian pillars. From the National History Museum, it's a short walk to the **River Dâmboviţa**. An old saying has it that whoever drinks the "sweet waters" of the Dâmboviţa will never wish to be parted from Bucharest, to which one nineteenth-century traveller retorted that anyone who ever did "would be incapable of leaving the city for ever afterwards". Always prone to flooding, the Dâmboviţa was canalized in the 1880s and now passes underground at Piaţa Unirii. The river marks the abrupt transition from the organic fabric of the old city to the arbitrarily imposed pattern of the Centru Civic.

Northern Calea Victoriei

Heading north from Piaţa Revoluţiei towards Piaţa Victoriei along the quieter, northern end of Calea Victoriei, you'll pass a couple of museums of interest. The early nineteenth-century Ghica Palace at no. 111 houses the **Museum of Art Collections** (Muzeul Colecţiilor de Artă; Sat–Wed May–Sept 11am–7pm; Oct–April 10am–6pm; €2) – a rich hoard of artwork garnered from across the world. Refreshingly, the museum largely eschews the standard presentation of works by Romania's foremost artists (Grigorescu, Pallady), and instead offers a superb collection of Persian and Turkish rugs, icons on wood and glass, and decorative pieces from Asia. At no. 141, a superb, early twentieth-century, clamshell-shaped *porte-cochere* topped with fluttering cherubs shades the entrance to the Cantacuzino Palace, one-time residence of Romania's national composer, George Enescu (1881–1955). It now houses the small **George Enescu Museum of Music** (Tues–Sun 10am–5pm), a handful of rooms packed with memorabilia and personal effects – photos of Enescu with his peers, batons, manuscripts, concert programmes and suchlike. For more on Enescu, see the box on p.459.

Piaţa Victoriei and around

Continuing north along Calea Victoriei, you eventually reach **Piaţa Victoriei**, a vast circular space around which crazed drivers manically jockey for position. On the east side of the square stands the main government building, the hulking Palaţul Victoria, completed in 1944 but even then already showing a chilly Stalinist influence in its design. On the north side, along Sos. Kiseleff, there is a cluster of museums. At no. 1 is the **Grigore Antipa Natural History Museum** (Muzeul de Istorie Naturală; Tues–Sun 10am–6pm; €2), named after the conservationist and founder of Romanian icthyology. A small aquarium aside, the museum's collection consists of some 300,000 items, including a 4.5-metre-high skeleton of a dinosaur unearthed in Moldavia, over 80,000 butterflies and moths, and the obligatory selection of stuffed animals.

Next door, at no. 3, is Bucharest's finest museum, the **Museum of the Romanian Peasant** (Muzeul Ţăranului Român; Tues–Sun 10am–6pm; €3). On show is a wonderful display of traditional peasant artefacts from all regions of Romania, including colourfully woven linen and textiles, carvings, ceramics, and a superb collection of wood and glass-painted icons. Of the several impressively reconstructed buildings dotted around the museum, the most eye-catching is an eighteenth-century **windmill** from Haţeg county, an enormous contraption that took three years to piece back together. Similarly, a thick-set peasant dwelling from Gorj county, comprising three rooms and a loft for storage, and originally displayed at the Village Museum up the road, took around a year to reconstruct. There is an incomplete timber church from Hunedoara, around which lie some of its furnishings – altar doors, a holy table, church bells and so on. A wooden church, typical of those found in Maramureş, stands on a neat patch of grass at the rear of the museum. Located here, too, is the museum shop, which sells a beautiful assortment of rugs, costumes and other folksy objects. The entire premises were actually occupied by the Museum of Communist Party History until 1990, and there are still remnants from this time in the small basement, which contains a curious collection of paintings and busts of former communist leaders. On one wall, as if displayed reluctantly, is a rare picture of Ceauşescu – most images of the dictator were destroyed following his execution.

Directly opposite, at Şoseaua Kiseleff 2, the **Geological Museum** (daily 10am–6pm; €2) contains an exhaustive collection pertaining to Romania's great mineral riches; however, it couldn't be duller if it tried, the dusty cabinets and absence of English captions not exactly conducive to an entertaining visit. The collection of luminescent rocks in an otherwise unlit basement room is just about worth a look.

Southeast of here, in between B-dul. Lascăr Catargiu and B-dul. Iancu de Hunedoara at Str. V. Alecsandri 16, the fabulous **Storck Museum** (Tues–Sun

9am–5pm; €2) is one of Bucharest's lesser-known delights. Inside is a superb collection of sculpted works by Frederic Storck (1872–1942), whose father, Karl, was the first Romanian teacher of sculpture, as well as numerous paintings and murals by his wife Cecilia. They actually lived in the house next door; the museum building was originally built as a workshop.

The Centru Civic

In 1971, Ceauşescu visited North Korea and returned full of admiration for the grandiose avenues of Kim II Sung's capital, Pyongyang. Thirteen years later, inspired by what he had seen, Ceauşescu set out to remodel Bucharest as "the first socialist capital for the new socialist man", and to create a new administrative centre which was to be "a symbolic representation of the two decades of enlightenment we have just lived through". In truth, of course, this **Centru Civic** was meant to embody the state's authority and that of Ceauşescu himself. Implementing this megalomaniac vision entailed the demolition of a quarter of Bucharest's historic centre (about five square kilometres), said to be slums damaged by the 1977 earthquake, but in fact containing nine thousand largely undamaged nineteenth-century houses, whose forty thousand inhabitants were relocated in new developments on the outskirts of the city. There was worldwide condemnation of this vandalism, particularly since many old churches were to be swept away. Though some of the churches were in the end reprieved, they are now surrounded by huge modern apartment blocks and are separated from the urban context that gave them meaning. The core of the complex was largely completed by 1989, just in time for the dictator's overthrow.

Uniting the two halves of the Centru Civic is **Bulevardul Unirii**, at 4km long and 120m wide, slightly larger – intentionally so – than the Champs-Élysées after which it was modelled. The western end of the development, which extends from Piaţa Unirii to the Palace of Parliament, remains eerily desolate, its vacant shops and apartments and bone-dry fountains making the area seem a virtual ghost town. Although the longer eastern extension is still blighted with unfinished projects, most notably a colossal building that was to have been a cultural centre (a wasteland now referred to by the locals as "Hiroshima"), the area does at least seem human, thanks to the presence of a few shops and banks, and a heavy stream of traffic.

The Palace of Parliament

Dominating the entire project from the western end of B-dul. Unirii is the colossal **Palace of Parliament** (Palatul Parlamentului; daily 10am–4pm; tours €6, plus €10 for use of cameras), claimed to be the second-largest administrative building in the world – after the Pentagon – measuring 270m by 240m, and 86m high. It epitomizes the megalomania that overtook Ceauşescu in the 1980s; here he intended to house ministries, Communist Party offices and the apartments of high functionaries. Built on the site of the former Spirei Hill, which was razed for this project, the sheer size of the building can only be grasped by comparison with the toy-like cars scuttling past below. It has twelve storeys, four underground levels (including a nuclear bunker), a one-hundred-metre-long lobby and 1100 rooms, around half of which are used as offices while the remainder are redundant. The interiors are lavishly decorated with marble and gold leaf, and there are 4500 chandeliers (11,000 were planned), the largest of which weighs 1.5 tonnes, but the decoration was never finished due to the Ceauşescus' ever-changing whims. They were demanding patrons, allowing little more than a technical role to the architects, of which there were around seven hundred – one

▲ The Palace of Parliament

staircase was rebuilt three times before they were satisfied. Meanwhile, the floor pattern – which mirrors the layout of the building itself – was, apparently, designed that way so Ceaușescu wouldn't get lost.

This huge white elephant was officially known as the Casa Republicii, then as the Casa Poporului, but more popularly as the Casa Nebunului ("Madman's House"), before taking on its present name. The new government spent a long time agonizing about an acceptable use for it, and in 1994 it was finally decided to house the Senate and Parliament here; it is now also used for international conferences. You can visit from entrance A3 (right-hand side as you face it; metro Izvor), although you may have to wait until there are enough people to make up a tour group. The 45-minute tour takes you through ten of the most dazzling, most representative or simply the hugest of the halls, such as the extraordinary, glass-ceilinged **Sala Unirii** ("Unification Hall"), where legendary Romanian gymnast Nadia Comaneci was married in 1996. One of the last rooms you're led to is the Alexandru Ioan Cuza room, whose balcony offers defining views of the city. Although Izvor is the nearest metro stop, the approach along Piața Unirii gives you the most impressive view of the building.

National Museum of Contemporary Art

Located in the building's west wing (to the rear of the Palace) is the **National Museum of Contemporary Art** (Muzeul Național de Arta Contemporana; Wed–Sun 10am–6pm; €2). Accessed via a specially constructed glass annex and external elevators (which, as they take you up, give you some idea of the breathtaking scale of this building), it's a superbly designed space. The works on display are exclusively by Romanian artists, and mostly take the form of sculptures, collages and montages – there's also a rare print from 1978 entitled *Removing Mihai Vodă Church*, in reference to the repositioning of the church when Ceaușescu set about demolishing the area (see below). Up on the third floor, an enormous darkened room holds a series of curious multi-media installations, including several large screen projections, one of which has a woman serenely desecrating her kitchen, and another of a naked man balancing on a circle of chairs. It's a bit of a slog to get here, as you have to walk round the palace – walk up Calea 13 Septembrie and it's the second entrance on the right.

The churches of the eastern Centru Civic

Hidden away among the rows of new buildings that make up the Centru Civic are numerous tiny Orthodox churches thankfully reprieved from demolition. In Bucharest, you'll frequently find churches in inappropriate places – such as the courtyards of apartment buildings – where the city planners have built around them, but here the churches seem even more disregarded and incongruous than elsewhere. The most striking example of this is the **Sf Nicolae–Mihai Vodă Church** (Biserica Mihai Vodă), built by Michael the Brave in 1591; to make way for the Centru Civic development, in 1985 the church was moved 279m east on rails to Str. Sapienței 4, which entailed the demolition of the church's medieval cloisters and ancillary buildings. What's more, as it's now standing on a concrete platform, the church will probably collapse when the next major earthquake hits Bucharest. A similar fate probably awaits the wretched-looking **Sf Apostoli Church** (Biserica Sfinții Apostolii), five minutes south of here at Str. Sf Apostoli 33A; this grey, largely seventeenth-century structure was embellished in 1715 with a fine little steeple by Stefan Cantacuzino, a portrait of whom is just about visible inside the almost pitch-black interior. Located in slightly more civilized surrounds a further five minutes east, at Calea Rahovei 3, is the late nineteenth-century **Domnița Bălașa Church** (Biserica Domnița Bălăsa), one of the most popular churches in the city. Named after Constantin Brâncoveanu's sixth daughter, Doamna – a statue of whom stands in the garden in front of the church – this orange brick edifice is actually the third church on this site, the previous two having burnt down in the eighteenth century. The interior, one of the most complete in the city, features a beautiful wooden cross-shaped chandelier.

On the southern side of B-dul. Unirii, at Str. Justiției 64, is the **Antim Monastery** (Manastirea Antim), a large, walled complex dating from 1715 with a high-domed church and a small chapel, but minus half its eastern wing. At the top of Dealul Mitropoliei stands the **Patriarchal Cathedral** (Patriarhia), built from 1655 to 1668 and seat of the Romanian Orthodox Church. The interior contains the most dazzling of the city's iconostases, as well as a couple of exquisitely carved side altars. Completing the set of buildings here is the Brâncoveanu-commissioned campanile, the **Patriarchal Palace** (built in 1875) and the former **Palace of the Chamber of Deputies** (1907). East of the cathedral, on the other side of B-dul. Dimitrie Cantemir, a couple of other churches lie in wait: at Str. Radu Vodă 24A, the **Radu Vodă Church** (also known as Holy Trinity, or Sf Treime) was founded in 1568 and once laid claim to being the richest monastery in the country with 8342 properties, while directly opposite, wedged between an apartment block and a glass high-rise on a mound above a high wall, is the forlorn-looking **Bucur Monastery** (1743).

Piaţa Unirii and south

Midway along B-dul. Unirii, **Piaţa Unirii** ("Square of Union") is an oversized expanse of concrete dominated by traffic, notable only as a key metro interchange, as the site of the city's main department store – the slicked-up Unirea – and as the best place to view the Palace of Parliament. From the square, B-dul. Dimitrie Cantemir runs south about 1km to the much older Calea Şerban Vodă. The two roads cover the site of Podul Şerban Vodă, destroyed by a fire in 1825. This was the route taken by merchants and Turkish officials heading for the Sublime Porte of Constantinople, the Sultan's Court. The two roads meet at the north end of **Tineretului Park** ("Youth Park"), which contains a fairground and a lake, as well as the Uman crematorium, a strange, rather Masonic chapel filled with caskets of ashes. To the west is the more popular and formal **Carol I Park**; its tatty southern end, site of an ugly monument which once held the remains of Gheorghiu-Dej and other communist leaders, gives way to a lovely green space bisected by a long promenade and a smaller lake – here, during the summer, you can hire rowing boats (daily 10am–8pm; €2 for 1hr). A short walk north of the lake is the **Museum of Technology** (Muzeul Tehnic; Tues–Sun 9am–4pm), an oddball place intended to assert Romania's technological fecundity, particularly several "firsts", such as the metal-bodied aeroplane (1912) and the streamlined motor car (1923). Ironically, it's the names of British, French and German firms that dominate the collection.

Ten minutes' walk south along Calea Şerban Vodă, at the junction of the highways to Olteniţa and Giurgiu and opposite the Eroii Revoluţiei metro, is the **Heroes of the Revolution Cemetery**; buried here, in neat rows of identical white marble graves, are more than 280 "Heroes of the Revolution", gunned down by "terrorists" in 1989. Despite the traffic roaring by, it's an affecting place, and even more poignant given that some of the victims were as young as 14. To the left of the cemetery stands the Church of the Martyr Heroes. From here, you can see the minaret of Bucharest's working mosque, at Str. C. Mănescu 4. Next to the Heroes of the Revolution Cemetery is the **Bellu Cemetery**, resting place of Romania's greatest writers, including Mihai Eminescu (see p.290), and opposite, on the Şoseaua Giurgiului, is the **Sephardic Jewish Cemetery** (closed on Saturdays) and the **Lutheran Cemetery**.

The Ceauşescus are buried in **Ghencea Cemetery**, southwest of the city along Drumul Sării; you can get here by bus from Eroii Revoluţiei metro station (#173, Mon–Fri only) and from Piaţa Unirii (#385; nearest stop at the junction of Drumul Sării and Calea 13 Septembrie). They were originally buried under pseudonyms, but their graves are now marked with their own names. Nicolae's, surrounded by a small black fence, is on the left side of the central alley before the chapel; Elena's grubby little plot is on the opposite side of the alley, and that of their playboy son, Nicu, is on the left side behind the church. Ask one of the guards to show you if you can't find them. Note that photos are not permitted. Next door is a military cemetery, a surreal forest of propeller blades marking the graves of airmen.

Piaţa Unirii to Piaţa Universităţii

Occupying a large chunk of the eastern side of Piaţa Unirii is the Unirea department store (see p.95), from where it's a short walk up B-dul. Corneliu Coposu to the junction of Str. Sf Vineri; a few paces along to the left, at no. 9, is the **Jewish Choral Temple**, a red-brick structure built in 1857 and which still serves the city's dwindling Jewish community (services daily 8am & 7pm). A five-minute walk to the right along Str. Sf Vineri brings you to the **Great Synagogue**, at Str. Mămulari 3, which now houses a **Museum of Jewish History** (Muzeul de Istorie al Evreilor din Romania; Mon–Wed, Fri & Sun 9am–1pm, Thurs 9am–4pm; free). There's a fairly comprehensive collection of books and paintings, as well as a handful of Jewish ritual objects, though the most impressive exhibit is an elegant sculpture commemorating the lives of some 350,000 Jews deported in 1944.

The historic quarter

Just north of Piaţa Unirii, Str. Franceză leads west off B-dul. I. C. Brătianu into the maze of streets and pleasantly decrepit houses that surround the oldest part of Bucharest. Mercifully, this picturesque and agreeably tatty little quarter was spared Ceauşescu's bulldozers, and it now offers a welcome respite from the concrete monotony of the Centru Civic. The area is undergoing a major regeneration project – which will inevitably take years to complete – but visitors can expect to see a gradual cleaning up of the many crumbling and hollowed-out buildings that comprise large parts of the quarter.

It was here that Prince Vlad ţepeş ("Vlad the Impaler", otherwise known as Dracula – see p.471) built a **citadel** in the fifteenth century. The building was severely damaged during ţepeş's attempt to regain the throne in 1476 (in which he succeeded, only to be murdered a few months later), and was further damaged by various earthquakes and fires over the following centuries; it was subsequently auctioned off as wasteland. Thus, little remains of the ancient citadel – just some of the walls, arches and shattered columns of the **Curtea Veche** ("Old Court"), at Str. Franceză 60 (Tues–Sun 9am–5pm), most of which was uncovered during excavations in the late 1960s. It's not really worth paying the (admittedly very small) entrance fee, as you can see pretty much all there is to see through the fence. The adjoining **Old Court Church**, established by Mircea Ciobanul ("Mircea the Shepherd") from 1546–58, is the oldest church in Bucharest. It is a typical example of sixteenth-century Wallachian church architecture, with horizontal bands of brick facing and rows of small niches beneath the cornice. The interior frescoes, sadly, are almost blackened beyond recognition. A few doors east from the Curtea Veche, at Str. Franceză 62, an austere white wall with barred windows conceals Bucharest's most famous hostelry, **Hanul lui Manuc** ("Manuc's Inn"). Built as a *caravanserai* in 1808 by a wealthy Armenian, Manuc-bey Mirzaian, it was for years a dodgy state-run hotel and restaurant, but is now under new ownership, with plans to reopen as a classy hotel complex.

From Str. Franceză, pick your way through a warren of small streets to Str. Lipscani, a narrow thoroughfare named after the merchants from Leipzig who traded here in the eighteenth century. It now holds a lively Gypsy street market (Mon–Sat 8am–4pm), selling Turkish jeans, pirated cassettes and all manner of other goodies. This whole area is a labyrinth of little shops and cafés, interspersed with arcades, such as the Hanul cu tei at no. 63. Beware of pickpockets in this area.

A couple of streets further north, on Str. Doamnei, stands the brazenly colourful, corkscrew-domed **Russian Church** (1905–09). The church, faced with yellow brick, Art Nouveau green tiling and pixie-faced nymphs, has a small interior, with frescoes blackened with age and smoke.

Piaţa Universităţii and around

Piaţa Universităţii is the focus of city life and traffic, and was one of the key sites of the 1989 revolution, as evinced by the numerous memorials (note the ten stone crosses in the road island) to those killed at Christmas 1989 and in June 1990. The latter marks the date on which miners, under Iliescu's orders, drove out students who had been on hunger strike since April 30, causing the square to be nicknamed Piaţa Tiananmen. The most poignant of the memorials is the black cross and wall plaque at B-dul. Bălcescu 18, some 200m north of the *Intercontinental* – this marks the spot where the first victim, Mihai Gătlan, aged 19, fell, at 5.30pm on December 21.

West of the square, occupying the first block on B-dul. Republicii, is **Bucharest University**. Its frontage is lined with statues of illustrious pedagogues and statesmen, as well as a regular crop of bookstalls. Established in 1859 after the union of Wallachia and Moldavia, the university equipped the sons of bourgeois families to become lawyers and men of letters until the communists took over in 1949. Technical skills and education for women were subsequently given top priority, but since the revolution business studies and foreign languages have overtaken them in popularity. The university continues to have an excellent reputation.

Just north of the square, adjacent to the *Intercontinental* hotel, is the **National Theatre of Bucharest**, which resembles an Islamicized reworking of the Colosseum; it was a pet project of Elena Ceauşescu, who had the facade rebuilt twice, and the roof once, before she was satisfied. Opposite is the **School of Architecture**, built between 1912 and 1927 in the neo-Brâncovenesc style – ornate pillars, prominent, richly carved eaves and a multitude of arches. On the southwest corner of Piaţa Universităţii, the **Bucharest History Museum** (Muzeul Municipal Bucureşti; Tues–Sun 9am–5pm) traces the city's evolution, with a limited but reasonably enlightening collection of old documents, coins, photographs and prints – there are also some rusting street signs from old Bucharest. The neo-Gothic building was built as the Suţu Palace in 1834; its superb *porte-cochere* was added later in the century.

Across the road from the museum lie two ancient and much-loved churches: in front of the hospital of the same name and period is the **Colţea Church** (Biserica Colţea), dating from the beginning of the eighteenth century and with a recently restored richly ornamented interior. Some 200m further south, the late sixteenth-century **New St George's Church** (Biserica Sf Gheorghe Nou) was the largest church to be built in the city during the reign of Constantin Brâncoveanu, who, it is alleged, was reburied under the church in 1720 after his wife brought him back from Istanbul. The grey-brick interior is enlivened by paintings, murals and sculptures by Mutu, Popp and Caragea. A suitably grand bronze statue of Brâncoveanu, completed by Karl Storck (see p.78), stands in the garden in front of the church.

West of Piaţa Universităţii

Heading west from Piaţa Universităţii, there are several appealing attractions, all within close proximity to each other. If you're looking to relax, head to the

Cişmigiu or Botanical Gardens, while there's more culturally oriented fare in the shape of the grand Cotroceni Palace and the National Military Museum.

Cişmigiu Gardens

West of Piaţa Universităţii, midway along B-dul. Regina Elisabeta, the lovely **Cişmigiu Gardens** (Gradina Cişmigiu) were laid out as a park on land bequeathed to the city in 1845. Originally belonging to a Turkish water inspector, the gardens now fittingly contain a serpentine lake upon which small rowing boats and pedalos glide, rented by couples seeking solitude among the swans and weeping willows (rental daily 10am–9pm June–Sept; about €3 per hour, plus €1.50 deposit, from a kiosk by the waterside). Otherwise, the gardens provide a tranquil space, with workers snoozing beneath the trees at lunch times and pensioners meeting for games of chess. At the park's northern end, a Roman garden contains busts of some of Romania's literary greats while, for kids, there's an attractive little playground next to the lake.

Opera Română and Casa Radio

A few hundred metres beyond Cişmigiu, on B-dul. Kogălniceanu, stands the mint-green **Opera Română**, a drab 1950s building containing a collection of operatic costumes, scores, photographs and posters. Although these are not particularly interesting, do try and catch one of the highly regarded performances here if you get the chance (see p.93). Looming over the Opera building is the monstrous **Casa Radio** ("Radio House"), another of Ceauşescu's unfinished projects. Initially intended to house the National History, Army and Communist Party museums, as well as Ceauşescu's tomb, it has long been rumoured that it will become, as the name implies, a radio centre. However, given the speed (or rather lack of speed) at which things move round here, this is highly unlikely, and the building seems destined to remain in architectural limbo for many years to come.

Cotroceni Palace and the Botanical Gardens

From the Opera Română, buses and trolley buses trundle south across the river along B-dul. Eroilor Sanitari to the Cotroceni Palace and the Botanical Gardens, passing an area of lovely bourgeois villas, each one individually designed. The **Cotroceni Palace** was built as a monastery by Şerban Cantacuzino between 1679 and 1682 and served as base for the Austrian army in 1737, the Russian army in 1806, and Tudor Vladimirescu's rebels in 1821. Damaged by numerous fires and earthquakes over the course of its history, the original building was demolished in 1863 and the palace rebuilt from 1893 to 1895 to provide a home for the newly wed Prince Ferdinand and Princess Marie. Under communism, it served as the Palace of the Pioneers – the "Pioneers" being the Soviet-bloc equivalent of the Boy Scouts. A new south wing was added during restoration following the 1977 earthquake, and this is now the presidential residence. In 1986, Ceauşescu had the church demolished, apparently because it spoilt the view. Enter the palace by a small door in the north wall at Şoseaua Cotroceni 37 (Tues–Sun 9am–5.30pm; €4; advance booking necessary on ☎021/221 1200). Tours pass first through the remains of the monastery, where the Cantacuzino family gravestones are kept, then through the new rooms from the 1893–95 rebuild, decorated in an eclectic variety of Western styles.

On the other side of Şoseaua Cotroceni lie the university's well-tended **Botanical Gardens** (Grădina Botanică; daily 8am–7pm; €2), which contain pine trees and lily ponds, as well as glasshouses and a museum of botany (Tues, Thurs & Sun 9am–1pm).

The National Military Museum

A short way north of the Opera Română, in a former army barracks at Str. Mircea Vulcănescu 125, is the **National Military Museum** (Tues–Sun 9am–5pm; €2). The first part of the museum is an intermittently interesting trawl through Romania's military history, featuring an impressive array of weapons, banners and uniforms. The one section of the museum that really merits a visit, however, is the exhibition on the 1989 revolution. It's a deeply moving presentation, comprised mainly of personal belongings donated by families of soldiers and civilians killed during the fighting – from glasses, watches and medals to more sobering items such as torn and blood-splattered clothing and bullet casings. The main exhibit is the pistol, walkie-talkie and blood-soaked uniform of **General Vasile Milea**, Minister of Defence at the time of the revolution, who was executed for refusing to carry out orders to shoot upon the civilians. There are also some rare English-language newspaper editions from that time, including many graphic images of the dead and those mourning the dead. Despite the voluminous display of memorabilia on view in the remainder of the museum, Romania has rarely gone in for martial adventures; from 1958, it was the only Warsaw Pact country without Soviet troops on its soil. Ceauşescu called vociferously for disarmament, announcing peace proposals and cuts in the defence budget. Post-communist Romania has become more involved in international concerns, contributing a chemical-warfare unit to the Gulf War forces, a military hospital to the UN in Somalia, and peace-keeping troops to Albania and the former Yugoslavia. In 1999, Romania allowed NATO – of which it is now a member – to use its air space to fly bombing missions across Serbia.

North of the museum, towards the Gara de Nord, is a village-like neighbourhood of tiny street-corner churches and dimly lit workshops. Ivy and creepers cloak the residential houses – all outwardly run-down, but often concealing parquet-floored apartments with elegant antique furniture and other relics of pre-war bourgeois life.

The northern suburbs

The **Şoseaua Kiseleff**, a long, elegant avenue lined with lime trees, extends north from Piaţa Victoriei towards the Herăstrău Park and the Village Museum, one of Romania's best open-air museums, before heading out towards the airports and the main road to Transylvania. Modelled on the Parisian *chaussées* – though named after a Russian general – Şoseaua Kiseleff is a product of the Francophilia that swept Romania's educated classes during the nineteenth century; it even has its own Arc de Triumf.

The Skopţi

The **Skopţi coachmen**, who worked along the Şoseaua Kiseleff until the 1940s, were one of the curiosities – or grotesqueries – of Bucharest. Members of a dissident religious sect founded in Russia during the seventeenth century – and related to the Lipovani of the Danube Delta – the Skopţi ritually castrated themselves in the belief that the "generative organs are the seat of all iniquities", interpreting literally Christ's words on eunuchs in the Gospel of St Matthew. This was done after two years of normal married life – a period necessary to ensure the conception of future Skopţi. Driving *droshkys* pulled by black Orloff horses, the coachmen wore caftans sprouting two cords, which passengers tugged to indicate that the driver should turn left or right.

East of Şoseaua Kiseleff, beyond B-dul. Aviatorilor at Str. Muzeul Zambaccian 21, the **Zambaccian Museum** (Muzeul Zambaccian; Wed–Sun 11am–6pm, €1.50) is another little gem. This little-known museum houses a small but terrific collection of art accumulated by wealthy businessman Krikor H. Zambaccian (1889–1962), and is notable for its paintings by established Romanian artists such as Grigorescu, Andreescu and Lucian, and French artists Renoir and Matisse; it is also home to the only painting in the country by Cézanne, as well as a few pieces of sculpture from Brâncuşi and Storck.

About 1km north along Şoseaua Kiseleff you'll come to the **Arc de Triumf**, built in 1878 for an independence parade, and patched together in 1922 for another procession to celebrate Romania's participation on the winning side in World War I and the gains achieved at the Versailles peace conference. Originally made of wood, it was more fittingly rebuilt in stone from 1935 to 1936, in the style of the Arc de Triomphe in Paris.

Herăstrău Park

Immediately beyond the Arc is **Herăstrău Park**, which is best reached by metro – the Aviatorilor stop is at its southeastern corner. Paths run past formal flowerbeds to the shore of **Lake Herăstrău**, one of the largest of a dozen lakes strung along the River Colentina. These lakes, created by Carol II to drain the unhealthy marshes that surrounded Bucharest, form a continuous line across the northern suburbs. Arched bridges lead via the small and fragrant Island of Roses to numerous lakeside snack bars and restaurants, from where rowing boats can be rented (€2 per hour). Alternatively, you can take a thirty-minute lake cruise (€1.50); tickets for both must be bought from the windows opposite the departure point (May–Sept for boats and lake cruise). Also located within the park is the **Expo-market** – a vast indoor shopping arena selling mostly clothes – and a creaky old fairground. These are located near the park's other entrance, which is at the northern end of Şoseaua Kiseleff, near Piaţa Libere.

The residential area east of the park is one of Bucharest's most exclusive neighbourhoods. It is where the communist elite once lived, cordoned off from the masses they governed; the Ceauşescus lived in the Vila Primavera, at the east end of B-dul. Primăverii. The area is still inhabited by technocrats, favoured artists and members of the elite.

The Village Museum

Another of Bucharest's worthwhile sights is the **Village Museum** (Muzeul Satului: daily: May–Oct 9am–7pm; Nov–April 9am–5pm; €2.50) on the

The Băneasa bridge

The bridge immediately north of Băneasa Station, where the DN1 crosses the River Colentina, was the scene of a **crucial battle** in August 1944. The success of the August 23 coup against Marshal Antonescu (see p.438) meant that Hitler's oil supplies were more than halved, which is reckoned to have shortened the war in Europe by at least six months. However, at the time just 2800 Romanian troops faced between twenty thousand and thirty thousand Germans, mostly at Băneasa and Otopeni. King Mihai offered the Germans safe passage out of Romania, but they responded by bombing Bucharest. The bridge was held by a Romanian lieutenant and a handful of men until August 25, when Romanian reinforcements began to arrive from Craiova. Allied help finally came the following day when four hundred American planes bombed the German positions, and by August 27 Bucharest had been cleared of German forces (only to be occupied by the Red Army four days later).

shores of Lake Herăstrău – the entrance is on Şoseaua Kiseleff, just up from the Arc de Triumf. Established in 1936, this wonderful ensemble of over three hundred dwellings, workshops, churches, windmills, presses and other structures from every region in the country illustrates the extreme diversity of Romania's folk architecture.

The most interesting are the oak houses from Maramureş with their rope-motif carvings and shingled roofing, and their beamed gateways carved with animals and hunting scenes, Adam and Eve and the Tree of Life, and suns and moons. Other highlights are the heavily thatched dwellings from Sălciua de Jos in Alba county; dug-out homes, or "pit" houses (with vegetables growing on the roof) from Drăghiceni and Castranova in Oltenia; colourfully furnished homesteads from Moldavia; and windmills from Tulcea county in the Delta. Keep an eye out,

▲ The Village Museum

too, for the beautiful wooden church from the village of Dragomireşti in Maramureş. Mud-brick dwellings from the fertile plains ironically appear poorer than the homes of peasants in the less fertile highlands where timber and stone abound, while the importance of livestock to the Székely people of Harghita county can be seen by their barns, which are taller than their houses. The terrific souvenir shop here is the best place in the city to buy folk art objects, including textiles and costumes, ceramics and woodenware.

The museum has had a pretty rough time of it in recent years, suffering two serious fires: the first, when several houses were subject to an arson attack by an embittered ex-employee; and the second time, in 2002, when more than a dozen houses burnt down in less suspicious circumstances. Understandably, then, this is a no-smoking museum.

Piaţa Presei Libere

Şoseaua Kiseleff ends at **Piaţa Presei Libere** ("Free Press Square"), in front of **Casa Presei Libere** ("Free Press House"), a vast white Stalinist building, which was once the centre of the state propaganda industry. Little seems to have changed, as the free publishing industry is still largely corralled into this one building. Romania's Commodities Exchange is also based here. Until 1989, the pedestal in front of the building accommodated a huge statue of Lenin, before he was carted off to Mogoşoaia Palace (see p.100) and unceremoniously dumped there.

Some 500m further north of here, by the Băneasa train station just off the Bucureşti–Ploieşti Highway, are Bucharest's two least-known museums. Both of these eccentric buildings on Str. Dr Minovici were constructed in the early twentieth century, specifically to hold the private collections of the oil-rich Minovici family. Built in 1905 in the style of a fortified manor house, the **Museum of Popular Arts** (Tues–Sun 9am–5pm; €1.50) at no. 2 exhibits woven blankets, Transylvanian blue pottery, painted Easter eggs, spinning wheels, musical instruments, furniture and beautiful peasant garments – there's also a tiny Orthodox chapel with eighteenth-century icons. Next door at no. 3, constructed in 1910 in a bizarre fusion of English Tudor and Italian Renaissance styles, the **Minovici Museum of Old Western Arts** (Thurs–Sun 9am–5pm; €1.50) is filled with hunting trophies and weapons, Flemish tapestries, Florentine furniture, German and Swiss stained-glass windows, and a fine rug from Mosul in Iraq.

Eating, nightlife and entertainment

Between the wars Bucharest was famed for its bacchanals, its gourmet cuisine and its Gypsy music – but all this ended with the puritanical postwar regime of communism. However, the situation has improved distinctly in recent years, with a burgeoning, and still remarkably cheap, **restaurant** scene. The city's nightlife is also on the up, and there are now some terrific **bars** and **clubs** scattered around town.

The best places for **snacks** are the street stalls, pizzerias, kebab and burger bars on the main avenues, around the Gara de Nord and in the Piaţa Universităţii underpass; these are generally open Monday to Saturday from 9am until around 7pm, though many of those near the station are open around the clock. **Patisseries** are also a good bet for a quick snack; most of them dispense freshly baked sweet and savoury pastries, cakes and confectionery. Look out, too, for the kiosks doling out *gogoş*, large, elongated doughnuts that come with a choice of fillings.

There are at least half a dozen **markets** (see shopping, p.95) in the city, where you can select from a huge and colourful selection of fruit and vegetables, which vary depending on the season.

Cafés and patisseries

Bucharest is now home to some genuinely enjoyable **cafés**, many of which offer sandwiches, snacks and alcoholic beverages. Note that a lot of the **patisseries** often have stand-up counters instead of seats.

Ana Pan Str. Radu Beller 8. Clean and modern sit-down/takeaway patisserie with more than a dozen outlets around the city, serving croissants, sweet and savoury pastries, tarts and yoghurts. Mon–Sat 8am–8pm, Sun 9am–1pm.

Café Boheme Str. Caderea Bastilliei. A short walk from hectic Piaţa Romană, this is a lovely spot to come and relax. Aside from the prolific range of coffees (including flavoured, iced, Turkish), this is one of the best places in town for a hot toasted sandwich or omelette breakfast. Mon–Thurs 8am–1am, Fri–Sun until 2am.

Caffe and Latte B-dul. Schitu Măgureanu 35. In a lovely leafy location across from the Cişmigiu Gardens, this is one of the city's most enjoyable cafés, run by happy smiling staff. Excellent coffees, fruit and chocolate shakes, and pastries. Daily 8am–10pm.

Casandra B-dul. Magheru 32. A friendly sit-down place serving savoury bites, fancy biscuits and cakes (including strudel and baklava), and small cups of coffee.

Chocolat Calea Victoriei 12a (located on Str. Stavropoleos). Kick back in one of *Chocolat's* comfortable cushioned wooden chairs and select from a prodigious list of chocolate-flavoured drinks, cakes and mousses. There's even an in-house chocolatier. It's also a good spot for brunch, with cold cuts of meat and salads on offer. Mon–Fri 8am–3am, Sat & Sun 9am–1am.

IO Bar Str. Demetri Dobrescu 5. This former Securitate hideout, gutted during the revolution – as evidenced by the superb wall-length black-and-white prints depicting these events – has been stunningly revamped into offices and a café. It's a friendly and relaxing venue, perfect after an afternoon at the National Art Gallery across the road. Daily 9am–midnight.

Market Café Str. Stavropoleos 8. Another recent funky addition to the old-town area, this adventurously designed café features mauve painted walls, ceiling mirrors and lamps, complemented by beautiful wood, leather and glass furnishings. Fine coffee and cakes too. Daily 9am–midnight.

Panipat B-dul. Bălcescu 24 (24hr), Gara de Nord (24hr), Str. M Rosetti 15, B-dul. Brătianu 44, Şos. Ştefan cel Mare 48 and B-dul. Kogălniceanu 55. Established franchise patisserie with good takeaway buns, pizzas and cakes, including strudel.

Picasso Café Str. Franceză 2–4. Cool, relaxing and beautifully lit café, the perfect coffee stop after trooping around the National History Museum just up the road. Can get a bit smoky, however. Daily 9am–1am.

Rendez-vouz Str. Tudor Stefan 7–9. Bucharest's only teahouse is a mellow affair, offering an extensive range of teas from around the world, albeit at rather inflated prices. Daily 8am–11pm, Fri & Sat until midnight.

Saga Café Str. Radu Beller 6. The best of several fashionable coffee shops sited along this hip little street in Dorobanţi; wicker chairs on the pavement terrace, leather seats in the loungey interior, and a decent selection of coffees, ices, ice-cream cakes and fruit salads. Daily 8am–11pm, Fri & Sat until midnight.

Scala B-dul. Bălcescu 36 (at Str. Rosetti). Small shop but with a huge choice of chocolates and cakes; the baklava is especially good.

Turabo Str. Episcopiei 6 and Str. Ion Ghica 3. Cool, classy café that draws a moderately posey crowd, but that doesn't mean it isn't one of the best coffee houses in town – deep burgundy seats, spotlights and large bay windows that allow for unalloyed people-watching pleasure. Daily 8am–1am.

Snack and sandwich bars and fast food

Frufru Str. Batiştei 1–3. Directly behind the *Intercontinental* hotel, this funky little place doles out tubs of fresh pasta, either to eat in or take away.

Gregory's B-dul. Magheru 32–34, Str. Lipscani 27, and Universităţii metro underpass. Decent enough sandwich and deli outlets, though not in the same league as *Snack Attack* (see p.70).

Pizza Hut Calea Dorobanţilor 1 and B-dul. Regina Elisabeta 17. Reliably the same as anywhere else in the world, with smoking and no-smoking sections. The branch at Dorobanților also has a rather pleasant side terrace.

Snack Attack Piața Dorobanți, Calea Victoriei 224, Str. Ion Câmpineanu 10, and Piața. Amzei 7–9. Bright and fashionable outlets serving the freshest and tastiest sandwiches, baguettes, soups and salads, as well as juices and desserts (yoghurt, panacotta, cheesecake).

Spring Time B-dul. N. Titulescu 6, Str. Academiei 35, and Calea Floreasca 131. It's not sophisticated, but this Lebanese-run fast-food chain has a wide range of foods to take away or eat in.

Restaurants

Bucharest's **restaurant** scene is changing fast, and for the better. In recent years, there's been a welcome diversification in the types of cuisines available, from Belgian and French to Lebanese and Fusion, while it's now also possible to find decent Asian or South/Central American food. Al fresco dining is extremely popular, and a healthy number of restaurants have terraces, handy in a city that can be stifling in the summer. While restaurants in Bucharest are marginally more expensive than elsewhere in the country, dining out remains a fantastically cheap pastime. As a general rule, expect to pay around €9 for a two-course meal with wine, around a third more for the very best establishments. **Credit cards** are also now widely accepted. Telephone numbers have also been given where it's best to reserve a table. Note that many of the restaurants listed here can be quite tricky to find, as they tend to be secreted away down leafy side streets in residential areas or in anonymous-looking buildings.

Around Piața Revoluției and Piața Universității

Bistro Atheneu Str. Episcopiei 3 ☎ 021/313 4900. Across from the Atheneum concert hall, this homely little restaurant – its walls cluttered with bells, instruments and old Bucharest street signs – has been keeping pre- and post-concert punters happy for over a decade with its tasty Romanian and continental food. Daily noon–midnight.

Burebista Str. Batiștei 14. You can eat as cheaply or as expensively as you wish in this convivial place, named after the great Dacian ruler, located 200m east of the *Intercontinental* hotel. The prodigious menu offers some of the best-value Romanian food in town – the white bean soup and *sarmalute* (Moldavian stuffed cabbage) are especially recommended. Daily noon–midnight.

Byblos Str. N Golescu 14–16. Located right behind the Atheneum, this is just about the friendliest and most relaxing place to eat in the area – superb Italian fare, including first-rate risottos, in either the informal bar-style area or the posher restaurant proper. Daily noon–midnight.

La Mama Str. Episcopiei 9, Str. Barbu Văcărescu 3, and Str. Delea Veche 51. Absurdly popular restaurant chain doling out enormous, and very cheap, portions of wholesome Romanian food (grills, stews and cabbage dishes), while waiters scuttle about at optimum speed. They also do take-outs. No shorts allowed inside after 6pm, but, in summer, the terrace is equally as enjoyable. Daily 10am–2am, Fri & Sat until 4am.

La Taifas Str. Gh. Manu 16. Well-established, popular and personable restaurant with a large terrace and two salon-style rooms, each brightly painted and warmly decorated. The menu – notable for its delicious grilled and fried meats (the lamb mix is very good) – is chalked up on a board and brought to your table. Daily noon–1am.

East of Bulevardul G. Magheru and Bulevardul N. Bălcescu

Amigos Str. Tunari 67–69. Bright, funky and friendly Mexican venue, whose specialities – tacos, burritos, enchilladas, quesedillas and the like – are made from the freshest, most authentic ingredients imported from Mexico. Rather helpfully, the dishes are coded according to their spiciness. Daily noon–midnight.

Balthazar Str. Dumbrava Rosie 2 ☎ 021/212 1460. Superb contemporary fusion restaurant offering an intriguing Franco-Asian (Japanese, Thai, Vietnamese, Chinese) menu – featuring exotic dishes like salmon in banana leaves and tuna cigars. In addition, the great-looking surrounds (burgundy walls, white drapes and glitterballs) and impeccable service make the expense worth it. Daily noon–midnight.

Bolivar Str. Salcâmilor 9 ☎021/211 4848. Classy South American restaurant offering a range of dishes from Peru, Argentina and Brazil (with meat imported from these countries), with some superb Chilean wines to boot. Three elegantly minimalist, and very colourful, rooms with tall, leather-backed chairs, as well as a fabulous shaded terrace. Daily noon–midnight.

Mediterraneo Str. Icoanei 20 ☎021/211 5308. Cramped, but warm and hospitable restaurant whose mainly Italian menu is complemented by some interesting Turkish dishes. They also do an excellent three-course lunch menu for around €5. Hugely popular, so get there early. Daily 10am–2am.

Mesogios Str. Calderon 49 ☎021/313 4951. This beautifully turned-out restaurant is *the* place to come for seafood. Cuttlefish, octopus, red snapper and squid are just a few of the dishes on offer – but it's not cheap. Daily 12.30pm–12.30am.

Smarts Str. Al. Donici 14 ☎021/211 9035. Just around the corner from *Mediterraneo*, this tightly packed restaurant – all chunky tables and thick wooden beams – veers heavily towards Belgian food; their steaks are among the best in the city, while the freshwater-fish pancakes make for an unusual entrée. Neat little inn-style bar downstairs, too, where you can sample Belgian beers. Daily 11am–midnight, bar until late.

Sterling Str. Calderon 41. Although well regarded for its steaks, this quiet and friendly place just along from *Mesogios* also offers a very creditable pasta menu, along with crepes and salads. There's a very polished indoor dining area or the more informal side terrace. Mon–Sat noon–11.30am, Sun 4–11.30pm.

The historic quarter and around

Carul cu Bere Str. Stavropoleos 3. A change of hands has transformed this popular tourist hangout into a thoroughly enjoyable eatery; the fabulous surrounds, featuring splendid neo-Tannhauser decor and high Gothic vaulted ceilings, makes for the perfect spot to tuck into *mititei* (grilled spicy sausages), Moldavian *tochitură* (pork stew) and *mămăligă* (polenta). The daily set menu (€6; between noon and 4pm) is terrific value. Daily noon–midnight.

Count Dracula Club Spl. Independenţei 8a, 200m west of Calea Victoriei. You'll not be surprised to learn that everything here is themed: the furniture, the food, even the waiters. But it's not as tacky as it sounds, and there's solid Romanian food at good prices. Daily 12.30pm–1am.

Locanta Jaristea Str. George Georgescu 50–52. ☎021/335 3338. Some of the best and most unusual Romanian food in the city, such as grilled pigeon, boiled goat and roast boar or bear is on offer here. The room is styled on early twentieth-century Bucharest, while the lush red carpets, tall-backed chairs and smartly attired waiters add to the overall sense of effortlessness. It's a little tricky to find as there's no sign – it's the white villa-style building on the corner with Str. Justiţiei. Daily 11am–2am.

St George Str. Franceză 44. A complimentary shot of Tuica to start things off, followed by a delicious and wholesome plate of typically calorific Hungarian fare – thick dumpling soup, Hortobagy pancakes (beef-filled crepes), goose liver – and, finally, a pancake dessert accompanied by a glass of sweet Tokaj Aszu. The authentic Magyar decor and resident Gypsy band (neither too loud or invasive) round things off superbly. Daily 9am–11pm.

Whispers Str. Ion Brezoianu 4. Upscale, yet informal, American-style diner, serving burgers, hot sandwiches and salads. Suffices equally for a lunch stop-off or a more hearty evening meal. A plethora of sports on the big screens while you eat. Daily 10am–midnight.

North of the centre

Angel's Str. Paris 52. This immensely popular huge terrace restaurant rustles up some of the best pizzas in town. In addition, there's a diverse choice of Italian meals, ranging from pastas and risottos to grilled octopus and boiled lobster and, for veggies, options like baked mushrooms with mozzarella. Daily noon–1am.

Barka Saffron Str. Av. Sănătescu 1 ☎021/224 1004. Located near the *Butterfly Vila* hostel (bus #82 from Gara de Nord), this informal and enchanting little Indian–fusion restaurant has an appealing choice of chicken- and lamb-based curries, alongside some spicy Sri Lankan and Caribbean dishes. Bus #82 from Gara de Nord. Daily noon–11.30am.

Casa Doina Şos. Kiseleff 4 ☎021/222 3179. Occupying a prime location on the edge of a wooded park, this late nineteenth-century building accommodates an elegant and formal restaurant (no shorts allowed inside), serving an upscale, and expensive, take on Romanian dishes; good vegetarian options, too. Live music most nights from 6pm. Daily 11am–midnight.

Die Deutsche Kneipe Str. Stockholm 9. Terrific, family-run restaurant in a quiet residential street off Calea Dorobanţilor; gut-busting portions of succulent German sausages served with lashings of sauerkraut and washed down with German Pils or keg beer. Mon–Sat 3–11.30pm.

Piccolo Mondo Str. Clucerului 16. One of a handful of good Lebanese eateries recently established in Bucharest, this handsome restaurant lists a long menu of salads, kebabs (including a good choice for vegetarians), yoghurt-based dishes, and cured meats. Post-meal, enjoy a smoke on a hookah pipe. A good place for al fresco dining in the summer. Daily 11.30am–1am.

Thai Moods Str. Petre Creţu 63 ☎021/224 6851. Housed in a handsome white villa in the northern suburbs, this is the capital's best ethnic restaurant by some stretch; superb stir-fry and curry options, each packed with the freshest, most colourful ingredients and coated in delicious sauces. Afterwards, take your pick from an exquisite selection of fruit-based desserts. The restaurant itself looks fantastic, as does the summery Orchid Garden terrace with its outdoor bar. Daily noon–midnight.

Uptown Bar and Grill Str. Rabat 2. Another pleasantly secluded place just off B-dul. Aviatorilor (or a ten-minute walk from Piaţa Dorobanţilor). Delicious crepes, salads, pastas, risottos and grilled meats – try and grab a table in the elegant horseshoe-shaped conservatory. Daily 10am–midnight.

Bars and clubs

Bucharest does not immediately strike visitors as a place where **nightlife** abounds, but this is partly because, like the best of the city's restaurants, many places are discreetly tucked away or concentrated in unlikely areas of the city. Indeed, Bucharest is currently experiencing a new vibrancy, with **bars** springing up all over the city on a regular basis, coming and going according to the latest trends. The **club** scene, too, is fast improving, and in addition to the growing number of bars that double up as clubs there are now some choice venues scattered around town, increasingly catering to a more discerning range of musical tastes. Bucharestians, however, have long been starved of decent **live music**, a situation reflected in the dearth of venues.

Backstage Str. Gabroveni 14. You can count on a relaxed vibe and a good mix of retro tunes at this perennially popular club, a long-standing favourite on the local disco scene. The upstairs bar, meanwhile, has a couple of table footballs. Daily 6pm–5am.

Champions Sports Bar Calea 13 Septembrie 90, on the first floor of the *Grand Marriott* hotel. Thoughtfully designed, American-style bar and diner with an impressive array of superstar memorabilia, including George Foreman's gloves and Dan Marino's helmet, as well as items belonging to local heroes Ilie Nastase, Gheorghe Hagi and Nadia Comaneci. The bar also has large plasma screens for all your sporting kicks. Daily 1pm–midnight.

Club A Str. Blănari 14. The "Young Architects' Club", as it is popularly known, is something of a Bucharest institution; an energetic, pro-active venue with good (often live) music, cheap drinks and a happy youthful crowd. Occasionally features drama, foreign films and jazz. Mon–Fri 10am–5am, Sat & Sun 9pm–5am.

Coyote Café Calea Victoriei 48–50 (Pasajul Victoriei). One of the very few decent live music

venues in town, *Coyote* lays on a varied programme of rock concerts, but is otherwise a cool place to down a few beers. Mon–Thurs 4pm–2am, Fri–Sun until 5am.

Dubliner B-dul. N. Titulescu 18. The original expat hangout, ten minutes' walk west of Piaţa Victoriei, this is as close to a good old-fashioned boozer as you'll find, offering a decent range of beers, in addition to pies and steak sandwiches. Daily 9am–2am.

Green Hours 22 Club Calea Victoriei 120. *Green Hours* remains Bucharest's jazz club of choice; an intimate cellar bar with live turns most evenings and, in summer, gigs taking place in the leafy courtyard, itself a lovely place to kick back and sup a beer. Daily until 3am.

The Harp Str. Bibescu Voda 1, on the south side of Piaţa Unrii. The sister pub of *Dubliner*, but larger and more lively, and attracting a predominantly Romanian crowd. Serves the usual expensive Irish beers: Guinness, Murphy's and Kilkenny. Daily 9am–2am.

Lăptăria Enache on the 4th floor of the National Theatre, B-dul. Bălcescu 2. Massive outdoor terrace bar invariably packed to the gills, and which occasionally has live jazz and film screenings on the huge projector. Daily noon–2am, Fri & Sat until 4am.

Music Club Str. Baratiei 31. There aren't many, but this is just about Bucharest's premier live music venue. In addition to the hugely enjoyable resident house band, you're likely to find some of Romania's leading musicians taking a bow here. Daily 9pm–4am.

The Office Str. Tache Ionescu 2. Consistently one of the hottest club venues in town, with banging tunes, good-time atmosphere and a hip crowd. Drinks are not cheap though. Thurs–Sat 9.30pm–5am, Sun 10pm–2am.

Offside Pub Str. Gabroveni 14. Located right next door to *Backstage*, this football-themed pub is one of the best places in town to catch both foreign and domestic games. An impressive sprinkling of Romanian football stars' shirts (Hagi,

Chivu, Mutu) adorns the large, dark interior, though the staff could use a lesson or two in courtesy. Daily noon–2am.

Salsa III Str. Mihai Eminescu 89. Fabulous party place where the locals (and exponents of all abilities) indulge in a more sophisticated mode of dancing – Latino and Salsa. Mon–Sat 10pm–5am.

Tipsy B-dul. Schitu Măgureanu 13. A three-in-one pub, club (a "plub", apparently) and restaurant; have a bite in the very good restaurant before moving on to the busy pub, or, at weekends (Thurs–Sat), the cellar club, which hosts one of the best discos in town. Restaurant and pub open daily 6pm–4am.

Yellow Bar Str. Edgar Quinet 10. Funky café/bar with plush leather sofas, tunes just on the right side of loud, and a good-looking crowd. Mon–Fri 10am–3am, Sat & Sun 4pm–5am.

Entertainment

Bucharest's cultural forte is undoubtedly **classical music**, and it's possible to catch some top-drawer, and incredibly cheap, concerts in several locations around town. Operatic and ballet performances, too, are invariably excellent, with ostentatious sets and huge casts. Note that many **theatres** and **concert halls** close during the summer, but over the rest of the year check *Bucharest In Your Pocket* (see p.61) for the most up-to-date listings.

Classical music, opera and ballet

Several internationally acclaimed musicians have cut their teeth with the **George Enescu Philharmonic Orchestra**, which plays in the architecturally and acoustically superb **Romanian Atheneum** at Str. Franklin 1, near Piaţa Enescu (box office Mon–Fri 10am–6pm; ☏021/315 2567). There are concerts most days of the week (though usually not Mondays), including a matinee concert on Sundays. The **Romanian National Opera (Opera Română)**, at B-dul. Kogălniceanu 70 (box office daily 10am–1pm & 2–7pm; tickets €2–8; ☏021/313 1857, ⓦwww.operanb.ro), is the principal venue for operatic and ballet performances, with other productions taking place at the **Teatrul Operetă** (☏021/313 6348) next to the National Theatre, at B-dul. Bălcescu 2. There are also high-quality concerts at the **Sala Radio**, at Str. Berthelot 62 (box office daily 10am–6pm; tickets €2–5; ☏021/314 6800), which is home to

Casinos

There's a rash of **casinos** in Bucharest, which pander unashamedly to the pretensions of travelling businessmen and the city's nouveaux riches, with overpriced drinks and underclad hostesses. Some of them are in very beautiful historical buildings, and they often have genuinely good restaurants, open well into the early hours. The most attractive are the Palace Casino, incorporating the *Casa Vernescu* restaurant, in the Lenş-Vernescu Palace at Calea Victoriei 133 (☏021/231 0220), the Grand Casino (☏021/659 4913) in the basement of the *Athénée Palace Hilton* hotel at Str. Episcopiei 1, and the Casino Bucharest (☏021/310 2020) in the *Intercontinental* hotel at B-dul. N. Bălcescu 4. In general, you can gamble with US dollars or lei.

the National Radio Orchestra. Occasional **outdoor concerts** are held in Cişmigiu Gardens and Tineretului Park during the summer.

Drama

The huge **National Theatre**, at B-dul. Bălcescu 2 (box office Mon 10am–4pm, Tues–Sun until 7pm; ☎021/314 7171), with its three auditoriums, is the premier venue for domestic and foreign theatre productions (unfortunately, none in English). Other venues with productions that might just surmount linguistic barriers are the Tăndărică Puppet Theatre, at Str. E. Grigorescu 24 (☎021/211 4014); the two music halls at Calea Victoriei 33 and 174; the Comedy Theatre at Str. Măndineşti 2, and the State Jewish Theatre, at Str. I. Barasch 15 (☎021/323 3970). The **circus** is at Aleea Circului 1 (Metro Ştefan cel Mare; ☎021/211 4195), with performances at 10am and 3pm on Saturdays and 3pm and 6pm on Sundays – it's usually closed through the summer months. The circus is also the venue for Micul Paris ("Little Paris"), a lively **cabaret** show set in 1930s Bucharest featuring superb singing and music, much fancy footwork and extravagant costumes; it's a terrific evening's entertainment. Micul Paris is staged every Saturday at 10pm and tickets (€15–40) can be purchased from the circus box office (Tues–Sun 10am–2pm and two hours before the performance). Note that the show finishes just after midnight when most public transport has shut down – if you need a taxi, contact one of the reputable companies (see p.63).

Cinemas

Cinemas are plentiful, both in the centre and the suburbs, showing films from all over the world, though, predictably, subtitled Hollywood flicks are the most popular fare. Prices are cheap at around €3–7. The two major multiplexes are the Movieplex at the Plaza Romania Mall (see opposite) and the Hollywood Multiplex in the Bucharest Mall (see opposite) – both have up to ten screenings at any one time. The best of the city-centre cinemas (where films are slightly cheaper) are Patria and Scala, on B-dul. Magheru 12 and 2 respectively, and Corso, at B-dul. Elisabeta 1. The Elvira Popesco Hall, in the French Institute at B-dul. Dacia 77 (☎021/211 3836), is usually a good place to catch world films,

Bucharest's Festival Year

Bucharest is not traditionally known for its **festivals**, but this is slowly changing, partly due to the increased willingness of Western acts to perform in the country. The highlight of the city's cultural offerings – and it's a world-class event – is the bi-annual George Enescu Festival (⊛www.festivalenescu.ro) in September, which features three weeks of classical concerts by some of the world's finest musicians. Throughout this period, there is a full programme of concerts at the Atheneum and Sala Palatalui, as well as recitals, movie screenings, events on Piaţa Revoluţiei and exhibitions on Enescu. There's also a festival of piano music, named after Romania's greatest pianist, Dinu Lipatti, in early May. In the second week of November, the Ion Luca Caragiale Festival, dedicated to Romania's best-known playwright, brings to town the best of the year's drama from the provincial theatres. Long starved of top-drawer live music, the city now has B'Estival (⊛www.bestival.ro), a three-day music-fest that takes place at the end of June at the Romexpo pavilion, featuring rock and dance acts such as the Prodigy, Faithless and Marilyn Manson. Now that Romanian film is becoming better known, there's a chance to see the best of it at the DaKino Bucharest International Film Festival (BIFF) in November, which features an impressive roster of both new domestic and foreign (mainly European) movies.

while the Cinematecă, at Str. Eforie 2 (☎021/313 0483), shows a good selection of screen classics – programmes are posted outside.

Sports and activities

Bucharest's only major spectator sport is **football**, with four clubs resident in the city: by far the most famous club is the army team and former European Cup winners, **Steaua Bucureşti** (B-dul. Ghencea 35; tram #8 or #47, trolley bus #69), followed by the one-time Securitate team, **Dinamo Bucureşti** (Şos. Ştefan cel Mare 9; Metro Ştefan cel Mare). Next in the pecking order comes the rail-workers team, **Rapid Bucureşti** (Şos. Giuleşti 18; Metro Cringaşi), and then the real minnows, **Naţional**, who play at the Cotroceni Stadium, behind the *Grand Marriott* hotel. Tickets (between €2–4) can be bought at the stadia before each game.

The best of the city's relatively few **sporting facilities** are the Diplomatic Club, Str. Al Minovici (daily 9am–10pm), which has tennis, swimming pools (including one for kids), and Bucharest's only golf course (albeit just seven holes); and the Herăstrău complex, at Şos. Nordului 5–7 (tennis, sauna and massage facilities). In the summer, Strandul Tineretului, at Aleea Ştrandului 1, offers water sports and tennis. The Diplomatic club aside, the best **swimming** pool is Blue Ciel, a large open-air venue north of the city at Str. Giuseppe Verdi 2 (daily 9am–9pm). Other options include the (small) pools at the *Athénée Palace, Ramada Majestic* and *Intercontinental* hotels, and the city lakes – Floreasca (Metro Aurel Vlaicu), Strauleşti (western terminus of trolley bus #97) and Băneasa (bus #131 or #205). The students' swimming pool is at Ştrandul Tei, off B-dul. Lacul Tei.

Shopping

Bucharest's range of **shops** has expanded considerably in recent years, with many international names appearing in the city's handful of new and refurbished shopping malls. The city's largest **shopping complex** is Plaza Romania, west of the centre at B-dul. Timisoara 26 (daily 10am–10pm), followed by the Bucureşti Mall, south of the centre at Calea Vitan 55–59 (daily 10am–10pm). More convenient is the Unirea department store at Piaţa Unirii 1 (Mon–Sat 9am–10pm, Sun 9am–6pm). Otherwise, there's the posh Grand Avenue (daily 10am–8pm), a small precinct inside the *Grand Marriott* hotel (see p.66) housing a few designer and boutique shops.

For **antiques**, head for the streets around the historic quarter, and in particular Str. Lipscani and Str. Covaci; two of the best places are Craii de Curtea Veche, at Str. Covaci 14 (Mon–Fri 10am–6pm, Sat 10am–3pm), and the Hanul cu Tei bazaar, at Str. Lipscani 63–65 (same times). For craftwork and traditional **souvenirs**, try Romartizana, at Calea Victoriei 16–20 (Mon–Fri 10am–8pm, Sat 9am–1pm) or, better still, make your way out to the Museum of the Romanian Peasant (see p.77) or the Village Museum (see p.86).

For Romanian **music**, Muzica at Calea Victoriei 43 (Mon–Fri 9.30am–7pm, Sat 9.30am–2.30pm) is a good bet, as are the Diverta shops at Str. Rosetti 14 (daily 10am–10pm) and up on the third floor of the Unirea department store (see above). The best place to get hold of English-language **books** – including Romanian history and politics, fiction and non-fiction, and some excellent children's books – is Cărtureşti, at Str. Pictor Arthur Verona 13 (Mon–Fri 9am–9pm, Sat 11am–8pm, Sun 1–9pm). Librăria Noi, at B-dul. Bălcescu 18

(Mon–Sat 9.30am–8.30pm, Sun 11am–7pm), carries a decent range of English-language books, translated Romanian literature, and CDs – it's also the best place to pick up **guidebooks and maps**. Humanitas, next to the Crețulescu church at Calea Victoriei 45 (Mon–Sat 10am–7pm, Sun 10am–5pm), has a varied selection of titles on Romania, while secondhand books can be found on the streets around the University and in the Piața Universității underpass. Foreign newspapers and magazines are tricky to come by, but the kiosks in the higher-end hotels might have same-day foreign editions.

For food, the best **supermarkets** are La Fourmi in the Unirea department store (Mon–Fri 8.30am–9.30pm, Sat 8.30am–9pm, Sun 10am–6pm) and at B-dul. 1 Mai (Mon–Sat 9.30am–8.30pm); Mega Image at B-dul. N. Titulescu 39–49 (Mon–Sat 8.30am–9.30pm, Sun 8.30am–6pm), and at Șos. Ștefan cel Mare 226; and Nic, on Piața Amzei (24hr) – all of these have good deli counters. The 24-hour grocery store at Calea Griviței 142, opposite the Gara de Nord station, is a useful place to stock up on foodstuffs before embarking on a long journey.

The best of the city's **markets** – where you can pick up fresh produce and a variety of other knick-knacks – are Piața Amzei, near Piața Romană, and Matache, behind the CFR office near the Gara de Nord. There's also a vast Sunday-morning **flea market** (Trgul Vitan) on Calea Vitan, fifteen minutes' walk south of the Dristor I metro station, alongside the Dâmbovița embankment. Beware of pickpockets at all these places.

Listings

Airlines The main Tarom office is at Spl. Independenței 17 (Mon–Fri 9am–7pm, Sat 9am–1pm; ☎021/337 0400, ⌨www.tarom.ro), with additional offices at Str. Buzești 59, just off Piața Victoriei (Mon–Fri 9am–7.30pm, Sat 9am–1pm; ☎021/204 6464). Carpatair is based at Băneasa Airport (☎021/204 1093, ⌨www.carpatair.com), as is WizzAir (⌨www.wizzair.com). Air France, Str. G-ral Praporgescu 1–5 (☎021/312 0085); Austrian Airlines, B-dul. Magheru 16–18 (☎021/312 0545); British Airways, Calea Victoriei 15 (☎021/303 2222, ⌨www.ba.com); KLM, Aleea Alexandru 9a (☎021/231 5619); Lufthansa, B-dul. Magheru 18 (☎021/204 8410); Malev, Calea Vitan 6 (☎021/326 8072).

Airport information Henri Coândă ☎021/204 1000; Băneasa ☎021/232 0020.

Banks and exchange Exchange counters are on all the main streets, and most of them are open until late in the evening. Usually they do not charge commission, but be wary of those that do and be sure you know what the rate might be. Changing travellers' cheques is a relatively painless process; among the quickest and most efficient places is the Bank Austria Creditanstalt on Piața Revoluției, and the BCR at B-dul. Regina Elisabeta 5.

British Council Calea Dorobanților 14 (Mon 3–7pm, Tues–Fri 11am–7pm, Sat 10am–1pm; ☎021/307 9600, ⌨www.britishcouncil.ro/kls). Library, newspapers and Internet.

Buses Atlassib, B-dul. Gh. Duca 4 (☎021/222 4735); Eurolines Touring, B-dul. Al. Ioan Cuza (☎021/210 0890) for buses to Germany; Murat, B-dul. D. Golescu 31 (☎021/222 7307) or Toros, Calea Griviței 136–138 (☎021/223 1898) for buses to Istanbul; Anesis, Str. Poterași 20–22 (☎021/330 9176) for buses to Athens.

Car rental Avis, at Str. Mihail Moxa 9 (☎021/210 4344, ⌨www.avis.ro) and at the *Intercontinental* hotel (☎021/314 1837); Budget, Str. Polonă 35 (☎021/210 2867, ⌨www.budgetro.ro); Europcar, Calea Calarasilor 44 (☎021/320 8554, ⌨www.europcar.com); and Hertz, at Str. Ion Bianu 47 (☎021/222 1256, ⌨www.hertz.com.ro) and at the *Grand Marriott* hotel (☎021/403 2956). All these companies have outlets at Henri Coândă Airport.

Car repairs ACR has its head office at Str. Tache Ionescu 27 (☎021/315 5510) and technical assistance centres at Calea Dorobanților 85 (☎021/211 1835) and Spl. Independenței 204 (☎021/212 6433). These should be open 24hr.

Embassies and consulates Australia, B-dul. Unirii 74 ☎021/320 9826, ⌨www.romaniaaustralia.ro; Bulgaria, Str. Rabat 5 ☎021/230 2150, ⌨bulembassy@pcnet.ro; Canada, Str. N. Iorga 36 ☎021/307 5000, ⌨www.dfait-maeci.gc.ca /bucharest; Hungary, Str. Prof. Dr. Dimitrie Gerota 63–65 ☎021/312 0073; Moldova, Aleea Alexandru 40 ☎021/230 0474; Serbia, Calea Dorobanților 34

021/211 9871; UK, Str. Jules. Michelet 24 021/201 7300, www.britishembassy.gov.uk /romania; Ukraine, Calea Dorobanţilor 16 021/211 6986; US, Str. Filipescu 26 021/210 4042, www.usembassy.ro.

Emergencies Ambulance 961; police 955; fire service 981.

Hospitals For emergency treatment, you should go to the Emergency Clinic Hospital (Spitalul Clinic de Urgenţa), at Calea Floreasca 8 (Metro Ştefan cel Mare; 021/317 0121), or the private Biomedica International Medical Centre, Str. M. Eminescu 42 (Mon–Sat 8am–8pm; 021/211 9674, for emergencies, 230 8001). Your embassy can recommend doctors speaking your language. There's excellent, Western-standard dental treatment at the German-run B.B. Clinic, Str. Ionescu Gion 4 (021/320 0151).

Internet access Places offering online services come and go on what seems like a daily basis, but the best of the current bunch are: Acces Internet, B-dul. Catargiu 6 (daily 24hr); Biblioteca GDS, Calea Victoriei 120 (daily 24hr); British Council, Calea Dorobanţilor 14 (Mon 3–7pm, Tues–Fri 11am–7pm, Sat 10am–1pm); Cyber Espace, inside the French Institute at Dacia 77 (Mon–Sat 10am–8pm); Cyber Club, B-dul. Carol I 25 (daily 10am–10pm); Sweet Internet Café, Str. Maria Rosetti 79 (daily 24hr). Expect to pay around €1 for an hour online. Wi-Fi is available in many of the upmarket hotels, as well as all KFC and Pizza Hut outlets.

Laundry Immaculate Cleaners, Str. Polonă 76 (Mon–Fri 9am–10pm, Sat 9am–4pm; 021/211 4413); Nufărul, Calea Moşilor 276 (Mon–Fri 7am–8pm, Sat 9am–1pm; 021/210 1441); Nuf Nuf, Calea Şerban Vodă 76–78 (021/335 0168).

Pharmacies There is at least one 24hr pharmacy in each sector of the city. Sensiblu have a number of pharmacies throughout Bucharest, including central outlets at Calea Dorobanţilor 65, Str. G. Enescu 36–40, B-dul. Titulescu 39–49, B-dul. Bălcescu 7 (there's a good optician here, too), and in the Unirea department store. Helpnet pharmacy has 24hr outlets at B-dul. Ion Mihalache 92 and B-dul. Unirii 24.

Police Each sector has its own police station, but the most central is at B-dul. Lascăr Catargiu 20 (entrance on Str. Daniel; 021/659 2046). Traffic accidents (with damage) should be dealt with at Str. Logofăt Udrişte (021/323 3030).

Post office The main post office is at Str. Matei Millo 10 (Mon–Fri 7.30am–8pm). To receive mail here, make sure it is addressed c/o Officiul PTTR no. 1, Bucureşti. There's another, much bigger, office near the train station on Str. Gara de Nord (Mon–Fri 7.30am–8pm, Sat 8am–2pm).

Trains Agenţie CFR's advance booking offices are at Str. Domniţa Anastasia 10–14 (Mon–Fri 7.30am–7.30pm, Sat 8am–noon; 021/313 2642), and next to the IBIS hotel at Calea Griviţei 139 (same times; 021/212 8947); to be sure of a seat in summer, you should book tickets one day in advance. You can also buy national and international tickets from Wasteels in the Gara de Nord (Mon–Fri 8am–7pm, Sat 8am–2pm; 021/222 7844, www.wasteelstravel.ro); foreign currencies are accepted here.

Travel agents Atlantic Tours, Calea Victoriei 202 (021/212 9232); Dacia Tour, B-dul. Magheru 1–3 (021/310 2547); European Travel Services, Str. Orzari 5 (021/323 6187, www.european -travel-services.com); J'Info Tours, Str. Jules Michelet 1 (021/222 5010); SimpaTurism, Str. Puţu cu Plopi 18 (021/312 7495, www .simpaturism.ro) and Str. Calderon 1 (021/314 0323) for city tours; Paralela 45, B-dul. Regina Elisabeta 29–31 (021/311 1958, www .paralela45.ro) for ski and spa bookings.

Around Bucharest

There's a fine selection of places to visit in Bucharest's immediate surroundings. The city is ringed by some superb monasteries, such as **Căldăruşani** and **Snagov**, country houses – most notably **Mogoşoaia** – and interesting villages, such as **Clejani**, which is home to some of the country's finest Gypsy music. However, without your own transport, many of these places are quite hard to reach, the only option in most cases a painfully slow and crowded bus ride.

North of Bucharest

If you travel to Snagov by road, you'll pass through the area most notoriously affected by Ceauşescu's **systematization** programme (see box, pp.98–99).

Baloteşti, just north of Henri Coandă Airport, consists of stark modern apartment buildings housing people displaced from villages such as Dimieni, which lay just east of the airport. Vlădiceasca and Cioflinceni, just off the DN1 on the road to Snagov, were bulldozed in 1988, and the inhabitants resettled in Ghermăneşti, on the western outskirts of Snagov.

Four kilometres east of Baloteşti is **Căciulaţi**, built as a planned estate village by the Ghica family, whose villa – now the property of the Romanian Academy – was occupied by the Securitate; over three hundred bodies, unrecorded victims of the communist police state, were found buried in its run-down park in the mid-1990s. Seven **trains** a day from Bucharest (to Urziceni) stop here, and, of these, five continue on to **Greci**, another 10km east. A couple of kilometres south of Greci is the **Căldăruşani Monastery**, which is beyond the reach of public transport from Bucharest. This inconvenience didn't stop the world press from mobbing it when tennis stars Mariana Simionescu and Bjorn Borg were married here in 1980. The church where the wedding took place was built in 1638 (in exactly 100 days) by Matei Basarab and is noted for its school of icon painting, established in 1787. Among the many icons on display here are eight by the juvenile Grigorescu (see box, p.111), who studied at the school from 1854 to 1855. The monastery is now home to some thirty monks and over 150 boys attending the priest school. Father Calinic may be able to

Systematization

Systematization was Ceauşescu's policy to do away with up to half of the country's villages and move the rural population into larger centres. The concept was first developed by Nikita Krushchev in the Soviet Union in 1951, to combat the movement of younger people to the towns by **amalgamating villages** to raise the standard of rural life. Similar plans were put forward in Hungary, and in 1967 Ceauşescu reorganized Romania's local government system and announced a scheme to get rid of up to 6300 villages and replace them with 120 new towns and 558 agro-industrial centres.

His declared aim (based on an original idea in Marx and Engels' *Communist Manifesto*) was "to wipe out radically the major differences between towns and villages; to bring the working and living conditions of the working people in the countryside closer to those in the towns". Ceauşescu thought that by herding people together into apartment buildings so that "the community fully dominates and controls the individual", systematization would produce Romania's "new socialist man". Thankfully, the project was forgotten while Ceauşescu was preoccupied by other projects such as the Danube–Black Sea Canal and Bucharest's Centru Civic, but he relaunched it in March 1988, when he was becoming obsessed with increasing exports and paying off the national debt.

Since collectivization, Romania's agricultural output had declined steadily, and this on fertile land with one of the longest growing seasons in Europe. In 1985, the minuscule private sector produced twenty-nine percent of the country's fruit, fourteen percent of its meat and almost twenty percent of its milk. Ceauşescu was determined to **revolutionize agriculture** by increasing the growing area, while also further increasing centralization and reducing the scope and incentive for individual initiative. While the peasants had previously been able to support themselves with their own livestock, there was to be no accommodation for animals in the new blocks. To add insult to injury, the peasants were to receive derisory compensation for their demolished homes and then be charged rent.

The model development was to be the **Ilfov Agricultural Sector**, immediately north of Bucharest, where the first evictions and demolitions took place in August 1988.

give you a short guided tour of the church and also take you down to the ossuary, where a large number of monks' skulls are held.

Snagov

SNAGOV, a small sprawling village 40km north of Bucharest, is the most popular weekend destination for Bucharestians: its beautiful sixteen-kilometre-long lake has water-sports facilities and a reserve for water plants, such as Indian waterlily, arrowhead and oriental beech. In the centre of the lake is an island occupied by a **monastery** built in 1519. King Mihai and later Ceauşescu and other high functionaries had their weekend villas around the shore, and the lake was also the scene of the summit which saw Yugoslavia's expulsion from the Warsaw Pact in 1948. Bălcescu and other revolutionaries of 1848 were held in the monastery's prison, as was the Hungarian leader Imre Nagy following the Soviet invasion of 1956.

Visitors now come here principally to seek the **tomb of Dracula**, sited in front of the church altar. Though lacking identifying inscriptions, it's likely that this is indeed the burial place of Vlad the Impaler: the richly dressed corpse exhumed in 1935 had been decapitated, as had Vlad, whose head was supposedly dispatched, wrapped and perfumed, as a gift to the Sultan. Vlad's murder

Only two or three days' notice was given before shops were closed down and bus services stopped, forcing the people into the designated villages. Entire communities were removed to blocks in Otopeni and Ghermăneşti, where up to ten families had to share one kitchen and the sewage system had not been completed. At the same time, the villagers of Buda and Ordoreanu, just south of Bucharest on the River Argeş, were relocated to Bragadiru to make way for a reservoir for the proposed Bucharest–Danube Canal. In other villages across the nation – including, fittingly, Scorniceşti, Ceauşescu's birthplace in Wallachia – ugly **concrete Civic Centre buildings** began to appear in the centres of the planned New Towns.

Repairs were banned in all the doomed villages and on all single-storey buildings, but these regulations were interpreted differently by the various counties. In Maramureş, the authorities, aware that greater distances to the agricultural land would be a disadvantage, allowed repair work on outlying farms and also permitted attics to count as a second storey. In the Banat, efforts were made to attract migrants to houses left by emigrating Schwabs (a German ethnic group), although these should in theory have been demolished.

There was widespread condemnation of this scheme that was set to uproot half of the rural populace; in August 1988, the Cluj academic **Doina Cornea**, one of the country's few open dissidents, wrote an open letter (published in the West) in protest, pointing out that the villages, with their unbroken folk culture, are the spiritual centre of Romanian life, and that to demolish them would be to "strike at the very soul of the people". She was soon placed under house arrest, but the campaign abroad gathered pace. Although the Hungarian view that the plan was an attack on their community was widely accepted, it does seem clear that Ceauşescu's aim was indeed a wholesale assault on the rural way of life.

Approximately eighteen villages had suffered major demolitions by the end of 1989, when the scheme was at once cancelled by the FSN, the new ruling party following the revolution; new buildings are going up all over the country, and those people uprooted by Ceauşescu's scheme are returning to the sites of their villages and starting all over again.

is believed to have occurred in the forests nearby, and the monks would have been predisposed to take the body, since both Vlad and his father had given money to the monastery. Indeed, Vlad is thought to have had quite a hand in its development, insisting that several features be added, including, appropriately enough, a prison and torture chamber. To get across to the island, you can hire a rowing boat (€5 from the jetty on the southern shore of the lake, just past the Complex Astoria (see below); follow the reeds round to the left until the monastery comes into view. Give yourself a good couple of hours to make the trip over and back. Note that you must be appropriately dressed to gain admittance to the monastery.

Nine **buses** a day make the rather long-winded trip from the Băneasa bus station – located 500m west of Băneasa Airport on B-dul. Ionescu de la Brad 1 – to Snagov. Get the driver to drop you off at the fork in the road 1km beyond the village, and walk the remaining half a kilometre or so to the **Complex Astoria**, a large and crowded leisure park on the lake's southern shore; there's a small entrance fee payable to enter the complex (€1 per person and €4 for cars). Although it's unlikely you'll need, or want, to stay here, the complex contains the overpriced *Snagov Minihotel* (☎021/313 6782; ⑤), and an unofficial **campsite** with the most basic facilities. There's better accommodation in the village of **Ghermăneşti**, 2km south of Snagov, namely the roadside *Pension Galanton* at Ghermăneşti 18 (☎0722/222 353; ⑤), which has a dozen smartly furnished rooms, restaurant and pool. The bus to Snagov stops in the village.

Mogoşoaia

The lovely **palace** at **Mogoşoaia** (Tues–Sun 10am–6pm), 10km northwest of Bucharest along the DN1, is perhaps Wallachia's most important non-religious monument. Designed by Constantin Brâncoveanu (see p.131) between 1698 and 1702 as a summer residence for his family, it's a two-storey building of red brick with a Venetian-style loggia overlooking a lake. After Brâncoveanu's execution, the palace became an inn, then, after a fire destroyed the interior, a warehouse. Towards the end of the nineteenth century, the palace was passed to the Bibescu family (descendants of Brâncoveanu), before finally being handed over to the state in 1956.

At the end of the long drive, which extends from the main road up to the palace, you pass the small St George's Chapel (built in 1688) before entering the complex proper through the entry tower; to the left is the L-shaped great house, to the right, the old kitchen, and straight in front, the main palace building. Its interior is now given over to a series of rather dull, furniture-less rooms (thanks to Ceauşescu, who requisitioned it all), occasionally brightened up with tapestries, vestments and icons, while the fine vaulted cellar to the left of the entrance contains a stack of stoneworks. The lush gardens, and the lake behind the main building, do, however, make a visit worthwhile, and there's some good rambling to be had in the nearby woods. Hidden away on waste ground behind the old kitchen wall is a huge statue of Lenin, removed from Piaţa Presei Libere and dumped here after the 1989 revolution; next to the prostrate Russian leader is the statue of the former communist prime minister Petru Groza. The easiest way to get to Mogoşoaia is by **maxitaxi** (heading for Buftea), or **bus** #460 from the Laromet tram terminus. A less enticing option is to take one of the five daily local **trains** (to Urziceni), although this entails a three-kilometre walk back along the tracks into the village.

▲ Remains of Lenin Statue, Mogoşoaia

Clejani

Some 40km southwest of Bucharest is the small village of **CLEJANI**, renowned throughout the region as a centre for **Gypsy music**; the world-famous band Taraf de Haidouks (see p.461) hails from here, as well as a number of other very talented musicians. If you're a fan of such music, or if you're just interested in experiencing Gypsy culture close up, then take half a day to visit the village – and, if you're lucky, you may get to hear some of the spellbinding music first-hand.

The village itself is unremarkable, but the Gypsy settlement – little more than a dusty, mud-dried street lined with crumbling, one-roomed homes – is easily found; upon arriving at the village from Vadu Lat (see below), take the first left, continue walking for 400m and you'll find the Gypsy settlement on your right. Strangers are few and far between here, and you may initially feel a little intimidated, but for every pair of eyes fixed on you there will be a barefooted, grinning child tagging along, eager to have their photo taken. While you're here, there's a good chance that you'll find a group happy to put on an impromptu **performance**; ask around for Sandin Marin, also known as Zis Tagoia, who should be able to gather together the Taraf de Plugări band. It's expected that you'll offer some money in return for the band's efforts (€10–15 would be appropriate), and a few bottles of beer wouldn't go amiss either. While at the settlement, have a wander around; it's likely you'll get invited into someone's house, which will give you the opportunity to witness first-hand the paucity of Gypsy life.

To get to Clejani from Bucharest, take one of the five daily **trains** from the Gara Basarab to Vadu Lat (the last train back to Bucharest is at 10pm). From the station, it's a three-kilometre walk: turn right and continue along the tracks for 100m until you come to some steps set into an embankment; from here, walk along the path across the field until you come to the main road, then turn left and carry on walking for 2km – there's also a good chance you'll be able to hitch a ride.

Travel details

Trains

Bucharest to: Baia Mare (2 daily; 11–13hr); Braşov (every 45–60min; 2hr 30min–4hr 45min); Cluj (6 daily; 7hr–11hr 15min); Constanţa (8–15 daily; 2hr 30min–5hr 30min); Craiova (hourly; 2hr 30min–4hr 45min); Galaţi (5 daily; 3hr 30min–5hr 15min); Giurgiu Nord (8 daily; 1hr 30min); Iaşi (5 daily; 5hr 30min–7hr 45min); Mangalia (4–7 daily; 3hr 45min–5hr 15min); Oradea (2 daily; 11hr); Piteşti (10 daily; 1hr 30min–3hr); Ploieşti (every 40–60min; 45min–1hr 45min); Satu Mare (2 daily; 13–14hr); Sibiu (5 daily; 4hr 45min–11hr 30min); Sighişoara (10 daily; 4hr–7hr 30min); Suceava (4 daily; 5hr 30min–6hr 30min); Târgovişte (5 daily; 1hr 15min–2hr 15min); Timişoara (6 daily; 7hr 30min–10hr 30min); Tulcea (2 daily; 5hr 45min–6hr 45min).

Buses and maxitaxis

Bucharest (Băneasa) to: Snagov (9 daily; 45min). Bucharest to: Bacau (10 daily; 4hr 30min); Braşov (every 30min; 2hr 45min); Craiova (every 30min; 4hr); Piatra Neamţ (10 daily; 5hr 30min); Piteşti (every 45min; 1hr 45min); Sibiu (2 daily; 4hr 30min); Sinaia (every 30min; 2hr); Târgu Mureş (7 daily; 5hr 30min).

Flights

Bucharest to: Arad (12 weekly; 1hr); Baia Mare (5 weekly; 1hr 15min); Cluj (2–3 daily; 1hr); Constanţa (4 weekly; 1hr); Iaşi (3 daily; 1hr 10min); Oradea (6 weekly; 1hr 20min); Satu Mare (6 weekly; 1hr 15min); Sibiu (10 weekly; 45min); Suceava (2–3 daily; 1hr 45min); Timişoara (3–4 daily; 55min).

International trains

Bucharest to: Belgrade, Serbia (1 daily; 12hr 30min); Budapest, Hungary (4 daily; 12–13hr); Chişinău, Moldova (1 daily; 12hr 30min); Istanbul, Turkey (1 daily; 19hr); Kiev, Ukraine (1 daily; 30hr); Moscow, Russia (1 daily; 45hr); Prague, Czech Republic (2 daily; 23hr); Ruse, Bulgaria (3 daily; 2hr 30min–3hr); Sofia, Bulgaria (2 daily; 10hr 30min); Thessaloniki, Greece (1 daily; 23hr); Vienna, Austria (2 daily; 17hr).

International buses

Bucharest to: Chişinău Moldova (1 daily; 8hr); Istanbul, Turkey (3 daily; 11hr).

2

Wallachia

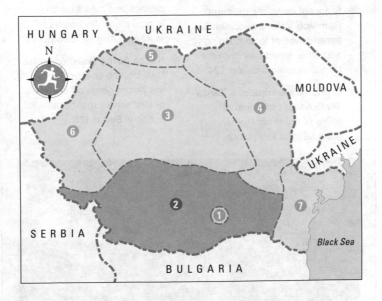

CHAPTER 2   # Highlights

✱ **Curtea de Argeş** Attractive small town with two of the region's most striking ecclesiastical monuments – the Princely Church and Episcopal Church. See p.121

✱ **Dracula's Castle** Continue on Vlad's trail up to the dramatically sited Poienari Castle – the real Dracula's castle. See p.123

✱ **Bujoreni open-air museum, Râmnicu Vâlcea** Fascinating assemblage of local buildings and other structures from the Olt valley region. See p.124

✱ **Brâncuşi's sculptures, Târgu Jiu** Outdoor collection of some of the great Romanian's most famous sculptures, including the *Endless Column*. See p.127

✱ **Horezu Monastery** Brâncoveanu's marvellous seventeenth-century complex, featuring the Great Church replete with Byzantine frescoes. See p.130

✱ **Tismana garden festival** Listen to shepherds' panpipes and check out traditional clothes and rugs at this annual music and crafts festival in August. See p.132

✱ **Kazan gorge** Bisected by the Danube, the sheer cliffs of the Kazan gorge offer some of Wallachia's most dramatic scenery. See p.136

▲ Episcopal Church, Curtea de Argeş

2

Wallachia

Centuries before the name "Romania" appeared on maps of Europe, foreign merchants and rulers had heard of **Wallachia**, the land of the Vlachs or Wallachs, known in Romanian as Ţară Romaneasca ("Land of the Romanians"). A distant outpost of Christendom, it succumbed to the Turks in 1417 and was then largely forgotten until the nineteenth century. Occasional travellers reported on the region's backwardness and the corruption of its ruling boyars, but few predicted its sudden union with Moldavia in 1859 – the first step in the creation of modern Romania. Today, in the highlands and on the Bărăgan Steppe – where pagan rites such as the festivals of Ariet and Căluş are still practised – peasant life largely follows the ancient pastoral cycle, but industrialization and collective farming have wrought huge changes to the plains around **Ploieşti**, **Piteşti**, **Craiova** and the Jiu Valley, all places that now have little to recommend them. The region is mainly comprised of flat and featureless agricultural land, and is in many ways the least interesting of Romania's three principal provinces, but as it is home to the nation's capital, **Bucharest**, people will invariably find themselves passing through en route to Transylvania, the coast, or Bulgaria.

The most rewarding part of Wallachia is its western half, known (after its chief river) as Oltenia, which stretches from Bucharest to the Iron Gates on the Danube. Here, the foothills of the Carpathians are largely scenic and unspoilt, and possessed of the region's most attractive and historically interesting towns, such as **Curtea de Argeş**. Both **Poienari Castle**, north of Curtea de Argeş, and the town of **Târgovişte** have strong connections with Vlad Ţepeş – better known as Dracula – who once ruled Wallachia, even though modern myth links him with Transylvania. In addition, a string of fine monasteries, such as **Horezu** and **Arnota**, runs along the foothills; most were razed at the behest of "progressive" despots (who otherwise spent their time fighting the Turks and repressing their own peasantry), but were rebuilt in the late seventeenth century in the distinctively Romanian style developed by Constantin Brâncoveanu. The remainder of the region is dominated by large industrialized centres, such as **Ploieşti**, **Piteşti**, **Craiova** and **Târgu Jiu**, the last of which does at least have the work of Romania's world-renowned sculptor Constantin Brâncuşi as a major inducement to visit. Otherwise, there's a fine excursion to be had up along the **Kazan gorge**, where the Danube marks the border with Serbia.

Wallachia is renowned for its **festivals**. During the third week in February, folk musicians gather for the Izvoare Fermecate festival at Târgu Jiu, while Polovragi to the east is the setting for a big fair in July. Another fair, devoted to pottery, coincides with the Songs of the Olt festival at Calimăneşti during the first week in August; and on August 15, pan-pipers congregate at Tismana. For

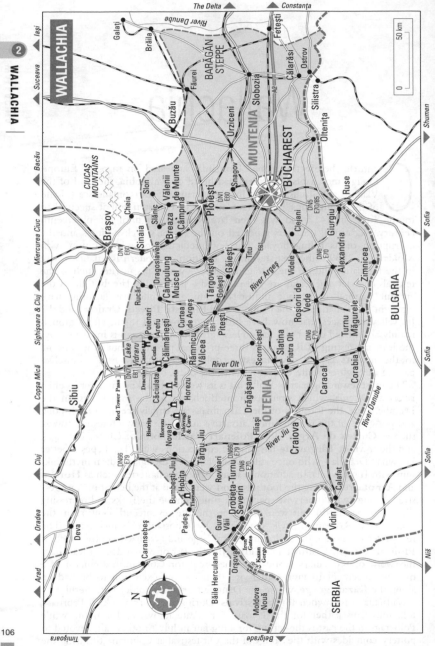

WALLACHIA

The Delta ▲   ▲ Constanţa

River Danube

BARĂGĂN STEPPE

Galaţi
Brăila
Fetești
Călărași
Ostrov
Silistra
Făurei
Buzău
Slobozia
Urziceni
A2
MUNTENIA
BUCHAREST

CIUCAȘ MOUNTAINS

Cheia
Sinaia
Brașov
Slon
Vălenii de Munte
Slănic
Breaza
Câmpina
Ploiești DN1 E60
Snagov
Ruse
DN5 E70/85
Giurgiu
Dragoslavele
Câmpulung Muscel
Rucăr
Târgoviște
Golești
Găiești
Titu E81
Clejani
River Argeș
Videle
DN6 E70
Alexandria
Poienari
Arefu
Curtea de Argeș
Cozia
Dracula's Castle
Lake Vidraru
Călimănești
Râmnicu Vâlcea
DN7 E81
Pitești
Roșiori de Vede
Zimnicea
Turnu Măgurele
Red Tower Pass
Cozia
Horezu
River Olt
Scornicești
Slatina
Piatra Olt
DN6 E70
Căciulata
Horezu
Bistrița
Drăgășani
Caracal
Corabia
Novaci
Polovragi & Cave
Filiași
Târgu Jiu
Craiova
River Jiu
DN66 E79
Rovinari
DN66 E79
Bumbești-Jiu
Hobița
Tismana
Drobeta-Turnu Severin
DN6 E70
Calafat
Padeș
Gura Văii
Iron Gates
Orșova
Kazan Gorge
Vidin
Moldova Nouă

OLTENIA

MUNTENIA

SERBIA

BULGARIA

◄ Iași
◄ Suceava
◄ Bacău
◄ Miercurea Ciuc
◄ Sighișoara & Cluj
◄ Copșa Mică
◄ Cluj
◄ Oradea
◄ Arad

Sibiu
Deva
Caransebeș
Băile Herculane

▼ Timișoara
▲ Belgrade
▼ Niš
▼ Sofia
▼ Sofia
▼ Sofia
▼ Shumen

N

0   50 km

more information on the region's festivals, see p.42. **Getting around** the region is easy enough: trains fan out from Bucharest in all directions, serving most places listed here, while regular maxitaxis shuttle between towns and link the capital to destinations as far afield as Craiova and Târgu Jiu.

Ploieşti, Târgovişte and Piteşti

The large industrial towns of **Ploieşti** and **Piteşti** are typical of much of Wallachia as a whole, and while neither is very attractive nor possesses much in the way of sights, they do serve as useful springboards for more enticing destinations in the region. Ploieşti lies on the principal road and rail line between Bucharest and Transylvania, with a couple of sites of interest to the north, while Piteşti is situated astride the main routes from Bucharest to Câmpulung and the Argeş and Olt valleys. The most worthwhile of the three major towns north and northwest of Bucharest is **Târgovişte**, the old capital of Wallachia, boasting several ancient churches and the ruins of Vlad Ţepeş's court.

Ploieşti and around

An oily smell and the eerie night-time flare of vented gases proclaim **PLOIEŞTI** as Romania's biggest oil town. In 1857, the world's first oil wells were sunk here and in Petrolia, Ontario; the first ever refinery was built in Ploieşti, and in 1858 Bucharest became the first city in the world to be lit by oil lamps. By the outbreak of World War I, there were ten refineries in the town, all owned by foreign oil companies; these were wrecked in 1916 by British agents to deny them to the Germans, and patched together again only to be destroyed once more, this time by the retreating German forces in 1918. However, it was the townsfolk who really paid the price, when Allied aircraft carpet-bombed Ploieşti in 1944 – hence the town centre's almost total concrete uniformity today. The main reason to come to Ploieşti is to take advantage of the excellent **transport links** to the more interesting parts of Wallachia.

Arrival and information

Generally speaking, **trains** to and from Transylvania use Ploieşti Vest station, southwest of town at the end of Str. Mărăşeşti, while those to and from Moldavia use Ploieşti Sud, 1km south of town on Piaţa 1 Decembrie 1918; thus trains from Bucharest may arrive at either. The two stations are linked by bus #2, which passes close to the centre of the town. The CFR office, for **rail bookings**, is next to the department store at B-dul. Republicii 17 (☎0244/195 620), while TAROM, for flight enquiries, is at B-dul. Republicii 141, Bloc 31 C1 (☎0244/595 620).

The **bus station** is 200m west of the Sud train station. There are frequent maxitaxis from the station to Bucharest that will set you down at Otopeni Airport if you're flying onwards from there; going in the other direction, from the airport to Ploieşti, is rather more hit-and-miss unless you have a reservation. To make a reservation call Millennium Trans (☎021/9441, 0743/001 000; ⒺCobrescu@gmail.com). Car rental from Cronos Car, on Str. Cantacuzino 115 (☎0721/251 070, ⓦwww.cronoscar.ro), is far cheaper than at Otopeni Airport.

The Town

There's little to detain you in Ploieşti, though the town does have several moderately interesting museums. The most enjoyable is the **Art Museum** at

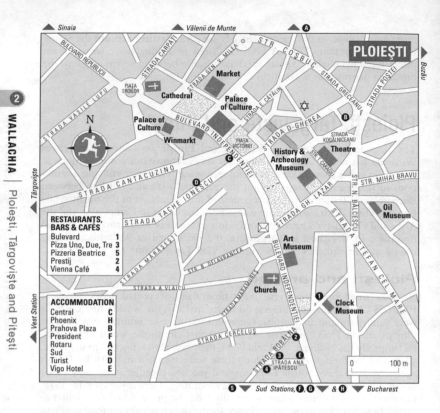

B-dul. Independenţei 1 (Muzeul de Artă; Tues–Sun 10am–6pm), a fine, recently restored Neoclassical building holding a healthy collection of paintings by many of Romania's foremost artists, including Aman, Luchian, Pallady, Petrascu and Grigorescu. In the huge Neoclassical Palace of Culture at Str. Cătălin 1, the **Museum of Human Biology** (Muzeul de Biologie Umană; Tues–Fri 9am–5pm, Sat & Sun 9am–1pm) has eye-catching displays on evolution, anatomy and ecology which make it one of the most striking museums of its kind in Romania. In the same building, the **Ethnography Museum** (Muzeul de Etnografie; Tues–Fri 8am–4pm, Sat & Sun 9am–1pm) houses more conventional displays of peasant costumes and artefacts, mostly from the Carpathian foothills. The intermittently interesting **Oil Museum** at Str. Bagdazar 10 (Muzeul Naţional al Petrolului; Tues–Sun 9am–5pm) has a comprehensive account of the oil industry's origins in Romania, while the **History and Archeology Museum**, nearby at Str. Toma Caragiu 10 (Muzeul de Istorie şi Arheologie Prahova; Tues–Sun 9am–5pm), displays relics from the Neolithic to Roman periods, as well as sixteenth-century armour, nineteenth-century furniture and portraits (including one each by Mişu Popp and Sava Henţia, and a few Grigorescu sketches), plus a room on postal history including fascinating 1920s postcards. Ploieşti's most unusual museum is the **Clock Museum** (Muzeul Ceasului; Tues–Sun 9am–5pm) at Str. Simache 1, where you can view (and listen to) an engagingly varied collection of clocks and timepieces.

Accommodation

Hotels

Central B-dul. Republicii 1 ☎0244/526 641, ⓦwww.thr.ro. Faded communist-era hotel with Wi-Fi. ❼–❽

Phoenix Str. Fat Frumos 15 ☎&ⓕ0244/510 094, ⓔhotel.phoenix@yahoo.com. On a residential street three blocks north of the Gara Sud, with Wi-Fi throughout and a Jacuzzi. ❼

Prahova Plaza Str. Dobrogeanu-Gherea 11 ☎0244/526 850, ⓕ526 309, ⓔhotelprahova @yahoo.com. A high-rise block that's had a very glitzy makeover and offers cable-only Internet access in all rooms. ❽–❾

President Str. Bobâlna 88 ☎0244/596 376. Close to the train and bus stations. The six garishly coloured and eccentrically furnished rooms here are worthy of an Austin Powers movie – and believe it or not, the mini-bar is free. ❻

Rotaru Str. Patriei 8 ☎0244/594 255, ⓦwww .rotaru.com.ro. A ten-minute walk north of the centre, this small, rustic pension has ornate but boxy wood-furnished rooms (and Wi-Fi). To get there, head up Str. E. Cătălin, across Str. G. Coşbuc, then right on Str. Gheorge Doja – Str. Patriei is the first street on the left. ❻

Sud Str. Depoului 4 ☎0244/597 411. Convenient for the Sud train and bus stations, this hotel is clean, modern and relatively cheap. ❹

Turist Str. Tache Ionescu 6 ☎&ⓕ0244/590 441, ⓔturisthotel@yahoo.com. A rather dated communist-era hotel with Wi-Fi and a/c rooms. ❻

Vigo Hotel Str. Independenţei 28 ☎0244/514501, ⓔreservation@vigohotel.ro. Aimed squarely at Romania's nouveau riche, with sauna, Jacuzzi and an international restaurant, as well as Wi-Fi in the lobby only. ❾

Campsites

Maxitaxis towards Bucharest will drop you at the *Popas Româneşti* campsite (11km south on the DN1 at km48.5), but you really need your own transport to reach the others at *Pădurea Păuleşti* (8km north on the DN1 to km68.5 and then 3km east) and *Paralela 45* (with rooms, 19km north on the DN1 at km79).

The Ploieşti ploy

In 1940 it was feared that Germany would occupy Romania – as in World War I – to guarantee oil supplies from what was then Europe's second-largest producer (after the Soviet Union). The neutral Romanian government gave tacit support to Anglo–French plans to **sabotage the oil wells**, thus making a German invasion pointless, but technical problems and bad luck meant that these never went ahead. The back-up plan, to stop the oil barges reaching Germany along the Danube by sinking barges in the Iron Gates gorge and blocking the navigable channel, was a greater fiasco: the Germans soon found out about the British barges making their way upstream from Galaţi, supposedly in secret, and forced the Romanian authorities to expel the crews (naval ratings ill-disguised as art students).

A third plan involved the RAF bombing the oil wells from its bases around Larissa in Greece. However, the 660-kilometre route would have taken the early Wellington bombers over Musala, the highest peak in southeastern Europe, at close to their maximum altitude. Following severe maintenance problems, the plan was abandoned. It wasn't long before the Allies were driven out of Greece, allowing the Axis powers access to Romania's oil wells, from which they subsequently obtained a third of their aviation fuel. On August 1, 1943, 178 new American Liberator B-24Ds took off from bases in North Africa to strike **Ploieşti** in the **longest-range bombing raid** yet attempted; although 440 aircrew were killed and 220 captured, a heavy blow was dealt to the Nazi war machine. By 1944, continuing raids from Italy had succeeded in halving oil production, despite terrible Allied losses.

2

Eating and drinking

Choices for **eating** in Ploieşti are limited to the very good restaurant in *Hotel President*, which has a surprisingly eclectic mix of Indian and Mexican cuisine; *Pizza Uno, Due, Tre*, a ten-minute walk south along B-dul. Independenţei at Str. Bobâlna 9; and, across the road in a beautiful villa at Str. Ana Ipǎtescu 3, the *Vienna Café*, which covers the whole gamut of soups, salads, pastas and grilled meat dishes – they've also got a great little bar menu available until 4pm. This area of pre-World War I villas just southwest of the Clock Museum also happens to be home to the town's liveliest pubs and *terasas*, such as the upmarket *Bulevard* opposite the museum, *Prestij* at Bobâlna 1, and the *Pizzeria Beatrice* at Bobâlna 52.

For quick snacks, try the market behind the Palace of Culture. The massive *Winmarkt* shopping centre has a food court (with Wi-Fi and toilets), but the *Billa* supermarket just north of Ploieşti Vest station (Mon–Sat 8am–10pm, Sun 9am–6pm) is better for buying supplies.

North of Ploieşti

From Ploieşti, the DN1 and the DN1A head north towards Braşov, the gateway into Transylvania. The DN1 is the main route, passing through the small towns of **Câmpina**, **Breaza**, Sinaia (see p.149) and Buşteni (see p.154), and the rail line follows the road closely right through to Braşov. The DN1A, a much quieter and more relaxing route, runs along the lovely **Teleajen valley** into the foothills of the Carpathian mountains; public transport along this route is poor, but it is well worth considering if you have your own car or bike.

Câmpina

CÂMPINA, another of Romania's key oil towns, lies on the DN1, 32km north of Ploieşti (linked by a maxitaxi every fifteen minutes), just before the Prahova valley enters the mountains. Like Ploieşti, Câmpina was heavily bombed during the war and hence is not an attractive place, though it does have two tourist sights that just about make a stop-off worthwhile. Around 1km north of the centre, across the rail tracks and up by the bend in the road, the unassuming **Nicolae Grigorescu memorial house** (Tues–Sun 9am–5pm) at B-dul. Carol I no. 166, was where the eponymous artist spent the last years of his life (see box, opposite); it's a modest yet enjoyable collection of his works, including a self-portrait and the painting he was completing when he died. Five minutes' walk further along the road, at no. 145, is **Hasdeu Castle** (Tues–Sun 9am–4.30pm), an odd cruciform structure with battlements and buttresses, built between 1894 and 1896 by historian and linguist Bogdan Petriceico Hasdeu (1838–1907), one of the progenitors of the nationalist and anti-Semitic philosophy that infected Romanian politics throughout the twentieth century. He built the castle as a memorial to his daughter Julia, to plans he claimed were transmitted by her in séances. After finishing high school, Julia went to study in Paris, and would have been the first Romanian woman to receive a doctorate from the Sorbonne had she not died of tuberculosis in 1888, aged just nineteen. Among the many items retained within the castle is the desk she used in France. She also left three volumes of plays and poetry, all published after her death.

The **train** station is 3km west but is connected to the centre by frequent maxitaxis, while the **bus** station is south of town on Str. Bǎlcescu. It's nicer to sleep in Breaza, but if you're stuck in Câmpina, the unappealing choices are the youth hostel on the south side of the *Casa Tineretului*, in front of the bus station at Str. Bǎlcescu 50 (☎0244/334 540; ❷); the refurbished and somewhat overpriced *Hotel Muntenia* at B-dul. Carol I no. 61 (☎0244/333 090,

Nicolae Grigorescu

Romania's most famous painter, **Nicolae Grigorescu**, was born in 1838 and came to Bucharest at the age of ten to train as a church painter; his earliest signed works, dating from 1853, are in the church of Sf Constantine and Helena in Baicoi (near Ploieşti). Grigorescu subsequently worked in Căldăruşani (1854–55), in Zamfira (1856–58), and in Agapia (1858–60), where his work represents the high point of **Romanian classicism**. Here he met Kogălniceanu, who arranged a grant for him to study in Paris, where he became a friend of Millet, joining the Barbizon group and beginning to paint *en plein air*. In 1869 he returned to Romania, where he painted society portraits, but also toured the Prahova, Dâmboviţa and Muscel counties painting local characters in a mobile studio in an adapted coach. From 1877–78, he accompanied the army in the War of Independence, producing, among others, major works of the battle of Griviţa. His first solo exhibition in 1881 was a great success, and from 1881 to 1884 he lived in Paris, developing a more Impressionist style. He kept a studio there until 1894, although from 1890 he spent increasing amounts of time with his companion Maria Danciu in **Câmpina**, where he died in 1907.

Ⓕ333 092; ❺); or the newer *Motel Club Montana*, 600m south of the bus station at Str. Sălaj 11 (☎0244/337 581).

Breaza

The small town of **BREAZA**, just a few kilometres north of Câmpina on a loop road off the DN1, is ideal for a quiet stopover en route towards Sinaia and Braşov. There are some excellent examples of the local architectural style – many houses have carved wooden verandas – but Breaza's one real sight is the small Orthodox **Church of Sf Nicolae**, just south of the centre of town. Finished in 1777, the church's interior is totally covered in paintings; of special note is that of the *Last Judgement* in the porch.

Arriving by **train** entails a two-kilometre walk (500m of which is a steep climb) on Str. Căpriou into town; **maxitaxis** to Bucharest (every 2hr) leave from the park in the centre of town, and there are others to Sinaia and Câmpina (every 10–15min respectively). The best of the several **pensions** in town is *Casa Ionuş* at Str. Morii 7 (☎0788/780 453; ❹), which has a handful of funkily designed en-suite rooms. To find it, walk north of the park for 400m to the *Terasa Rustick* (which offers Internet access) at Str. Republicii 102, turn right on Str. Morii, then left down the driveway after 200m. *Pensiunea Speranţa*, to the north of town at Str. Talii 46 (☎0744/586 707, Ⓦwww.pensiuneasperanta.com; ❷–❸) offers youth hostel discounts, but only for a minimum two-night stay. There are also double rooms (❻), suites (❼–❽) and apartments (❾) at the *Lac de Verde* **golf club** (☎0244/343 525, Ⓦwww .lacdeverde.ro), 1.5km west of town at Str. Caraiman 57 (it's signposted). The short but very scenic nine-hole course (€20 for nine holes, €30 for eighteen holes) is one of the few in Romania.

For **food**, there's a mini supermarket, the *Eldiv Pizzeria*, at the junction to Lac de Verde and Adunaţi at the south end of the park, and a couple more pizzerias just south of the centre.

Continuing northwards from Breaza, trains and maxitaxis take you to Sinaia and Buşteni in the magnificent Prahova valley (see p.148) and on into Transylvania.

The Teleajen valley

The main place to stop along the secondary DN1A route to Braşov is **VĂLENII DE MUNTE**, served by trains from Ploieşti 30km to the south; the town's train and bus stations are just south of its two **hotels**, both on the main thoroughfare, B-dul. N. Iorga. The first is the smart *Hotel Capitol* at no. 50 (☎0244/281 965; ❹) and the second the grim but cheap *Ciucaș* at no. 77 (☎0244/280 425; ❸). A few hundred metres north of the latter, at Str. Enescu 3, is a fine **memorial house** (Tues–Sun 9am–5pm) dedicated to the great historian and former prime minister Nicolae Iorga, who lived here from 1910 until his murder by the Iron Guard in 1940. Ironically, Iorga founded the National Democratic Party, a predecessor of the Guard. As well as some beautiful furniture, many of Iorga's personal effects – books, handwritten letters, family photos and portraits – have been neatly preserved. There's also a good ethnographic collection next door (at Str. Enescu 1), featuring some superb icons painted on glass and wood.

From Vălenii, a minor road heads west for 11km to **SLĂNIC** (sometimes known as Slănic Prahova, to distinguish it from Slănic Moldova, to the north). Here, the Muntele de Sare, or Salt Mountains – a product of the salt mining that has taken place in the area since at least 1532 – stand between two lakes in which you can swim in summer. The town's salt-working heritage is displayed in the tiny **Museum of Salt** (daily 9am–7pm), housed in the Casa Cămărășiei (the former Salt Chancellery built in 1800) at Str. 23 August no. 9. More worthwhile is the **Unirea Mine Complex** (Tues–Sun 9am–3pm), a ten-minute walk east of town across the bridge, which displays scenes from Romanian history carved in salt. A lift drops 210m below the surface to the former salt mine, converted in 1970 into a sanatorium for lung disorders and a tourist attraction, with sculptures of Roman and Dacian gods and of historical figures such as Mihai Viteazu and Mihai Eminescu carved from the salt walls. The central chamber is 54m high and has been used for model flying contests. Slănic lies at the end of a rail line from Ploiești Sud via Ploiești Vest; three of the four daily trains do the distance in 80–90min, but the early afternoon train (in each direction) stops for 35min in Plopeni. The only **hotel** in Slănic is the run-of-the-mill *Slănic* at Str. 13 Decembrie 15 (☎0244/240 131; ❹).

North of Vălenii, a minor road forks east off the DN1A, and about 7km along that another minor road strikes off north, running parallel to the DN1A and ending at the small village of **SLON**, 22km north of Vălenii. Five buses a day run from Ploiești via Vălenii to this woodworking centre, which produces barrels, spindles, spoons and shingles; it is very much a working village, but you may be able to invite yourself into one of the workshops.

The DN1A continues north along the Teleajen valley past the Suzana nunnery (built in the eighteenth century and rebuilt in 1835–38 with icons by Tattarescu) to the pleasantly relaxed resort of **CHEIA**, 35km north of Vălenii, at the foot of the Ciucaș mountains; minibuses to the resort meet trains at Măneciu, 17km north of Vălenii. Cheia has a good stock of *agroturism* guesthouses that make useful bases for exploring the surrounding area; you can either take pot luck by wandering around looking for signs, or book ahead through the Prahova branch of Antrec (☎0244/192 915, ✉prahova@antrec.ro). There are also hotels here, including the *Cheia* (☎0244/294 331; ❹), a giant A-frame construction with a restaurant and sauna. From Cheia, the DN1A continues due north into the **Ciucaș mountains**, a compact range of weirdly eroded conglomerate outcrops and pillars, with fine open walking country all around.

The Bratocea Pass is away to the northwest, between the Roșu and Ciucaș mountains. At the foot of the mountains, 7km from Cheia, is the *Muntele Roșu* cabana (☎0244/294 370; ❶), from where it's a two-hour walk, marked with yellow stripes, up to the friendly but basic *Ciucaș* cabana (❶). From the pass the road leads downhill all the way past the *Babarunca* cabana (☎0268/274 885; ❶) into Săcele and Brașov.

Târgovişte

TÂRGOVIŞTE, 50km west of Ploieşti on the DN72, was the capital of Wallachia for more than two centuries, vestiges of which can be seen in the old Princely Court complex, the town's principal attraction and the one major reason for coming here. In recent times, the town has been best known as an industrial centre, producing equipment for the oil industry, but gained notoriety when Nicolae and Elena Ceauşescu were executed in its army barracks on Christmas Day, 1989.

The town and around

The **Princely Court** (Curtea Domnească; Tues–Sun 8am–5pm, approx May–Sept until 7pm) lies north of the centre on Calea Domnească (on some maps this is still shown as Str. Bălcescu). Now a mass of crumbling ramparts, with a few well-preserved sections, it was once the royal seat of Wallachia (from 1415–1659), from where 33 *voivodes* (princes) exercised their rule – all of whom are denoted on the inside wall of the southern gate, the entrance to the complex. The Princely Court figured large in the life of **Vlad the Impaler** (see p.471), who spent his early years here, until he and his brother Radu were sent by their father to Anatolia as hostages. Following the murder of his father and

his eldest brother, Mircea, who was buried alive by Wallachia's boyars, Vlad returned to be enthroned here in 1456, and waited three years before taking his revenge. Invited with their families to feast at court on Easter Sunday, the boyars were half-drunk when guards suddenly grabbed them and impaled them forthwith upon stakes around town, sparing only the fittest who were marched off to labour on Vlad's castle at Poienari (see p.123). Dominating the complex is the 27-metre-high **Sunset Tower** (Turnul Chindiei), built during the fifteenth century and originally used as a watchtower for Vlad's soldiers. It now houses an exhibition, albeit in Romanian, charting his life and times; there are also some terrific views of the complex and the rest of the town from the top of the tower. Nearby stands the **Princely Church**, built in 1583 and painted in 1698, where Vlad's successors used to attend services, sitting upstairs in a special section screened from the congregation. The interior contains a vast

▲ Princely Church, Târgovişte

iconostasis, as well as dozens of frescoes of Wallachian princes, such as Basarab, Cantacuzino and Brâncoveanu.

Due south of the Princely Court, along Calea Domnească, is a trio of museums, the first two of which are the **art gallery** (Muzeul de Artă; Tues–Sun 9am–5pm) and **History Museum** (Muzeul de Istorie; Tues–Sun: winter 9am–5pm; summer 10am–6pm). The latter was set up in the former Law Courts by Ceauşescu in 1986, and the first floor, now used for temporary art shows, was devoted to his achievements. At the same time, he removed the heating from the art gallery, housed in the former prefecture opposite, which, as a consequence, is now in a terrible condition – at the time of writing, it was closed for extensive renovation. To the rear is the unlikely sounding **Museum of the Romanian Police** (Muzeul Poliţei Române; Tues–Sun 9am–5pm), not surprisingly the only one of its kind in the country. As well as charting the history and evolution of the Romanian police, it also exhibits costumes garnered from numerous forces from around the world, including an old-fashioned British bobby's uniform. Just south, at Str. Justiţei 7, the **Museum of Printing and Old Books**, and the **Museum of Local Writers** (Muzeul Tiparului şi al Cărţii Vechi Romaneşti and Muzeul Scriitorilor Dâmboviţeni; both Tues–Sun 9am–5pm) display old texts by the score, though neither is hugely interesting.

A couple of minutes' walk west of here, along Str. Stelea (with the newly restored fifteenth-century Church of Sf Nicolae Geartoglu on your right), you'll come to the **Stelea Monastery**, a striking building in the same Moldavian Gothic style of the famous Church of the Three Hierarchs in Iaşi (see p.286), its exterior carved with chevrons and rosettes studded with green discs. Built in 1645 by Moldavia's Basil the Wolf as part of a peace agreement with the Wallachian ruler, Matei Basarab, it inspired the design of many Wallachian churches. The monastery was closed from 1863 to 1992 (although it served as a parish church), but is once more in use. It houses a rare seventeenth-century iconostasis and Byzantine-influenced frescoes, of which the more interesting were painted from 1705–06 under Constantin Brâncoveanu.

Three kilometres northeast of town (bus #7), the graceful bulk of **Dealu Monastery** rises upon a hill. Built in 1501, it set the pattern for much of Wallachian church architecture – with its towers above the pronaos and cornice arcades separated by cable moulding – until the advent of the Brâncovenesc style at the end of the seventeenth century. Inside, beneath a marble slab topped by a bronze crown, lies the **head of Michael the Brave** – severed within a year of his conquest of Transylvania and Moldavia, which put paid to the unification of Romania for another 250 years. The inscription reads: "To he who first united our homeland, eternal glory".

Practicalities

Târgovişte's **train station** is southwest of town on Piaţa Gării, from where it's a pleasant fifteen-minute walk along B-dul. Carol I, lined with trees and attractive villas, to the centre; alternatively, bus #4 will take you into town. Now largely screened by trees, the barracks to the right of the station as you exit is where the Ceauşescus were executed, but be warned, it's forbidden to take any pictures. Maxitaxis for Bucharest arrive and depart every half-hour from a point 200m to the left of the station as you exit, and less often from immediately east of the *Hotel Valahia*. The large and disorganized **bus station** is 1km west of town by the Romlux train halt and linked to the centre by buses and maxitaxis along Calea Câmpulung. The best way to reach Piteşti is usually to take a maxitaxi to Găieşti, from just east of the railway bridge, and then a train or bus from there. The **CFR** office is at B-dul. Carol I no. 2. There's 24-hour Internet access at Computer Fun, in front of the *Hotel Valahia*.

Of the town's three **hotels**, the best value is the tidy *Pensiunea Dracula* (☎0245/620 013; ❷), with four rooms above a café-bar opposite the Princely Court at Calea Domnească 200. The two other hotels are on the north side of the Parcul Central: the *Dâmboviţa*, at B-dul. Libertăţii 1 (☎0245/613 961, ❼www .hoteldambovita.ro; ❻), has smart rooms overlooking the park; and 200m further along at B-dul. Libertăţii 7, the cheaper *Valahia* (☎0245/634 491, ☏021/312 5992; ❺) is fine, if a little dull. Hostel-style rooms are available at *Calea Câmpulung 88* (☎0723/266 774, 0766/417 167; ❷). The Priseaca **campsite** is 7km out along the Câmpulung road, reached by bus #18. The best of the very few **places to eat** in town is the *Bistro Alexu*, on the north side of the Sunset Tower, serving pizza and chicken indoors or in attractive garden pavilions.

Piteşti and around

Situated at the end of what was for a long time Romania's only freeway, just 100km northwest of Bucharest, **PITEŞTI** is another of Wallachia's industrial towns, though it's far from the grimmest and does make a useful base for forays up into the Argeş valley. Much of the town's architectural charm has been lost to earthquakes and subsequent rebuilding, and these days it's dominated by the woodworking and petrochemical industries, and by the Renault (formerly

Piteşti prison

For older Romanians, Piteşti is synonymous with its **prison**, the scene under the early Stalinist regime of some of the most brutal psychiatric abuse anywhere in the Soviet bloc. In May 1948, there were mass arrests of dissident students, and from December 1949 about a thousand of them were brought here, to the "Student Re-education Centre", for a **programme** aimed at "re-adjusting the students to communist life" and eliminating the possibility of any new opposition developing. In fact, it simply set out to destroy the personality of the individual: by starvation, isolation, and above all by forcing prisoners to torture each other, breaking down all distinctions between prisoner and torturer, and thus between individual and state. "United by the evil they have both perpetrated and endured, the victim and the torturer thus become a single person. In fact, there is no longer a victim, ultimately no longer a witness", as Paul Goma put it in his book *The Dogs of Death*. Sixteen students died during this atrocious "experiment".

The programme was extended to Gherla and other prisons and the Danube–Black Sea Canal labour camps, but security was looser here and the torture stopped when word got out. The experiment was abandoned in 1952, when the Stalinist leader Ana Pauker was purged; it was claimed that the authorities had not been involved, and in 1954, those running the Piteşti prison were tried secretly for murder and torture. The leader of the "Organization of Prisoners with Communist Convictions", Eugen Ţurcanu, was executed along with several of his henchmen, while others were sentenced to forced labour for life. Nevertheless, because of the guilt of all involved – both prisoners and guards – there followed a conspiracy of silence, which only began to break in 1989. By that time the controversial Stanford Prison Experiment of 1971 was well known, in which volunteer guards had displayed such sadism towards their volunteer prisoners that the roleplay was abandoned after only six of the planned fourteen days. The intention of the experiment had been similar to that of the Piteşti programme: depersonalization and submission to perceived authority. It had proved how easily human rights abuses such as those perpetrated at Piteşti might re-occur under parallel conditions.

Dacia) factory – origin of most of Romania's cars – 11km north in Mioveni. If you are planning to stop en route to western Wallachia, come on a Friday or Saturday, when Piteşti fulfils its traditional role as a **market** town for the country folk of the Argeş valley.

The Town

The heart of the town is Str. Victoriei, a broad, pedestrianized throughfare lined with shops, cafés and hotels, with a couple of minor sights located at either end. Standing on a solitary patch of grass at its eastern end is the seventeenth-century **Princely Church** of Constantin Şerban, and at the opposite end, on Pasajul Victoriei, are the theatre and a Roman Catholic church. Just before the theatre, through the park at B-dul. Republicii 33, is the town's main **art gallery** (Galeria de Artă; Tues–Sun 9am–5pm), which houses a good sample of works by some of Romania's finest painters – Grigorescu, Pallady and Iser – as well as some intriguing wooden pieces by Gheorge Călineşti, one of the country's foremost sculptors.

South of B-dul. Republicii on the parallel Str. Călinescu, the **County Museum** (Muzeul Judeţean; Tues–Sun 9am–5pm), housed in the turn-of-the-twentieth century prefecture building, offers a standard review of the region's history, as well as a dull natural history section. In front is the odd conjunction of anti-tank guns and a small botanical garden, and to its east a new wing housing the **Naïf Art Gallery** (Galeria de Artă Naivă; Tues–Sun 9am–5pm), featuring a typically exuberant collection of works by unschooled local painters. A synagogue survives nearby at B-dul. Noiembrie 1. The seventeenth-century **Trivale Hermitage**, southwest of the centre in Trivale Park, is nothing special, but it's a lovely twenty-minute, traffic-free walk to it up Str. Trivale through fine oak woods. Alternatively, maxitaxis and bus #8 run from the station up Str. Smeurei just to the east, leaving you in the midst of modern apartment blocks immediately above the hermitage. The **Ştrandului Argeş Park**, facing the gigantic new Euromall shopping centre across the Argeş, contains a sports centre, outdoor pool and small beach area, all of which get very crowded in the warmer months.

Practicalities

The town's **train station** is 1km to the southeast, linked to the centre by buses #2, #8 and #19 and frequent maxitaxis; trains serving Curtea de Argeş also call at Piteşti Nord, in the northern suburbs. The disorganized **bus station** is to the northwest of the train station on Str. Târgul din Vale. **Tourist information** is available from the county's Centru de Informare Turistică at Pasajul Victoriei 89 (☏0248/21230, @cjarges@ro), and you can also ask at the Muntenia tourist agency (Mon–Fri 8am–7pm, Sat 9am–1pm; ☏0248/625 463), next to the hotel of the same name on Piaţa Muntenia. There's **Internet access** at the IQ Club (daily 9am–1am), on the corner of Str. Victoriei and Str. Justiţiei, and at Republicii 65, just southeast of the centre.

There's plentiful **accommodation** in town, all of it very central. Easily the best-value hotel is the colourful and modern *Metropol* (☏&℉0248/222 407; ❹), just off B-dul. Republicii at Str. Panselelor 1, followed by *Carmen* at B-dul. Republicii 84 (☏0248/222 699, ℉290 433; ❹), which has a mix of older and newer rooms (❺), some of which overlook the park. Facing each other across Piaţa Muntenia are two communist-era hotels, the very cheap and very basic *Argeş* at no. 3 (☏0248/625 450, ℉214 556; ❸), which has singles and doubles with and without bathrooms; and, at no. 1, the *Muntenia* (also ☏0248/625 450, ⓦwww.turism-muntenia.ro; ❹–❺), an ugly concrete mass with a range of

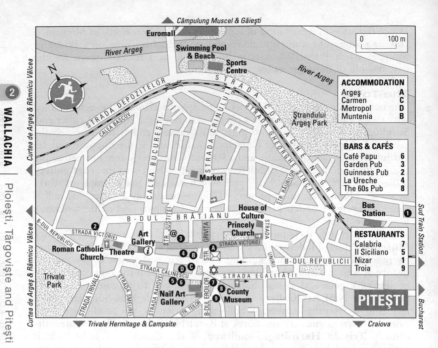

rooms of varying quality. There are also chalets (❷) in the Trivale Park **campsite** (☏0248/634 190).

There are a couple of highly commendable **restaurants** in town: the *Calabria*, across from the County Museum at Str. Eroilor 5, is an atmospheric Italian place dishing up pasta and spaghetti, as well as good pizza, and just around the corner, at Str. Primăverii 11, is *Troia*, a classy little Greek establishment. There's simpler fare at *Il Siciliano* at Str. Călinescu 38, and at *Nizar*, a nonstop Turkish restaurant opposite the bus station to the east. The liveliest **drinking** spots are *La Ureche* at B-dul. Republicii 39, the *Garden Pub* at Str. Victoriei 76, and the *Guinness Pub* at Str. Victoriei 30. *Café Papu*, at Str. Călinescu 44, is in an attractive neo-Brâncovenesc house with a *terasa* and thumping music; below *Troia* on Str. Primăverii, *The 60s Pub* plays its music more quietly.

Goleşti

The village of **GOLEŞTI**, 8km east of Piteşti just off route 7 (the road running parallel to the Bucharest–Piteşti highway), is the junction from the Bucharest–Piteşti railway to the branch to Câmpulung Muscel. It was once the fiefdom of the Golescus, one of the leading liberal families of nineteenth-century Wallachia – not only were they active members of both the 1821 and 1848 revolutions, but they also worked in favour of Romanian union in 1859 and Romanian independence in 1877. Their home – now at the heart of a very enjoyable open-air **Museum of Fruit and Vine Growing** (Muzeul Viticulturii şi Pomiculturii; May–Sept Tues–Sun 8am–4pm) – is in fact a *conac* or summer residence (winters would be spent in Bucharest or Paris), and is beautifully cool, with authentic furnishings and historical displays. The museum itself is behind the house, settled among plum and pear orchards, and comprising over one hundred structures from Romania's fruit- and vine-growing communities, mainly dwellings (including dug-out homes, or "pit houses"), but also churches, wine presses and wells. The oldest structure is the wooden church of Drăguteşti, built in 1814. Over the gateway is the immaculately restored *foişor* or watchtower of Tudor Vladimirescu, leader of the 1821 peasant revolt, who was captured here and taken to Târgovişte to be executed. Beside this stands an early nineteenth-century schoolhouse, which still retains some original fixtures and fittings, including German, Greek and Latin textbooks, and a sandbox that was used for practising writing. There's also an interesting little **Ethnographic Museum** (same times) in the grounds, exhibiting various viticultural implements, peasant costumes and craftworks. The village church, across the road from the museum's main gate, dates from 1646; if you want to look around, you'll need to ask in the village for the caretaker who will let you in to the church.

Câmpulung Muscel and north to Transylvania

Câmpulung, or **CÂMPULUNG MUSCEL** (as it is properly known), 53km north of Piteşti, is overshadowed by mountains to the north, and begrimed by pollution from its factories. However, the town dates back to pre-Roman times and has played an important role in Wallachia's history, including a stint as the region's first capital after the *voivodate* was forged around 1300. Today, there are a couple of minor attractions to while away an hour or two, and it's a convenient place to break a journey to Transylvania. About 500m north of the train station on Str. Negru Vodă, Câmpulung's main drag, is the town's major sight, the **Negru Vodă Monastery**, attributed to its namesake, Romania's legendary thirteenth-century Black Prince, but largely rebuilt following several earthquakes. The present building, incorporating stonework from the original, was completed in 1837; the infirmary chapel to its rear dates from 1718. The monastery's most striking feature is the massive seventeenth-century gate tower, with its heavy beech gates, and a twelfth-century stone carving of a doe to the left as you enter; this was brought from a nearby Dominican monastery and is remarkably Western European in style.

Continuing north, Str. Negru Vodă brings you to Str. Republicii, which forms the southbound stretch of the centre's one-way system (Str. Negru Vodă forms the northbound). Housed in a fine seventeenth-century building at Str. Republicii 5 is a fabulous little **Ethnographic Museum** (Muzeul de Etnografie; Tues–Sun 9am–5pm), containing some exquisitely crafted furniture, colourful regional costumes, and a stock collection of farming and cooking implements. Beyond here is the town centre, with some wonderful neo-Brâncovenesc buildings on the west side of Str. Negru Vodă, and the town hall and the main hotel, the *Muscelul*, to the east. Strs. Negru Vodă and Republicii meet (continuing as the north- and southbound sides of one divided main road) at the Bărătei complex, where the fourteenth-century **Roman Catholic Church of St James** houses the tombstone of Count Laurentius of Campo Longo, the inscription on which, dating from 1300, is the oldest Romanian document. It's also worth seeing the mid-seventeenth-century parish house and the bell tower, built in 1730 and raised at the end of the nineteenth century.

The **town museum** (Muzeul Câmpulung Muscel; Tues–Sun 9am–5pm) is just north at Republicii 119, opposite the *Hotel Muscelul*. It offers a fairly standard overview of the region's history, in Romanian only, in addition to a dusty collection of artwork by the likes of Grigorescu and Luchian, plus a

couple of sketches by Pallady. There's also coverage of the **Roman fort**, or
castrum, of Jidava, part of the Limes Transalutanus defensive line, which was
destroyed by the Goths in 244 AD. The fort's remains, by the Pescăreasa rail halt
6km south of town en route to Piteşti, have been preserved and can be visited
(Tues–Sun 9am–5pm); there's also a small museum here housing a few excavated
fragments and a mock-up of how the camp would have looked.

Practicalities

Trains from Goleşti (just east of Piteşti) terminate at Câmpulung Station, 2km
south of town, and are met by maxitaxis. Otherwise, there are regular maxitaxis
to and from Piteşti at the following locations: the main bus station, located to
the east of town across the river at Str. I.C. Frimu; just north of the Negru Vodă
Church; and a small terminal by the bridge just south of the town centre. Cars
can be rented at Full-Contact, at Str. Bălcescu 122A (☎&ⓕ0348/401 153,
Ⓦwww.full-rent.ro).

The town's main **hotel** is the *Muscelul* at Str. Negru Vodă 117 (☎0248/511 330,
ⓕ512 990, Ⓦwww.muscelul.ro; ❸–❹), a drab 1970s-style place with dated, plastic
furniture. *Pensiunea Elyon*, nicely set back at Str. Negru Vodă 104 (☎&ⓕ0248/511
839, Ⓦelyon.muscel.ro; ❷–❸), has a lively *terasa* and weekend disco but is
probably quiet enough during the week; rooms have private bathroom and
TV but there's no breakfast. The *Restaurant-Pensiunea Casa Blanca* at Str. Matei
Basarab 95 (go west up Str. Istrate Rizeanu from just south of the *Muscelul* and
left at the top; ☎0248/512360; ❷) is quiet and offers meals. A more distant alternative is the *Motel Flora* (☎0744/520 709; ❸), 3km north of town on the Braşov
road, at the turn-off to the village of Lereşti. There are also several agrotourism
programmes in the area, the oldest of which centres on **Lereşti**, 8km north of
town (and reached by regular maxitaxis). **Homestays** here (and in equally attractive villages such as Rucăr, Dâmbovicioara and Dragoslavele) can be booked
through the local Antrec office in Rucăr (☎0248/542 230, Ⓔarges@antrec.ro),
or you can just try your luck where you see a sign for *Agroturism* or *Cazare*.

The best **place to eat** here is the *Brâncovenesc* restaurant, behind the Bărătiei
Church at Str. C. Brâncoveanu 50; the *Casa Regală*, in a courtyard almost opposite
the *Pensiunea Elyon*, serves decent Romanian food, notably a good-value lunch;
and there's the good little *Iepuraşul* patisserie opposite the *Hotel Muscelul*.

North to Transylvania

The scenery becomes increasingly dramatic on the road north from Câmpulung
into Transylvania. Eight kilometres beyond Câmpulung (at the junction of a
lovely road to Târgovişte, to the right), a road branches left to the village of
Nămăesti (served by maxitaxis), site of a gorgeous little rock church complete
with an ancient icon (said to miraculously cure ailments) and cells hewn from
sandstone by sixteenth-century monks. Today, the small monastery complex is
inhabited by a handful of nuns.

Some 3km further along the road to Braşov, the austere, lighthouse-shaped
Mateias Mausoleum marks the spot where Romanian troops managed to
repel a major German offensive over 45 days in 1916. More than two thousand
Romanians lost their lives, their remains now kept in a large glass chest in the
ossuary. The walls and ceiling of the mausoleum, meanwhile, are beautifully
decorated with mosaics, depicting scenes of war as well as some of Romania's
most prominent historical figures, including Mircea the Old, Constantin
Brâncoveanu and Vlad Ţepeş. There's also a small **museum** (daily 9am–5pm)
up the steps, containing artefacts, photographs and a working diorama retelling
the events of the battle.

Beyond the monument, the road continues to the villages of **Dragoslavele** and **Rucăr**, with their traditional wooden houses and verandas. Dragoslavele also has an eighteenth-century wooden church, and there's a campsite just beyond Rucăr; homestays are available at both villages (see opposite for the Rucăr Antrec office). From Rucăr, the road continues up in a series of hairpin bends towards the Bran (or Giuvala) Pass, encountering the **Bridge of the Dâmboviţa**, a spectacular passage between the Dâmboviciorei and Plaiu gorges to the north and the yet narrower Dâmboviţei gorges to the south (see p.167 for the continuation of the route beyond the Bran Pass).

Curtea de Argeş, Arefu and Poienari Castle

After the Old Courts of Bucharest and Târgovişte (see p.82 and p.114 respectively), Wallachia's Dracula trail continues west via the small town of **Curtea de Argeş**, another former princely capital that still boasts some interesting churches and palace ruins, to the remains of **Dracula's Castle** at **Poienari**. Although the tourist industry focuses on Bran castle in Transylvania (see p.167), which has almost no connection to the Dracula myth, the castle at Poienari was once Vlad the Impaler's residence, and its location in the foothills of the Făgăraş mountains makes for a wonderfully dramatic setting.

Curtea de Argeş

CURTEA DE ARGEŞ, Wallachia's second capital (after Câmpulung and before Târgovişte), lies some 36km northwest of Piteşti, and is easily accessible by road or rail. It's an attractive small town, strung out along its one main street, that doesn't see too many coach parties. Not far north of the centre, enclosed by a wall of river boulders, is the **Court of Argeş** and the oldest church in Wallachia. The thirteenth-century complex (Tues–Sun 10am–6pm) was rebuilt in the fourteenth century by Radu Negru, otherwise known as Basarab I, the founder of Wallachia. Its **Princely Church** (in which the early Basarab rulers are buried) was constructed in 1352 and its interior decorated with frescoes in 1384; later restoration work has now been largely removed to reveal the original frescoes, which are fully in the Byzantine tradition but wonderfully alive and individual, reminiscent of Giotto rather than the frozen poses of the Greek masters. To its east are the remains of a palace and tower, and to the north those of the later palace of Neagoe Basarab. Across the square, in the pink and white-painted villa at Str. Negru Vodă 2, the **town museum** (Muzeul Municipal; Tues–Sun 9am–4pm) displays a rather mundane collection of local artefacts. Across the main road to the east are the ruins of the fourteenth-century Church of San Nicoara, and up the hill beyond, the equally ruinous seventeenth-century Olarie (Potters') church.

More visually impressive is the monastery, or **Episcopal Church** (daily 8am–7pm), about 1.5km north of the court along the main through road, B-dul. Basarabilor, reached by maxitaxis from the town centre. Resembling the creation of an inspired confectioner, it's a boxy structure enlivened by whorls, rosettes and fancy trimmings, rising into two twisted, octagonal belfries, each festooned with little spheres and the three-armed cross of Orthodoxy. Next to a restaurant in the park across the road, **Manole's Well** is a spring said to have been created by the death of **Manole**, the Master Builder of Curtea de Argeş.

Legend has it that Manole was marooned on the rooftop of his creation, the Episcopal Church, when Prince Neagoe Basarab, who had commissioned him to build it, ordered the scaffolding to be removed, to ensure that the builder could not repeat his masterwork for anyone else. Manole tried to escape with the aid of wings made from roofing shingles – only to crash to his death, whereupon a spring gushed forth immediately. The story is perhaps that of a crude form of justice, for legend also has it that Manole had immured his wife within the walls of the monastery – at the time it was believed that *stafia* or ghosts were needed to keep buildings from collapse.

The current Episcopal Church is not Manole's original creation of 1512–17 but a re-creation of 1875–85 by the Frenchman Lecomte de Noüy, who grafted on all the Venetian mosaics and Parisian woodwork; he wanted to do the same to the Princely Church, but the historian Nicolae Iorga managed to get legal backing to stop him. Inside the garish red, green and gold painted interior lie the tombs of the church founder and kings Carol I (1866–1914) and Ferdinand (1914–27).

Practicalities

It's just five minutes to the old town centre from the ornate Mughal-style **train station** and the adjacent **bus station** – turn left out of the stations on Str. 1 Mai (which bypasses the town centre) and then right up Str. Traian and left on Str. Negru Vodă. This continues as B-dul. Basarabilor; it's one-way northbound, so maxitaxis loop south on Str. 1 Mai. Unusually, all the town's sights are very well signposted, starting at the station, so you'll have no trouble finding your way around. Moving on by train, your only option is one of the five daily services to Piteşti; there's more choice at the bus station, with services to Arefu, Bucharest, Câmpulung, Braşov, Râmnicu Vâlcea and Sibiu. **Maxitaxis** run from outside the Princely Church (every 15min) as far as Bascov – get another maxitaxi there on to Piteşti, 10km to the south.

Most of the town's **accommodation** options are on or just off B-dul. Basarabilor, including the badly maintained but reasonably good-value *Posada* hotel, midway between the Princely Church and the monastery at B-dul. Basarabilor 27 (℡0248/721 451, ℉506 047, ⓦwww.posada.ro; ❸–❹), and the new *Pensiunea Montana* at B-dul. Basarabilor 72 (℡0248/722 364; ⓦwww.montanatop.ro; ❹). To the north, 2km along the Câmpulung road, the *Hotel Venus*, on Str. Valea Iaşului 73 (℡0248/723 292, 0722/673 393; ❸), is a large block that's best for groups.

There are precious few places to **eat and drink** in town, other than the hotels: two good beer gardens face each other across B-dul. Basarabilor just north of the Princely Church, and the *No Comment Pizza* sits next to a *cofetărie* a little further north. The *Restaurant Laura*, by Manole's Well, has a nice *terasa* around a pool and serves adequate Romanian food as well as pizza. Taking the first road east south of the monastery and turning right at the end on to Str. Episcop Nichiţa, you'll come to the *Restaurant Sârbesc*, serving Serbian food. You can buy food at the *Supermarket Posada*, near the Hotel Posada, or the *Plus* supermarket on Str. 1 Mai.

Arefu and Poienari Castle

Twenty-five kilometres north of Curtea de Argeş is **AREFU** (or Aref), a long, ramshackle village 3km west of the valley road – note that, if you're travelling by car, it's a very rough surface from the main road to the village. It was to here, in 1457, that the survivors of Vlad the Impaler's massacre in Târgovişte (see p.114) were marched to begin work on his castle. This is the real Dracula's Castle, which

Vlad began work on in 1457 (see Contexts, p.471) – his only connection with the better-known one at Bran is that he may have attacked it once (see p.167). Situated on a crag north of the village, the moody **POIENARI CASTLE** (daily 9am–5pm), 4km north on the road from Arefu, can only be reached by climbing 1400 steps (about a 30min walk) from the hydroelectric power station (and a kiosk selling refreshments), which proves a powerful disincentive to most visitors. There are plenty of maxitaxis from Curtea de Argeş, but only as far as Arefu, so you'll need to walk (or have your own transport) beyond there. Struggle to the top and you'll find that the citadel is surprisingly small, one third having collapsed down the mountainside in 1888. Entering by a narrow wooden bridge, you'll come across the crumbling remains of two towers within; the prism-shaped one was the old keep, Vlad's residential quarters, from where, according to legend, the Impaler's wife flung herself out of the window, declaring that she "would rather have her body rot and be eaten by the fish of the Argeş" than be captured by the Turks, who were then besieging the castle. Legend also has it that Vlad himself escaped over the mountains on horseback, fooling his pursuers by shoeing his mount backwards – or, according to some versions, by affixing horse-shoes that left the impression of cow prints. Simple **private rooms** (❶) are available both in Aref village – contact the *Vilă Aref* on ☎0726/906 249 or Gheorghe Tomescu on ☎0248/730 102 – and in the two villages preceeding Arefu, Corbeni and Căpăţânenii Pământeni, where you can try places (advertising *camere* or *cazare*) at random, or ask at the *primaria* (mayor's office).

You can continue up the twisting road to **Lake Vidraru**, held back by a spectacular dam (165m), 4km from Poienari. Four hundred metres beyond the dam is the *Casa Argeşeana* cabana (☎0248/730 315; ❶), essentially a **restaurant** but with a few **beds** available too. A further 8km on, above the main road beside the lake, is the *Cabana de Pesti* (☎0248/730 250; ❺), an attractive hotel popular at weekends with local fishermen; comfortable rooms are complemented by an outstanding fish restaurant. Beyond the lake, the **Transfăgărașan Highway** continues across the **Făgăraş mountains** and into Transylvania (see p.171).

The Olt valley

The **River Olt** runs south from its source in Transylvania through the Red Tower Pass below Sibiu, carving a stupendous fifty-kilometre gorge through the Carpathians down into Wallachia, where it passes through **Râmnicu Vâlcea**, 34km west of Curtea de Argeş, and continues south to the Danube. In Wallachia, the valley can best be approached by road from Piteşti and Curtea de Argeş or from Târgu Jiu further to the west. From Târgu Jiu, the route is long but very scenic, while the one from the *autostradă* at Piteşti is very busy, as the difficulty of travelling through Serbia has made this the main truck route between Turkey and Western Europe. **Trains** from Piatra Olt, midway between Piteşti and Craiova, head north up the valley to Podu Olt and Sibiu, with slower services stopping at the villages in between; there's also an increasing supply of buses following the valley between Râmnicu Vâlcea and Sibiu.

Râmnicu Vâlcea

There are more interesting places further north up the Olt valley but it's worth pausing in **RÂMNICU VÂLCEA**, west of Piteşti, to buy food, get local information and check festival dates for the surrounding area. Sprawling across successive terraces above the River Olt, it's a typically systematized town, with many communist-era apartment blocks and more modern malls, but there are half a dozen attractive old churches as well as an excellent open-air museum here.

The town's main street, Calea lui Traian, runs along the western side of Piaţa Mircea cel Bătrân; to the south of this square lies the daily fruit and veg market, and to the north, opposite the *Alutus* hotel, is the sixteenth-century **Church of the Annunciation** (Buna Vestire). This was established between 1545 and 1549 by Mircea the Shepherd and rebuilt in 1747 by the citizens of Sibiu. Going a block west to reach Calea lui Traian at the fantastic Palace of Justice (Palatul de Justiţei) and heading north, you'll pass two more old churches: **St Paraschiva**, built between 1557 and 1587, and **All Saints**, built between 1762 and 1764 in a post-Brâncovenesc style with distinctive oblique cable mouldings that make the towers seem twisted. Not far north at Calea lui Traian 143 you'll come to the **County Museum** (Muzeul Judeţean; Tues–Sun 10am–6pm), which holds a better-than-average hoard of local archaeological finds. Behind the museum at Str. Carol I no. 25 is a modern villa housing the **art gallery** (Muzeul de Artă; Wed–Sun 10am–6pm), with works by the customary Romanian artists, Grigo-rescu and Pallady. Another five minutes north, at Str. Carol I no. 53, is the **Bishopric** (Episcopiei), a wonderfully tranquil complex, with three small churches set in well-kept lawns. It dates from the sixteenth century, although the main church, with its Tattarescu paintings, was only built in 1856, after a fire destroyed the original. Further north, at Calea lui Traian 351, the **Citadel Church** (1529) still stands amid the remains of its fortifications.

At the northern town limits is the superb **Bujoreni open-air museum** (Tues–Sun 10am–6pm), a fine ensemble of some eighty structures laid out as per a typical village from the Vâlcea region. It's possible to enter a good cross-section of these units, including a splendidly preserved inn (1899), one of the village's largest buildings and its social focus, a perfectly furnished village school (1904), complete with period books and maps, and a *cula* or watchtower, dating from 1802. The oldest building is the church (1785), complete with a candela-brum featuring wooden eggs hanging below wooden birds, and some original icons. To get here, take a **maxitaxi** from town, or walk south for fifteen minutes from the Bujoreni train station.

Practicalities

The **train station** is east of the centre on Str. V. Popescu, from where it's a ten-minute walk along Str. Regina Maria (50m to the left of the station as you exit) to Piaţa Mircea cel Bătrân and Calea lui Traian. From the **bus station**, south of the river on Str. G. Coşbuc, it's a short walk to the left along Str. Dacia and right on Calea lui Traian to cross the bridge into the centre. Your best bet for **infor-mation** is the Vâlcea Tourism Association at Str. Regina Maria 7 (℡0250/733 449). The **CFR** office is on Calea lui Traian by Piaţa Mircea cel Bătrân (Mon–Fri 7am–8pm). You can get online at Internet Club 20, Str. Bălcescu 1 (just east of Calea lui Traian to the north of the centre).

Accommodation

The best of the town's hotels is the modern ⚘ *Castel*, at Str. Praporgescu 5 (℡0250/730 003, 0748/291 111, ✉rezervari@hotel-castel.ro; ❺), beautifully decorated and with a Romanian-Mediterranean restaurant (and a sports bar across the road) and air-conditioned rooms with large TVs, Internet access and balcony. The most central is the *Alutus* at Scuarul Mircea cel Bătrân 2 (℡0250/736 601, 🖷0250/737 760, 🖳www.alutus.home.ro; ❹), while more restful alternatives are located on the slopes of the hills immediately west of town. The *Capela* (☎0250/738 906, ℉737 760; ❹), which also has chalets (❷), is a good twenty-minute walk from the centre along Calea lui Traian and left past the Bishopric onto Aleea Castanilor; while the slightly pricier *Gemina* (☎0250/735 101, ℉731 949; ❹), a ten-minute walk past the art gallery to the top of Str. Pinului, is basic but acceptable, with lumpy beds compensated for by good views. On the other side of town at Str. Petrarche Poenaru 2, two blocks south of the bus station, the *Restaurant-pensiunea Supca* (☎0250/713 857, ⓦwww.supca2001.home.ro; ❸) has decent en-suite rooms with TVs, as well as a restaurant and terrace. Located on the southern outskirts (served by the Halta Ostroveni rail halt) is the *Popas Ostroveni*, a basic **campsite** with chalets (❶).

Eating and drinking

Save for the cracking *Boromir* patisserie at Str. Târgului 2, a modern circular building on the east side of Piaţa Mircea cel Bătrân, and the adjacent *Ariel* at Scuarul Mircea cel Bătrân, a pretty slick pizzeria and *terasa*, there's nowhere great to eat and you're just as well buying your food. You can do this at the central **market** (behind the *Galeriile Romarta* on the south side of Piaţa Mircea cel Bătrân) or the *Diana* and *Anabella* supermarkets, on the east and north sides of the Piaţa respectively.

Călimăneşti–Căciulata

The twin settlements of **CĂLIMĂNEŞTI–CĂCIULATA** mark the entrance to the Olt valley, a deep, sinuously twisting gorge of great beauty and the site of several monasteries, the most notable of which are **Cozia** and **Turnul**. Although the river was notoriously wild and dangerous here, it has now been tamed, with a project to build a series of dams; viaducts carry the road in places. While the main road runs along the Olt's west bank, a lesser road (as far as Cozia) and the rail line follow the other side of the defile.

The sleepy spa town of **CĂLIMĂNEŞTI**, 15km north of Râmnicu Vâlcea, is home to the **Songs of the Olt folklore festival**, with musical groups from all over Oltenia, usually combined with a **pottery fair** during the first week in August. The nearest **train station** is actually in the village of Jiblea just to the south, although the station itself takes Călimăneşti's name; buses run every twenty minutes from here into Călimăneşti, then to its twin town of Căciulata and onwards as far as Cozia Monastery. In fact the station is only 1km from Călimăneşti, and it takes just ten minutes, walking beside the train tracks, then turning left along Str. Vlahuţă, to reach the dam that carries the main road across the Olt into town. A bridge opposite the *Hotel Central*, just north of the centre, leads to **Ostrov island**, a municipal park and the site of a tiny **hermitage**, built from 1520–22 for Despina, wife of Neagoe Basarab, with painted frescoes dating from 1752–60. The hideous green-faced women in the porch are no indication of the beautiful paintings inside.

The only **hotel** in Călimăneşti itself is the *Central* at Calea lui Traian 398 (☎0250/750 990, ℉751 138; ❶), a classic, and ridiculously cheap, spa hotel, built in 1886 and remodelled 24 years later by the same architect; they have more modern rooms in the *Pensiunea Pescăruş* across the road. The *Pensiunea Călimăneşti Varianta* (☎0250/751 179; ❹), at a petrol station 1km south of the town, is worth considering, as is the *Seaca* **campsite**, on the main road north of the centre. There's stacks more accommodation immediately to the north of Călimăneşti (take the paved path on the river embankment rather than the road) in **CĂCIULATA**, a one-street spa town lined with villas, many of which advertise *cazare* or *camera* (rooms). The most prominent hotel here is the trade union-owned *Traian* (☎0250/750 780, ⓦwww.hotel-traian.ro; ❷), with clean and good-value rooms that belie the grim exterior; just behind it there's the *Vila Flora* (☎0250/750 164; ❹), a small villa complete with spa facilities. Rather grander is the modern *Orizont* at Calea lui Traian 495 (☎0350/805 993; ⓦwww.hotel-orizont.ro; ❻). There is also a **campsite**, the *Ștrand*, across the road from the *Traian* hotel; the trio of ghastly hotels to the north is best avoided.

Cozia and Turnul

Beautifully pitched amidst elegant pine trees and fragrant rose bushes, **Cozia Monastery**, 1km north of Căciulata (4km from the centre of Călimănești), is the earliest example of Byzantine architecture in Wallachia. Built by Serb architects in 1388 – thanks to the patronage of Vlad Țepeș's grandfather, Mircea the Old (who is buried within the monastery) – the church's principal architectural features include alternating bands of brick and stone, filigree latticework and fluted, false pillars. The church portico was added by Constantin Brâncoveanu in the early eighteenth century, although it's not a particularly striking example of the Brâncovenesc style. The monastery also houses a small **museum of religious art**, exhibiting a dazzling collection of church treasures – mostly seventeenth- to nineteenth-century icons. Across the road is the impossibly slender Bolnița, or **Infirmary Church**, built between 1542 and 1543, with murals dating from the same period. About 300m south of the church stands the *Hanul Cozia* motel (☎0250/751 909; ❷), where maxitaxis from the south terminate; opposite it are the *Vila Liliacul* (☎0250/750 440; ❸), which has refreshingly clean and colourful rooms, and the similarly bright *Hotel-Pension International* (☎0250/751 294, 0722/176 892; ❸), a few metres north. Unusually, breakfast costs extra in these establishments. The *Restaurant Coziana*, also opposite the Han, is a more modern but less popular eating place. Just to the north, a dam takes you across the Olt to the reconstructed Arutela *castrum*, a fort built in 137 AD as part of the Limes Alutanus, the Romans' defensive line along the Olt.

About 3km north of Cozia Monastery, on the east bank of the River Olt near the Mânăstirea Turnu train halt, is **Turnul Monastery**, based around rock cells hewn by hermits from Cozia at the end of the sixteenth century. From here, it's a five- to six-hour walk up a steep trail marked by red stripes to the *Cozia* cabana (❶), situated near the summit of the **Cozia massif**. Sheltered from northeasterly winds by the Făgăraș mountains, this has the mildest climate of all Romania's ranges, enabling oak, walnut and wild roses to grow at altitudes of up to 1300m. Both sides of the Olt north of Căciulata are now protected as part of the new Cozia National Park (ⓦwww.cozia.ro).

Târgu Jiu and around

Forewarned about **TÂRGU JIU** and the surrounding **Jiu valley**, visitors often decide to ignore them completely – but the town does merit a visit on the strength of its association with Romania's foremost sculptor, Constantin Brâncuși. Ranged along the valley, from Petroșani (see p.213) to Rovinari, are the **coal and lignite mines** that traditionally supported all the country's other industries. For the most part, this is a bleak landscape made grimmer by slag heaps, pylons and the mining towns themselves, while the sandbanks in the river are almost solid coal dust. Under communism, the **miners** were lauded as the aristocrats of the proletariat, but had to be placed under **martial law** in 1985, when Ceaușescu demanded ever higher output and halved their pay

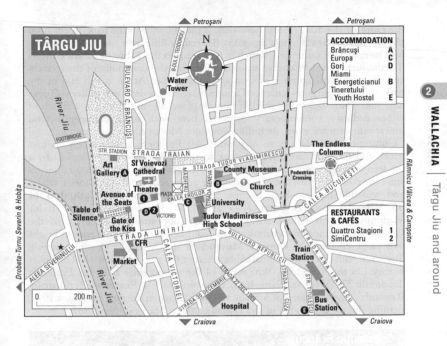

when quotas weren't achieved. After the revolution of 1989, the miners were used as Iliescu's **shock troops**, rushed on special trains to Bucharest to terrorize the opposition as required, and even to precipitate the resignation of prime minister Petre Roman himself (see p.443). Târgu Jiu is known for its great winter music gathering, the **Festival of Enchanted Water Springs** (*Izvoare Fermecate*), normally staged during the third week of February – a pretty uninviting time of year.

The Town

Although Târgu Jiu has no links with coal mining, it still suffered the gross "modernization" imposed by Ceauşescu on Romania's coal-mining centres, with homes knocked down to make way for unattractive and impractical concrete blocks. Nevertheless, this busy, dusty town, dominated by windswept, concrete buildings, does hold one singularly important attraction (or attractions) – namely the monumental sculptures that **Constantin Brâncuşi** (see box, p.128) created in the late 1930s as a war memorial for the town of his boyhood. He offered a series of twelve sculptures, but completed only four before he died. The most iconic of his works, in a park at the eastern end of Calea Eroilor, is the recently restored **Endless Column** (*Coloană Infinita*), a vast thirty-metre-high totem pole of smooth rhomboidal blocks, whose rippling form is emulated in many of the verandas of the old wooden houses throughout the region. Brâncuşi actually began working on variations of the column in 1918, though this structure wasn't installed until 1937, following a request from the local authorities to create a memorial for those killed during World War I.

Brâncuşi's other sculptures lie at the opposite end of Calea Eroilor, which runs 1.7km west from the *Endless Column* to the park on the banks of the Jiu river:

the **Gate of the Kiss** (*Poarta Sărutului*), at the entrance to the park, opens onto the **Avenue of Seats** (*Aleea Scaunilor*), flanked by lime trees and 27 stone chairs (not intended for sitting on), which in turn leads to the **Table of Silence** (*Masa Tăcerii*), surrounded by twelve stools representing the continuity of the months and the traditional number of seats at a funeral feast. At the north end of the park, in a villa purpose-built for Ceauşescu, is the modern **art gallery** (Tues–Sun 9am–5pm); Brâncuşi's work is now unaffordable, so there's just a clutch of rather ordinary contemporary paintings here with some eighteenth- and nineteenth-century icons, including one from Mount Athos in Greece.

Cutting through the centre of town, Calea Eroilor is a surprisingly narrow street, and the vista east from the park to the *Endless Column* is blocked by a modern and ugly church. However, there are some striking architectural pieces amid the concrete, most notably around the pedestrianized Piaţa Victoriei, where you will find the neo-Brâncovenesc prefecture and the tiny **Cathedral of SS Voievozi**, built between 1749 and 1764. On Str. Unirii, the Tudor Vladimirescu high school stands diagonally opposite the Rectorat of the Constantin Brâncuşi University, both splendid neo-Brâncovenesc piles in bright new paint schemes. The **County Museum** at Str. Geneva 8 (Muzeul Judeţean; Tues–Sun 9am–5pm) is unremarkable, offering the standard view of Romanian history. On the main road, 3km north of the town centre at B-dul. Ecaterina Teodoroiu 270 (Wed–Sun 9am–4pm), is the birthplace of **Ecaterina Teodoroiu**, Romania's answer to Joan of Arc; she was only 23 when she died in August 1917, fighting disguised as a man in the crucial battle of Mărăşeşti (see p.267).

Constantin Brâncuşi

One of the greatest sculptors of the twentieth century, **Constantin Brâncuşi** was born in 1876 in a peasant cottage at Hobiţa, some 28km west of Târgu Jiu. He came to town at the age of nine to work as an errand boy, and later learnt the techniques of the local wood carvers, who chiselled sinuous designs on rafters, verandas and wells in the region. Through the sponsorship of local boyars, he was able to attend an art college in Craiova and went on to the **National School of Fine Arts** in Bucharest, before arriving at the Ecole des Beaux Arts in Paris in 1904, with a government scholarship of 600 Lei. He stayed in France for over fifty years, helping create a revolution in sculpture with his strikingly strong and simple works. With a circle of friends that included Picasso, Gide and Pound, he was at the centre of the intellectual ferment of Paris at its height.

He worked briefly in Rodin's studio, then, in company with Amadeo Modigliani, discovered the primitive forms of African masks and sculptures, concentrating thereafter on stripping forms down to their fundamentals. In 1907, he claimed that "what is real is not the exterior form but the essence of things", a credo which he pursued for the rest of his career. In 1920, his *Prinţesa X* was removed by police from the Salon des Independents because it was considered obscenely phallic; it was bought by Fernand Leger and Blaise Cendrars, but Brâncuşi never exhibited in Paris again. A different sort of scandal followed in 1926 when Brâncuşi took his *Măiastra* (*Magic Bird*) with him to New York. US Customs classified it as "a piece of metal" and levied import duty of $10; Brâncuşi appealed against the decision, thereby starting a furore which made him a household name in America. During that same trip, the photographer Edward Steichen gave credibility to Brâncuşi's work by publicly announcing that he had bought one of the sculptor's bronze *Birds in Flight* for $600 – by 1967, it was worth $175,000. Brâncuşi died in 1957, with his series of sculptures for Târgu Jiu unfinished, and is buried in Montparnasse cemetery in Paris. You'll find examples of his work in Craiova and Bucharest as well as Târgu Jiu, and also in London, New York and Philadelphia; his last studio is preserved in Paris.

Practicalities

The **train** and **bus stations** are just a stone's throw apart on Str. Titulescu, a twenty-minute walk east of town. Târgu Jiu is on the Simeria–Petroşani–Craiova train line, with a few trains continuing to Arad, Cluj, Craiova, Deva and Bucharest. Buses and maxitaxis run to Bucharest, Cluj, Horezu, Râmnicu Vâlcea, Drobeta-Turnu Severin, Sibiu, Timişoara and most surrounding villages. **Rail bookings** can be made at the CFR office at Bloc 2, Str. Unirii (Mon–Fri 7am–8pm).

The town's **hotels** are nothing special, but they all offer reasonable value for money: the best is the new *Europa* at Calea Eroilor 22 (℡0253/211 810; ⓌWwww.hotelrestauranteuropa.ro; ⑤), where all rooms are non-smoking and come with Internet access and huge TVs. The bizarrely named *Miami Energeticianul* at Calea Eroilor 24 (℡0253/218 407, Ⓕ213 449; ④) is modern, with small rooms while the tacky *Brâncuşi*, at B-dul. C. Brâncuşi 10 (℡0253/215 981, Ⓕ211 167, Ⓦwww.hotelbrancusi.ro; ⑥), has tidy, albeit gaudy, rooms. At the *Tineretului Youth Hotel*, a block south of the bus station at Str. Titulescu 26 (℡0253/238 353; ②), the lights are dim and the water's usually cold; but rooms are even cheaper at the *Gorj* at Calea Eroilor 6 (℡&Ⓕ0253/214 814; ②), as grim inside as out. **Homestay accommodation** in the area (❶) can be arranged through the Guardo Tours agency, just behind the cathedral at Str. Tudor Vladimirescu 17 (℡0253/223 081, Ⓔgorj@antrec.ro).

There's a paucity of **places to eat** in town. The best restaurant is in the *Hotel Europa*, serving Romanian-Italian food; the *Quattro Stagioni*, opposite the *Gorj* on Calea Eroilor, serves a good range of pizzas. For **drinking**, try the *SimiCentru*, a decent little bar with a busy outdoor garden on the west (older) side of Piaţa Victoriei. There's **Internet** access in the building next to the theatre and upstairs in the *Anairo* bar, immediately south of the station.

East of Târgu Jiu

Away from the industry of the Jiu valley, there are plenty of tranquil villages where traditional customs are still a part of everyday life. The area east of town has particularly impressive **cave formations** and important **monasteries**, notably those at Horezu. Unfortunately, the more remote sights are poorly served by buses from Târgu Jiu and Râmnicu Vâlcea. Six buses a day serve Polovragi from Târgu Jiu and there are less regular buses to Horezu on the Târgu Jiu–Râmnicu Vâlcea route. There are also several mountain hikes north into Transylvania, towards Voineasa and the Cindrel mountains (see p.196) and the Parâng range (see p.196).

Polovragi and around

POLOVRAGI, 48km east of Târgu Jiu and dominated by the Căpăţânii mountains, is home to one of the great Wallachian fairs: the *Nedeia*. An occasion for highlanders to dress up, dance and do deals face-to-face in the old fashion, the *Nedeia* usually occurs on the Sunday between July 14 and 20. If your visit doesn't coincide with the fair, the main sites of interest are north of the village, where a forestry road runs into the 1.6-kilometre-long **Olteţu gorges**, beyond which, 3km from the main road, you'll find the **Polovragi Monastery and cave**. The small monastery was originally built in 1470, then rebuilt by Brâncoveanu in 1647; the later **Bolniţa Church** (1736), on the same site, is definitely worth the trip for its fine frescoes. Further on, lurking behind the eastern rockface at the mouth of the gorge, is the Polovragi cave, once believed to be the abode of Zalmoxis, the Dacians' chief deity. Now fully illuminated and open for guided tours (daily 9am–5pm), it was first explored in 1860 by the French naturalist Lancelot, and is renowned for the stalactites in its "Candlesticks Gallery".

From Baia de Fier, 7km west of Polovragi and 5km north of the main road from Târgu Jiu to Râmnicu Vâlcea, a road leads 3km north to a beautiful grotto in the smaller **Galbenul gorges**. Although only two passages out of the ten kilometres of convolutions that make up the so-called **Women's Cave** (Peştera Muierilor; daily 9am–5pm) have been illuminated, it's an impressive sight nonetheless; halfway in, multicoloured stone columns resemble petrified wood, while in the lower passage the skeletons of 183 cave bears have been discovered. The cave gets its name from the human skeletons – mainly those of women and children, and dating from prehistoric times – found on its upper levels. From the cave and nearby *cabana*, a footpath leads up to the **Rânca tourist complex** (☏0244/461 542; ❸) 15km away in the Parâng mountains in Transylvania; the basic accommodation is useful mainly for hikers in the summer. Just to the west, **NOVACI** marks the start of the forestry road to Rânca (18km) and on to Sebeş (see p.199). There are two ordinary motels in Novaci, on Str. Tudor Vladimirescu, and in Baia de Fier there is the *Hotel Peştera Muierilor* (☏0744/790 730; ❸).

Horezu and the monasteries

Set amid apple and plum orchards, sweet chestnut trees and wild lilac, 16km east of Polovragi on the main road to Râmnicu Vâlcea (which is another 42km east), is the small town of **HOREZU** – so-called after the numerous owls (*huhurezi*) that reside here (the town is also shown as Hurez on some maps). Although wooden furniture and wrought-iron objects are also produced here, Horezu is best known for its **pottery**, especially its plates, which by tradition are given as keepsakes during funeral wakes. The Cocoşul de Horezu **pottery fair**, held on the first Sunday of June, is one of the year's biggest events in the area – though if you miss it, you can still see many wares displayed outside houses along the road just east of the centre. Four kilometres south in **Măldăreşti** (on the main bus route from Târgu Jiu) stand two *culas* or tower houses, built in the eighteenth and nineteenth centuries, when punitive raids by Turkish troops were still a possibility.

▲ Horezu Monastery

Constantin Brâncoveanu

Constantin Brâncoveanu (1654–1714) became ruler of Wallachia in 1689 after the usual Byzantine family intrigues, and was instrumental in bringing about a cultural renaissance by establishing a printing press in Bucharest and a school of architecture and sculpture at the monastery of Horez. He created an **architectural style** that was a fusion of Western (especially Venetian) Renaissance and Ottoman elements, characterized by a harmonious layout and fine ornamental stone carving, especially on balconies, external staircases and arcades. In the early twentieth century a neo-Brâncovenesc style was very popular, especially in Wallachia and Moldavia, as an expression of the new nation's cultural identity.

Politically, he sought to distance Wallachia from its Ottoman overlords (partly because he wanted to keep for his building projects some of the massive taxes they demanded). At the outbreak of a Russo-Turkish War in 1710 he sought alliances with the Russians, as well as the Hapsburgs, while also being prepared to fight on the Turkish side if they seemed likelier winners. However he was arrested, tortured and (with his four sons and grand treasurer Enache Văcărescu) executed in 1714 in Constantinople. He was succeeded by his cousin Ştefan Cantacuzino, who was soon deposed and executed by the Ottomans and replaced by Nicolai Mavrocordat, the first Phanariot ruler of Wallachia (having already been the first Phanariot ruler of Moldavia).

In 1992 he, and those executed with him, were declared saints and martyrs by the Romanian Orthodox Church, honoured as protectors of the Orthodox faith against Islam. Nevertheless, to the outside world it is his artistic and cultural achievements that are his lasting legacy. Mogoşoaia Palace, 15km from Bucharest, built by him between 1698 and 1702, now houses the **Muzeul Brâncovenesc**.

The real attraction, however, lies near the village of Romanii de Jos, around 3km northeast of town, turning off the main road 2km east of town. Built between 1691 and 1697, and now a UNESCO World Heritage Site, **Horezu Monastery** is the largest and finest of Wallachia's Brâncoveanu complexes, and is the site of the school which established the Brâncovenesc style. The complex is centred around the **Great Church**, built in 1693 and entered via a marvellous ten-pillared porchway and doors of carved pearwood. Inside, the **frescoes**, once tarnished by the smoke from fires lit by Turkish slaves who camped here, are slowly being restored, but you can still make out portraits of Constantin Brâncoveanu and his family, Cantacuzino and Basarab, as well as scenes from Mount Athos and the Orthodox calendar. To the right of the church as you enter is a vacant tomb, which was Brâncoveanu's intended resting place – as it is, he is buried in St George's Church in Bucharest (see p.83).

Opposite the church is the nuns' refectory, which contains some more but poorly preserved frescoes and, to the left, another Brâncoveanu porch, featuring a splendid stone balustrade carved with animal motifs. Set apart to the north and west are the small hermitages of the Holy Apostles and of St Stephen, built in 1700 and 1703 respectively. The chapel of St Michael outside the gates was built by Brâncoveanu for the local villagers.

There's **accommodation** in the centre of Horezu at the *Hanul Turistic Horezu* (T0250/861 040, @coophorezu@yahoo.com; ❷), the motel by the bus station, which has tennis courts and offers youth hostel discounts. There are also guesthouses, such as *Pensiunea Criveanu*, behind the motel at Str. Căpitan Maldăr 5 (T0250/860 038, 0729/103 929; ❷); *Pensiunea Dana*, to the north at Str. Olari 15 (T0250/860 113, 0723/978 255, @pensiuneadana@k.ro; ❷); and *Pensiunea Steldan*, on the eastern edge of town at Str. Tudor Vladimirescu 4

(☎0250/861 110; ❷). The *Trei Stejarii* campsite, right at the west end of the town, also has tiny, bunker-like huts sleeping two (☎0250/860 570; ❶).

Six kilometres on towards Râmnicu Vâlcea on the DN67, a left turn at Coşteşti leads another 6km north to **Bistriţa Monastery**, funded by the boyars of Craiova in the fifteenth century. You will, however, need your own transport, as bus services no longer run here. As well as three churches, dating from the sixteenth and seventeenth centuries, there is a cave containing two more chapels, in one of which the relics of St Gregory the Decapolite were hidden during the Turkish wars; a nun can lead you to the cave along the precipitous cliffside path. The seventeenth-century **Arnota Monastery** stands on a hill, 4km north of Bistriţa beyond a large quarry; by financing the construction of this monastery, *voivode* Matei Basarab guaranteed himself a tasteful burial place within its church surrounded by his chattels and murals of his wife, of which only fragments remain. As so often in this area, the porch is the work of Brâncoveanu.

West of Târgu Jiu

The small scenic towns and villages to the west of Târgu Jiu are a complete contrast to the flat, grimy mining areas to the east and south. Buses run from Târgu Jiu along the DN67d, stopping close to most of the sites of interest. From Peştişani, 21km west of Târgu Jiu, it's 3km south to the small village of **HOBIŢA**, birthplace of Constantin Brâncuşi (see p.128). The sculptor's childhood home has been turned into a small **museum** (Wed–Sun 9am–5pm); if it's closed, you can ask in the shop at the crossroads for the museum's custodian to let you in. It's an attractive, traditional cottage, surrounded by plum and cherry trees, in which you'll learn relatively little about Brâncuşi, but it's worth seeing the ceramics and textiles displayed inside, and the intricate spiral motifs on the veranda posts. One hundred metres away on the same road is the *Popas* pension, where you can sleep in *căsuţe* (wooden cabins; summer only; ❶) by a ford which leads into a wood dotted with Brâncuşi-esque sculptures left by a 1981 summer-school group. Further south, at the edge of the same wood, but reached by the main road through the village, is the village cemetery, with a tiny wooden chapel; even if it's closed, it's possible to enter the chapel's roof space by a ladder from the open porch to admire the skill of the local carpenters. There's also accommodation at the east end of Peştişani at the modern *Pensiunea Casa Brâncuşi* (☎0253/374 321; ❷).

TISMANA, just north of the DN67d another 7km west, harks back to the region's traditional pastoral ways. **Tismana Monastery**, 3km to the north of the village, is the oldest in Romania, founded in 1375 by St Nicodim, a member of the Basarab royal family, whose hermit-like cave is just to the right of the monastery gate, and whose tomb is to the right as you enter the church porch. Surrounded by a high wall during the reign of Matei Basarab, the monastery served as a meeting place for rebels in the 1821 rising led by Tudor Vladimirescu. Tismana is the setting for the annual **Tismana Garden Festival** of music and crafts on August 15, where the most popular instrument is the *nai* or shepherds' panpipes. You'll find wooden utensils, sculptures, embroidered clothing and Oltenian rugs on sale during the festival, but the quality and range of goods has declined in recent years; there are also stalls all year in the car park, selling good ceramics as well as trashy souvenirs. The monastery has a modern guesthouse (❶), and the *Gura Plaiului* youth hostel (☎0253/374 238, ✉gorunhoratiu@yahoo.com, ⊛www.e-tineret.ro; ❶) is right at the entry to the car park, with a sign in English. Tismana also has some good **homestay** possibilities – contact the Guardo Tours Agency in

Târgu Jiu (see p.129) or scout around the village, where *Pensiunea Magnolia* (☎0251/461 106, 0744/197 088; ❷), about 1km north of the main road, is a bar with rooms.

Buses for Călugăreni and Cloşani turn north off the main road about 12km west of Tismana, stopping after 5km in **PADEŞ,** where the 1821 peasant revolt, led by Tudor Vladimirescu, began. Some old men still wear folk costume – narrow white homespun trousers piped with braid and voluminous cloaks – which resemble the uniforms worn by Vladimirescu's soldiers. Picturesque **karst formations** abound in the region, particularly around Cloşani and Ponoarele, 7km south of the main road just west of Baia de Aramă (another 9km west of Padeş); here, the **Giant's Bridge**, 25m wide by 50m long, was formed when the ceiling of a large cave collapsed.

Drobeta-Turnu Severin and the Danube

Drobeta-Turnu Severin lies in the far west of the region, on the north side of the **River Danube**, the country's natural border with Serbia and Bulgaria. The river narrows below Moldova Veche before surging through the **Kazan gorge** towards Orşova, only to be tamed and harnessed by the dam at the mighty **Iron Gates**, before reaching the town. Motorists driving down from Moldova Veche can see something of this magnificent panorama (the rail journey is less scenic); but if you're coming from Târgu Jiu, the real landscape feast doesn't start until you reach Drobeta-Turnu Severin. The shortest route from Târgu Jiu is via the badly surfaced DN67, usually crowded with trucks. By train, you'll have to travel down to the unappealing town of **Filiaşi** to join the Craiova–Drobeta-Turnu Severin line.

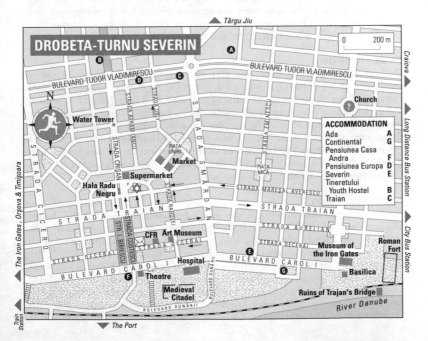

Drobeta-Turnu Severin

Dubbed the "town of roses" for its beautiful parks, notably the archeological park around the Museum of the Iron Gates, with its lovely roses and walnut trees, the modern appearance of **DROBETA-TURNU SEVERIN** (usually known simply as Severin) belies its origins as the Dacian settlement of Drobeta, more than two thousand years ago. Its Roman conquerors left more enduring landmarks, however, notably the ruins of **Trajan's bridge**, which Apollodorus of Damascus built to span the Danube at the order of the emperor in 103–105 AD. As the travel writer Patrick Leigh Fermor put it, "two great stumps of his conglomerate masonry still cumbered the Romanian side", and these can be seen from the train or from the grounds of the **Museum of the Iron Gates** (Muzeul Porţile de Fier; Tues–Sun 9am–5pm) at the southern end of Str. Independenţei on the east side of town. Nearby, within the museum precincts or *Parc Arheologic*, are the remains of a Roman bath and the foundations of both the fort that guarded Trajan's bridge and the fourteenth-century **Metropolitan's Basilica**. The museum itself is divided up into several sections which, overall, are a bit hit-and-miss: the most enjoyable is the ethnographic section, featuring a lovely assortment of rugs, costumes, ceramics and painted chests, while the aquarium, with tanks full of unusual species from the Danube, will keep kids happy. Otherwise, the natural science, archeological and historical departments are eminently missable, if only because all captions are in Romanian. The small **art museum** (Muzeul de Artă; Tues–Sun 10am–6pm) at Str. Rahovei 3 holds a few works by important Romanian painters, including several still-life paintings and nudes by Pallady.

A few minutes' walk south of the art museum, across B-dul. Carol I and down past the hospital, stand the tower and walls of a **medieval citadel** dating from the thirteenth century. Heading back north, the lively daily market is on Piaţa Unirii, while just to the west are a **synagogue** (finally being refurbished) and the site for a new Orthodox cathedral, and the *Hala Radu Negru* market hall, which now houses a huge furniture and textile store.

Practicalities

Drobeta-Turnu Severin's main **bus station** is on Str. D. Ghiaţa, to the east of the centre at Str. Topolniţei (buses #1 and #45), with services west to Băile Herculane and Timişoara in the Banat and east to Târgu Jiu and Râmnicu Vâlcea. Minibuses from here to Motru and Târgu Jiu also pick up in Piaţa Unirii. From the **train station** it's a fifteen–minute walk east along B-dul. Carol I to the centre; train tickets can be booked at the **CFR** office at Str. Decebal 43 (Mon–Fri 9am–4pm). The best source of **information** on the area is the *Hotel Continental*'s tourist agency, who can also arrange riverboat trips upstream from Orşova (see p.136) to Moldova Veche (see p.137).

Accommodation

Easily the best **hotel** in town is the smart *Pensiunea Europa* at B-dul. Tudor Vladimirescu 66 (℡0252/333 737, ℱ325 281, ⓦwww.pensiunea-europa .ro; ⑤–⑥), which has comfortable air-conditioned rooms and apartments with Internet access. The *Pensiunea Casa Andra*, at Str. Coşbuc 2 (℡&ℱ0352/401 444, ⓦwww.casa-andra.ro; ④), has simple air-conditioned rooms, all with Internet access, in a nice old building above a large restaurant. The *Hotel Ada* at B-dul. Tudor Vladimirescu 125 (℡0252/326 123, Ⓔadahotel@petrostal .ro; ④–⑤) is very friendly but has only eight air-conditioned rooms, all with Internet access. The alternatives, *Continental* at B-dul. Carol I no. 2, *Severin* at

Str. Eminescu 1 and *Traian* at B-dul Tudor Vladimirescu 74, are unappealing and only really worth trying if all of the above are full. The budget choice is the *Tineretului* youth hostel, just north of the *Europa* at Str. Crişan 25 (T&F0252/317 999; ●). The *Vatra Haiducilor* (Outlaws' Hearth) **campsite** is 3km north along Str. Crişan in the Crihala forest. Antrec, at Str. Avram Iancu 38 (T0252/318 076, ●mehedinti@antrec.ro), can arrange **homestay accommodation** (●) in the county.

Eating and drinking

There are few dining options in Drobeta-Turnu Severin. The classy little restaurant in the *Pension Europa* serves upscale Romanian fare and is without doubt the best place to eat. *Casa Andra*, which also does good traditional Romanian dishes, is a decent alternative.

The Iron Gates

The **Iron Gates** is a cliff-lined stretch of the River Danube which once had a formidable reputation, owing to the navigational hazards (eddies, whirlpools and rocks) which formerly restricted safe passage during the two hundred days of the year when the river was in spate, meaning that boats had to take aboard a pilot at Moldova. The blasting of a channel in 1896 obviated these terrors, and the building of the largest **hydroelectric dam** in Europe (excluding the former Soviet Union) at Gura Văii, 10km upstream of Drobeta-Turnu Severin, finally tamed the river.

Conceived in 1956, the Porţile de Fier I hydroelectric project was undertaken as a joint venture; Romania and Yugoslavia (as it was then) each built a 1GW turbine plant and locks for shipping on their respective banks, linked by a slipway dam and an international road crossing. That task took from 1960 until 1972 and raised the river level by 33m. Romantics have deplored the results, which, in the words of Patrick Leigh Fermor, "has turned 130 miles of the Danube into a vast pond which has swollen and blurred the course of the river beyond recognition", turning "beetling crags into mild hills". The damming has submerged two places worthy of footnotes in history – the island of **Ada Kaleh** and old **Orşova** – and reduced the Danube's peak flow, so that the pollution of Central Europe is no longer flushed out to sea but gathers here, killing fish and flora. Near the dam is the *Continental Motel Porţile de Fier* (T0252/342 144, Wwww.continentalhotels.ro; ●), with comfortable rooms that mirror those of the other hotels in the *Continental* chain – there is also a swimming pool and tennis courts. On the E70 (DN6) 10km west of Drobeta-Turnu Severin, the dam can be reached by bus #3 (*Baraj*) from the local *autogara* at the junction of Str. Traian and Str. Calărasi, just east of the Roman

---

A Turkish outpost

Legend has it that the Argonauts discovered the olive tree on **ADA KALEH**, an island that was famous at the beginning of the twentieth century for its Turkish community, complete with mosques, bazaars and fortresses. Their presence here at so late a date arose from a diplomatic oversight, for at the conference where the Ottoman withdrawal from the region was negotiated in 1878, Ada Kaleh was forgotten about, enabling it to remain Turkish until the Trianon Treaty officially made it part of Romania in 1920. Before Ada Kaleh's submersion by the Danube, Eugene of Savoy's citadel was removed and reconstructed on the island of **Ostrov Şimian**, 5km east of Turnu Severin. Unfortunately, being a military base, the island is inaccessible.

fort in Severin. Since 2000 the Iron Gates have in theory been protected by the Parc Natural Porțile de Fier (⟨W⟩www.portiledefier.ro), which has information centres in the Museum of the Iron Gates at Drobeta-Turnu Severin and at Orșova, Berzasca and Moldova Nouă.

Orșova

Before 1918, **ORȘOVA**, 23km upstream from Drobeta-Turnu Severin, was the frontier crossing into the Magyar-ruled Banat, and it was nearby that Kossuth buried the Crown of St Stephen on his way into exile after the failure of the 1848–49 revolt in Hungary (it has since been returned to Budapest). However, the town was flooded by the dam, and replaced by the new Orșova, 3km east of its train station. There's nothing particularly worth stopping off for, but if for some reason you do want to stay, there are a couple of good-value **hotels** available: the modern and bright *Hotel Meridian*, just across from the bus station at Str. Eroilor 12 (⟨T⟩0252/362 800, ⟨F⟩362 810; ⑤), and the marginally cheaper *Hostel Flora*, close by at B-dul. Porțile de Fier 26 (⟨T⟩&⟨F⟩0252/362 081; ④).

The Kazan gorge, Moldova Veche and Moldova Nouă

Sixteen kilometres beyond Orșova, on both sides of the village of **DUBOVA**, the sheer cliffs of the **Kazan gorge** (Cazanele Dunării) fall 600m into the tortuous river. Rather than attempt to cut a path through the rock, the Romans bored holes in to the side of the cliff to hold beams upon which they laid planks, roofing over the road to discourage Dacian ambushes. The first proper road was created on the northern side of the gorge on the initiative of the nineteenth-century Hungarian statesman Count Szechenyi, but had not long been finished when the 1920 Trianon Treaty transferred it to Romania, whereupon it was neglected and finally submerged in the 1970s by the rising

▲ The Kazan Gorge

waters. Since the building of the dam, modern roads have been built on both sides of the river, and the dramatic landscape makes this an excursion not to be missed. The authorities aren't keen on tourists canoeing down the Danube (mainly because of the industrial barges using the river and the proximity of the border with Serbia), but it's a great drive. If you don't have your own transport, tour boats – which closed during the Yugoslav wars – are soon to restart. It's 77km upstream (either by car or one of the two buses a day that leave from Orşova) to the small port of **MOLDOVA VECHE**, its old quarter largely inhabited by Serbs, while the high-rise blocks to the west are dominated by Romanians brought in during the communist period, when the port was developed to serve the copper and molybdenum mines inland. There is, though, nothing of interest here now. Similarly, the communist-era mining community of **MOLDOVA NOUĂ**, 4km inland from the port, is in a state of terminal decline, with both its hotel and museum now closed.

Before Moldova Veche, within sight of the port, the river divides around an island near the isolated **rock of Babakai**. According to legend, the Turkish governor of Moldova marooned Zuleika, one of his seven wives, here because she had attempted to elope with a Hungarian noble. Admonished to "Repent of thy sin!" (*Ba-ba-kai*) and left to die, Zuleika was rescued by her lover, who later had the joy of taunting the mortally wounded governor with the news that Zuleika was alive and had become a Christian. Another legend refers to the caves near the ruined fortress of **Golubac**, just downstream on the Serbian bank of the river, where St George is said to have slain the dragon. Thereafter, its carcass has reputedly fed the swarms of bugs that infest the town of the same name.

Southern Wallachia

In many respects, **southern Wallachia** is tedious, uninviting terrain, for while the Subcarpathians provide varied scenery and picturesque villages, below them stretch kilometres of featureless plains, dusty or muddy according to the season, with state farms lost amid vast fields of corn or sunflowers. Although the large industrial town of **Craiova** has a few rewarding museums, the only obvious reason for venturing into this region is to cross the **border to Bulgaria**: there are crossing points at Calafat, 87km southwest of Craiova, and Giurgiu, some 60km south of Bucharest.

Craiova

Almost every locomotive on the tracks of Romania originally emerged from the Electroputere workshops of **CRAIOVA**, which also exports to Hungary, Bulgaria, China and even Britain. The city is also a centre for the Romanian automobile industry, the Oltcit works having produced many of the country's cars first in collaboration with Citroën, then, as Rodae, with Korea's Daewoo conglomerate. After Daewoo's worldwide collapse in 2002, the government bought back the factory and in 2007 sold it to Ford; Electroputere was also sold in 2007, to a Saudi company. These industries are here because of the ready availability of oil, whose presence is attested to by the derricks surrounding what is now the chief city of Oltenia and capital of Dolj county. Craiova does have a longer history than it might appear from its industrialized heritage, having begun its life as the Roman town of Pelendava, and **Michael the Brave** (see p.435) began his career here as deputy governor. Today it's a sprawling and

The Răscoala

Despite its rich soil, the southern plain has traditionally been one of Romania's poorest areas, as the boyars – and, worse still, their estate managers – squeezed the peasants mercilessly with extortionate land taxes. The amount of available land diminished as the peasant population, taxes and rural unemployment increased, building up to the explosive **1907 uprising**, the *Răscoala*. Triggered near Vaslui in Moldavia where Jews, believed to exploit peasants, were the first targets, the uprising raged southwards into Wallachia. Panic-stricken boyars flooded into Bucharest, demanding vengeance for the burning of their property – and the army obliged, quelling the ill-armed peasantry with cannon fire, and then executing "ringleaders" by the thousand. Though there's a **Museum of the Uprising** at Str. Dunării 54 (Tues–Sun 10am–5pm) in Roşiori de Vede (Teleorman county), the English translation of Liviu Rebreanu's novel *Uprising* (see Books, p.482) is a more gripping exposition of the subject.

hectic place, but you may find yourself breaking a journey to or from Bulgaria here, in which case there is a cluster of impressive museums to while away the time, and on the southern edge of the city (down Calea Unirii) the superb **Romanescu Park**, laid out by French architects in 1901–03, with a zoo and lake and the first cable suspension bridge in Europe.

The Town

Built from 1900–08 by a French architect for one of Romania's richest men, the elegant neo-Baroque **Mihail Palace**, at Calea Unirii 15, was home to Nicolae Ceauşescu in the early 1950s when he was local party secretary, and since 1954 has housed an excellent **art gallery** (Muzeul de Artă; Tues–Sun 10am–5pm). At the core of the museum's collection are two rooms housing half a dozen pieces by Brâncuşi (including versions of *Mlle Pogany* and *The Kiss*), a room of paintings by local artist Theodor Aman (1831–91), and two dozen paintings by Grigorescu. There's also plenty of French decorative art, including Sèvres porcelain, and some Italian paintings, including works by Bassano and Bellotto.

Continuing south, Calea Unirii becomes the pedestrianized axis of the modern city centre; immediately to the right on the main plaza, at Str. Popa Şapcă 4, is the **Natural History Museum** (Muzeul Ştiinţele Naturii; Tues–Sun 9am–5pm), offering the usual grim assortment of stuffed animals. Southwest of the museum, on Str. Madona-Dudu, is the **History Museum** (Muzeul de Istorie şi Arheologie; Tues–Sun 9am–5pm). Displays include Oltenia's oldest archeological remains, medieval ornaments and frescoes, good coverage of the War of Independence (1877–78) and World War I, and some Brâncovenesc art. Opposite this is the **Madona Dudu Church**, rebuilt in 1936 to house an icon of the Virgin.

Immediately to the south on Str. Matei Basarab is the **cathedral of Sf. Dumitru-Băneasa**, built in 1652 but thoroughly transformed in 1889 by Lecomte de Noüy – it's less gloomy than most Orthodox churches, with a gorgeous golden glow to its frescoes. Occupying the former governor's residence, or *Casa Băniei* (dating from 1699), at Str. Matei Basarab 16, is the very worthwhile **Ethnographic Museum** (Muzeul de Etnografie; Tues–Sun 9am–5pm, closed for refurbishment in 2007), with a fabulous assortment of local costumes, ceramics from Horezu, porch pillars and some exquisitely carved staffs; the stunning cellar holds a superb assemblage of agricultural and viticultural implements, all with English captions.

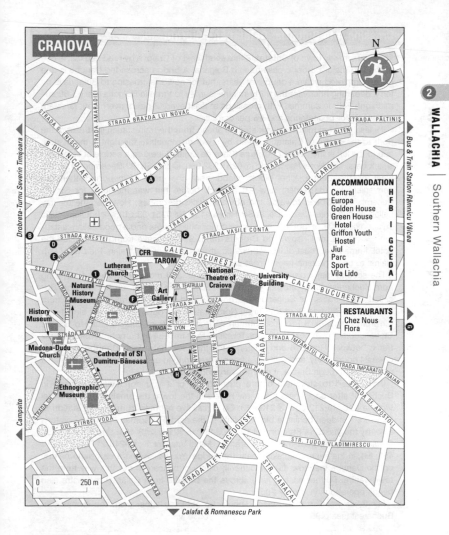

CRAIOVA

Campsite

STRADA G. ENESCU
STRADA AMARADIEI
STRADA BRAZDA LUI NOVAC
STRADA ŞERBAN VODĂ
STRADA PĂLTINIŞ
STRADA PĂLTINIŞ
STR. OLTENI
B-DUL NICOLAE TITULESCU
STRADA C. BRÂNCUŞI
STRADA ŞTEFAN CEL MARE
STRADA ŞTEFAN CEL MARE
B-DUL CAROL I
STRADA BRESTEI
STRADA BRESCU
STRADA VASILE CONTA
CALEA BUCUREŞTI
STRADA MIHAI VITEAZUL
CFR
TAROM
Lutheran Church
Natural History Museum
National Theatre of Craiova
University Building
CALEA BUCUREŞTI
STR. POPA SAPCA
Art Gallery
STR. TEATRULUI
STRADA A.I. CUZA
STRADA A.I. CUZA
History Museum
STRADA BRESCU
STRADA THEODOR AMAN
STRADA LYON
STRADA ARIEŞ
Madona-Dudu Church
STRADA M. DUDU
Cathedral of Sf Dumitru-Bâneasa
STR. FRAŢII BUZEŞTI
STRADA IMPĂRATUL TRAIAN
STRADA IMPĂRATUL TRAIAN
Ethnographic Museum
ST. DUMITRU
STR. M. KOGĂLNICEANU
STRADA MITROPOLIT FIRMILIAN
STR. EUGENIU CARCADA
STRADA SF. APOSTOLI
B-DUL ŞTIRBEI VODĂ
STRADA MATEI BASARAB
CALEA UNIRII
STR. TUDOR VLADIMIRESCU
STRADA ALEX. MACEDONSKI
STRADA CARACAL

0   250 m

ACCOMMODATION

Central	H
Europa	F
Golden House	B
Green House Hotel	I
Griffon Youth Hostel	G
Jiul	C
Parc	E
Sport	D
Vila Lido	A

RESTAURANTS

Chez Nous	2
Flora	1

▼ Calafat & Romanescu Park

Practicalities

Craiova's **train** and **bus stations** are located side by side northeast of the centre on Str. Dacia, from where it's a twenty-minute walk along B-dul. Carol I (or minibuses #1, #5, #12 and #29) to the main through road, Calea Bucureşti. There are two train lines between Craiova and Bucharest: the main route crosses the southern plains by way of Caracal, Roşiori de Vede and Videle (with express trains continuing to Timişoara), while the second is a non-electrified line via Piteşti (see p.116). From B-dul. Decebal 3, on the east side of the bus station, *C&I* maxitaxis (☎0788/142 310, ⓦwww.cdy.ro) leave on the hour for Piteşti and Bucharest, and *Ognivia* international buses run to western Europe; *Dacos* buses to Râmnicu Vâlcea, Sibiu and Cluj leave from B-dul. Decebal 13. The **CFR** (Mon–Fri 7am–7.30pm) and **TAROM** (Mon–Fri 9am–5pm; ☎0251/411 049) offices are at Calea Bucureşti 2, in the

Crossing into Bulgaria: Calafat and Giurgiu

The neat, orderly town of **Calafat**, 84km southwest of Craiova by road and rail, is one of the two major border crossings into Bulgaria. A bridge across the Danube is due to be completed within a couple of years, but for now the crossing to Bulgaria is by ferry, departing hourly for the thirty-minute journey to **Vidin** in Bulgaria (daily 5.30am–midnight; 24hr in summer, with crossings at least every 3 hours overnight); fares are around €2 for pedestrians and €6 per car.

It's less than ten minutes' walk straight ahead from the train station (just east of the port) to the centre of Calafat, marked by a war memorial; to the right is the market, and to the left is the House of Culture (Casa de Cultură), next to a couple of cafés and snack bars. The *Hotel Panoramic* (①0251/232 960; ③), at Str. 22 Decembrie 1, is just west of the centre, one block inland from the port (*Vama*), and therefore convenient for the ferries; turn left a block before the war memorial for Str. 22 Decembrie and head towards the obvious dockside cranes. However, the friendly Italian-owned *Hotel Casa Italia*, at Str. Horea 41 (①&①0251/333 135, ⑥ hotelcasaitalia @yahoo.com; ④), is much nicer, with air-conditioned rooms and a good Italian restaurant. Maxitaxis for Craiova and Drobeta-Turnu Severin leave from right outside the hotel. Immediately east of the *Panoramic* at the corner of Str. Traian, the *Daniel Pub* claims to be a "pizzeria-bar-internet-sala biliard".

The second major crossing point into Bulgaria, and more convenient if travelling from Bucharest, is at **Giurgiu**, 64km due south of the capital, on the Danube. So-called rapid trains for Bulgaria take an hour and a half to crawl the 85km from Bucharest's Gara de Nord to Giurgiu Nord Station just outside the town; slow trains run from Bucharest's Progresu Station and continue from Giurgiu Nord to Giurgiu Station, in the town next to the bus terminal. Built in 1954 to carry both road and rail traffic between Romania and Bulgaria, the three-kilometre-long **Danube Bridge** is open 24 hours a day, and with most people preferring to enter Bulgaria from Romania rather than through Serbia, it can get very congested.

If you need to stay here before pushing on, or if you don't want to arrive in Bucharest after dark, there are a few **hotels** in the town: the small and basic *Hotel Victoria* (①0246/212 569, ①213 453; ③) is just five minutes from Giurgiu station at Str. Gării 1, hidden behind a block of flats to the right. For something more comfortable, try the *Vlaşca* at Str. Portului 12 (①0246/215 321, ①213 453; ⑤), or the *Steaua Dunării*, a vaguely post-modern pile at Str. Mihai Viteazul 1 (①0246/217 270, ①213 453; ⑦), in the eastern outskirts near the bridge. You'll also find a **campsite** nearby on the Danube meadow (Lunca Dunării); plenty of buses run out this way from the town centre. Further east, a ferry across the Danube from Călăraşi to Silistra also began operation in October 2007.

For those needing them, **visas** should be obtained either from the embassy in Bucharest (see p.96), or from home before you leave.

Unirea shopping complex opposite the *Hotel Jiul*. The airport (7km east on Şoseaua Craiova-Bucureşti) is used only by Carpatair, with three flights a week from Timişoara via Craiova to Constanţa; tickets are available through agencies such as the friendly Mapamond, just off Calea Unirii at Str. Olteţ 2 (Mon–Fri 8am–5pm, Sat 8am–1pm; ①0251/415 071, ⑥ travel@mapamond .ro). Mapamond also acts as an Antrec agent booking **homestay accommodation** (①) in the surrounding villages, and is the best source of **tourist information**. Cars can be rented from Romnicon Rentacar, at Str. A.I. Cuza 55 (①0251/553 947, ⑩ www.romnicon.ro). The *Pădurea Satului* **campsite** is a long way east, beyond the airport on the DN65.

Accommodation

Central Str. Mitropolit Firmilian 1 ☎0251/534 895, ✉hotelcentral@rds.ro. Simple but friendly, with basic facilities and no breakfast. **❸**

Europa Calea Unirii 10A ☎0251/412 321, ✉cmitrita@yahoo.com. A new three-star place, very central but set back from the main road; rooms are a/c and with satellite TV and Internet access. **❽**

Golden House Str. Brestei 18 ☎0251/406 270, ⓦwww.goldenhouse.ro. The most luxurious place in town, with a/c rooms, Internet access, swimming pool and a good restaurant. **❾**

Green House Hotel Str. Fraţii Buzeşti 25 ☎&ⓕ0251/411 352, ⓦwww.green-house.ro. A modern building with comfortable, sunny rooms and good service. **❻**

Griffon ☎0251/804 902, ✉dtjdolj@yahoo.com, ⓦtineret_dolj.ro. A youth hostel a couple of kilometres east at Str. Electroputere 21 bis, in the industrial area. **❶**

Jiul Calea Bucureşti 1 ☎0251/414 166, ⓕ412 462. A very ordinary communist-era block, but centrally located and decently refurbished. **❹–❻**

Parc Str. Bibescu 12 ☎0251/417 257, ⓕ418 623, ⓦwww.hotelparc.go.ro. Once the Communist Party's guesthouse, now well renovated; rooms have a/c and cable TV, and there's a nice terrace restaurant at the rear. **❻**

Sport Str. Brestei 25 ☎0251/412 022, ⓦwww .hotel-sport.ro. Only a few years old but a typical Romanian sport hotel, with small rooms and basic bathrooms. **❺**

Vila Lido Str. C. Brâncuşi 10 ☎0251/590 332, ⓕ595 799. The best-value hotel in town has a quiet, pleasant location and a swimming pool. **❺**

Eating, drinking and entertainment

There's a dire shortage of **places to eat** in Craiova, though the restaurants in the *Golden House Hotel* (French) and *Green House Hotel* (Romanian) are good. For more traditional Romanian fare, try *Chez Nous* at Str. Traian Demetrescu 8 or *Flora* at Str. Mihai Viteazul 18. A few of the city's 25,000 students meet at the bars on Str. Arieş near the university. The *Teatrul Naţional Marin Sorescu*, just west of the university at Str. A.I. Cuza 11 (tickets ☎0251/413 677), is home to one of Romania's leading theatre companies. Performances are in Romanian only but are visual enough that you won't need to understand the language to get a sense of the plot.

Travel details

Trains

Câmpulung to: Goleşti (5 daily; 1hr 5min–1hr 50min).

Craiova to: Bucharest (20 daily; 2hr 30min–4hr 30min); Calafat (5 daily; 2hr 45min–3hr); Drobeta-Turnu Severin (12 daily; 1hr 35min–3hr 10min); Filiaşi (27 daily; 25min–1hr); Piatra Olt (12 daily; 45min–1hr 20min); Piteşti (5 daily; 2hr 15min–4hr); Sibiu (4 daily; 4hr–7hr 20min); Târgu Jiu (10 daily; 1hr 25min–3hr); Timişoara (10 daily; 4hr 50min–7hr).

Curtea de Argeş to: Piteşti (6 daily; 45min–1hr 5min).

Drobeta-Turnu Severin to: Băile Herculane (11 daily; 45min–1hr 5min); Caransebeş (11 daily; 2hr 5min–3hr 15min); Craiova (12 daily; 1hr 40min–3hr 10min); Orşova (11 daily; 25–40min); Timişoara (11 daily; 3hr 15min–5hr 45min).

Piatra Olt to: Călimăneşti (5 daily; 1hr 50min–3hr 15min); Râmnicu Vâlcea (11 daily; 1hr 5min–2hr 30min); Sibiu (5 daily; 3hr 10min–6hr); Turnu Monastery (3 daily; 3hr 15min–3hr 30min).

Piteşti to: Bucharest (10 daily; 1hr 20min–2hr 40min); Câmpulung Muscel (4 daily; 1hr 55min–2hr 10min); Curtea de Argeş (6 daily; 45min–1hr 5min); Goleşti (10 daily; 10min); Titu (7 daily; 45min–1hr 20min).

Ploieşti to: Braşov (every 30min–1hr; 1hr 40min–2hr 45min); Bucharest (every 20min–1hr; 40min–1hr 35min); Iaşi (5 daily; 5–6hr); Slănic Prahova (4 daily; 1hr 20min–2hr); Suceava (8 daily; 5hr 30min–7hr); Târgovişte (4 daily; 1hr 35min–1hr 50min); Văleni (3 daily; 56min).

Râmnicu Vâlcea to: Călimăneşti (10 daily; 25–30min); Craiova (4 daily; 1hr 50min–3hr 55min); Piatra Olt (11 daily; 1hr–2hr 45min); Podu Olt (6 daily; 2hr–2hr 45min); Sibiu (6 daily; 2hr–3hr 25min).

Târgovişte to: Bucharest (5 daily; 1hr 15min–2hr); Ploieşti (4 daily; 1hr 35min–1hr 50min); Titu (8 daily; 30–45min).

Târgu Jiu to: Filiaşi (10 daily; 1–2hr); Petroşani (9 daily; 1hr 10min–1hr 45min); Simeria (5 daily; 2hr 45min–3hr 25min); Subcetate (3 daily; 2hr 20min–2hr 50min).
Titu to: Târgovişte (9 daily; 30–55min).

Buses and maxitaxis

Călimăneşti to: Bucharest (2 daily); Cluj (5 daily); Curtea de Argeş (1 daily); Polovragi (1 daily); Sibiu (14 daily); Târgu Jiu (1 daily); Voineasa (6 daily).
Câmpina to: Bucharest (every 2 hours); Sinaia (every 15min); Ploieşti (every 15min); Târgovişte (1 daily).
Câmpulung to: Braşov (5 daily); Bucharest (14 daily); Craiova (2 daily); Curtea de Argeş (2 daily); Lereşti (hourly); Piteşti (4 daily); Ploieşti (2 daily); Râmnicu Vâlcea (2 daily); Rucăr (8 daily, weekends 5 daily); Târgovişte (4 daily).
Craiova to: Băile Herculane (3 daily); Braşov (2 daily); Bucharest (every 45min); Calafat (12 daily); Câmpulung (2 daily); Drobeta-Turnu Severin (8 daily); Hunedoara (1 daily); Orşova (1 daily); Piteşti (every 45min); Ploieşti (2 daily); Porţile de Fier (1 daily); Râmnicu Vâlcea (10 daily); Sibiu (2 daily); Târgovişte (4 daily); Târgu Jiu (14 daily); Timişoara (6 daily).
Curtea de Argeş to: Arefu (up to 12 daily); Braşov (1 daily); Bucharest (9 daily); Câmpulung (2 daily); Râmnicu Vâlcea (3 daily); Sibiu (2 daily).
Drobeta-Turnu Severin to: Baia de Aramă (1 daily); Baile Herculane (8 daily); Calafat (5 daily); Craiova (8 daily); Hunedoara (2 daily); Orşova (10 daily); Râmnicu Vâlcea (4 daily); Târgu Jiu (6 daily); Timişoara (6 daily).
Giurgiu to: Bucharest (every 30min).
Horezu to: Braşov (1 daily); Bistriţa monastery (3 daily); Bucharest (3 daily); Craiova (1 daily); Haţeg (4 daily); Horez monastery (5 daily); Cluj (2 daily); Râmnicu Vâlcea (hourly); Sibiu (4 daily); Târgu Jiu (5 daily); Timişoara (3 daily).
Orşova to: Caransebeş (9 daily); Drobeta-Turnu Severin (7 daily); Moldova Nouă (2 daily); Reşiţa (1 daily); Timişoara (1 daily).
Piteşti to: Braşov (3 daily); Bucharest (every 30min); Câmpulung (every 30min); Cluj (3 daily); Craiova (3 daily); Găieşti (every 45min); Râmnicu

Vâlcea (every 30min); Sibiu (4 daily); Târgovişte (1 daily); Târgu Jiu (1 daily).
Ploieşti to: Bucharest (every 30min); Buzău (hourly); Câmpulung (2 daily); Constanţa (2 daily); Craiova (2 daily); Sinaia (every 30min); Slanic Prahova (up to 4 daily); Slon (4 daily); Târgovişte (20 daily).
Râmnicu Vâlcea to: Bistriţa monastery (6 daily Mon–Fri, 3 daily Sat–Sun); Braşov (2 daily); Bucharest (every 30min); Câmpulung (3 daily); Cluj (6 daily); Cozia (15 daily); Craiova (7 daily); Curtea de Argeş (7 daily); Drobeta-Turnu Severin (3 daily); Horezu (hourly); Piteşti (every 30min); Sibiu (14 daily); Târgovişte (1 daily); Târgu Jiu (9 daily); Timişoara (4 daily); Voineasa (3 daily).
Târgovişte to: Braşov (3 daily); Bucharest (hourly); Câmpulung (4 daily); Piteşti (1 daily); Ploieşti (20 daily), Sinaia (3 daily).
Târgu Jiu to: Baia de Aramă (3 daily); Baia de Fier (3 daily); Bucharest (6 daily); Cluj (7 daily); Craiova (6 daily); Drobeta-Turnu Severin (3 daily); Horezu (12 daily); Petroşani (7 daily); Piteşti (5 daily); Polovragi (6 daily); Râmnicu Vâlcea (11 daily); Reşiţa (1 daily); Sibiu (2 daily); Timişoara (5 daily); Tismana (8 daily).

Flights

Craiova to: Constanţa (3 flights weekly); Timişoara (3 flights weekly).

International trains

Craiova to: Belgrade (1 daily; 9hr 45min); Budapest (1 daily; 13hr).
Drobeta-Turnu Severin to: Belgrade (1 daily; 8hr).
Giurgiu Nord to: Istanbul (1 daily; 16hr); Kiev (1 daily; 29hr); Moscow (1 daily; 42hr); Ruse (4 daily; 30min); Sofia (2 daily; 7hr 30min–8hr 15min); Thessaloniki (1 daily; 15hr 30min).

International ferries

Călăraşi to: Silistra, Bulgaria (6 daily).
Calafat to: Vidin, Bulgaria (hourly 5.30am–midnight daily; 24hr in summer, with crossings at least every 3 hours overnight).

Transylvania

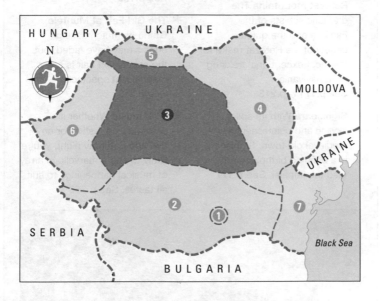

CHAPTER 3 — # Highlights

* **Braşov** Wander the beautiful Baroque streets of Braşov's old town, whose medieval ramparts contain a variety of modern restaurants and bars. See p.157

* **Wildlife-watching in the Carpathians** Take to the woods on the trail of the brown bear, lynx, chamois and grey wolf. See p.170

* **Hiking in the Făgăraş and Retezat mountains** The dramatic schists of the Făgăraş and the quieter beauty of the Retezat make for the most exceptional trekking in Transylvania. See p.171 & p.213

* **Sighişoara** With its spiky skyline and quintessentially medieval old town, Sighişoara is a befitting birthplace for Vlad the Impaler. See p.177

* **Saxon fortified churches** Set high up on a hill, Biertan's Saxon church is the most prominent of the massive and austerely fortified churches that dominate many of the region's villages. See p.184

* **Sibiu** With its gorgeous cobbled squares, outstanding museums and colourful festivals, this is the most engaging of Romanian cities. See p.186

* **The Girl Fair at Muntele Găina** Its matchmaking origins may have faded, but the annual Girl Fair is still a magnificent spectacle. See p.248

* **Folk music** Whether it's an organized festival or an average Saturday night, you're likely to find a marvellous array of musical happenings to suit all tastes. See p.253

▲ The Black Church and Old Town, Brasov

Transylvania

hanks to Bram Stoker and Hollywood, **Transylvania** (from the Latin for "beyond the forest") is famed abroad as the homeland of Dracula, a mountainous place where storms lash medieval hamlets, while wolves – or werewolves – howl from the surrounding woods. The fictitious image is accurate up to a point: the scenery is breathtakingly dramatic, especially in the Prahova valley, the Turda and Bicaz gorges and around the high passes; there are spooky Gothic citadels, around Braşov and at Sibiu, Sighişoara and Bran; and there was a Vlad, born in Sighişoara, who earned the grim nickname "The Impaler" and later became known as **Dracula** (see p.471).

But the Dracula image is just one element of Transylvania, whose near 100,000 square kilometres take in alpine meadows and peaks, caves and dense forests sheltering bears and wild boars, and lowland valleys where buffalo cool off in the rivers. The **population** is an ethnic jigsaw of Romanians, Magyars, Germans and Gypsies, among others, formed over centuries of migration and colonization, with high feelings in both Hungary and Romania routinely exploited by politicians. Most Hungarians view Erdély ("the forest land", their name for Transylvania) as a land first settled by them but "stolen" in 1920 (with the signing of the Trianon Treaty) by the Romanians, who continue to oppress some two million Magyars. Romanians, who call it Ardeal, assert that they appeared first in Transylvania and that for centuries it was the Magyar minority who oppressed them. Since 1920, the Romanian majority has been boosted by peasants brought in from Moldavia and Wallachia to form a new industrial proletariat. The revolution of 1989 enabled Transylvania's German population to return to their ancestral homeland, leaving the Hungarians as the region's main minority group. Meanwhile, Transylvania's Gypsies (Ţigani) still go their own way, largely unconcerned by growing prejudice against them. The result is an intoxicating brew of characters, customs and places that is best taken in slowly.

For the visitor, most striking of all are the *stuhls*, the former seats of Saxon power, with their medieval streets, defensive towers and fortified churches. **Sighişoara**, the most picturesque, is their greatest legacy and an ideal introduction to Transylvania, followed by the citadels and churches of **Braşov** and **Sibiu**, and smaller settlements like **Cisnădioara**, **Hărman**, **Prejmer**, **Viscri** and **Biertan**. The other highlight of this southeastern corner is the castle at **Bran**, which looks just how a vampire count's castle should: a grim facade, perched high on a rock bluff, its turrets and ramparts rising in tiers against a dramatic mountain background. Travelling west, routes towards the Banat and Hungary pass through southwestern Transylvania, a region of peaks and moorland peppered with the citadels of the Dacians, rulers of much of Romania before the Roman conquest. To the north and east, Transylvania has a more Hungarian

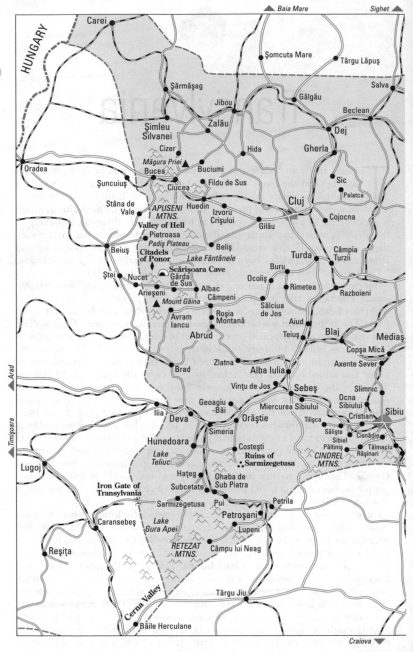

HUNGARY

▲ Baia Mare   Sighet ▲

Carei

Şomcuta Mare   Târgu Lăpuş

Şărmăşag

Jibou   Gâlgău   Salva

Zalău   Beclean

Şimleu
Silvanei   Dej

Cizer   Hida   Gherla

Oradea   Măgura Priei ▲   Buciumi   Sic
        Bucea   Palatca
        Ciucea   Fildu de Sus
Şuncuiuş   Cluj

Stâna de   Huedin   Izvoru   Cojocna
Vale   APUSENI   Crişului
        MTNS.   Gilău
Valley of Hell   Pietroasa
        Padiş Plateau   Beliş
Beiuş   Citadels   Lake Fântânele   Turda   Câmpia
        of Ponor   Turzii
Ştei   Scărişoara Cave   Buru
        Nucet   Gârda   Ocoliş
                de Sus   Rimetea   Razboieni
Arieşeni   Albac   Sălciua
        Câmpeni   de Jos   Aiud
        Mount Găina   Roşia
        Avram   Montană   Teiuş   Blaj
        Iancu   Mediaş
        Abrud   Alba Iulia   Copşa Mică
                                Axente Sever
        Brad   Zlatna   Sebeş   Slimnic

        Vinţu de Jos   Ocna
                        Sibiului   Sibiu
        Geoagiu   Miercuria Sibiului
        -Băi   Cristian
Ilia   Deva   Orăştie   Tilişca
        Simeria   Sălişte   Cisnădie
                        Sibiel   Păltiniş
Lugoj   Hunedoara   Costeşti   Tălmaciu
        Lake   Ruins of   CINDREL   Răşinari
        Teliuc   Sarmizegetusa   MTNS.

        Haţeg   Ohaba de
        Subcetate   Sub Piatra
Iron Gate
of Transylvania   Pui   Petrila
        Sarmizegetusa   Petroşani
Caransebeş   Lupeni
        Lake
Reşiţa   Gura Apei   Câmpu lui Neag
        RETEZAT
        MTNS.

        Cerna Valley   Târgu Jiu

        Băile Herculane   Craiova ▼

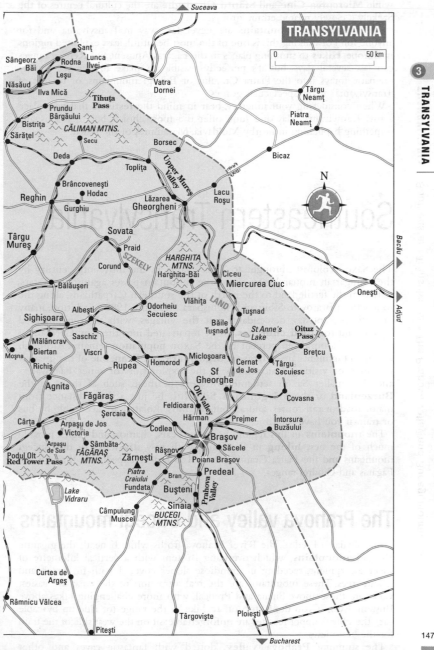

TRANSYLVANIA

flavour: cities such as **Cluj** and **Târgu Mureş** have a strong Magyar influence, while **Miercurea Ciuc** and **Sfântu Gheorghe** are the cultural centres of the Székely, a closely related ethnic group.

The **Carpathian mountains** are never far away in Transylvania, and for anyone fond of walking this is one of the most beautiful, least exploited regions in Europe. **Hikes** to stunning places in the Făgăraş, Apuseni and Retezat ranges can last several days, but it's perfectly feasible to make briefer yet equally dramatic forays into the Piatra Craiului or Bucegi mountains, or to one of Transylvania's many spectacular gorges.

When considering your itinerary, bear in mind the **festivals** that take place across Transylvania: May and June offer the most choice, but there's usually something happening in nearby Moldavia, Maramureş or the Banat.

Southeastern Transylvania

The Saxon colonists, brought to Transylvania in the thirteenth century by the Hungarian monarchy to guard the mountain passes against the Tatars, settled in the fertile land to the north of the southern Carpathians, along the routes from Braşov to Sibiu and Sighişoara. After the 1989 revolution, many of their present-day descendants left the villages, with their regimented layouts and **fortified churches**, to be repatriated into the new Germany – today, only around ten percent of the Saxon population remains. Although the main highlights are at **Braşov**, **Sighişoara** and **Bran**, one of the greatest pleasures of visiting Transylvania is the exploration of quiet backwaters and the smaller Saxon settlements. Many of these, such as those in the **Burzenland** or the **Mărginimea Sibiului**, lie just a short distance from major road or rail routes, and all but the most isolated are accessible by bus or train if you have the time.

The **mountains** in this region, home to bears, chamois and eagles, provide much of the best **hiking** in Romania, with easy day-walks in the Bucegi mountains and the Piatra Craiului, as well as longer expeditions through the Făgăraş and Cindrel ranges.

The Prahova valley and Bucegi mountains

From Sinaia to Predeal, the River Prahova froths white beneath the gigantic **Bucegi mountains**, which overhang Buşteni with a vertical kilometre of sheer escarpment, receding in grandiose slopes covered with fir, beech and rowan trees. These mountains are the real attraction of the area: the easiest walks are those above Sinaia and Predeal, with more challenging hikes above Buşteni. Even if you don't stop off to hike in the range (or ride up by cable car), the valley's upper reaches are unforgettable: sit on the west side of the train for the best views.

The stunning **Prahova valley**, dotted with fantastic caves and other karstic phenomena, is shadowed by the DN1 (E60) highway and the

Most walks in the **Bucegi mountains** (Munţii Bucegi) are easy day-walks, with cable cars an alternative on the steeper sections. There are plenty of **mountain cabanas**, which in theory aren't allowed to turn hikers away, and if you're really stuck, maps can locate refuges and sheepfolds (*refugiu* and *stână*), where you may find shelter.

Snow covers **Mount Omu**, the highest point of the Bucegi (2505m), for two hundred or more days a year. Elsewhere the snow generally retreats during April, and soon after the meadows are covered with **wildflowers** such as ladies' gloves, grape-ferns and edelweiss. The forests shelter woodcock, hazel grouse and nightingales from the circling golden eagles, while other **wildlife** includes the Carpathian stag (around Bran) and wild boar. The last, like wolves and bears, are only a potential threat during the winter (when food is scarce) or if their litters are endangered. Above the forest, on the cliffs to the north of the massif, you may well see chamois.

A good **map** to get hold of if hiking in the region is the oddly titled *Five Mountains from the Carpathians Bend* (it also covers the Piatra Craiului – see p.169), which has English-language notes. Otherwise, the Romanian-language **maps** of the mountains shouldn't be hard to understand if you refer to our vocabulary in *The great outdoors* colour section.

③

Bucharest–Braşov **rail line**: express services take two and a half hours to Braşov, stopping en route at Ploieşti (see p.107) and the resorts of **Sinaia**, in northern Wallachia, and **Predeal**, in Transylvania proper. There are also plenty of slower trains that stop at the smaller towns and villages – change at either Sinaia or Predeal for a Personal train to **Buşteni**, also served by some Accelerats. The DN1 has been largely modernized in recent years, and construction of a Bucharest–Braşov–Târgu Mureş–Cluj–Oradea motorway should be under way within the next couple of years. Frequent local buses and maxitaxis link Ploieşti, Sinaia, Buşteni and Azuga.

Sinaia

SINAIA, 122km from Bucharest, is famed for its magnificent mountain scenery and royal castle. Originally the preserve of a few hermits and shepherds, then an exclusive aristocratic resort, it is nowadays full of holidaymakers here to walk or ski in the dramatic **Bucegi mountains**. Though technically in the province of Wallachia, it has much in common with the neighbouring Transylvanian towns and has been included in this chapter for convenience.

Arrival and information

Steps lead up from Sinaia **train station** to the main street, B-dul. Carol I, and beyond it the **Dimitrie Ghica Park**; turn left along the boulevard for the town centre. The **tourist information centre** is in front of the town hall at B-dul. Carol I 47 (Mon–Fri 8.30am–4.30pm ☏0244/315 656, ✉contact@infosinaia .ro). In addition to the plentiful **buses** and **maxitaxis** along the DN1, local **minibuses** run up to the hillside areas of Platoul Izvor and Furnica, and occasion-ally to Cota 1400, the roadhead at the mid-station of the Bucegi cable car.

The **post office** (Mon–Fri 7am–8pm, Sat 8am–1pm) is at B-dul. Carol I 33, and there's **Internet access** about 150m south in the basement of the shopping centre (opposite the *Bucegi* restaurant). **Ski gear** can be bought or rented at the excellent Snow shop, located by the cable-car terminal at Str. Cuza Vodă 2 (daily 9am–6pm); they also **rent bikes** (€12/day). The only **cinema** is the *Perla*, opposite the *Sinaia* hotel.

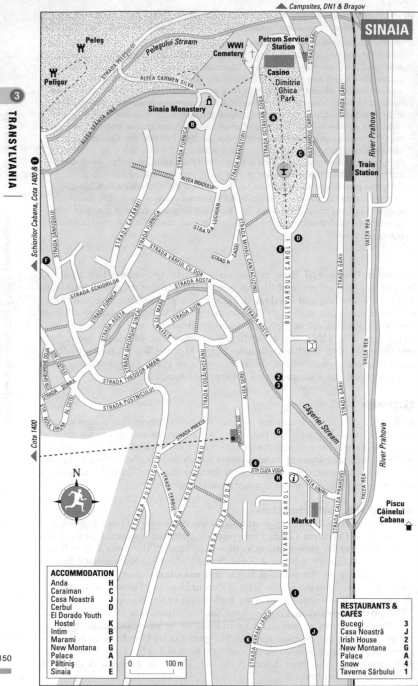

SINAIA

Campsites, DN1 & Braşov

Peleş

Pelişor

Peleşului Stream

STRADA PELEŞULUI

ALEEA CARMEN SILVA

WWI Cemetery

Petrom Service Station

Casino

Dimitrie Ghica Park

Sinaia Monastery

ALEEA SFÂNTA ANA

STRADA FURNICA

ALEEA BRADULUI

STRADA MANĂSTIRII

STRADA DA. LUCHIAN

STRADA OCTAVIAN GOGA

BULEVARDUL CAROL I

STRADA GĂRII

STRADA GĂRII

STRADA GĂRII

River Prahova

Train Station

STRADA CAZARMII

STRADA FURNICA

STRADA VARFUL CU DOR

STRADA MIHAI CANTACUZINO

STRADA ZAMFIR

STRADA M

VALEA REA

Schiorilor Cabana, Cota 1400 & 1

STRADA SĂNIUŞULUI

STRADA SCHIORILOR

STRADA FURNICA

STRADA AOSTA

ŞTEFAN CEL MARE

STRADA SION

STRADA AOSTA

BULEVARDUL CAROL I

STRADA GĂRII

Căşeriei Stream

VALEA REA

River Prahova

Cota 1400

STR GHEORGHE DOJA

STR COSTILEI

STRADA ŞOIMUL

STRADA GHEORGHE ŞINCAI

STRADA THEODOR AMAN

STRADA KOGĂLNICEANU

ALEEA SERBI

STR. ORZAH

AL. CITEI

STRADA PUSTNICULUI

STRADA PINULUI

N

STRADA PUSTNICULUI

STRADA KOGĂLNICEANU

STRADA CERBUL

STR CUZA VODĂ

PIAŢA UNIRII

Market

Piscu Câinelui Cabana

STRADA CUZA VODĂ

BULEVARDUL CAROL I

STRADA CALEA PRAHOVEI

VALEA REA

STRADA AVRAM IANCU

0   100 m

ACCOMMODATION

Anda	H
Caraiman	C
Casa Noastră	J
Cerbul	D
El Dorado Youth Hostel	K
Intim	B
Marami	F
New Montana	G
Palace	A
Păltiniş	I
Sinaia	E

RESTAURANTS & CAFÉS

Bucegi	3
Casa Noastră	J
Irish House	2
New Montana	G
Palace	A
Snow	4
Taverna Sârbului	1

Ploieşti & Bucharest

Accommodation

The town is extremely well served with **hotels**, a good number of which cater to package tourists. The *El Dorado* **youth hostel**, at Str. Avram Iancu 14 (☏0244/312 667; ❶), has utilitarian rooms (some with bathroom and TV), but is basically fine. There are also a number of **villas** located inside Peleş Park (☏0244/310 353, 🗗311 150; ❹–❻), while touts at the station and on the way into town offer **private rooms** (❶) – before agreeing to anything, though, insist upon knowing exactly where the location is, as some of the rooms are far from the centre. There are two **campsites** north of Sinaia; *Izvorul Rece*, at km118, and, 8km further on, *Vadul Cerbului*. Finally, the **cabanas** at the *Piscu Câinelui* (☏0244/315 492; ❶) and *Schiorilor* (☏0244/313 655; ❶) at Drumul Cotei 7 are small but right on the outskirts of town.

Anda B-dul. Carol I 30 ☏0244/306 020, 🌐www .hotelanda.ro. Typical of the ski hotels in town, this is a polished, modern and comfortable place. Very pleasant wine-cellar restaurant, too. ❼

Caraiman B-dul. Carol I 4, in Dimitrie Ghica Park ☏0244/312 051, 📧palace@rdslink.ro. Sinaia's first hotel, opened in 1881, is a decent enough place, even if the rooms are a little cramped and the furnishings somewhat dated. ❹

Casa Noastră B-dul. Republicii 9 ☏0244/314 556. Peculiar-looking, narrow high-rise wooden construction, with simple wood-furnished rooms, including triples and quads. Also houses a restaurant and deli. Breakfast is extra. ❷

Cerbul B-dul. Carol I no. 19 ☏0244/312 391, 📧hotelcerbul@gmail.com. Renovated and good-value hotel with modern (if not particularly stylish) rooms, some with communal showers. Breakfast is extra. ❹

Intim Str. Furnica 1 ☏0244/315 557. No frills here; antique (as in ancient) furnishings, lumpy beds, and cold-tile flooring in the bathrooms, but it's cheap, reasonably cheerful, and offers lovely views into the monastery grounds. Breakfast is extra. ❸

Marami Str. Furnica 52 ☏0244/315 560, 🌐www .marami.ro. One of the town's more welcoming hotels, the *Marami* has large, well-equipped rooms, each furnished in a different colour. Sauna, Jacuzzi, gym, and a very good bar-pizzeria. ❼

New Montana B-dul. Carol I 24 ☏0244/312 751, 🌐www.newmontana.ro. This large hotel on the main street is as slick as you'd expect from a hotel catering in the main to big ski groups. Facilities include pool, sauna and gym. ❾

Palace Str. Octavian Goga 4 ☏0244/312 051, 📧palace@rdslink.ro. In the park by the casino, this gem of a building, opened in 1912, has retained much of its Edwardian style. Two categories of room, but worth paying the minimal extra for the more modern ones. ❻–❼

Păltiniş B-dul. Carol I 67 ☏0244/314 651, 📧receptie@hotelpaltinis.ro. Hulking grey neo-Brâncovenesc pile built atop two floors of treatment rooms; rooms with and without bath. ❹–❺

Sinaia B-dul. Carol I 8 ☏0244/302 900, 🌐www .hotelsinaia.ro. Along with the *New Montana*, this is the town's main ski hotel; its rooms, either with bath or shower, and some with balconies, have all the standard comforts. ❼

The Town

Sinaia's **train station** is a historical site in itself; here, the Iron Guard murdered the Liberal leader Ion Duca in 1933, just three weeks after he had taken office as prime minister. From here, steps lead to **Dimitrie Ghica Park**, which contains several fine buildings in neo-Brâncovenesc style. Beyond the park, a World War I military cemetery also houses a poetic **memorial** to the US airmen killed over Romania in World War II; a footpath leads off Str. Mănăstirii up to **Sinaia Monastery**, founded by Prince Mihai Catacuzino in 1690, following his return from a pilgrimage to Mount Sinai. The original **Old Church** (Biserica Veche), decorated with a fine *Last Judgement* soon after it was built, is not the one before you as you enter, but is hidden through a passageway to the left – though it's currently closed pending renovation. The latter addition, the so-called **Great Church** (Biserica Mare), is distinguished by a fine Brâncovenesc-style porch, and also features an unusual green enamel belt with a twisted rope motif encircling the building. Four of the five fresco portraits adorning the west wall of the interior are of King Carol I as an officer,

Queen Elisabeta, her youngest daughter Maria, and Catacuzino himself. There are currently around a dozen monks here.

Just behind the monastery, a long cobbled path lined with souvenir stalls leads up to one of Romania's most popular and rewarding sights, **Peleş Castle** (Muzeul Naţional Peleş; Wed 11am–5pm, Thurs–Sun 9am–5pm; €4 and €10 for use of camera). Set in a large park landscaped in the English fashion, and named after the River Peleş which flows nearby, the castle outwardly resembles a Bavarian Schloss. Built between 1875 and 1883 for Carol I, and largely decorated by his eccentric wife Elisabeta (better known as the popular novelist Carmen Sylva), it contains 160 rooms, richly decorated in ebony, mother of pearl, walnut and leather – all totally alien to the traditional styles of Romanian art – and stuffed solid with antiques and copies of paintings housed in Bucharest's National Art Museum. To **visit the castle**, follow signs to a ticket window and then to the separate entry for foreigners. You then wait in the entry hall for a guide to take you on a forty-five minute tour of eighteen rooms on the ground floor – the stairs and upper floors are in poor condition. Note that there are no toilets available.

The first room (the Reception Hall) is startling, awash with fantastic walnut carvings, alabaster reliefs and French tapestries, to say nothing of the sixteen-metre-high glass ceiling that opens up in summer. Thereafter, you proceed through several more extravagantly decorated rooms, including the Florentine Hall, with kitschy Murano chandeliers; a Moorish hall based on the Alhambra and containing a Carrera marble fountain; and the Louis XIV room (with paintings by a young Gustav Klimt) housing Romania's first cinema. How a man of such reputedly austere tastes as Carol managed to live here is something of a mystery, and indeed it hasn't been lived in since his death in 1914. Following the monarchy's demise, Peleş was opened to the public in 1953, with a temporary interruption when the Ceauşescus appropriated it as a "state palace". In 2006, the government decreed that the castle would be returned to King Michael I, thus reuniting the Romanian monarch with his birthplace and childhood home.

A short walk up the hill stands **Pelişor Palace** (Little Peleş; same times and price), built between 1899 and 1903 for Ferdinand and Marie, Carol I's heirs. Although its exterior is also in the German Renaissance style, the interior is far more restrained and mostly Art Nouveau. The one exception is the dazzling Gold Room, covered in 24-carat stucco gold leaf and home to a Tiffany lamp from Chicago. Although Ceauşescu used Pelişor Palace to host foreign dignitaries – on one occasion Colonel Gadaffi – he much preferred the seclusion afforded him at the **Foişor Lodge**, located a little above Pelişor. Finished in 1878, it was home to Queen Elisabeta from 1914, and then to Prince Carol (later King Carol II) and Princess Helen from 1921; here, Carol met the Jewish Magda Lupescu, who for thirty years remained his mistress and the power behind the throne, outraging Romanian society, which tended towards anti-Semitism. The lodge is now used for government protocol, but the park is open to the public (Wed–Sun 9am–4pm).

Across the DN1 from the lower gate of the Peleş park, signs lead to the **George Enescu Memorial House** (Tues–Sun 9am–4pm; Ⓦ www.casa-enescu.ro; €2), in Cumpătu, 2km north of the town centre. Known as the **Vila Luminiş** (Sunshine House), it was built for the great composer-violinist from 1921 to 1926 in the style of a *conac* (Turkish administrator's house); he spent his summers here until 1946, when he left the country for good. The ground floor contains Oriental, Biedermeyer and traditional Romanian furnishings, and Enescu's Ibert piano; upstairs are his simple bedroom (as well as student Yehudi

Menuhin's more conventional room) and his workroom, looking west to the peaks of the Bucegi mountains, and home to photos, posters and scores of his works. Tours of Enescu's house are accompanied by his lushly romantic music, CDs of which are sold at the ticket desk. The house also plays host to numerous concerts, recitals, exhibitions and workshops throughout the year.

Eating and drinking

Eating and drinking options in town are reasonable, if a little limited. The best and most interesting food in Sinaia, as long as you're not a vegetarian, is at the *Taverna Sârbului*, a ten-minute taxi ride north of town en route to Cota 1400 at Calea Codrului 39 (daily 11am–11pm). This hugely popular and convivial Serbian restaurant dishes up gargantuan portions of meat-heavy Serbian cuisine, typically *čorba pasulj* (bean soup with smoked meat), *čevapi* (grilled rissoles of meat) and *pljeskavica* (oversized beefburger). Otherwise, in the centre of town, the *Bucegi* at B-dul. Carol I 22 (daily 11am–9.30pm) has very good pizza, game (roast bear, boar and venison) and excellent vegetarian choices. Next door at no. 18, the *Irish House* (daily 8am–midnight) offers a predictable Irish slant to its dishes, namely Dublin chicken's liver, Irish breakfast and "Irish salad", as well as Romanian dishes and pizza and pasta. Other decent options are *Snow* (next to the shop of the same name – see p.149), an après-ski-type place doling out big bowls of steaming soup and mixed grills, and, to the south of the centre at B-dul. Republicii 9, the *Casa Noastră* (see p.151) which has excellent *crama*, *terasa* and deli. Other hotels offering good **dining** include the *Palace* and *New Montana*.

For a **drink**, most people congregate at the *Irish House* (with draught Guinness and Sheridans, and Jameson's whiskey) and *Snow*. There's also the *Old Nick Pub*, at B-dul. Carol I 22, or a low-key Irish pub in the *New Montana*. The *Disco Diana*, under the *Sinaia* hotel, keeps kicking until 4am.

Around Sinaia

From its terminal on Str. Cuza Vodă (behind the *New Montana*), a **cable car** (*telecabina*; summer Tues–Sun 8.30am–5pm; €4 single, €6 return) whisks you to an altitude of 1400m (**Cota 1400**) at the roadhead halfway up the hill, site of the *Alpin* hotel and numerous cabanas. From here, there's another cable car (Tues–Sun 8.30am–5pm) to **Cota 2000**, and a chairlift (Wed–Mon 9am–5pm) to **Cota 1950**, both just a five-minute walk from the *Miorița* cabana (☏0244/311 211; ❶) on Mount Furnica. This is the start of the taxing **Papagul ski run** back down to Cota 1400. To the south, below Cota 1950, is the *Valea Dorului* cabana (☏0244/313 531; ❶), from where there's a three-hour circular walk down the Dorului valley to the beautiful tarns of **La Lacuri**, following a path marked with yellow crosses and red stripes.

Heading north, an attractive and easy half-hour walk takes you from Mount Furnica to **Piatra Arsă**, behind Mount Jepi Mari, where the cabana (❶) has been joined by the National Centre For Sports Training at Altitude. Here, blue triangles indicate the route downwards to Bușteni (2hr maximum) via **La Scari**, a spectacular "stairway" hewn into rock, while another path (marked with blue stripes) drops westwards into the central depression of the Bucegi, reaching the *Peștera* hotel (☏0245/311 094; ❷) and monastery in about an hour (for routes north of the *Peștera*, see p.156). Just west of the *Peștera*, past the **Ialomița cave** – a 400-metre-long grotto with a walkway in awful condition (bring a flashlight) – is an unmarked path leading up through the Batrâna valley past several waterfalls, the "Gorge of the Bear" and two natural bridges. Half an hour to the south lies the *Padina* cabana (☏0244/314 331; ❶), from where a very rough road leads further south past more caves and gorges to a camping spot near **Lake Bolboci**, eventually emerging from the Izvoraşu valley just south of Sinaia.

Buşteni

Ten kilometres up the valley from Sinaia is **BUŞTENI**, a small, bustling resort overshadowed by the sheer peaks of Caraiman (2384m) and Coştila (2498m),

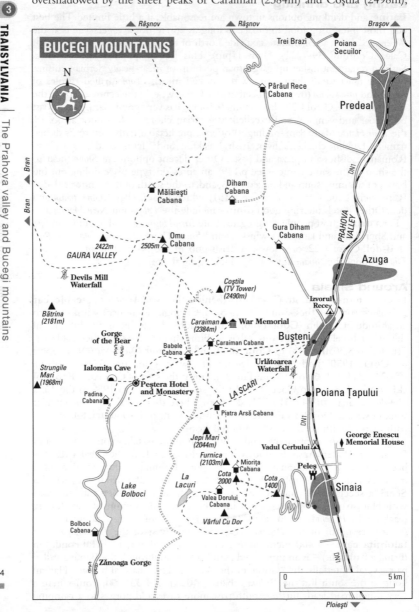

BUCEGI MOUNTAINS

N

Râşnov | Râşnov | Braşov

Trei Brazi | Poiana Seculor

Pârâul Rece Cabana

Predeal

Mălăieşti Cabana

Diham Cabana

2422m | 2505m
GAURA VALLEY | Omu Cabana

Gura Diham Cabana

PRAHOVA VALLEY

Azuga

Devils Mill Waterfall

Coştila (TV Tower) (2490m)

Izvorul Recei

Bătrina (2181m)

Caraiman (2384m) | War Memorial

Buşteni

Gorge of the Bear

Babele Cabana | Caraiman Cabana

Strungile Mari (1968m)

Ialomiţa Cave

Urlătoarea Waterfall

Poiana Ţapului

Padina Cabana

Peştera Hotel and Monastery

LA SCARI

Piatra Arsă Cabana

Jepi Mari (2044m)

George Enescu Memorial House

Furnica (2103m)

Vadul Cerbului

Miorița Cabana

Peleş

Cota 2000

Cota 1400

Sinaia

La Lacuri

Lake Bolboci

Valea Dorului Cabana

Vârful Cu Dor

Bolboci Cabana

Zănoaga Gorge

0 | 5 km

DN1

Ploieşti

▲ Buşteni cable car

separated from each other by the dark Alba valley and the highest conglomerate cliffs in Europe. Caraiman is identified by a huge cross (a war memorial erected in the 1920s), and Coştila by a TV tower that looks like a space rocket. There's nothing much to Buşteni itself, other than the house of writer **Cezar Petrescu** (1892–1961), located in a handsome villa north of town on Str. Cezar Petrescu, and a church founded by Carol I and Queen Elisabeta in 1889, but it's a good base for the excellent walking routes in the surrounding mountains.

Practicalities

The **train station** is in the centre of town on the main DN1, from where it's just a few hundred metres south to the main clutch of **hotels**. The first of these is the *Caraiman* at B-dul. Libertăţii 89 (℡0244/320 156; ❸), which has small but decently furnished rooms, including triples and quads. Several hundred metres further south (past the Internet café and to the right at the country's oldest paper mill), at Str. Telecabiniei 36, is the *Silva* (℡0244/320 027, ℮office1@hotelsilva.ro; ❻–❼), a large package tourist place that has a mixed bag of two- and three-star rooms. Back down on the same road, at no. 22 (it's set back from the road and has no sign), the *Villa Laura* guesthouse (℡0241/552 858, ℮paradis@rdsct.ro; ❸) has clean and comfortable en-suite double rooms, some with a little kitchen area. North of the station, at B-dul. Libertăţii 153, the very conspicuous, grey-brick *Hotel Alexandros* (℡0244/320 138, ⓦwww .hotel-alexandros.ro; ❼) is another of the town's more comfortable places. The friendly and informal *Motel Maximilian* is across the tracks to the southeast (in the Zamora quarter), at Str. Pescariei 8 (℡0244/323 297; ❶); it's most easily reached by car (take the first turning on the left south of Str. Telecabinei). Strada Valea Albă, just north of the station, leads to the *Hotel-Restaurant Marietta* at Str. Buştenilor 32 (℡0244/323 297; ❹) and to the Calinderu ski slope and quad chairlift. It's also worth enquiring at the **tourist agency** (daily 10am–6pm; ℡244/320 027) at B-dul. Libertăţii 202, 150m north of the train station, about **villas** and **private rooms** (❶); you'll also see *Oferim cazare* signs on houses that offer accommodation.

The best of a rather poor bunch of **restaurants** is *Bistro Armando*, a friendly little place opposite the *Caraiman* serving grills, pasta and salads – the *Caraiman* itself has the cosy *Rustic* restaurant, with a similar menu. The *Cofetăria Roza*, opposite the train station, sells snack-sized pizzas as well as coffee and cakes. You may find **events** taking place at either the Casa de Cultura or the Maison Franco-Roumaine opposite at B-dul. Libertăţii 158. There's **Internet** access at Str. Libertăţii 39 (daily 10am–11pm).

Around Buşteni

From the *Hotel Silva* on Str. Telecabinei, 1.5km south of the train station, an easy path marked with red dots leads to the **Urlătoarea waterfall** and back to the road at **Poiana ţapului** (2hr). A harder footpath, marked with blue crosses, and a **cable car** (Mon–Fri 8am–3.45pm, Sat & Sun 8am–4.45pm in summer; €6 return) ascend the Jepi valley to the **cabanas** at *Caraiman* (☎0244/320 817; ●) and *Babele* (☎0244/314 450; ●). The latter offers a panoramic view, and is only five minutes' walk from an impressive skull-like rock formation, the **Babele Sphinx**. From here, you can walk (1hr) or ride the cable car (daily 8am–4pm) down to the *Peştera* hotel and monastery (see p.153). North of the *Babele* cabana, a path marked by yellow stripes leads to **Mount Omu** (4hr); alternatively, from *Peştera*, a blue-striped path takes you up the Ialomiţa valley to **Omu** (1–2hr). There's a small hut here (☎0244/320 677; closed winter), without running water; many hikers prefer to stay (unofficially) in the Omu meteorological station.

Though completely cloudless days are rare in the vicinity of **Mount Omu**, it is possible to see the **Burzenland**, the ridge of the Piatra Craiului, to the west and the **Făgăraş range** beyond. From Omu, a path marked with blue stripes descends a glacial valley past eroded rock "chimneys" to the **Mălăieşti** chalet (2–3hr); two other paths lead down to **Bran** in about six hours – the route indicated by yellow triangles is easier going, while the path marked with red crosses drops down the superb Gaura valley past the **Cascada Moara Dracului** ("Devil's Mill Waterfall"), a fitting approach to "Dracula's Castle" in the village below (see p.123).

There's plenty more accommodation in the village of **AZUGA**, a couple of kilometres north of Buşteni, which is known mainly for its brewery and bottle factory but also has a couple of ski runs. It's also the location for the **Rhein Azuga Cellar**, owned by the British winemakers Halewood; specializing in sparkling wines from an area just south of the Prahova Valley, they offer wine-tasting sessions along with a tour of the cellars (€5). There's a shop here (daily 10am–5pm) and a super pension, with restful, rustically styled rooms ☎0722/530 955, ✉rezervari@halewood.com.ro; ●). Otherwise, there's the *Hotel Azuga*, on the main DN1 at Str. Victoriei 87 (☎&☏0244/327 406; ●); the *Pensiunea Căprioara*, at Valea Azugii 38 (☎0244/326 318; ●) and *Pensiunea Flora*, at Florilor 50 (☎0722/354 718; ●).

Predeal

PREDEAL, sitting on the 1038-metre pass of the same name and marking the official border of Transylvania, is further from the more spectacular peaks that dominate Sinaia and Buşteni to the south, but is a popular centre for winter sports and easy strolls. There's also a wide choice of **accommodation** in town, which can be booked through the **tourist office** (Mon–Fri 8am–4pm, Sat 9am–2pm; ☎0268/455 330, ⊛www.predeal.ro) in a striking modern building outside the train station, itself a decent piece of communist modernism. There's a good chance that you'll be offered a room while near the station. The best option in the centre is the *Carmen*, just south of the station at B-dul. Săulescu

121 (☎0268/456 517, 🖷455 426; ❺); although it might look a little unkempt from the outside, the rooms are tidy and brightly furnished. There are several other options further north, on Str. Trei Brazi, the road that leads up to the mountainside *Trei Brazi cabana* (see below); the first of these is the *Orizont* (☎0268/455 150, Ⓦwww.hotelorizont.ro; ❺), a good modern hotel with a pool, sauna and tennis courts. Better still are the *Relax Comfort Suites* (☎0268/455 795, Ⓦwww.predealcomfort-suites.ro; ❾) a little further up the hill, whose fabulous rooms are fitted with wrought-iron furnishings and huge corner baths. Moving further up, as the road deteriorates, the *Vila Select* (☎0268/456 579, Ⓦwww .vila-select.ro; ❺) makes for a quiet, pleasant stopover. The welcoming *Fulg de Neà* at Str. Teleferic 1 (☎0268/456 089; ❸), on the way to the Clăbucet chairlift, has fairly rudimentary, but perfectly acceptable, accommodation.

A couple of half-decent **restaurants** are *Casa Ana*, B-dul. Săulescu 2 bis (☎0268/456 572), and *Căprioara*, Str. Libertăţii 90 (☎0268/456 964), which both serve Italian food. The 24-hour Casa de Ana store at Str. Libertăţii 127 has good supplies for a long hike, and there's a well-stocked supermarket along from the train station (Mon–Sat 7am–8pm, Sun 8am–4pm). The best **bar** in town is at the *Fulg de Neà*, and it has pretty good food too; in a similar vein there's the *Green Club* (or *Guinness Pub*), at B-dul. Săulescu 32. **Ski equipment** can be rented at the *Fulg de Neà* (which also has mountain bikes – €15 per day), or the Clăbucet-Sosire chairlift terminal.

Around Predeal

There's good **walking** in these hills, not as dramatic as in the Bucegi but with fine views to the high peaks and cliffs, and plenty of **cabanas** to aim for. *Gârbova* (☎0744/160 103; ❶) and *Susai* (☎0268/457 204; ❶) are within a few kilometres of Clăbucet-Plecare, and there are others northwest of Predeal in the foothills of the Bucegi massif. These include the hotel-like *Trei Brazi*, 5km west of Predeal at the top of Str. Trei Brazi (☎0722/372 998; ❹); the *Poiana Secuilor* (☎0740/752 579; ❶), a short walk east; and the *Pârâu Rece* complex, 2km west of *Trei Brazi* just off the Predeal to Râsnov road (73A), which also has camping (☎0268/456 491; ❶). The *Diham* cabana (☎0788/608 161) is higher up and further south, with a slalom run nearby.

Braşov

The medieval Saxons, with an eye for trade and invasion routes, sited their largest settlements within a day's journey of the Carpathian passes. One of the best placed, **BRAŞOV** (Kronstadt to the Saxons and Brassó to the Hungarians), grew prosperous and fortified as a result, and for many centuries the Saxons there constituted an elite whose economic power long outlasted its feudal privileges. During the 1960s, the communist regime drafted thousands of Moldavian villagers to Braşov's new factories, making it Transylvania's second-largest city. The economic collapse in the 1980s led to the **riots** of November 15, 1987 and again in December 1989, the casualties of which were claimed as martyrs by the new regime.

The town's proximity to a host of attractions, such as the **Piatra Craiului mountain range**, the alpine resort of **Poiana Braşov**, the fortified **Saxon churches** of **Hărman** and **Prejmer**, and "**Dracula's Castle**" at **Bran**, make it an excellent base.

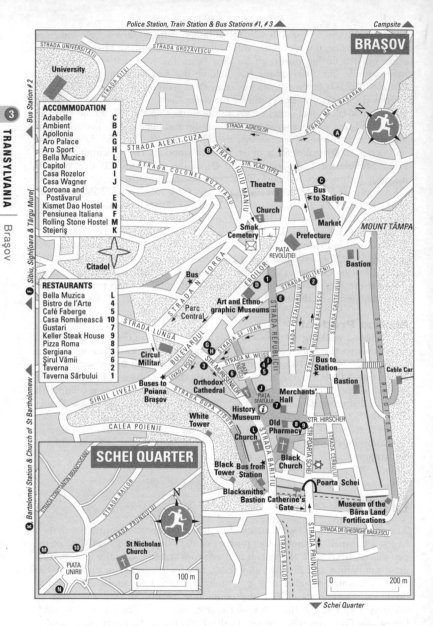

Arrival and information

Braşov is a major rail junction, served by long-distance **trains** from every corner of the country. The **train station** is situated more than 2km northeast of the old town, right in the heart of the concrete drabness of Braşov's new suburbs. Bus #4 will take you down to **Parc Central** (also known as Titulescu), and on to the Schei quarter in the old town. Buy a **day pass** (€1.50) if you expect to make several bus trips. Local trains from Zărneşti and Sibiu also call at the **Bartolomei station**, northwest of the centre at the end of Str. Lungă.

The town has three **bus stations**: international services and most long-distance buses arrive at **Autogară 1**, by the train station (T0268/427 267); maxitaxis also arrive here. Buses from Piteşti and Râmnicu Vâlcea use both this terminal and **Autogară 2** at Str. Avram Iancu 114 (T0268/426 332), which also serves Bran and Curtea de Argeş, while services from the Székely Land use **Autogară 3**, 1km northeast of the main train station at Str. Harmanului 47 (T0268/332 002). Bus #12 runs from Autogară 2 to the centre, and bus #10 runs from the train station to Stadion Tineret (Youth Stadium), from where you can cut through to Autogară 2. From Autogară 3, trolley bus #1 runs into town. Braşov has hordes of **taxis**, but you're best sticking to the following: Martax (T0268/313 040), Rey Taxi (T0268/411 111), RoTaxi (T0744/319 999) or Tod (T0744/321 111).

The city **tourist office** is located inside the Council House (in the same building as the History Museum) on Piaţa Sfatului (daily 9am–5pm; T0268/419 078, Wwww.brasov.ro), though it's of rather limited help. A more useful source of information is Roving Romania (T0268/326 271, Eroving@deltanet.ro).

Accommodation

There is stacks of accommodation in Braşov, from some very characterful **hotels** and **pensions** to a couple of smart little **hostels** and lots of private offerings. There are also a number of decent places to stay outside the city, in particular on the road out towards Poiana Braşov.

Hotels

Adabelle Str. Pieţii 5 T0268/411 080, Wwww.adabelle.ro. Despite its hostel-like appearance, this tidy youth hotel has modern, well-equipped en-suite rooms, with plasma TV and minibar. The price includes breakfast and dinner, so it's good value. ❺

Ambient Str. Aninoasa 5 T0268/470 856, Wwww.hotelambient.ro. This large glass cylindrical tower, just north of Str. Iuliu Maniu, has shiny, spacious rooms – the service, meanwhile, is warm and personal. ❼

Apollonia Str. Neagoe Basarab 7 T0268/476 163, Wwww.hotelapollonia.ro. Smart, unassuming little hotel in a pleasant, peaceful location close to the centre. Sauna, massage and fitness facilities. ❼

Aro Palace B-dul. Eroilor 27 T0268/478 800, Wwww.aro-palace.ro. Boasting what must be the country's largest hotel lobby, *Aro Palace* has the most luxuriously furnished and most expensive rooms in the city; ask for a room with a view across to Mount Tâmpa. A pool and spa centre is planned for completion in 2009. ❾

Aro Sport Str. Sfântu Ioan 3 T0268/478 800, Eoffice@aro-palace.ro. On a narrow side street behind *Aro Palace*, this is a very basic, hostel-like place, with shared toilet and shower facilities. However, it's cheap, reasonably cheerful and very central. No breakfast available. ❸

Bella Muzica Piaţa Sfatului 19 T0268/477 956, Wwww.bellamuzica.ro. Occupying a lovely 400-year-old Neoclassical building, this gem of a hotel has modestly sized but sumptuously furnished rooms, each of which has been assigned some thoughtful little touches, such as wood-framed mirrors, pictures and plants. Its superb restaurant is a few steps down the road (see p.163). ❽

Capitol B-dul. Eroilor 19 T0268/418 920, F472 999. A bit dreary, with cluttered rooms and zero atmosphere – the best thing going for it is its location opposite Parc Central. ❼

Casa Rozelor Str. Michael Weiss 20 T0268/475 212, Wwww.cazarozelor.ro. Converted from an old salt warehouse, the "House of Roses" has three (more are planned) magnificent apartment-style rooms; the original bare brick walls remain, while each room – differently configured – features an outstanding fusion of contemporary and period furnishings and original artwork. ❽

Casa Wagner Piaţa Sfatului 5 T0268/411 253, Wwww.casa-wagner.eu. This understatedly elegant pension has twelve beautifully furnished rooms – fitted with lots of wood and brass – some of which overlook the square itself. Very good value. ❼

Coroana Str. Republicii 62 T0268/544 330, Wwww.aro-palace.ro. A muddy grey building concealing two rather careworn and rudimentary hotels – the only difference between the one-star *Postăvarul* and the two-star *Coroana* is that the *Coroana* has larger rooms with bathrooms. ❸–❼

🏃 **Pensiunea Italiana** Str. Lungă 70 ☏0268/476 001, 🅦www.pensiunea-italiana.ro. An easy 15min stroll west of the centre, this homely, welcoming pension has six tastefully designed – and Italianate influenced –

rooms. Breakfast is on a self-catering basis and there's secure off-street parking. ❹

Pension Montana Stejeris 2A ☏0268/472 731. Excellent bed and breakfast (no other meals available), on the road up to Poiana Braşov, with marvellous views over the city. ❻

Stejeriş Str. Stejerişului 15 ☏0268/476 249. Very comfortable and personable six-room guesthouse 2km along the Poiana Braşov road. Pleasant restaurant and wine cellar, too. ❹

Hostels, private rooms, camping and cabanas

There are two **hostels** in Braşov, both located in the Schei quarter – from the train station take bus #51 to the quarter's main square, Piaţa Unirii (last stop), and it's a two-minute walk to either. The clean and welcoming *Rolling Stone*, at Str. Piatra Mare 2a (☏0268/513 965, 🅦www.rollingstone.ro), has modern dorms (❶) as well as three very comfortable double rooms (❸), one of which is en-suite; there's also a pleasant terrace with pool and basement bar. Just a short walk away, at Str. Democratiei 2b, is the *Kismet Dao* (☏0268/514 296, 🅦www.kismetdao.com; ❷–❸), which also has dorms (❶) and private rooms (❶). Both hostels have laundry facilities and all prices include breakfast and Internet access.

Closer to the centre or the station, your best option may be a **private room** (❶), likely to be in a modern apartment block; there are many people offering these on arrival at the train station, the most likely suspects being Maria and Grig Bolea (☏0744/816 970); the helpful Eugene (☏0722/542 581, 🅔ejrr68@yahoo.com); the Beke family (☏0268/461 888); the Babes family (☏0268/543 728); Gigi and Diana Borcea (☏0268/416 243); and Gabriel Ivan (☏0744/844 223). Most of these will happily arrange local excursions.

The **Dârste campsite** (☏0268/339 967, 🅦www.campingdirste.ro) is about 7km from Braşov's centre, on the Bucharest highway, the DN1. Take trolley bus #3 or bus #6 from the centre to the Saturn/Autocamion terminus (also known as Roman or IABV) on Calea Bucureşti, and then bus #21 (for Săcele, every 10min) out along the main highway until it turns off; the campsite is ten minutes' walk further south along the DN1. The site has reasonable facilities plus bungalows sleeping two to four people (❷–❹) with 24-hour hot water.

The Town

Most visitors make a beeline for the largely Baroque **old town**, coiled beneath Mount Tâmpa and Mount Postăvaru. Essentially, this begins at **Str. Republicii** – the hub of the city's social and commercial life – which opens up onto **Piaţa Sfatului**, a strikingly handsome, quintessentially Germanic town square dominated by the **Black Church**. Close by are the medieval ramparts and, beyond here, the Schei quarter.

Piaţa Teatrului and around

Buses from the train station will set you down near busy **Piaţa Teatrului**, from where it's a short walk to the major sights. Close to the square are some stark reminders of the events that took place during December 1989; in a small park next to the post office stand thirty headstones, in memorial to those gunned down, including a young girl of six caught in the crossfire. Across the road, at the head of Str. Republicii, stands the heavily pockmarked **Volksbank building**, which is now the only edifice exhibiting any damage. From here, it's a pleasant stroll down pedestrianized **Str. Republicii**

(Purzengasse), a wide boulevard that's at its best during the warmer months when it's lined with cafés and bars.

A two-minute walk southwest of the Volksbank building along B-dul. Eroilor, at no. 21, is the **Ethnographic Museum** (Muzeul de Etnografie; Tues–Sun: summer 10am–6pm; winter 9am–5pm; €1), which has a modest but enlightening display on the regional textile industry and local costume – the pick of the exhibits is a still-functioning Jacquard weaving loom from Germany (ask the guardian for a demonstration). There's also a neat selection of craftworks for sale, together with books and CDs. Next door, the **Art Museum** (Muzeul de Artă; same times and admission) has a large selection of canvases by Grigorescu, Aman and Tattarescu, as well as works by Braşov-born **János Máttis-Teutsch** (1884–1960), one of the most influential of modern Romanian artists. Máttis-Teutsch was a painter, sculptor, writer and teacher who exhibited with avant-garde groups in Berlin, Budapest and Bucharest before returning to figurative art. The decorative arts collection in the basement – with English Wedgwood, Zsolnay vases from Pecs in Hungary, and lots of Chinese porcelain – is also worth a peek.

Piaţa Sfatului

Local legend has it that when the Pied Piper enticed the children from Hamelin in Germany, they vanished underground and emerged in Transylvania near the site of Braşov's main square, now called the **Piaţa Sfatului** (Council Square). It is lined with sturdy merchants' houses, their red roof tiles tilted rakishly, presenting their shop fronts to the Casa Sfatului (Council House) in the centre of the square, which was built by 1420, rebuilt in the eighteenth century, and now houses the tourist office and **History Museum** (Tues–Sun 10am–6pm). The dusty exhibits tell the story of the Saxon guilds – locksmiths, goldsmiths, milliners and so on – who dominated Braşov and met in the Hirscher Haus or **Merchants' Hall** (Casa Negustorilor) on the eastern side of the square. Built in the "Transylvanian Renaissance" style, this now contains craft shops, a wine cellar and the *Cerbul Carpatin* restaurant. Through an archway (which actually looks like the cathedral's frontage) at Piaţa Sfatului 3, you'll find the **Orthodox cathedral**, built in Byzantine style in 1896; its dark, richly painted interior features an eight-metre-high iconostasis and marble paved flooring from 1963, while the brightly coloured wall paintings in the courtyard are of more recent vintage, dating from 2003. Across the road, and similarly hidden away down an alley at Str. Bariţiu 12, the eighteenth-century **Sf Treime (Holy Trinity) Church** also features an elaborately decorated altar screen.

To the southwest, the square is dominated by the pinnacles of the town's most famous landmark, the **Black Church** (Biserica Neagră; Mon–Sat 10am–3.30pm), stabbing upwards like a series of daggers. Allegedly the largest Gothic church between Vienna and Istanbul, it took almost a century to complete (1383–1477) and is so-called for its once soot-blackened walls – the result of a great fire started by the Austrian army that occupied Braşov in 1689. It's a classic example of a three-nave hall church, though its interior is largely devoid of colour or ornamentation and the main altar is memorable only for its size. The exceptions to this are the mostly seventeenth-century **Turkish prayer mats** hung in isolated splashes of colour along the balconies and walls of the nave – a superb collection built up from the gifts of local merchants returning from the east. The main altarpiece is nothing special, but there's an older triptych on the north wall, and a fine tympanum of the *Virgin and Child* with two saints in the inside of the south porch. The four-thousand-pipe organ is one of the largest in southeastern Europe, and it's worth trying to catch one of the church's regular recitals – check with the tourist office. On the last pillar to your left as you enter, look out for the four bullet holes, the result of shots fired through the nearby wooden door as people cowered inside during the fighting in 1989. To the south and west of the church are the buildings of the **Honterus Gymnasium**, the still-prestigious Saxon school named after the apostle of Luther's Reformation in Transylvania.

A short walk east of Piaţa Sfatului, at Str. Poarta Schei 27, is Braşov's Moorish-style **synagogue** (Mon–Fri 9am–1pm), built in 1901 and now beautifully restored.

The fortifications and Mount Tâmpa

With the threat of Turkish expansion in the fifteenth century, Braşov began to fortify itself, assigning the defence of each bastion or rampart to a particular guild. A length of **fortress wall** runs along the foot of Mount Tâmpa, beneath a maze of paths and a cable car running up to the summit – good **views** of the old town can be had from Str. Brediceanu, the semi-pedestrianized promenade beyond the lower cable-car terminal, but the best views are from the forested heights of **Mount Tâmpa** (967m), accessible by cable car (Tues–Sun 9am–6pm; €2) or by the various paths which wind up to its summit.

Of the original seven **bastions**, the best preserved is that of the Weavers (Bastionul Ţesătorilor), on Str. Coşbuc, which has three tiers of wooden galleries and meal-rooms in which the townsfolk stocked bread, meat and other provisions in case of siege. The top two floors are now too weak to be used, but the ground floor now contains the **Museum of the Bârsa Land Fortifications** (Tues–Sun 10am–6pm; €2), where displays recall the bad old days when the surrounding region was repeatedly raided by Tatars, Turks and, on a couple of occasions, by Vlad Ţepeş. The **Blacksmiths' Bastion** (Bastionul Fierarilor) and the **Black and the White Towers** (1494) on Calea Poienii (best seen from Str. Dupa Ziduri, squeezed between stream and walls) all managed to survive these onslaughts, but the inhabitants didn't always fare so well. When Ţepeş attacked Braşov in 1460, he burnt the suburbs and impaled hundreds of captives along the heights of St Jacob's Hill to the north of the city. Referring to allegations that Vlad dined from a holy icon surrounded by his suffering victims, his hagiographer Stoicescu wrote that "being on campaign … the terrible Prince may not have had the time to take his meals otherwise".

The Schei quarter

During the heyday of Saxon rule, the Romanian-speaking population was compelled to live beyond the citadel walls, in the southwestern district of **Schei**. They could only enter the centre at certain times, and had to pay a toll at the gate for the privilege of selling their produce to their neighbours. The Poarta Schei, the gate on the street of the same name, was built in 1825 by Emperor Franz I, next to the splendid **Catherine's Gate** (Poarta Ecaterinei) of 1559, which bears the city's coat of arms. Today, Schei is a peaceful residential dead end whose main sight is the **Church of St Nicholas**, on Piaţa Unirii, ten minutes' walk from Poarta Schei. A fetching amalgam of Byzantine, Baroque and Gothic, it was the first Orthodox church to be built in Transylvania by the voivodes of Wallachia, between 1493 and 1564; it was extended and the clocktower added in 1751 – the interior frescoes were realized by the master Romanian painter Misu Popp. On the left as you enter the churchyard is the first **Romanian-language school**, established in the fourteenth century; it is now a museum (daily 9am–5pm; €2), exhibiting the first Romanian-language textbooks.

The Pageant of the Juni

The **Pageant of the Juni** (Sărbătoarea Junilor) is held on the first Sunday of May, traditionally the one day of the year that Romanians could freely enter the Saxon city. The name derives from the Latin for "young men", and on this day the town's youths dress up in costumes and, accompanied by brass bands, ride through town in groups named after famous regiments – the Dorobanţi, or the Roşiori – while the married men, or Old Juni, bring up the rear. Some of the elaborate Juni costumes (now in the Schei Church Museum) are more than 150 years old, while one of the Roşiori wears a shirt sewn with 44,000 spangles that weighs 9kg – the product of four months' work by Braşov's women each year.

The parade assembles in the morning on the **Piaţa Unirii**, which forms the historic heart of Schei. It then marches to Piaţa Sfatului, returns to the Schei backstreets, and finally climbs a narrow valley northwest to the **Gorges of Pietrele lui Solomon**. Here, spectators settle down to watch the Round Dances (Horăs), which for the dancers are something of an endurance test. The Horă, which still has the power to draw onlookers into its rhythmically stepping, swaying and stamping circles, used to serve as a sanction in village society – local miscreants seeking to enter the circle (and so re-enter society) were shamed when the dancing immediately ceased, resuming only when they withdrew.

Eating and drinking

Outside Bucharest, Braşov has the best selection of **restaurants** in Romania. **Drinking** options, too, are plentiful, particularly during the warmer months when the cafés and bars spill out onto Piaţa Sfatului and along Str. Republicii.

Restaurants

Bella Muzica Str. Gheorghe Bariţiu 2 ☎0268/477 956. Located deep inside a gorgeous, low-ceilinged cellar, this is unquestionably Braşov's classiest restaurant. The food is a curious mix of Mexican and Hungarian cuisines, while the surrounds – dim table lamps and soft background music – are delightful. Perfect for a romantic evening out. Daily noon–11pm.

Bistro de l'Arte Piaţa Enescu 11 ☎0268/473 994. Tucked away in a little courtyard, this cosy, low-key place offers a limited menu of excellent French-influenced food, but is worth a visit just for its delicious fondue. Cracking breakfast options, too. Mon–Sat 9am–1am, Sun noon–midnight.

Café Faberge Piaţa Enescu 13 ☎0268/478 590. Just a few paces from *Bistro*, this stylish restaurant specializes in high-end French cuisine (shrimp à la Provencal, tartlets with foie gras), including a gourmet menu for two – the large plasma TV screen is a bit of an annoyance, though. Daily 12.30pm–midnight.

Casa Românească Piaţa Unirii 15. The only really decent place to eat in the Schei quarter (and handily located if staying at either of the hostels) – there's nothing fancy about it, but the tasty Romanian food is inexpensive and there's regular live music. Daily noon–midnight.

Gustări Piaţa Sfatului 14. Though far from the flashiest restaurant on the main square, *Gustări* is the place to plump for if you fancy eating around here, as any local will tell you. Wholesome Romanian food, served with a smile. Daily 8am–11pm.

Keller Steak House Str. Apollonia Hirscher 2. One of the country's few genuine steak houses, this well-turned-out establishment also has a terrific Romanian menu and a very good wine list. Highly recommended. Daily 11am–midnight.

Pizza Roma Str. Apollonia Hirscher 2. A friendly, no-smoking, Italian place next to *Keller*, serving up decent pizzas and big bowls of fresh salad on its genial street-side *terasa*. Daily 11am–midnight.

Sergiana Str. Mureşenilor 27. Set in an attractive maze of bare-brick and stone cellars, with lots of hidden alcoves, the *Sergiana* has a large menu of traditional and modern Romanian dishes – a fun place to eat. Daily 11am–midnight.

Şirul Vămii Str. Mureşenilor 18 ☎0268/477 725. Second only to *Bella Muzica*, this handsome-looking restaurant offers high-class (Belgian, French and Italian) food, fine wines and impeccable service. Expensive. Daily noon–midnight.

Taverna Str. Politechnicii 6 ℡ 0268/474 618. Intimate, warm and classy restaurant serving plates of spicy mixed meats and fish, with lots of choices for veggies – mushroom stew with sour cream, and spinach puree with egg are just two of several options. Daily noon–midnight.

Taverna Sârbului Str. Republicii 55. Set back from the main street and through a small indoor courtyard, this cellar-like space, with thick wooden tables and bench seating, is where you can indulge in fantastically tasty, gut-busting portions of meat-heavy Serbian food. Daily 11am–11pm.

Cafés and bars

The **cafés** along Str. Republicii and around Piaţa Sfatului are much of a muchness, but more than suffice for a relaxed evening's drinking; the pick of the pavement cafés hereabouts is *Mado*, Str. Republicii 10, a colourful coffee house that also has a good selection of cakes and ices. The queen of Braşov's cake shops, however, is the old-style *Vatra Ardealului*, Str. Bariţiu 14 (Mon–Sat 8.30am–10pm, Sun 10.30am–8.30pm), which has a tremendous selection of sticky things, and good coffee too.

The most popular **bars** are *Deane's*, Str. Republicii 19, a decent Irish boozer that puts on some varied entertainment including live jazz, stand-up and karaoke; and the *Auld Scots Pub* on Str. Apollonia Hirscher, with big glass doors that open up on to the street and an impressive range of English draught beers. Other possibilities include *Festival 39*, Str. Mureşenilor 23, which boasts a long cocktail list and weird decor and, nearby at no. 13, the big, open-fronted *Saloon* which also has bar food. The *For Sale Pub*, B-dul. 15 Noiembrie 24, has bargain beer and unusual cocktails, but its eccentricity is rather forced, while the *Formula Pub* at B-dul. Eroilor 29 can pass the time while you're waiting for a bus at Livada Postei, or if you're a fan of Formula 1 – most of these places stay open until around 2am.

Entertainment

Classical concerts are held at the Braşov Philharmonic, Str. Hirscher 10 (℡ 0268/477 813); tickets are inexpensive but usually sell out well in advance – the box office (such as it is) is through the front door and up the stairs at the back of the theatre (Mon–Fri 10am–5pm). The municipal **theatre** is on Piaţa Teatrului, at the east end of B-dul. Eroilor (℡ 0268/418 850; box office Tues–Fri 11am–7pm, Sat & Sun 3–7pm); the less appealing **Lyric Theatre** – which mainly stages operettas and musicals – at Str. Bisericii Romăne 51 (℡ 0268/415 990); and the **puppet theatre** inside the Centrul Cultura Reduta next to the Philharmonic. Note that between mid-June and mid-September there's unlikely to be much happening at any of these. There are no **cinemas** near the city centre; the main ones are the *Patria* (B-dul. 15 Noiembrie), *Cosmos* (Str. Uranus 1) and *Bulevard* (B-dul. Griviţei 47).

The **Pageant of the Juni Festival** aside (see p.163), Braşov doesn't really have any other significant festivals. That said, smaller-scale events include the **Springtime Jazz and Blues Festival** in early May; the **International Chamber Music Festival** in the first week of July; the **Golden Stag** pop music extravaganza, which takes over Piaţa Sfatului in late August or early September; and the rather anonymous **Beer Festival** in early October, which brings a range of near-identical lagers to town.

Shopping

Braşov is a good place to buy books and outdoor gear, and the food markets are fine, but it's hardly a shopper's dream. The STAR **department store** is at Str. Bălcescu 62 (Mon–Sat 9am–8pm, Sat 10am–3pm), and there are some fascinating **antique** and **junk** shops on Str. Coresi. English-language books can be found at the Coşbuc bookshop, Str. Republicii 29 (Mon–Fri 8am–8pm, Sat 10am–4pm), and at the Şt. O. Iosif bookshop, Str. Mureşenilor 14 (Mon–Fri 8am–8pm, Sat 10am–4pm), which also sells some useful **maps**. Himalaya, Str. Republicii 23, is an excellent **mountain-gear** shop. The central food **market** is next to the STAR department store, and there's another behind the apartment blocks opposite the train station. Also near the station, on B-dul. Victoriei, is the Rapid **supermarket** (24hr). For the greatest selection, head to one of the two big hypermarkets – Selgros, at Calea Bucureşti 231 and Metro, 8km west at km174 of the DN1 towards Sibiu; show your passport on arrival to get the temporary membership form needed to shop here.

Listings

Banks and exchange There are plenty of ATMs around the centre, and private exchange offices at the junction of Piaţa Sfatului and Str. Mureşenilor that accept travellers' cheques; others on B-dul. Eroilor and at the top of Str. Bariţiu charge commission. You can also change money at the CEC offices (Mon–Fri 8am–3pm) in the police headquarters at Str. Titulescu 28 and at the corner of Piaţa Sfatului and Republicii, or at the Banca Commerciala Romană at Str. Republicii 45 (Mon–Fri 8.30am–noon).

Car rental Avis, through Sun Tours, Piaţa Sfatului 19 (☏ 0268/474 179); Budget, *Hotel Aro Palace* (☏ 0268/474 564); CarpaTour, B-dul. 15 Noiembrie 1 (☏ 0268/471 057); Europcar through Astra Tours, Str. Bariţiu 26 (☏ 0268/336 264); Hertz, Str. 15 Noiembrie 50A (☏ 0268/471 485); Sixt, through Contempo, Dârste DN1 km160 (☏ 0268/339 446).

Football FC Braşov play at Stadion Tineret on Str. Stadionului.

Hospitals County Hospital, Calea Bucureşti 25–27 (☏ 0268/135 080); Emergency Military Hospital, Pietei 9 (☏ 0268/416 393); Clinica Romano Americana, Str. Traian 10 (☏ 0268/332 023).

International bus tickets Amad Turistik, c/o Sun Tours (see above), & Str. Vlahuţă 32 (☏ 0268/329 364); Armin-Meyer Reisen, Str. M. Weiss 2 (☏ 0268/143 131); AtlasSib, Str. Lungă 1; Civic Trans, at the station (☏ & ☏ 0268/472 498 or 152 774); Double-T, Piaţa Sfatului 25 (☏ 0268/410 466); Kaiser, Republicii 25 (☏ 0268/416 871); Kessler, c/o Dialect Tour, Str. Toamnei 9 (☏ 0268/327 041); MegaSoy, Str. Mureşenilor (☏ 0268/470 816); Micomis, Str. Republicii 53

(☏ 0268/470 472); Mihu Reisen, Str. Cerbului 34 (☏ 0268/142 257); Pletl, Piaţa Teatrului 4 (☏ 0268/150 387); Simpa Turism (see below); Tavi Reisen, Str. Vlahuţă 38 (☏ 0268/416 378); Touring-Eurolines, Piaţa Sfatului 18 (☏ 0268/474 008); Wasteels, at the train station (☏ 0268/424 313, ⓦ www.wasteelstravel.ro). Budapest tickets can be bought from *Autogară* 1.

Internet access Club Internet, Str. Toamnei 17; Hip Internet C@fe, Str. 15 Noiembrie 1; Cybercafe, Str. Apollonia Hirscher 12; Internet Café, Str. Michael Weiss 11; Internet Caffé, Str. Republicii 41 (24hr); Internet Club, B-dul. Victoriei 10; and on the mezzanine floor of the train station.

Pharmacy Aurofarm, Str. Republicii 27 (daily 8am–midnight ☏ 0268/143 560).

Police The county police headquarters are at Str. Titulescu 28 (☏ 0268/407 500). This is also the place to go for visa extensions.

Post office Str. Iorga 1. Poste restante available. Mon–Fri 7am–8pm, Sat 8am–1pm.

Telephone office B-dul. Eroilor 23 (Mon–Fri 7am–9pm).

Tour and travel agents TAROM, Str. Mureşenilor 22 (☏ 0268/406 373); KronTour, Str. Bariţiu 12 (☏ 0268/410 515, ⓦ www.krontour.ro); Simpa Turism, Piaţa Sfatului 3 (☏ 0268/475 677, ⓦ www .simpaturism.ro); Paralela 45, Str. Mureşenilor 20 (☏ 0268/473 399); and J'Info Tours, Piaţa Sfatului 12–14 (☏ 0268/414 701).

Train tickets CFR, B-dul. 15 Noiembrie 45 (☏ 0268/477 018); Wasteels (see above); and Civic Trans, on the station mezzanine.

Around Braşov

Braşov sits right at the foot of the mountains, and there are opportunities for hiking and skiing just a few kilometres from the city at **Poiana Braşov**. The most popular bus excursion is to the castle of **Bran**, and in spite of the crowds it's well worth a visit. Better still, though, is the ruined fort at **Râşnov**, located approximately halfway between Braşov and Bran. Further to the south, the Bucegi mountains (see p.148) are within easy reach, and to the west the Făgăraş range (see p.171), containing Romania's highest peaks, can be accessed by train. Between these two ranges lies the very distinctive ridge of the **Piatra Craiului**, a single block of limestone that offers a marvellous, if tiring, day's walking.

Poiana Braşov

The rustic resort of **POIANA BRAŞOV** is set at an altitude of 1000m, on a shoulder of the spectacular Mount Postăvaru, 12km south of Braşov (20min by bus #20, every 30min from Livada Postei, by the Parc Central). It's Romania's premier **ski resort**, and while it's a great place to learn to ski, with lots of English-speaking instructors, the experienced are likely to get bored. **Skiing equipment** can be rented at several places, as can **mountain bikes**; **horse-riding** is also available.

The town's **hotels** are usually filled by package groups, but they may have space outside the season, and the tourist office can try to find you an inexpensive room in a villa. The *Alpin* (☎0268/262 343, ⓦwww.hotelalpin.ro; ➌) has the best facilities and serves a heavy buffet breakfast, but the most attractive place, and ideally located for the slopes, is the *Sport* (☎0268/262 313; ➌); the *Poiana Ursului* (☎0268/262 216; ➋) is a youth hotel that's open to all ages and offers simple facilities. One of the best of the many **villas** dotted around the resort is the welcoming *Vila Zorile*, Str. Poiana Ruia 6 (☎0268/262 286, ⓦwww.vila-zorile.ro; ➐). There's also a fair chance that you'll be approached by locals offering **apartments** (➌–➏), which can work out to be good value.

The resort's **restaurants** go in for folk architecture and local cuisine, as you'd expect with names like *Şura Dacilor* (Dacians' Barn) and *Coliba Haiducilor* (Outlaws' Hut), both of which are open from 11am until midnight and offer pretty authentic pork-heavy cuisine.

Râşnov

Thirty minutes from Braşov by bus or train, and 12km west of Poiana Braşov by a back road, is **RÂŞNOV** (Rosenau), where a **ruined fort** (Mon–Fri 10am–5pm, Sat & Sun 9am–6pm; €3), founded around 1225 by the Teutonic Knights, crowns the fir-covered hill that overlooks the town. Such has been the fort's resolve that it was only ever conquered once, by the Hungarian prince, Gabriel Báthory, around 1600. It last saw action during the 1848 revolution, after which it was abandoned, only to undergo extensive restoration work in recent years. One of the more curious tales surrounding the fort concerns the 143-metre well, which was supposedly dug by two Turkish prisoners in return for their eventual release – however, some thirty years after completing their task, they were summarily executed.

A small **museum** inside the fort holds mostly weaponry and implements used for torture, along with a seventeenth-century skeleton of a female, discovered inside the citadel during excavations; there is also a small **taverna** serving simple refreshments. The best reason for visiting the fort, however, is to take in the glorious mountain **views** across to Piatra Craiului.

To get there on foot, head through the archway and up the steps opposite the BCR bank on Piaţa Unirii, just south of the Lutheran church. You can also get there by car or bike, along a road that starts at the **hotel** *Cetate* (☎0268/230 266; ➌), which is on Str. Cetăţii (the Poiana Braşov road) – this can be accessed from the southern end of Piaţa Unirii. Another, much better, place to stay in town is the terrific-value *Pension Ştefi*, just a few paces from the steps leading up to the fort, at Piaţa Unirii 5 (☎0268/231 618, ⓦ www.hotelstefi-ro.com; ❸).

Bran and around

Situated 28km southwest of Braşov, the small town of **BRAN** (Törzburg) commands the entrance to the pass of the same name, once the main route into Wallachia. The Saxons of Kronstadt (Braşov) built a castle here between 1377 and 1382 to safeguard this vital trade artery, and although what's now billed on every tourist brochure as **Dracula's Castle** (Muzeului Castel Bran; Mon

▲ Dracula's Castle, Bran

noon–6pm, Tues–Sun 9am–6pm; Ⓦwww.brancastlemuseum.ro; €4) has only tenuous associations with Vlad the Impaler – it's likely he laid siege to it in 1460 when he attacked the Burzenland – Bran does look rather like a vampire count's residence, perched on a rocky bluff and rising in tiers of towers and ramparts from the woods against a glorious mountain backdrop.

After lengthy restoration, the castle now looks much as it would have done in the time of its most famous resident, **Queen Marie of Romania**. A granddaughter of Queen Victoria and married to Prince Ferdinand in 1893, Queen Marie soon rebelled against the confines of court life in Bucharest – riding unattended through the streets, pelting citizens with roses during the carnival, and appointing herself a colonel of the Red Hussars. Her popularity soared after she organized cholera camps in the Balkan war and appeared at the Paris peace conference in 1919, announcing that "Romania needs a face, and I have come to show mine". Marie called Bran a "pugnacious little fortress", but whether because of her spirit pervading the rooms or the profusion of flowers in the yard, it seems a welcoming place, at odds with its forbidding exterior. Inside it's a warren of spiral stairs, ghostly nooks and rooms stuffed full of Renaissance, Biedermeier and neo-Baroque furnishings. Not surprisingly, it can get horribly crowded: the trick is to arrive as the castle opens – the bus parties will be arriving as you leave.

In the grounds, the open-air **Village Museum** (Muzeul Satului; same hours and ticket as castle) comprises some fine examples of local architecture, including a sawmill, fulling mill (used to help in the manufacture of wool) and, most impressively, a large house dating from 1843, comprising a dwelling place – living room, hall and cellar, and stables.

By the road south, the **Ancient Customs House Museum** (Vama Medievală; same hours and ticket), in the former *vama*, predictably stresses the trade links from the earliest times between the Vlachs on either side of the Carpathians, and displays examples of foreign goods, including an English clock and a Canadian travelling trunk. There's a hectic **crafts market** at the castle gate, but inevitably there's lots of Dracula tack among the authentic folk art on sale. Bran holds its village **festival** on August 9 (the Feast of St Pantelimon).

Aside from its castle, Bran is a good base for **hikes** into the Bucegi mountains to the east (see p.148) and onto the narrow ridge of the **Piatra Craiului**, the eastern extremity of the Făgăraş mountains, to the west (see p.171).

Bran practicalities

Buses run from Braşov's *Autogară* 2 south via Râşnov and Bran to Moeciu de Jos, 3km south of Bran (Mon–Fri every 30min, Sat & Sun hourly); the two or three buses from Braşov south to Piteşti and Câmpulung Muscel will also stop off at Bran. Note that, if **parking** here, you will pay over the odds. There's no tourist **office** in Bran, but you can get (scant) **information** from Antrec at Str. Dr. Aurel Stoian 395 (daily 8am–5pm; ☎0268/362 355), or the Centrul Agroturistic agency a few steps further on at Str. Principala 504C (daily 9am–5pm; ☎0268/238 308, Ⓦwww.turism-bran.ro) – both of these agencies can also set you up in **private accommodation** (❷–❹), which is big business in Bran.

The best **hotel** is the *Hanul Bran*, a five-minute walk north of the castle at Str. Principală 363 (☎0268/236 556; ❷–❺), which has a new wing to supplement the older, now mostly antiquated rooms. One kilometre from the centre (back on the road towards Braşov), and 100m up a turning, there's the pleasant *Villa Bran*, Sohodol 271A (☎0268/236 866, Ⓔvilabran@xnet.ro; ❷), which is actually a complex of several new villas, each containing en-suite rooms.

Another reasonable place, with its own pool, is the *Popasul Reginei*, across the small park near the castle on Str. Dr. Aurel Stoian (℡0268/236 834; ❸). Just outside the village, 3km out on the road towards Braşov, the *Hotel Wolf* complex (℡0268/419 576, ✉complexulwolf@gmail.com; ❸) has fresh, modern rooms. There are also a few independent **guesthouses** around the village, the best of which is the British-run *Villa Jo* (℡0745/179 475; 🌐www.jocompany.ro; ❸), opposite the *Hanul Bran at Str. Principală 395A* (the sign reads *Jo & Co*). Other good ones are *Pension Iulia*, nearby at Bologa 20 (℡0268/236 966; ❷); and the slightly smaller and cheaper *Casa Laura* (℡0268/236 684; ❷), at Str. Dr. Iancu Gontea 48 – 1km to the left beyond the bridge 1.5km south of Bran.

The *Taverna Lupilor* **restaurant** in the *Wolf* complex (see above) is easily the best place to eat hereabouts, with lots of hunter-style dishes (deer stew and roast boar) available in its heavily rustic setting – there's a large **supermarket** here, too (Mon–Sat 8am–9pm, Sun 9am–7pm). Otherwise, the restaurant in the *Popasul Reginei* is good, or there's the *Cheile Castelului* for pizza, below the castle near the *vama*.

Fundata

In **MOECIU**, immediately south of Bran, there are plenty of **guesthouses**, all very clean with lots of stripped pine and big breakfasts. **Buses** terminate just beyond the junction at km105; there's a group of three good guesthouses 2.5km up the Moeciu de Sus road. Call in advance at *Olteanu*, Cheia 427A (℡0268/419 477; ❷), *Urzica*, at no. 433 (℡0268/237 233, ✉ovyonut@yahoo.com; ❷), or *Camelia*, no. 436 (℡0268/236 233, ✉golteanu@just.ro; ❷), and they'll pick you up. In Moeciu de Sus (Upper Moeciu) itself, 8km south of the junction, the best **place to stay** is the *Casa Orleanu*, also known as the *Centru de Ecologie Montană*, at no. 125 (℡0745/978 023; ❷), in the centre of the village; you can get information on local wildlife here.

Fourteen kilometres south of Bran, **FUNDATA**, one of the highest villages in Romania, sits atop the spectacular **Bran** or **Giuvala Pass** (1290m) and is served only by occasional Braşov–Câmpulung buses. Little more than a scattering of small farmhouses, it is host to the popular **Mountain Festival** (Nedeia Muntelui) on the last Sunday of August. The underlying purpose is to transact business: exchanges of handicrafts, livestock and (formerly) of pledges of marriage. As Fundata straddles the border between Transylvania and Wallachia, the festival was important as a means of maintaining contacts between ethnic Romanians in the two provinces.

Zărneşti and the Piatra Craiului

Mountains dominate the skyline around Bran. To the east is the almost sheer wall of the **Bucegi range** – it takes about eight hours to climb the path from Bran to Mount Omu, where there's a cabana. To the west, gentler slopes run up to the national park of **Piatra Craiului**, a narrow ridge at the eastern extremity of the Făgăraş mountains, the forested hills around which were the setting for 2003's Hollywood blockbuster *Cold Mountain*. This twenty-kilometre-long limestone ridge, punctured with karst caves along its eastern face, is known as the Royal Rock, and is home to Carpathian bears (see box, p.170), lynx and chamois, as well as the endemic Piatra Craiului pink.

The gateway to the park, and a good starting point for hikes, is the anonymous town of **ZĂRNEŞTI**, some 25km west of Braşov and reachable by bus and train. About 1.5km east of the town centre, along a gravel road heading up the Bârsa Mare Valley (see p.170), is the new **Piatra Craiului Visitor Centre** (℡0268/223 008, 🌐www.pcrai.ro), an overly conspicuous structure where you

Wildlife-watching and other activities

The **Piatra Craiului National Park** offers endless possibilities for wildlife-watching and other leisurely pursuits. Organized by a number of different agencies – all of whom are members of the **Association of Eco-tourism in Romania**, a collective dedicated to nature conservation and sustainable tourism development in the region – there is a multitude of things to see and do, from observing wild animals in their natural habitat to sporting activities and guided walks.

The most popular of these is **bear-watching**, which gives visitors a rare chance to observe these animals in their natural habitat – gathering at dusk, you are taken up to one of the forest hides, where the chances of seeing a brown bear are rated at around eighty to ninety percent (€35, plus €25 for the use of cameras; Carpathian Tours; ☎0745/512 096, ⍟www.cntours.ro). While the chance of seeing wolves is far more remote, **wolf-tracking** is another popular activity and can be arranged through the excellent Transylvanian Wolf (☎0744/319 708, ⍟www.transylvanianwolf.ro). It's also possible to visit two semi-tame wolves, rescued from a fur farm in 1996 and raised in a large enclosure just beyond the park visitor centre – contact Carpathian Tours or Roving Romania (☎0744/212 065, ⍟www.roving-romania.co.uk). Other companies with similar programmes include Absolute Carpathian (☎0788/578 796, ⍟www.absolute-nature.ro) and Discover Romania (☎0268/472 718, ⍟www.discoverromania.ro).

Equus Silvania (☎0268/228 601, ⍟www.equus-silvania.com), 50km west of Braşov in the village of Sinca Noua, offer **horse-riding** lessons and guided one- and two-day trips.

can pick up lots of useful information on the surrounds, and which also has a cabana (❷). They can also point you towards the various agencies in the area offering **wildlife-watching** trips, such as bear-watching and wolf-tracking, as well as a host of other leisure pursuits and guided tours (see box above).

Of the several **guesthouses** in town, the homely *Pensiunea Mosorel*, Str. Dr Ioan Şenchea 162 (☎0745/024 472; ❸), offers super home cooking – they'll also allow camping in the large back garden. You can also stay in the spectacular *Wolf House*, Str. I. Metianu 108 (❹), a family guesthouse owned by the people who run Transylvanian Wolf (see box above). They serve traditional and regional home cooking, made using local produce and fresh herbs, and all meals are included in the room price. *Elena*, Str. Piatra Craiului 43 (☎0268/223 070; ❸), is another good option.

From Zărneşti, it's less than three hours' walk up the Bârsa Mare valley to the *Plaiul Foii* cabana (☎0268/231 465; ❶), the main centre for **hiking** in this area. The hut has single, double and triple-bedded rooms, some with showers, and a restaurant; note, though, that the water isn't safe to drink. The best day hike from here leads to the *Curmătura* cabana at 1470m (☎0745/995 018; ❶), where camping is also available – there's good food here, too. It begins with a stiff climb (3–4hr, following red cross markings, and using fixed cables in places) to the main ridge 1400m above, and continues north along its knife-edge (following red dots), finally descending (following yellow stripes) to the right to the *Curmătura* cabana or to the left to Zărneşti. The route is demanding and you should be properly equipped with boots, waterproofs and plenty of water. The ridge offers fantastic **views** west towards the Făgăraş range and east towards the Bucegi.

In the foothills southwest of Zărneşti, between the Piatra Craiului and the Bran–Fundata road, hide tiny settlements where new *agroturism* pensions are springing up all the time. The pick of the bunch is the *Montana* cabana in Măgura, at no. 44 (☎0744/801 094; ❶) – phone ahead and they'll meet you from the bus in Zărneşti.

Făgăraş and around

FĂGĂRAŞ (Fogarasch), 54km west of Braşov, is scarred by chemical works and communist attempts at town planning. Nevertheless, it's a good jumping-off point for hikes in the mountains to the south, and for exploring the Saxon villages just north – thanks to a wide range of small, cheap hotels – and it does have some small-town charm in places. Founded by Hungarians and Saxons, from 1366 it and the surrounding duchy of Amlaş were under Wallachian rule; when Vlad the Impaler was deposed in 1460, he set out on a murderous rampage from the Olt Valley towards the Burzenland, razing the citadel of Făgăraş en route. The sturdy **fortress** that dominates the town centre today was built in the late sixteenth century on its ashes.

From the **train station** 1km south of the centre, turn left along Stradă Negoiu, and you'll pass between the market and an abandoned synagogue to reach the modern town centre and the fortress, which today houses a moderately good **museum** of local history (Tues–Fri 9am–4pm, Sat & Sun 9am–3pm) in its cellars. One block west is Piaţa Republicii, the old town centre; this forms the heart of social life in the town.

Local **buses** run from next to the train station to and from Agnita, Ucea and Sâmbata de Jos. For **information**, the local NGO Fundaţia Culturală Negru Vodă, Piaţa Republicii 6 (℡0268/211 193; ⓦwww.negruvoda.ro), is very

Hiking in the Făgăraş mountains

The **Făgăraş mountains** are composed mainly of crystalline schists with occasional limestone outcrops, a series of pyramidal crests, linked by narrow ridges, that harbours more than seventy **lakes** at heights of 1800 to 2250m. Up to about 2000m the mountainsides are covered with spruce forests sheltering deer, bears, chamois and other **wildlife**; above this level there may still be snow as late as June.

Most **hiking routes** are well marked and fairly simple to follow with a *Hartă Turistică Munţii Făgăraşului* map, which can be bought in Braşov, Bran, Făgăraş or Sibiu, or in the cabanas in the mountains. It's useful, but rarely essential, to **reserve accommodation**. Always carry ample food and water, and wear boots and waterproofs – the weather is very changeable on the ridge.

Almost invariably, the starting point is one of the settlements along the Olt valley, where marked routes lead from the train stations to the mountains. All trains stop at **Ucea**, where passengers clamber onto buses south to **Victoria**, a town dominated by its chemical works, the siren of which is audible on the main ridge of the Făgăraş. From the bus station, follow the main road uphill to the works gates and then the route marked with red triangles round to the right (west). A forestry track bypasses the *Arpaş* cabana (℡0268/241 433; ❶) and continues as a steep trail past the *Turnuri* cabana (℡0744/936 809; ❶) and up to the basic *Podragu* cabana (℡0745/319 766; ❶) at 2136m, reached in eight to ten hours. From the *Podragu*, follow the **ridge path** marked with red stripes, either eastwards past Romania's highest peak, **Moldoveanu** (2544m), descending by the Sâmbata valley to the friendly *Valea Sâmbatei* cabana (℡0722/760 840; ❶) and the *Complex Turistic Sâmbăta* (with a monastery and accommodation; ❶), from where occasional buses head to Făgăraş and Victoria, 11km west; or west to **Bâlea Lake** (2034m); the *Bâlea Lac* hotel (℡0788/609 930; ❸) also has dorms, a decent restaurant-bar, and an attractive *terasa* by the lake. From *Bâlea Lac*, you can descend either by the Trans-Făgăraş Highway (usually June–Sept) or by a cable car to the *Bâlea Cascada* cabana (℡0269/524 255; ❶), and from there to the *Vama Cucului* cabana (℡0269/524 717; ❶), Cărtişoara and the Cărţa rail halt.

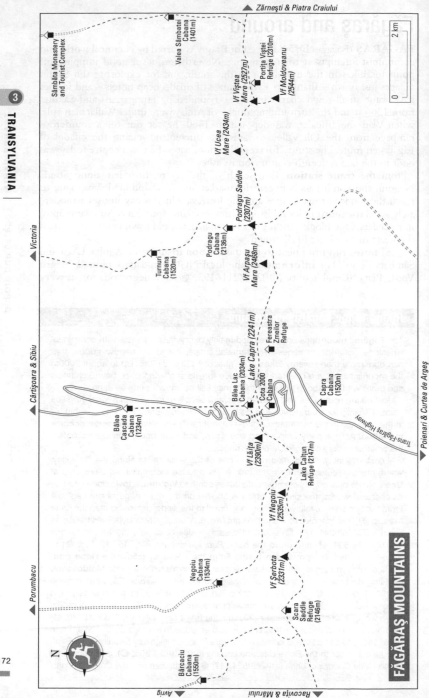

▲ Zărneşti & Piatra Craiului

0   2 km

FĂGĂRAŞ MOUNTAINS

N

Sâmbăta Monastery and Tourist Complex

Valea Sâmbetei Cabana (1401m)

Portiţa Viştei Refuge (2310m)

Vf Viştea Mare (2527m)

Vf Moldoveanu (2544m)

Vf Ucea Mare (2434m)

▲ Victoria

Podragu Saddle (2307m)

Podragu Cabana (2136m)

Turnuri Cabana (1520m)

Vf Arpaşu Mare (2468m)

▲ Cârţişoara & Sibiu

Fereastra Zmeilor Refuge

Lake Capra (2241m)

Bâlea Lac Cabana (2034m)

Cota 2000 Cabana

Bâlea Cascada Cabana (1234m)

Capra Cabana (1520m)

Trans-Făgăraş Highway

▲ Poienari & Curtea de Argeş

Vf Lăiţa (2390m)

Lake Caltun Refuge (2147m)

Vf Negoiu (2535m)

Negoiu Cabana (1534m)

Vf Şerbota (2331m)

Scara Saddle Refuge (2146m)

Bârcaciu Cabana (1550m)

▲ Porumbacu

▲ Avrig

▲ Racoviţa & Mârului

helpful. The best **hotel** is the *Montana*, just north of the station at Str. Negoiu 98 (☎0268/212 327; ❸); opposite the station at no. 125, the *Meridian* (☎&℻0268/212 409; ❷) is simple, clean and friendly. In the centre, the basic *Progresul*, Piaţa Republicii 15 (☎0268/211 634; ❷), is very cheap and welcoming enough; there's a shared bathroom where hot water is provided as required. For better facilities, head for the warm and friendly *Roata*, at the east end of the new town centre at Str. V. Alecsandri 10 (☎0268/212 415; ❸). The best **places to eat** in town are the *Don Giovanni* pizzeria, just east of Piaţa Republicii, and the *Cetate*, a fairly classy restaurant near the museum.

Around Făgăraş

Wallachian rule gave rise to characteristic local art forms still evident in the villages surrounding Făgăraş, such as the icons on glass in the gallery at **Sâmbata Monastery**, founded in 1696 by Constantin Brâncoveanu, 27km southwest of the town, while the fifteenth-century church at **Vad**, reached by buses east to Şinca, also has a collection. Just beyond Arpaşu, the ruined Cistercian monastery of **Cârţa** is the oldest Gothic building in Transylvania, founded in 1202 and rebuilt after the Tatar attack of 1241; it was dissolved in 1474, but the choir remains intact and in use as the village church.

To the north of Făgăraş, buses to Agnita and Rupea (via Lovnic) pass through Saxon villages with fine **fortified churches**. Villagers still dress up in embroidered costumes for **New Year celebrations** – particularly at Şercaia, Arpaşu, Porumbacu de Jos and Porumbacu de Sus – and gather en masse together with Saxon dancers from Tilişca for the **Flowers of the Olt Festival** (Florile Oltului) at **Avrig** on the second Sunday of April. The Saxon village of **Şoarş** (Scharosch) offers good **homestays**; contact Mihai Patrichi, Str. Principală 155 (☎0268/267 415, ✉patrichimihai@yahoo.com), or Viorica Bica, in Făgăraş at Str. Gheorghe Doja 53 (☎0268/215 170); bikes and excursions are also available.

Beyond Avrig, the road forks: the DN1 heading to the right to Sibiu, the other branch veering south to Tălmaciu and the Red Tower (Turnu Roşu) Pass, and on into Wallachia. Travelling by train, you may need to change at Podul Olt to reach Piatra Olt in Wallachia; these services pass several of the monasteries in the Olt valley (see p.123).

From Braşov to Sighişoara

Southern Transylvania was the heartland of the **Saxon community**, and although the Saxons have almost all departed to Germany following the end of communism, the landscape is still dotted with the vestiges of their culture. In 1143, King Géza II of Hungary invited Germans to colonize strategic regions of Transylvania; their name for Transylvania was Siebenbürgen, derived from the original "seven towns" that divided the territory between them, of which Hermannstadt (**Sibiu** to the Romanians) became the most powerful. In-between them, hundreds of farming villages grew up that developed a distinctive culture with a vernacular style of architecture. Although the Székely, immediately to the north, put low walls about their places of worship and the Moldavians raised higher ones about their monasteries, it was the Saxons who perfected this type of building; their Romanesque and early Gothic churches were initially strengthened to provide refuge from the Tatars, and then surrounded by high walls and towers to resist the more militarily sophisticated

Turks. These **fortified churches**, some of which house warrens of storerooms to hold stocks of food sufficient to survive a siege, are highly individual.

Alas, for the Saxons, their citadels were no protection against the tide of history, which steadily eroded their influence from the eighteenth century on and put them in a difficult position during World War II. Although many bitterly resented Hitler's carving-up of Transylvania in 1940, which gave its northern half to Hungary, there were others who, relishing their new status as Volksdeutsche, embraced Nazism and joined the German army. As a collective punishment after the war, all fit Saxon men between the ages of 17 and 45, and women between 18 and 30 (30,000 in all), were deported to the Soviet Union for between three and seven years of slave labour; many did not return, and those who did found that much of their property had been confiscated.

Though **road** and **rail** routes diverge in places, it's fairly easy to reach the settlements along the Olt valley in particular; however, there are many more in the side valleys that are well worth discovering and can only be reached by occasional buses, by car, bike or on foot. In summer, many Saxons return from Germany to their home villages, but at other times you're likely to be the only visitor.

Hărman

Visiting the Saxon villages around Braşov on the eve of World War II, the writer Elizabeth Kyle found churches prepared for siege as in the times of Sultan Süleyman and Vlad the Impaler. **HĂRMAN** (Honigberg), 12km northeast of Braşov, still looks much as she described it, situated "in a wide and lovely valley, its houses arranged in tidy squares off the main street which sweeps towards the grim fortress that closes the vista". Erected in the fifteenth century, the immense **fortification system** surrounding the church once consisted of three concentric walls (the outermost wall has since gone), with the inner wall, standing some 12m high, having been reinforced with seven towers. Entered via a long narrow passageway, the **church** (Tues–Sun 9am–noon & 1–5pm) itself dates from 1293 and displays clear Cistercian influences, its high vaulted ceiling looking down on rows of rudimentary wooden pews – of particular importance are the fifteenth-century chapel frescoes (discovered in the 1920s), with scenes depicting the *Last Judgement* and the *Crucifixion*.

Hărman is served by regular **buses** (Mon–Fri hourly, Sat & Sun every 2hr) from Braşov's *Autogară 3*; in addition, buses from *Autogară 1* towards Târgu Secuiesc and Sfântu Gheorghe, and maxitaxis to Prejmer, will drop you by Hărman **train** station, 1.5km from the centre along Str. Gării and served by the same five trains a day that go on to Prejmer. While it's unlikely that you'll need to stay here, there is **accommodation** at the *Dynasty Club* (☎0744/560 287; ❹), just down from the church, and the unmarked *Country Hotel* at Mihai Viteazul 441 (☎0268/367 051, ✉mcosnean@yahoo.com; ❻), which has a small swimming pool.

Prejmer

PREJMER (Tartlau), 7km to the east, and off the main road (but on the railway), is the most comprehensively fortified and perhaps the most spectacular of all the region's **churches** (May–Oct Tues–Fri 9am–5pm, Sat 9am–3pm; Nov–April Tues–Sat 9am–3pm) – one that's now on UNESCO's World Heritage list. Access to the inner precinct and church is through a thirty-metre-long vaulted gallery, in the centre of which is a sliding portcullis. The church was originally built in the form of a Greek cross (completed by 1225), but from the mid-thirteenth century was adapted to the Cistercian style. The crossing and choir are old, with splendidly worn rough stone, while the nave has late-Gothic vaulting, and there's a fine Gothic altarpiece depicting *The Passion* (1450–60).

After the Turkish campaign of 1421, the church was surrounded by a five-towered wall, 12m high, lined two centuries later with four tiers of rooms, used variously for storage and refuge – many of these have been cleaned up and can now be viewed, including one that contains a mocked-up classroom. Two of the four towers on the exterior of the outer wall have since been demolished, and, as at Hărman, the moat has been filled in. There is even a small **museum** (same hours – ask the caretaker if closed), boasting fine examples of Saxon costume and a view of the inner wall gateway's portcullis, up the covered stairs in the first court.

Prejmer is served by frequent **maxitaxis** from Braşov's Str. Harmanului, at the east end of B-dul. Gării, and by **buses** from *Autogară* 3 to Vama Buzaului (6–8 daily). There are also five **trains** a day in each direction; note that the Ilieni train stop is closer to the town centre than Prejmer station proper (and nowhere near the village of Ilieni). Prejmer's Lutheran parish, across the main road from the church at Str. Mică 6, has a few **beds** in a couple of very basic dorms – call ahead to check if it's open (☎0268/362 042; ❶). There are no restaurants or cafés here.

The Olt valley

Further north, towards Sighişoara along the River Olt, there are many more Saxon villages with fortified churches; **trains** between Braşov and Sighişoara (4 daily) stop at most, including **FELDIOARA** (Marienburg), where the Teutonic Knights built a citadel, refashioned into a basilica after 1241; **ROTBAV** (Rothbach); **MAIERUŞ** (Nussbach); and **APAŢA**, just across the Olt from **AITA MARE** (Nagyajta). The DN13 (E60) now bypasses Maieruş, swinging left across the wooded Perşani mountains.

A few kilometres north of Aita Mare, the sixteenth-century castle of the Kálnoky family in the remote village of **MICLOŞOARA** (Miklósvar) is a rare example in Romania of the Italian Renaissance style. Count Kálnoky's three renovated **guesthouses** here (☎0742/202 586, ⓦwww.transylvaniancastle .com; ❼) are beautifully furnished in Székely and Saxon style; meals are also available, and there's a full programme of activities – including cultural and wildlife tours, riding and hiking trips – to choose from. Upon request, guests can be collected from Braşov or Henri Coandă airport in Bucharest. Micloşoara can be reached by daily **buses** from Sfântu Gheorghe and Braşov to Baraolt.

Around 17km north of Micloşoara is the Almaş cave in the gorge of the Vârghis (Vargyas) river, a system that continues for a total of 7.5km on four levels and where the **Pied Piper** legendarily surfaced with the children of Hamelin (who became the Saxon colonists of Transylvania).

Rupea and Viscri

The small industrial town of **RUPEA** (Reps), about 60km northeast of Braşov on the main E60, might not have a Saxon church, but it does possess the impressive ruins of a **medieval fortress**, its jagged walls and crumbling towers spread across a mound of volcanic rock – it's accessible by both and car and, from the Baroque church in the centre of town, by foot (the path is marked *cetate pietoni*).

Twelve kilometres east of Rupea, off the main E60 and north along an awful, unsurfaced road, is the village of **VISCRI** (Deutsch-Weisskirch), a designated World Heritage Site. Set, gleaming white, upon a small hill and screened by a bank

The Mihai Eminescu Trust

Established during Ceauşescu's dictatorship to give dissidents a lifeline to literary civilization, the **Mihai Eminescu Trust** (☏0265/506 024; in London ☏020/7603 1113, ⊛www.mihaieminescutrust.org) – named after Romania's national poet – also helped save hundreds of towns and villages from destruction by alerting the West to Ceauşescu's plans to bulldoze Romania's rural architecture. Since then, the Trust has continued to play a prominent role in the country's cultural rebirth, one aspect of which is evident in the Saxon villages of Transylvania, where they have renovated more than a hundred medieval buildings using traditional methods, in order to help resurrect local income after the country's agricultural collapse and revive a sense of community. Already, more than a thousand Saxons have returned, with incoming Romanians and gypsies being integrated into the communities. These successes are influencing regional conservation policy and serving as a model for threatened communities elsewhere in Romania.

of trees, its **citadel** is one of the most impressive and celebrated in Romania. It's largely thirteenth-century Gothic, with fortified walls added in 1525, and an assortment of towers from the fifteenth, seventeenth and eighteenth centuries. The interior is surprisingly small, its rickety pillars now barely supporting the wooden lofts, themselves painted with red, seventeenth-century motifs.

Another noteworthy feature is the **Lard Tower**, so-called because this is where – thanks to its coolness – ham and bacon would be kept (and permanently guarded), the pieces stamped with the house number of each villager in order to ascertain whose was whose. There's also an interesting little **museum** within one of the towers, featuring a collection of costumes and other personal effects donated by Saxons who've since left the village. If the **church** is closed, the key is available from house no. 141, just a few steps away.

The village – overwhelmingly populated by Roma, and with around just two dozen Saxons left – has been at the forefront of recent efforts by the Mihai Eminescu Trust (see above) to restore many of the buildings in the region, as evidenced by the many renovated, brightly painted houses fronting the wide, rambling main street. The village is also prospering thanks to a somewhat more unlikely source, namely **sock making**. What started a few years back as a small-scale operation involving a handful of people has grown into a fairly substantial cottage industry, and now there are more than one hundred villagers participating in the manufacture of socks and other woollen goods, many of which are exported to Germany.

There are plenty of **homestays** (❶) here, largely co-ordinated through the Eminescu Trust – this also essentially functions as the village's **tourist office**. There's also a simple yet homely little **café** on the main street, although, as a charitable organization, it relies solely on donations.

Cloaşterf and Saschiz

The road north out of Viscri rejoins the main E60, from where it's a further 20km to a left turn and the village of **CLOAŞTERF** (Klosdorf) where many restored houses have been the beneficiaries of Eminescu Trust funds. Standing within a simple square wall in the centre of the village is the **Church of St Nicholas**, a modest Saxon construction finished in 1524 and with three of its four original towers remaining – the free-standing bell tower, meanwhile, dates from 1819. The key can be obtained from no. 99, about 200m back down the road near the entrance to the village. The former bell-ringer's house just inside the church entrance has been converted into a simply furnished **guest**

room, complete with a small fridge and two-ring stove – contact the Eminescu Trust for details (see box opposite).

Seven kilometres north of Cloașterf, the E60 bisects the village of **SASCHIZ** (Keisd), where around fifty Saxons still reside. The roadside church is unusual in that it's not surrounded by walls, while its magnificent bell tower is an almost identikit version of the Clock Tower in Sighișoara (see p.180). From the church, across the small covered bridge and following the signs, it's a lovely thirty-minute walk up to the ruins of a fourteenth-century **castle**, from where there are superb views of the surrounding countryside.

Just across from the church is the **tourist office** (daily: summer 10am–7pm, winter 10am–4pm; ℡0265/711 635, ⓦwww.fundatia-adept.ro), whose helpful and knowledgeable staff can advise on any aspect of visiting the surrounding villages. Established by the British-run, non-profit organization **Fundatia Adept** – themselves responsible for the promotion of rural development projects in the region – they organize a variety of excursions, from visiting a *stână* (sheepfold), to meeting local beekeepers and sampling delicious wildflower meadow honey.

Sighişoara

A forbidding silhouette of battlements and needle spires looms over **SIGHIŞOARA** (Schässburg to the Saxons and Segesvár to the Hungarians) as the sun descends behind the hills of the Târnava Mare valley; it seems fitting that this was the birthplace of Vlad Ţepeş, "The Impaler" – the man known to so many as **Dracula**. Visually archaic even by Romanian standards, Sighişoara is on UNESCO's World Heritage list and makes the perfect introduction to Transylvania, especially as the eastbound Dacia and Pannonia express trains stop here, making a convenient break in the long journey between Budapest and Bucharest.

During the last weekend of July, sometimes later, a lively **Medieval Arts Festival** takes over the streets of the citadel, starring costumed musicians and street performers. There's also an Inter-ethnic Cultural Festival in August. On **national holidays** a brass band often plays in Piaţa Cetăţii.

Arrival, information and accommodation

The **train and bus stations** are fifteen minutes' walk north of the centre, across the Târnava Mare river; outside the train station you'll see an antique locomotive that once ran on the Sibiu-Agnita-Sighişoara line. Run by the Romanian branch of the Mioritics Association – an organization dedicated to the development of regional cultural tourism – the terrific, and extremely well-informed, **tourist information centre** is down in a little cellar room opposite the Clock Tower. The **post office** (Mon–Fri 7am–8pm) is in the lower town on Str. 1 Decembrie, near the CFR office at Str. Octavian Goga 6 (Mon–Fri 8.30am–3.30pm). There's **Internet access** in the Catacombe (Mon–Fri 11am–7pm, Sat noon–4pm), in the basement of the House on the Rock, on Piaţa Cetăţii, and in the *Burg Hostel* (see p.178).

Accommodation

Over the last few years, numerous **hotels and pensions** have opened up in restored buildings in the citadel, while there are many more options to choose from in the lower town. There are several **hostels** near the station, which is where you'll also find people offering **private rooms** (around €10 per person),

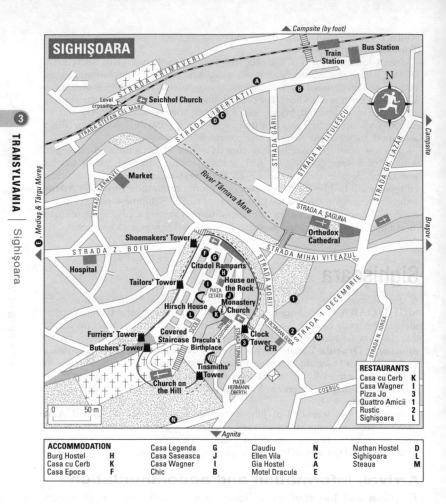

SIGHIȘOARA

Campsite (by foot)

Train Station
Bus Station

Level crossing — Seichhof Church

STRADA PRIMĂVERII

STRADA ȘTEFAN CEL MARE

STRADA LIBERTĂȚII

STRADA GĂRII

STRADA N. TITULESCU

STRADA GH. LAZĂR

Campsite

River Târnava Mare

Brașov

Market

STRADA ȚARNAVEI

STRADA A. ȘAGUNA

Orthodox Cathedral

Shoemakers' Tower

STRADA Z. BOIU

STRADA MIHAI VITEAZUL

Hospital

Citadel Ramparts

Tailors' Tower

House on the Rock
PIAȚA CETĂȚII
Monastery Church

Hirsch House

STRADA MORII

STRADA 1 DECEMBRIE

STRADA N. IORGA

Furriers' Tower
Butchers' Tower

Covered Staircase
Dracula's Birthplace

STRADA OCTAVIAN GOGA

Clock Tower
CFR

STRADA TURNULUI

Tinsmiths' Tower

Church on the Hill

PIAȚA HERMANN OBERTH

COȘBUC

0   50 m

RESTAURANTS	
Casa cu Cerb	K
Casa Wagner	I
Pizza Jo	3
Quattro Amicii	1
Rustic	2
Sighișoara	L

Agnita

ACCOMMODATION							
Burg Hostel	H	Casa Legenda	G	Claudiu	N	Nathan Hostel	D
Casa cu Cerb	K	Casa Saseasca	J	Ellen Vila	C	Sighișoara	L
Casa Epoca	F	Casa Wagner	I	Gia Hostel	A	Steaua	M
		Chic	B	Motel Dracula	E		

some of which will be in the citadel – one of these is Cristina Faur's lovely family house at Str. Cojocarilor 1 (☎0744/119 211, ✉cristinafaur2003@yahoo .de) – there's a dorm room sleeping six, plus en-suite doubles together with kitchen and laundry facilities. The *Dealul Gării* **campsite** (with cabanas and a restaurant; ☎0265/771 046, ℱ164 149) is on the hilltop overlooking the train station: turn left from the station, cross the tracks by a bridge, and then follow Str. Dealul Gării up the hill.

Youth hostels

Burg Hostel Str. Bastionului 4–6 ☎0265/778 489, ⓦwww.ibz.ro. Located in the citadel, this place has a wide range of rooms, from dorms with shared facilities to single, double and triple en suites. Laundry and breakfast available for an extra charge. ❶–❸
Ellen Villa Str. Libertății 10 ☎0265/776 402, ✉office@elenvillahostel.com. Very pleasant

hostel with a pretty, shaded garden just five minutes' walk from the stations; four- and eight-bed dorms, free Internet and laundry, but breakfast is extra. ❶
Gia Hostel Str. Libertății 41 ☎0265/772 486, ⓦwww.hostelgia.ro. Very accommodating place with clean and colourful four- to eight-bed dorms as well as singles, doubles and triples. No

breakfast, but there's a kitchen available for self-catering. ①–③

Nathan Villa Str. Libertatii 8 ☎ 0265/772 546, ⓦ www.nathansvilla.com. Right next door to the *Ellen Villa*, this is of a similar standard, but is a much more lively place; large dorms as well as some doubles. Breakfast included. ①–②

Hotels

🏃 **Casa cu Cerb** Str. Şcolii 1 ☎ 0265/774 625, ⓦ www.ar-messerschmitt-s.ro. Named after the painting of the stag on its corner, this classy, warm and welcoming hotel has ten beautifully furnished rooms, with wrought–iron beds, sofas and corner tubs. Breakfast is extra. First-class restaurant, too (see p.183). ⑥

🏃 **Casa Epoca** Str. Tâmplarilor 4 ☎ 0265/773 232, ⓦ www.casaepoca.com. This sublime pension, located on the quieter northern side of the citadel and housed inside a fifteenth-century Gothic building, oozes character; the original wooden doors and timber ceilings have been splendidly preserved, while furnishings are almost entirely fashioned from thick oak. There are even beds styled for kids. Breakfast is extra. ⑥

Casa Legenda Str. Bastionului 8 bis ☎ 0744/632 775, ⓦ www.legenda.ro. Along an alley just north of Piaţa Cetăţii, this low-key pension offers five very attractive, highly individual, themed rooms. Good value. ④–⑥

Casa Saseasca Piaţa Cetăţii 12 ☎ 0265/772 400, ⓔ office@casasaseasca.com. Another fine addition to the ranks of accommodation in the citadel, this lovely sky-blue pension has good-looking rooms,

its furnishings hand-painted with pretty floral motifs. ④

Casa Wagner Piaţa Cetăţii 7 ☎ 0265/506 014, ⓦ www.casa-wagner.com. A nicely restored hotel with antique decor – the rooms are large, comfortable and tastefully decorated, but the staff can be a bit surly. The restaurant's not bad either (see p.183). ⑥

Chic Str. Libertăţii 44 ☎ 0265/771 046, ⓕ 164 149. Simple place opposite the station, with clean and modernish rooms with and without bathrooms. The downstairs restaurant/bar can get a little noisy, though. ②–③

Claudiu Str. Ilarie Chendi 28 ☎ 0265/779 882, ⓦ www.hotel-claudiu.com. Lovely, restful little hotel just south of the citadel with colourfully furnished rooms and friendly staff. Guarded parking. ⑤

Motel Dracula ☎ 0265/772 211, ⓔ dracula .danes@email.ro. Six kilometres to the west of town, near the village of Daneş, this motel is better than the name might lead you to imagine, with a fabulous swimming pool and horse-riding on offer. ④

Sighişoara Str. Şcolii 4 ☎ 0265/771 000, ⓔ rezervare@sighisoarahotels.ro. Located in the former Bishop's Palace, the *Sighişoara* has four floors (there is no lift) of big, bright rooms (some with a/c), a very good restaurant and pleasant *terasa* at the rear (see p.183). ⑦

Steaua Str. 1 Decembrie 12 ☎ 0265/771 930. The town's longest-established hotel is, for the most part, a pretty desperate affair, but it does possess a handful of decently renovated rooms, some with TV and bathroom, and is very cheap. ③

The Town

Of overwhelming interest to most is the old town or **citadel**, which dominates the newer quarters from a rocky massif whose slopes support a jumble of ancient, leaning houses, their windows overlooking the steps leading up from

Draculaland

One of the juiciest scandals of recent years in Romania has been the project to build a **Draculaland theme park**, on the southwest edge of Sighişoara – complete with blood-red candyfloss, garlic-flavoured ices, amusement rides and a centre for vampirology research – with a kilometre-long chairlift linking it to the citadel. The project received immediate opposition, including from UNESCO, and even the Transylvanian Society of Dracula, which manages to tread the tightrope between academic accuracy and sensationalism, backtracked on its initial support and came out against it. To make matters worse, it turned out that Greenpeace Romania, which supposedly supported the park, was a fake, and that its so-called foreign investors were nothing more than paper-front companies. Above all, it was obvious that the sums were wrong and the whole thing was a scam. Rumours persist that the park may yet be built at Snagov (see p.99), Vlad Ţepeş's burial place.

▲ Sighişoara

Piaţa Hermann Oberth to the main gateway. Below here, the **lower town** holds little of note, though is useful for things of a practical nature.

Clock Tower

Above the gateway rises the mighty **Clock Tower** (Turnul cu Ceas), where each night as the bell chimes midnight one of seven wooden figures emerges from the belfry to gaze over the lower town; two figures, representing day and night, face the upper town. The tower was raised in the thirteenth and fourteenth centuries when Sighişoara became a free town controlled by craft guilds, each of which had to finance the construction of an eponymous bastion and defend it during wartime. The Clock Tower, however, was different in that it belonged to the public authority, serving as the city council headquarters. It was subsequently rebuilt after earthquakes and a fire in 1676. In 1894 the roof was replaced and covered in glazed shingle tiles and topped with a grand, onion-domed spire.

Originally a Saxon town known as Castrum Sex (Fort Six), Sighişoara grew rich on the proceeds of trade with Moldavia and Wallachia, as the **history museum** in the tower attests (Mon 10am–4.30pm, Tues–Fri 9am–6.30pm, Sat & Sun 9am–4.30pm). Most of the burghers were Magyar or Saxon, and the Romanians – or Vlachs as they were then called – became inferior citizens in Transylvanian towns following edicts passed in 1540. In what constitutes a curious and somewhat random collection – Gothic furniture, pharmaceutical objects and the like – the best display is about **Hermann Oberth**, one of the fathers of space travel, born in Sighişoara in 1894. In 1923, his book *The Rocket into Interplanetary Space* introduced the notions of a space station and a cosmic mirror. He worked in Berlin – launching his first rocket there in 1931 and teaching Werner von Braun – and at Peenemünde, on the V2 rocket, and in the 1950s and 1960s on the American equivalent. The main reason for climbing the tower, though, is for the marvellous **views** of the crooked lanes and orange-roofed houses below, and the thickly forested hills of the Târnava Mare valley out into the distance.

Sited under the Clock Tower stands an old **torture chamber** (same times as history museum), a simple, blackened room containing a handful of devilish implements – note the innocuous-looking ladder, upon which victims were tied and stretched while being roasted alive. A few paces across from the tower, on the corner with Str. Cositorarilor, there's a small **museum** of medieval weapons (same times as history museum).

Vlad's birthplace

In around 1431, in or near a three-storey house at Piaţa Muzeului 6, within the shadow of the old town's Clock Tower, a woman whose name is lost to posterity gave birth to a son called Vlad, who in later life earned the title of "The Impaler". Abroad, he's better known as **Dracula**, derived from Dracul or The Devil – referring to his father, **Vlad Dracul**, whom the Holy Roman Emperor Sigismund of Hungary made a knight of the Order of the Dragon in 1431. At this point, Vlad Dracul was merely the guard commander of the mountain passes into Wallachia, but in 1436 he secured the princely throne of Wallachia and moved his family to the court at Târgovişte. Vlad's privileged childhood there ended several years later, when he and his brother were sent by their father as hostages to the Turkish Sultan in Anatolia; there, as the brothers lived in daily fear of rape and of the silken cord with which the Ottomans strangled dignitaries, Vlad observed the Turks' use of terror, which he would later turn against them. Nowadays, his birthplace contains a tacky, and not particularly good, restaurant.

The rest of the citadel

To the north of the Clock Tower stands the Dominican or **Monastery Church** (Tues–Sat 10am–5pm, Sun 11.15am–3pm), now Lutheran, which has a stark, whitewashed interior hung with colourful carpets similar to those in the Black Church at Braşov, and an altar that resembles a wooden carpet-beater. The church was established by 1298, but was progressively rebuilt between 1484 and 1680. In summer, there's also an organ recital on Fridays at 6pm.

From Piaţa Muzeului, it's a short walk through to **Piaţa Cetăţii** (Citadel Square), the heart of the upper town and a particularly lively spot in the summer when a clutch of cafés spills out into the square. The square is surrounded by some fine, recently restored sixteenth-century buildings, such as the **Hirsch House** – more commonly known as the *Stag House* and now a fine pension and restaurant – and the House on the Rock opposite it, itself housing a super little café.

Heading south from Piaţa Cetăţii, up Strada şcolii, you reach an impressive, steep, covered wooden **staircase (the Scholars' Stairs)** consisting of 175 steps and 29 landings that date from 1642. At the top, the fine murals and wooden balconies of the Bergschule, or School on the Hill, built in 1619, are being restored. Dominating the hill is the main Saxon church, aptly named the **Church on the Hill** (daily 10am–5pm) – founded in 1345 and finished in 1525, it has been beautifully restored, with scraps of murals and memorial stones surviving in an otherwise bare interior, as well as three Gothic altars. Massively buttressed and with few windows, it is a cool and restful place. Opposite the Church on the Hill's door is the main entrance to the **Saxon cemetery** (daily 9am–4pm), a weed-choked mass of graves spilling over the hilltop beside the ruined citadel walls.

Of the citadel's original fourteen **towers**, named after the guilds responsible for their upkeep, nine survive, the most impressive being the hexagonal Shoemakers' Tower (Turnul Cizmarilor), the Tailors' Tower (Turnul Croitorilor) and the Tinsmiths' Tower (Turnul Cositorarilor); the last of these, best viewed from the gateway of the Pfarrhaus, below the Church on the Hill, has a fine wooden gallery and still shows traces of its last siege in 1704.

The lower town

The **lower town** has little of the character of the citadel, but there's a nice ambience around **Piaţa Hermann Oberth**, where townsfolk gather to consume coffee, beer or pizza, conversing in Romanian, Magyar and, occasionally, antiquated German. **Strada 1 Decembrie** has a fine array of Baroque facades, and there's a striking synagogue at Tache Ionescu 13. The **Mill quarter**, between the citadel and the river, was partially cleared before 1989 for redevelopment as a Civic Centre, and the area is still in limbo. Taking the footbridge over the Mare river, you come to the Romanian **Orthodox Cathedral**, built in the Byzantine style in 1937. Its gleaming white, multifaceted facade is in striking contrast to the dark interior.

The **market**, off Str. Târnavei, sells food daily but is particularly recommended on Wednesdays and Saturdays, when crafts such as carved wooden spoons are sold for far less than in the citadel's stalls.

Eating and drinking

The best **restaurants** are in the hotels and pensions. During the summer Piaţa Cetăţii is taken over by **cafés**, most of them linked to the various hotels and pensions surrounding the square. The best is the *International Café*, in the House on the Rock at Piaţa Cetăţii 8 – it's a great place for a snack, too, with a delicious range of home-made cookies, cakes and quiches available – their organically produced apple juice and spiced cider are great refreshers in hot weather. Hidden away at the southern end of the citadel, at Str. Cositorarilor 9, the lovely *Casa Cositorarilor* is the place to go to enjoy coffee and cake or a glass of wine in quieter surrounds.

Drinking options are rather more limited, and most people end up congregating in one of the several convivial pizzerias scattered around. The *Culture Pub*, in the basement of the *Burg Hostel*, has **live music** and stays open until 3am, and if you fancy a spot of dancing, there's the *Office*, beneath the Clock Tower, and the *City Club*, next to *Rustic* on Str. 1 Decembrie.

Restaurants

Casa cu Cerb Str. Şcolii 1. The *Stag House*, in the hotel of the same name, is the most enjoyable place in town to eat; high-class and beautifully presented international and Romanian food, gorgeous surrounds and impeccable service.

Casa Wagner Piaţa Cetăţii 7. Another polished restaurant, along the lines of *Casa cu Cerb*, this bright, handsome-looking place offers an upscale take on Romanian dishes.

Pizza Jo Piaţa Hermann Oberth. Lively, popular pizzeria situated on a raised terrace in-between the Clock Tower and the lower town. Good place to sup a beer, too.

Quattro Amicii Str. Octavian Goga 12. Next to the small scruffy field in the lower town, this is the best pizzeria going; the large terrace is a good venue from which to enjoy the crisp, oven-baked pizzas and fresh salads.

Rustic Str. 1 Decembrie 58. Low-key, enjoyable restaurant whose traditional Romanian food – such as *mittitei*, *sarmalute* and Transylvanian goulash – is very good. Non-smokers have one table secreted away behind a glass partition. Good breakfasts, too.

Sighişoara Str. Şcolii 4. As classy as the hotel it's located in, the Romanian food on offer here is top-notch. You can choose to eat in the large, green terrace or the very attractive cellar restaurant – the service is spot-on, too.

From Sighişoara to Sibiu

The main **approach to Sibiu** is to follow the Târnava Mare river west from Sighişoara. From the train or the DN14, you'll see water buffalo pulling wagons or wallowing in the river, watched by their drovers, and glimpse the towers of fortified Saxon churches in villages situated off the main road. The area south and west of Sighişoara is particularly good for leisurely exploration, its villages all accessible by bus from Sighişoara.

Mălâncrav

Around 7km west of Sighişoara, along the main DN14, a side road heads south through Laslea to **MĂLÂNCRAV** (Malmkrog), a picturesque little village nestling at the head of a narrow wooded valley. Its diminutive stone-built

---

The Kirchenburgenschutzverein

The **Kirchenburgenschutzverein** (the Union for Protection of the Fortified Churches) is a group dedicated to the preservation of the **fortified churches** and associated aspects of Saxon culture. In addition to raising money among the Saxon diaspora in Germany, it has set up a network of Gästehäuser or small **guesthouses** (❶), so that those interested in seeing the churches can contribute financially to the cause, and vice versa. These generally charge for a bunk or a bed and a basic bathroom; breakfast may be available by arrangement, but you shouldn't rely on it. The caretakers tend to be elderly and prefer pre-booked groups rather than independent travellers. The **coordinators** are Kilian Dörr, at the Lutheran parish house (Evangelisches Pfarrhaus) in Sibiu at Piaţa Huet 1 (☏0269/213 141, ✉evang.kirche@logon.ro), and Hugo Schneider, at Str. Gh. Doja 23 in Mediaş (☏0269/828 605); there are also local contacts, listed with the villages in question. An excellent and inexpensive **guide** to the Gästehäuser and to walks in the area south of Mediaş can be bought at the parish houses of Sibiu and Mediaş.

church, idyllically set on a small hillock, was built in the late fourteenth century and surrounded by low walls in the fifteenth century; it is noted for its altarpiece (*c*.1520) and lovely frescoes from the late fourteenth century and the second half of the fifteenth century – the most outstanding of these, on the north wall, depict the *Genesis* and the *Life of Christ*. The church is usually shut, but the key can be obtained from no. 140, on the main street just below. Across from the church stands a seventeenth-century Hungarian **manor house**, an unusual presence given that it was uncommon for such buildings to be found in Saxon villages at that time. The house is currently being renovated with funds donated by HRH the Prince of Wales (a patron of the Eminescu Trust), the idea being that it will eventually serve as a guesthouse, though probably for groups only. The Mihai Eminescu Trust does, however, have a **guesthouse** at no. 139 (see p.176 for booking details), as well as an organic orchard with ancient varieties of apple, pear, plum and walnut, producing wonderful apple juice.

Biertan

Continuing west along the DN14, a turning at **Şaros pe Târnave**, 26km from Sighişoara, leads to **BIERTAN** (Birthälm); if you're travelling by train, you'll need to get off at Mediaş for a local bus to Biertan; otherwise, it should cost no more than €10 to take a taxi from Sighişoara. The best approach to the village, however, is the four-hour hike through fields and wooded ridges from Brateiu (Pretai), the first rail halt east of Mediaş, via the tiny villages of Aţel (Hetzeldorf) and Dupuş (Tobsdorf), both with fortified churches; Aţel has a functional Gästehaus (☎0269/204 865, ext 114; ❶) should you want to stop over.

Biertan itself contains the best known of all the Saxon **fortified churches** (Mon–Sat 10am–7pm, Sun 9–11am & 2–7pm), set high on a hill within two-and-a-half rings of walls linked by a splendid covered staircase, not dissimilar to the one in Sighişoara (see p.182). Completed as late as 1522 on the site of a Catholic basilica, and now on UNESCO's World Heritage list, this was the seat of the Lutheran bishops from 1572 to 1867, and their fine upright gravestones can be seen inside the Bishops' Tower – one of the church's seven towers. The interior is a classic example of a late-Gothic hall church, with some superb masonry and intricate stone-ribbed vaulting. Other notable features are the altarpiece with a classic triptych dated 1483–1515; the sacristy door, with an extraordinary locking mechanism comprising no fewer than nineteen locks, and a room where couples wanting to divorce were supposedly shut up together for two weeks. Once done with the church, it's worth a wander around this pretty village, which has more or less retained its medieval layout. There are some particularly fine Baroque houses around the main square, with the oldest houses located on the eastern side.

There's some **accommodation** in Biertan, the most restful place being the *Casa Dornröschen* (☎0269/868 293, ✉cucausbuc@gmail.com; ❸), which is actually within the church grounds – it's down the path beginning by the archway at the church entrance. There are further guesthouses on Str. 1 Decembrie, including *Pension Otto* at no. 29 (☎0742/352 368; ❷). Just below the church, the medieval themed *Unglerus* **restaurant** is good for a hearty meal, though it's rather group-oriented. Homemade cheese can be bought at the private dairy (*lăptărie*) on the Copşa Mare road, while good white wine costs next to nothing at the factory set back from the Richiş road. The village is the site of the **Sachsentreffen** or Saxon Meeting, when many Saxons return from Germany to meet up, drink and dance on the second or third Saturday of September.

Mediaş

The main town between Sighişoara and Sibiu is **MEDIAŞ** (Mediasch), which, despite being home to the tanneries and chemical works fed by the Târnava Mare valley's methane reserves, gets more attractive the further in you venture. Originally an Iron Age and then a Roman settlement, Mediaş was a predominantly Saxon town for many centuries, walled and with gate towers, two of which remain on Str. Cloşca, east of the bus station. After 1918, it began to develop an industrial and Romanian character, stemming from political changes after World War I and the construction here of Transylvania's first gas pipeline.

From the **train station** on Str. Unirii, turn right to reach the **bus station**, a few minutes' walk away, opposite the synagogue; from here, head left up Str. Pompierilor and then take a right down Str. Roth to the town centre, **Piaţa Regele Ferdinand I**, an attractive triangular space ringed by brightly painted two-storey town houses and pavement cafés.

Just up from the square, along Str. Johannes Honterus, is the fifteenth-century **Evangelical Church of St. Margaret**, its seventy-metre bell tower slightly askew; the church (daily 10am–3pm) is a true citadel, surrounded by store rooms, high ramparts and towers (one of which, the Tailors' Tower, served as a jail for Vlad the Impaler in 1467). The church interior is one of the region's most ornamented, with Anatolian carpets, superbly preserved frescoes, a colourful Baroque organ (used for recitals at 7pm on Mondays from June to Sept), and two superb Gothic altarpieces, including a Crucifixion with a view of Vienna painted in 1474 to 1479. If the church is closed, pop over to the parish office at the top of the courtyard. The **Schuller House** (Schullerhaus), on the same square at no. 25, was built in 1588 and once housed the Transylvanian Diet but now serves as a guesthouse (see below). For a limited insight into the history of the town, and a better wildlife display, visit the **town museum** (Tues–Sun 9am–5pm) in a former monastery east of the centre at Str. Mihai Viteazul 46.

There's some good **accommodation** in town, by far the best of which is the *Hotel Traube*, Piaţa Regele Ferdinand I 16 (℡0269/844 898, ℮traube@dafora .ro; ❼) – whose fantastically comfortable rooms feature an appealing mix of wrought-iron and handcrafted wooden furnishings; in addition, there's the small but pleasant *Select*, 50m away at Str. Petófi 3 (℡0269/834 874, ℻835 743; ❹), and there are also simple but clean rooms in the friendly *Schullerhaus*, Piaţa Regele Ferdinand I 25 (℡0269/831 347, ℻832 390; ❸). **Internet** access is available at *Intim*, near the Schullerhaus. Buses run from the bus station to Agnita, Sibiu and Târgu Mureş, and to all the surrounding villages. Some especially picturesque villages with fortified churches lie along the road to Agnita, notably **Moşna** (Meschen), whose church, built in 1491, has a fifty-metre tower.

Copşa Mică and Ocna Sibiului

Filthy **COPŞA MICĂ** (Kleinkopisch), 13km west of Mediaş, is probably Romania's most polluted town – and if you're unlucky with connections you may have to change trains for Sibiu here rather than in Mediaş. Life expectancy here is nine years below the national average.

There are good fortified churches in **Valea Viilor** (Wurmloch, 4km south of Copşa Mică), **Axente Sever** (Frauendorf) and **Agârbiciu** (Arbegen) – these last two visible just east of their rail halts. It's possible to follow easy hiking trails from Agârbiciu to Valea Viilor and Moşna to Biertan. Otherwise, there's little worth stopping for en route to Sibiu other than **OCNA SIBIULUI** (Salzburg), a bathing resort with fizzy, salty water, which bubbles up in four lakes formed in abandoned salt-workings. The grand fin-de-siècle spa building is very slowly being restored. The nearest train stop to the spa is Băile Ocna Sibiului, 2km north of Ocna Sibiului station proper, with a decent **campsite** adjacent.

Sibiu

"I rubbed my eyes in amazement," wrote Walter Starkie of **SIBIU** in 1929. "The town where I found myself did not seem to be in Transylvania, for it had no Romanian or Hungarian characteristics: the narrow streets and old gabled houses made me think of Nuremberg." Nowadays, the illusion is harder to sustain, in a city surrounded by high-rise suburbs and virtually abandoned by the Saxons themselves, but the old town is still a startling sight, with many of its houses painted sky blue, red, apricot or pea green, and home to some of Romania's best museums. Split into a **historic centre** and a lower **new town**, Sibiu has many fine old **churches**, as well as the remains of the original **Saxon**

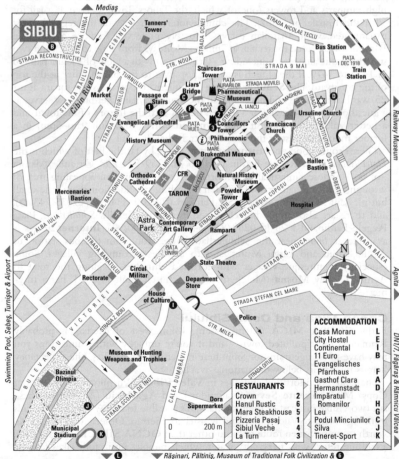

ACCOMMODATION

Casa Moraru	L
City Hostel	E
Continental	I
11 Euro	B
Evangelisches Pfarrhaus	F
Gasthof Clara	A
Hermannstadt	D
Împăratul Romanilor	H
Leu	G
Podul Minciunilor	C
Silva	J
Tineret-Sport	K

RESTAURANTS

Crown	2
Hanul Rustic	6
Mara Steakhouse	5
Pizzeria Pasaj	1
Sibiul Veche	4
La Turn	3

Bastions that formed the town's fortifications. The town's **pottery fair** is held on the first weekend of September.

Some history

Sibiu, known in German as Hermannstadt and in Hungarian as Nagyszeben, was founded in the 1190s and grew to be the chief city of the **Transylvanian Saxons**. Clannish, hard working and thrifty, its merchants dominated trade between Transylvania and Wallachia by the Olt gorge route, and by 1367 formed exclusive guilds under royal charter. They were envied by others and knew it; their literature and proverbs are marked by admonitions to beware of outsiders, and Sibiu's plethora of fortifications testifies to their historical caution. As early as 1241 their first citadel was destroyed by the Tatars, leaving only a hundred survivors; the townsfolk surrounded themselves with three rings of walls by 1350 and a fourth (which included the new lower town) in 1452. Behind these defences, mighty enough to repel the Turks three times, the people of Sibiu linked their buildings and streets with tunnels and gateways, and set heavily grated windows to cover the stairways and corners where they might ambush intruders. Parts of the walls were demolished, and new gateways opened up in the nineteenth century, but much remains. Now, the wheel has turned, and Sibiu has stronger trading links with Germany than any other Transylvanian town, and has even elected a Saxon mayor.

Arrival and information

Sibiu's **bus and train stations** are next to each other on the northeast side of town. The rail service is poor, but bus services are increasingly taking up the strain, reaching as far afield as Bucharest, Cluj, Constanţa and Timişoara. To reach the centre, cross Piaţa 1 Decembrie 1918 (still generally known as Piaţa Gării) and follow Str. General Magheru up the hill. The **airport** (℡0269/229 161) is on the western edge of town, served by buses #11 and #20 or trolley bus #T8; a taxi will cost around €5.

The **tourist information office** is in the town hall on the north side of Piaţa Mare (Mon–Fri 9am–5pm, Sat 9am–1pm; ℡0269/208 913, ⊛www.sibiu .ro), though an equally good source of information and help is Kultours, Piaţa Mică 16 (daily 9am–7pm; ℡0269/216 854, ⊛www.kultours.ro) – they offer city sightseeing tours, as well as city audio guides (€8–14), and have **bikes for hire** (€12/day). The **Lutheran Pfarrhaus**, Piaţa Huet 1 (℡0269/211 203), sells a leaflet (currently in German only, with summaries in English) describing the town's new Kulturweg circuit of information signs, as well as a book listing accommodation and walks in the Saxon villages to the north.

Accommodation

Sibiu has a decent, if largely uninspiring, range of **hotels** and **guesthouses** to choose from, most of which are fairly central. The *City Hostel* (℡0269/216 445, ⊛www.hostelsibiu.ro; ❶), in a fabulous location at Piaţa Mică 26, has three large, bright dorms, laundry facilities and Internet access – breakfast is not included but there is a kitchen. There's a good-quality **campsite** (℡0269/214 022, ℻228 777) in the Dumbrava forest 4km to the south (trolley bus #T1 from the train station), with the *Parc Dumbrava* **motel** next door (same contact details as the campsite; ❹), and a former **han**, now upgraded to the three-star *Palace Dumbrava* (℡0269/218 086; ❺), nearby. In the same direction (bus #5) the well-run *Valea Aurie* cabana (℡0269/242 696; ❸) has a good restaurant.

Casa Moraru Str. A. Vlahuță 11A ☎0269/216 291, ☏215 490. A private hotel with good facilities, including fitted hair dryers and alarm clocks in all rooms, a good restaurant and bar, plus a sauna and pool. ❼

Continental Calea Dumbrăvii 2 ☎0269/218 100, ✉reservation@continentalhotels.ro. High-end, but really rather bland, chain hotel with all the stock comforts. ❽

11 Euro Tudor Vladimirescu 2 ☎0269/222 041, ✉contact@11euro.ro. Daftly named, unmissable yellow and orange brick building in a quiet spot across from the Cibin River; it's a decent place, with two categories of room, the only difference between them being that some rooms have been refurbished. ❷–❹

Evangelisches Pfarrhaus Piața Huet 1 ☎0269/0269/211 203, ✉gast@evang.ro. The Lutheran parish house provides clean, simple hostel-style accommodation. Breakfast is not available. ❸

Gasthof Clara Str. Răului 24 ☎0269/222 914, ⊕www.gasthofclara.ro. Across the Cibin River from the market, identifiable by its fake half-timbering, this is a pleasant, restful small hotel with six rooms, all with Wi-Fi. ❼

Hermannstadt Str. Blănarilor 13 ☎0269/212 368, ⊕www.pensiuneahermannstadt-sibiu.ro. The only

place in the vicinity of the station (but also very close to the centre), this breezy little place has modern, a/c rooms. Breakfast is extra. ❸

Împăratul Romanilor Str. Bălcescu 4 ☎0269/216 500, ✉office@imparatulromanilor.ro. The city's most opulent, and expensive, hotel, which also benefits from a great location – yet still feels somewhat underwhelming. ❽

Leu Str. Moș Ion Roată 6 ☎0269/218 392, ☏213 975. Secreted away at the bottom of the "Passage of Stairs", this simple, hostel-style pension has double and triple en-suite rooms, all with TV. ❸

Podul Minciunilor Str. Azilului 1 ☎0269/217 259, ⊕www.ela-hotels.ro. The "Liars' Bridge" guesthouse, just down from the bridge and first on the left, is a friendly, old-fashioned place with six simple en-suite rooms. Breakfast not available. ❹

Silva Aleea Eminescu 1 ☎0269/243 985, ⊕www.hotelsilvasibiu.com. Pleasant, welcoming hotel in an agreeable parkside location, with spacious well-furnished rooms. ❼

Tineret-Sport Str. Octavian Goga 2 ☎0269/233 673. Not exactly the best location – next to the football stadium – but the rooms are relatively modern, with bathroom and TV, and cheap. Breakfast is extra. ❸

The Old Town

The old town centres on three conjoined squares – the **Piața Mare** (Grosser Ring), the **Piața Mică** (Kleiner Ring) and the **Piața Huet** (Huetplatz). Heading south from the train station, along Strada Magheru (Sporergasse), you'll pass an old **synagogue** (which is still used in the summer by Sibiu's remaining handful of Jews) and the **Ursuline church** (1474–78) at the junction with Str. Avram Iancu and now shared by Greco-Catholic and Roman Catholic congregations. One block south, on Str. Șelarilor, is the **Franciscan church**, also dating from the fifteenth century, although it was rebuilt in the Baroque style after its roof collapsed in 1776. Forking right onto Str. Avram Iancu brings you to no. 16, one of the oldest houses in town, built in the first half of the fourteenth century and now being restored.

Piața Mare

Traditionally the hub of public life, the resplendent-looking **Piața Mare** (Large Square) is surrounded by the renovated premises of sixteenth- and seventeenth-century merchants, whose acumen and thrift were proverbial. Its north side is dominated by a Roman Catholic church (1726–33); to its left, at Piața Mare 5, the eighteenth-century **Brukenthal Palace** was the home of Samuel von Brukenthal (see box, p.190), the imperial governor of Transylvania from 1777 to 1787. Built between 1778 and 1785 by a Viennese architect in a refined Late Baroque style, the palace now houses Transylvania's finest art collection, partly assembled by von Brukenthal himself and opened to the public in 1817, three years before the Louvre in Paris. Before you enter, take a look up at the splendid portal, dating from 1777 and incorporating a gilded coat of arms (in the centre) and two large urns atop the side pillars.

As well as an extensive array of Romanian and Western art, the **Brukenthal Museum** (Muzeul Brukenthal; Tues–Sun: May–Oct 10am–6pm, Nov–April 11am–5pm; €5) includes fifteenth- and sixteenth-century Transylvanian wooden religious sculptures and eighteenth-century Romanian icons. While the first floor is something of a disappointment – gloomy family portraits, French and German illustrated bibles and suchlike – the real treasures lie on the second floor, namely the masterpieces; beautifully presented in spotlit glass cases, the chief paintings are Antonello de Messini's *The Crucifixion*, Pieter Brueghel's *Massacre of the Innnocents*, and the collection's signature piece, Jan van Eyck's exquisite *Man in Blue Turban*.

Heading from here towards Piaţa Huet, you'll pass near the **History Museum** (same hours), housed in the Old City Hall (Primăria Veche; 1470–91) at Str. Mitropoliei 2 (Fleischergasse); the arcaded courtyard is worth a look even if you choose not to go inside to view the interesting exhibits on local history or the collection of silverware.

Piaţa Huet and Piaţa Mică

In the **Piaţa Huet**, the massive **Evangelical Cathedral** (daily: summer 9am–8pm, winter 9am–3pm), built in three phases between 1320 and 1520, dominates its neighbours, the Saxons' Brukenthal Gymnasium (Grammar School; 1782) and Pfarrhaus (Parish House; 1502) – confirming the town's pre-eminence as a centre of the Lutheran faith. There's a fresco of the *Crucifixion* (1445) by Johannes von Rosenau on the north wall of the choir, showing Italian and Flemish influences, and the **tomb of Mihnea the Bad**, Dracula's son, is in the crypt; Mihnea was voivode of Wallachia for just three years before being stabbed to death in 1510 outside the cathedral after attending Mass (the building was still a Catholic place of worship at that time). There's also a fine collection of funerary monuments here, including a well-tended memorial to the dead of World War I. The cathedral **tower** (visits Mon–Sat noon & 4pm) is worth the climb for the expansive views it gives over the city. By the cathedral, an alley leads to the thirteenth-century **Passage of Stairs** (Pasajul Scărilor), which descends into the lower town overshadowed by arches and the medieval citadel wall. The cathedral houses Romania's largest church organ, and in summer there's a regular programme of concerts – check the posters outside or contact the Pfarrhaus just across the way.

From Piaţa Huet it's a short hop into **Piaţa Mică (Small Square)**, where a miniature urban canyon runs down from the northwest corner under the elegant wrought-iron Iron Bridge (Podul de Fier). Dating from 1859, this bridge is nicknamed the **Liars' Bridge** (Podul Minciunilor), the story being that if someone tells a lie while standing on it the bridge will collapse. Ceauşescu managed to give a speech from it and survive, although he disliked the town and never returned.

By the bridge, at Piaţa Mică 21, stands the arcaded **House of the Butchers' Guild** (Fleischerhalle), a handsome, mint-green structure now hosting temporary art exhibitions. On the eastern side of the square, at no. 26, the **Pharmaceutical Museum** (Muzeul Farmacie; Tues–Sun 10am–6pm) preserves the interior of an ancient pharmacy – beautiful walnut carved fittings of the shop front and a laboratory stuffed with flutes, scales and copper pans – and also commemorates Samuel Hahnemann, founder of homeopathy, who lived in Sibiu in the 1770s (see box, p.190). The Casa Hermes (Hermeshaus), at no. 11, houses the **Franz Binder Museum of Ethnology** (Muzeul de Etnografie Universale Franz Binder; Tues–Sun 10am–6pm), based on the collection of Franz Binder (1820–75), who spent thirty years in Africa as

The roots of homeopathy

Baron **Samuel von Brukenthal**'s achievements in his time as governor of Transylvania were many, but his role in the development of **homeopathy** was the widest-ranging and ultimately most important.

It was Brukenthal who paid for **Samuel Hahnemann** (1755–1843) to complete his medical degree in Germany and who then brought him to Sibiu to be his private doctor. In recompense, Hahnemann spent the best part of two years (1777–79) cataloguing Brukenthal's immense library of 280,000 books, including a large collection of rare manuscripts and books by medieval alchemists and physicians such as Paracelsus and Rumelius; it was his study of these authors that laid the basis of his lifetime's work.

In 1779, Hahnemann returned to Germany, married and had children – although desperately poor, he pursued his studies, driven on by his dissatisfaction with the conventional medicine that he was obliged to practise at the time, while gradually formulating his own theories. Although homeopathy was eventually marginalized by conventional (allopathic) medicine, by the 1870s this had itself absorbed key homeo-pathic principles, such as the abandonment of complex mixtures of drugs and the adoption of theories of disease based upon infectious agents.

In recent times, Romania was one of the first countries to legitimize homeopathy, due to the shortage of medicines and medical equipment under Ceauşescu. From 1995 only qualified doctors were allowed to practise homeopathy (although those already registered as homeopaths were permitted to continue).

a merchant and plant collector – as well as items from Africa, Binder garnered all manner of objects from far-flung places, such as Chinese vases and Japanese statuettes. At the rear of the Casa Hermes, the **Emil Sigerus Museum of Saxon Ethnography** on Piaţa Huet (Tues–Sun 10am–6pm) has a rather limited collection of household goods. To get back to Piaţa Mare from Piaţa Mică, cut through the gate below the **Councillors' Tower** (Turnul Sfatului; daily 10am–6pm), built in the early thirteenth century as part of the city's second ring of fortifications, and rebuilt in 1588; climb the 111 steps and you'll be rewarded with fine **views** of the city.

Alternatively, a passageway leads down through the **Staircase Tower** (Fingerlingsstiege) at Piaţa Mică 24 via Piaţa Aurarilor to Str. Movilei, a street pockmarked with medieval windows, doorways and turrets. Down in the rambling lower town northwest of the squares are the octagonal brick **Tanners' Tower** (Turnul Pielarilor), on Str. Pulberăriei, reached via Str. Valea Mare, and a busy food **market** beside the river on Piaţa Cibin – the site of the first settlement in Sibiu.

Over to the east, near the train station, the enjoyable **Railway Museum** (Muzeul Locomotivei; daily 8am–8pm) is an open-air collection of more than thirty steam locomotives, as well as snow ploughs and steam cranes – rail enthusiasts will love it. To get there, turn left from the station, ascend to the road bridge, cross the tracks and descend the steps to the right, turning left along Str. Dorobanţilor at the bottom; after 300m or so (at house no. 26), turn sharp right to the rail tracks and go through the arch to the left.

The New Town

In Saxon times, Sibiu's promenade was the Heltauergasse, now **Strada Bălcescu**, which heads south from Piaţa Mare to Piaţa Unirii, and this is still the heart of the modern city. At the northern end of the street is Sibiu's oldest hotel, the **Împăratul Romanilor**, still recognizable as the grand establishment once patronized by the likes of Liszt, Johann Strauss and Eminescu. The design of the hotel, which dates from 1895, was a reaction against the militaristic architecture that had previously dominated the town; this can be seen to the southeast in the three rows of **ramparts and bastions** on either side of B-dul. Coposu, where three mighty **towers** were built in the late fourteenth century and manned by contingents of the Carpenters', Potters' and Arquebusiers' (later the Drapers') guilds. To the east, the **Powder Tower** (Pulverturm) was converted to a theatre in 1788 and is slowly being restored to this role. Just beyond it, at Str. Cetății 1, the **Natural History Museum** (Tues–Sun 9am–5pm) has the standard collection of stuffed wildlife. The **Haller Bastion** (1552) at the northern end of Str. Cetății, and the Soldisch or **Mercenaries' Bastion** (the last to be built, in 1627) further west on Str. Bastionului also survive.

Sibiu developed as a centre of intellectual and cultural life during the nineteenth century, and the first congress of **ASTRA** – The Association for the Propagation of Romanian Culture in Transylvania – was held in October 1861 on **Strada Mitropoliei**, a street east of the Mercenaries' Bastion that is full of significance for Romanian nationalists. No. 19 was the home of Zaharia Boiu (1834–1903), poet and founder of the first Romanian-language school in Sibiu, while Avram Iancu and Mihai Eminescu both stayed in houses here. Furthermore, opposite the **post office** is the **Orthodox Cathedral** (1902–06), which was based on the Aya Sofya in Istanbul and is embellished with all manner of neo-Byzantine flourishes and frescoes, plus mosaics from Munich. South of the cathedral is the **ASTRA Park**, lined with busts of Romanian worthies. In 1905, ASTRA opened a library and museum overlooking the park in a fine building at Str. Lupaş 5; from here, Str. Lupaş takes you east to Piaţa Unirii. A block east from the park, at Tribunei 12, you'll find the Brukenthal Museum's **Contemporary Art Gallery**.

Two blocks southwest of Piaţa Unirii, at Str. Şcoala de Înot 4, the **Museum of Hunting Weapons and Trophies** (Tues–Sun 10am–5pm), once the home of a Habsburg general, still shelters his collection of weapons, medals and stuffed animals, and is worth a brief visit.

Outside the centre

Southwest of the centre along Calea Dumbrăvii (trolley bus #T1 from the train station), on the edge of the Dumbrava Forest, the superb **Museum of Traditional Folk Civilization** (daily: May–Oct 10am–8pm, Nov–April 10am–6pm; €5) is the best open-air museum in Romania. Set against a mountain backdrop, it offers a fantastic insight into Romanian rural life, comprising an ensemble of more than 350 structures. Divided up into themed areas, highlights include the many neatly thatched or wooden-roofed homesteads with their adjoining workshops (such as blacksmiths', wheelwrights', weavers' and potters'), several Dutch-style windmills, and two wooden churches, both of which are still functioning. You'll also notice scattered around numerous *troiţas*, stone crosses used as places of worship in those villages where no church existed. It's worth buying the excellent guiding leaflet.

The grounds of the museum are the venue for a couple of annual **festivals**, namely, the Craftsmen's Fair in mid-August (usually around the 15th) and, in September, the Festival of National Traditions, featuring folk costumes from the country's multifarious regions, music, dance and much merriment. There's also an excellent little **information office** (daily 9am–3pm) in one of the converted huts near the entrance, and a good **restaurant** (see p.192).

About 1km back along the road to Sibiu is the city **zoo** (daily 9am–7pm), a predictably dispiriting affair, with brown bear, wolves and tigers pacing nervously about their grubby cages. On the adjoining lake you can rent pedaloes and rowing boats (€2.50/30min).

Bus #8, from the bridge south of the train station on B-dul. Coposu, takes you to **Turnişor**, where it will drop you outside the *Pfarrhaus* at Str. Bielz 62 (Kirchgasse). To Romanians, Turnişor is simply a suburb of Sibiu, but to its German populace it's a distinct village, Neppendorf. Originally Saxon, its population was boosted in the eighteenth century by an infusion of Austrian Protestants, expelled by their Catholic neighbours. Although the two groups never mixed in other villages throughout the region, here the Saxons and Landler intermarried – yet they are still seated separately in the church, with Landler women on one side of the nave and Saxon women on the other. The **church** was never fortified – the villagers fled to Sibiu when the Turks came to burn their settlement in 1493 – but the interior is typical of Saxon village churches, with lovely paintings on the gallery, and a Turkish rug; ask at the *Pfarrhaus* for the key. There's also an excellent **museum** in the north transept, mapping the history of the village, with lots of old photos and plenty of text (all in German). Today, there are only about 200 Germans in Turnişor, compared to some 4000 before World War II. Visible from trains to the north of Turnişor station is an amazing Gypsy palace, resembling a Japanese castle with multiple Gothic spikes.

Eating and drinking

While there are plenty of them, Sibiu's **restaurants** are not particularly varied and there's often little to distinguish one from another. For faster food, there's *Papa Giulio's*, Piaţa Mare 5, a super little takeout place offering hot sandwiches and pizza slices, with several *rotisseries* serving roast chicken.

There's a healthy spread of places to **drink** on the two main squares, **Piaţa Mare** and **Piaţa Mică**, though the latter has the better ones, such as *Atrium* at no. 16. The squares aside, the greatest concentration of cafés and bars is along **Strada Bălcescu**, most of which have convivial *terasas* for daytime or evening drinking. At no. 11, the smart and relaxing *Turabot Café* has comfy red chairs and huge bay windows through which to people-watch. For a quiet cup of tea, make your way to *Teea*, at General Magheru 10. Away from here, decent venues include the vaguely bohemian *Art Café*, beneath the Philharmonic at Str. Filarmonicii 2, which has occasional jazz gigs; and *Trei Stejari*, Str. Fabricii 2, where big jugs of beer on the enormous rambling *terasa* are the order of the day, thanks to the brewery next door. Best of all is the cute and classy *Imperium Pub*, Str. Bălcescu 24, where regular evenings of quality jazz, piano and stand-up will ensure a most enjoyable evening. **Other bars** which stay open later include *Chill Out*, Piaţa Mică 23 (playing house and techno music to a partly gay crowd until 6am), and *Liquid*, behind the Dumbrava department store at Str. Dobrun 1 – here, you'll find a diverse programme of club nights and musical happenings.

Restaurants

Crown Piaţa Mică 29. Comfortable, cosy and inexpensive restaurant with a bright *terasa* overlooking the square; the menu also includes a hearty meat and cheese snack plate (€5). Daily 11am–11pm.

Hanul Rustic Museum of Traditional Folk Civilization. This place does a roaring trade with locals and tourists alike; the entrance is on the Răşinari road, about 1km or so beyond the museum's main entrance (see p.191). Daily noon–midnight.

Mara Steakhouse Str. Bălcescu 21. Just about the best restaurant along this busy street, this pleasingly simple and convivial joint also has Romanian staples, including game (deer, wild boar and bear). Decent breakfast menu, too. Daily 10am–midnight.

Pizzeria Pasaj Str. Turnului 3. Sprightly pizzeria with a cool brick interior, offering a varied selection of green salads, pizzas and spaghetti dishes, as well as chicken and beef options. Good vegetarian possibilities, too. Daily noon–midnight.

Sibiul Veche Str. Papiu Ilarian 3. Located just off Str. Bălcescu, this claustrophobic *crama*, with walls strewn with objects from the region, offers some of the most authentic Romanian food (*sarmale*, *mamaliga*) in town. As befits its rather touristic bent, there's regular live folk music. Daily noon–midnight.

La Turn Piața Mare 1. Nothing out of the ordinary, but the setting, in a quiet cobbled corner next to the Councillors' Tower, and the juicy mixed grills, makes a visit worthwhile. Daily 11am–midnight.

Entertainment

Classical concerts are held in the House of Culture on Str. Şaguna and the adjacent Army House (Cercul Militar; B-dul.Victoriei 3), as well as in the **state theatre** at B-dul. Corneliu Coposu 2 (☎0269/217 577); tickets can be bought at the Agenţie Teatrala, Str. Bălcescu 17 (Mon–Fri 11am–7pm, Sat 11am–3pm), or at the theatre one hour prior to performances.

Sibiu has one of the liveliest and most varied **festival** rosters in Romania. The best of the year's gatherings is the superb **International Theatre Festival**, usually beginning at the end of May and lasting around two weeks – the focal point is an open-air stage on Piața Mare upon which there are nightly happenings (classical, rock and world music concerts, contemporary dance), with a multitude of different events (installations, films, plays and photographic/art exhibitions) taking place on the other squares and in various venues around town. Elsewhere, there's a **Jazz Festival** at the beginning of May and, in October, the **International Festival of Documentary Film and Anthropology**.

Shopping

While not as good as Braşov or Cluj, Sibiu can meet most shoppers' needs, usually on Str. Bălcescu: the best for imported foodstuffs is Nic at no. 30; slide film is available at Foto Universal, no. 17. The main **department store**, the Dumbrava (Mon–Fri 8am–8pm, Sat 9am–2pm), is on the far side of Piața Unirii, opposite the *Continental* hotel. There are two food **markets**, Piața Cibin, by the river on Str. Turnului, and Piața Teatrului, by the theatre on B-dul. Coposu. For outdoor gear, go to Action Sports, Str. Avram Iancu 25; for crafts, it's best to head out to the open-air museum south of town (see p.191). The Metro cash-and-carry is at Şoseaua Alba Iulia 79A (Mon–Sat 6am–9pm, Sun 8am–6pm).

The excellent Schiller bookshop, Piața Mare 7 (Mon–Fri 10am–7pm, Sat 10am–6pm, Sun 11.30am–6pm), sells **maps and guides** (including the authoritative Fabini series on Saxon churches), postcards, calendars, and books (many in German) on Transylvanian architecture and culture. The Humanitas bookshop, Str. Bălcescu 16 (Mon–Sat 10am–7pm, Sun 11am–5pm), also has a good stock of maps and guides, as well as books on Romania in English.

Listings

Airlines TAROM, Str. Bălcescu 10 (Mon–Fri 9am–5pm; ☎0269/211 157).

Banks and exchange Prima, Str. Cetății 1, and Olt Vegas and TransEuropa, on Str. Bălcescu, offer good rates for cash. IDM, Str. Papiu Ilarian 12 (off Str. Bălcescu) and Piața Mică 9, accepts credit cards and travellers' cheques, but at poor rates.

Buses Services to Germany and elsewhere in Western Europe are operated by: AtlasSib, Str. Tractorului 14 (☎0269/229 209 or 224 101, ⓦwww.atlassib.ro) and c/o the agency at the *Hotel Bulevard* (☎&ⓕ0269/218 125); Amad Turistik, Calea Poplăcii 58 (☎0269/212 227, ⓕ233 127) and Piața Mare 6 (☎0269/216 997);

Andronik Reisen, Str. Blănarilor 2 (at Str. 9 Mai, opposite the station); Double-T, Str. Bălcescu 1 (☎0269/217 497); Kessler, Str. Bieltz 22 (☎0269/228 118, 🖷229 011) and Str. Bălcescu 6 (☎0269/243 820); Mihu Reisen, Şelimbăr (☎0269/560 127); Pletl, Str. Brukenthal (☎0269/228 007); Touring-Eurolines, B-dul. Milea 13 (☎0269/212 248, 🖷sibiu @eurolines.ro); and TransEuropa, Str. Bălcescu 19 (☎0269/211 296, 🖷rezervari@transeuropa.ro) and Str. Fraţii Grachi 5 (☎0269/431123). Tickets to Italy with Ognivia can be booked at the Prima agency, Str. Cetăţii 1.

Car rental Elite, Str.Bălcescu 22 (☎&🖷0269/228 826 or 0721/219 196); Toro, Str. Filarmonicii 5 (☎0269/232 237 or 0745/514 441, 🖳www .tororent.ro).

Hospital On B-dul. Spitalelor, opposite the Haller Bastion.

Internet access There's 24hr Internet access at Str. Bălcescu 27 and 52. Others include Click Internet Café, Str. Ocnei 13, and Silence Internet Café, Mitropoliei 27 (daily 10am–10pm).

Libraries The British Council library is administered by the central library (Biblioteca Centrala) at the University Lucian Blaga, B-dul. Victoriei 10 (☎0269/446 077).

Pharmacy Farmasib at Str. Bălcescu 53 (daily 9am–10pm) has an urgent night-time service.

Police Str. Revoluţiei 4 (☎0269/430 929).

Post office Str. Mitropoliei 14 (Mon–Fri 7am–8pm, Sat 8am–1pm).

Sport Facilities are clustered around the open-air swimming pool, the Ştrand, on Şos. Alba Iulia, while there's an indoor, Olympic-sized swimming pool on B-dul. Victoriei. At Str. Şaguna 2, the Baia Neptun (Tues–Sun 8am–8pm) has a 20m pool and sauna and massage. Sibiu's football team, FC InterSibiu, plays in the Municipal Stadium in the Parc sub Arini.

Train tickets The CFR office is at Str. Bălcescu 6 (Mon–Fri 7am–8pm).

Travel agencies Eximtur, Str. Bălcescu 6 (☎0269/245 508, 🖷sibiu@eximtur.ro); Paralela 45, Calea Dumbrăvii 12, at the rear of the *Hotel Continental* (☎0269/216 109, 🖷paralela45sibiu @hotmail.com).

Around Sibiu

Buses from the terminal by the train station serve many of the **old Saxon settlements** around Sibiu. Many of these villages have sizeable Romanian and Gypsy populations, now far outnumbering the Germans, but most have fortified churches and rows of houses presenting a solid wall to the street – hallmarks of their Saxon origins. "They have existed for seven hundred years, a mere handful, surrounded by races that have nothing in common with them, and yet they have not lost those customs that attach them to their fatherland", observed Walter Starkie in the 1920s. This remained largely true of the Saxon communities until 1989 – for example **Cisnădioara**, where the sight and feel of the place suggested Bavaria two hundred years ago – but the Saxons are disappearing fast, and it won't be long before their culture too has vanished from the area.

The villages south of Sibiu lie in the foothills of the **Cindrel** (or **Cibin**) mountains, where enjoyable day walks and longer hikes can be taken from the small ski resort of Păltiniş. To the east and north of Sibiu, there are more Saxon villages with doughty fortress-churches, including Vurpăr (Burgberg), Şura Mare and Şura Mică (Gross-Scheuern and Klein-Scheuern) and Slimnic (Stolzenburg), all accessible by bus, a pretty excursion through rolling hills and orchards. **Slimnic** is particularly interesting because the church, begun in 1450, was never finished, but the ruins of a substantial fortress around it survive.

Cisnădie and Cisnădioara

Two or three buses an hour (or roughly one every two hours at weekends) leave Sibiu's bus station for **CISNĂDIE** (Heltau), 12km to the south. Cisnădie's modern outskirts quickly give way to the old Red Town (so-called by the Turks both for the colour of its walls and the blood that was shed attempting to breach them) – a long square leading to the largely Romanesque **church** (daily 9am–2pm & 3–6pm), a formidable bulk protected by a double wall and a moat. You can also ascend the massive thirteenth-century **tower**; the climb takes you up a succession of lofty vaults linked by creaking ladders and narrow stairways to the four turrets, medieval symbols of civic status, which crown the tower. From the belfry, the view of Cisnădie's angular courtyards and red rooftops is superb, while just visible in the distance below the Cindrel mountains is the conical rock that overlooks the village of Cisnădioara. The church grounds are also the unlikely setting for a small **Museum of Communism** (daily 9am–2pm & 3–6pm), containing newspaper clippings and objects belonging to former party members, as well as the public, such as a calendar used for bread rationing – there's also a rare picture of Ceauşescu. There's no **accommodation** in town itself, but one option if you have your own transport is to head 2.5km south along Strada Cetăţii towards Sadu, and the comfortable and friendly *Cerbul Carpatin* (℡0269/562 937; ❹).

From central Cisnădie, it's a three-kilometre walk west along Str. Măgurii and the valley road, lined with poplars and orchards, towards the striking seventy-metre-high rock that looms over **CISNĂDIOARA** (Michelsburg), also reached by around eight buses a day (Mon–Fri only) from Sibiu. Crowning the summit of the hill is the tiny **Romanesque church**, built in 1223 and which frequently withstood Tatar attacks; the villagers defended it by hurling down rocks which had previously been carried into the citadel by aspiring husbands, the custom being that no young man could marry until he had carried a heavy rock from the riverbed up the steep track (the villagers were anxious to prevent weaklings from marrying in case they spoiled the hardy race). Save for a tiny stone altar, the interior is completely bare, but the **views** over the two-metre-high stone wall surrounding the church across to the snow-streaked peaks of the Făgăraş mountains are superb. The stiff fifteen-minute climb up to the church begins near the bus stop in the centre of the village – there's usually someone present to collect the €2 fee, but if there's no one there (and the gate is shut), go to house no. 202 or call ℡0269/564 332.

Follow the main road down through the village and you will pass a few shops and rows of neat, unmistakably German houses, now used as holiday homes. The best **accommodation** in the village is the *Pension Subcetate* (℡0740/220 049; ❹), just down from the path leading up to the church – a lovely, homely place with bright rooms and furniture carved and painted in traditional local style, it also has a very good **restaurant** (Tues–Sun noon–10pm). Alternatively, beyond the lower church towards the end of the village, there's a guesthouse at no. 32 (℡0269/566 066; ❷) – they've also got huts (❶–❷) and holiday houses for rent (❸–❺) a short way up the road.

Răşinari and Păltiniş

From Sibiu, hourly buses make their way to **RĂŞINARI**, 12km distant and on the road to Păltiniş. It's a tight-packed village with a painted Orthodox church built in 1752, and an **ethnographic museum** (Tues–Sun 10am–5pm), showing the usual range of local costumes and pottery. However, it's more noteworthy for the annual **Pastoral Album Folklore Festival**, held on the third Sunday of April, as well as the large Gypsy population at the southern end of town. There are several appealing **guesthouses** in the village, all on Str. Octavian Goga, including the *Phoenix* at no. 777 (℡0745/308 034; ❷), and the *Badiu* at no. 786 (℡0269/557 359; ❷). Further possibilities extend along the Păltiniş road, including the *Casa Mai* (℡0269/572 693; ❼), an Austrian-style pension with smart rooms, a good restaurant and a swimming pool. Răşinari is

3

Ambiguous philosophers

Răşinari was the birthplace not only of the anti-Semitic prime minister and poet Octavian Goga, but also, in 1911, of the philosopher **Emil Cioran**. In 1934, Cioran published *Pe Culmile Disperarii* (*On the Heights of Despair*), setting out the **nihilist anti-philosophy** that the only valid thing to do with one's life is to end it. He continued, with a total lack of humour, to expound this view in a succession of books, but never quite managed to actually do away with himself, dying only in 1995. In the 1930s, he supported the Legion of the Archangel Michael, better known as the Iron Guard, but, after moving to Paris in 1937, became less extreme in his views.

Another philosopher, **Constantin Noica** (1908–87), spent the last years of his life in nearby **Păltiniş**. In the 1930s, he too was a supporter of the Iron Guard, although he later retreated to the mountains to translate detective stories; in 1949, he was arrested (supposedly for writing a study of Goethe) and exiled to Câmpulung Muscel, and from 1958 to 1964 he was imprisoned (for writing to Cioran, and in effect for *Letters to a Distant Friend*, which Cioran published as a reply in Paris) – this case contributed to the founding of Amnesty International in 1961. He made his name with *Romanian Philosophical Speech* in 1970, and *The Romanian Sense of Being* in 1978. In 1974 he settled in a one-room cabin (Thurs–Sat 10am–6pm) in Păltiniş.

Noica remains an ambivalent figure. With a Platonic distrust of democracy and a fascination with "the Romanian soul" and with "pure" intellectual rigour, he preferred to criticize Western decadence rather than Ceauşescu's dictatorship, and his admirers included both prominent supporters and opponents of the regime. A romantic nationalist, he was opposed to materialist ideologies and saw culture as the only means of survival for a people's soul. Since 1989, his influence has been generally positive, but Romanian intellectual life in the twentieth century was tainted by anti-Semitism, and he said little to help counter this.

also connected to Păltiniş by a path (marked with red stripes) leading over the mountains; the walk takes six to seven hours. About an hour before Păltiniş, near Mount Tomnaticu, a path marked with blue triangles turns right to the Şanta cabana (❶), a few kilometres east of the resort.

PĂLTINIŞ (Hohe Rinne; 1442m), 22km from Răşinari, is primarily a minor (and overpriced) **ski resort**, but also attracts summer hikers. Three **buses** a day (#22) come here from Str. 9 Mai, near the train station in Sibiu. The Păltiniş travel agency has an office in Sibiu at Str. Tribuniei 3 (Mon–Fri 8am–4pm; ☎0269/223 860, ✉paltinis@bmfms.ro) and can book villa **accommodation** (❶) in Păltiniş; backpackers should ask for a bed at the *Kloster Schitu*. You should phone directly to book a bed at the *Pensiunea Bufniţa* (☎0744/494 440; ❸), the central *Casa Turistilor* cabana (☎0269/216 001; ❸), or the *Hotel Cindrel* (☎&⑲0269/574 057; ❹), which has decent rooms.

The Cindrel and Lotrului mountains

Păltiniş makes a good starting point for walks into the **Cindrel and Lotrului mountains**, one of the lesser-known sections of the Transylvanian Alps; the mountains offer high open hikes on quiet trails, and easier terrain than the **Parâng range** to the west. It's only two or three hours' walk north from Păltiniş, predominantly downhill, through the **Cibin gorges** (Cheile Cibinului), past Lake Cibin, to the *Fântânele* cabana (❶), following the red dots beyond the *Casa Turistilor*. From here, you can push on in a couple of hours either to **Sibiel** village (see p.198) following blue dots, or direct to Sibiel rail halt following blue crosses.

However, the route barely takes you above the tree line, so it's worth trying some **longer hikes** of two or three days. A two-day route, marked with red triangles, leads south via the *Gâtu Berbecului* cabana (2–3hr; ❶) and a forestry road along the Sadu valley and the Negovanu Mare (2135m) in the Lotrului mountains to Voineasa in the Lotru valley. If you take this route, you will need to camp, but the more popular route is to the west, into the Parâng mountains, east of **Petroşani** (see p.213), which has well-spaced cabana accommodation. This second route, indicated by red stripes, follows a mountain ridge to the *Cânaia* refuge (5–6hr; ❶) and then continues over open moorland (poorly marked with red stripes and red crosses – be careful not to lose your way) to the *Obârşia Lotrului* cabana (another 9–10hr; ❶), at the junction of the north–south DN67C and the east–west DN7A, both unsurfaced and open only to forestry traffic. This is the gateway to the **Parâng mountains**, an alpine area with beautiful lakes; the red crosses continue up to the main ridge, from where red stripes lead you west to Petroşani.

The Mărginimea Sibiului and Sebeş

West of Sibiu, the DN1/7 (E68/E81) and the rail line pass through the **Mărginimea Sibiului** (Borders of Sibiu) towards Sebeş. This area is fairly densely populated, mostly by Romanians rather than Saxons, with a lively folklore recorded in small ethnographic museums in most villages. There are many sheep-raising communities here, and you'll see flocks on the move, with donkeys carrying the shepherds' belongings. Personal trains between Sibiu and Vinţu de Jos (a few kilometres beyond Sebeş) halt a short distance from several settlements en route.

The first of the accessible villages, reached from Sibiu by Personal trains and bus #20 (hourly), is **CRISTIAN**, where a double wall protects the fifteenth-century Saxon church of Grossau, with its massive towers. An earthquake in 1850 partially destroyed the church, and it was at this point that the tower was extended with the addition of four turrets – there are superb views from the top. Since the mid-eighteenth century, when some 150 Austrian migrants arrived, the village has been largely dominated by a Protestant population, who fled here to avoid Catholic oppression. Indeed, there were still some three thousand Germans living here in the mid-1970s, but that number has dwindled considerably and there are now fewer than fifty. The entrance is on Str. X, at no. 40, but if it's closed contact ☎0269/579 350. Around May or June the village becomes the resting place for dozens of storks, who construct their impressive, and improbably bulky, nests atop telegraph poles and chimneys – these afford fabulous photo opportunities. The one place to **stay** in the village is the *Spack* hotel (☎0269/579 262; ❸), just north of the **train** station (walking towards the church) at Str. II 9; it's a clean, homely little place owned by a Saxon family, but it has no restaurant. The main road passes to the north of all of the villages after Cristian, and some of the train stations – notably those for Sălişte and Tilişca – lie several kilometres north of the villages they serve, which makes using public transport slightly problematic here; however, there are good guesthouses in every village.

ORLAT, with its medieval castle ruins, is about 6km south of Cristian, and is served by buses (to Gura Râului) ten times a day (though just twice at weekends) as well as by the Personal trains. There are a couple of lovely guesthouses here: the *Angela*, Str. Noua 759 (☎0745/003 980; ❸), and *Ileana*, Str. Noua 771 (☎0744/542 365; ❸), which also has space for a few tents. It's 2km west to the Sibiel train station, from where an even smaller road leads west past **Fântenele** (an attractive hamlet with a charming little museum) and, 3km from its station, the village of **SIBIEL**, a sheep-raising community with a strong tradition of **witchcraft**. Perhaps understandably, witches and ghosts are more feared for their attacks on livestock than on people. The villagers blow horns to prevent witches (*strigoi*) from stealing their ewes' milk on St George's Day, but also credit witches with occasional good deeds, such as magically shutting the jaws of wolves intent on ravaging their flocks. Located in the grounds of the eighteenth-century Orthodox church, the rather good **Museum of Icons Painted on Glass** (daily 8am–8pm) has more than 700 icons, most of which were painted by naïve (or peasant) artists from Transylvania and Moldavia; from here, a footpath leads uphill past a ruined citadel to the Fântânele cabana (1) and through the Cibin gorges to Păltiniş in eight hours (see p.196). Just down from the museum, the welcoming pension *Adriana* (☎0269/552 573; ❷) has several cheap and cosy rooms, with dinner available upon request – the family also produce their own painted icons, which you can buy.

Continuing north from Sibiel, the road meets the route east back to the main DN1/7 at **SĂLIŞTE**, famous for its peasant **choir**, which performs occasionally in the community centre, and for its cooperative, which produces carpets and embroidered costumes, the latter worn during Sălişte's **Meeting of the Youth Festival** (December 24–31). From a distance, the village church could almost be Saxon, but it is in fact firmly Orthodox. Just beyond it, on Piaţa Eroilor, is the **ethnographic museum**, which can only be visited by booking a day in advance (☎0269/553 086); it houses costumes and artefacts specific to the area. Near a watermill in excellent condition, ten minutes' walk along the Tilişca road, lives Radu Ilies, who makes the distinctive black felt hats worn by men in this area and lets visitors watch him as he works. Costumes are more likely to appear during the course of everyday life at the compact little village of **TILIŞCA**, about 3km west; this is a less spoilt settlement than Sălişte and one that can trace its origins back to Dacian times. Standing in the heart of the village is the late eighteenth-century **church**, painted a lovely sky blue and decorated, just under the rim of the roof, with a belt of exterior frescoes depicting various saints. A two-minute walk down from the church, at Str. Şcolii 535, is the smart *Pensiunea Irina* (☎0269/554 009 or 0744/313 102, ✉irina_raceu@hotmail.com; ❸). There are also OVR **homestay** schemes in both Sălişte (contact Maria Cazan, Str. I. Moga 1266; ☎0269/553 357) and Tilişca (contact Elena Iuga, Str. Principală 561; ☎0269/554 012, ✉horeacazan@hotmail.com).

North of Sălişte, the main road takes a direct route west through the attractive village of **Apoldu de Sus** (Grosspold), settled by Austrian Landlers in 1752 and maintaining its traditional architecture, while the railway crawls through beautiful oakwoods, loops south around Apoldu de Sus, and passes through the Hungarian village of **Apoldu de Jos** (Kisapold). Road and rail are reunited at **MIERCUREA SIBIULUI** (Reussmarkt), a village whose name derives from the Romanian word for Wednesday, the traditional market day – there is still a market here on this day. In the centre of the village is a small, well-preserved thirteenth-century basilica, fortified during the fifteenth century like other Saxon churches, with food stores on the inside of its oval ring wall. Trains and buses also stop 5km further on at **BĂILE MIERCUREA**, a modest spa resort with a run-down campsite, tourist cabana (❶) and a hotel-restaurant on the main road. A few kilometres west, a handful of cabins (❶) stand at the junction to **CÂLNIC** (Kelling/Kelnek), 3km south of the DN1/7, where a massive keep, built around 1300, and a very simple Romanesque chapel of the same period, are enclosed within one-and-a-half rings of walls that resisted several Turkish sieges. The castle has recently been restored and opened to visitors; local trains halt at Cut, just northwest of the road junction.

Sebeş

The town of **SEBEŞ** grew up on the proceeds of the leather-working industry, trading mainly with Wallachia; as Mühlbach, it was the capital of the Unterwald, the westernmost zone of Saxon settlement. The German street names have recently been resurrected, but Italian influence is now dominant. In 1438, a Turkish army arrived, demanding that the town surrender; a number of inhabitants refused, barricading themselves in one of the towers of the **citadel**, which the Turks stormed and burned. The only survivor, a student aged 16, was then sold as a slave, but escaped twenty years later to write a best-selling exposé of the bogeymen of fifteenth-century Europe. The **Student's Tower** (also known as the Tailors' Tower), at Str. Traian (or Parkgasse) 6, is thus one of the main sights of Sebeş, although it's not actually open. Heading west from Parkgasse brings you to the large **Evangelical Church** (Tues–Sat 10am–1pm & 3–5pm, Sun 3–5pm), built in Romanesque style between 1240 and 1270, with a disproportionately large and grand Gothic choir added by 1382, followed by the upper part of the tower in 1664. The choir boasts the best Parleresque statues in Transylvania, as well as a large polychrome altar dating from 1518. Just to the north stands the cemetery chapel, built in 1400 and now used by the Uniates. A **museum** (Tues–Fri 8am–5pm, Sat & Sun 10am–4pm) featuring the standard ethnographic displays is housed on the north side of the square in the late fifteenth-century **House of the Voivodes**.

The **train** (Sebeş Alba) and **bus stations** are to the east, in the new town. From the stations, a pleasant route into town heads right on Str. Mărăşeşti, crossing the road to Daia Romană – with a view of the dramatic Red Cliffs (Râpa Roşie) to the north of town – and along Str. Mihai Viteazul to the main square. There's little incentive to linger, but should you need to **stay** overnight, the *Clasic* hotel (☎0258/733 016; ❻), just east on the DN1, has tidy air-conditioned rooms – it's also the best place in town to **eat**. A reasonable spot for a **drink** is the *Café River*, which is actually at the end of a small jetty on the large artificial lake next to Parkgasse. Note that if you're travelling the few kilometres north to Alba Iulia, you're best off catching one of the frequent buses from Sebeş, saving the lengthy wait for a train connection at Vinţu de Jos.

Southwestern Transylvania

Heading west from Mediaş or Sibiu, you soon leave the Saxon part of Transylvania and move into an area where Hungarian influence is more apparent. However, while a Hungarian ruling class lived here for centuries, the peasantry has always been Romanian. Over the course of millennia, the Stone Age tribes that once huddled around the caves and hot springs of the Carpathian foothills developed into a cohesive society, whose evolution was largely determined by events in the **southwest** of the region. The stronghold of the Dacian kingdom lay here, in the hills south of **Orăştie**, and these were ultimately conquered by Roman legions marching up from the Danube through the narrow passes known today as the Eastern Gate (Poarta Orientală) and the Iron Gate (Poarta de Fier) of Transylvania. The conquerors founded their new capital, **Sarmizegetusa**, in the Hațeg depression, and the area became one of the earliest centres of Romanian culture in Transylvania; it's now known for the *hațegana*, a quick dance (and the name of the local beer), and some of Romania's oldest and most charming churches. To the north, Hungarian churches and castles dominate the main route along the Mureș valley to and from Hungary – **Hunedoara** is the site of the greatest medieval fortress in Romania. **Alba Iulia**, one of the most important towns in this region, has been a centre of Romania's wine industry since the first century BC. By contrast, the smoggy mining towns at the feet of the Retezat mountains, in the far southwest of Transylvania, belie the beauty of the range, whose peaks feed dozens of alpine lakes, making this one of the most beautiful of the Carpathian ranges and deservedly popular with hikers.

Alba Iulia and around

The tension between the Hungarian and Romanian communities is symbolized in **ALBA IULIA**, 14km north of Sebeș, by the juxtaposition of the Roman Catholic and Orthodox cathedrals in the heart of its citadel. This hill top was

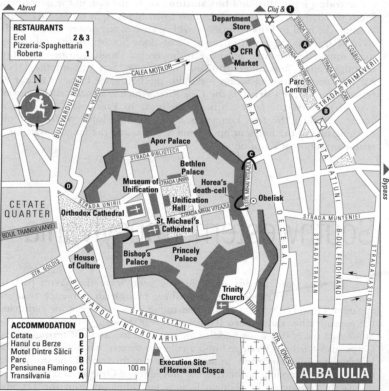

fortified by the Romans and then by the Romanians, before the Hungarian ruler, István I, occupied it and created the bishopric of Gyulafehérvár – the Magyar name for Alba Iulia – in the early part of the eleventh century, to consolidate his hold on Transylvania. Only after World War I did the Romanians take over the levers of power here and build their own cathedral. The town is dominated by its huge **citadel**, in effect the **upper town**, laid out in the shape of a wonky star; east of this, the **lower town** has been tidied up since it was partly cleared for "rationalization" in Ceauşescu's last years, and is home to a scattering of low-key Art Deco buildings.

Arrival and information

Alba Iulia's **bus** and **train** stations are both 1.5km south of the centre on B-dul. Ferdinand I (DN1), reached by buses #3 and #4, looping via the lower town and the Cetate quarter every ten minutes (10–20min at weekends), one in each direction. Strada Iaşilor, parallel to the DN1, makes a pleasant walk from the stations into town; turn left at the police station and Romtelecom (which also houses the **post office**) for the citadel. The CFR agency, for **train tickets**, is at Calea Moţilor 1 (Mon–Fri 7am–8pm). **Internet** is available at Parc Net opposite the *Hotel Parc*, Domino, B-dul. Horea 42, and a couple of places on B-dul. Transilvaniei. **Bike** repairs are possible at Str. Moţilor 21 (☎0745/880 744).

Accommodation

Accommodation in Alba Iulia is limited and pricey, except for the *Pensiunea Flamingo* and a couple of places by the river 4km south of the centre on the DN1 (bus #12 or #13). There's also a small motel to the north of town at km384.

Cetate Str. Unirii 3 ☎0258/811 780, ⓔ cetate @cristalsoft.ro. West of the centre, in the new town, this unattractive high-rise offers drab, colourless rooms with careworn furniture. **❼**

Hanul cu Berze Str. Republicii 179 ☎&ⓕ0258/810 129. A friendly, family-run place, on the north side of the river 2km south of the bus and train stations. **❷**

Motel Dintre Sălcii Str. Republicii ☎0258/812 137. Just over the bridge from the *Hanul cu Berze* (and almost as nice), this is a very cheap but pleasant motel. **❷**

Parc Str. Primăverii 4 ☎0258/811 723, ⓦ www .hotelparc.ro. The best hotel in town has a mix of

two- and four-star rooms – the former with twin beds only. It's worth paying the little extra for the higher category. **❻–❽**

Pensiunea Flamingo Str. Mihai Viteazul 6 ☎0258/816 354, ⓔ pensiunea_flamingo@yahoo .com. The only central budget option, with seven simple rooms (including triples and quads) and a bar serving basic meals. **❸**

Transilvania Piaţa Iuliu Maniu 21 ☎0258/812 052, ⓕ806 282. The ugly exterior of this large hotel belies some perfectly agreeable and modern (if a little cramped) rooms. **❻**

The Town

Between 1715 and 1738, twenty thousand serfs, under the direction of the Italian architect Visconti, built the Vauban-style **citadel**, which was named Karlsburg in honour of the reigning Habsburg monarch. Imperial levies on the countryside did much to embitter the Romanian peasants, who turned on their (mainly Hungarian) landlords in the 1784 uprising led by Horea, Cloşca and Crişan. After the uprising had been crushed, Horea and Cloşca were tortured to death, a martyrdom commemorated both at the execution site south of the citadel walls, and by a twenty-two-metre-high **obelisk** pitched on the eastern side of the citadel up beyond the newly restored first gateway, itself flush with statues and reliefs. At the top of the cobbled path lie the remains (fragments of pillars) of the second gateway, which was demolished at the end of the nineteenth century in order to reduce the incline of the road up to the citadel. Beyond here is the richly carved Baroque main (third) gateway, currently being restored and above which is Horea's death-cell. Crişan cheated the excecutioner by committing suicide. To the south of the gateway, the **Trinity church** is a modern wooden structure, in traditional Romanian style.

Within the citadel, the Act of Unification between Romania and Transylvania was signed in the ornate marble **Unification Hall** (Sala Unirii; Tues–Sun 10am–5pm) on December 1, 1918, as the Austro-Hungarian Empire commenced its death throes; built between 1898 and 1900, it served as the officers' mess until 1968, and now holds a small ethnographic collection. Facing the hall, a military accommodation block (1853) houses the exhaustive **Museum of Unification** (Muzeul al Unirii; same hours and ticket), which embodies the credo that Romania's history has been a long search for national unity and glorifies the Wallachian prince **Michael the Brave**, who united Wallachia, Transylvania and Moldavia, and made Alba briefly capital of Romania in 1599–1600. In a fit of pique, the Magyars demolished his Coronation Church in 1713, so, unsurprisingly, the Romanians built a vast new **Orthodox Cathedral** in 1921, in which King Ferdinand and Queen Marie were crowned the next year. Entered via a fifty-eight-metre-high tower, the colourful peach- and cream-coloured, neo-Brâncovenesc cloister belies the medieval style of the cathedral, filled with neo-Byzantine frescoes, including portraits of Michael and his wife, Stanca. The Catholic **St Michael's Cathedral** on the south side of Str. Mihai Viteazul testifies to the Hungarian connection. The foundations of the eleventh-century church have been preserved, as has a superb Maiestas carving above a blind door in the south aisle. What you see now was mostly built between 1247 and 1256, in late Romanesque style, with the Gothic choir added in the fourteenth and fifteenth centuries; of the later accretions, the most notable are the Renaissance László and Váraday chapels, built in 1512 and 1524 respectively. The **tomb of Hunyadi**, the greatest of Transylvania's warlords, is in the middle of the three to the right of the west door; a century after his death, the tomb was vandalized by the Turks, still bitter at their defeats at his hands. Having been neglected for much of the twentieth century, the cathedral has recently been restored; if it's closed, ask for the key at the Bishop's Palace, flanking the gate to the new town. To the south of the Catholic cathedral stands the former **Princely Palace**, where the Transylvanian Diets met between 1542 and 1690. Leaving the citadel to the west, you'll come to the modern **Cetate quarter**, where the liveliest watering holes can be found, as well as the Artists' Union Gallery on B-dul. 1 Decembrie 1918.

Eating and drinking

There are pretty slim pickings when it comes to **eating and drinking** in Alba Iulia. In addition to the hotel restaurants, the popular *Pizzeria-Spaghettaria Roberta* is 150m north of Calea Moţilor on Str. Tudor Vladimirescu, and also has a branch on B-dul. Transilvaniei, in Cetate; *Erol*, sprawling either side of the pedestrian subway under Calea Moţilor by the market, is pleasant enough, serving reasonable pizza. For drinking, there are several *terasas* on the lively pedestrianized B-dul. Transilvaniei, including the two-storey *Blue Hours* and the *Terasa Dakota* opposite it. Just inside the citadel, across from the obelisk, *Pub 13* makes a pleasant alternative.

Around Alba Iulia

Many of the towns around Alba Iulia bear witness to the centuries of Hungarian rule, including **Aiud**, which has a pleasant ambience, while **Blaj** is of historical interest as the cradle of Romanian Nationalism only. The area is easily visited on public transport: there are buses more or less hourly from Alba Iulia heading into the Apuseni highlands and good train links to Blaj and Aiud.

Blaj

Thirty-five kilometres east of Alba Iulia on the DN14b to Sighişoara, the small town of **BLAJ** stands at the junction of the main Sighişoara–Cluj rail line and the branch to Sovata and Praid (see p.218). Blaj's main claim to fame is its historical status as the ark of Romanian Nationalism, though it is now run-down; the town still produces good wine, however – notably the dry white Feteasca Regală – and Bergenbier is brewed here. The centre lies about 1km east of the train station (where buses also pull in); heading east through communist-era blocs you'll come to Str. Republicii, the main drag, with the **History Museum** (Tues–Fri 9am–4pm, Sat & Sun 10am–2pm) to the right in Avram Iancu park. In addition to temporary art shows upstairs, the museum covers Blaj's history as headquarters of the **Uniate Church** (see box below) and that of the many intellectuals who taught here at the end of the eighteenth

---

The Uniate Church

In 1596, the Austrian government persuaded the Orthodox Church in Galicia (now southern Poland and Ukraine) to accept the authority and protection of the Vatican, hoping to detach them from eastern, and above all Russian, influences and to tie them more firmly to the western fold. Thus was born the **Uniate Church**, also known as the Catholic Church of the Eastern Rite, or the Greco-Catholic Church. However, the new Church failed to attract most Romanian Orthodox believers, and was further marginalized when Romania's Orthodox Church gained autonomy in the 1920s. Even so, its leading figures exercised great influence. At the end of the eighteenth century, the **Transylvanian School** (Şcoala Ardeleana), a group of clerics and teachers in Blaj, played a key role in making Romanian a literary language, revitalizing Romanian culture and instilling a sense of nationhood into the Romanian people. The Uniate Church stood for independence of thought and self-reliance, as opposed to the more hierarchical and conformist Orthodox Church, so the communist regime called its million-plus adherents "agents of imperialism" and forcibly merged them with the Orthodox Church. Uniates remained a harassed and often imprisoned minority, with no status under the 1948 and subsequent constitutions (although these recognized the existence of fourteen other denominations or "cults"), until the overthrow of communism.

The Uniates accept four key points of Catholic doctrine: the Filioque clause in the creed (according to which the Holy Spirit proceeds from the Father and the Son, as opposed to the Orthodox doctrine by which the Holy Spirit proceeds only from the Father); the use of wafers instead of bread in the Mass; the doctrine of Purgatory (unknown in the East); and, above all, the supremacy of the pope. All the other points of difference – the marriage of priests, a bearded clergy, the cult of icons, different vestments and rituals – remain identical to Orthodox practice. In certain areas, such as Maramureş, there is now a considerable revival in the fortunes of the Uniate Church, although hopes that it can again revitalize the country as it did around 1800 under the Transylvanian School appear misplaced. The Iliescu government has also supported, and been supported by, the Orthodox Church, and the Uniates have found it a long, hard struggle to reclaim even their buildings.

century and beginning of the nineteenth; they are also remembered by numerous plaques around town.

Continuing east on Str. Republicii you'll come to the hotel, and, on Piaţa 1848 behind it, the Uniate (or Greco-Catholic) **cathedral** (1749–79), the first Baroque building in Transylvania. To its south is the school where classes were held in the Romanian language from 1754; the great botanist Alexandru Borza (1887–1971) taught here. East of the town centre is the **Field of Liberty**, a famous rallying point in 1848 and 1868 for tens of thousands of Romanians protesting against Hungary's demands to reincorporate Transylvania within the "lands of Stephen". The sole **hotel** in town is the central *Târnavele* (☎0258/710 255, ⓕ714 246; ❸), at B-dul. Republicii 1, which has twin rooms only.

Aiud

Some 25km north of Alba Iulia, on the DN1 (E81), lies **AIUD** (Nagyenyed). It's an attractive town, despite the grim reputation of its prison, which was used to hold Soviet spies during World War II, and Iron Guardists after the communist takeover – it remains Transylvania's largest prison, housing the country's most serious offenders. The town's centre has one of the oldest **fortresses** in Transylvania, dating back to 1302, and still boasting a full ring of walls and eight towers. It shelters two Hungarian churches (the first Lutheran and built in the late nineteenth century on a medieval groundplan; the second Calvinist and dating from the early fifteenth century) and a **History Museum** (Tues–Fri 8am–4pm, Sat & Sun 8am–noon); there's a display of stuffed animals at the **Natural Sciences Museum** (Tues–Sun 10am–5pm) upstairs in the Bethlen College across the road. Behind the fortress, the landmark, turn-of-the-century **Industrial School** rises up like a huge Renaissance palace. From the **train station**, it's a twenty-minute walk to the centre – head up Str. Coşbuc, just to the left of the station, and after the stadium turn left to pass the Conti **Internet café** and turn right up Str. Iuliu Maniu to the market; the road continues as Str. Trandafirilor to Str. Băilor. Alternatively, you can turn right after the stadium, cross the bridge, passing the prison and then the **bus station** on Str. Băilor (hidden behind an ugly new church). The only decent place to **stay** in town is the *Mobis* pension at Str. Transilvaniei 120 (☎0258/862 772; ❸), about 1km north of town out on the road to Cluj – this smart, fresh place also has a pool and accommodates the town's best **restaurant**. Otherwise, there is the *Luk* restaurant by the market at Str. Libertăţii 9.

Orăştie, Deva and Hunedoara

South of Alba Iulia, in the mountains between Timişoara and Sibiu, are a number of **Dacian citadels**, six of which were placed on UNESCO's World Heritage list in 1999; the most interesting, **Sarmizegetusa**, is accessible from **Orăştie**, a quiet town 38km southwest of Sebeş on the main road and rail line west towards Timişoara and Arad. There are also two striking medieval structures in this part of Transylvania: the ruined fortress on the **Hill of the Djinn**, overlooking **Deva**, and the huge, practically undamaged, Gothic castle of the Corvin family at **Hunedoara**. Deva lies west beyond Orăştie on the main road and rail lines, while Hunedoara is accessible by rail from **Simeria** on that same line, or by bus from Deva. The Dacian citadels, however, are further off the beaten track and you'll have to walk or hitch to reach them.

Orăştie and around

ORĂŞTIE, first recorded in 1224 as the Saxon *stuhl* of Broos, is a pleasant small town in which to break a journey along the Mureş valley. From the **train station**, 3km west of the town, trains are met by buses for the town centre (buses to the station depart from stops along the DN7 and are less predictable – roughly half-hourly – so you'll need to allow a bit of leeway). Heading into

▲ Sarmizegetusa

town, buses turn right at the Piaţa Europea roundabout; get off here, cross the main road and follow Str. Armatei south to Piaţa Victoriei – marked by a 1930s Orthodox cathedral – and the main street, Str. Bălcescu. The town **museum** (Tues–Sun 9am–5pm), at Piaţa Aurel Vlaicu 1, whose exhibits include textiles, old clocks and Dacian relics, is off Str. Bălcescu to the right, as is the old **citadel** (not open to the public) immediately south, with large German Evangelical and Hungarian Reformed churches crammed close together.

There are three, almost identically priced, **hotels** in town, the best of which is the *Dacor*, set amidst a jumble of apartment blocks at Str. Muresul 7 (☎0254/244 646; ❸), whose clean and sunny rooms are terrific value. There's also the *Mini-Hotel Jorja*, Str. Bălcescu 30 (☎0254/241 574, ✉jorjaconstantin @yahoo.com; ❸), a quirky, privately run littled guesthouse with neon-strip lighting in the rooms; and the *Sura*, just off Bălcescu at Str. Stadionului 1A (☎0254/247 222, ✉rezervari@sura.ro; ❸), which has rooms with and without bathrooms – it also possesses the town's best **restaurant**. There are also half a dozen cabins (❶) attached to the *Hanul Margareta* restaurant, just over 1km west of town on the DN7.

Cetatea Costeşti and Sarmizegetusa

Cetatea Costeşti, the first of the Dacian citadels, lies south of Orăştie along the Grădiştie valley. Several buses a day cover the 20km to the village of Costeşti, but from there you'll have to continue on foot for about 1km to the Popas Salcâmul campsite and Costeşti cabana (❶), then a further 3km west to the citadel – cross the river at the bridge and turn right past the sign to the citadel, then left at the junction and sharp left at the farm to reach the three rows of earthworks, grazed by cows and surrounded by birch and cherry trees.

The largest citadel, **Sarmizegetusa**, lies deeper into the mountains. Without your own transport, you'll have to walk or hitch; continue south from Costeşti along the valley road through the hamlet of Grădiştea de Munte and travel a further 8km over the roughest stretch of the road to Sarmizegetusa. Situated 1200m above sea level and covering an area of 3.5 hectares, it was the Dacian capital from the first century BC to 106 AD, though it requires some imagination now to conjure up a picture of its grandeur from the weathered walls and stumps of pillars that remain. That said, it's clear that Sarmizegetusa was divided into two distinct quarters: the citadel, used as a refuge during times of war; and the sacred area, dominated by the great sanctuary, a stone circle containing a horseshoe of wooden columns where ritual sacrifices were performed. The Romans, shrewd imperialists as they were, rebuilt Sarmizegetusa after its capture in 106 AD, stationed a detachment of the IV Legion here and appropriated the shrines, rededicating them to members of their pantheon. The Roman capital was southwest of here, near the modern town of Sarmizegetusa – and took its name from the Dacian citadel.

Deva

The capital of Hunedoara county, **DEVA**, 30km west of Orăştie, lies on the east side of a **citadel** built in the thirteenth century and transformed into one of Transylvania's strongest fortifications on the orders of the warlord, Hunyadi, in the fifteenth century. It crowns a volcanic hill in the shape of a truncated cone – supposedly the result of a stupendous battle between the djinns (spirits) of the Retezat mountains and of the plain, hence the nickname **Hill of the Djinn**.

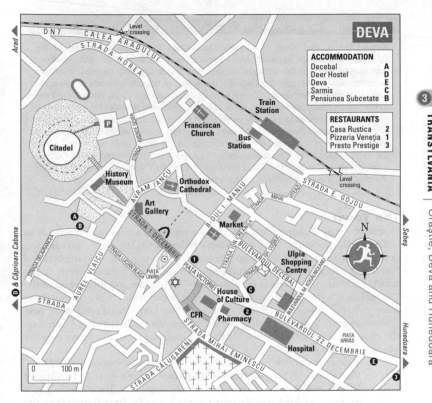

Arrival, information and accommodation

All **trains** on the main line from Arad stop at Deva, making it a good place to pick up services to Budapest or the further corners of Romania; from the station, the town centre is just five minutes south along B-dul. Iuliu Maniu. From the **bus station**, next to the **train station**, five services a day head for the Apuseni mountains, while buses leave frequently for Hunedoara, Simeria and Orăştie. Maxitaxis for Călan and Simeria wait to the right of the train station. **Train bookings** can be made at the CFR agency at Str. 1 Decembrie, Bloc A (Mon–Fri 7am–8pm).

There are a few **hotels** in town, all less than inspiring; the most pleasant place, though, is the *Pensiunea Subcetate*, a homely little guesthouse with a lovely, flower-filled garden, at Str. Delavrancea 6 (⌕0254/212 535, ⒺofficeⓉcazaredeva.ro; ❹). The pick of the hotels is the accomplished *Deva* at Str. 22 Decembrie 110 (⌕0254/225 920, Ⓔ deva.deva@unita-turism.ro; ❼), with the other two options being the ghastly *Sarmis* at Piaţa Victoriei 3 (⌕0254/214 731, Ⓕ213 730; ❼) and the lifeless *Decebal*, just across from the *Pensiunea Subcetate* at B-dul. 1 Decembrie 37 (⌕0254/212 413, Ⓕ219 245; ❹). The *Deer* **youth hostel** (⌕0354/803 494, Ⓔturism_hunedoara@yahoo.com; ❶), 4km west of town up in the hills, is clean and well run, but caters largely to groups of young students – the only way to get here is by car (or taxi), though the owners will pick up from the stations upon request.

③

The Festival of the Călușari

Around the second week of January, Deva hosts the colourful **Festival of the Călușari** (Călușerul Transilvănean). Ensembles from Wallachia and southern Transylvania perform the intricate dances and rituals originally devised to ensure good harvests and dispel the Rusalii – the spirits of departed friends or relations, who, according to Romanian folklore, would take possession of the living should any of the taboos associated with the Week of Rusalii (following Whitsun) be violated. The rite was also intended to promote fertility, and in the old days the dancers (all male) were accompanied by a mute who wore a huge red phallus beneath his robes and muttered lewd invocations. Under communism, such antics were discouraged and the mute carried a more innocuous wand covered in rabbit fur. Contact the Cultural Inspectorate in Deva (Str. 1 Decembrie 28; ℗0254/213 966) to confirm the exact dates of this and other festivals in Hunedoara county.

The Town

Despite the mason charged with building it reputedly immuring his wife in its walls in order to guarantee his creation's indestructability, Deva's **citadel** was destroyed in 1849 when the magazine blew up, leaving only the ramparts and barracks standing. A sizeable portion remains, including a small cavern, inside which is a memorial to David Ferenc (1520–79), founder and first bishop of the Uniate Church (see p.203) who was martyred in the castle's prison. If you don't fancy the stiff 184-metre climb to the top, then you can take the new (and Romania's first) **funicular** (*telecabina*; daily 9am–9pm; €2), which is located on the eastern side of the hill by the football stadium; the expansive views over the Mureş valley are superb.

In the park at the bottom of the hill – beneath the Hollywood-style "Deva" sign on the citadel – is the **Magna Curia palace**, rebuilt in 1621 by Voivode Gábor Bethlen, under whom Deva was briefly capital of Transylvania. Since 1882, it has housed a **History Museum** displaying archeological finds from the Orăştie mountains; following restoration, the exhibits are scheduled to be in place by 2009, until when you can see some Roman stonework languishing in the long grass outside. There's also a tiny **art gallery** in the prefecture opposite, on the corner of Str. Avram Iancu. Heading down this street, you'll come to the Orthodox **cathedral of St Nicolae**, dating from 1893. To the north, on Str. Progesului, is the Franciscan church. Alternatively, head east to the modern centre via the pedestrianized Str. 1 Decembrie, passing the country's only Ecological University in the former *Hanul Mare*, the inn where Alexandru Ioan Cuza slept on his way into exile in 1866.

Eating and drinking

The best of a limited bunch of **restaurants** is *Presto Prestige*, located on a horribly busy intersection at Str. Carpati 1, but whose outdoor hammock-type seating is, nevertheless, an enjoyable place to try risottos, pastas and Mexican dishes, as well as toasted sandwiches and breakfast options. There are two bright and modern pizzerias; *Casa Rustica*, on B-dul. 22 Decembrie, which offers crispy thin-crust pizzas and has a no-smoking section, and the larger *Pizzeria Venetia* on B-dul. Iuliu Maniu (between B-dul. Decebal and Str. 1 Decembrie), which also has a terrace. There is a string of pavement **cafés** along Str. 1 Decembrie, the most appealing of which is *Arta*, thanks chiefly to its delectable selection of cakes and ices. The Ulpia shopping centre (Mon–Fri 9am–9pm, Sat 9am–7pm, Sun 10am–2pm), on B-dul. 22

Decembrie, has a very good **supermarket**, although there's better fresh fruit and meat in the market.

Hunedoara

HUNEDOARA (Vajdahunyad/Eisenmarkt), 16km south of Deva, would be dismissed as an ugly, smoggy, industrial town were it not also the site of **Corvin Castle** (May–Sept Mon 9am–3pm, Tues–Sun 9am–6pm; Oct–April Mon 9am–3pm, Tues–Sun 9am–4pm; €2), the greatest fortress in Romania. The travel writer Patrick Leigh Fermor found its appearance "so fantastic and theatrical that, at first glance, it looks totally unreal". It's moated to a depth of 30m and approached by a narrow bridge upheld by tall stone piers, terminating beneath a mighty barbican, its roof bristling with spikes, overlooked by multitudes of towers. Founded during the fourteenth century and rebuilt in 1453 by **Iancu de Hunedoara**, with a Renaissance-style wing added by his son, Mátyás Corvinus, and Baroque additions by Gabriel Bethlen in the seventeenth century, it was extensively and tastefully restored in 1965–70. Within, the castle is an extravaganza of galleries, spiral stairways and Gothic vaulting, most impressively in the Knights' Hall, with its rose-coloured marble pillars. On the second pillar a carved Latin inscription reads "this work has been performed by the great and handsome Iancu de Hunedoara in the God's year 1452" – clearly a man not given to modesty. The hall also accommodates a display of weaponry, while it's just about possible to make out some medallion portraits of the Bethlen family and their acquaintances.

Legend has it that Iancu de Hunedoara, the warlord known in Hungarian as János Hunyadi, was the illegitimate son of King Sigismund, who gave the castle to Hunyadi's nominal father, Voicu, a Romanian noble, in 1409. Hunyadi, the "White Knight", rose largely by his own efforts, winning victory after victory against the Turks, and devastatingly routing them beneath the walls of Belgrade in 1456. Appointed voivode of Transylvania in 1441, Hunyadi later became regent of Hungary and a kingmaker (responsible for the overthrow of Vlad Dracul and the coronation of the Impaler, see p.471), while his own son, Mátyás Corvinus, rose to be one of Hungary's greatest kings.

The reserves of iron ore in the hills to the west of Hunedoara were known in Roman times; they were exploited on an industrial scale from 1884 and then after World War II, when the communists deliberately built a huge and ugly steel plant right in front of the castle.

Practicalities

Buses between Deva and Hunedoara run every twenty minutes; you pay on board. There are also **trains** from Simeria and five minibuses a day from Hațeg, 45 minutes to the south (look out for the huge Gypsy palaces on entering Hunedoara from Călan). From the **train** and **bus stations**, it's a twenty-minute walk south to the castle: turn right onto the main road, B-dul. Republicii, and then right again onto B-dul. Libertății, passing the town hall and Ghelari church, until you reach a bridge on the right; cross this and follow the signs for the remaining five-minute walk to the castle.

Once you've seen the castle there's no reason to remain in Hunedoara; if you do get stuck, the *Rusca* **hotel** at B-dul. Dacia 10 (⊤0254/717 575, Ⓦwww .hotelrusca.ro; ❻), is a fifteen-minute walk south of the station; head down Str. Avram Iancu then turn right along B-dul. Dacia. Alternatively, there's the private *Termorep* at Str. Ștefan cel Mare 1 (⊤0254/712 449, Ⓕ712 050; ❹), well south of the centre, near the market. There are other accommodation options at the popular resort of **Lake Teliuc**, an artificial body of water 7km southwest of Hunedoara where lies the modern *Cinciş* hotel (☎0254/738 844, ⓦwww .cincis.ro; ➎) – which also has apartments (➏) and bungalows (➐).

Haţeg and around

Twenty kilometres southeast of Hunedoara, **HAŢEG** is the gateway to Transylvania's greatest Roman remains and one of the most convenient approaches to the Retezat mountains. In addition to the ruins, you'll find a number of interesting **Romanesque churches** in the surrounding area, all of which can, with a little difficulty, be reached by local buses from the terminal at Str. Caragiale 14, off Str. Mihai Viteazul by the market. For accommodation, the town's two **hotels** are the small but modern *Art Motel*, smack-bang in the centre at B-dul. Tudor Vladimirescu 15 (☎0254/772 344; ⓦwww.geraico.ro; ➍), and the much less appealing, but cheaper, *Belvedere* (☎0254/777 604; ➌), at the Abator bus stop, 1km south on Str. Progesului, the Petroşani road; this is served by buses to Subcetate. The *Hanul Bucura*, at the northern entrance to town, has no accommodation, but its **restaurant** has great views across the town to the Retezat mountains.

The Romanesque churches

Fifteen kilometres northwest of Haţeg is **Prislop Monastery** – near Silvaşu de Sus, at the head of the Silvaşului valley in the foothills of the Poiana Ruscă mountains. Founded in 1400, this is one of the oldest convents in Romania but is remarkably little known and very tranquil, and the nuns are happy for you to go in and look around. It lies just off the direct road from Hunedoara to Haţeg, but most traffic goes via **Călan**, on both the rail line and the DN66 (E79) south from Simeria, though the road is terrible in places. Călan itself is quite a sight, its eerily redundant steelworks – closed more than a decade ago now – an appalling spectacle; however, there is a more pleasant spa (dating from Roman times) across the river to the east, with the lovely twelfth-century **church of Streisângeorgiu** on its southern fringe, with frescoes dating from 1313. A couple of kilometres south of Călan (beyond the Hunedoara turning), a similar church at **Strei** dates from the thirteenth century and has fine fourteenth-century frescoes.

Three kilometres south of Haţeg (an easy stroll from where the Subcetate bus turns off the main road), you'll come to **SÂNTĂ MĂRIA-ORLEA** (Oraljaboldogfalva), site of another late thirteenth-century church, which marks the transition from the Romanesque to Gothic style and has a fine collection of fourteenth-century frescoes; from the tower, there's a great view of the Retezat range. An eighteenth-century mansion, just across the road from the church and up the path, is now a **hotel**, the *Castell Sânta Maria Orlea* (☎0254/777 768, ⓕ772 200; ➌), a sombre place that provides nothing more than an adequate stopover.

Twelve kilometres west of Haţeg, in **DENSUŞ**, a very strange little church has been cannibalized from the mausoleum of a fourth-century Roman army officer – most of what you see dates from the early thirteenth century, with frescoes from 1443. Ask at no. 15 on the main road, east of the statue of the etymologist Ovid Densuşianu, for someone to let you in.

Roman Sarmizegetusa

SARMIZEGETUSA, 15km southwest of Hațeg, is the site of one of the key Roman settlements. Today, the town's fame still derives from the **Roman ruins** east of the centre, whose excavated portions are only part of the original municipality. You can see the remains of the forum, the palace of the Augustales, and the elliptical brick and stone amphitheatre, this last one forming the bulk of the extant remains – although it doesn't look like it, it could seat more than five thousand spectators. Start by visiting the **museum** (Tues–Sun 9am–5pm) across the road from the ruins, which avoids mentioning the likelihood that most of the Roman colonists believed to have interbred with the Dacians to create the ancestors of today's Romanians were actually of Greek or Semitic origin.

You can get here on the daily Hațeg–Reșița **bus** or on the twice-daily service (weekdays only) from Deva to Zeicani. About 500m along the main road, a left turn brings you to a couple of good **pensions**; the very smart *Sarmis* at no. 82 (☎0254/776 572; ✉office@pensiuneasarmis.ro; ❸), which has an indoor pool, and the *Ulpia Traiana* (☎0254/762 153; ❷), a short walk further on.

The Iron Gate of Transylvania

It's only about 6km from Sarmizegetusa to Zeicani at the entrance to the **Iron Gate of Transylvania** (Poarta de Fier a Transilvanei), a narrow pass 700m above sea level. A monumental mace erected near the village commemorates the defeat of 80,000 Turks by 15,000 Transylvanians under the command of Hunyadi in 1442. Further up the pass, in 106 AD, the Dacians had their final clash with the Romans; as recorded by Roman scribes, this battle was a disaster for the Dacians – their forces were crushed, and their ruler Decebal committed suicide rather than be ignominiously paraded through the streets of Rome. The pass itself is 10km long, and accessible by road (the DN68); minimal rail services resume at the mining village of Băuțar on the far side.

The Retezat mountains

Road and rail routes southeast from Hațeg skim the northern reaches of the **Retezat mountains**. Access is slightly harder here than in the other Transylvanian mountain ranges, though whereas in the Făgăraș or Piatra Craiului you find yourself for the most part following a ridge walk, with little opportunity to step aside and view the summits from a distance, here you'll find yourself surrounded by well-defined peaks, often reflected in clear alpine lakes. There is a large network of **hiking routes**, so you'll meet fewer walkers and have a better chance of seeing **wildlife** such as chamois and eagles. Note that the northwestern part of the massif is a scientific reserve (Ceaușescu treated it as a private hunting ground) and entry is restricted.

The **Retezat National Park** (☎0254/218 829, ⓦwww.retezat.ro) itself was set up in 1935, becoming a UNESCO Biosphere Reserve in 1980. To enter, you need a permit (€2 for a week plus a tent fee of €1 per night), available from an entry post (see p.213) or from a patrol; you'll be given a rubbish bag and a ticket with a basic map – it's worth buying a more detailed one in advance. **Entry posts** are at Râu de Morii, Cârnic and Câmpu lui Neag; boards here and elsewhere give **information** in English and German on the trails and the park's dozen camping sites. **Guides** can be booked through the National Park,

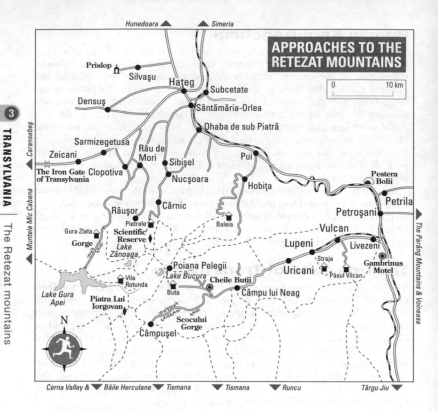

APPROACHES TO THE RETEZAT MOUNTAINS

or through New Horizons, an American-led charity in Lupeni (☎0254/564 471, ⓦwww.new-horizons.ro).

Approaches to the Retezat

There are three main **approaches** to the Retezat: from Râu de Mori, a bus ride from Haţeg and on the west side of the massif; from various points along the Subcetate to Petroşani road and rail line to the northeast; and from the West Jiu valley to the south.

From **Râu de Mori** (where you can stay in the *Mara* or *Turbopin* pensions), it's at least a three-hour walk south along the Râul Mare valley (passing the *Pensiunea Dumbrăviţa* after 5km and the *Pensuinea Anita* 2km further on) to the *Gura Zlata* cabana (see opposite) and campsite, from where you can strike out for the high peaks. Continuing south you'll come to Lake Gura Apei; beyond its eastern end, 5km from Gura Zlata, is Ceauşescu's former Vila Rotonda.

From the northeast, tracks and roads lead from villages along the rail line between Subcetate and Petroşani. From Ohaba de sub Piatră, it's 18km (a five-hour walk, following blue stripes then blue triangles) to the *Pietrele* cabana (❶) and campsite. The 2pm bus from Haţeg follows the route via Sălaşu de Sus (where there are guesthouses) as far as Nucşoara, 7km short of the cabana, and summer services, which meet trains at Ohaba, go a few kilometres further to Cârnic; alternatively, an information board at the Ohaba station gives phone numbers for taxis. Two-thirds of the park's visitors arrive this way, so the trail

212

and cabana both get quite crowded. Some hikers therefore prefer to start from either the *Complex Turistic Râuşor* (a two-hour hike from Râu de Mori, following red triangles; with a motel, a guesthouse, camping and a basic ski-drag) or the campsite at Pui, east of Ohaba, hiking for six-and-a-half hours up a steep and winding mountain road (marked with red stripes) to the cabanas at Baleia (16km) and Stâne de Râu (6km further) – see the box below for hikes beyond these points.

The final approach to the mountains is from the **mining towns of the West Jiu valley** to the east, but these are grim places with little in the way of accommodation.

From Petroşani to Voineasa

The largest of the mining towns is **PETROŞANI**, served by trains between Simeria and Târgu Jiu; these are desperately slow, and you may prefer to travel by maxitaxi. The only reason to stop here is to stock up on food before hiking in the Retezat mountains, and most people head straight on to the cabanas above **Vulcan** and **Lupeni** in the West Jiu valley by train, bus or frequent maxitaxis.

Hiking in the Retezat

From Gura Zlata
Some popular hikes start from *Gura Zlata* cabana (❶), south of Sarmizegetusa along the Râul Mare valley. A succession of coloured symbols marks successive phases of the trail east from here to the *Pietrele* cabana (❶), going by way of Lake Zănoaga (campsite), Lake Tăul Portii and the Bucura Saddle. This is a nine- to ten-hour hike, which is closed in winter. The road through Gura Zlata continues 12km south to the Lake Gura Apei, from whose western extremity well-equipped hikers can follow a trail west across the mountains to the *Muntele Mic* cabana (❶) in the vicinity of Caransebeş, or south to Băile Herculane; allow two days for each. Heading east along the reservoir and up the Lăpuşnic valley takes you to either the *Buta cabana* (❶) or the Bucura valley in four hours.

From Câmpu lui Neag
Also leading to the cabana at Buta are two of the most popular trails from Câmpu lui Neag and the *Cheile Butii* hotel in the south of the region. Red crosses mark the quickest route to the cabana (6–7hr), which runs through a fir forest and up to the La Fete sheepfold, offering great **views** of the "karst cathedrals" en route. Red triangles indicate the longer trail (10–12hr) to the cabana, which goes via the strange formations of the Scocului gorge, and the plateau of Piatră lui Iorgovan, where you can sometimes spot chamois. A forestry road continues southwest over the watershed from the Jiu valley into the Cerna valley, and on towards **Băile Herculane**, a good two days' walk (see p.382); another path, marked with blue triangles, heads south to Tismana in roughly six hours (see p.132).

Buta lies in the **Little Retezat**, the limestone ridge south of the great glacial trough of the Lăpuşnic valley, which has an almost Mediterranean flora and fauna. However, the best hikes take you into the crystalline **Great Retezat** to the north, past serried peaks and alpine lakes. There are two trails into the Great Retezat from Buta; the first, marked by blue stripes, follows a switchback path to the *Pietrele* cabana (❶; 7hr), dropping into the Lăpuşnic valley, and leading up past the wonderful lakes of the Bucura valley before coming down from a pass of 2206m past the Genţiana club's hut; the second, marked by red stripes then blue triangles, follows a trail to the *Stâne de Râu* cabana (❶), by way of the Bărbat springs and the Ciumfu waterfall (9hr; forbidden during winter).

▲ Mountain stream, Retezat mountains

From Lupeni, buses continue every two hours up the valley to **Câmpu Lui Neag**, starting point for some good hikes into the mountains (see box, p.213). In summer, the buses continue about 3km further west to the excellent *Cheile Butii* **hotel** (☏0722/210 278; ❷), and there are various guesthouses nearby.

From Petroşani, the main road and railway – the latter built by political prisoners in the late 1940s – follow the Jiu valley south to **Târgu Jiu** (see p.126), cutting through a scenic cleft between the Vâlcan and Parâng mountains and passing **Lainici**, whose motel (☎0253/463 502, ℱ214 010; ❷) stands near a fine eighteenth-century monastery with a striking new church. A newly paved road, the DN7A, heads 83km east from Petroşani to **Voineasa**, passing the decent *Gropa Seaca* cabana (☎0254/542 246 or 0744/136 555; ❶) at km18; this is very rustic and peaceful, and marks the start of a fabulous day-hike into the Parâng range.

The Székely Land and the eastern Carpathians

In the ethnic patchwork of Transylvania, the eastern Carpathians are traditionally the home of the **Székely**, a people closely related to the Magyars who speak a distinctive Hungarian dialect and cherish a special historical identity. For a long time it was believed that they were the descendants of Attila's Huns, who had entered the Carpathian basin in the fifth century. However, most modern historians and ethnographers believe that the Székely either attached themselves to the Magyars during the latter's long migration from the banks of the Don, or are simply the descendants of early Hungarians who pushed ever further east into Transylvania. Whatever the truth of their origins, the Székely feel closely akin to the Magyars who, in turn, regard them as somehow embodying the finest aspects of the ancient Magyar race, while also being rather primeval – noble savages, perhaps. Today, their traditional costume is close to that of the Romanian peasants, the chief difference being that Székely men tuck their white shirts in while Romanians wear them untucked and belted.

For visitors, the chief attractions of the region are likely to be the **Székely culture** and the scenery. Religion plays an important part in Székely life, as shown by the fervour displayed at the **Whitsun pilgrimage to Miercurea Ciuc**, the continuing existence of Székely mystics, and the prevalence of **walled churches** (less grimly fortified than the Saxon ones). Traditional Székely **architecture** is well represented throughout the Székely Land (Székelyföld); it is epitomized by tiny hilltop chapels and blue-painted houses with carved fences and gateways, incorporating a dovecote above, the best examples of which can be found in Corund. The **landscape** gets increasingly dramatic as you move through the Harghita mountains, particularly around the Tuşnad defile and St Anne's Lake to the south, and Lacu Roşu and the Bicaz gorges just before the borders of Moldavia.

Into the Székely Land

From Sighişoara and **Odorheiu Secuiesc**, the region's western capital, you can either head east to **Miercurea Ciuc**, the capital of the eastern Székely Land, or take a shorter loop to **Târgu Mureş** via the spa town of **Sovata Băi**. It's possible to make the approach from Braşov by rail; after passing the showpiece Saxon villages of **Hărman** and **Prejmer**, the route follows the Olt and Mureş valleys through **Sfântu Gheorghe**, Miercurea Ciuc and **Gheorgheni**, looping around to Târgu Mureş.

Odorheiu Secuiesc

ODORHEIU SECUIESC (Székelyudvarhely) lies more or less 50km from Sighişoara, Miercurea Ciuc and Sovata; it's an unusually prosperous town, thanks to textile companies producing 1.5 million men's suits per year, as well as the furniture, leather and print industries (factory outlets can add a whole new dimension to visits here). The town hosts a series of crafts, food and beer **festivals** throughout the spring and summer, while the excellent Szejke festival in mid-June is held out at the spa of the same name, 4km north by the Sovata road, when folk dance groups put on displays to a picnicking audience. There's also a rock festival at Szejke on the fourth weekend of July, featuring a predominantly Balkan line-up.

Arrival and information

The **bus** and **train stations** are about 1km north of the town centre; trains stop first at Odorhei Sud halt (actually on the road north to Sovata), which is nearer the centre. Turning left out of the bus station on Str. Târgului and then right onto Str. Bethlen (with the main train station to the left), you'll come in a couple of minutes to Str. Tompa László, which leads south to the citadel. **Information** is available from TourInfo, Piaţa Márton Áron 6 (Mon–Fri 9am–5pm; ☏0266/217 427, ⓦwww.tourinfo.ro), while Robert Roth of Herr Travel, opposite at Piaţa Márton Áron 2 (Mon–Fri 9am–5pm, Sat 9am–1pm ☏0266/211 342 or 0722/201 997, ⓦwww.herrtravel.ro), offers **walking tours** of the town.

The **Internet** café at Str. Petófi 17 also serves as a bar (8am–midnight), and there's Wi-Fi at the *Opium bar* (see opposite). Note that you can use **Hungarian forints** in some establishments.

Accommodation

By some distance, the town's best **hotel** is the *Gondüző*, a five-minute walk east of Piaţa Márton Áron at Str. Sântimbru 18 (☏0266/218 372, ⓦwww.gonduzo .ro; ❻); this newly built red-brick building has large, fabulously comfortable rooms with lovely wood furnishings, thick carpets and corner baths. Other central options include the *Târnava* (the *Küküllő* to Magyars) at Piaţa Primariei 16 (☏0266/213 963, ⓦwww.kukullo.ro; ❻), which has decent, if a little cramped, rooms, gym and sauna facilities; the *Korona Panzió*, Piaţa Primăriei 12 (☏0266/218 061, Ⓔoffice@koronapanzio.ro; ❹); and the *Maestro Panzió*, Piaţa Primariei 3 (☏0266/215 600; ❸), both of which are very simple and functional. There's **hostel** accommodation available in July and August at the school at Budvár 8A (☏0266/218 428). For **camping** there's *Camping Calypso* at the end of Str. Parcului, as well as wild camping 4km north at Szejke.

The Town

The busy and attractive town centre is essentially made up by two conjoined squares, **Piaţa Primăriei** (Városháza tér) and **Piaţa Márton Áron**, where three churches stand in a row: to the west, the former Franciscan monastery (1730–79); on the island between the two squares, the Reformed church (1780–81); and, on the hill beyond, the Catholic church of Sf Miklós (1787–93), set between the Jesuits' building of 1651 and the huge Tamasy Aron Gymnasium or high school, established in 1593 and now in a Secession building dating from 1911 to 1912. From Piaţa Primariei, Str. Cetăţii leads to the fifteenth- and sixteenth-century **citadel**; since 1891 this has housed an agricultural college, but you can go inside to stroll along the walls.

On the Sighişoara road, at Str. Kossuth 29, the town **museum** (Muzeul Haáz Rezsó; Tues–Fri 9am–4pm, Sat & Sun 9am–1pm) has a fine ethnographic collection, with ceramics and Székely funerary posts, which may hark back to the days when a Magyar warrior was buried with his spear thrust into the grave. Used only by Calvinists and Unitarians, these bear carvings of the tools of the deceased's trade and a ring for each decade of life; a man's post is topped with a star and a woman's with a tulip. There's also a superb wooden gate on show, typical of those found throughout the region. Two kilometres further down the same road is the **Jesus chapel** (Jézus-kápolna), one of the oldest buildings in the area, built in the thirteenth century, with a coffered ceiling – a distinguishing feature of Hungarian churches – fitted in 1667.

Eating and drinking

The town is blessed with several top **restaurants**, the best of which is the one in the *Gondüző* hotel, a good-looking place with a high-class Hungarian and Romanian menu. Two more superb Hungarian places are the *Gizi Csárda*, Str. József 3, which serves Székely food only, and *Pethö*, south of town beyond Str. Kossuth at Str. Rákóczi 21. Good pizzerias abound, including *Jungle*, in a lovely, leafy setting in the park behind the Casa de Cultura (just across the river beyond the *Târnava* hotel) – they've also got dark Ciuc beer on tap; *Pizza Diablo*, near the train station at Str. Szabok 43; and *Pizza 21* at the junction of Bethlen Gabor and Eötvös Jószef, near the Poliklinika. *Alexsandra*, Piaţa Márton Åron 1, is a fabulous, old-fashioned Hungarian-style *cukrászda* (patisserie) with marvellous coffee and cake, and *Lehel*, Str. Kossuth 56, is a great Székely pastry shop. Two hugely enjoyable and idiosyncratic places to **drink** are the *G Café*, a mellow affair next to the *Gondüző* hotel, furnished with dinky wooden tables and bare-brick walls adorned with prints; and *At the Hat*, on Str. Kossuth, a genial little place which has two-and-a-half-litre tubes to guzzle beer from. An older, posier crowd frequents the designer-furnished *Opium bar*, opposite *At the Hat*.

Around Odorheiu Secuiesc

The Unitarian village of **DÂRJIU** (Székelyderz), 17km southwest of the town, has a particularly fine fortified church, now on UNESCO's World Heritage list, with frescoes that date from 1419. As in some Saxon villages, ham and grain are still stored inside the church walls, a tradition dating back to the time when there was risk of siege. The key to the church is held next door, and the priest offers accommodation.

MUGENI (Bögöz) village, 9km west of Odorheiu by road and rail, has a fine fourteenth-century church with wonderful frescoes and a coffered ceiling. There is a fair sprinkling of **accommodation** in the village, such as the *Székelykapu Panzió* at no. 176 (☎0741/992 892, ⓦwww.szekelykapupanzio .com; ❷), which also has space for tents, and the *Ilyés Panzió* at no. 383 (☎0266/245 505, ✉ilyespanzio@yahoo.com; ❷). Continuing west from here will eventually bring you to Sighişoara, passing on the way the larger village of **CRISTURU SECUIESC** (Székelykeresztúr), whose excellent **museum** (Tues–Fri 10am–5pm, Sat & Sun 10am–1pm) on the elongated square tells the story of the ceramic industry, established here since 1590, in addition to a natural history display. Through-buses stop in the main square, but those terminating here arrive at the bus terminal, which, like the train station, is ten minutes' walk east of the centre.

East of Odorheiu Secuiesc, en route to Miercurea Ciuc, several little resorts with low-key accommodation make good options for breaking your journey. Passing through Satu Mare (Marefalva), you'll come to **BĂILE HOMOROD** (Homoródfürdó), which has hot springs that you can bathe in and the good *Lobogo Panzió* (☎0266/247 545, ⓦwww.lobogo.ro; ❸). A little further on, **VLĂHIŢA** (Szentegyházasfalu) also has mineral springs, as well as a campsite and guesthouses. About 13km beyond Vlăhiţa, at the *Brădet* cabana (❶), a turning to the north leads up to **HARGHITA BĂI** (Hargita-fürdó), located in the beautiful, thickly forested Harghita mountains, renowned for their wildlife. Here you'll find the isolated *Hotel Ozon* (☎0266/124 770; ❷) and a cabana (❶). There are two buses a day from Miercurea Ciuc rail station, or it's less than an hour's walk from the Brădet cabana. In the village of **SUBCETATE** (Zetevárajla), on a road that loses itself in the Harghita mountains northeast of Odorheiu, the village priest (at no. 96) has set up a good rural tourism infrastructure; *Balász Panzió* at no. 60 (☎0744/644 812, ⓔbalaszpanzio@pont.ro) is a decent guesthouse.

Corund, Praid and Sovata Băi

CORUND (Korond), 25km north of Odorheiu, is famed for its green and brown pottery, as well as the cobalt blue introduced by the Germans in the eighteenth century. You'll see it for sale everywhere, but for the best choice poke around the town's backstreet workshops or visit the colourful market held every year on the weekend closest to August 10.

For a complete change of atmosphere, push on to **PRAID** (Parajd), a small but popular holiday centre 12km to the north where there's a visitable salt mine. It's served by local buses from both Odorheiu and Sovata and by the rail branch from Blaj; the helpful **tourist office**, at Str. Principală 211 (daily: mid-May to mid-Sept 9am–6pm; rest of year 9am–3pm; ☎0266/240 272, ⓦwww.praid.ro), can arrange **accommodation** in private rooms (❶). There's also a fairly standard motel just north of the tourist office at Str. Principală 221 (☎0266/240 272; ❷), which offers cheaper beds to youth hostellers, as well as the basic *Hotel Omega* (☎0266/240 088; ❶) on the same road at no. 141. The fine *Casa Telegdy* **restaurant**, just north of the centre, serves up mid-priced Székely-influenced food. Seven kilometres further north by road and rail is **SOVATA** (Szováta), which has the *Ursul Negru* hotel at Str. Principală 152 (☎0265/570 987; ❷), and the *Vasskert* campsite (no cabins) at Str. Principală 129 (☎0265/570 902). **SOVATA BĂI** lies 1km to the east, a **bathing resort** surrounded by beautiful forests on the shore of **Lacul Ursu** (Medvetó or Bear Lake). A surface layer of fresh water, 1m deep, acts as an insulator keeping the lower saltwater at a constant temperature of 30–40°C year round; it rains a lot here, in short showers, but bathing is still pleasant. Its mineral waters are supposedly particularly effective for infertility. The resort's most distinctive feature is the array of wooden buildings that line the main street, Str. Trandafirilor: huge, extravagantly balconied villas and twee Hansel and Gretel churches.

Sovata Băi's **bus station** is on Str. Trandafirilor. The resort is dominated by the triumvirate of *Danubius*-owned **hotels**; the *Danubius*, Str. Trandafirilor 82 (☎0265/570 151, ⓦwww.danubiushotels.com; ❻), the *Făget* and the *Bradet* (same address and contacts; ❻). All are of a uniformly high standard, and each has its own pool and treatment facilities, while the *Danubius* also has an indoor

Kós Károly

Kós Károly (1883–1977) was the leading architect of the Hungarian National Romantic school, which derived its inspiration from the village architecture of Transylvania and Finland. The Transylvanian style is reflected in the wooden roofs, gables and balconies of his buildings, while the Finnish influence appears in the stone bases and trapezoidal door frames. Fine examples of Kós's work can be seen in Sfântu Gheorghe and Cluj (notably the Cock Church), as well as in Budapest.

After the separation of Transylvania from Hungary, Kós, a native of Timişoara, was one of the few Hungarian intellectuals to accept the new situation, choosing to remain in Cluj (and in his country home just north of Huedin) and to play a leading role in Hungarian society in Transylvania. While continuing to work as an architect, he also travelled around Transylvania, recording the most characteristic buildings (of all ethnic groups) in delightful linocuts; these were published in 1929 by the Transylvanian Artists' Guild (co-founded by Kós himself), with Kós's own text outlining the historical influences on Transylvanian architecture. In 1989, an English translation of the book, *Transylvania*, was published by Szépirodalmi Könyvkiadó in Budapest, although the Hungarian edition is well worth having just for the linocuts.

saltwater pool. The *Villa Klein*, Str. Trandafirilor 81 (℡0265/577 686, 📠411 457; ❹), is a good guesthouse. As you continue east along the same road, a left turning, just beyond a strikingly modernist Catholic chapel, takes you onto Str. Tivoli and brings you in about ten minutes to the excellent *Tivoli* hotel (℡0265/570 493; ❺), surrounded by woods with deer foraging outside the windows. Strada Tivoli continues to Lacul Tineretului (Lake of Youth), a five-minute walk, where you can rent pedaloes from the kiosks serving snacks. Another 700m along Str. Trandafirilor, you'll come to the *Stâna de Vale* **campsite** (℡0265/571 048) and, a couple of kilometres further still, the appealing *Edelweiss* hotel (℡0265/577 758, 🌐www.hoteledelweiss.ro; ❻), situated in quiet grounds and with bright, colourful rooms – there's a decent restaurant here too.

Sfântu Gheorghe

SFÂNTU GHEORGHE (Sepsi-Szentgyörgy), 30km northeast of Braşov, is a drab industrial town which, following Ceauşescu's demise, has become the heart of the Székely cultural revival. The highlight is the **County Museum** (Tues–Fri 9am–4pm, Sat 9am–1pm, Sun 9am–2pm) at Str. Kós Károly 10, south of the centre; take bus #1 to the central park and walk south. Built in 1910 to the design of **Kós Károly** (see box above), it covers the archeology, history and ethnography of the area, focusing on the revolution of 1848–49 (see p.436).

The museum lies to the south of the town centre, which is focused on the large green space of **Piaţa Libertăţii**, with a technical college designed by Kós, and (behind the statue of Mihai Viteazul) the Casa de Cultură to the west, and the **Arcaded House**, the oldest building in town (1820–21), to the east. At the north end of the square, the **Art Gallery** (Tues–Fri 9am–4pm, Sat & Sun 10am–2pm) is in a big mustard-yellow block with a tower, built in 1870 as a department store and now hosting temporary art shows. North of the square, beyond the defunct *Bodoc* hotel, Str. Kossuth leads past a Kós Károly house (no. 19) to the cobbled Str. Şoimului and the old town, with a fine fifteenth-century walled Reformat **church** at the top of Piaţa Kalvíny. In its cemetery, behind a Székely beamgate raised in 1981, you'll find stone versions of traditional wooden Székely graveposts.

Practicalities

Both the **train** and **bus stations** are 2km east of the centre; follow Str. 1 Decembrie 1918 to reach Piaţa Libertăţii. There's a **tourist office** at Str. 1 Decembrie 1918 no. 2 (Mon–Fri 9am–5pm; ℡0267/316 474). The town's best **hotel** is the charming little *Sugás*, behind the restaurant of the same name on Str. 1 Decembrie 1918 (℡0267/312 171; ⓦwww.sugaskert.ro; ❻). Alternatively, there's the rather dour *Park*, up behind the technical college at Str. Gábor Áron 12 (℡0267/311 058; ❹). Two good small private hotels are the *Korona* (℡0267/351 164; ❶) opposite the station; and the *Consic* (℡0267/326 984; ❷) at B-dul. Bălan 31 – take bus #5 from the station, or walk north from the BTT office at the junction of B-dul. Bălan and Str. 1 Decembrie 1918. Sfântu Gheorghe's BTT branch (℡&⒡0267/351 902) is particularly active in agrotourism, arranging **homestays** in nearby spas and villages; this is also the place to book long-distance bus tickets and flights.

The choice **place to eat** in town is the restaurant of the *Sugás* hotel, which serves fine Transylvanian food; otherwise there are plenty of pizza places, of which the *Tribel* (actually a cafeteria with a self-service counter), next to the tourist office at Str. 1 Decembrie 1918 no. 2, is best. The *Tein*, next to the Art Gallery, is a delightful and very mellow coffee- and teahouse.

The **post office** (Mon–Fri 7am–8pm, Sat 8am–1pm) is on Str. 1 Decembrie 1918, in the early twentieth-century *Hotel Hungaria*, and the CFR office (Mon–Fri 8am–4.30pm), for **train tickets**, is 50m further along at Str. Grof Miko Imre 13. **Internet** access is available at Internet Klub, Str. Ciucului 47. The town holds a **festival** on Saint George's day, April 23.

Covasna and around

Trains east from Sfântu Gheorghe to Târgu Secuiesc and Breţcu pass close to **COVASNA** (Kovászna), 30km away, although the DN11 (E574) lies well to the north. The "spa of the thousand springs", or Valea Zânelor (Fairies' Valley), east of here, is popular with walkers, and there's easy access to the Vrancea and Penteleu mountains. The main attraction is an amazing inclined plane, built in 1886 as part of Romania's first narrow-gauge **forestry rail line**, a UNESCO World Heritage Monument, where wagons of timber were lowered down a 1232-metre slope, before continuing to the main-line transfer sidings in Covasna.

From the **train station**, buses take you the 3km to the modern centre of town, and then continue 5km to the hospital in Valea Zânelor. The **bus station** is behind the market at Str. Ştefan cel Mare 48, just east of the road to the station; **train tickets** can be booked at the CFR office at Str. Libertăţii 24. For access to the mountains, the best place to stay is the *Hotel Bradul* (℡0267/340 081, ⒡340 030; ❹), an excellent modern hotel opposite the hospital at Valea Zânelor 10; otherwise try the *Turist* (℡0267/340 573, ⒡340 632; ❶) at Str. Gării 2, a small, friendly place with limited facilities. There are also plenty of guesthouses, such as the *Lux* at Str. Ştefan cel Mare 106. A little further up the valley is a **campsite** (℡0267/340 401), which has both cabins (❶) and tent space.

Around Covasna

TÂRGU SECUIESC (Kezdivásárhely), thirty minutes beyond Covasna by train, is something of a backwater – it's a stronghold of Székely culture, with little Romanian spoken – but it was a major trading centre in medieval times and the first Székely town to be granted a charter in 1427 (its Romanian name means Székely Market); people still flock to its Thursday **market** today. Through buses from Braşov stop on the ring road, Str. Fabricilor, just north of the bus station. From the **train** and **bus stations**, it's about a ten-minute walk north along Str. Gării to the central Piaţa Gábor Arón, lined with nineteenth-century merchants' houses, one of which, at Curtea 10, contains the **Museum of the Guilds** (Tues–Fri 9am–4pm, Sat 9am–1pm, Sun 9am–2pm) – in addition to the history of the guilds, there are temporary art shows and a surprisingly good display of costumed dolls. If you're looking for somewhere to **stay**, the *Hotel Oituz* (☎0267/363 798; ❷), opposite the museum at Piaţa Gábor Arón 9, is small and friendly, with shared bathrooms. The *Hotel Fortyogo*, Str. Fortyogo 14 (☎0267/362 663; ❸), is more comfortable, though a couple of kilometres out of town to the east. The *Bujdosó* **restaurant**, by the park at the southern end of Curtea 33, serves Székely specialities, such as goulash and *kohlrabi*.

In the other direction, 10km down the Braşov road, it's well worth a detour to take a look at the **Bod Peter Museum of Székely Life and Culture** (daily 8am–late) at the northern end of the village of **CERNAT DE JOS** (Alsó-csernáton); to get there, take the asphalt road signposted to Cernat de Sus, and fork left about 100m beyond the church – the museum is almost 1km along this road, at no. 330. A number of village houses have been moved here and there are excellent collections of wooden implements, decorated wooden dowry chests, and ceramics; unfortunately, information is only in Hungarian. Five **buses** run from Târgu Secuiesc to Cernat de Sus on weekdays; the last one returns at 1.30pm, but if you want to stay over, the museum has a couple of **rooms** (❶).

Băile Tuşnad and St Anne's Lake

To the north of Sfântu Gheorghe, the River Olt has carved the beautiful **Tuşnad defile**, at the far end of which is **BĂILE TUŞNAD** (Tusnádfürdő), a bathing resort set amid larch and fir woods, with a campsite, the *Popas Turistic Univers* (☎0266/335 087; May–Sept), offering bungalows (❶), easily spotted just south of the train station.

The main road, Str. Oltului, heads south from the Petrom garage near the train station to Univers Tourist (daily 8am–6pm; ☎0266/335 415, ⓔuniverstourist @kabelkon.ro), where **information** is available, as well as **accommodation** in villas (❷–❹) and at the *Lacul Sf. Ana* cabana (see below), and excursions. A **swimming pool**, with bathing in mesothermal waters (9am–7pm from early May), operates opposite the Casa de Cultură, which houses temporary exhibitions. Further down Str. Oltului are a library and an Ecotourism Information Centre, and the *Hotel Tuşnad* at no. 87 (☎0266/335 202, Ⓕ335 108; ❹), which has **Internet** service. North of the station, the new guesthouses are concentrated on Str. Apor, including *Panzió Csomad* at no. 17 and *Panzió Iris* at no. 22 (☎0266/335 586; ❷), a grander place with a **restaurant**. South of town, from the village of Bixad, a road leads east to **St Anne's Lake** (Lacu Sf Ana), a two-hour walk from Băile Tuşnad following blue dot markings. Set in a crater on Mount Ciumatu, the lake is the only intact volcanic lake in Europe and is run by an NGO that charges a fee to visit; note that the Univers Tourist agency (see above) runs an excursion to the lake at 3pm daily. It's spectacularly twee and is the site of a fervent **festival** on St Anne's day (July 26). The *Lacul Sfânta Ana* cabana is set on the east rim of the crater, near the rare Tinovul Mohuş peat bog (in a secondary crater, with glacial relicts such as Drosera insectivorous plants). A few kilometres beyond, on the Târgu Secuiesc road, the tiny spa of **BĂILE BALVANYOS** (Bálványos-füred) makes a good stop, with both cabana-type accommodation (❶), pensions (❷), and the upmarket *Hotel Carpaţi* (☎0267/360 310, ⓔbalvanyos@bestwesternhotels.ro; ❼), built as a sanatorium in 1938 and now part of the *Best Western* chain.

Miercurea Ciuc

The industrial city of **MIERCUREA CIUC** (Csíkszereda/Szeklerburg), 100km north of Braşov, is capital of Harghita county, though it possesses little of the charm of Odorheiu Secuiesc. Its main claim to fame these days is as the home of Ciuc, one of Romania's most popular beers.

Arrival, information and accommodation

Miercurea Ciuc's **bus** and **train stations** are both west of the centre, south of the Odorheiu road; Ciceu station, one stop north, is the junction for the rail line across the Eastern Carpathians to Adjud. Trains between Cluj and Moldavia stop here without passing through Miercurea Ciuc; if there's no connecting train, take bus #22 (roughly hourly). Long-distance bus tickets can be bought

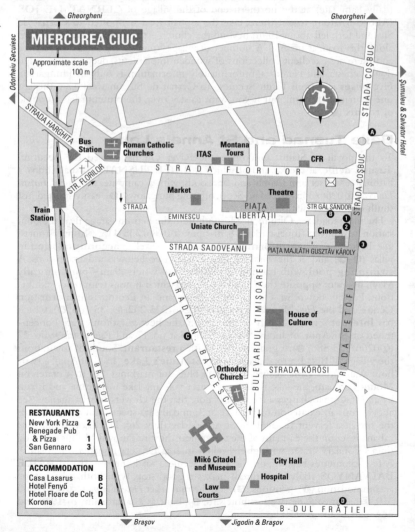

MIERCUREA CIUC

Approximate scale
0   100 m

N

▲ Gheorgheni   Gheorgheni ▲

◄ Odorheiu Secuiesc

STRADA HARGHITA

STRADA COŞBUC

Şumuleu & Salvator Hotel ►

Bus Station

Roman Catholic Churches

ITAS

Montana Tours

CFR

STR. FLORILOR

S T R A D A   F L O R I L O R

Train Station

STRADA

Market

Theatre

PIAŢA LIBERTĂŢII

STR GÁL SÁNDOR

STRADA COŞBUC

EMINESCU

Uniate Church

STRADA SADOVEANU

PIAŢA MAJLÁTH GUSZTÁV KÁROLY

Cinema

STRADA N. BĂLCESCU

STR. BRAŞOVULUI

BULEVARDUL TIMIŞOAREI

House of Culture

STRADA PETŐFI

Orthodox Church

STRADA KÖRÖSI

STRADA KŐRÖSI

Mikó Citadel and Museum

City Hall

Hospital

Law Courts

B - D U L   F R Ă Ţ I E I

RESTAURANTS
New York Pizza — 2
Renegade Pub & Pizza — 1
San Gennaro — 3

ACCOMMODATION
Casa Lasarus — B
Hotel Fenyő — C
Hotel Floare de Colţ — D
Korona — A

▼ Braşov   ▼ Jigodin & Braşov

from Montana Tours, Str. Florilor 22–24 (Mon–Fri 9am–5pm; ⓣ&ⓕ0266/317 122), and ITAS, Str. Florilor 26 (Mon–Fri 8am–4pm, Sat 8am–noon). The post office is at Str. Florilor 5 (Mon–Fri 7am–8pm, Sat 8am–1pm), and there's a CFR office, for train tickets, at Str. Florilor 12 (Mon–Fri 7.30am–6pm; ⓣ0266/317 007). There are supermarkets on the south side of Str. Florilor, plus a market at the rear. Internet access is available at Str. Petófi 3 (24hr).

The town's most appealing accommodation is the *Korona* pension, Str. Coșbuc 38 (ⓣ0266/310 993, ⓦwww.korona.panzio.ro; ❺), a lovely building concealing fifteen large, delightfully coloured rooms. South of the centre, there's the *Hotel Fenyó* at Str. Bălcescu 11 (ⓣ0266/311 493, ⓦwww.hunguest-fenyo .ro; ❼), with adequate yet unspectacular rooms, a gym, sauna and massage, and the *Hotel Floare de Colț*, at B-dul. Frătiei 7 (ⓣ0266/372 068, ⓕ312 533; ❷), which is a bit tatty, with shared showers, but very cheap. The excellent *Casa Lasarus* youth hostel, at Str. Gál Sándor 9 (ⓣ0266/310 497, ⓦwww.lasarushostel.ro; ❷), has very tidy, en-suite four-bed rooms with TV – it also has laundry facilities, Internet and a kitchen for self-catering. There's also a campsite in Băile Jigodin, 2km south on the main road and served by buses #10 and #11; you can walk there by following the blue-dot hiking markings.

The Town

The city centre, with the windswept Piața Libertății at its heart, was extensively rebuilt in communist concrete, a situation made worse by a rash of ugly modern churches, and aside from the Mikó citadel, south of the centre, and the adjacent 1890s Law Courts and City Hall, there is little of architectural interest here. The citadel itself was built in 1611–21 then rebuilt in 1716 and now contains an excellent county museum (Tues–Sun 9am–5pm), with exhibits on Székely churches. Two kilometres further south in the suburb of Jigodin (Zsögödfürdó) the Nagy Imre Gallery (daily except Tues 9am–5pm) displays a rotating selection of the forceful paintings of the Székely artist Nagy Imre (1893–1976); his former home, at the rear of the gallery, contains local textiles and Corund ceramics, as well as photos of the artist. Near the rail and bus stations, the Roman Catholic church on Str. Florilor was built in 1751–58 in a simple Baroque style; behind it, the utterly weird Millennium Templom, also Catholic, is a vision of what the Magyar nomads might have built a millennium ago if they'd had modern materials.

The city's only other attraction is the great Székely pilgrimage to Şumuleu, well worth the trip if you're looking for a flavour of the Székely culture. It takes place on Whit Sunday at Şumuleu (Csiksomlyó), a Franciscan monastery 2km northeast of the city (buses #11, #21, #40, #41, #42 from the station forecourt towards Păuleni and Şoimeni). Largely rebuilt in 1804, the complex was founded in 1442 by Iancu de Hunedoara in thanks for the Székely victory at Marasszentimre; the festival, however, commemorates the 1567 victory of Catholic Székely over János Sigismund Báthori's, who was attempting to impose Calvinism on them. At least 200,000 black-clad pilgrims attend, singing hymns and queuing up to touch the wooden statue of the Virgin in the sanctuary, before processing on to the three small chapels on the nearby hilltop. From here, there's a good view of the plain, dotted with Székely villages.

Eating and drinking

There are several reasonable restaurants running the length of Str. Petófi, the best of which is *San Gennaro*, a good-looking place which has some cracking pizzas, in addition to pastas, risottos and fish options. Also worth trying along here is the *Renegade Pub & Pizza* and the *New York Pizza*. A popular fast-food option – sit-down or takeaway – is *Big Boss*, at the junction of Str. Gál Sándor and Str. Coşbuc. This being the home of Ciuc beer, you'll be offered little else in the town's **pubs** and **bars**, most of which are congregated along Str. Petőfi. This includes the *Hockey Klub*, with loud music and lots of surprisingly impressive ice hockey memorabilia, and *Rodeo Saloon* close by.

The Upper Mureş valley

From Miercurea Ciuc, a semicircular route, by both road and rail, crosses a low pass from the Olt valley to the Mureş valley and curves around to the great Hungarian city of **Târgu Mureş**. It's a leisurely route taking in the tranquil **Lacu Roşu**, the untamed **Căliman mountains** and a plethora of attractive villages, including Gurghiu and Hodac, both of which hold renowned **festivals**. Travelling by train, you may need to change at Deda for Târgu Mureş; with your own transport you can take a shortcut via Sovata, but there are next to no buses on this route.

Gheorgheni and around

GHEORGHENI (Gyergyószentmiklós) is jumping-off point for **Lacu Roşu** (see opposite). **Trains** arriving at Gheorgheni are met by buses to spare passengers the twenty-minute hike east into the town centre. Getting back to the station is not so easy, and you'll probably end up having to walk or take a taxi. The **bus station** is immediately south of the train station, but you can also board eastbound buses on B-dul. Lacu Roşu, just north of the centre; the only bus west on the DN13B leaves at 6.45am (except Wed & Fri) for Sovata and Târgu Mureş.

The road from the station meets the DN12 at a well-conserved synagogue and continues east as B-dul. Lacu Roşu; one block south is the triangular Piaţa Libertăţii, ringed with tatty buildings redolent of the Austro-Hungarian era. To the north of the square, the pedestrianized Str. Miron Cristea leads to B-dul. Lacu Roşu and the splendid high school, completed in 1915; Str. Márton Áron leads east from the square past the Catholic church to Piaţa Petőfi and the **museum** (Tues–Fri 9am–4pm, Sat & Sun 9am–1pm), on the far side of the square at Str. Rácóczi 1. Housed in a former Armenian merchants' inn, it contains some fascinating artefacts, including weatherboards carved with shamanistic motifs brought by the Magyars from Asia.

Practicalities

The town's **tourist office** (Mon–Fri 9am–5pm) is on the south side of the square, and the **post office** (Mon–Fri 8am–6pm, Sat 8am–1pm) is on the west side, with the Calvinist church. There are three simple **hotels** in Gheorgheni; at Piaţa Libertăţii 17, the *Szilagyi* (☎0266/367 591; ❷) has en-suite rooms with between two and six beds and is relatively overpriced; at the south end of Str. Doua Poduri (opposite the Catholic church) the *Astoria* (☎0266/363 698; ❶) offers simpler en-suite rooms above a pizzeria. The *Sport Hotel Avântul* (☎0266/361 270; ❶) at Str. Stadionului 11, off Str. Bălcescu (the Topliţa road), has rooms with shared showers. There's also a **campsite** 4km east of town on the Lacu Roşu road, near the newish *Motel Patru* (☎&⨍0266/364 213; ❷). The best **restaurant** is the *Mukátli*, halfway to the station, while other options are the *Sárkány* Chinese restaurant on Str. Gabór Áron just south of the square, and the pizzeria at the *Astoria* hotel.

Lacu Roşu

Lacu Roşu, or the **Red Lake** (Gyilkostó, or Murderers' Lake, in Hungarian), lies in a small depression 25km east of Gheorgheni. It was formed in 1838 when a landslide dammed the River Bicaz; you can still see the tips of a few pines protruding from the water, which is rich in trout. Surrounded by lovely scenery and blessed by a yearly average of 1800 hours of sunshine, this is an ideal (and busy) stopover if you're crossing the Carpathians into Moldavia through the wild Bicaz gorges (p.280). The area is a national park, and the **Eco-Info-Center** (Tues–Sun 10am–6pm), on the main road near the lake at the western end of the resort, offers information on walks.

At km26, in the centre of the resort, a track crosses a bridge to the north and climbs to the simple *Bucur* **hotel** (℡0266/362 949; ❷). The more atmospheric *Casa Ranova* (℡0266/364 226; ❷) is right by the lake (next to the boat rental shack), and there are also guesthouses such as the *Capra Neagră* (℡0740/455 515), *Combucur* (℡0266/364 049) and *Turist* (℡0745/601 113). The **campsite**, with cabins, is at the eastern end of the resort, although nobody seems to mind if you just pitch a tent anywhere.

Lăzarea

Six kilometres north of Gheorgheni on the DN12 (one stop by train), the village of **LĂZAREA** (Szárhegy) is worth a visit to see **Lazăr Castle**, situated just below the Franciscan monastery whose white tower is visible from the station and passing trains. The fifteenth-century castle's fine Renaissance hall and frescoed facade are being gradually restored by artists who hold a summer camp here each year. The **castle gallery** (Tues–Sun 9am–5pm) exhibits the work of artists attending the camp, and there is also now a well-stocked sculpture park, open all year, in the castle grounds. The OVR office (℡&℻0266/164 191) can provide information about their work as well as details of **homestay** schemes in the area.

Topliţa and the Căliman mountains

The train line continues north for a further 30km from Lăzarea to **TOPLIŢA** (Maroshévíz), a third-rate spa and logging town whose only real sights of interest are two wooden churches – the church of Sf Ilie, 1km north on the main road, built in 1847 and moved here in 1910, and the Doamnei Church in a lovely nunnery 10km further on, dating from 1658 – and a covered bridge south of town. A road runs through the eastern Carpathians from Topliţa into Moldavia, served by buses to Borsec, Poiana Largului and Târgu Neamţ.

From Topliţa, the road and rail routes head west along the Mureş valley, which is lined with various **places to stay**, such as the *şoimilor* cabana (❶) 2km west of the Stânceni Neagră train halt, 16km west of Topliţa; the *Doi Brazi* motel (❷) in Sălard, a further 9km west and 3km west of Lunca Bradului station; and a homestay in Androneasa (Str. Principală 160; ❶), a further 6km west of Sălard. The wild, unpopulated Căliman mountains rise steeply to the north of this narrow, rugged defile, in which retreating German soldiers made a vain attempt to ambush the Red Army in 1944. Today, the Căliman range – the main volcanic zone of the Carpathians – is a paradise for hikers. The best route in is probably from Răstoliţa, 30km west of Topliţa. There's plenty of road traffic as far as the new dam at Secu, from where paths head northeast to the volcanic peaks and the settlements in the huge crater beyond, leading ultimately to Vatra Dornei in Moldavia (see p.320).

South to Târgu Mureş

From Topliţa roads and railtracks lead to Deda (the junction for Beclean and Cluj), and then south towards Târgu Mureş. **BRÂNCOVENEŞTI** (Marosvécs), 13km south of Deda and served by slow trains only, was founded on a Roman site and has the fine Kemény castle (visible across the river from the train) dating from the fourteenth century and best known for housing disabled children judged too sick or traumatized to recover during Ceauşescu's regime. **REGHIN** (Szászrégen/Sächsisch Reen), 10km beyond Brâncoveneşti, is ringed by factories, including an amazingly successful violin factory, located here because of the wealth of the very grainy curly sycamore (also known as flamed maple) in the Gurghiu valley. The main reason to stop here, though, is to make bus connections to Gurghiu and Hodac from immediately outside the train station, so there's little reason to venture into town, 1.5km west. **GURGHIU**, 14km east, and **HODAC**, 8km further, are traditional shepherding communities. Gurghiu is known for its **Girl Fair** (Târgul de fete) on the second Sunday of May, similar to that of Muntele Găina (see box, p.248). At Hodac, there's a **Measurement of the Milk festival** (see p.252) on the first Saturday of May, while the second Sunday in June sees the **Buying Back of the Wives Festival**, reaffirming the economic underpinnings of matrimony. To guard against a wasted journey, check dates at the tourist office in Târgu Mureş (see below). During the festivals, special **buses** are laid on from Reghin; at other times, both villages can be reached by buses bound for Dulcea and Toaca, while Gurghiu is also served by buses to Glăjărie and Orşova.

Târgu Mureş

TÂRGU MUREŞ is still at heart **Marosvásárhely**, one of the great Magyar cities of Transylvania, although the Magyar influence has been diluted by recent Romanian and Gypsy immigration – that said, around half of the city's 180,000 population is Hungarian. The city was briefly notorious as a centre of ethnic tension, with riots in 1990, but is more reputably known as a centre of learning – its university is small, but both the medical and drama schools are renowned nationally. The city suffers from heavy pollution generated at the chemical plant by the main road and rail line to the southwest of town – it's liable to be an unpleasant experience entering or leaving town along this route.

Arrival and information

Târgu Mureş is on a secondary line between Razboieni and Deda and is served by several fast trains a day, with extra services in the summer; however, connections south are poor, and you're best off taking a bus or maxitaxi to Sighişoara, 55km south, and catching a train from there. The **train station** is a fifteen-minute walk south of the centre, with the **bus station** ten minutes further south on Str. Gheorghe Doja – upon exiting turn right, past the train station and on to Piaţa Victoriei and Piaţa Trandafirilor. Note that maxitaxi services to Sighişoara and Sovata leave from a stop on B-dul. 1 Decembrie 1918, in front of the Policlinic (no. 2). The **airport** (ⓦwww.targumuresairport.ro), a busy hub for daily flights to Budapest, is some 12km south of the centre – a taxi should cost around €6.

The **tourist office** (May–Sept Mon 8am–4pm, Tues–Fri 8am–8pm, Sat 8–11am; Oct–April Mon–Fri 8am–4pm; ⓣ0265/404 934; ⓦwww.mures.ro)

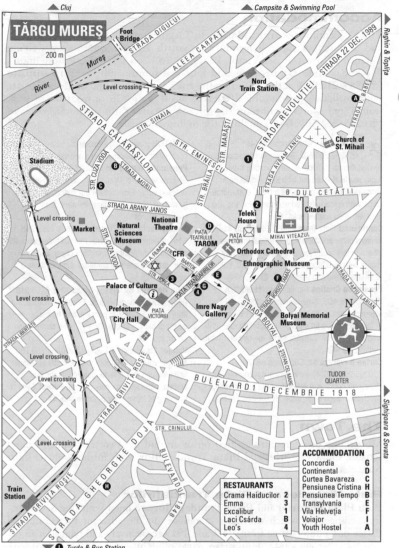

TĂRGU MUREŞ

0 — 200 m

ACCOMMODATION
Concordia	G
Continental	D
Curtea Bavareza	C
Pensiunea Cristina	H
Pensiunea Tempo	B
Transylvania	E
Vila Helveţia	F
Voiajor	I
Youth Hostel	A

RESTAURANTS
Crama Haiducilor	2
Emma	3
Excalibur	1
Laci Csárda	B
Leo's	4

is housed inside the Palace of Culture (the entrance is on Str. Enescu) and its extremely helpful staff can furnish you with a wealth of useful information on the city and surrounds. The **post office** is at Str. Revoluţiei 2 (Mon–Fri 7am–8pm, Sat 8am–1pm); the CFR office, for **train tickets**, is at Piaţa Teatrului 1 (Mon–Fri 7am–8pm); and the **TAROM** office is at Piaţa Trandafirilor 7 (Mon–Fri 9am–5pm; ☎0265/236 200). **Internet** access is available at Internet Club Europe at Piaţa Trandafirilor 43 (10am–midnight), through an alleyway behind the *Leo* restaurant, and Oz, B-dul. 1 Decembrie 1918 no. 11 (24hr).

Accommodation

There's plentiful **accommodation** in Târgu Mureş, including several hotels and a clutch of super pensions. The **youth hostel**, within easy walking distance of town at Str. Victor Babeş 11 (☎0265/257 057, ✉hostelmures @yahoo.com; ❶–❷), has two- and four-bed rooms; and there's a **campsite** (☎0265/212 009) at the Ştrand on the river at the north end of Aleea Carpaţi, with small, two-person cabins (❷); take bus #14 or #26, or maxitaxi, or walk from Târgu Mureş Nord train station. You can also camp at the *Stejeriş motel* (☎0265/233 509; ❷), 7km along the Sighişoara road.

Concordia Piaţa Trandafirilor 45 ☎0265/260 602, ⓦwww.hotelconcordia.ro. Terrific, top-class hotel accommodating fresh, funky rooms decked out with lush red carpets, zebra-print chairs and big, high beds. Bathrooms come with colourfully tiled walls and flooring and unusual, deep square sinks. ❾

Continental Piaţa Teatrului 6 ☎0265/250 416, ⓦwww.continentalhotels.ro. Identical to all the others in this countrywide chain of hotels; tidy rooms with nice fittings, and efficient staff, but ultimately bland and overpriced. ❽

Pensiunea Cristina Str. Piatra de Moară 1/A ☎0265/266 490, ✉pensiunea.cristina @muresonline.ro. It's nothing fancy, but the rooms in this welcoming little pension are bright and tidy, with a/c – it's also convenient for the bus and train stations. ❹–❺

Curtea Bavareza Str. Cuza Vodă 68–70 ☎0265/265 466, ⓦwww.curtea-bavareza.ro. The "Bavarian Court" is a delightful little guesthouse, which has seven large, superbly equipped rooms

(with DVD player), and immaculate bathrooms with complimentary accessories. Good value. ❻

Pensiunea Tempo Str. Morii 27 ☎0265/213 552, ⓦwww.tempo.ro. Upscale yet very affordable pension with eleven simple but stylish, smoothly furnished rooms – terrific restaurant, too (see p.230). ❹

Transylvania Piaţa Trandifirilor 46 ☎0265/265 616, ✉helvetia@rdslink.ro. This old hotel conceals a range of different rooms, from cheap and grubby one- and two-stars to some far superior three-stars. ❸–❻

Villa Helveţia Str. Borsos Tamăs 13 ☎0265/216 954, ⓦwww.villahelvetia.ro. Extremely cordial, if a little pricey, Swiss-run pension with homely, comfortable a/c rooms. They've got a terrific wine cellar, too. ❼

Voiajor Str. Gheorghe Doja 143 ☎0265/250 750, ⓦwww.voiajor.ro. Modern and perfectly agreeable hotel located in the same building as the bus station, although it's really only convenient if you're planning to leave early or arrive late. ❹

The Town

Most things of interest are centred on or around the two traffic-filled central squares, **Piaţa Victoriei** and **Piaţa Trandafirilor**, with further sights a short walk east of here.

Piaţa Victoriei and Piaţa Trandafirilor

Both **Piaţa Victoriei** and **Piaţa Trandafirilor** are lined with fine Secession-style edifices, of which the most grandiose are the adjacent Prefecture and Palace of Culture, dating from 1907 and 1913 respectively and typical of an era when a self-consciously "Hungarian" style of architecture reflected Budapest's policy of "Magyarizing" Transylvania.

The Prefecture's rooftops blaze with polychromatic tiling, as do those of the **Palace of Culture** (Palatul Culturii; Tues–Fri 9am–4pm, Sat & Sun 9am–1pm; €2), whose facade is richly ornamented with bronze bas-reliefs, ornately carved balconies and a splendid mosaic. Inside, the gloomy corridors are relieved by floral painted walls and stained glass, and 50kg of gilding – working your way up the marble stairs, take a look at the many stained-glass windows illustrating eminent Hungarians, such as the composer Franz Liszt, politician Lajos Kossuth and the poet Sándor Petófi. One flight up by the right-hand staircase is the most spectacular room of all, the **Hall of Mirrors** (Sala de Oglinzi), with stained-glass windows illustrating local myths. Another flight up is the **history section**, little more than a dull collection of archeological pieces. Two flights up the left-hand staircase, a door gives you a free glimpse from the gods of the city's concert hall; the huge organ is often used for recitals. Another floor up is the museum's **art section**, focusing on the Hungarian Revival of the late nineteenth and early twentieth centuries. Classical **concerts** take place inside the palace every Thursday, with tickets available from the same ticket office (Mon–Fri 10am–1pm & 5–7pm). Back on Str. Enescu, a gallery houses free shows by local artists (Tues–Fri 10am–4pm, Sat 10am–1pm).

Two blocks north of the Palace of Culture, in the fine Baroque Toldalagy House at Piaţa Trandafirilor 11, is the **Ethnographic Museum** (Muzeul Etnografic; Tues–Fri 9am–4pm, Sat 9am–2pm, Sun 9am–1pm); it's a rather dry presentation, but the displays on local industry, together with a collection of colourful regional costumes and icons on glass, are intermittently interesting. Beside the museum stands a tower raised in 1735 – all that remains of the Minorite (Franciscan) monastery – and behind this, the concrete plaza of Piaţa Teatrului, with its undistinguished modern sculptures. A short walk up behind Piaţa Teatrului, beyond the city's synagogue, the **Natural Sciences Museum** (Muzeul de Ştiinţele Naturii; same hours) at Str. Horea 24 exhibits a series of large dioramas of stuffed beasts.

The neo-Byzantine **Orthodox Cathedral** (1925–34) marks the northern end of Piaţa Trandafirilor. The Romanian riposte to the imperialistic Magyar administrative buildings dominating the southern end of the square, it pushes aside the more modest Baroque church of the Jesuits (1728–64) on its eastern flank; for good measure, the new masters added a statue of Avram Iancu on the cathedral's southern side, not to mention the Greek-Catholic Catedral Mică, or Little Cathedral (1926–36), at the south end.

East of Piaţa Trandafirilor

East from Piaţa Trandafirilor, on the corner of Str. Bolyai and Str. Kóteles Sámuel, the **Imre Nagy Gallery** (Mon–Fri 9am–4pm, Sat & Sun 9am–1pm) displays the oeuvre of the eponymous Székely artist, whose paintings were heavily influenced by the Transylvanian countryside. Despite its long-standing role as a garrison town, Târgu Mureş also takes pride in its intellectual tradition; the mathematician Farkas Bolyai (1775–1856) and his son János (1802–60), founders of non-Euclidean geometry, receive their due in the **Bolyai Memorial Museum** at Str. Bolyai 17 (Tues–Fri 10am–6pm, Sat & Sun 10am–1pm), beyond a high school built in 1909 in the Hungarian Art Nouveau (flippantly known as Art Noodle) style. The museum houses Târgu Mureş's greatest treasure, the **Teleki–Bolyai library** (Biblioteca Bolyai–Teleki). Amassed by the chancellor of Transylvania, Count Samuel Teleki (1739–1822), the collection consists of some 40,000 volumes, including more than 60 incunabula (books printed before 1500), as well as the works of the philosophers of the French Enlightenment, first translations of the Bible in both Hungarian (1590) and Romanian (1688), and the only copy of the first Hungarian encyclopedia.

A ten-minute walk north from here, beyond Str. Mihai Viteazul, stands the **citadel**, whose walls shelter the Calvinist church built for the Dominicans in 1430 and later used by the Transylvanian Diet; there's a small history display in a gate tower (built in 1613). After years of neglect, parts of the citadel have been renovated, including the former Austrian barracks that line the eastern side, while the spacious grounds are also becoming a focus for live events – open-air theatrical performances and the like – during the summer months. Two blocks east of the citadel, along B-dul. Cetăţii, Str. Şaguna heads north to the **wooden church** of Sf Mihail (1793–94). Set in a large cemetery, the church has a shingled onion-dome, while there are still some traceable frescoes in the largely blackened interior. The porch is a virtual shrine to the national poet, Mihai Eminescu, owing to the fact that he slept in it in 1866 because there was no room at the inn.

Eating and drinking

There are two particularly fine Hungarian **restaurants** in town; the *Laci Csárda*, inside the *Tempo* pension (see p.228), which replicates a Hungarian-style inn (*csárda*) to impressive effect with lots of rustic trappings and great food, particularly the homemade soups and bread; and *Emma*, Str. Horea 3, a more traditional Hungarian restaurant (*vendéglő*) offering lots of goulash and dumpling dishes, as well as good cooked breakfasts. Otherwise, there are a few reasonable options on or just off Piaţa Trandafirilor, such as *Leos* at no. 44, a popular, informal place whose food is solid rather than spectacular; *Crama Haiducilor*, Str. Poştei 12, a reasonable cellar pizzeria; and, north of Piaţa Trandafirilor, at Str. Revoluţiei 29, *Excalibur*, a vaguely medieval themed restaurant whose menu mainly consists of meat-heavy platters.

The best **fast-food** options are the *LactoBar* at Piaţa Trandafirilor 5, which serves big plates of canteen-style grub, and *Panda Pui* at no. 15, which is open round the clock. Excellent doughnuts (*gogoşi* or *langoş*) are served till 10pm at the rear of the Cinema Arte on the south side of Piaţa Trandafirilor, with another counter selling *covrigi ardeleneşti* (Transylvanian bread rings) close by.

By far the most characterful place to **drink** is *Teatrul 74*, tucked away in the Butcher's Bastion in the northwestern corner of the citadel – with its bare brick walls, colourful artwork, wicker chairs and leather sofas, it's a relaxing place for a daytime coffee or evening beer, and also stages a cracking programme of music, theatre and comedy. Another underground-style venue is *Ariel*, Str. Postei 2, where you can listen to jazz, poetry and acoustic music. Elsewhere, the main drinking venues are ranged along or just off Piaţa Trandafirilor; the *Gallery Café* at no. 17 is a cool, somewhat posey, place with pavement seating and a cellar incorporating separate smoking and no-smoking sections and Wi-Fi. Across the road, the pavement café of the *Concordia* hotel is as pleasant as anything else along here. There are several possibilities up along Str. Bolyai, the best of which is the *Dancing Shiva* teahouse at no. 16, where you can kick back on low stools and indulge in a marvellous selection of world teas.

Cluj and northern Transylvania

Cluj was the great Hungarian capital of Transylvania and remains a natural gateway to the region, just six hours from Budapest by train. There is more buzz to its café life than in other towns, maybe due to the seventy thousand students resident here.

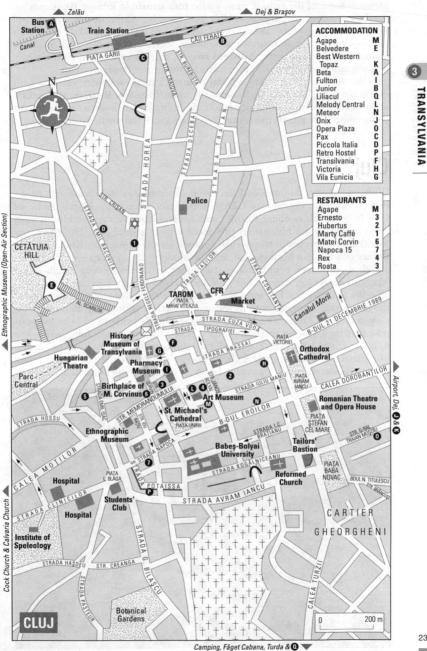

▲ Zalău   ▲ Dej & Brașov

Bus Station A
Canal
Train Station   CĂII FERATE   B
PIAȚA GĂRII   C

N

STR. TRAIAN

STRADA DECEBAL

STRADA TRAIAN

STRADA HOREA

STR. CRIȘAN

STRADA EMIL RACOVIȚĂ

Police

STR. BURIBISTA

ACCOMMODATION

Agape	M
Belvedere	E
Best Western Topaz	K
Beta	A
Fullton	I
Junior	B
Liliacul	Q
Melody Central	L
Meteor	N
Onix	J
Opera Plaza	O
Pax	C
Piccola Italia	D
Retro Hostel	P
Transilvania	F
Victoria	H
Vila Eunicia	G

RESTAURANTS

Agape	M
Ernesto	3
Hubertus	2
Marty Caffé	1
Matei Corvin	6
Napoca 15	7
Rex	4
Roata	3

CETĂȚUIA HILL

AL. SCĂRILOR

Ethnographic Museum (Open-Air Section) ▲

D

E

1

STRADA REGELE FERDINAND

STRADA ȚĂILOR

TAROM
PIAȚA MIHAI VITEAZUL

CFR

Market

STRADA CUZA VODĂ

Canalul Morii

B-DUL 21 DECEMBRIE 1989

STRADA TIPOGRAFIEI

STRADA

PIAȚA VICTORIEI

History Museum of Transylvania

F   G

STRADA BRASSAI

Orthodox Cathedral

CALEA DOROBANȚILOR

Hungarian Theatre

Pharmacy Museum
J

2

STRADA IULIU MANIU

H

PIAȚA AVRAM IANCU

Parc Central

Birthplace of M. Corvinus
3   6

5

STRADA EMIL ISAC

STR. MEMORANDUMULUI

STRADA BOLYAI

L
4

Art Museum
M

N

Romanian Theatre and Opera House

B-DUL EROILOR

PIAȚA ȘTEFAN CEL MARE

STR. G-RAL TRAIAN MOȘOIU

O

STRADA HOSSU

Ethnographic Museum

St. Michael's Cathedral
PIAȚA UNIRII

STRADA NAPOCA

7

Babeș-Bolyai University

STRADA I.C. BRĂTIANU

Tailors' Bastion

PIAȚA BABA NOVAC

BOUL. N. TITULESCU

STR. BRÂNCUȘI

CALEA MOTILOR

PIAȚA L. BLAGA

P

STRADA POTAISSA

STRADA KOGĂLNICEANU

Reformed Church

CARTIER

GHEORGHENI

Hospital

STRADA CLINICILOR

Students' Club

Hospital

STRADA AVRAM IANCU

Institute of Speleology

STRADA HAȘDEU

STR. CREANGA

STRADA G. BILAȘCU

STRADA PASTEUR

Botanical Gardens

CALEA TURZII

CLUJ

0   200 m

◀ Cock Church & Calvaria Church

Airport, Dej ▶ J & K

Camping, Făget Cabana, Turda & Q ▼

The area surrounding Cluj, particularly the **Transylvanian Heath** to the east, harbours some of the richest, most varied **folk music** in Europe. Weekends are the best time to investigate villages such as **Sic**, **Cojocna**, **Rimetea** and **Izvoru Crişului**, where almost every street has its own band and there are rich pickings to be had at spring and summer festivals. The town itself is also a natural base for visiting the **Apuseni massif**, with its wide green pastures, easy walking and caving opportunities, particularly on the **Padiş plateau**.

To the north of the Apuseni is **Sălaj county**, a rural backwater scattered with quaint wooden churches. Further east, the historic town of **Bistriţa**, once centre of an isolated Saxon community (and today more widely known for its Dracula connections), still guards the routes into Maramureş and northern Moldavia.

Cluj

With its cupolas, Baroque and Secession outcroppings and weathered *fin-de-siècle* backstreets, downtown **CLUJ** (sometimes known by its full name of Cluj-Napoca; Klausenburg to the Germans and Kolozsvár to the Hungarians) looks every bit the Hungarian provincial capital it once was. The town was founded by Germans in the twelfth century for the Hungarian King Geza, on the site of a Roman Municipium, and the modern-day Magyars – now less than a fifth of the city's population – still regret its decline, fondly recalling the Magyar *belle époque*, when Cluj's café society and literary reputation surpassed all other Balkan cities. For most Romanians, however, Kolozsvár was the city of the Hungarian landlords until its restoration to the national patrimony in 1920; they consider Ceauşescu's addition of Napoca to its name in 1974 as recognition that their Dacian forebears settled here 1850 years ago, long before the Magyars entered Transylvania. It's rightly said that Romanians live in Cluj and Hungarians – who comprise around twenty percent of the population – still live in Koloszvár, with separate schools, theatre and opera, though relations

▲ Pavement café on Piaţa Unirii, Cluj

between the two communities are healthy. Cluj is also the birthplace of the Unitarian creed and its centre in Romania, further adding to the multiethnic, multifaith cocktail.

Under communism, Cluj was industrialized and, with a population of more than 330,000, became Transylvania's largest city. Nonetheless it retained something of its old languor and raffish undercurrents, as well as a reputation for being anti-Ceauşescu. From 1992 to 2004, the city was run by Gheorghe Funar, the "Mad Mayor" of Cluj, a former leader of the Romanian National Unity Party, and a man notorious for his anti-Hungarian stance – park benches and litter bins were painted in the colours of the Romanian flag, while a number of absurdly expensive monuments were raised, the last of which are still very much in evidence. With a clutch of fine museums, churches and buildings, and buzzing nightlife, Cluj could quite easily detain you for a couple of days.

Arrival and information

From Cluj's **train station**, it takes about twenty minutes to walk down Str. Horea, across the Little Someş river, where the road becomes Str. Regele Ferdinand (until recently Str. Gheorghe Doja), and into the spacious **Piaţa Unirii**, the focus of the city's life. Across the road from the station, trolley buses #3, #4 and #9 stop on their loop route into the centre, going south on Str. Traian and returning along Str. Horea. The **bus station** is just across the tracks/bridge to the north of the train station (bus #31 or #42). The **airport** (Ⓦ www.airportcluj.ro) is 5km east of the city at Calea Traian Vuia 149, connected by bus #8 to Piaţa Mihai Viteazul, node of the city's public transport system, in the centre just east of Str. Regele Ferdinand. A taxi to the centre should cost no more than €4, but check the price before getting in. The terminal, built in 1969, has been modernized but has no carousel; just wait in the hall until your bags appear.

Cluj's buses, trolley buses and trams provide frequent and reliable **city transport**, though stops are often far apart; buy tickets at kiosks (€1 for two rides). The most reliable **taxis** are operated by Pritax (Ⓣ942), Diesel (Ⓣ953), Pro Rapid (Ⓣ948), Terra (Ⓣ944) and Nova (Ⓣ949).

Disappointingly, the city is still without a **tourist office**, but a very good source of information is the *Retro Youth Hostel* (see p.234). An excellent **map** of Cluj (including public transport routes) is published by Top-o-Gráf/Freytag & Berndt and can be found in most bookshops as well as kiosks around Piaţa Unirii. There are also free weekly **listings magazines**, *Zile şi Nopţi* and *Şapte Seri* (Ⓦ www.sapteseri.ro), but only in Romanian.

Accommodation

As befits Romania's second-largest city, Cluj has a wide range of accommodation, with a varied selection of **hotels** and **pensions**, a terrific **hostel** and, during the summer, a range of other student accommodation.

Hotels

Agape Str. Iuliu Maniu 6 Ⓣ 0264/406 523, Ⓦ www.hotelagape.ro. Quiet, central hotel accommodating big, brightly coloured rooms with large armchairs, fluffy rugs, wall lamps and pictures, and gleaming white bathrooms. Reception is up on the second floor. ❼

Belvedere Str. Călăraşilor 1 Ⓣ 0264/432 071, Ⓔ belvedere.cluj@unita-turism.ro. Upscale modern place overlooking the town from Cetăţuia hill. The renovated rooms are not much more impressive than the standard ones. Main access by foot (up dilapidated steps, not safe at night), or by taxi – nearest bus is #37/38, stopping not too far north at Str. Gruia. ❼—❽

Best Western Topaz Str. Septimiu Albini 10 ☎0264/414 021, ⓦwww.bestwesterntopaz.ro. A few steps away from the *Onix*, this is a rather staid and characterless choice, but its facilities are as good as anything else around. ❻

Beta Str. Giordano Bruno 1 ☎0264/455 290. Refurbished hotel inside the bus station, though the rooms are dull and a little poky. Convenient, if somewhat overpriced. ❹

🏃 **Fullton** Str. Sextil Pușcariu 10 ☎0264/597 898, ⓦwww.fullton.ro. Extremely elegant hotel tucked away on a quiet, narrow street a few steps from Corvinus' birthplace; the warm rooms – some with four-poster beds – are smartly furnished with thick pile carpets and arty, striped painted walls. ❻

Junior Str. Căii Ferate 12 ☎0264/432 028, ⓔoffice@pensiune-junior.ro. Clean and quiet, if a little scruffy, hostel-type place just 200m east of the train station, with double and triple rooms. ❸

Liliacul Calea Turzii 251A ☎0264/438 129, ⓦwww.hotelliliacul.com. Located out of town on the DN1, just before the Făget campsite turning, this is a reasonable option, with well-appointed rooms, including some triples. ❹—❻

Melody Central Piața Unirii 29 ☎0264/597 465, ⓦwww.centralmelody.com. There's been a hotel of sorts here for more than a century, and despite its great central location it's quite noisy and now somewhat lacking in character. ❺—❻

Meteor B-dul. Eroilor 29 ☎0264/591 060, ⓦwww.hotelmeteor.ro. A decent hotel in a very central location (set back from the street), with satellite TV, parking and buffet breakfast, but it can get a little noisy thanks to the downstairs bar. ❺

Onix Str. Septimiu Albini 1 ☎0264/414 076, ⓦwww.hotelonix.ro. A short way east of the centre (trolleys #2, #3, #25; bus #33), this place has some four-star rooms, with PCs and free Internet access, and considerably dingier three-stars, which are not a whole lot cheaper. Sauna, massage and hairdresser also available; along with a nightly "erotic show" at the nightclub. ❺—❼

Opera Plaza Str. G-ral Traian Moșoiu 10 ☎0264/428 164, ⓦwww.operaplaza.ro. While the building/exterior of the city's sole five-star establishment looks very ordinary, the rooms are as luxurious as you'd expect, from the smooth oak-wood bureaus and rich green carpets, down to the sumptuous square beds and immaculate, handsomely equipped bathrooms. Sauna, pool and fitness suite, and underground parking. ❾

Pax Piața Gării 1 ☎0264/432 927, ⓦwww.hotelpax.ro. Smack-bang opposite the train station, the fourteen rooms – with and without bathrooms – here are a touch sprightlier than the exterior might suggest. ❸—❹

Piccola Italia Str. Emil Racoviță 20 ☎0264/536 110, ⓦwww.piccolaatalia.ro. Homely little guesthouse on a quiet residential street, with breezy, modern rooms, including several triples. ❹—❺

Transilvania Str. Regele Ferdinand 20 ☎0264/594 429, ⓦwww.hoteltransilvaniacluj.ro. A rare city-centre budget option, though the grey, spartanly furnished rooms (some with baths) are pretty dated – the entrance is through the passage off the main street. ❹

Victoria B-dul. 21 Decembrie 1989 54 ☎0264/597 963, ⓦwww.hotel-victoria.ro. Decent central hotel whose spacious rooms have modern fittings. ❼

Vila Eunicia Str. Emile Zola 2 ☎0264/594 067, ⓔoffice@vilaeunicia.ro. The bright yellow, flower-bedecked facade of this central guesthouse conceals modern, slightly cluttered rooms with cable TV and Internet connections. Free parking. ❺

Hostels, camping and cabanas

Cluj has one of Romania's best **youth hostels** in the 🏃 *Retro*, Str. Potaissa 13 (☎0264/450 452, ⓦwww.retro.ro; ❶—❸); possessing a great central location, it's an immaculately clean, friendly and well-run place, with singles, doubles, triples and dorm rooms – breakfast and laundry are both available for a small extra charge, and there's free Internet/Wi-Fi access. As well as being a useful source of information, the hostel sells bus tickets to Budapest, can organize car hire, and also runs excursions to places such as the Turda Gorge and Salt Mine (see p.243). In July and August, you could also try the **student accommodation** at Str. Brașov 2 (☎0264/586 616, ⓔdoremi@hihostels-romania.ro; check-in 9am–1pm & 6–10pm; ❶), near the Turda road (bus #3 to Piața Ciprariu) – it has three-bunk dorms, with the showers down the corridor, and cooking facilities.

The *Făget* **campsite** (year-round; ☎0264/596 234; ❶) is 4km south along the DN1 and a further 1.5km off the main road towards Turda (turn off at km472.5, by the *Liliacul* hotel); bus #40A goes there from Aleea Învaţatorului, on the south side of Piaţa Ştefan cel Mare, every hour or two in season, or failing that take any of the frequent buses for Feleacu and Turda to the *Liliacul* and then walk the remaining 1.5km. The site's facilities include simple two-bed cabins (❷), a restaurant and bar, and nonstop hot water (during the summer); there's also plenty of space for tents and caravans. Across the road from the campsite is the *Silva*, a nice private bar-restaurant, recommended for its tripe soup.

About fifteen minutes' walk beyond the campsite is the *Făget* **cabana** (☎0264/596 880; ❶); there are others at Cheile Baciului – take the train or buses #31 or #42 west on the DN1F to *Calea Baciului* (☎0264/435 454; ❶), and at Făget-Izvor turn left onto Str. Primăverii at the Mănăştur roundabout, and then after 1km or so turn left at a signed turning, from where it's a further kilometre to the cabana (☎0264/562 991; ❶).

The City

Unlike almost every other Romanian city of comparable size, Cluj has no Civic Centre, thus avoiding a widespread demolition of its old central zone, which remains largely unspoilt within the line of the **city walls**, now almost entirely gone. The focal point of the city is **Piaţa Unirii**, surrounded by shops, cafés and restaurants and dominated by the monumental **St Michael's Cathedral**. Located around and close to the square is the core of the city's museums, the best of which is the marvellous **Ethnographic Museum**. South of Piaţa Unirii is the widely dispersed **university area**, sprinkled with several impressive buildings, and a short walk further east there's more fine architecture on display, notably the **Romanian National Theatre and Opera House** on Piaţa Ştefan cel Mare.

Piaţa Unirii

Dwarfing **Piaţa Unirii** is **St Michael's Cathedral**, built between 1349 and 1487 in the German Gothic style of the Saxons who then ruled unchallenged over the city. It's a superb example of a Central European hall-church – not dissimilar to the Black Church in Braşov (see p.161) – comprising three capacious naves separated by mighty pillars that curve into austerely bare vaulting. To this great church the Hungarian aristocracy later added a sacristy – the door of which (dated 1528) encapsulates the Italian Renaissance style introduced under Mátyás Corvinus – a wooden Baroque pulpit flush with sculptures and bas-reliefs, and a massive tapering bell tower raised in 1859. Note, too, the fifteenth-century frescoes on the south wall, to the right as you enter.

South of the cathedral, a clumsy but imposing equestrian **statue of Mátyás Corvinus** (raised in 1902) tramples the crescent banner of the Turks underfoot. His formidable Black Army kept the Kingdom of Hungary safe from banditry and foreign invasion for much of his reign (1458–90), but just 36 years later the nation was more or less wiped off the map at the battle of Mohács. A popular lament that justice departed with his death highlights Mátyás's political and military achievements, but the leader's reputation derives equally from his Renaissance attributes, for which his wife **Beatrix of Naples** should share the credit. By introducing him to the Renaissance culture of Italy and selecting foreign architects and craftsmen, and humanists like Bonfini to chronicle events and speeches, Beatrix was a catalyst for Hungary's own fifteenth-century Renaissance, and she personally commissioned many volumes in the Corvin Library.

Beyond the statue, in the southwestern corner of the square, stand seven elongated bronze cylinders, known as the **Shot Pillars** – these elegant sculptures were erected in 2003 to commemorate those gunned down in the 1989 revolution, some 26 in total. Across the road from the pillars, the now defunct **Hotel Continental** stands out in the array of late nineteenth-century buildings: built in 1895 in an eclectic style combining Renaissance, Classical and Baroque elements, it later served as the German military headquarters in Transylvania at the end of World War II. Across the road, the University Bookshop is another fine building, bearing two plaques to those killed on and December 21 and 22 1989.

On the northern side of the square, on the corner of Str. Regele Ferdinand, the Hintz House served as Cluj's first apothecary, opening in 1573 and finally closing in 1949. Inside, the **Pharmacy Museum** (Mon–Sat 10am–4pm; €2) displays a beautiful collection of ancient prescriptions, jars and implements, as well as Baroque furnishings and glass cabinets. Down in the pharmacy basement – something akin to a medieval dungeon – is the old laboratory, complete with an assortment of tools, pestles and containers.

East of the cathedral, at Piaţa Unirii 30, stands the **Art Museum** (Wed–Sun noon–7pm; €2), which, alongside its counterpart in Bucharest (see p.69), offers the best survey of Romanian art in the country. It is housed in the Baroque Bánffy Palace, built in 1774–91 to the design of Johann Eberhardt Blaumann for the Bánffy family. The collection is dominated by works of the largely French-influenced artists of the nineteenth and twentieth centuries, with the best stuff here by Romania's foremost painter, Nicolae Grigorescu (1838–1907); as well as his superb landscapes, look out for some wonderful character paintings, such as *Turkish Prisoner* and *Gypsy with Bear*, and a rare self-portrait. Also well represented are Theodor Aman (1831–91) and Theodor Pallady (1871–1956), who spent several decades in Paris and was clearly inspired by Matisse. Some of Hungary's greatest painters, such as Istvan Nagy and Imre Nagy, also get a look-in. However, there's nothing by Romania's great sculptor, Brâncuşi, and virtually no abstract or truly modern art. In summertime, there's an open-air bar in the courtyard (see p.241), and concerts performed by anyone from Moldavian Gypsy brass bands to the Cluj Philharmonic.

North of Piaţa Unirii

From the northwest corner of Piaţa Unirii, Str. Matei Corvin leads to the small fifteenth-century mansion at no. 6, also known as the **birthplace of Mátyás Corvinus**, Hungary's greatest king. Born in 1440, Corvinus was the son of Iancu de Hunedoara, and thus a Romanian, as a plaque added by Funar (see p.233) in 1999 makes clear (however, Magyar myth makes his father the illegitimate son of the Hungarian King Sigismund, and this was virtually a place of pilgrimage for Hungarians in Habsburg days). The mansion is now an art college, but it's worth a peek inside to view the original stone door entrance and vaulted Gothic ceiling – there are also occasional free exhibitions down in the basement.

Continuing north, Str. Corvin leads into Piaţa Muzeului, where Roman ruins have recently been excavated (and covered again) in the centre. Just to the left of the square, at Str. Daicovici 2, is the **History Museum of Transylvania** (Tues–Sun 10am–4pm; €2). On the first floor, strange skulls and mammoth tusks are succeeded by arrow- and spearheads, charting progress from the Neolithic and Bronze Ages to the rise of the Dacian civilization, which reached its peak between the second century BC and the first century AD. On the floor above, the story continues up to World War I, but overall this is a desperately dull display, and with information in Romanian only.

At the east end of the square, the **Franciscan church** was built after the Tatar attack in the thirteenth century and handed over to the Dominican order by Iancu de Hunedoara in 1455; it was transferred to the Franciscans in 1725 and subsequently rebuilt in the Baroque style. Inside, the fanciful main altar features a painting of the Virgin Mary, flanked by statues of the great Hungarian kings, St Joseph and St Stephen.

Adjoining the church to the north, a fine Gothic house is home to a music school, and there are more Roman foundations opposite this. By the river, to the north, the Tranzit art centre (fairly inactive in summer) has taken over a former synagogue at the rear of Str. Bariţiu 18. To the west is the city's park, with pedaloes on a lake and a casino at its far end; near the river, the Academy of Visual Arts occupies an orange building with a few statues outside.

North of here is **Piaţa Mihai Viteazul**, a traffic-laden square dominated by a large statue of Michael the Brave, and a new eternal flame. To the east of the square and the busy market (see p.242), a disused synagogue at Str. Croitorilor 13 now houses the university's centres for Jewish Studies, Holocaust Studies, Gender Studies and the like; it's a plain building, almost like a Methodist chapel. Heading further north, across the river and along Str. Horea towards the train station, brings you to the Mughal-style Neologue **synagogue**, built in 1886, sacked by the Legionaries in 1927, demolished in 1944 and rebuilt in 1951.

Across to the east, atop Cetăţuia Hill, stand the remains of a fifteenth-century **citadel**, which still surround the *Belvedere* hotel. The Securitate used the hotel as its power base, and twelve people were supposedly gunned down on the steps in the 1989 revolution. The plinth of the massive cross, raised here by the Uniate Church in 1993–97 (replacing one demolished in 1948), is the best place to **view** the city. Behind the hotel is a tower that looks something like a dock for airships but was in fact built for testing parachutes.

The university area

From Piaţa Unirii, Str. Napoca leads west to the **Students' Club** and the old library on Piaţa Blaga, and Str. Universităţii heads south past the Baroque church of the Piarist Order (1718–24) to the **Babeş-Bolyai University**. Since its foundation in 1581, as a Jesuit Academy, the university has produced scholars of the calibre of Edmund Bordeaux Székely (translator of the Dead Sea Scrolls), but has also served as an instrument of cultural oppression. Long denied an education in their own language, the Romanians promptly banned teaching in Hungarian once they took over in 1919, only to hurriedly evacuate students and staff when Hitler gave northern Transylvania back to Hungary in 1940. After liberation, separate universities were created to provide education in the mother tongues of the two main communities, and for a while it seemed that inequality was a thing of the past. However, in 1959 the authorities decreed a shotgun merger, enforced by a then little-known cadre called Nicolae Ceauşescu, which led to the suicide of the Bolyai's pro-rector, and, more predictably, a rapid decline in its Hungarian-language teaching. This and a similar running-down of primary and secondary schooling convinced many Magyars that the state was bent on "de-culturizing" them. In 1997, it was decided to demerge the university, but this time it has found a genuinely multicultural vocation, with teaching in both languages as well as the first Jewish Studies courses in Romania.

Outside the university's main door stand statues of Samuil Micu, Gheorghe Şincai and Petru Maior, the leaders of the **School of Transylvania** (Şcoala Ardeleana) whose philological and historical researches in Blaj fuelled the Romanian cultural resurgence of the nineteenth century and the resistance to

Magyarization. They inspired the "generation of 1848", including Avram Iancu, who lived as a student in 1841–44 at Str. Avram Iancu 17; nearby, flower and coffin shops mark out the gate of the **cemetery** at no. 26 (daily: March–Oct 6.30am–7.30pm; Nov–Feb 8am–5.30pm); the cave scientist Emil Racoviţa and his family lie on the left as you go up to the graves of Kós Károly (see box, p.219) and the writer Emil Isac, both on the right. Cutting across below Károly's final resting place to the next avenue east, you'll find the grand grave of the composer Nicolae Bretan at the junction, and the dramatist Szentgyörgy István (1842–1931) on the right just below.

At Str. Bilaşcu (formerly Republicii) 42, just south of the university, are the **Botanical Gardens** (daily 9am–7pm; €2), one of the largest in southeastern Europe, with more than 10,000 species. They contain a museum and herbarium, greenhouses (to 6pm) with desert and tropical plants including Amazon waterlilies 2m across, and a small Japanese garden.

East to Piaţa Ştefan cel Mare

The tree-lined Str. Kogălniceanu runs east from the university to the Calvinists' **Reformed church**, built in 1486–1516 for Mátyás Corvinus, with a pulpit added in 1646. Outside the church stands a copy of the statue of St George and the Dragon in Prague's Hradčany castle – one of the world's most famous equestrian statues – made in 1373 by the masters Martón and György of Kolozsvár (Martin and George of Cluj). The church's interior features plain late Gothic stonework above the stalls and wooden panels, decorated with the coats of arms of all the leading Hungarian families of Transylvania. The ornate organ (1766) in the gallery, added in 1912, above the west door, is used for recitals. If the church is closed, the key is available at Str. Kogălniceanu 21.

Just east of the church, on Piaţa Baba Novac, is the restored fifteenth-century **Tailors' Bastion** (Turnul Croitorilor), which once guarded southern access to the city. North of the bastion, the elongated square of Piaţa Ştefan cel Mare is dominated by the apricot-and-white facade of the **Romanian National Theatre and Opera House**, built in 1906 by the ubiquitous Viennese theatre architects Fellner and Helmer. Inaugurated in 1919, the building has hosted the great and good of Romanian theatre and opera, as testified by the many photos on the walls of the lobby.

Unitarianism

The **Unitarian Church** was founded in Cluj in 1556 by the hitherto Calvinist minister Dávid Ferenc (1510–79), and by 1568 it was already accepted as one of the four official churches of Transylvania. Unitarianism had its origins among the Italian and Spanish humanists and some of the more extreme Anabaptists, and one of its Italian leaders, Faustus Socinus (1539–1604), came to Cluj in 1578, before moving on to Kraków in 1580.

Unitarianism derives its name from its rejection of the doctrine of the Trinity, as well as of other basic doctrines such as the divinity of Christ, his atonement for the sins of the world, and thus the possibility of salvation. However, its significance lies in its undogmatic approach – adherents are conspicuous for their devotion to reason in matters of religion, and to civil and religious liberty, and their exercise of tolerance to all sincere forms of religious faith.

Unitarianism spread worldwide, and by the 1830s had mutated to become the religion, for instance, of the Boston/Harvard establishment, with an emphasis on scientific progress and material success. In Romania, there are now around 75,000 Unitarians, almost all among the Hungarian community.

Across the road, in Piaţa Avram Iancu, is the notorious statue of Avram Iancu – leader of the 1848 revolt against the Hungarians – commissioned by Funar in 1993. Looming behind the statue is the huge and startling **Orthodox Cathedral** (Tues–Fri & Sun 6am–8pm, Mon & Sat 6am–1pm & 5–8pm), built in 1921–33 and looking as if it fell through a time warp from Justinian's Constantinople. It was raised to celebrate the Romanians' triumph in Transylvania, and the neo-Byzantine stone facade hides a concrete structure. Inside, amidst the cold, grey concrete and fading frescoes, are many elaborate and colourful adornments. In 2001, the narthex, sections of the nave walls, and a spot just above the interior entrance, were decorated with Murano mosaic from Venice – more than one hundred hues, including twenty different shades of gold, were used in these beautiful compositions. Meanwhile, the huge iconostasis – bearing the unmistakeable stamp of Brâncoveanu – comprises three rows of icons featuring scenes from the life of Christ and images of revered saints. Note, too, the fabulous twisted rope motif around the narthex. The enormous chandelier was a gift from King Carol I.

From here, the most direct route back to the centre is along B-dul. Eroilor, at the east end of which is another of Funar's absurd monuments – the ugly *Memorandum* monument, commonly known as "*The Guillotine*". It was raised in memory to Romanians imprisoned for protesting in the 1892 *Memorandum* against Hungarian chauvinism.

At B-dul. Eroilor 10 you'll see the Greco-Catholic cathedral of the Transfiguration, a Baroque pile built for the Minorites in 1775–79; other fine buildings are the Cinema Victoria (at the east end of the street) and nos. 42 and 49. Alternatively, you can take B-dul. 21 Decembrie 1989, starting by the fine Secession prefecture and passing Unitarian and Evangelical churches, both Baroque, to end up at the Pharmacy Museum (see p.236).

West of Piaţa Unirii

The city's main east–west axis runs across the northern edge of Piaţa Unirii – to the east of the square as B-dul. 21 Decembrie 1989 and westwards as Str. Memorandumului. At Str. Memorandumului 21, the palace where the Transylvanian Diet met in 1790–91 (and where the 1894 trial of the Memorandumists was held) now houses the main branch of the superb **Ethnographic Museum** (Tues–Sun 9am–5pm; €2), by some distance the city's finest museum. The exhibition starts with the history of shepherding in the region, featuring some finely crafted staffs, cattle horns used for storing gunpowder, and ferocious-looking bear traps. The importance of traditional crafts is manifest most colourfully in a collection of carved gates from Maramureş, painted Saxon chests and wardrobes, and some exquisite glazed pottery. There's also an outstanding assemblage of traditional musical instruments, such as flutes, alpenhorns and clarions, the latter used by peasants throughout the Apuseni region to ward off undesirable prey.

Up on the second floor is probably Romania's finest collection of traditional carpets and folk costumes – from the dark herringbone patterns of the Pădureni region to the bold yellow, black and red stripes typical of Maramureş costumes. While blouses and leggings might be predominantly black or white, women's apron-skirts, and the waistcoats worn by both sexes for special occasions, are brilliantly coloured. Peacock feathers serve in the Năsăud area as fans or plumes, and the love of complicated designs spills over onto cups, masks, distaffs (used as an application for marriage) and linked spoons (used as a charm against divorce). Afterwards, you can have a drink in the pleasant courtyard café (see p.241).

The museum also has an excellent **open-air section** (Tues–Sun 9am–4pm; €2) to the northwest of town on the Hoia hill, with peasant houses and three wooden churches from the surrounding areas; it's a thirty-minute walk from the centre, or you can take bus #27 from the station or #30 from Piaţa Unirii to Str. Haţeg (Cartier Grigorescu), and then head ten minutes north from there up Str. Tăietura Turcului.

Strada Memorandumului continues west from the museum to the splendidly towered city hall, where it becomes Calea Moţilor. At no. 84 is the beautiful Calvinist **Cock Church**, built in 1913 by Kós Károly (see box, p.219), who designed everything down to the light fittings, all with a cock motif symbolizing St Peter's threefold denial of Christ before cock's crow; ask for the key at the parish office behind the church. The architectural conservation group Utilitas is accommodated in Kós's first house, built for his parents at Str. Breaza 14, north of the train station. Further west is the **Mănăstur** quarter, the oldest part of Cluj, although you wouldn't know it from the serried ranks of 1980s apartment blocks – the best **views** are from the Calea Mănăstur flyover, where you can see ancient earthworks to the south and a relatively modern shrine and belfry atop them. Behind these is the **Calvaria Church**, built by the Magyars in the twelfth century and rebuilt by the Benedictines in 1466; it's a Gothic hall-church, simple but surprisingly high, recently restored and with a new belfry.

Eating, drinking and entertainment

Cluj has a reasonable bunch of **restaurants**, including several upmarket, though not expensive, ones, and lots of fast-food options and snack bars, especially on Str. Napoca and Piaţa Blaga, to fuel the needs of the city's students. **Café** life in Cluj ranks only second to that of Bucharest, as does the **bar** and **club** scene, thanks in part to the city's large student population.

Restaurants

Agape Str. Iuliu Maniu 6. Terrific self-service restaurant (Mon–Fri 11am–9pm) offering cheap and cheerful snacks, mains and desserts. There's also a regular pizzeria upstairs (noon–midnight).

Ernesto Piaţa Unirii 23. The accent at this intimate, formal cellar restaurant on the north side of the square is on fancy, with starters such as lobster cream soup and mains such as duck breast mignon, red tuna and veal ragout – however, with no a/c it can get rather stifling when busy. Daily noon–11pm.

Hubertus B-dul. 21 Decembrie 1989 22. This is the city's most refined dining option, where a well-presented English menu offers the likes of spit-roast game, boar-meat rolls and pheasant ragout. Dark orange walls, beautifully laid tables and cloth-backed chairs round off the experience superbly. Daily 10am–midnight.

Marty Caffe Str. Horea 5. Toasted sandwiches, pastas, soups and cooked breakfasts form the mainstay at this bright and breezy restaurant. Two other branches at Str. Traian Moşoiu 28 and Str. Victor Babeş 39.

Matei Corvin Str. Matei Corvin 3. Along with the *Hubertus*, this relatively small place is the city's most elegant restaurant, specializing in Hungarian food (goulash and beef-filled Debrecen pancakes), in addition to, rather curiously, some Mexican options. Terrific wine, too. Mon–Sat 11am–11pm.

Napoca 15 Str. Napoca 15. The appealing and wide-ranging menu here features salads, pastas, chicken, beef and filled pancakes – choose from the formal indoor seating area or the more relaxed terrace to the rear. Daily 11am–11pm.

Rex Str. Bolyai 9. Ordinary-looking but popular side-street pizzeria with a standard pizza menu plus a decent choice of pasta dishes. Daily 10.30am–10.30pm.

Roata Str. Alex Ciura 6A. Located just off Str. Isac, this cosy, rustically styled restaurant – Transylvanian costumes and textiles draped over the walls – offers some of the city's best Romanian food; add to the mix sharp service and a convivial atmosphere, and you've got a most enjoyable place to eat. Daily 1–11pm.

Cafés and bars

Cluj has a nice spread of **cafés** around town, many of which double up as places to drink as the hours wear on. *Flowers*, Piaţa Unirii 25, is a bijou little teahouse, while next door, the infinitely posier *Crema* is a pleasant place to relax and watch the world go by. Terrace gardens (*gradinas*) are few and far between in Cluj, but two worth visiting are *Etno*, in the leafy courtyard of the Ethnographic Museum, and the *Terasa Muzeu*, in the courtyard of the Art Museum. A more bohemian place is the *Art Club*, Piaţa Ştefan cel Mare 14, whose walls are plastered with yellowing posters from past performances at the theatre across the road – you're also likely to find Cluj's leading actors hanging out here.

In the evenings, two worthwhile places are the colourful *Insomnia*, Str. Iuliu Maniu 4, with terrific service, and *Bulgakov*, Str. Klein 17, an arty joint named after the Russian novelist. *Café Umbra*, Str. Georges Clemenceau 7, is a Gothic-styled bar with lots of dark nooks and crannies, while *Euphoria,* Str. Muzeul 4, good for a relaxing daytime drink, ups the tempo come night-time. For late-night **music**, one of the hottest **clubs** around is *H2O*, Calea Turzii 203A; otherwise, there's the *Diesel Jazz Bar*, in the cellars of Piaţa Unirii 17, a decent, if posey, lounge bar/club; *Autograf*, Str. Memorandumului 23, featuring folk, rock and jazz; and the pub-like *Roland Garros*, Str. Horea 2, with a riverside balcony and live rock music at weekends.

Entertainment

Cluj has a strong cultural suit, thanks in part to the healthy mix of both Romanian and Hungarian communities. Tickets for the **Romanian Theatre and Opera** can be bought across the road from the theatre at Piaţa Ştefan cel Mare 14, next to the *Art Club* (box office daily 11am–5pm; ☎0264/595 363). The **Hungarian State Theatre**, Str. Emile Isac 26, is the venue for a prolific number of theatrical and operatic productions, the overwhelming majority of which are in Hungarian (box office daily 10am–1pm & 4.30–6.30pm; ☎0264/593 468, ⓦwww.huntheater.ro). The **Cluj Philharmonic** is at Str. Kogălniceanu (box office Mon–Fri 11am–5pm; ☎0264/430 060). For kids, there's the fabulous Puck **Puppet Theatre** at Str. I.C. Braţianu 23 (☎0264/595 992). Note that performances at most of these venues are suspended from around early July to mid-September.

Cinema in Cluj

Cluj is the unofficial capital of Romanian **cinematography** – it was here, in 1905, that the first film studio was inaugurated, and the city has the highest number of cinema-goers of any Romanian city. Moreover, it's one of the few places where city-centre **cinemas** are still flourishing, the best being: Republicii, Piaţa Mihai Viteazul; Arta-Eurimages, Str. Universităţii 3; Victoria, B-dul. Eroilor 51; and Favorit, Str. Horea 6. Cluj is also home to the country's premier film festival, the **Transylvanian International Film Festival** (TIFF), a ten-day jamboree at the beginning of June that features a superb mix of domestic and world films shown at those cinemas listed above.

Romanian **film** is currently enjoying something of a renaissance, thanks in part to a clutch of recent award-winners. Three highly acclaimed movies are *The Death of Mr Lazarescu* (2005), a darkly humorous tale of an elderly man's experience being trawled round Bucharest's hospitals as he faces imminent death; *12:08 East of Bucharest* (2006), a fabulous deadpan comedy surrounding the events of the 1989 revolution; and the Palme d'Or-winning *4 Months, 3 Weeks and 2 Days* (2007), a tragic story of illegal abortion set during the final days of the Ceauşescu regime.

Shopping

Cluj's main **department store**, the Central, is at Str. Regele Ferdinand 22 (Mon–Sat 9am–8pm, Sun 10am–3pm), while the arcaded Sora shopping precinct, 21 Decembrie 1989 5, has a decent **supermarket** in the basement. The daily food **market** is on Piaţa Mihai Viteazul, and on Thursdays there's also a craft market here selling wood carvings and embroidery from the Apuseni highlands and the Transylvanian Heath. The AgroFlip delicatessen, Piaţa Mihai Viteazul 9a (Mon–Fri 7.30am–9pm, Sat til 6pm), has a fair choice of imported goods; and the Napolact shop, Piaţa Mihai Viteazul 8 (Mon–Fri 6am–7pm, Sat 7am–3pm), sells some superb dairy products and other foods.

Two excellent **outdoor gear** shops are Polartek Sports, Str. Universităţii 8 (Mon–Fri 10am–6pm, Sat 10am–2pm), and Atta, Str. David Ferenc 34 (Mon–Fri 10am–6pm, Sat 10am–2pm). For English-language **books**, try the university bookstore (Mon–Fri 8am–8pm, Sat 9am–4pm) at the corner of Piaţa Unirii and Str. Universităţii, which also has good dictionaries and books on Romanian ethnography and arts, and some French-, German- and Hungarian-language titles. Gaudeamus, Str. Iuliu Maniu 3, has books and maps in English (Mon–Fri 10am–7pm, Sat 11am–2pm).

Listings

Airlines TAROM, Piaţa Mihai Viteazul 11 (Mon–Fri 8am–6pm, Sat 9am–1pm; ☎0264/432 669); Carpatair, at the airport (☎0264/416 016, ⓦwww .carpatair.ro); Happy Tour, Str. Horea 2 (☎0264/433 933; ⓔcluj@happytour.ro); Lufthansa, Str. Horea 1 (☎0264/536 926, ⓦwww.aerotravel.ro).
Car rental Avis, *Hotel Victoria*, B-dul. 21 Decembrie 1918 54 (☎0264/439 403) and at the airport (☎0720/111 605, ⓦwww.avis.ro); Hertz, at airport (☎0364/401 722, ⓦwww.hertz.com. ro). An excellent local company is PanTravel, Str. Grozăvescu 13 (☎0264/420 516, ⓦwww .pantravel.ro); Rodna Rentacar, Str. Traian Vuia 62 (☎0264/450 711, ⓦwww.rodna-trans.ro).
Internet access Club Internet, Str. Bariţiu 2 & B-dul. Eroilor 37; Computer Zone, Str. Cuza Vodă 40; Ghost Internet, Str. David Ferenc 19; KetNet, Str. Raţiu 4; Millenium, Piaţa Mihai Viteazul 39 and Str. Şaguna 15; Net Zone, Piaţa Muzeului 5; Internet, Str. Iuliu Maniu 17 (24hr); Total Net, Str. Isac 2 (24hr).
International bus tickets Amad Turistik, Str. Titulescu 4 (☎0264/414 483); AtlasSib, Piaţa Mihai Viteazul 11, bloc D, ap. 1, Str. Voiteşti 3 (☎0264/433 432); Avetour, Str. Şincai 2 and B-dul. 21 Decembrie 1989 8 (☎0264/596 257); Axis Travel, B-dul. Eroilor 47; Bohoris Express, *Hotel Napoca* (☎0264/580 715); Calibra, Piaţa Unirii 11 (☎0264/590 808); Eurolines, *Hotel Victoria*, B-dul. 21 Decembrie 1989 54 (☎0264/431 961); Mihu-Reisen, c/o Napoca Tours, *Hotel Napoca* (☎0264/580 927), and c/o Unifix-Tour, Str. Poştei 5 (☎0264/430 425); TransEuropa, B-dul. Eroilor 10 (☎0264/590 090); Kameleon Trans, Str. S. Micu 6 (☎0264/591 697);

Optimus, Str. Gen. Grigorescu 12 (☎0264/584 966); Tihanyi Travel, Str. S. Micu 6 (☎0264/439 385); TransEuropa, B-dul. Eroilor 10 (☎0264/211 296).
Libraries British Council Library, Str. Arany Janos 11 (Mon, Wed & Thurs 1–7pm, Tues & Fri 10am–4pm; ☎0264/594 408); American Library, Deutsches Institut and French Cultural Centre, Str. Brătianu 22; American Cultural Centre, Str. Iuliu Maniu 22.
Pharmacy The weekend rota is posted in the southeast corner of Piaţa Unirii; Cynara, Calea Floreşti 75 (☎0264/426 272) is open 24hr. Sensiblu, Str. Clinicilor 8 (8am–10pm) is a good modern place by a hospital. For medicinal plants, try Hypericum, Str. Horea 4, or B-dul. Eroilor 7.
Police Str. Decebal 28 ☎112.
Post office Str. Regele Ferdinand 33 (Mon–Fri 7am–8pm, Sat 8am–1pm).
Telephone office Directly behind the post office and also on the south side of Piaţa Unirii (daily 7am–10pm).
Train tickets Agenţia CFR at Piaţa Mihai Viteazul 20 (Mon–Fri 7am–8pm).
Travel agents and tour operators Agrotrip, Str. Campului 63 (☎0264/406 363, ⓦwww.agrotrip .ro); Air Transilvania, Piaţa Ştefan cel Mare 14 (☎0264/593 245, ⓔoffice@airtransilvania.ro); Eximtur, Str. Şaguna 34 (☎0264/433 569, ⓦwww.eximtur.ro); Marshal Turism, B-dul. Eroilor 51 (☎0264/484 945, ⓦwww.marshal.ro); Pan Travel, Str. Grozăvescu 13 (☎0264/420 516, ⓦwww.pantravel.ro); Linea Blu Travel, B-dul. 1 Decembrie 1918 54 (☎0264/591 037, ⓦwww .lineablutravel.ro).

The Apuseni mountains

The **Apuseni mountains** are bordered to the south by the Arieş valley and to the north by the Crişul Repede valley, enabling public transport to reach a variety of access points into the range. From Turda, the **Arieş valley** runs west, between the Apuseni massif to the north, and various smaller ranges such as the Trascău and Metaliferi (Metal Bearing) mountains to the south. The DN75 follows the valley as far as Câmpeni – capital of the **Moţi highlanders** – where one road heads west into the Bihor, and another runs south to Brad and Alba. Having successfully resisted the Roman conquest, the Moţi moved from the valleys into the hills in the eighteenth century when the Habsburgs attempted to conscript them into the army, and they now live all year round at up to 1400m, some of the highest settlements in Romania, in scattered groups of high-roofed, thatched cottages. **Buses** run east along the valley to Turda and on to Cluj in the early morning and return west more or less hourly through the afternoon; there are also plenty of services from Alba Iulia to Câmpeni. Along the **Crişul Repede valley**, most Accelerat trains stop only at Huedin, Ciucea and Aleşd, but the less frequent Personal services give opportunities for exploration by stopping at every hamlet along the line.

Despite opposition from the forestry and other industries – the uranium mines are now closed, but Europe's largest opencast gold mine is now being planned beneath Roşia Montana (see p.248) – the **Apuseni Nature Park** (Ⓦwww.parcapuseni.ro) has recently been established within the mountains, alongside the creation of an excellent network of hiking trails.

Turda

Thirty kilometres south of Cluj along the main DN1 (€60/81), **TURDA** (Torda) was once one of the wealthiest towns in the country, thanks to salt mining. The modern Turda, with its 60,000 mainly Magyar inhabitants, and a large Roma minority, is ringed by filthy factories, but beyond these is still a surprisingly elegant centre. The salt mine aside, the main reasons to come are to visit the spectacular **Turda gorge**, 8km to the west, and to explore the Arieş valley beyond, in the foothills of the Apuseni mountains.

The **Salt Mine** (*Salina Turda*; daily 9am–5pm, last entry 3.30pm; €3) is sited on the northern edge of town at Str. Salinelor 54. Take bus #10 or #42 or walk for fifteen minutes along Str. Avram Iancu (which becomes Str. Mureşanu beyond the hospital) to a lovely leafy park shading another attractive Calvinist church to the east. From here, Str. Basarabiei heads past the north side of the church and (as Str. Tunel) to the mine. Entrance to the mine is via a three-hundred-metre-long tunnel, its sodium-encrusted walls marked every 10m, just in case you think it's never going to end. Gradually excavated over 250 years, the mine is comprised of several huge hangar-like chambers, the most impressive of which is the cavernous **Rudolf Mine**, some 80m long and 50m wide, and reached via a series of stout wooden staircases leading ever further downwards. You'll also pass through the Joseph Mine, known as the echo chamber owing to some twenty or so echos, and the so-called "altar room", the centrepiece of which is an extraordinary altar-shaped monument sculpted from salt, created for the purposes of religious service and prayers before miners began their shifts. It's just under 10°C degrees in the mine, so warm clothing is advisable.

Back in town, on the broad main street, Piaţa Republicii, stand two Gothic churches: the lower one, built between 1387 and 1437, is Calvinist, and the upper

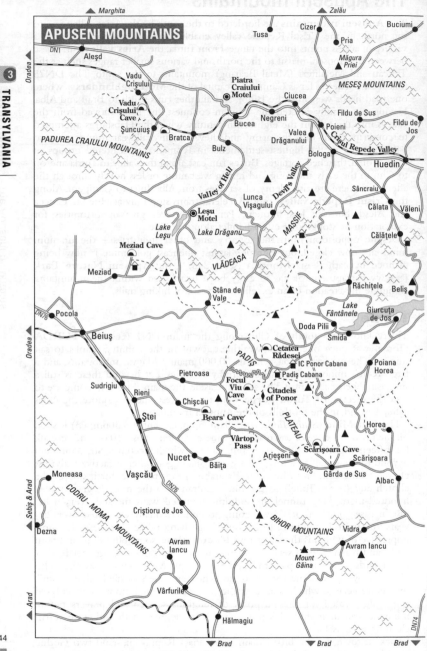

APUSENI MOUNTAINS

▲ Marghita   ▲ Zalău

Tusa   Cizer   Buciumi

DN1   Aleşd   Pria

Vadu   Măgura
Crişului   Priei

Piatra   MESEŞ MOUNTAINS
Craiului
Motel   Ciucea

Vadu   Fildu de Sus   Fildu de
Crişului   Negreni   Jos
Cave   Poieni
Şuncuiuş   Bucea   Valea   Crişul Repede Valley
Bratca   Drăganului
PADUREA CRAIULUI MOUNTAINS   Bologa   Huedin
Bulz

Valley of Hell   Devil's Valley   Sâncraiu

Leşu   Lunca   Călata   Văleni
Motel   Vişagului

Lake   MASSIF   Călăţele
Leşu   Lake Drăganu

Meziad Cave   VLĂDEASA

Meziad   Răchiţele   Beliş

Stâna de   Lake
Vale   Fântânele   Giurcuţa
DN76   Pocola   de Jos
Doda Pilii
Beiuş   Smida

Cetatea   Poiana
Rădesei   Horea
Pietroasa   PADIŞ   IC Ponor Cabana
Focul   Padiş Cabana
Sudrigiu   Rieni   Viu   Citadels
Chişcău   Cave   of Ponor
Ştei   Bears' Cave   PLATEAU   Horea

Vârtop   Scărişoara Cave
Pass
Nucet   Arieşeni   Scărişoara
Băiţa   DN75
Moneasa   Vaşcău   Gârda de Sus   Albac
DN76
CODRU - MOMA MOUNTAINS
Criştioru de Jos   BIHOR MOUNTAINS   Vidra
Dezna   Avram Iancu
Avram   Iancu
Mount
Vârfurile   Găina

Hălmagiu

DN74

▼ Brad   ▼ Brad   Brad ▼

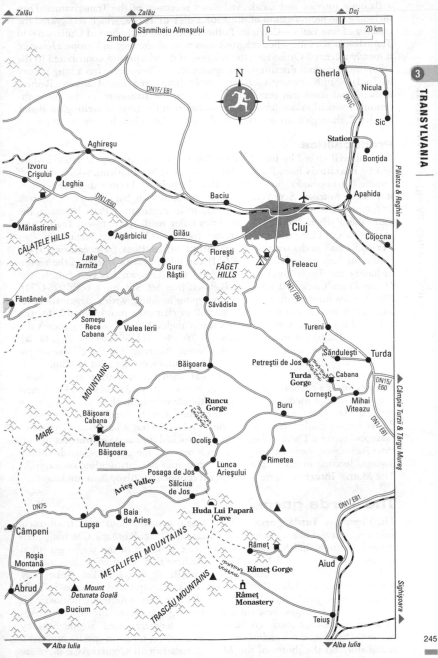

one is Roman Catholic (built in 1478–1504 and rebuilt in 1822 after a fire), with a Baroque interior and facade. It housed meetings of the Transylvanian Diet, including the promulgation of the 1568 **Edict of Turda**, which recognized the equality of four faiths – Calvinist, Lutheran, Roman Catholic and Unitarian – in Transylvania at a time when religious wars were all the rage in Europe. However, it merely tolerated Orthodoxy, the religion of the Vlachs, and contributed to the ethnic and religious discrimination against them. Christianity has a long history in Turda – fifth-century Christian tombs have been found among Roman remains, and these can eventually be seen in the **museum** in the fifteenth-century Voivodal Palace (closed for renovation at the time of writing) at B-dul. Haşdeu 2, through a small park behind the Calvinist church.

Practicalities

Turda is well served by **buses** from Cluj, picking up at Piaţa Ştefan cel Mare, and by **maxitaxis** from Piaţa Ştefan cel Mare at Str. Brătianu, which drop off outside the Leonardo shoe shop on Piaţa Republicii. Longer-distance services stop at the Autogara Sens Vest (Mon–Fri 6.30am–9pm, Sat & Sun 6.30–9am & 1–7.30pm; ☎0264/313 431) below the town centre near Piaţa Romana, the roundabout where the DN75 (the Arieş valley road) leaves town. **Trains** stop at the town of Câmpia Turzii, 9km east; take bus #20 to Piaţa Republicii.

Friendly staff at the **tourist information office**, Piaţa 1 Decembrie 1918 1 (Mon–Sat 8am–6pm; ☎0264/314 611), can inform on all aspects of the region including the Turda gorge and the Apuseni. The town has two **hotels**; the *Hunter Prince Castle*, just off Piaţa Republicii at Str. Sulutiu 4/6 (☎0264/316 850; Ⓦwww.huntercastle.ro; ❻), is a pompous building, with a jagged roof line and pointy turrets, but the rooms are full of character, mostly notable for the colourful stone walls jutting out at various angles. More prosaically, there's the downbeat *Potaissa*, at Piaţa Republicii 6 (☎0264/311 691, Ⓕ311 771; ❸–❹), which has rooms with and without shower. Alternatively, there's the simple *Imperial* (☎0745/259 194; ❷), at no. 65A in Tureni, on the road to Cluj.

If you're looking for somewhere to **eat**, then the restaurant in the *Hunter Prince Castle* is a cut above anything else in town; despite its obvious kitschiness – an overcooked medieval/Dracula combination – both the food and service are first class. You can also eat on the raised terrace overlooking the pretty, flower-strewn garden. Next door, the *Rosalca* café has a fabulous selection of cakes and pastries. There's a large and well-stocked fruit and veg **market** just off Piaţa Republicii – enter through the arch opposite the church – worth visiting if you're looking to stock up before heading into the surrounding countryside. The Matrix **Internet** centre is at Piaţa Republicii 16 (daily 8am–midnight).

The Turda gorge

The impressive **Turda gorge** (Cheile Turzii) is a two-hour walk from town, following red and blue cross markings west from Piaţa Romana. Catching a bus towards Corneşti and Moldoveneşti will take you part of the way – get off at the turning 2km beyond Mihai Viteazu (where there's a small Gothic church and a restaurant-pension) and continue north on foot for 5km. Either way, you'll end up at the *Cheile Turzii* cabana (❶) and campsite (there's also a simple restaurant here) just before the gorge itself. From here, a footpath, marked with red stripes and crosses, heads north up the gorge, overshadowed by three-hundred-metre-high cliffs containing caves formerly used as hideouts by outlaws. The unique microclimate provides a habitat for plant species otherwise found only on the shores of the Mediterranean or in Central Asia; there are more than a thousand here, as well as 111 bird species, including golden eagles and rock vultures. After around 3km, the path ends at **Petreştii de Jos**, from where there are occasional buses back to Turda.

The Arieş valley

West of Turda, the main DN75 follows the north bank of the River Arieş, passing through a succession of small villages including **BURU**, the setting of the **Babaluda festival** on April 23 (St George's Day), when six young men dress up: two as Babaluda and his wife, clad in cherry bark and birch leaves; two as soldiers; and two all in black, who smear black dye over everyone, forcing evil spirits to leave. With the help of the rest of the populace, Babaluda and his wife set about throwing all the young girls of the village into the river (a typical fertility rite), while everyone also tries to touch Babaluda for good luck; the soldiers' task is to prevent them from touching him, unless they pay.

Eight kilometres south of Buru is the attractive village of **RIMETEA** (Torockó), where traditional dress is worn for festivals on February 22 and the first Sunday of March. Costumes can also be seen on display in the village **museum** (Tues–Sun 9am–5pm). The Transylvania Trust has restored a number of houses here and there are several guesthouses.

Just to the west of Buru, a road turns north to the tiny village of **BĂIŞOARA**, from where it's 14km west to the single-slope **Muntele Băişorii** ski resort; here, you can stay at the *Băişoara* cabana (☎0264/314 569; ❶), *Pensiunea Mini* (☎0264/595 285; ❷) or the *BTT Băişoara hostel* (book through BTT, Piaţa Ştefan cel Mare 5, Cluj; ☎0264/598 067, ✉bttcluj@zortec.ro; ❶). Continuing north from Băişoara, the road passes through **SĂVĂDISLA** (Turdaszentlászló), where the *Tamás Bistro* **restaurant** at no. 153 offers the best Magyar cuisine in the area, and finishes at Luna de Sus, just west of Cluj.

Back on the Arieş valley road, it's 14km from Buru to the turn-off for **Ocoliş**, 4km north of the main road (don't confuse this with the Ocolişel turning), and, a little further up from that, the **Runcu gorge**; from the latter, an eight- to ten-hour hike, marked with blue crosses, cuts through the gorge to the Muntele Băişorii ski resort (see above). Four kilometres beyond Ocoliş, the valley road runs past an unmarked junction at km126.5, where a road leads over a bridge to **LUNCA ARIEŞULUI**, where you can stay at the *Vila Ramona* (☎0264/147 742; ❶); a couple of kilometres west is the turning north to **POŞAGA**. The next stretch of road is lovely, with beech woods, conglomerate boulders, and at km121.5 a small waterfall to its south. Almost 5km west of the Poşaga turning, a footbridge signals the start of a day-walk south past watermills to the **Huda lui Papară cave** and the **Râmeţ gorge**; the route takes you either on a goat track along the cliff, or through the stream itself. At the far end of the gorge, tourists can stay in the *Râmeţ* cabana (❶), near the fourteenth-century **Râmeţ monastery**, where the festival of St Ghelasie is celebrated on June 30. From here, three buses a day head south to Teiuş and Alba Iulia.

In **LUPŞA**, 75km west of Turda, the well-regarded **Ethnographic Museum** (daily 8am–noon & 2–6pm) stands below a stone church raised on its hillock in 1421 and recently restored. Across the river to the south, reached by a footbridge or a new road bridge 1km west, is the village of **Hădărău**, which boasts a similar Gothic church. **Lupşa monastery** is another 2km west along the main road at km90; it has a lovely little church dating back to 1429.

Câmpeni and around

It's another 12km west to **CÂMPENI** (Topánfalva), capital of the Ţara Moţilor and a possible base for forays into the mountains. The town is well

The Girl Fair of Muntele Găina

The **Girl Fair** (Târgul de fete) of Muntela Găina takes place on the Sunday before July 20 on the flat top of Mount Găina, roughly 33km west of Câmpeni, near the village of **AVRAM IANCU**, named after the leader of the 1848 revolt against the Hungarians who was born here in 1824 (his birthplace can be visited). It is the region's largest festival, and was originally a means of allowing young men who were often away shepherding for two-thirds of the year to meet young women from other communities and to pursue matrimony. Naturally, prospective spouses made every effort to enhance their appeal, the girls being displayed in their finest attire, surrounded by linen, pottery and other items of dowry – even to the extent of carting along rented furniture. Nowadays, this aspect of the fair has all but disappeared, but thousands still come for the music and spectacle.

A special bus service transports visitors from Câmpeni to the fair, which is a large and lively event, but the real action is on the hill top, and you should really camp the night before to catch the local's dawn chorus on *tulnics* (alphorns). A rough forestry road takes an 8km loop to reach the hilltop, but you can find more direct routes on foot. The biggest names in popular traditional Romanian music appear here, with local dance ensembles, and there's plenty of food and drink; there is little drunkenness, however, and everyone behaves well, with unarmed Jandarmaria troops in attendance.

served by buses, which arrive at the station just east of the centre beyond the market. The best **hotel** is the *Hanul Moţilor* at Piaţa Avram Iancu 1 (T0258/771 824; ❷), which has a *crama* and pizzeria. The town's **Avram Iancu Museum**, in his old headquarters by the river on the corner of Str. Revoluţiei 1848, is decrepit but functional, though opening times are erratic. There's a good supermarket opposite, and two simple **restaurants** and a **post office** on the semi-pedestrianized square west of the *Tulnic* hotel.

From Câmpeni, the DN74A leads 10km south to Abrud, passing on the way a turning for **ROŞIA MONTANĂ**, 7km to the east. Transylvania was a major source of gold throughout history, with the Dacians the first to dig here, then the Romans; others followed more or less continuously and, in the 1970s, Ceauşescu's opencast mining demolished the entire Cetate massif. Now there are plans to create Europe's largest opencast gold mine beneath Roşia Montana, which is to be largely demolished, along with its attractive Baroque houses and historic mining tunnels; however, a campaign against the project is gathering momentum. Roman lamps, tombstones and wax tablets recording operational details can be seen in the **museum** at the mine, 2km before the village beside the Orlea hill.

From here, there's a one-hour walk (marked by red triangles) south to **ABRUD**. The old town, whose Baroque buildings incorporate stones from earlier Roman structures and are liberally adorned with plaques commemorating the many notables who visited when Abrud was the Moţi capital, is tatty but far more attractive than Câmpeni. From Piaţa Eroilor, the centre of the old town, there are buses to **BUCIUM POIENI**, 13km east and the centre of a *comuna* of six small mining villages; there's a Belgian-owned hostel here, and it's also the starting point for an hour's climb to two basalt towers known as the **Detunata**.

Gârda de Sus and around

From here, the DN75 continues another 15km through a gorge to **GÂRDA DE SUS**, a pretty village with a part-wooden church built in 1792, with naïve paintings inside; accommodation is available at the *Mama Uţa* pension-restaurant-camping (T0258/627 901; ❷). More notably, it is the starting point

Romania's religious architecture

Romania's entangled history of competing faiths accounts for the country's extraordinary diversity of church architecture, ranging from the lofty wooden churches of Maramureş and the magnificent painted monasteries of Bucovina to the austere fortified churches raised by the Saxons around Braşov and Sibiu. Many Romanian Orthodox churches are in fact monasteries, with a small residence alongside housing a few monks or nuns. The churches are built on the classical Byzantine plan, with porch, nave, domed crossing and altar, and have small windows and smoke-blackened icons and frescoes. The grandest of the monasteries, such as Horezu and Polovragi, are found in Wallachia: rebuilt, expanded and given their distinctive Romanian style by Constantin Brâncoveanu at the end of the seventeenth century.

Wooden churches

Priest blessing worshippers outside ▲
Bârsana monastery, Maramureş

Fresco of Christ being crucified, Mara church,
Maramureş ▼

Although there has long been a tradition of building **wooden churches** throughout Eastern Europe, by far the most spectacular examples are found in the beautiful, isolated region of **Maramureş** (see p.327) in northern Romania. Of the forty or so wooden churches that remain, many are in a parlous state, though many more have been renovated in recent years, and eight are on UNESCO's World Heritage list. Built in response to a thirteenth-century Hungarian prohibition on the construction of Orthodox stone churches, the wooden churches reached their artistic peak during the eighteenth century, following the last of the Tatar raids. They were constructed by locally trained carpenters, who adopted and refined the Gothic style hitherto prominent in the churches of Transylvania. Their distinguishing features are a steeply sloping shingled roof (in many cases a double roof), which enabled windows to be built high up in the nave to increase illumination, a porch (*privdor*) at the western end, and a slender bell tower adorned with miniature turrets – the churches at **Şurdeşti** and **Bârsana** are perhaps the finest examples in the region.

The small, low-ceilinged interiors are usually very dark, a black film of soot the legacy of centuries of candlelit devotion, though, unfortunately, this only serves to further obscure the marvellous, if mostly decaying, frescoes. These wall paintings, so characteristic of medieval Orthodox churches, are naïf in style, especially compared to those of the painted monasteries, and were usually executed at the hands of unknown local artists. In most cases they conform to the universal Orthodox pattern, depicting scenes from the Old and New Testaments, the most common iconographical themes being the *Last Judgement* and the *Passion*.

Saxon churches

During the middle of the twelfth century, at the behest of Hungary's King Geza II, a wave of Saxon immigrants arrived from the Moselle and Rhine regions of northern Europe, colonizing villages across southern Transylvania. Trade prospered and settlements grew during the thirteenth and fourteenth centuries, but villagers were obliged to build fortifications in order to withstand the constant threat of Ottoman and Tatar raids. In all, more than two hundred citadels were raised, collectively representing a form of architectural heritage unique in Europe today.

Invariably sited on a hillock in the centre of the village, the key component of any **fortification** was the church, either a Romanesque basilica or a single-nave Gothic structure, some with Baroque accretions. With solid walls and tiny windows, these were further adapted for defensive purposes, typically with a massive ring wall (in some cases a double wall) and towers, together with storerooms for food. Indeed, the compound would usually be large enough to accommodate an entire village in times of danger.

The most important and powerful Saxon settlements were the cities of **Braşov** (see p.157) and **Sibiu** (see p.186) and the wonderful medieval town of **Sighişoara** (see p.177), but it's the fortifications in the smaller villages that exert the greatest pull. For example, there's **Prejmer** (see p.174), the largest citadel in Transylvania; **Biertan** (see p.184), a fine, prepossessing structure set in two and a half rings of walls; and the delightful church of **Mălâncrav** (see p.183), one of the few villages in the region to retain a sizeable Saxon population, around 150.

▲ Interior of wooden church, Budeşti, Maramureş

▼ Saxon fortified church at Hărman, near Braşov, Transylvania

Painted monasteries

Ceiling fresco ▲ and porch ▼ at Horezu monastery, Wallachia

Fresco of the *Last Judgement*, Voroneţ monastery, Bucovina ▼

While Maramureş's evocative wooden churches and Transylvania's imposing Saxon citadels are rightfully proclaimed as masterpieces of religious art and architecture, they are little match for the painted monasteries of **Bucovina** (see p.302), in Moldavia. Scattered in gorgeous sloping valleys sheltered by thick forests of beech and pine, these magnificent monuments rank among Europe's most revered artistic and architectural treasures. Predominantly built during the second quarter of the sixteenth century, they follow the pattern of earlier Byzantine churches like **Horezu** in Wallachia (see p.131), with a large fortified enclosure with thick-set walls and an imposing entrance gate, offering refuge from Turkish invaders.

Above all, though, it's the exterior wall paintings that stand out – startlingly detailed compositions depicting mythological beliefs and biblical events, the most striking being the *Siege of Constantinople* at **Moldoviţa** (see p.310), the *Ladder of Virtue* at **Suceviţa** (see p.311), and most splendid of all, the *Last Judgement* at **Voroneţ** (see p.306). Even after nearly half a millennium of exposure to the elements, the colours remain incredibly fresh and strong. The diligent artists, now mostly unknown, employed classic fresco techniques and could complete four square metres or more in a day. They used dyes derived from various minerals, such as red from lead oxide and blue from copper carbonate, mixed with lampblack and charcoal as well as vinegar, egg and honey.

Many of the monasteries remain active, so there's every possibility of chancing upon a service, the start of which is signalled by a nun striking a *toaca* – a long wooden board – with a mallet as she circles the church.

for several excellent hikes, the most popular of which, marked with blue stripes, begins near the **campsite** and leads north through the Ordâncuşa gorges, past a mill and into a forest, ending after three hours at the village of **GHEŢARI**. This is named after the **Scărişoara ice cave** (Peştera gheţarul; daily 9am–5pm), a few minutes west of the village; filled with 70,000 cubic metres of ice, 15m thick, it has preserved evidence of climatic changes over the last 4000 years. At the back of the main chamber is the "church", so-called because of its pillar formations.

Marked walking routes in this area link the cave with **Albac** and Horea's birthplace in **Fericet**, where a festival occurs in mid-August in the village of **Horea** itself (reached by three buses a day from Câmpeni).

The Padiş plateau

The **Padiş plateau** (Plateul Padiş) is in the heart of a classic karst area, with streams vanishing underground and reappearing unexpectedly, and dips and hollows everywhere, all promising access to the huge cave and river systems that lie beneath the plateau. Two or three buses during the week (but none at weekends) depart Huedin for Răchiţele and Poiana Horea, from where it's an easy day's hike to the *Padiş* cabana (℡0788/561 223; ❶), which lies at the crossroads of the plateau and is the focal point for the Apuseni region's trails. Note that the *Padiş* has an open-air disco; a quieter (and cleaner) place to stay is the *Varişoaia* cabana (℡0788/601 815; ❶), about 2km northwest on the road towards Stâna de Vale.

Homestays are available in Răchiţele (bookable through Green Mountain Holidays – see p.251), while further south, 3km from Lake Fântânele in the village of **DODA PILII**, is the excellent (and aptly named) *Hotel Rustic* (℡0788/591 890; ❻ half-board), with trout fishing available. The comfortable *Agroturism IC Ponor* cabana (℡0744/272 465, ✉agroturism_icponor@yahoo .com), with eight biggish *casuţe*, is at IC Ponor, two hours' walk up the road from Padiş towards Răchiţele.

Hikes on the plateau

Of the various **trails** starting from the *Padiş* cabana, the most popular, marked with blue dots, is a three-hour hike south to the underground complex of **Cetăţile Ponorului** (Citadels of Ponor), where the Ponor stream flows through a series of sinkholes up to 150m deep. There's a good camping spot en route at Glavoi, a one-hour walk away, and the *Cetaţile Ponorului* cabana (℡0740/104 838; ✉zonapadis@yahoo.com; ❶) is just beyond Glavoi. A trail from the third hollow of the Ponor Citadels (marked by yellow dots) leads for 2km to the **Focul Viu** ice cave, and then (marked with red stripes) back to *Padiş*. Alternatively, you could head south from Ponor to Arieşeni (see p.367) in three hours following red triangles, or west from Focul Viu to Pietroasa (see p.367) in two-and-a-half hours, following yellow dots and triangles.

North of the *Padiş* cabana, you can hike to the **Cetatea Rădesei** cave; follow red stripes along a track to the forestry road and head north. Ten minutes beyond the Vărăşoaia pass, take another path (red dots) to the right of the citadel itself. Here you follow the stream through a cave – slightly spooky but quite safe, although a flashlight helps – and follow the overground route back (marked by red dots) to see the various skylights from above.

Other hikes simply follow forestry roads, west to Pietroasa (marked by blue crosses), east to Răchiţele or Poiana Horea (unmarked), or northwest to **Stâna de Vale** (red stripes). This last route continues from Vărăşoaia, climbing to the

Cumpănatelu saddle (1640m) and eventually turning right off the main ridge to descend through the forest to the resort (see p.367). Unlike most trails in the area, this six-hour walk is quite safe in winter.

The *Padiş* is also a five-hour hike southeast of Scărişoara (see p.249) along a marked track.

③ The Crişul Repede valley

From Cluj, the DN1 (E60) heads west along the verdant **Crişul valley**, shadowed for much of the way by the railway line. Ten trains a day run west to Oradea; buses are less frequent. **Cyclists** can take two lovely back roads through the valley that run parallel to the main DN1 to the south: from Leghia to Bologa, and from Bucea to Tileagd.

You'll find a rich choice of accommodation and camping options along or just off this route, including in **Gilău**, **Gura Răştii** (where the *Lui Pui* cabana offers hiking, kayaking, mountain-biking and tennis), **Valea Ierii** and **Izvoru Crişului** (Körösfő) – this last village is essentially one big bazaar selling Magyar arts and crafts, and also has a seventeenth-century walled Calvinist church with an eighteenth-century painted ceiling.

Huedin and Sâncraiu

HUEDIN (Bánffyhunyad), to the north of the Apuseni range and 46km west of Cluj, is a small town with a largely systematized centre; it's also known for its huge Gypsy palaces, which line the main street as you enter from the west. The chief reason for stopping here is to pick up buses to the surrounding valleys. Huedin's **train and bus stations** are just east and west respectively of the Zimbor road's level crossing, a five-minute walk north of the town centre. Most

The culture of the Kalotaszeg

The area immediately west of Cluj is known to Hungarians as **Kalotaszeg** and, since the great Hungarian Millennium Exhibition of 1896, it has been revered as the region where authentic Magyar culture has survived uncorrupted. It's common to see local people selling handicrafts by the roadside here – particularly to Hungarian tourists on pilgrimages to the wellsprings of Magyar culture.

The local **embroidery** is particularly famous, usually consisting of stylized leaves and flowers, in one bold colour (usually bright red) on a white background; the style is known as *írásos*, meaning "drawn" or "written", because the designs are drawn onto the cloth (traditionally with a mixture of milk and soot) before being stitched. The Calvinist churches of these villages are noted for their **coffered ceilings**, made up of square panels (known as "cassettes"), beautifully painted in the eighteenth century, along with the pews and galleries, in a naïve style similar to the embroidery. The architects of the National Romantic school, led by Kós Károly, were strongly influenced by Transylvanian village architecture, as well as by that of the Finns, the Magyars' only ancestral relations.

The composers **Béla Bartók and Zoltán Kodály** amassed fine collections of Transylvanian handicrafts, and Bartók's assortment of carved furniture from Izvoru Crişului (Körösfő) can be seen in his home in Budapest. The composers' main project, however, was to collect the **folk music** of Transylvania. Starting in 1907, they managed to record and catalogue thousands of melodies, despite local suspicion of the "monster" (the apparatus for recording onto phonograph cylinders). Through the project, they discovered a rich vein of inspiration for their own compositions; Bartók declared that a genuine peasant melody was "quite as much a masterpiece in miniature as a Bach fugue or a Mozart sonata".

of the surrounding villages are served by two or three buses a day during the week, but the service is virtually nonexistent at weekends.

If you need to stay, Huedin's only **hotel** is the *Motel Montana* (☎0264/253 090; ❷) at the eastern edge of town, though **homestays** are a better option, with at least two dozen (❶) available just on the main street of **SÂNCRAIU** (Kalotaszentkirály), known for its strong Magyar folklore and its thirteenth-century church, just 6km south; Green Mountain Holidays (see below) can arrange bookings and transfers, and bikes can be rented here.

Around Huedin

From Huedin, a minor road heads 9km south to the village of **Călata** (Nagykalota), where on Sundays the Magyar population still wear their home-made **folk costumes**, and on to the nearby village of **Călățele** (Kiskalota), where you'll see carved wooden homesteads. Sixteen kilometres beyond (connected to Huedin by three buses on weekdays) is **BELIŞ** (Jósikafalva), a village moved (along with its lovely wood church) from the valley when the artificial Lake Fântânele was created; there's now a small lakeside resort comprising two identical two-star hotels (both ☎0264/354 183), and a handful of homestays. Hostel accommodation is also available at the *Popas Turistic Brădeţ* (May–Sept only; ☎0264/147 206; ❶). There's no campsite, but the hotels will allow you to pitch a tent.

MĂNĂSTIRENI (Magyargyerómonostor) lies to the southeast of Huedin, on a minor road south from the DN1. The village has a lovely thirteenth-century walled Calvinist church whose gallery, pews and ceiling were beautifully painted in the eighteenth century. It's also important as the location of Green Mountain Holidays, at no. 277 (☎0264/418 691, ❿www .greenmountainholidays.ro), a Belgian-run company that organizes a range of activities (hiking, cycling, kayaking and horse-riding) and customized trips, such as photo safaris and excursions on steam locomotives; they can also provide information, sell maps, and arrange homestays throughout the Apuseni. Just west of here is **Văleni** (Magyarvalkó), where many of the houses have decorated mouldings. Another thirteenth-century Calvinist church has a wonderful hilltop setting and a collection of carved wooden graveposts, more typical of the Székely Land.

In the valleys to the north of Huedin you will find half a dozen villages with striking **wooden churches** – examples of the Gothic-inspired ones that once reared above peasant settlements from the Tisa to the Carpathians. The most spectacular, and the nearest to Huedin, towers over **Fildu de Sus** (Felsőfüld), a small village reached by a ten-kilometre track west from Fildu de Jos (Alsófüld) on the Huedin–Zalău road. Built in 1727, the church was painted in 1860, with scenes of Daniel in the den with some wonderful grinning lions. Two buses a day run from Huedin to Fildu de Sus, and the Huedin–Zalău bus passes through Fildu de Jos.

Ciucea

Twenty kilometres west of Huedin, by road and rail, the village of **CIUCEA** (Csucsa) is notable for a **museum** (Tues–Sun 9am–5pm) dedicated to the poet and politician **Octavian Goga**, prime minister in 1937 for six chaotic weeks. This house belonged to the wife of **Endre Ady**, the great figure of early modernist poetry in Hungary, who lived here until 1917; Goga bought it after his death in 1919 and had a sixteenth-century **wooden church** from Gălpâia brought here in order to preserve it – you can still enter through the tiny door to view the faintly traceable frescoes in an otherwise blackened interior. Later still, Goga's own **mausoleum**, an ostentatious piece of work decorated with bright blue mosaics set against a silver and gold background, was built in the grounds. The museum is located at the east end of the village next to the church. There's a small, faded little roadside **pension**, the *Romanța* (☎0264/255 064; ❶), by the road and train halt.

Valea Drăganului and Valea Iadului

Two dramatically named valleys run south into the Apuseni mountains on either side of Ciucea, meeting at Stâna de Vale. To the east, the **Valea Drăganului** (Devil's Valley) runs from the train halt and tourist complex of the same name, passing through Lunca Vișagului, from where you can follow the forestry road south past a reservoir before tracing the track marked with blue crosses west to Stâna de Vale (see p.367). The road down the **Valea Iadului** (Valley of Hell) turns off the DN1 at the Piatra Craiului train station, by the wooden church of Bucea, and just east of the *Munți Piatra Craiului* motel (☎0259/341 756; ❷). Civilization ends after 25km, at the *Leșu Lake guesthouse* (☎0722/468 664; ❸), by the artificial lake of the same name; it's another 20km, past the Iadolina waterfall, to Stâna de Vale.

Northern Transylvania

The two counties of Sălaj and Bistrița-Năsăud, covering the swath of ranges from the Apuseni mountains to the Eastern Carpathians, are historically referred to as **Northern Transylvania**. If you're travelling from Cluj to Maramureș, or eastwards over the Carpathians into Moldavia, road and rail routes are fast and direct, but it's well worth considering detours in this little-visited region. To the west, the chief attraction is the idyllic rural scenery of unspoilt Sălaj county, with its many old wooden churches.

Trains into Maramureș run via Jibou to Baia Mare, about two hours from Dej. The quickest road north is the DN1C to Baia Mare. Trains from Cluj into Moldavia run via Năsăud and the Ilva valley to Vatra Dornei and past several of the painted monasteries (see p.302). The DN17 heads east from Dej to Bistrița and through the Bârgău valley to Vatra Dornei. Bistrița and Năsăud, 22km apart, are linked by frequent buses, so it's easy to hop from one route to the other.

Bonţida, Gherla and Sic

From Cluj, both the DN1C (E576) and a rail line head north to nearby Gherla and Dej, passing **BONŢIDA** (Bonchida), site of a great Baroque **palace**, visible from the road and railway. Its last owner was Miklos Banffy, a diplomat who was sent in 1944 to make peace with the advancing Red Army; in revenge, the retreating Germans virtually destroyed the palace. In 1999, the World Monuments Fund placed Bonţida on its list of the world's 100 most endangered monuments, and a Built Heritage Training Centre was established here, whereby craftsmen and architects could be trained while rebuilding the palace. Much progress has since been made, but the main building remains almost totally hollowed out. One of the few completely renovated buildings is the old kitchen block, which now accommodates a pleasant little **café** (daily 10am–6pm). The **train station** is near the main road at the entrance to the village, from where it's a long (about 2.5km), but very pleasant, walk to the palace. The palace has no opening times as such, but the entrance – though a small gateway – is usually always open.

GHERLA (Szamosujvár/Neuschloss) has been a centre of Armenian settlement since 1672; carved Armenian family crests are still visible over many doorways, but the population is now assimilated with the local Hungarians. The town is also synonymous for its prison, which, during the communist era, was used for political detainees; in one notorious incident in 1977, the town (and the prison) flooded, but wardens refused to open the cells, resulting in the deaths of a number of inmates. From the **train station**, it's a five-minute walk west along Str. Avram Iancu to Piaţa Libertăţii and the Baroque Armeno–Catholic **cathedral** on the south side. Built between 1748 and 1798, its greatest treasure is a painting of the *Descent from the Cross* by Rubens (though this has never actually been verified), which can be seen in a small chapel to the left of the choir – you may have to ask to see it. The tower, meanwhile, has had a colourful existence, having been destroyed on no less three occasions. There's a pleasant park across the DN1C from the square, and just to the northeast, at Str. Mihai Viteazul 6, the town **museum** (Mon–Fri 9am–4pm) houses its collection of Armenian manuscripts and icons on glass behind the superb gateway of a seminary, built in 1859. The only place to **stay** in town is the *Pensiunea Ioana*, a decent, quiet place fifteen minutes' walk south at Str. Clujului 4 (℡0264/243 451; ✉office@pensiuneaioana.ro ❷), next to the petrol station.

One of the best villages to hear **traditional music** in this area is **SIC** (Szék), 20km southeast of Gherla, with which it is linked by bus (7 daily). Sic spreads over several hills, with a number of churches and municipal buildings testifying to its former importance as a centre of salt mining. There's a high proportion of Magyars here, who wear costumes the like of which have long disappeared into museums – the men in narrow-brimmed, tall straw hats and blue waistcoats and the women in leather waistcoats, red pleated skirts and black headscarves embroidered with flowers. Every street in Sic seems to have its own band (normally consisting of just three musicians – on violin, viola and double bass), typically playing traditional ancient Magyar and Romanian melodies woven in with Gypsy riffs.

Dej

DEJ, 46km north of Cluj, lies at the junction of the two branches of the Someş River and the routes from Cluj to Maramureş and Bucovina. The town centre is a good kilometre to the north of the main **train station**, Dej Călători (bus #2, #3, #8 or #9); the **bus station** is almost as far on the other side of town.

The Vienna Diktat

On August 30, 1940, Hitler, needing Hungarian support in his new offensive against the Soviet Union, forced Romania to cede 43,492 square kilometres and 2.6 million people in northern Transylvania to Hungary in the **Vienna Diktat** (or Belvedere Treaty). The new border ran south of Cluj, Târgu Mureş and Sfântu Gheorghe and then more or less followed the watershed of the eastern Carpathians north to the border of what is now Ukrainian Transcarpathia. The border is still a living memory in these areas, and locals will be able to show you the earthworks that used to mark it.

More than 10,000 Romanians, mostly members of the educated classes, such as civil servants, teachers, lawyers and priests, were expelled in cattle trucks, some at just two hours' notice, and others after being subjected to mock executions. Atrocities were committed in the appropriated region by the Horthyist police, with 89 killed in the village of Treznea and 157 in Ip, both in Sălaj county, a pattern of cruelty that was repeated after the more extreme Sztójay Döme government took power in Budapest in March 1944 and the Hungarians, Hitler's last allies, retreated before the Red Army.

To reach the centre, take the path left across the rail line, cross the main road before the Peco station to Str. Pintea Viteazul and the footbridge across the Someş River to Str. Aleco Russo, and go through the park, heading for the spire of the **Reformed Church**, dominating the main square, Piaţa Bobâlna. The square itself is an attractive space, its pretty flower-filled park framed by a number of tidy and colourful buildings. The **Municipal Museum** (Tues–Sun 9am–3pm), at Piaţa Bobâlna 4 (the entrance is through a bookshop), has good coverage of the nearby salt mines that drove the medieval economy here, as well as a small ethnographic display. Fifty metres down the road, and a right turn into Str. Petru Rareş, is the **Military Museum** (Tues–Fri 9am–4pm), exhibiting a range of items from the Roman to the communist periods.

Dej has two **hotels**: the *Someş*, a dismal communist-era relic, near Piaţa Bobâlna at Piaţa Mărăşeşti 1 (☎0264/213 330, ℱ216 982; ❹); and the much better *Parc-Rex*, by the river at Str. Aleco Russo 9 (☎0264/213 799, ℱ211 325; ❺), which has good-sized rooms with private bath and cable TV. There's an **Internet café** by the local bus terminal on Piaţa 16 Februarie, at Str. Titulescu, just east of the centre.

Năsăud and the Someş Mare valley

Twenty-five kilometres east of Dej lies the small town of **BECLEAN** (Bethlen), at the junction of routes north into Maramureş; this is the ancestral seat of the Bethlen family, which provided several distinguished governors of Transylvania. The road and rail routes to Vatra Dornei and Suceava in Moldavia also divide here, drivers heading southeast to Bistriţa while the train runs further north via Năsăud.

From **Salva**, 24km northeast of Beclean, road and rail routes head north to Maramureş; 9km along this road is the village of **COŞBUC**, named after its most famous son, **George Coşbuc** (1866–1918), poet and activist for Romanian cultural revival. His simple family home is now a **museum** (Tues–Sun 9am–5pm). **NĂSĂUD** (Nussdorf), 6km east of Salva, is at the heart of a region where villagers still wear their traditional embroidered waistcoats and blouses, and hats decorated with peacock feathers. A selection of these is on display in the **museum** at Str. Granicerilor 25. The sole **accommodation** in town is with Ancuţa Nistor of Transylvania Travel, Str. Valea Caselor 22a (@www.transylvaniatravel.from.ro; ❹), who also offers student reductions and tours. Just 5km south of town along the Bistriţa road is the birthplace of **Liviu**

Rebreanu (1885–1944), whose novels *Ion, Uprising* and *The Forest of the Hanged* give a panoramic view of Romanian society before World War I.

The Someş Mare valley

Twenty kilometres east of Năsăud lies Ilva Mică, the junction of a minor branch line that provides access to the shabby spa town of **SÂNGEORZ-BĂI**, a good starting point for hikes north into the Rodna mountains (see p.355). The refurbished *Vila Lotus* on Str. Izvoarelor provides the best-value **accommodation**; otherwise, there's the large but rather impersonal *Hebe*, Str. Izvoarelor 94 (☎0263/370 228, ⓕ370 035; ❷), and guesthouses such as *Pensiunea Bradul* on Str. Someş (☎0263/370 441). The branch line ends at the mining town of **Rodna Veche**, where you can see the ruins of a tenth-century fort and a thirteenth-century church; buses then continue the 7km to **ŞANŢ**. This attractive village of wooden houses with open verandas and shingled roofs is noted for its elaborate wedding celebrations, lasting all weekend. **Homestays** are available – at *Pensiunea Grapini*, Str. Morii 65 (☎0263/379 124), where there's a kitchen, cable TV and Internet access, and *Pensiunea Nechiţa* (☎0263/379 019).

The main railway line to Vatra Dornei runs to the south of the branch line up the Ilva valley. **LEŞU**, eight minutes up the line from Ilva Mică – from the stop, it's a four-kilometre walk east up the valley to the village – is home to one of the best festivals in the region, the **Rhapsody of the Trişcaşi Festival**, held on the first Sunday of September and bringing together pipers from three counties.

It's another 25km to **LUNCA ILVEI**, the last settlement before the pass into Moldavia. Three kilometres east of the village centre and station, the British-run Ştefan cel Mare **horse-riding** centre, at Str. Bolovan 340 (☎0263/378 470, ⓦwww.riding-holidays.ro), offers a range of one- and two-week **riding tours** (April–Oct), as well as day-rides and carriage driving tours – they've also got some good en-suite **accommodation** (❷–❸).

Bistriţa and the Bârgău valley

BISTRIŢA (Bistritz), 40km east of Beclean, and the forested **Bârgău valley** beyond, are the setting for much of Bram Stoker's **Dracula**; his Dracula's castle lies in the Bârgău valley and it was in Bistriţa that Jonathan Harker received the first hints that something was amiss. Remains of **Neolithic settlements** have been found near Bistriţa, although the earliest records of the town coincide with the arrival of Saxon settlers, who built fine churches in many villages (less fortress-like than those further south). The bulk of the Saxon population left after World War II.

Arrival and information

Trains run from Cluj via Beclean to Bistriţa Nord, but you may have to change trains at Sărăţel, just southwest of Bistriţa on the Dej–Braşov line. Just north of the junction is the small village of **Sărata**; from here, bus #10 will take you to Bistriţa. The busy **bus station** is also a major hub for maxitaxis.

The **Tourist Information Centre** in the Casa de Cultura at Str. Albert Berger 10 (Mon–Fri 9am–5pm; ☎0263/219 919) gives free information (including maps) and can arrange all sorts of outdoor activities. The CFR office (Mon–Fri 7am–8pm) is right by the Coroana tourist agency at the top of B-dul. Republicii, and TAROM (Mon–Fri 8am–4pm; ☎0263/216 465) is inside the *Coroana de Aur* hotel. The Clubnet **Internet café** (daily 10am–midnight) is on the corner of B-dul. Decebal and Str. Ursului, under the external staircase.

The **County's Folk Tradition Centre** (☎0263/212 023), in Ceauşescu's former villa on Piaţa Petru Rareş by B-dul. 1 Decembrie, has a gallery and will

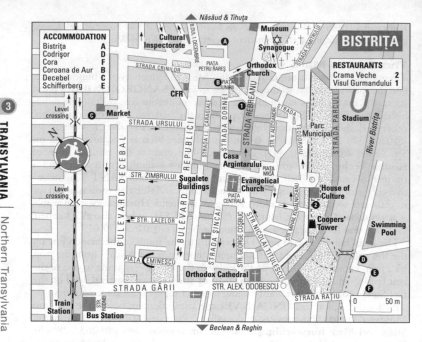

▲ Năsăud & Tihuța

ACCOMMODATION

Bistrița	A
Codrișor	D
Cora	F
Coroana de Aur	B
Decebel	C
Schifferberg	E

RESTAURANTS

| Crama Veche | 2 |
| Visul Gurmandului | 1 |

▼ Beclean & Reghin

be able to confirm the dates of **festivals** at Leșu and the Bârgău villages; Bistrița's own **International Folklore Festival** is held in the second week of August. The Union of Plastic Artists also has a **gallery** at Piața Centrală 24 (closed Mon).

Accommodation

There are plenty of **hotels** in town, though none is particularly special. Of interest to Dracula fans is the *Coroana de Aur* (Golden Crown) at Piața Petru Rareș 4 (☎0263/232 470, 🌐www.hotel-coroana-de-aur.ro; ❺), where Jonathan Harker stayed en route to the Borgau Pass. Just across the way, the *Bistrița*, Str. Petru Rareș 2 (☎0263/231 154, 🌐www.hotel-bistrita.ro; ❹–❺), has renovated rooms far superior (and not that much more expensive) to the older ones, while the very basic *Decebel*, further west at Str. Cuza Vodă 9 (☎0263/212 568, 🆎233 541; ❸), is reasonable enough. Across the river to the south of town are three lower-profile, and cheaper, hotels: the *Codrișor* at Str. Codrișor 28 (☎0263/233 814, 📧hotelcodrisor@coroana.ro; ❸); the *Cora* at no. 23 (☎0263/221 231, 🆎227 782; ❸), which, though not the most attractive place, is extremely welcoming; and the *Schifferberg* next door (☎0263/236 071, 📧schifferberghotel@yahoo.com; ❸), which offers the smartest rooms of these three.

The Town

From the train and bus stations, it's about ten minutes' walk to the centre; heading southeast on Str. Gării you'll pass a typically hideous Centru Civic, but as you turn northeast onto Str. Șincai you enter a more attractive townscape, with pedestrian alleys linking mostly north–south streets. The main square, **Piața Centrală**, is dominated by a great Saxon Evangelical **church** (Tues–Sat 10am–noon & 2–5pm, Sun 3–5pm, service 10am). Built in the Gothic style in the fourteenth century, the church was given Renaissance features in 1559–63 by Petrus Italus da Lugano, who introduced the style to Moldavia. A few decades later, a seventy-six-metre tower was added, the highest stone church tower in Transylvania.

On the northwest side of Piaţa Centrală, the arcaded **Şugălete** buildings (occupied by merchants in the fifteenth century) give a partial impression of how the town must have looked in its medieval heyday. At Str. Dornei 5 you'll find the Renaissance **Casa Argintarului** (Silversmith's House), now accommodating an art college, and continuing northeast, on Piaţa Unirii, an Orthodox church, built for the Minorites in 1270–80, just to the northwest is the synagogue and beyond that is the **County Museum** (Tues–Sun 10am–6pm), which has a collection of Thracian bronzeware, Celtic artefacts, products of the Saxon guilds, mills and presses, as well as a smallish wooden church at the far end of the courtyard. From the museum, you can head back down **Strada Rebreanu**, the town's main, and recently pedestrianized, thoroughfare; with its tree-shaded cafés, and sunny lemon and mint-green coloured townhouses, it's a pleasant place for a stroll, and also contains some interesting buildings, the most notable of which is the **House of Ion Zidaru**, located at the far southern end. Named after a local stonemason, this late Gothic house (built around 1500) was restored in the Transylvanian Renaissance style – note the fine stone portal and balcony – though it's been criminally neglected and now lies boarded up and empty.

Like Braşov and Sibiu, Bistriţa used to be heavily fortified, but successive fires during the nineteenth century have left only vestiges of the fourteenth-century citadel along Str. M. Kogălniceanu and Str. Teodoroiu, including the **Coopers' Tower** (Turnul Dogarilor) – housing the **Galeria de Măşti şi Papuşi**, a collection of folklore masks and puppets (ask at the County Museum for admission). Outside the walls is the Municipal Park, which ludicrously claims to have one of just three *Gingko biloba* or maidenhair trees in Europe.

Eating and drinking

There's precious little to inspire in Bistriţa eating-wise; the most atmospheric **restaurant**, thanks to its riverside location and vast terrace surrounded by neatly clipped bushes, is the *Crama Veche*, behind the House of Culture – the food, mostly Romanian grilled meats, is superb, too, with waitresses scuttling around at optimum speed. Elsewhere, two very commendable pizzerias are *Visul Gurmandului*, Str. Rebreanu 4, and the rather more prosaically named *Pizza Tonight*, B-dul. Independenţiei 16 – its garden terrace is also a good place to sup a draught beer.

For a snack, you can't beat the great *plăcinte* (pies) filled with cheese, cabbage, apple or plum, sold from a hatch at Str. Şincai 37. There are a couple of interesting and lively **bars** in medieval basements, such as *Any Time*, Piaţa Centrală 1, and *Iris*, Str. Rebreanu 2. *Metropolis*, at Piaţa Eminescu (10pm–6am), is one of the biggest **clubs** in Transylvania, with dance floors on two levels, as well as bars, pizza and videogames.

The Bârgău valley

Four buses a day head east up the valley to Vatra Dornei in Moldavia (see p.320). Trains follow this route only as far as Prundu Bârgăului, from where it's another 60km to Vatra Dornei, including the 1200-metre Tihuţa Pass, crossed by two daily buses. The scenery of the Bârgău valley is dramatic, with huge hills draped in forests of fir trees, and villages appearing as living monuments to a way of life unchanged for centuries. In **LIVEZELE**, a long and attractive roadside village 8km from Bistriţa (local bus #3), the **Saxon House Museum** (Muzeul Casa Sasească), at Str. Dorolea 152, demonstrates a way of life that is still commonplace in other villages further up the valley. Dating from around 1870, the house

▲ Typical Saxon village, Transylvania

has two large rooms, kept exactly as they've always been and stuffed with Saxon ceramics, folk dress, furniture, books and photos, and out back there's a large barn with several wine presses – to get to the museum, head down the gravel path leading away from the roadside Lutheran church; the key is kept by the curator at Str. Dorolea 197 (☎0263/270 109). There are now only half a dozen Saxon families left in the village.

In **JOSENII BÂRGĂULUI**, 8km beyond Livezele, black pottery is manufactured and old fulling mills and cottages remain in use. **PRUNDU BÂRGĂULUI**, 6km east of Josenii, is the venue for the **Raftsmen's Festival** on the last weekend of March, when unmarried men crown their usual attire of sheepskin jackets with a small hat buried beneath a plume of peacock feathers.

One kilometre on from Prundu Bârgăului is **TIHA BÂRGĂULUI**, occasional host to the interesting **Festival of Regele Brazilor** (King of the Fir Trees). This is an opportunity to hear the traditional songs, and the part-improvised lamentations (*bochet*) of relatives and friends of the deceased, telling of the deceased's deeds in this life; if the festival runs at all, it's on the third Sunday of June. The *Motel Cora* is at the west end of Tiha Bârgăului, and at km97 (35km from Bistriţa, beyond Mureşeni Bârgăului) is the *Bradului* cabana, where you can **camp**. Climbing steadily eastwards, the DN17 (E576) reaches the scattered settlement of **Piatra Fântânele** and at km108 the *Hotel Castel Dracula* (☎0263/265 192; ❻), where staff delight in hiding in a coffin from which they try and scare guests. Note that the map of hiking trails outside is incorrect; some trails don't exist, while some that do aren't shown. There are cabanas offering *camere de inchiriat* (private rooms) in the village; the *Pensiunea Bubulea* (☎0263/238 563), behind the hotel on a short-cut to the Dornişoara road, is recommended, particularly for its cooking.

Just beyond, at km113, lies the **Tihuţa Pass**, which may be blocked by snow for a day or two between late October and mid-May. Although the country is relatively densely settled near the main road, the surrounding mountains harbour more **bears** than in any other part of Europe, as well as red deer, boars and **wolves**; the **view** from the pass of the green "crests" of Bucovina to the northeast and the volcanic Căliman mountains to the southeast is marvellous.

Travel details

Trains

Alba Iulia to: Arad (5 daily; 2hr 45min–3hr 45min); Braşov (3 daily; 3hr 15min–3hr 35min); Cluj (8 daily; 1hr 45min–2hr 40min); Deva (8 daily; 1hr 5min–1hr 30min); Hunedoara (1 daily; 1hr 55min); Sibiu (4 daily; 1hr 45min–2hr 30min); Sighişoara (3 daily; 1hr 30min–1hr 50min); Târgu Mureş (3 daily; 1hr 30min–3hr); Timişoara (4 daily; 4hr 35min–5hr).

Bistriţa to: Cluj (3 daily; 3hr); Sărăţel (14 daily; 15min).

Braşov to: Bucharest (every 40–60min; 2hr 30min–4hr 45min); Cluj (5–7 daily; 4hr 30min–6hr 15min); Deva (5 daily; 4hr 15min–5hr 30min); Făgăraş (10 daily; 1hr–1hr 30min); Miercurea Ciuc (11 daily; 1hr 30min–2hr 30min); Sfântu Gheorghe (13 daily; 30–55min); Sibiu (8 daily; 2hr 20min–3hr 40min); Sighişoara (17 daily; 1hr 45min–2hr 30min); Sinaia (every 30–60min; 50min–1hr 20min); Târgu Mureş (4 daily; 5hr 15min–7hr 45min); Zarneşti (6 daily; 40min).

Cluj to: Bistriţa (3 daily; 2hr 45min–3hr); Deva (3 daily; 3hr 15min–3hr 30min); Miercurea Ciuc (1 daily; 4hr 40min); Oradea (14 daily; 2hr 15min–4hr 50min); Sfântu Gheorghe (1 daily; 5hr 40min); Sibiu (2 daily; 3hr 35min); Sighişoara (7 daily; 2hr 50min–3hr 25min); Târgu Mureş (1 daily; 2hr 20min).

Făgăraş to: Braşov (10 daily; 55min–1hr 35min); Sibiu (10–11 daily; 1hr 10min–2hr 10min).

Hunedoara to: Simeria (9 daily; 30min).

Miercurea Ciuc to: Baia Mare (1 daily; 7hr 30min); Braşov (11–12 daily; 1hr 35min–2hr 40min); Dej (2–3 daily; 4hr 5min–5hr); Gheorgheni (11 daily; 55min–1hr 10min); Sighet (1 daily; 8hr 20min); Suceava (1 daily; 6hr 20min).

Petroşani to: Cluj (2 daily; 5hr 30min); Craiova (7 daily; 2hr 40min–4hr 10min); Deva (8 daily; 1hr 50min–2hr 50min); Simeria (11 daily; 1hr 35min–2hr 30min); Târgu Jiu (8 daily; 1hr 10min–1hr 40min).

Sibiu to: Arad (1 daily; 5hr); Braşov (9 daily; 2hr 20min–3hr 40min): Cluj (2 daily; 3hr 35min); Deva (4–5 daily; 2hr 20min–2hr 45min); Mediaş (4 daily; 1hr 20min–1hr 35min); Râmnicu Vâlcea (5 daily; 2–3hr); Timişoara (3 daily; 5hr 15min–6hr).

Sighişoara to: Alba Iulia (3 daily; 1hr 35min–1hr 45min); Braşov (17 daily; 1hr 45min–2hr 30min); Cluj (6 daily; 2hr 55min–3hr 20min).

Sinaia to: Braşov (every 30–60min; 50min–1hr 20min); Bucharest (every 30–60min; 2hr 45min).

Târgu Mureş to: Cluj (2 daily; 2hr 10min–2hr 20min); Deda (10 daily; 1hr–1hr 30min); Deva (1 daily; 3hr 40min); Razboieni (10 daily; 1hr–1hr 45min).

Zalău to: Jibou (8 daily; 40min).

Buses & maxitaxis

Abrud to: Alba Iulia (7 daily); Câmpeni (10 daily); Cluj (3 daily); Oradea (1 daily).

Alba Iulia to: Aiud (3 daily); Blaj (5 daily); Bucharest (6 daily); Câmpeni (6 daily): Cluj (12 daily); Deva (2 daily); Oradea (2 daily); Sebeş (every 20–30min); Sibiu (2–4 daily); Târgu Jiu (3 daily); Târgu Mureş (3 daily); Timişoara (3 daily).

Bistriţa to: Baia Mare (2 daily); Braşov (5 daily); Borşa (1 daily); Cluj/Oradea (5 daily); Năsăud (Mon–Fri 11 daily; Sat & Sun 6 daily); Rodna (Mon–Fri 2 daily); Sibiu (3 daily); Sighişoara (4 daily); Suceava (5 daily); Târgu Mureş (5 daily); Vatra Dornei (6 daily).

Braşov (Autogară 1) to: Agnita (1 daily); Bacău (7 daily); Bistriţa (5 daily); Bucharest (every 30–60min); Buzău (4 daily); Câmpulung Muscel (2 daily); Făgăraş (1 daily); Gheorgheni (2 daily); Iaşi (1 daily); Odorheiu Secuiesc (1 daily); Piatra Neamţ (1 daily); Prejmer (Mon–Fri 7 daily, Sat & Sun 3 daily); Sibiu (2 daily); Târgovişte (2 daily); Târgu Mureş (6 daily); Târgu Neamţ (1 daily); Târgu Secuiesc (10 daily).

Braşov (Autogară 2) to: Bran (Mon–Fri every 30min, Sat & Sun hourly); Câmpulung Muscel (4 daily); Curtea de Argeş/Râmnicu Vâlcea (1 daily); Piteşti (2 daily); Zărneşti (Mon–Fri hourly, Sat 8 daily, Sun 2 daily).

Braşov (Autogară 3) to: Bacău (3 daily); Buzău (1 daily); Hărman (Mon–Fri 6 daily); Prejmer (Mon–Fri 8 daily, Sat & Sun 2 daily).

Câmpeni to: Abrud (10 daily); Alba Iulia (7 daily); Arad (1 daily); Arieşeni (4 daily); Brad (4 daily); Bucharest (1 daily); Cluj (4 daily); Deva (2 daily); Oradea (2 daily); Sebeş (1 daily); Timişoara (2 daily).

Cluj to: Abrud (2 daily); Alba Iulia (11 daily); Baia Mare (6 daily); Bistriţa (8 daily); Braşov (1 daily); Câmpeni (4 daily); Cojocna (3 daily); Deva (1 daily); Gheorgheni (3 daily Mon–Fri); Huedin (2 daily); Hunedoara (1 daily); Oradea (5 daily); Râmnicu Vâlcea (6 daily); Reghin (1–4 daily); Satu Mare (2 daily); Sibiu (8 daily); Sighet (3 daily); Târgu Jiu (2 daily); Târgu Lăpuş (2 daily); Târgu Mureş (6 daily); Turda (15 daily); Zalău (8 daily).

Covasna to: Sfântu Gheorghe (3–4 daily); Târgu Secuiesc (4 daily).

Deva to: Brad (14 daily Mon–Fri, 8 daily Sat & Sun); Câmpeni (2 daily); Cluj (2 daily); Hunedoara (every 20min); Oradea (2 daily); Sarmizegetusa (2 daily Mon–Fri); Sibiu (4 daily); Târgu Mureş (2 daily); Timişoara (7 daily).

Gheorgheni to: Braşov (2 daily); Cluj (3 daily); Lacu Roşu (3 daily); Odorheiu Secuiesc (1 daily); Piatra Neamţ (3 daily); Târgu Mureş (3 daily); Târgu Neamţ (1 daily).

Haţeg to: Cluj (2 daily); Densuş (2 daily); Hunedoara (5 daily); Reşiţa (1 daily); Sarmizegetusa (3 daily Mon–Fri); Timişoara (1 daily); Târgu Jiu (2 daily).

Hunedoara to: Cinciş (7–9 daily); Cluj (6 daily); Craiova (1 daily); Deva (3 hourly); Drobeta-Turnu Severin (1 daily); Haţeg (5 daily).

Mediaş to: Agnita (1–3 daily); Făgăraş (1 daily Mon–Fri); Sibiu (5 daily); Târgu Mureş (5 daily Mon–Fri, 4 daily Sat & Sun).

Miercurea Ciuc to: Băile Tuşnad (4 daily); Braşov (2 daily); Frumoasa (11 daily Mon–Fri, 4 daily Sat & Sun); Odorheiu Secuiesc (5–7 daily); Piatra Neamţ (2 daily); Sovata (3 daily); Târgu Mureş (3 daily); Târgu Neamţ (1 daily); Târgu Secuiesc (2–3 daily).

Odorheiu Secuiesc to: Braşov (1 daily); Covasna/Târgu Secuiesc (1 daily); Gheorgheni (1 daily); Miercurea Ciuc (2 daily); Praid (10 daily); Sf. Gheorghe (1 daily); Sighişoara (1 daily); Sovata/Târgu Mureş (5 daily).

Reghin to: Bistriţa (1 daily); Cluj (1–4 daily); Hodac (17 daily); Sighişoara (1 daily); Sovata (2 daily); Târgu Neamţ (1 daily); Vatra Dornei (1 daily).

Sebeş to: Alba Iulia (2 hourly); Câmpeni (1 daily); Cluj (8 daily); Sibiu (12 daily); Timişoara (2 daily).

Sfântu Gheorghe to: Braşov (2 daily); Bucharest (1 daily); Covasna (3 daily Mon–Fri, 1 daily Sat & Sun), Odorheiu Secuiesc (1 daily); Piatra Neamţ (2 daily); Târgu Neamţ (1 daily); Târgu Secuiesc (2 daily).

Sibiu to: Agnita (4 daily); Bistriţa (3 daily); Braşov (4 daily); Bucharest (4 daily); Cisnădie (every 20–30min Mon–Fri, 10 daily Sat & Sun); Cluj (8 daily); Cristian (hourly Mon–Fri, 5 daily Sat & Sun); Deva (4 daily); Galaţi (2 daily); Gura Râului (10 Mon–Fri, 2 daily Sat & Sun); Mediaş (3–5 daily); Oradea (1 daily); Păltiniş (3 daily); Râmnicu Vâlcea (4 daily); Sighişoara (8 daily); Slimnic (3 daily); Târgu Jiu (1 daily); Târgu Mureş (4 daily); Timişoara (2 daily).

Sighişoara to: Agnita (1 daily); Bistriţa (3 daily); Braşov (1 daily); Făgăraş (1 daily); Odorheiu Secuiesc (1 daily); Sibiu (5 daily); Sovata (3 daily); Târgu Mureş (hourly).

Sovata to: Cluj (1 daily); Miercurea Ciuc (3 daily); Odorheiu Secuiesc (5 daily); Reghin (2 daily); Sighişoara (1 daily); Târgu Mureş (6–10 daily).

Târgu Mureş to: Alba Iulia (3 daily); Bistriţa (6 daily); Braşov (6 daily); Cluj (4 daily); Mediaş (5 daily); Miercurea Ciuc (2 daily); Odorheiu Secuiesc (8 daily); Piatra Neamţ (1 daily); Sibiu (5 daily); Sighişoara (Mon–Fri 12 daily, Sat & Sun 6 daily); Sovata (Mon–Fri hourly, Sat & Sun 8 daily); Târgu Neamţ (3 daily); Vatra Dornei (2 daily).

Târgu Secuiesc to: Bacău (5 daily); Covasna (4 daily); Miercurea Ciuc (2 daily).

Zalău to: Baia Mare (1 daily); Cluj (5–6 daily); Huedin (1 daily); Jibou (3 daily); Oradea (2 daily); Şimleu-Silvanei (4 daily); Timişoara (2 daily).

Planes

Cluj to: Bucharest (Mon–Fri 4 daily, Sat & Sun 2 daily; 1hr).

Sibiu to: Bucharest (4 weekly; Carpatair; 45min).

Târgu Mureş to: Bucharest (4 weekly; 1hr 30min).

International trains

Braşov to: Budapest, Hungary (4 daily; 10hr 30min–12hr); Prague, Czech Republic (1 daily; 22hr 30min); Vienna, Austria (1 daily; 15hr 30min); Krakow, Poland (1 daily; 22hr).

Cluj to: Budapest (2 daily; 6hr 30min).

Deva to: Budapest (2 daily; 5hr 30min–7hr 10min); Prague (1 daily; 17hr); Vienna (1 daily; 9hr 30min); Krakow (1 daily; 17hr).

Miercurea Ciuc to: Budapest (1 daily; 12hr).

Sighişoara to: Budapest (3 daily; 8hr 30min–9hr 30min); Krakow (1 daily; 19hr 30min); Prague (1 daily; 18hr 30min); Vienna (1 daily; 12hr).

International buses

Braşov to: Budapest (Tues, Thurs & Fri); Chişinău, Moldova (Mon–Fri); Germany (several daily); Istanbul, Turkey (Thurs & Sun).

Cluj to: Athens, Greece (2 weekly); Budapest (2 daily); Germany (1 daily); Thessaloniki, Greece (2 weekly).

Deva to: Germany (several daily).

Gheorgheni to: Budapest (1 daily).

Miercurea Ciuc to: Budapest (2 daily).

Odorheiu Secuiesc to: Budapest (2 daily).

Reghin to: Budapest (Thurs & Sun).

Sebeş to: Germany (several daily).

Sfântu Gheorghe to: Budapest (1 daily).

Sibiu to: Germany (several daily).

Sighişoara to: Budapest (1 Mon & Fri); Germany (daily).

Târgu Mureş to: Budapest (1 daily).

Moldavia

HUNGARY

UKRAINE

MOLDOVA

UKRAINE

SERBIA

Black Sea

BULGARIA

CHAPTER 4

Highlights

✳ **Ghimeş** An isolated Hungarian enclave perched on the old Habsburg-Ottoman border, this quiet village is surrounded by rolling green hills. See p.268

✳ **Agapia Convent** This picture-perfect convent, where over four hundred nuns live in trim cottages, is one of the spiritual centres of the Romanian Orthodox Church. See p.276

✳ **The Neculai Popa Museum** A delightful collection of folk sculpture and other curiosities, set in the rugged village of Tărpeşti, south of Târgu Neamţ. See p.277

✳ **The Ceahlău massif** Bucovina is the most forested region of Romania, and the hills and rock formations of the massif offer wilderness on an impressive scale. See p.279

✳ **Iaşi** In spite of Ceauşescu's best efforts to crush its spirit, the old Moldavian capital is full of surprises; Iaşi's vibrant restaurant scene is especially impressive. See p.281

✳ **Bucovina pensions** Stay at least a night in one of the dozens of hospitable Bucovina guesthouses such as *Casa Buburuzan* in Humor; guests are served lavish traditional meals made from home-grown products. See p.309

✳ **The Ladder of Virtue, Suceviţa Monastery** This splendid, richly detailed ensemble is just one of the unforgettable frescoes of Bucovina's painted monasteries. See p.311

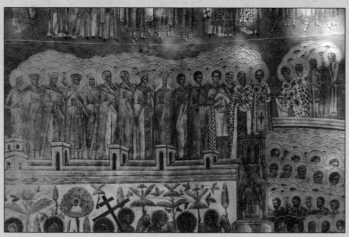

▲ Frescoes in Voroneţ Monastery

Moldavia

F or travellers, Moldavia gets more interesting the further north you go, and the difficulty of some journeys can, perversely, add to the attraction of your final destination. This is particularly true of the jewels in the Moldavian crown, the **painted monasteries of southern Bucovina**. Secluded in valleys near the Ukrainian border, their medieval frescoes of redemption and damnation blaze in polychromatic splendour – Voroneţ and Suceviţa boast peerless examples of the Last Judgement and the Ladder of Virtue, while Moldoviţa is famous for its fresco of the Siege of Constantinople. The unpainted Putna Monastery, final resting place of Stephen the Great, draws visitors interested in Romanian history. Though all are more or less accessible from Bucovina's regional capital, **Suceava**, many visitors opt for ONT tours from Bucharest, although it's far less expensive to make your own way to Suceava and book a tour there (see p.296).

As in Wallachia, most towns and cities in Moldavia have been marred by hideous concrete apartment blocks and factories. Only **Iaşi** holds any great appeal – with numerous churches and monasteries retained from its heyday as the Moldavian capital, it has a charm that puts Bucharest to shame. In contrast to the new-town developments, the countryside looks fantastic, with picturesque villages dwarfed by the flanks of the Carpathians. Just over halfway to Suceava, Neamţ county contains the eclectic **Neculai Popa Museum**, as well as Moldavia's largest **convents** – Agapia and Văratec – and the weirdly shaped **Ceahlău massif**, a paradise for hikers and climbers. Backwaters such as **Ghimeş** in the Magyar-speaking **Csángó region** are worth investigating if you're interested in rural life, and there are also numerous local **festivals** (see box, p.301). The main festivals are at Ilişeşti (July), Durău (August), Iaşi (October) and Odobeşti (November).

Moldavia's complex **history** is best understood in relation to the cities of Iaşi and Suceava, the former capitals of the region, and you'll find more details under the individual city accounts. Moldavia used to be twice its present size, having at various times included Bessarabia (the land beyond the River Prut) and Northern Bucovina (on the edge of the Carpathians). Both territories were annexed by Stalin in 1940, severing cultural and family ties; these have been revived since the fall of communism, especially between Moldavia and the former Bessarabia (now the sovereign Republic of Moldova).

Motorists heading along the DN2 into northern Moldavia should note that although the road is designated on maps as Euro-route 85, it's actually a country road where horse-drawn wagons without lights are a major hazard at night.

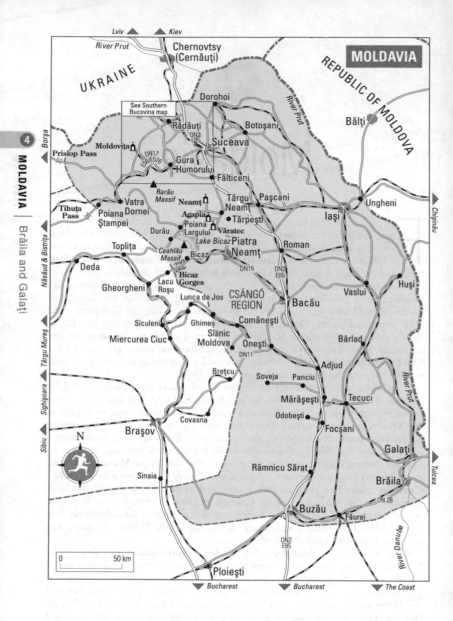

Brăila and Galaţi

Lying well off the main route through Moldavia, close to the region's south-eastern border and the Danube Delta, **Brăila** and **Galaţi** are seldom visited by tourists, and only then while en route to or from Tulcea, the Delta capital. Both were once ports where the Orient and Occident colluded in exporting Romania's agricultural wealth; now they are backwaters and monuments to economic failure. Brăila's docks are largely silted up – though its old town has retained more nineteenth-century architecture than most other Romanian cities – while Galaţi is blighted by bankrupt industries. There are no bridges across the Danube in the vicinity, and now that ferries and hydrofoils to Tulcea and the Delta have ceased operating, the only way to get to Galaţi from Tulcea is by bus (5 daily; 2hr) or maxitaxi (5 daily; 1hr 15min). The same applies to Braila, with buses from Tulcea running to Smârdan for a ferry connection. Fast trains run from Galaţi to Bucharest via Brăila, and slower services, as well as buses and maxitaxis, connect to northern Moldavia.

Brăila

BRĂILA has the air of a restful, pleasantly gone-to-seed Danubian town about it, laid out in concentric streets radiating from the port esplanade. As the region's principal harbour, Brăila shipped the harvests of the Bărăgan Plain to the rest of Europe in the nineteenth century, creating huge fortunes for a few landlords who built elegant villas here, using members of the local Gypsy population – at the time, the largest of any town in Europe – as domestic slaves. The villas have long crumbled, while the Gypsies remain; the vestiges of wealth and splendour give the place a romantic, even Bohemian, feel.

The old town, rebuilt after being liberated from the Turks in the war of 1828–29, in which it was heavily damaged, is centred on **Piaţa Traian**, a leafy square on which stands the **Church of the Archangel Michael**, built as a mosque by the Turks, probably in the eighteenth century, with a freestanding belfry added later. Sepia photos of Brăila in its heyday appear in the town's **museum** (Muzeul Brăila; Tues–Sun 9am–5pm), at Piaţa Traian 3.

From the far side of Piaţa Traian, the lively axis of Calea Călăraşilor leads towards the **Centru Civic**, passing villas housing restaurants and banks, as well as a large **Greek Orthodox church** built by the community that dominated the shipping business before World War I.

From the bottom of Piaţa Traian, Str. Imperator Traian leads to the dismal **waterfront** with its mournful array of rusting freighters and patrol boats; when Ceauşescu visited here, they even had to paint the grass green.

Practicalities

Brăila's **bus station** is about 200m left of the train station, on Str. Siret. **Maxitaxis** to and from Galaţi call at the intersection of B-dul Dorobanţi and Calea Galaţi, 1km north of the centre. Take the ferry from the waterfront to Smârdan for buses and maxitaxis east to Tulcea or Constanţa. To reach town from the **train station**, take maxitaxi #4 or walk 1km down Str. E. Grigorescu to B-dul A.I. Cuza; bear right as far as Str. Eminescu, the pedestrianized street which leads left to Piaţa Traian, centre of the old town. The most convenient **supermarket**, Plus, is at Calea Călăraşilor 104.

The best **place to stay** in terms of value for money and convenient location is the nondescript but recently renovated *Hotel Sport* (☎0239/611 346; ❸), which has clean and modern en-suite rooms. It's at Str. D. Bolintineanu 4, down the first turning to the right off Calea Galaţi, leading from Piaţa Traian. Standards are a bit higher at the *Traian* (☎0239/614 685, ⓕ612 685, ⓦwww .unita-turism.ro; ❹), a dull high-rise with English-speaking staff at Piaţa Traian 4. There are also adequate rooms at *LMS* (☎0239/611 900, ⓔlms@braila.astral .ro; ❸), a pizzeria-restaurant at Calea Galaţi 9 that is the most stylish **place to eat** in the centre. The *Old City Café*, at Calea Călăraşilor 14, also has good food, a pleasant terrace and an English menu, and *Cool Café*, at Calea Călăraşilor 57, serves pizza and salads until midnight and has Wi-Fi. Most of the best **bars** are also found along this road.

Galaţi

GALAŢI, 32km north of Brăila by road and rail, grew up as a port at the confluence of the River Danube with Moldavia's inland waterways, the Siret and the Prut. In Bram Stoker's *Dracula*, Jonathan Harker and Godalming come here to catch a steamer up the Siret and Bistriţa rivers, heading for Dracula's castle at the Bârgău Pass. Galaţi swelled to its present size during the 1960s, when Romania's largest **steelworks** were constructed here. For Gheorghiu-Dej and Ceauşescu, this enterprise was the prerequisite for Romania's emergence as a fully industrialized nation, and a symbolic and concrete assertion of independence from the Warsaw Pact, which preferred Romania to remain a largely agricultural country. Although virtually bankrupt, the steelworks were bought by Mittal Steel in 2001, a deal that is supposed to have secured British backing for Romania's accession to the EU.

Galaţi is a fair-sized city, with plenty of shops, hotels and restaurants, most found along the main avenue, Str. Brăilei, but you'll probably pass through only to make a bus or maxitaxi connection to Tulcea. The city was badly bombed in 1944 and largely rebuilt as a series of numbingly identical apartment buildings. Nevertheless, there's an area of attractive nineteenth- and early twentieth-century buildings along Str. Domnească, between the centre and the train station. These include the Prefectura (a very grand Mauresque pile), the theatre (a very grand Neoclassical pile across the road), the neo-Brâncovenesc university building, and, a block south at Str. A.I. Cuza 80, the Casa Cuza Vodă, once home to independent Romania's first ruler, Alexandru Ioan Cuza.

Practicalities

Buses to or from Tulcea call not in Galaţi proper, but at the ferry slip in the village of I.C. Brătianu across the Danube. Regular ferries shuttle both foot passengers (€0.30) and cars (€3.50, including the driver) across to Galaţi, a fifteen-minute ride. The final ferry sails around 10pm, well after the arrival of the last bus from Tulcea. From the small terminal on the Galaţi side, 3km south of town, take a taxi into the centre (going the other way, ask the driver to take you to the *debarcader* or *trecere bac*). Alternatively, you can turn right for a very pleasant walk through a riverside park, with a wide cycling/rollerblading track and modern sculptures. Galaţi's **train station** – adjacent to the **bus station** – lies 1km northeast of the town centre on Str. Gării. **Maxitaxis** to Brăila (much faster and more frequent than trains) are to be found south of the centre; take local maxitaxi #19 to the last stop. Buses to northern Moldavia also pick up at the Autogara Dunărea, by the Dunărea Stadium (behind the McDonald's), from where maxitaxis to Tecuci leave every ten minutes. For **car rental**, contact Autonom at Str. Brăilei 134 (☎0236/477 377, 0788/903 359, ⓔgalati@autonom.ro).

Accommodation

Dunărea Str. Domnească 21 ☎0236/418 041, ⓦwww.galtour-dunarea.ro. A refurbished communist-era block, with free Wi-Fi in its restaurant/*terasa*; good weekend rates. ❹–❺
Galaţi Str. Domnească 12 ☎0236/460 040, ⓦwww.hotelgalati.ro. Similar to the Dunărea

across the road, but with a/c, Internet access and friendly, competent staff. ❻
Hostel Galaţi Str. Portului 57 ☎0236/411 812, ⓔyouth_hostels_galati@yahoo.com. An HI-affiliated youth hostel by the river north of the Vega; entering by the first gate of the Grup Scolar

(a complex of colleges and dorms), go in the first door (on your left) and up to the third floor. It's wise to reserve in advance. ❶
Sport Str. A.I. Cuza 76 ☎ 0236/414 098, ℗ 415 672. Convenient for the train and bus stations, this is perhaps the best-value place in town, with small rooms but big modern bathrooms. ❸

Vega B-dul Marii Uniri 107 ☎ 0236/306 080, Ⓦ www.vegahotel.ro. A new high-rise hotel by the river, also with a/c and Internet access, as well as a sauna and gym. ❻
Vila Belvedere Str. Şoimului 1 ☎ 0236/499 780. A grand guesthouse 1km north, on the riverside cliff. ❺

Eating and drinking

There are a couple of attractive **restaurants** by the Danube: *Libertatea 2000*, a two-deck mock ship just north of the *Vega* hotel, offering mainly Romanian dishes and open from 9am until late, and further north, beyond the *Vila Belvedere*, the futurist *Pescărul* (specializing in fish).

From Buzău to Bacău

The main routes northeast from Bucharest through Moldavia, the DN2 and the Bucharest–Suceava train line, are a poor advertisement for the region, as one hideously modernized town succeeds another without even the sight of the Carpathians to lift your spirits until you reach Bacău, halfway to Suceava. There's little reason to stop along the way unless for a detour into the wine-growing or **Csángó** regions of the Subcarpathians; of princiapl interest is the village of Ghimeş, on the rail line to Miercurea Ciuc in Transylvania.

That said, you might consider visiting **Buzău**, 128km from Bucharest on the southern border of Moldavia, if you're around on the last Sunday in June, when it holds its kitsch **Drăgaica festival**. Once widespread in rural Romania, this Midsummer Day's custom required young girls wearing crowns and hoods to go singing and dancing into the fields to verify the readiness of the wheat for harvesting.

Focşani, 70km further north, has few reasons to stop other than bus and train links to the **wine-growing regions** of Panciu and Odobeşti, and routes northwest into the hills of Vrancea county. Immediately south of the rail junction of **Mărăşeşti** (20km north of Focşani), a huge mausoleum remembers the crucial battle in the summer of 1917, when German forces advancing on Iaşi were halted by Romanian troops, determined to preserve the last unoccupied region of their country.

At **Panciu** they make sparkling wines, while **Odobeşti** produces Galbena de Odobeşti, the yellow wine that was Ceauşescu's favourite tipple. Odobeşti is also noted for its **festivals**; the grape harvest is celebrated in late September, and on the third Sunday of November the shepherds of Vrancea county gather to entertain each other with performances on alpine horns and panpipes. Pension **accommodation** in Panciu, Odobeşti and elsewhere can be booked through the Vrancea County Antrec office (☎0237/673 049 or 0722 491 665, Ⓔvrancea@antrec.ro), located about 50km northwest of Focşani, in the village ofVidra. The spa of **Soveja**, 88km northwest of Focşani, is a base for visiting the hills to the west, with a museum and monastery (founded in 1645), various guesthouses and the *Zboina* hotel (☎0237/636 021; ❸).

The Csángó region

The name "Csángó" is thought to derive from the Hungarian for "wanderer", referring to those Székely (see p.215) who fled here from religious persecution in Transylvania during the fifteenth century, to be joined by others escaping military conscription in the seventeenth and eighteenth centuries. There is evidence that Hungarians have been present in this area for even longer than that, however; the true origin of the Csángó remains a subject of contentious debate. Once, there were some forty **Csángó villages** in Moldavia, a few as far east as present-day Ukraine, but today their community has contracted into a core of about five thousand people living between Adjud and Bacău, and in **Ghimeş** at the upper end of the Trotuş (Tatros) valley. Most rural Csángó are fervently religious and fiercely conservative, retaining a distinctive folk costume and dialect; their music is harsher and sadder than that of their Magyar kinsfolk in Transylvania, although their dances are almost indistinguishable from those of their Romanian neighbours.

Mutual suspicions and memories of earlier injustices and uprisings made this a sensitive area in communist times. While allowing them to farm and raise sheep outside the collectives, the Party tried to dilute the Csángó and stifle their culture by settling Romanians in new industrial towns like Oneşti. Things are a lot freer now, and the idyllic upper valley is frequently visited during the summer by tour groups from Budapest, as well as a few independent travellers. Tourist infrastructure in Ghimeş has developed apace, though shops are still very basic and there are no ATMs – bring what supplies and money you're going to need with you.

Practicalities

Adjud is the junction on the main Bucharest–Suceava line for the branch line west to Oneşti, Ghimeş and Transylvania. However, if you're coming to Ghimeş from the north, rather than riding all the way down to Adjud, it may be quicker to disembark at Bacău, catch a bus to Comăneşti (the last one leaves at 7.30pm), and wait there for the next train up the valley. The first major stop after Adjud is **Oneşti** (Onyest), which can also be reached by bus from Bacău, the last leaving at 6.30pm; dominated by the chemical industry, it is notable only as the birthplace of Nadia Comaneci (now resident in Norman, Oklahoma). From here or from **Târgu Ocna** (Aknavásar), a small spa 12km to the west that boasts the largest underground sanatorium in Europe, you can reach the larger spa of **Slănic Moldova** (Szlanikfürdo) which lies 20km southeast of Târgu Ocna.

Accommodation in Târgu Ocna is mainly found near the Saline station, 2km west, which is where the fast trains call; a good choice is *Casa Creangă* at Str. Gălean 33 (☎0234/341 795, ⓦwww.casacreanga.ro; ❹), which has an indoor swimming pool. In Slănic Moldova, try *Casa Albă*, at Str. Bălcescu 59 (☎0234/348 803, ⓦwww.pensiuneacasaalba.ro; ❸), or *Pensiunea Cristal*, at Str. Bălcescu 70 (☎0234/348 004; ❸). In Comăneşti there's the HI-affiliated *White Castle* youth hostel at Str Supanului 57 (☎0234/371 844, ⓔgraziela_dima@yahoo.com; ❶), as well as the *Hotel Bradul*, at Str. Republicii 6 (☎0234/374 303; ❹). In Oneşti the new *Hotel Sport*, at B-dul. Republicii 43 (☎0234/321 111; ❺), is far nicer than the *Hostel TransMoldova* in the bus station (☎0234/313 132; ❷).

Ghimeş

The quiet charm that is the real attraction of the beautiful Trotuş valley only begins to reveal itself on the far side of Comăneşti (Cománfalva), a coal-mining settlement that is also the junction for the decrepit oil town of Moineşti, birthplace of Dada founder Tristan Tzara (see box opposite). Beyond Comăneşti, industry is present only in the form of a few small-scale timber mills, and trains call at one picturesque village after another before finally reaching **Ghimeş** (Ghimeş-Făget or Gyimesbükk), the largest and most rewarding of the Csángó settlements, and the only one that can be visited with any ease. The rail line continues on to Miercurea Ciuc in Transylvania, and daily trains to and from Braşov and Timişoara make this an attractive stopping point en route to Neamţ County, Iaşi or Suceava.

Nearly all of the residents of Ghimeş are Hungarian, though there is a small Gypsy population, which, unusually, is well integrated into village life. This helps to account for the strong musical tradition, most in evidence at the **winter fair** held annually on January 20–21. Ghimeş' appeal lies in its tranquil setting, but the town does have a few modest sights. Its principal monument, at least for those who wish to contemplate the injustices of the Trianon Treaty after World War I, under which Hungary was forced to cede Transylvania to Romania, is the nineteenth-century customs house that marked the old border of Transylvania and Moldavia and, earlier, the Habsburg and Ottoman empires. It's just off the main road, 1.5km east of the station. The steps behind it lead up to the insubstantial ruins of **Rákóczi Castle**, built in 1626 by Prince Gábor Bethlen – more than the ruins, though, it's the **view** of the Trotuş valley from here that makes the climb worthwhile. This is also the beginning of the path that leads up the ridge of Papoj mountain (1271m). The area's remoteness makes it ideal for **hiking**, and a series of little-used trails, including several longer routes into Transylvania, is delineated on the 1:60,000 DIMAP map of the area, sold at Deáky Panzió (see p.270). The village itself, divided in two by the Trotuş River, is also an inviting place to take a walk – its houses are neat and colourful, with many boasting intricately carved eaves and flower gardens, and its streets are enlivened by the various farm animals wandering about. Opposite the train station, the **Gyimesi Házimúseum** (Ghimes Domestic Museum; daily in summer 10am–2pm) displays rural memorabilia. The main church, rebuilt in 1976, is 200m up from the station, but more interesting, and a good place to picnic, is the small wooden chapel that overlooks the town from a hilltop meadow across the river. Reaching it entails scaling a few fences, but nobody

My heart belongs to Dada

The magazine *Simbolul* ("The Symbol") was founded in 1912 by three Jewish schoolboys in Bucharest: Ion Vinea, Marcel Iancu and Samuel Rosenstock. All three were to play leading roles in the development of avant-garde art, but it was Rosenstock, calling himself **Tristan Tzara** (1896–1963), who was to achieve greatest fame. A poet and playwright, he was a central figure in the absurdist **Dada movement**, founded at Zurich's *Cabaret Voltaire* in 1916; he moved to Paris in 1920 but broke with Dadaism in 1923 when its French leaders, such as André Breton and Louis Aragon, turned to Surrealism. Iancu, better known as **Marcel Janco** (1895–1984), also went to Zurich, returning in 1922 to Bucharest and, with **Ion Vinea** (1895–1964), founding the magazine *Contimperanul* ("The Contemporary") which ran until 1932. Its manifesto (similar to that of the Dutch group De Stijl) was more constructivist than Dadaist. Janco also became the leading architect of Cubist and International Style buildings in Bucharest; after World War II he emigrated to Israel, dying there in 1984.

A younger artist, and perhaps the most important, was **Victor Brauner** (1903–1966) who was born in Piatra Neamţ and studied briefly at the Bucharest School of Fine Arts; he was involved with the Constructivists before leaving for Paris in 1930. André Breton saw him as "the quintessential magic artist"; a painter of premonitions, as well as a sculptor and print-maker, he was obsessed by blindness, painting figures without eyes, even in a self-portrait. Ironically, at a Surrealist party in 1938 a glass was thrown and smashed, putting out his left eye. He spent World War II in the French Alps, returning to Paris in 1945 and breaking from the Surrealists in 1948.

seems to mind. Just east of Ghimeş, 2km from the old customs house, is the down-at-heel Romanian logging town of Palanca. In the other direction, near the head of the valley, Lunca de Jos (Gyimesközéplok) and Lunca de Sus (Gyimesfelsólok) are Csángó villages just across the border in Transylvania.

Practicalities

Ghimeş's handful of commercial establishments are all in the centre of town, opposite the vast **train station**, built in the nineteenth century to handle customs and immigration formalities. There is a small **motel** (☎0234/385 765; ❶) 200m up the main road from the station, but it's better by far to stay at *Deáky Panzió* (☎0234/385 621, ✉deakyandras@xnet.ro; open May–Sept; ❶–❷), an attractive, comfortable **pension** on a converted farm by the river. It's run by the village

▲ Locals in Ghimeş

doctor, who speaks only Hungarian, Romanian and German, but his wife can communicate in English. From the station, turn left and follow the main road downhill for about 1km, past the post office and on past András Deáky's clinic until you see the sign for 🌟 *Deáky Panzió* on your right. As well as rooms with bath there are small but pleasant bungalows; it's best to book ahead, especially if arriving late. Food and wine, all from local farms, are both excellent and very reasonably priced; the communal dining room encourages conversation. If you stay for a few days, your visit is likely to coincide with a group of Hungarian tourists coming for dinner and an evening of wine, dancing and **Csángó and Gypsy music**. The singing, especially, is hauntingly beautiful, if a little overtly patriotic at times. The only place to eat, other than the pension, is a **restaurant** opposite the train station, with good food, slow service and a Hungarian/ Romanian menu.

Bacău

BACĂU, 60km north of Adjud along the main rail and road routes to Suceava, is a large industrial town with good transport services, but little else to recommend it. To reach the centre from the **train station**, head east up Str. Eminescu, to the right of the department store across the road, which leads after fifteen minutes to the *Hotel Moldova*, the high-rise that looms ominously over two Orthodox churches, including the half-built new cathedral. The town's two main axes, Str. Bălcescu and B-dul. Unirii, meet here, with the **bus terminal** ten minutes' walk east along Unirii, and maxitaxis linking it to the train station via the centre. Buses #18 and #22 pass 300m from the airport terminal every five minutes; otherwise it costs €2.50 to take a taxi into town. It's a surprisingly busy little airport, with TAROM (Str. Bălcescu 1; ☎0234/511 462) offering five flights a week to Bucharest and Suceava; Carpatair (Str. Aeroportului 1; ☎0234/575 335, ✉bacau@carpatair.com) flying to Timişoara daily Mon–Sat; and Blue Air (Str. Aeroportului 1; ☎0234/554 551, 🌐www .blueair-web.com) flying to Rome; Turin and Verona, each twice weekly, and once weekly to Barcelona.

Practicalities

Most facilities in town are on Str. Bălcescu. **Rail tickets** can be booked at CFR at no. 12 (Mon–Fri 8am–8pm), while the ACR tourist agency at no. 14 (Mon–Fri 9am–4pm) sells maps of the Bacău region. The local Antrec representative, Beatrice Grigoraş, also director of Bacău's British Centre, is well informed about rural tourism in Bacău county and can arrange pension and homestay accommodation in the Csángó region and elsewhere. Her office, at Mihai Viteazu 12 Bl. 2 (☎0234/337 797 or 0744/584 176, ✉bacau@antrec.ro), is on the far side of the block of flats behind the Casa de Cultură on Str. Bălcescu. **Cars** can be rented from Autonom at Str. 9 Mai 78 (☎0234/580 575, 🌐www.autonom.ro).

There's plenty of **accommodation** on offer, but none of it is good value, especially as there's no reason to stay. The best value is the *Dumbrava* (☎&📠0234/513 302, 🌐www.hoteldumbrava.ro; ❺), just south of the centre at Str. Dumbrava Roşie 2, a clean, modern place with a fridge in every room. It doesn't cost much more to stay at the sleek modern *Bistriţa*, at Str. Luminii 3 (☎&📠0234/547 031; 🌐www.hotelbistrita.ro; ❻), just off Str. Bălcescu by the Casa de Cultură. There are also various motels along the DN2, mainly to the south of town.

Decent **restaurants** include the Amarante, at Str. Spiru Haret 8, serving Italian and French cuisine, and the Villa Borghese, at Str. Gării 8, for Italian and traditional Romanian food.

Neamţ county

Neamţ county lies to the northwest of Bacău and is the best-known attraction between Bucharest and the old Moldavian capitals of Iaşi and Suceava. Although its towns – **Piatra Neamţ** and **Târgu Neamţ** – are nothing special, they serve as bases for the **historic convents** of Neamţ, Agapia and Văratec, set in wooded foothills that turn gloriously red and gold in autumn, and the delightful collection of naïve art and folk costumes at the **Neculai Popa Museum** in Tărpeşti. Further to the northwest rises the **Ceahlău massif**, whose magnificent views and bizarrely weathered outcrops make this one of Romania's most dramatic hiking spots.

On arriving, you'll be faced with the question of where to base yourself. The pensions around Agapia are best if you're travelling by car, but can be somewhat isolated if you're not. Of the towns, Târgu Neamţ is closer to the sights, but Piatra Neamţ, as the county seat, is livelier and offers a far better choice of places to stay and eat. The two are 40km apart and are linked by frequent **buses** and maxitaxis, almost all of which run via Coşere and Sacalauşeşti, the respective turn-offs for Văratec and Agapia. Buses also link the major towns with Durău, the jumping-off point for the Ceahlău massif, but all services are reduced (and overcrowded) on Sundays.

Piatra Neamţ

Sixty kilometres northwest of Băcau by road and rail, where the River Bistriţa emerges into the Cracau basin, lies **PIATRA NEAMŢ**. Hemmed in by the Carpathian foothills, it is one of Romania's oldest settlements, once inhabited by a string of Neolithic and Bronze Age cultures, and the Dacians, whose citadel has been excavated on a nearby hilltop. The town was first recorded in Roman times as Petrodava, and in 1453 under the name of Piatra lui Craciun ("Christmas Rock"); its present title may refer to the German ("Neamţ") merchants who once traded here, or may derive from the old Romanian word for an extended family or nation ("Neam"). As one of Moldavia's earliest industrial centres, the town later played a major role in the general strike of 1919, and was one of the few places where the communists were able to sabotage production during World War II. That said, Piatra has little to attract visitors beyond a medieval church and a better-than-average collection of prehistoric relics in its history museum.

Arrival and information

From the train and bus stations, it's a ten-minute walk up the tree-lined B-dul Republicii to Piaţa Libertăţii, passing the **tourist information** centre (Mon–Fri 9am–7pm), in the library opposite the *Hotel Central*. Railway tickets can be booked at the CFR office (Mon–Fri 9am–4pm) at Piaţa Ştefan cel Mare 10; for air tickets, TAROM is adjacent at Piaţa Ştefan cel Mare 18 (☏0233/214 268). Piatra Neamţ's 24-hour **pharmacy** is in the Mioriţa Complex, opposite the *Hotel Central*. The friendly, English-speaking staff at Neamţ county's Antrec office (☏0233/234 204, ✉neamt@antrec.ro; Mon–Fri 9am–6pm), up the stairs on the left side of the house at Str. Ştefan cel Mare 17, are knowledgeable about accommodation and sights and may be able to arrange a car with driver for day-trips in the area. To **rent your own car**, go to Autonom at Str. Fermelor 4 (☏0233/229 616, ⊛www.autonom.ro). **Internet access** is available at Nova Computer, at Str. Eminescu 2, and also at Str. Alexandru cel Bun 9.

Accommodation

Piatra Neamț's **hotels** (see list below) all have private bathrooms and include breakfast, but are otherwise fairly uninspiring. Accommodation at several pensions near the centre (all ❷) can be arranged through the Antrec office (see opposite). If you can't find a room in town, try *Pensiunea Nora* (☎0233/237 737; ❷), 2km west of the centre at Str. Petru Movilă 162A, or the motel-like *Pensiunea Agroturistică Troian* (☎0233/241 444; ❷), further west at no. 270, near the turning to the fifteenth-century Bistrița Monastery. There are also wooden cabins in Mix MusicLand (☎0730/880 926, ⓦwww.mixmusic.ro; ❶), a new leisure park across the river on Aleea Tineretului; to get there, head 1km west along Str. Bistriței until you reach the footbridge. They're fairly tight-packed and likely to be lively at summer weekends.

Bulevard B-dul. Republicii 38 ☎0233/235 010 or 235 020, ℉218 111. Dull but with clean, decent rooms. ❹

Ceahlău Piața Ștefan cel Mare 3 ☎0233/219 990, ⓦwww.hotelceahlau.ro. Newly refurbished; the twelfth-floor bar has good views and a pool table. ❺–❻

Central Piața Petrodava 1 ☎0233/216 230, ⓦwww.hotelcentral.ro. The best hotel in town, a recently renovated high-rise with modern comforts,

a good but lifeless restaurant, and a bar with billiards on the top floor. ❻

Hostel Cozla Str. Ștefan cel Mare 31 ☎&℉0233/213 069, ℮tineret.neamt@cscmail.ro. This HI-affiliated youth hostel has clean rooms with four to ten beds and private bathrooms, plus sports facilities. ❶

Lido B-dul. Republicii ☎0233/226 349. This new hotel by the train station is the best value in town, with clean, simple rooms with TVs. ❷–❸

The Town

Today, Piatra Neamț features every style of communist architecture, from dismal low-rises to the pseudo-malls that mushroomed in the 1980s. What's left of the old town is clustered around **Piața Libertății**. The spireless **Church of St John** originally formed part of a Princely Court (Curtea Domnească)

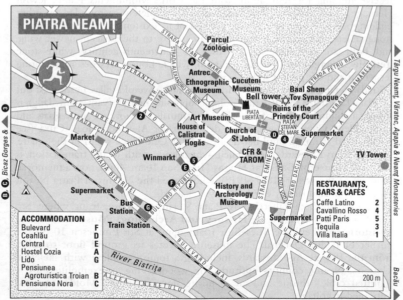

founded in 1468, of which only vestiges remain. Erected by Stephen the Great during 1497–98, hard on the heels of his seminal church at Neamţ Monastery, it set a pattern for Moldavian church architecture thereafter. The upper part is girdled by niches outlined in coloured brick, in which it was probably intended to paint saintly images. Beside the door, a votive inscription by his son Bogdan the One-Eyed presages a host of tacky modern paintings of Stephen inside the gloomy interior. A sturdy Gothic **bell tower** with a witch's hat brim, raised in 1499, stands to the northwest of the church. West of the bell tower, in a building that combines folk architecture with Art Nouveau, is the **Ethnographic Museum** (Muzeul de Etnografie; Tues–Sun 10am–4pm), and beside that a Brâncovenesc mansion, with ceramic studs echoing those on the church, housing the **Art Museum** (Muzeul de Artă; Tues–Sun 10am–4pm), showing work by local painters. If this is closed, ask at the Ethnographic Museum for it to be opened. Immediately north, at Str. Ştefan cel Mare 3, is the **Cucuteni Museum** (Muzeul de Artă Eneolitică Cucuteni; Tues–Sun 10am–4pm), housing a fine collection of relics, fertility charms and pottery from Iron Age culture (c.3000–2000 BC); the highlight is the curious figure dubbed the Scythian Rider (Cavalier Scit). Across the road on the northeastern side of the square, some vaulted **ruins of the Princely Court** have been laid bare by a shaft dug into the slope below the Colegiu Normal (a teacher-training college), but it's hard to see much through the locked gate; ask at the museums for entry.

Northeast of the Princely Court, on Str. Dimitrie Ernica, is the eighteenth-century wooden **Baal Shem Tov Synagogue**. Baal Shem Tov, the founder of Hasidism (a branch of Judaism based on the omnipresence of God and man's communion with Him), was for a short time supposed to have lived close to Piatra Neamţ, occasionally visiting to pray here. This is almost the only survivor of hundreds of similar buildings that were found across Eastern Europe until World War II. It's generally locked, but there are signs that the site may soon receive funding for restoration from the World Monuments Fund's Jewish Heritage Grant Program. The synagogue is completely surrounded by other buildings, so that you would have no idea of its existence were it not for the stone tablets on the roof. It seems like an annexe to the adjacent newer wing, and both are overshadowed by the late nineteenth-century white-stone **Temple Synagogue** (normally closed), which houses frescoes representing Jerusalem and the Holy Land.

Strada Ştefan cel Mare, dotted with several attractive old villas, heads west out of Piaţa Libertăţii; the Parcul Zoologic opposite no. 31 (9am–9pm daily) is mainly a children's playground – the only animals on show are some goats and sheep. Elena Cuza, widow of the deposed ruler Alexandru Ioan Cuza (see p.436), lived at no. 55 until her death in 1909. One block south of the square, set back from Bulevardul Republicii, which leads south to the train station, is the small **House of Calistrat Hogaş** (Tues–Sun 10am–4pm), now a memorial museum to the writer (1847–1918), who praised the charms of Piatra Neamţ when it consisted largely of Alpine-style chalets.

Just east of Piaţa Libertăţii is Piaţa Ştefan cel Mare, from where Str. Eminescu heads south to the **History and Archeology Museum** (Muzeul de Istorie şi Arheologie; Tues–Sun 10am–6pm) at Str. Eminescu 10 on the corner of B-dul. Decebal. The museum devotes its ground floor to relics from the Bronze Age onwards, including a tomb complete with skeleton. Upstairs, Neamţ county's aptitude for woodcarving is exemplified by a "knitted cable" throne and an exquisite door, with the Moldavian crest entwined in foliage.

Eating and drinking

The Italian community (linked to a synthetic fibres plant since the 1980s) has done wonders for Piatra Neamţ's **restaurant** scene. The best and most popular place to eat in the centre is *Cavallino Rosso*, in the mall opposite the *Hotel Ceahlău*. It's an unpretentious place with brick-oven pizzas and a few simple but good pasta dishes. Around 1km west of the centre at Str. Burebista 65 is the more upscale *Villa Italia* (noon–midnight daily), which has fine bruschetta and salads, and an extensive wine list. For dessert, more or less authentic *gelato* is on offer at *Patti Paris*, opposite the *Hotel Central*; there's also a big modern *cofetărie* here. West of the centre on B-dul. Decebal (opposite Str. Sadoveanu), *Caffe Latino* is a pleasant spot for a caffeine fix. The terrace at the *Hotel Ceahlău* is a nice place for a drink, with live music most nights in the summer. You could also cross the river to the large and flashy Mix MusicLand leisure park (open 24hr), where *Tequila* specializes in the eponymous product; there are three restaurants here, a weekend disco, and facilities for sports such as football, tennis, basketball, volleyball, handball, skating, skateboarding, swimming and horse-riding, with gear to rent, as well as kids' amusements. Cosmos, on Piaţa Kogălniceanu, and Fidelio, on Piaţa Ştefan cel Mare, are handy supermarkets to stock up at before heading out on a day-trip; nearby, at Str. Kogălniceanu 4, Crama Tohani is a smart little wine shop.

Văratec and Agapia

The rolling countryside west of the road between Piatra and Târgu Neamţ provides an idyllic setting for various monasteries and Romania's two largest convents: **Văratec** and **Agapia**, both with over four hundred nuns. Each has its own village – up the road from an agricultural village of the same name – where houses have lovely curvaceous porches, shingled or in metal. The nuns live in cosy houses with blue fretted eaves and glassed-in verandas. Note that taking photos within the convents is not allowed; on the other hand, they're not very strict about bare arms or shorts, or about removing beggars from the premises.

You can get to the convents by **bus** from Piatra Neamţ, Târgu Neamţ or Suceava; services normally wait thirty minutes before starting back. Transportation between the convents is provided by two daily buses between Piatra Neamţ and Agapia, calling at Văratec en route, and one at 6.30pm from Târgu Neamţ to Agapia and Văratec. However the landscape is so lovely you may prefer to walk from one to the other. If you're staying in Piatra Neamţ and miss the last bus back (which is quite possible if you don't get an early start), walk or hitch the 5km back to the main road, where the last buses between Târgu Neamţ and Piatra Neamţ pass at about 8pm. There are also plenty of charming guesthouses (❶–❷) in the villages.

Văratec Convent and around

Hedgerows, alive with sparrows and wagtails, line the narrow road winding through Văratec to the pretty nuns' village and Văratec Convent, its white-washed walls and balconies enclosing a lovely garden shaded by cedars. The novices inhabit two-storey buildings named after saints, while the older nuns live in cottages. There's a **museum of icons** (Tues–Sun 10am–6pm) to the south, and an **embroidery school** established by Queen Marie in 1934. It's an odd but not unfitting site for the **grave of Veronica Micle**, the poet loved by Eminescu, who couldn't afford to marry her after the death of her despised husband (see box, p.290); she killed herself two months after his death.

Văratec was founded in the eighteenth century, around a church that no longer exists; the site of its altar is marked by a pond with a statue of an angel.

The present **church**, built in 1808, is plain and simple, culminating in two bell-shaped domes. To cope with the harsh winters, the nuns have sensibly installed stoves by the columns dividing the narthex from the nave, so that both chambers are heated. The gilt pulpit and the gallery over the entrance to the narthex are unusual, but the interior painting is not great.

In fine weather, it's an agreeable **walk** through the woods from Văratec to Agapia; the seven-kilometre trail takes about an hour and a half, starting by house no. 219, back down the road from Văratec Convent. It's also possible to walk along the road connecting the two convents (from Văratec, walk about 1km back towards the main road, then turn left; from Agapia take the asphalt road across the bridge at the end of the nunnery village); picnic tables are provided, but camping is not allowed. The road passes through the pretty village of **Filioara**, where you'll find the finest of the local agrotouristic pensions, *Pensiunea Alina* (☎0233/244 861; ❹ including breakfast and dinner), a friendly place with dark wood furniture and excellent meals. Another beech-tree-lined trail from Văratec, marked by blue dots, leads west to **Sihla hermitage** (2hr), built into the cliffs near the cave of St Teodora, and hidden by strange outcrops. A back-road turns off the main road from Târgu Neamţ to the Ceahlău Massif, 2km west of the turn-off for Neamţ Monastery (see p.278), and passes the **Sihastria and Secu hermitages** en route to Sihla – an easy ten-kilometre hike, if you miss the one daily bus. The Sihastria hermitage was founded in 1655 and subsequently built over with a new stone church in 1734; the Secu hermitage dates from 1602 and has Renaissance-style paintings inside as well as the grave of Bishop Varlaam, who in 1634 printed *Canzania* ("Romania's teaching book"), the first book written in Romanian.

Agapia Convent and around

Agapia Convent actually consists of two convents a few kilometres apart; most visitors are content to visit only the main complex of **Agapia din Vale** ("Agapia in the Valley"), at the end of a village with houses with covered steps. The walls and gate tower aim to conceal rather than to protect; inside is a whitewashed enclosure around a cheerful garden. At prayer times a nun beats an insistent rhythm on a wooden *toaca* while another plays the panpipes; this is followed by a medley of bells, some deep and slow, others high and fast. The convent **church** was built in 1644–47 by Prince Basil the Wolf's brother, Gavril Coci. Its helmet-shaped cupola, covered in green shingles, mimics that of the gate tower. After restoration, the interior was repainted between 1858 and 1861 by Nicolae Grigorescu, the country's foremost painter at the time (see p.111); he returned to stay at Agapia from 1901 to 1902. Off to the right is a **museum** of icons and vestments from the seventeenth and eighteenth centuries (daily 10am–7pm), and to the left, past the nuns' cottages, is the **Casa Memorial Alexandru Vlahuță**, the house where the author (1858–1919) spent summers visiting his mother and sister, who were both nuns here. There are small traditionally furnished bedrooms, and books, photos and mementoes, plus a painting of Vlahuță's sister Elizabeta by Octav Băncila. Downhill by the Topolniţa stream stands a wooden church with three shingled domes and a modern gate tower. For a snack, try the fine bread stall at the entrance to the convent, where nuns also sell a pine syrup; further down the road a restaurant, *Cerbul Carpatin*, serves typical Romanian fare.

The older **Agapia din Deal** ("Agapia on the Hill"), otherwise known as Agapia Veche ("Old Agapia") is a smaller, more tranquil convent, high up a wooded slope about half an hour's walk from Agapia din Vale; ten minutes out, turn right at the unmarked junction. Another trail from the main convent leads to Văratec (see p.275). Several **pensions** have sprung up around Agapia in the last few years. *Casa Timofte* (☎0233/244 663; ❶), halfway between the main road and the convent, is simple but clean; nearby, *Pensiunea Andreea* (☎0233/244 760, ✉pens_andreea@yahoo.com; ❷), with a small shop and a garish restaurant attached, is modern enough but far from realizing its pretensions to glamour. Another option, back on the main road 1km south of the Agapia turn-off, is the pleasant *Pensiunea Lacramioara* (☎0233/247 012; ❷), and there are others just north of the turn-off. During the summer, it's also possible to stay in Agapia's theological seminary (❶), 100m down from the convent.

Tărpeşti

Two daily buses from Piatra Neamţ to Târgu Neamţ trace a leisurely semicircle along back roads east of the main route, first taking in the village of **Războieni**, where there is a spireless church (built by Stephen the Great in memory of the soldiers who died here in a 1476 battle with the Ottomans), and then, about 10km southeast of Târgu Neamţ, passing the turn-off to the ramshackle village of **TĂRPEŞTI**, home of the delightful **Neculai Popa Museum** (daily 9am–7pm; ⊛npopamuseum.netfirms.com). It's a pleasant but unshaded three-kilometre walk from the turn-off where the bus leaves you to the village, where signs will direct you to the museum; alternatively, Tărpeşti is served by two direct buses from Târgu Neamţ. There is no accommodation here, and trade is limited to a few basic shops that double as taverns.

Set in Popa's own yard, the museum's diverse works (all collected by Popa himself) are displayed with care and wit. The main building is devoted to Popa's folk art collections, including paintings by Romanian artists, an unusually good set of icons, and old Moldavian handicrafts such as thick leather belts and painted trousseaux. The colourful masks and folk costumes on display in the second building, many made by Popa's wife Elena, are occasionally used in children's pageants recounting legends such as that of Iancu Jianu, an eighteenth-century forest bandit known as the Robin Hood of Wallachia; performances featuring village children can be arranged with advance notice. In good weather, Popa can be seen in the sculpture garden using a timeworn chisel to fashion a new totem pole or menhir. His son now runs the museum, giving tours in Romanian and French, and there is also a gallery where folk art and icons are sold.

Târgu Neamţ

TÂRGU NEAMŢ, with its systematized concrete centre, is smaller and duller than Piatra, and therefore a less attractive stopover. The two museums facing each other on Str. Ştefan cel Mare – the **Historical and Ethnographic Museum** (Muzeul de Istorie şi Etnografie; Tues–Sun 10am–6pm) at no. 37, and the **House of Veronica Micle** at no. 34 (same hours) – are of no great interest, but the town's saving grace is the Neamţ **citadel** (Tues–Sun 10am–6pm), Moldavia's finest ruined castle. Visible from the road to Neamţ Monastery, but far more impressive at close quarters, the citadel is 1km west along Str. Ştefan cel Mare and then ten minutes north up an asphalt path equipped like a motorway with streetlights and crash barriers. Founded by Petru I Muşat in 1359, it was beefed up by Stephen the Great just in time to withstand a siege by the Turkish Sultan Mohammed II in 1496. Later it was partly demolished on the orders of the Turks, but again saw service in 1691 in the war between Moldavia and Poland. The approach to the citadel is over a long, curving **wooden bridge** raised on pillars high above a moat; the final stretch was originally designed to flip enemies down into an oubliette. Within the **bailey**, a warren of roofless chambers that used to be an arsenal, courthouse and baths surrounds a deep well, ringed by battlements that survey the Neamț valley for kilometres around.

Practicalities

Târgu's **bus station** is a few minutes from the centre on Str. Cuza Vodă, and the **train station** is a further fifteen minutes east on the same road. The best **hotel** in town is the three-star *Doina* at Str. Mihail Kogălniceanu 6 (☎0233/790 272, ⓦwww.hotel-doina.ro; ❹), a refurbished 1970s place behind the main church on B-dul. Ștefan cel Mare (just east of the central crossroads). At the exit to Suceava (1.5km north), the *Belvedere*, at Str. Mărășești 215 (☎0233/790 730; ❸), is a restaurant with good modern rooms. *Pensiunea Cassandra* (☎0233/791 191; ❷) is at Str. 9 Mai no. 1A, east of the centre near the train station. If you have a car, another option is the *Stațiunea Oglinzi* (☎0233/663 590; ❷), a balneo-therapeutic resort 4km north of town by the Suceava road and 4km west, with an excellent restaurant. The only decent place to eat in Târgu Neamț proper is the restaurant at the *Doina*. If you're heading to Iași by car, consider stopping 15km east of Târgu Neamț at *Hanul Ancuței* (☎0233/742 600, ⓔnusa@gavis.ro; ❸), an excellent if slightly kitsch roadside restaurant, which also has a few comfortable rooms.

Neamț Monastery

The twelfth-century **Neamț Monastery**, 12km northwest of Târgu Neamț, is the oldest in Moldavia and is the region's chief centre of Orthodox culture; it is also the largest men's monastery in Romania, with seventy monks and dozens of seminary students. It was founded in the twelfth century as a hermitage, expanded into a monastery in the late fourteenth century by Petru I Mușat, and then rebuilt in the early fifteenth century by Alexander the Good, with fortifications that protected Neamț from the Turks. It also had a printing house that spread its influence throughout Moldavia. The new church, founded by Stephen the Great in 1497 to celebrate a victory over the Poles, became a prototype for Moldavian churches throughout the next century, and its school of miniaturists and illuminators led the field.

Outwardly, Neamț resembles a fortress, with high stone walls and its one remaining octagonal corner tower (there used to be four). On the inside of the gate tower, a painted Eye of the Saviour sternly regards the monks' cells with their verandas wreathed in red and green ivy, and the seminary students in black tunics milling around the garden. The sweeping roof of Stephen's church overhangs blind arches inset with glazed bricks, on a long and otherwise bare facade. Its trefoil windows barely illuminate the interior, where pilgrims kneel amid the smell of mothballs and candlewax. At the back of the compound is a smaller church dating from 1826, containing frescoes of the Nativity and the Resurrection.

Outside the monastery stands a large, onion-domed **pavilion** for *Aghiastmatar*, the "blessing of the water", to be taken home in bottles to cure illness. The monastery's main festival is held on May 7.

The monastery can be reached by three daily **buses** from Târgu Neamț; you could also catch one of the frequent services along the main road to the turn-off at km33 and walk the remaining 4km to the monastery. There are **rooms** (❷) and a summer **campsite** with huts (❶) at the *Hanul Braniște*, 3km east of the turning to Neamț Monastery. Between here and Târgu Neamț is the delightfully unspoilt village of **Vânători Neamț**, known for its **Reserva de Zimbri** (aurochs or European bison), set up in 1970 when three of the primeval beasts, now extinct in the wild, were brought from Poland. There are also deer, bears and wolves here, though the closest you can get is looking over a fence.

The Ceahlău massif

West of Târgu Neamţ, 60km beyond the turning to Neamţ Monastery, looms the **Ceahlău massif**. Aptly designated on local maps as a *zona abrupt*, it rises above neighbouring ranges in eroded crags whose fantastic shapes were anthropomorphized in folk tales and inspired Eminescu's poem, *The Ghosts*. The Dacians believed that Ceahlău was the abode of their supreme deity, Zamolxis, and that the gods transformed the daughter of Decebal into the Dochia peak. The massif is composed of Cretaceous sediments – especially conglomerates, which form pillar-like outcrops – and covered with stratified belts of beech, fir and spruce, with dwarf pine and juniper above 1700m. Its **wildlife** includes chamois, lynx, capercaillie, bears and boars, and the majestic Carpathian stag. Ceahlău's isolation is emphasized by the huge, artificial **Lake Bicaz** (Lacul Izvoru Muntelei) that half-encircles its foothills.

A hydroelectric dam, built in 1950, rises at the southern end, 3km beyond the village of **BICAZ**. You can get to the dam from Piatra Neamţ by frequent maxitaxis, which terminate halfway between Bicaz and the dam. There are also a few trains (one each from Bucharest and Iaşi), and buses, mostly turning left here for Gheorgheni, 57km west in Transylvania. Bicaz's **History Museum** (Muzeul de Istorie Bicaz; Tues–Sun 9am–5pm), which has a display on the building of the dam and a small art exhibit, is at Str. Barajului 3, just north of the town's small systematized centre, where there are ATMs and a decent little supermarket.

Accommodation

The *Motel Ceahlău*, north of the centre, is a poor place to stay, but does have a terrace with a view of the dam (nicely lit at night). It's better to continue to the *Bicaz Baraj* cabana (☏0233/254 960; ❷), right below the dam, where you can also camp. The road continues over the dam, 500m beyond which, at the Portul Bicaz dock (6km from Bicaz), is the floating *Hotel Plutitor Lebăda* (☏0233/254 036, 0748/110 400, ⓦwww.bicazlac.ro; ❸), with fifteen air-conditioned rooms, and the more traditional *Pescăruş* (☏0233/254 080; ❹), which also has cabins (❶) and tent space. Pleasure boats sail from here in summer (€2.20 for 30min, or departures every hour including a meal for €55). Midway between here and the village of Potoci you'll find *Motel Cristina* (☏0233/254 456; ❷), with good **cabins** (❶) and rowing boats available at the pontoon jetty. In the village is the newish *Motel Potoci* (with cabins; ❶); along the road to the north are various guesthouses, some affiliated with Antrec, the national agrotourism body. The mountain road north to Vatra Dornei crosses the route from Târgu Neamţ to Durău and Transylvania at **Poiana Largului**, at the northern end of the reservoir, where it's feasible to **change buses** if you're prepared to wait a few hours. There are a few shops and souvenir stalls here, and the *Pensiunea Elvi* (☏0233/257 295, with a decent bar-restaurant) and *Pensiunea Teiul* are both small, cheap and adequate if you're stuck. The decent *Popas Petru Vodă* **campsite** is at the Argel Pass, 12km uphill towards Târgu Neamţ. In **Fărcaşa**, 10km out of Poiana Largului on the Vatra Dornei road, there's a fine eighteenth-century wooden church, and a small motel, the *Orizont* (☏0233/267 111, ⓔorizont@ambra.ro; ❸), which has a 24hr restaurant.

Hiking above Durău

The main base for hiking in the massif is **DURĂU**, on its northwestern side, which can be reached by bus from Piatra Neamţ or Târgu Neamţ. From the turn-off 7km west of Poiana Largului (and 67km east of Topliţa in Transylvania) it's 12km up a dead-end road to the resort, passing through the village of Ceahlău, where there are various guesthouses. Durău's major draw is the **Ceahlău Feast**, on the second Sunday in August, an opportunity for shepherds to parade their finery and an attraction for many tourists. It also boasts a small **hermitage** built in 1833, overwhelmed by a modern monastery. The three-star *Bradul* (ⓣ&ⓕ0233/256 501, ⓦwww.hoteluri-durau.ro; ❸), 300m to the left from the main crossroads, is the finest and best value of Durău's four **hotels**. There's also the *Ursuleţ* campsite (ⓣ0740 470825), 1km down the road, as well as a dozen or so pensions, of which *Vila Iris* at Str. Releu 1 (ⓣ0233/256531; ❷) and *Vila Albăstrica* at Str. Releu 3 (ⓣ0233/256 508, 0722/955 288; ❷) are above-average places with great views, up beyond the TV relay. Bikes can be rented at the *Bistriţa* hotel. From December to March, skiing (on a small scale, with just a few drags) replaces hiking as the main activity in the resort. The area is now protected by the Ceahlău National Park (ⓣ&ⓕ0233/256 600, ⓦwww .ceahlaupark.ro) and no motorized vehicles are allowed, so that the road from Durău to the Izvorul Muntelui cabana is now closed. You'll pay a fee (€2.20) for the duration of your stay in Durău and the park at the gate uphill from the resort or in the cabanas. You'll be given a leaflet map (and a garbage bag) at the gate, where they also sell a more detailed map.

From the resort, it's a 45-minute walk to the Fântânele cabana (1220m; ⓣ0233/678 078, 0744/186 360; ❶), on the steep, red-striped trail starting at the end of the road. A two-hour route (marked by blue crosses, then red crosses and finally yellow triangles) also runs there via the lovely Duruitoarea cascade, 2km from town, which falls a total of 25m in two stages. From Fântânele, the red-striped route (2hr) ascends within sight of the Panaghia rocks and Toaca peak to a plateau with glorious views and, in a further two hours, to the Dochia cabana (1750m; ⓣ0721/179 506; ❶). You can also follow red crosses direct from the cascade to Dochia. The route then continues south via several massive rock pillars, passing Ocolaşu Mare – at 1907m, the massif's highest peak – on its way to Poiana Maicilor, where the red-striped route turns downstream to the Izvoru Muntelui cabana, 7km by road from a turn-off between the Bicaz dam and cabana, while another, less frequented trail marked with blue crosses runs on to Neagra village, on the road to the Bicaz gorges. Both routes take about two hours from Dochia.

Into Transylvania and north to Vatra Dornei

To the north and south of the massif, narrow valleys enable two routes **into Transylvania**. The northern one crosses the 1112-metre-high Borsec pass beyond the alpine spa of Borsec, before descending to Topliţa, in the upper Mureş valley (see p.224). It's a scenic route, with buses heading west to Borsec and some continuing to Topliţa. There are also maxitaxis running from Suceava to Târgu Mureş. A better route runs through the **Bicaz gorges** (Cheile Bicazului), 25km upriver from Bicaz, past the lovely village of **Bicaz Ardelean**, which has a wooden church dating from 1829. Sheer limestone cliffs rise as high as 300m above the river, pressing so close around the Gâtul Iadului ("Neck of Hell") that the road is hewn directly into the rockface. The Cheile Bicazului cabana, amid the gorges, marks the start of several **hiking** trails, and a longer one ascends from Lacu Roşu (see p.225) to the *Piatra Singuratică* ("Lonely Rock") cabana. **Buses** from Piatra Neamţ, Târgu Neamţ and Bicaz travel this way en route to Gheorgheni (see p.224).

Alternatively, you can head north from Târgu Neamţ via Poiana Largului to **Vatra Dornei** (see p.320). By bus the 136-kilometre journey takes four hours, following the River Bistriţa through a narrow, twisting valley hemmed in by fir-covered peaks. About 20km before Vatra Dornei, you'll see the well-signposted Zugreni cabana (☎0230/574 548) across the river, from where a trail leads to the heart of the Rarău massif (see p.319).

Iaşi

IAŞI (pronounced "yash"), in the northeast of Moldavia, is the region's cultural capital and by far its nicest city, the only one where you're likely to want to stay a while. Its university, theatre and resident orchestra rival those of Bucharest – which was merely a crude market town when Iaşi became a princely seat – and give it an air of sophistication enhanced by a large contingent of foreign students. Cementing its place in the nation's heart, Romanians associate Iaşi with the poet Eminescu, Moldavians also esteem it as the burial place of St Paraschiva, and several million smokers remember it as the home of Carpaţi, the country's cheapest and roughest brand of cigarettes under communism.

Despite lying east of the main route northwards through Moldavia, Iaşi is accessible by direct **trains** from Bucharest, Cluj and several other major cities across the country, by **buses** and **maxitaxis** from most towns in Moldavia (and some in Transylvania) and by **flights** with TAROM (two daily) from Bucharest. Carpatair operates flights to Timişoara, with international connections (daily except Sun).

Some history

Iaşi's ascendancy dates from the sixteenth century, when the Moldavian princes (*hospodars*) gave up the practice of maintaining courts in several towns, and settled permanently in Iaşi. This coincided with Moldavia's gradual decline into a Turkish satellite, ruled by despots who endowed Iaşi with churches and monasteries to trumpet their earthly glory and ensure their eternal salvation. **Basil the Wolf** (Vasile Lupu, 1634–53) promulgated a penal code whereby rapists were raped and arsonists burned alive; he also founded a printing press and school, which led to the flowering of Moldavian literature during the brief reign, from 1710–11, of the enlightened **Dimitrie Cantemir**.

After Cantemir's death, Moldavia fell under the control of **Greek Phanariots**, originally from the Phanar district of Constantinople (Fener in modern Istanbul), who administered the region on behalf of the Ottoman Empire, chose and deposed the nominally ruling princes (of whom there were 36 between 1711 and 1821), and eventually usurped the throne for themselves. The boyars adopted Turkish dress and competed to win the favour of the Phanariots, the sole group that advised the sultan whom of the boyars he should promote. As Ottoman power weakened, this dismal saga was interrupted by the surprise election of **Prince Alexandru Ioan Cuza**, who clinched the unification of Moldavia and Wallachia in 1859 with the diplomatic support of France. In the new Romania, Cuza founded universities at Iaşi and Bucharest, introduced compulsory schooling for both sexes, and secularized monastic property, which at the time accounted for one fifth of Moldavia. Finally, his emancipation of the serfs so enraged landowners and military circles that in 1866 they overthrew Cuza and restored the status quo ante – but kept the union.

The latter half of the nineteenth century was a fertile time for intellectual life in Iaşi, where the Junimea literary circle attracted such talents as the poet **Mihai**

Moldavia and Iaşi have long been associated with the far right of Romanian politics. The most ardent member of Iaşi's League of Christian National Defence was **Corneliu Codreanu**, who went on, in the early 1930s, to found the Legion of the Archangel St Michael, better known as the **Iron Guard**. Wearing green shirts with bags of Romanian soil around their necks, the Legionari chased away village bailiffs to the delight of the peasantry, and murdered politicians deemed to be insufficiently nationalistic, until Marshal Antonescu jailed its leaders and Codreanu was shot "trying to escape". His followers fled to Berlin, returning with the Nazis to help carry out their genocidal "Final Solution" in Romania.

After the war, the communists employed ex-Legionari as thugs against the socialists and the National Peasant Party, whom they regarded as their real enemies. Following the 1989 revolution, fascism has been making a comeback with the **România Mare** ("Greater Romania") party of **Corneliu Vadim Tudor**, which ascribes all the nation's problems to a conspiracy of Jews, Magyars, Gypsies and everyone else who isn't a "pure" Romanian. Their headquarters in Iaşi is rather bizarrely shared with the Ecology Party.

Eminescu and the writer **Ion Creangă**, who, like the historian **Nicolae Iorga**, became national figures. This was also the heyday of Jewish culture in Iaşi (or Jassy, as it was called in Yiddish), and in 1876 local impresario **Avrom Goldfadn** staged the world's first Yiddish theatre performance at the Pumul Verde ("Green Tree") wine garden, facing the present National Theatre. The Junimea brand of nationalism was more romantic than chauvinist, but unwittingly paved the way for a deadlier version in the Greater Romania that was created to reward the Old Kingdom (Regat) for its sacrifices in World War I, when most of the country was occupied by the Germans, and the government was evacuated to Iaşi. With its borders enlarged to include Bessarabia and Bucovina, Moldavia inherited large minorities of Jews, Ukrainians and Gypsies, aggravating ethnic and class tensions in a region devastated by war.

During the 1920s, Iaşi became notorious for **anti-Semitism**, spearheaded by a professor whose League of Christian National Defence virtually closed the university to Jews, then over a third of the population, and later spawned the Iron Guard (see box above). Their chief scapegoat was **Magda Lupescu**, Carol II's locally born Jewish mistress, widely hated for amassing a fortune by shady speculations; in 1940 she fled abroad with Carol in a train stuffed with loot.

Arrival

Arriving at Iaşi's main **train station** on Str. Silvestru, or the large **maxitaxi station** across the street (both of which have toilets and left luggage facilities), you can either catch tram #3, #6 or #7 (buy a ticket from the driver or at one of the kiosks marked RATI), take a taxi or walk in ten to fifteen minutes to the central Piaţa Unirii, past the ornamental tower, up Str. Gării and right along Str. Arcu. Trains from Chişinău (in Moldova) arrive at the Gara Internaţională in Nicolina, south of the centre, where there's an ATM. By **bus** you might also arrive at the basic Autogara Iaşi Vest (℡0232/214 720), behind the Autocenter, 1km northwest of the train station on Şoseaua Moara de Foc (tram #2 or bus #30 to Iaşi centre), or the Autogara Eurovoyage (℡415 800/810, Ⓦwww .eurovoyage.ro), at Str. O.Teodoreanu 49, 100m south of Calea Chişinăului in an industrial wasteland to the southeast of the centre (trams #2, #7, #15). Be sure to ask about departure times here, as the posted timetables are long out of date.

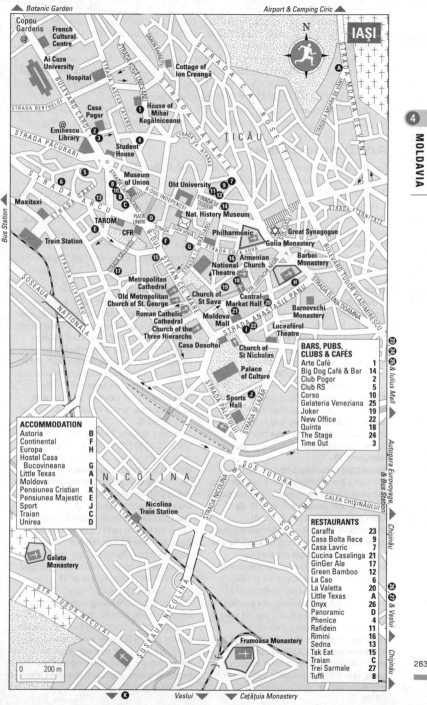

IAŞI

Botanic Garden
Airport & Camping Ciric

Copou Gardens
French Cultural Centre
Ai Cuza University
Hospital
Casa Pogor
House of Mihai Kogălniceanu **1**
Cottage of Ion Creangă
Eminescu Library
Student House **4**
Museum of Union
Old University
TICĂU
Maxitaxi
Bus Station
Nat. History Museum
TAROM
CFR
Train Station
Philharmonic
Great Synagogue
Golia Monastery
Barboi Monastery
National Theatre
Armenian Church
Metropolitan Cathedral
Old Metropolitan Church of St. George
Church of St Sava
Central Market Hall
Barnovschi Monastery
Roman Catholic Cathedral
Church of the Three Hierarchs
Moldova Mall
Luceafărul Theatre
Casa Dosoftei
Church of St Nicholas
Palace of Culture
Sports Hall

NICOLINA
Nicolina Train Station
Galata Monastery
Frumoasa Monastery
Vaslui
Cetățuia Monastery

MOLDAVIA **4**

Autogara Eurovoyage, & Bus Station
Chişinău
& Vaslui
Chişinău
& Iulius Mall

ACCOMMODATION
Astoria	B
Continental	F
Europa	H
Hostel Casa Bucovineana	G
Little Texas	A
Moldova	I
Pensiunea Cristian	K
Pensiunea Majestic	E
Sport	J
Traian	C
Unirea	D

BARS, PUBS, CLUBS & CAFÉS
Arte Café	1
Big Dog Café & Bar	14
Club Pogor	2
Club RS	5
Corso	10
Gelateria Veneziana	25
Joker	19
New Office	22
Quinta	18
The Stage	24
Time Out	3

RESTAURANTS
Caraffa	23
Casa Bolta Rece	9
Casa Lavric	7
Cucina Casalinga	21
GinGer Ale	17
Green Bamboo	12
La Cao	6
La Valetta	20
Little Texas	A
Onyx	26
Panoramic	D
Phenice	4
Rafidein	11
Rimini	16
Sedna	13
Tak Eat	15
Traian	C
Trei Sarmale	27
Tuffi	8

0   200 m

Iaşi's **airport** is 7km northeast of the centre; the only way to get there is by taxi (€18). See the Listings on p.294 for details of trains and air booking offices.

Trams rock and roll their way to most parts of the city every ten to fifteen minutes (6am–10pm); fares are €0.30 for a single ride, €0.60 for two, €1.20 for a day or €2.70 for ten rides. In general, **taxis** in Iaşi are metered and reliable, charging €0.33/km (€0.40/km after 10pm). Delta Taxi (℡0232/222 222) and Pro-Taxi (℡0232/211 211) are two good companies.

There is no tourist information office, but listings magazines such as *Zile şi Nopţi*, *24-Fun* and *Cityscape*, available in hotels, will tell you what's going on.

Accommodation

Iaşi has some reasonable mid-range and upscale **hotels**, but the budget options, though central, are less appealing. You might find a bed in one of the many student dorms (*camin de studenţi*) located around the university on B-dul. Copou, 1km northwest of the centre. The wooded *Camping Ciric* (℡0232/219 000; tents ❶, cabins ❷), by a lake 2km north of town, is only open in summer; buses run there hourly at weekends (and less frequently during the week) from the Târgul Cocului interchange, outside the Golia Monastery. Antrec's representative (℡0232/211 060 227, ✉iasi@antrec.ro) can arrange **homestay** accommodation outside the city.

Astoria Str. Lăpuşneanu 1 ℡0232/233 888, ✉reservation@hotelastoria.ro. A cheerful new place with comfortable beds, a/c and mini fridges. Next to the *Traian*. ❼

Continental Str. Cuza Vodă 4 ℡0232/211 846. Old-fashioned and dusty, with friendly, English-speaking staff. Some rooms have shared bathrooms, but it costs only a little more for rooms with good private facilities; there's also a lift. ❹–❻

Europa Str. Anastasie Panu 26 ℡0232/242 000, ✇www.hoteleuropa.ro. Soulless four-star mirror-glass tower attached to Iaşi's World Trade Center; with conference facilities, high-speed Internet, sauna and gym, room service and two restaurants. ❾

Hostel Casa Bucovineana Str. Cuza Vodă 30 ℡222 913. A good budget choice, in the centre and with clean, tidy little rooms with TV, basin and shared showers, or with shower but no toilet. ❷–❸

Little Texas Stradela Moara de Vânt 31 ℡&℻0232/222 545, ✇www.littletexas.org. Out on the road towards the airport. No longer the only luxury option, but this small and gracious American-run hotel (actually a charity venture) is still a cut above the rest. Rooms are all non-smoking with Internet access, furniture imported from the US and great views from the balconies; included is a typically hearty American breakfast in the superb restaurant (see p.292). ❽

Moldova Str. Anastasie Panu 29 ℡0232/260 336, ✇www.unita-turism.ro. A high-rise communist-era tower, now with a/c rooms, Internet access, a sauna, gym and indoor swimming pool, but still not very welcoming. ❻

Pensiunea Cristian Str. Cetăţuia 14A ℡&℻0232/242 363, 0745/456 416, ✇www.pensiunea-cristian.go.ro. Clean and friendly new pension with large a/c rooms with Internet access, digital TV and balconies. Good value (although breakfast is extra), but the drawback is the strange location, several kilometres south of the centre, with the Cetăţuia Monastery forest on one side and a disused tank factory on the other. From B-dul. Poitiers (bus #43) it's a 1km walk south on the east side of the railway; a taxi costs about €1.50. ❹

Pensiunea Majestic Str. Petru Rareş 7 ℡&℻0232/255 557, ✇www.pensiuneamajestic .ro. Ambitious new guesthouse, furnished in oak and bronze, with twelve twin rooms (with fridge and TV, some with balcony) and two apartments, as well as a lift, a restaurant with non-smoking room and a *terasa* with a good view. ❻

Sport Str. Sfântu Lazăr 76 ℡0232/232 800, ℻231 540. A few hundred metres downhill from the Palace of Culture near the Pod' Ros transit interchange. A good budget option, with passable rooms with bathrooms, hot water and cable TV, but often filled by athletic groups in summer. ❷

🏃 **Traian** Piaţa Unirii 1 ℡0232/266 666, ℻212 187, ✇www.grandhoteltraian.ro. Atmospheric establishment, designed by the Eiffel company in 1882, that's easily the most attractive building on Piaţa Unirii. Recently renovated in the grand style as a 4-star hotel with elegantly furnished rooms, with baths or showers, and friendly, very knowledgeable staff. Internet access in the lobby only. ❼–❾

Unirea Piaţa Unirii 5 ☎ 0232/205 000, ℱ 205 026, ⓦ www.hotelunirea.ro. Located on the main square, this large 1960s high-rise has been renovated, with a/c, Internet access, and Jacuzzis in all apartments. Friendly staff. ⓖ

The Town

Many of the sights of Iaşi can be found on the streets radiating from **Piaţa Unirii**. To the north, Str. Lăpuşneanu heads towards the university district of Copou and the residential district of Ţicău. Heading east, Str. Cuza Vodă leads towards ancient monasteries and the sole remaining synagogue, while B-dul. Ştefan cel Mare leads south towards the cathedral, the **Church of the Three Hierarchs**, easily the best-known building in Iaşi, and the huge **Palace of Culture**, housing a range of museums. Beyond this lies the Nicolina quarter, where you'll find the hilltop monasteries.

Around Piaţa Unirii

Str. Lăpuşneanu heads northwest from Piaţa Unirii to Cuza's mansion at no. 14, which now houses the **Museum of Union** (Tues–Sun 10am–5pm); among the exhibits is a coffee set emblazoned with an imperial "N", indicating Napoleon III's support for unification between Wallachia and Moldavia. Among the other items on display are various personal items of rulers and a good collection of coins. The rather comic tale of Cuza's downfall in 1866 is glossed over. Bursting into his bedroom, soldiers found Cuza making love to the King of Serbia's daughter-in-law; when pressed to sign a decree of abdication, he objected, "But I haven't got a pen." "We have thought of that," they said, producing a pen and ink, whereupon Cuza complained of the lack of a table. "I will offer myself," said a colonel, presenting his back to forestall further procrastination, and so Cuza signed and went into exile. He died in Heidelberg in 1873.

South along Bulevardul Ştefan cel Mare

Iaşi's traditional interplay of civil and religious authority is symbolized by a parade of edifices along B-dul. Ştefan cel Mare şi Sfânt (simply Ştefan cel Mare on most addresses), where florid public buildings face grandiose churches. Midway along the street, which (south of Str. Brătianu) is closed to traffic at weekends and holidays, is the huge, colonnaded **Metropolitan Cathedral**, begun in 1833 and completed in 1887, and now being refurbished. Still the largest Orthodox church in Romania, it dwarfs worshippers with its cavernous interior, painted by Tattarescu, and dominates the neighbouring Metropolitan's Palace and Theological College. In 1641, Basil the Wolf spent the country's entire budget for the next year and a half to acquire the **relics of St Paraschiva** of Epivat (c.980–1050), which were moved to the cathedral in 1889. Venerated as the patron saint of Moldavia, households, harvests, traders and travellers, St Paraschiva seems to be a conflation of four Orthodox martyrs of that name. There are pilgrims here throughout the year (some crawling the last 100m or so), but on October 14 (the saint's day) the cathedral overflows with thousands of worshippers who come to kneel before the blue and gold bier containing the relics. Immediately to the south stands the **Old Metropolitan Church of St George**, built in 1761; the pillars of its glassed-in porch are carved with symbolic animal reliefs, in the post-Brâncoveanu style of Wallachia. Inside it's like a mini-Sistine chapel, the large nave painted in a neo-Byzantine style and enhanced by effective uplighting. During 1999–2000 neo-Byzantine mosaics were added in the porch, with four scenes of paradise and one of the arrival of the relics of St Andrew the Apostle in Iaşi in 1996. Just south, the circular

Roman Catholic cathedral was completed in 2005; the white interior is set off by a lovely mosaic of the Virgin and angels behind the altar, and there's rich stained glass set into the roof on the upper level.

Across the road, and east of the elegant Pumul Verde Park, is the French-eclectic-style **National Theatre**, built by the Viennese architects Fellner and Helmer in the 1890s, with one of the most beautiful auditoriums in the country. The theatre is named after Vasile Alecsandri (1821–90) who co-founded the company in 1840 and, owing to a lack of plays in Romanian, had to write much of its initial repertory.

A few minutes further south along B-dul. Ştefan cel Mare from the Church of St George, you arrive at the famous **Church of the Three Hierarchs** (daily 9am–noon & 3–5pm), its exterior carved all over with chevrons, meanders and rosettes as intricate as lace. When it was completed in 1639 – perhaps by the Armenian master-builder Ianache Etisi – Basil the Wolf had the exterior gilded, desiring it to surpass all other churches in splendour. Aside from its unique carvings, the church follows the classic Byzantine trilobate plan, with two octagonal drums mounted above the *naos* and *pronaos* in the Moldavian fashion. Over the following two centuries, the church was damaged by fire and six earthquakes, but was rebuilt by the French architect Lecomte de Noüy during 1882–87; the interior decor is wholly his and quite missable. The church houses the **sarcophagi** of its founder Basil the Wolf, Dimitrie Cantemir and Alexandru Ioan Cuza. Since 1990 this has once more been a working monastery. The adjacent abbot's house, in which Basil the Wolf set up Moldavia's first printing press in 1644, contains a display of religious icons (officially Tues–Sun 10am–4pm; ask in the church if the door is locked).

From the Church of the Three Hierarchs, Str. Costache Negri heads east to the **Church of St Sava**, a contemporary yet quite different building whose red pantiles and massive, squat bell tower give it the look of an Andean village church. The tower is doubly impressive for being devoid of ornamentation. Immediately to the north the city's **Armenian church**, dating in part from 1385, is now being restored.

The Palace of Culture and around

At the southern end of Ştefan cel Mare, an equestrian **statue of Stephen the Great** and a cross commemorating the martyrs of the revolution are overshadowed by the stupendous **Palace of Culture** – a neo-Gothic pile built between 1906 and 1925 as a government centre, which now houses four of the city's **museums**, including the excellent Museum of Art (all Tues–Sun 9am–5pm). The palace's spired tower and pinnacled wings presage a vast lobby awash with mosaics, stained glass and armorial reliefs, dominated by a magnificent double staircase. You can admire the decor free of charge, but tickets are required for entry to the museums.

The corridor on the left of the lobby leads to the **Museum of Science and Technology**, displaying music boxes, symphonia and orchestrions; the curators might be persuaded to demonstrate the ingenious Popper's Bianca, a kind of projector that anticipated the cinema. To the right of the lobby, the **Moldavian History Museum** is strong on local archeology. Upstairs, casts of antique statues line the way to an **Ethnographic Museum**, whose collection includes a small windmill, two-metre-long Moldavian alpine horns, hollow trunks used as beehives, and oil-presses the size of trees. The **Museum of Art**, which is divided into Romanian and European galleries, has over two dozen paintings by Grigorescu, and a fine collection by the post-1919 Colourist painters, such as Luchian and Pallady. Portraits of bearded boyars in Turkish fur hats, and scenes of Jewish life by Octav Băncila (1872–1944), give more local colour. In the European section, Ludovic Starski's *The City of Iaşi in 1842* presents an unrecognizable vision of church spires not hemmed in by concrete. There's also a *Pieta* by Murillo and a Rubens of *Caesar Receiving Pompey's Head*. The vaulted Hall of Voivodes (*Sala Voievozilor*), containing the portraits of dozens of rulers, is used for temporary art shows.

Two much-restored relics of Iaşi's past stand between the Palace and the Centru Civic. The arcaded **Casa Dosoftei**, built between 1677 and 1679, is a fitting home for the dull **Museum of Old Moldavian Literature** (Tues–Sun

▲ Palace of Culture, Iaşi

10am–5pm) – it once housed a press that spread the words of the cleric and scholar Metropolitan Dosoftei, a statue of whom sits outside. The Phanariot policy of using Iaşi's presses to spread Greek as the language of Orthodox ritual had the unintended result of displacing the ossified Old Slavonic tongue from this position, clearing the way for intellectuals to agitate for the use of their own language, Romanian. Next door, at Str. A. Panu 28, is the **Courtly Church of St Nicholas**, in theory the oldest building in Iaşi, erected by Stephen the Great in 1492 but pulled down and rebuilt by Lecomte de Noüy during 1885–97; its svelte facade now masks a hermetic world of carved pews and gilded frescoes.

From the Centru Civic to Golia Monastery

From the south end of B-dul. Ştefan cel Mare, Str. Anastasie Panu leads east through the **Centru Civic**. Due to the array of administrative buildings already standing along Ştefan cel Mare, the architects of Iaşi's Centru Civic wisely focused on consumer aspirations instead. That consumer focus is more conspicuous now than ever: representative examples include the communist-era Moldova Magazin Universal and the more modern **Central Market Hall**, midway along Str. Anastasie Panu. Further east, opposite the new World Trade Center and next to an open park at Str. Ghica Vodă 26, you can catch a glimpse of the former **Barnovschi Monastery**, founded by Prince Miron Barnovschi in 1627; it's now reduced to a white church with a Baroque porch and two onion-shaped spires, flanked by a gate tower through which you enter the church. The **Bărboi Monastery**, at the far end of the main road, has fared better. Housed in a tranquil walled garden with a tall neo-Byzantine gate tower, it still bears the name of Urşu Bărboi, who founded it in 1613, although the present Church of Peter and Paul, with an overhead gallery for the choir, was built during 1841–44 by Dimitrie Sturdza, who is buried in the *pronaos* in a tomb covered with Greek inscriptions. It's a large open church, painted throughout, with a gilt iconostasis.

A little to the north, beyond the busy Str. Sărărie, you can see the Star of David atop the **Great Synagogue** – a sad misnomer for this low-domed edifice built between 1659 and 1671 and restored after an earthquake in 1977, shortly before most of its congregation left for Israel. Outside is an obelisk to the victims of the pogrom of June 28–29, 1941.

Just west, beyond the Târgul Cucu bus and tram interchange, is the **Golia Monastery**, a peaceful haven in the heart of Iaşi whose dozen monks enjoy a rose garden dotted with shrines and protected by a thirty-metre-tall gate tower and rounded corner bastions. Founded in the 1560s by Chancellor Ion Golia, when the capital was moved from Suceava, the monastery was rebuilt and fortified by Basil the Wolf, who began a new **Church of the Ascension** within the monastery's grounds, completed by his son Ştefăniţa in 1660. The walls and towers were built in 1668 (with the gate tower added in 1855); it was burnt three times and damaged by an earthquake, but survived to become the Metropolitan Cathedral in 1786; however by 1863 it was a ruin, being rebuilt only in 1947. A striking mixture of Byzantine, Classical and Russian architecture, with the traditional Moldavian domed plan but Corinthian capitals on the exterior, the church boasts of its associations with Tsarist Russia, since it was visited by Peter the Great in 1711, and serves as the burial place for the **viscera of Prince Potemkin**, Catherine the Great's favourite. These were removed so that the rest of his body could be preserved and returned home after he died in 1791, after catching a fever in Iaşi and defying doctors' orders by wolfing huge meals, starting at breakfast with smoked goose and wine. He actually died across the border in present-day Moldova. The interior was painted in 1838 and is being filled with wooden platforms as these are slowly restored; the arcaded eighteenth-century house to the east of the church was home to dean Ion Creangă from 1866 to 1871.

West along Bulevardul Independenţei

Bulevardul Independenţei, a drab thoroughfare linking the Golia Monastery with Piaţa Eminescu, has a few sights worth noting. Midway along the boulevard stands the **old university**, a Baroque edifice that was constructed between 1795 and 1806 as the Callamachi family palace, and given to the university in 1860; now overshadowed by newer wings, it is the centrepiece of the University of Medicine and Pharmacology. On the university's west side rises the **gate tower** of the Sf. Spiridion Monastery of 1786, which now houses a hospital; the monastery's old **church** contains the tomb of its founder, Grigore III Ghica, whose head was sent giftwrapped to the sultan in 1777, for harbouring treasonous thoughts. Opposite the university, at no. 16, the **Natural History Museum** (Muzeul de Istorie Naturală; closed Aug; Tues, Thurs & Sat 9am–3pm, Wed & Fri 9am–4pm, Sun 10am–4pm) occupies the eighteenth-century Ruset House, in whose Elephant Hall Cuza was elected Prince of Moldavia in 1859. At that time, the house belonged to the Society of Physicians and Naturalists, who had opened their collections to the public in 1834, making this one of the first such museums in Romania. From the street it now seems very run-down, but the entrance is in fact around the corner to the east; there are the usual dead birds and animals, fossils, shells, and a new conservation exhibit.

The boulevard leads to the **Independence Monument**, a statuesque woman striding forth ahead of billowing drapery, sculpted by Gabriela and Gheorghe Adoc in 1980, and finally to Piaţa Eminescu. From here, you can head towards the university district or return to Piaţa Unirii via the shopping precinct behind the *Hotel Unirea*.

The university district

Copou, the university district, lies northwest of the centre, out along the B-dul. Carol I, where trams (#1, #11 and #13) and buses (#28 and #41) toil uphill. The foot of the hill is distinguished by a Stalinesque **Student House** to the right, with bas-reliefs of musical youths, alongside a small park overlooked by statues of Moldavian princes, and the colonnaded **Eminescu Library** to the left. Working as a librarian in an earlier incarnation of this building, Eminescu could nip across the road (just where a statue of him now stands sage-like in a cloak) for meetings of the Junimea literary society (1863–85) in the **Casa Pogor**, just north of the Student House. Casa Pogor was built in 1850 by Vasile Pogor, a co-founder of the Junimea society, and now houses the **Museum of Romanian Literature** (Tues–Sun 10am–5pm; €1.80), with an art gallery (same hours) at the rear housing temporary shows.

It's a few minutes' walk further uphill to the A.I. **Cuza University**, an Empire-style edifice built in the 1890s, which acts as an umbrella for 26 faculties and eight research institutes of the Romanian Academy. Just to the north are the Titu Maiorescu Dendrological Park, then fine 1880s villas housing the Goethe Zentrum and Chamber of Commerce. Also here are the tranquil **Copou Gardens**, where Eminescu (see box, p.290) meditated under a favourite lime tree, now squat and ugly and boxed in by a low hedge. Nearby in the centre of the park is a cultural centre that houses a small museum on Eminescu (Tues–Sun 10am–5pm).

Further out on B-dul. Carol I is Romania's oldest **Botanic Garden**, at Str. Dumbrava Roşie 7 (mid-April–Oct 9am–8pm, Nov–mid-April 9am–5pm), founded in 1856 and moved in 1963 to this site, with a lake and a seventeenth-century church. The rose garden and the tropical greenhouses are particularly attractive.

Ticău

Țicău is a pretty, hilly, old residential quarter, east of the university area, with lime trees, some modernist houses (from the 1930s–50s), and two memorial museums that provide an excuse for a ramble. At no. 11 on the street that now bears his name, the **house of Mihail Kogălniceanu** (Wed–Sun 10am–5pm) commemorates the orator and journalist who was banned from lecturing for lambasting "oppression by an ignorant aristocracy". He fled to Habsburg Bucovina in 1848, returning in the 1850s to help secure Cuza's election and serve as foreign minister. More entertaining is the **cottage of Ion Creangă** (Bojdeuca), dating from 1850 at the latest, at Str. Simion Bărnuțiu 4 (Tues–Sun 10am–5pm), which displays first editions and prints of his works, including stills from films based on them. A defrocked priest and failed teacher, Creangă (1837–89) wrote *Recollections of Childhood* and fairy tales such as the *Giants of Irunica*, finally achieving success just before he died. From the cottage, you'll have a fine view of the vineyards and rolling hills that surround Iaşi.

The southern monasteries

A more ambitious way to stretch your legs is to visit the **monasteries** in the Nicolina district, south of the city centre, by the polluted stream of the same name. Catch bus #9 or a southbound maxitaxi downhill past the Palace of Culture and out along Str. Nicolina; cresting the flyover, you'll see the Cetăţuia and Galata monasteries on separate hilltops to the east and west, and a modern Roman Catholic church with a prow-like spire in the valley, which is where you should alight. From here, either follow Str. Tudor Neculai west up the hill and past a cemetery to Galata Monastery; or cross the main road and head east through apartment buildings and under the tracks to find Frumoasa Monastery and the trail south to Cetăţuia. If you're intending to visit all three, it's best to see Cetăţuia first and work your way back to the others, as the hike to Cetăţuia requires the most effort.

The **Galata Monastery** stands on Miroslavei hill and is entered by a fortified gate tower. To the right of the gateway, beside a newer building in use today, are the ruins of the original monks' quarters and a Turkish bath. The monastery's church was built between 1579 and 1584 to a typically Moldavian plan, with an enclosed porch and narthex preceding the nave, which was painted in 1811. Its founder, Prince Petru Şchiopul, is buried in the nave with his daughter, Despina.

Mihai Eminescu

Mihai Eminescu, Romania's national poet, was born in 1850 in Botoşani, east of Suceava, and schooled in Cernăuţi, the capital of Habsburg Bucovina. At the age of 16, he gave his surname, Eminovici, the characteristic Romanian ending -escu and became a prompter for a troupe of actors, until his parents packed him off to study law in Vienna and Berlin. Returning to Iaşi in 1874, he found a job as a librarian, joined the Junimea literary society, and had a tortured affair with Veronica Micle, a poet and wife of the university rector. After the rector's demise, Eminescu decided that he was too poor to marry her and took an editorial job in Bucharest to escape his grief. Overwork led to a mental breakdown in 1883, and from then on, until his death from syphilis six years later, periods of madness alternated with lucid intervals. He is best remembered for *Luceafărul* (*The Evening Star*), a 96-stanza ballad of love.

Frumoasa Monastery, on a hillock surrounded by low walls, was derelict for decades, but after restoration is close to living up to its name, meaning "beautiful", once more. Largely built by Grigore II Ghica from 1726 to 1733, Frumoasa differs from the other monasteries thanks to the ponderous form of Neoclassicism in favour when the complex was reconstructed in the 1830s. On the north side are Ghica's summer garden and court, beyond a grand marble Neoclassical tomb built in 1842 by Francesco Vernetta for the family of Prince Mihail Sturdza.

For the **Cetățuia Monastery**, turn left out of the gate onto Str. Cetățuia and (after five minutes) cross B-dul. Poitiers, along which runs bus #43; on the far side the road climbs through woods for 1.5km to a hilltop. You can turn off onto a short-cut path, which is more of a slog. It's well worth the hike, especially if you're not going to Bucovina. Here, the monastery (whose name means "citadel") seems remote from Iași; on misty days, the city is blotted out, and all you can see are the surrounding ridges. Its high walls conceal a harmonious ensemble of white stone buildings with rakish black roofs, interspersed by low conifers and centred on a church that's similar to the Church of the Three Hierarchs in town, but hardly carved, except for a cable moulding and Renaissance window frames. Prince Gheorghe Duca and his wife, now buried in the *pronaos*, founded the monastery in 1669, with a royal palace that served as a refuge for the ruling family in time of war.

Eating, drinking and entertainment

Monasteries and museums notwithstanding, it's worth visiting Iași for its increasingly sophisticated restaurant scene. A number of stylish but affordable places offering Romanian interpretations of various world cuisines have opened recently, but there are also still plenty of staid, traditional establishments where you can try Moldavian cooking, as well as a few genuinely ethnic eateries. New places open fairly regularly; the free publication *Iași: What, Where, When* – available in the better hotels – carries details of the latest restaurant openings.

Fast food is available in the guise of the various joints dispensing pizza, spicy sausages (*mititei*) and other **snacks** along B-dul. Ștefan cel Mare and in the university district. For a quick coffee or pastry, head for *Fast Food Amandina*, on Piața Unirii. Additionally, there are a couple of kebab and falafel outfits on Str. Sfântu Teodor, near the Rafidein (see p.292). The best ice cream in town is in the *Gelateria Veneziana*, at the Iulius Mall. While many of the restaurants double as drinking spots, notably *GinGer Ale* and *Casa Lavric*, there are also plenty of bars and summer-only terraces. In addition to the ones listed below, there are several flashy clubs 2km east of the centre, in the vicinity of the Iulius Mall. To get there, take tram #8, trolley-buses #42 or #43, or any maxitaxi marked *Tudor*.

Restaurants

Caraffa B-dul. Tudor Vladimirescu, Iulius Mall. Mexican and Italian venture with the same owners as *GinGer Ale*. The food is up to scratch, though you may not wish to dine in a shopping mall. Daily noon–midnight.

Casa Bolta Rece Str. Rece 10 ☏0232/212 255, ⓦwww.casaboltarece.ro. Legendary and still popular restaurant and wine garden that dates back over two centuries. Decent traditional food and slightly kitsch peasant decor, with live folk music most evenings. Daily 8am–midnight.

Casa Lavric Stradela Sf. Atanasie 21 ☏0232/229 960, ⓔcasa_lavric@yahoo.com. Fashionable and slightly pretentious new restaurant serving adventurous Romanian and international cuisine at reasonable prices. The *sarmale* are perfect; less traditional dishes are equally successful. Mon 3pm–midnight, Tues–Sun noon–midnight.

Cucina Casalinga Str. Costache Negri 6 ☏0232/210 288. Near the Moldova Mall, a decent Italian restaurant with a/c and a *terasa*. Mon–Sat 9am–11pm, Sun 4–11pm.

GinGer Ale Str. Săulescu 23 ☎0232/276 017. Some way behind the CFR office on Piața Unirii, this is one of the best restaurants in the city, with a long and varied menu of international cuisine, including risotto, magret de canard, loin of lamb and beef fillet. Moderate to expensive, unless you come between noon and 4pm, when food (but not drinks) is either half price (weekends) or 20 percent off (weekdays). Popular with expats. Daily 11am–1am.

Green Bamboo Str. Sf. Teodor 26. Classy Chinese place, with cheap dishes and free coffee for students. Daily 10am–11pm.

La Cao Str. Arcu 8 ☎0232/240 485. Basic but pleasant Chinese restaurant. Daily noon–11pm.

La Valetta Str. Anastasie Panu, adjacent to the Central Market Hall. Clean and modern Italian place with above-average pizza, strong espresso and floor-to-ceiling windows looking out over the concrete expanse of the Centru Civic. Daily 8am–11pm.

Little Texas Stradela Moara de Vânt 31 ☎&℉0232/272 545, 🌐www.littletexas.org. On the road towards the airport, at the hotel of the same name (see p.284). American establishment with impeccable service and exemplary Tex-Mex food (spice levels have been toned down to suit the Romanian palate); nachos (€2–3) are especially recommended, as is apple pie with vanilla ice cream (€2). There's a reasonable choice of vegetarian dishes, and Wi-Fi Internet access. You can dine inside, amid the more or less tasteful Wild West decor (smoking downstairs only, on the way to the toilets), or on the fabulous terrace. Well worth the €1 taxi ride. Mon–Thurs noon–11.30pm, Fri–Sat noon–midnight, Sun noon–10pm.

Onyx Șos. Bucium 7. Elegant and upscale local favourite south of the centre, with well-prepared and stylishly presented European and Romanian cuisine. Daily 10am–midnight.

Panoramic Piața Unirii 2. There's a restaurant with a terrace on the thirteenth floor of the Hotel Unirea, the only place on the square from which you can't see the hotel itself. Serves traditional Romanian fare.

Phenice Str. Lascăr Catargiu 9 ☎0232/222 239. A stylish new Lebanese place, with several vegetarian options.

Rafidein Str. Sfântu Teodor 22. Tiny Iraqi restaurant (look for the red awning) just east of the old university building. Informal, with good meat dishes and salads. Daily 9am–midnight but may close in the afternoon.

Rimini Str. Cuza Vodă 50. A cheap and agreeably informal place with friendly staff, serving simple but tasty Romanian food (despite its name). Daily 11am–11pm.

Sedna Str. Arcu 18 ☎0232/210 107. A small, pleasant place with a tiny balcony that's reached via a set of winding stairs. Serves pizza from a wood-fired oven. To midnight daily.

Tak Eat B-dul. Ștefan cel Mare 6. A snack bar where you can design your own salads and drink good coffee, beers and ices on the terrace; Wi-Fi Internet access.

Traian Piața Unirii 1. Cavernous echoing place from the days when waiters eavesdropped for the Securitate. The food is decent; the prices remarkably low for such a posh place. Daily 6am–midnight.

Trei Sarmale Șos. Bucium 52 ☎0232/237 255. Ten minutes south of the centre by car or maxitaxi. Classic, vineyard-themed establishment, where staff in peasant costumes serve typical Romanian food. Standards have slipped a bit, but it's still a good place to eat. Daily 9am–2am.

Tuffi Str. A Lapușeanu. Excellent pastries to eat at tables in a pedestrian street with piped classical music. Daily 8am–midnight.

Bars, pubs and clubs

Arte Café Str. M. Kogălniceanu 11. A classy coffee bar with paintings, Wi-Fi, and sofas outside; one side is non-smoking. Open Mon–Fri 9am–11.30pm, Sat–Sun 1–11.30pm.

Big Dog Café & Bar Str. Sf. Teodor. A small studenty place facing the east end of the street, fine for a drink before or after eating at the *Rafidein* or *Green Bamboo*.

Club Pogor Str. Vasile Pogor 4. A small terrace, pleasant for an afternoon drink, when you can feel at least vaguely in tune with Eminescu and his pals who held their literary meetings here. Daily 10am–2am.

Club RS Str. Fătu 2A 🌐www.clubrs.ro. Bizarre

Greek-owned restaurant and nightclub with tone-deaf lounge singers. Daily 8am–2am.

Corso Str. Lăpușneanu 11 🌐www.corsoterasa.ro. Massive, noisy, semicircular terrace bar that looks like an MTV dance set. Daily to midnight.

Joker Str. Sf. Sava 2. Unpretentious but very popular summer beer garden located on a small street between the National Theatre and the Central Market Hall.

New Office Str. A. Panu 1 🌐www.clubnewoffice .ro. Near the Central Market, a nightspot that for some reason also has Wi-Fi. Good music (hip-hop on Wed and Sun, karaoke on Thurs) and cocktails. Wed–Sun from 8pm (happy hour to 11pm).

Quinta Str. Sf. Sava 10. Pleasant, slightly louche café/bar in a lime-green Baroque mansion a few doors down from *Terasa Joker*. A good place for an afternoon drink or coffee; less agreeable Fri & Sat nights, when it's taken over by strutting teens. Open Sun–Thurs noon–1am, Fri–Sat noon–4am.

The Stage B-dul. Mangeron 71A. A bar-restaurant near the Chemistry Faculty that often hosts live music. Time Out B-dul. Copou 4. A nice terrace with comfortable wicker furniture to watch the traffic on the boulevard; serves coffee and sub sandwiches. Mon–Fri 8am–2am, Sat–Sun 10am–4am.

Entertainment

Lovers of classical music should try to attend a performance of the **Moldavian Philharmonic**, the country's best orchestra outside Bucharest. Its own venue was damaged in a recent fire, and for the next few years performances will be held in either the Luceafărul Youth Theatre (Str. G. Ureche 5), the Ateneu Tătărași (Str. Pictorului 4) or the Sala Studio Teofil Vâlcu of the National Theatre (the rest of which is also closed for refurbishment) on B-dul. Ștefan cel Mare. The same venues are all also used by the **Opera Națională Româna Iași**. Tickets are available from the ticket agency (Agenția Teatrală; Mon–Sat 10am–5pm) at B-dul. Ștefan cel Mare 8, near Piața Unirii.

Iași's big annual event is the **St Paraschiva festival week** (Sarbatorile Iașului) on October 14, when people from all over Moldavia flood into town to pay homage to the saint buried in the Metropolitan Church. The **Festival of the Three Hierarchs** is celebrated on January 30, when literally a million pilgrims come to worship in the presence of the church's relics. Traditional folklore festivals include the **Folk Music Festival** in mid-December, a **Festival of Winter Customs** on the first Sunday in January and a week-long **Ceramics Fair** (Târgul de Ceramicâ "Cucuteni 5000") in mid-June.

Shopping

Iași has a decent variety of **shops**, including some of the best **bookstores** and **antique** retailers in the region. The Galeriile Anticariat at Str. Lăpușneanu 24 (Mon–Fri 10am–8pm, Sat 11am–7pm, Sun 11am–5pm), selling antiques, icons and secondhand books in several languages, is easily the best shop of its kind in Moldavia, whilst the Galeriile de Artă at no. 7 is one of the few places where you can purchase genuine pieces of work by Iași's finest artists. There are outdoor Anticariat bookstalls (daily 9am–7pm) lined along the same street and on Piața Unirii, while the secondhand bookshop at Str. Cuza Vodă 15 is also worth a look. The best place for new books in English is the small Librăria Humanitas (Mon–Sat 10am–7pm, Sun 10am–3pm) directly opposite the *Hotel Traian* on Piața Unirii; nearby, facing the *Hotel Unirea*, the Librăria Junimea (Mon–Fri 8am–8pm, Sat 9am–4pm, Sun 9am–2pm) stocks books and maps. The Librăria Alexandria, on Piața Eminescu at the top of Str. Muzicescu, is a leading chain bookshop.

On the ground floor of the **Hala Centrala** (Central Market), on Str. Costache Negri, you'll now find G'Market, the most central of the modern supermarkets (8am–10pm daily); the actual market is on the basement level under a glass dome. At Str. Palat 1, just to the southwest, Moldova Mall is a modern shopping mall (daily 10am–10pm). The smaller old-style Unic supermarket (Mon–Sat 7am–8pm, Sun 8am–noon) is on Piața Unirii, while two 24hr places can be found on B-dul. Ștefan cel Mare. On the ground floor of the **Iulius Mall** (ⓦ www.iuliusmall.com), 1.5km east of the city centre, the Gima Superstore (Mon–Sat 9am–11pm, Sun 9am–10pm) is another good choice. The Selgros hypermarket is south of the centre at Șos. Nicolina 57A (west of the railway), and the similar Metro is 9km west on the Pașcani road.

Listings

Airport information ☎0232/278 510, ⓦwww .aeroport.ro/index-eng.htm.

Car rental Icar Tours, Str. Costache Negri 43 (Mon–Fri 8am–6pm, Sat 10am–2pm; ☎0232/216 319, ⓕ217 160, ⓦwww.icar.ro), are agents for Avis and rent cars with or without drivers on a daily or weekly basis. Autonom, at B-dul. Ştefan cel Mare 8 (☎0232/220 504, airport ☎0748/110 557, ⓦwww.autonom.ro), Borgomar, at Str. Codrescu 6 (☎0232/263 300, 0747/912 300, ⓦwww .borgomar.ro) and Total Car, at Str. Pallady 8 (☎0232/277 210, ⓦwww.totalcargrup.ro) all rent compact cars from €20/day (for a week or more),

Flights The TAROM office is at Str. Arcu 3–5 (Mon–Fri 9am–5pm; ☎0232/267 768, ⓕ217 027), with two–three flights a day to Bucharest. Carpatair, also near Piața Unirii at Str. Cuza Vodă 2 (Mon–Fri 9am–6pm; ☎0232/215 295, ⓔiasi @carpatair.com), has a daily flight (except Sun) to Timişoara for international connections. Austrian Airlines, at the airport (☎0232/241 144), has a flight to Vienna daily except on Sat.

Hospital Urgențe (emergency) admission is on the corner of Str. L. Catargiu and Str. G. Berthelot (☎112, 0232/216 584).

Internet access Blue Net, on a dead-end street off B-dul. just north of the Eminescu Library, is open 24hr, with a non-smoking room and English spoken; there's another place just north on the corner of B-dul. Carol I and Str. Maiorescu. Voodoo, at B-dul. Independței 25, scara C1, is just east of the centre. In the suburbs, try Raf-Caffe (24hr) facing the Frumoasa monastery, or the Internet café on B-dul. Primăverii just south of Calea Chişinăului.

Libraries The British Council library is at Str. Păcurari 4 (☎0232/316 159, ⓦwww.britishcouncil .ro/iasi; Mon, Tues & Thurs 1–7pm, Wed & Fri 10am–4pm, closed Aug).

Pharmacy Iaşi has two 24hr pharmacies, Farmacia Sf. Parascheva next to the Kodak shop at Piața Unirii 3 (☎220 549), and Rosmarin, at Str. Tudor Vladimirescu 44 (☎263 365); there's another that's open 8am–10pm daily opposite the BCR bank at the south end of Str. Sfântu Lazar.

Photography There are well-signposted Kodak outlets on B-dul. Ştefan cel Mare and on the corner of Piața Unirii and B-dul. Independenței, and an Agfa Image Center in the Hala Centrala.

Post office Str. Cuza Vodă 3 (Mon–Fri 8am–7pm, Sat 8am–1pm). There's a smaller branch in the arcade on Str. Muzicescu immediately south of Piața Eminescu.

Sports facilities The Ştrand athletic club, below the Palace of Culture on B-dul. Ştefan cel Mare (daily 8am–7pm), has a swimming pool and tennis courts. The Piscina Moldova covered pool is in the *Hotel Moldova* at Str. A. Panu 29 (opposite Pizza Hut).

Train tickets The CFR office is at Piața Unirii 10 (☎0232/147 673; Mon–Fri 7.30am–8.30pm); upstairs, you can make international bookings, including for the overnight *Prietenia* to Chişinău in Republica Moldova, for which some foreigners may need a visa, obtainable from the Moldovan embassy in Bucharest (see p.96).

Suceava and around

Crossing the industrial sprawl between the stations and the city centre, it's difficult to imagine **SUCEAVA**, 150km northwest of Iaşi, as an old princely capital. The city's heyday more or less coincided with the reign of **Stephen the Great** (1457–1504), who warred ceaselessly against Moldavia's invaders – principally the Turks – and won all but two of the 36 battles he fought. This record prompted Pope Sixtus IV to dub him the "Athlete of Christ" – a rare accolade for a non-Catholic, which wasn't extended to Stephen's cousin Vlad the Impaler (see p.471), even though he massacred 45,000 Turks during one year alone.

While Stephen's successors, **Bogdan the One-Eyed** and **Petru Rareş**, maintained the tradition of building a new church or monastery after every victory, they proved less successful against the Turks and Tatars, who ravaged Suceava several times. Eclipsed when Iaşi became the Moldavian capital in 1565, Suceava missed its last chance of glory in 1600, when **Michael the Brave** (Mihai Viteazul) completed his campaign to unite Wallachia, Moldavia and Transylvania by marching unopposed into Suceava's Princely Citadel. In terms of national pride, Suceava's nadir was the long period from 1775 to 1918, when the **Habsburgs** ruled northern Moldavia from Czernowitz (Cernăuţi), although Suceava was able to prosper as a trading centre between the highland and lowland areas.

Under communism, this role was deemed backward and remedied by hasty **industrialization** – the consequences of which long blighted the town. Its wood-processing and tanning plants poisoned the Suceava River for kilometres, while the "Suceava Syndrome" of malformed babies has been linked to air pollution from the artificial fibres factory. The paper mill, one factory that has seen some success in recent years, is responsible for the distinctive odours with which Suceava is too often enveloped. One positive result of Romania's drive for EU accession is that the dangerous emissions have been more or less eliminated.

For visitors, Suceava is primarily a base for **excursions to the painted monasteries** (see p.302), which are the only reason to spend much time here. Many of Suceava's churches are on the World Heritage list and are now being restored, but the town's sights can still be covered in a day.

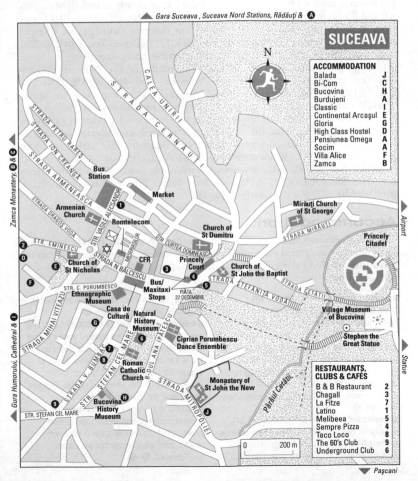

Arrival and information

The Suceava River and adjoining industrial areas separate the city's three train stations from the city centre and from each other. **Suceava Nord** (in the Iţcani suburb, 6km northwest) is the most useful and the one where most trains stop. It wasn't designed to be a main station, though, and there is no tunnel connecting the platforms, so getting to or from your train may involve climbing through carriages on the intervening tracks. The other useful station is Gara Suceava in Burdujeni, a similar distance north. The **bus station** is just northwest of the town centre on Str. V. Alecsandri. Suceava's **airport**, 12km east of town, is accessible only by taxi (€30). Public transport is provided by modern buses on key routes (notably to the train stations) and private **maxitaxis**. Buses #1 and #5 run from Iţcani (Suceava Nord station) to the southwestern suburb of Obcini; bus #2 (and occasionally #3) from Burdujeni (Gara Suceava) to Obcini; and bus #4 from Cinema Burdujeni via Str. Maraşeşti to Obcini. All these buses stop just east of Suceava's main square, Piaţa 22 Decembrie, between the Princely Court and the church of St John the Baptist, and all run roughly every ten minutes from 4.15am to 10.30pm (and #2 runs hourly at night). Maxitaxis #6 and #9 go from Burdujeni via the bus station to Obcini; maxitaxi #12 runs from Iţcani (Suceava Nord) via the bus station, the new cathedral (Str. Enescu) and Zamca to Obcini. Eurotaxi (☎0230/511 111), Canon Taxi (☎0230/522 222) and Cristaxi (☎0230/530 013) are respectable taxi companies.

The county's **Info Turism office** is currently in the Natural History Museum, at Str. Ştefan cel Mare 23 (Mon–Fri 8am–4pm; ☎&☏0230/551 241, ✉infoturism@suceava.rdsnet.ro), although it is expected to move. There's also a touchscreen information system plus leaflets at the airport. Nearby, at the north end of Str. Ştefan cel Mare, there's a cluster of **agencies** that can arrange tours of the city and the painted monasteries (as well as flights and beach holidays), such as Best Travel Bucovina (Str. Ştefan cel Mare 26; ☎0230/521 094, ⊛www.travelbucovina.ro); Gigi Turism (Str. Ştefan cel Mare 28; ☎0722/601 031, ⊛www.gigiturism.ro); Instant Travel (Str. Ştefan cel Mare 28; ☎0230/521 615); and West Travel (Str. Ştefan cel Mare 24; ☎0230/520 257, ⊛www.westtourism.ro).

Accommodation

There are several small, modern and comfortable private **hotels** operating alongside Suceava's staid communist-era establishments. There are also various **guesthouses** along the Gura Humorului road, in the light-industrial area to the southwest.

Balada Str. Mitropoliei 3 ☎0230/520 408, ⊛www.balada.ro. Smart, private hotel, one of the best in town, downhill from the Monastery of St John the New. Some rooms have double beds and balconies plus cable TV. Breakfast included. ❼

Bi-Com Str. Narciselor 20 ☎0230/216 881, ⊛www.bicom.ro. Modern but rather gloomy hotel in the quiet Zamca district. A 15min walk from the centre, or 5min by maxitaxi #12. Some rooms have balconies. ❺

Bucovina B-dul. A. Ipătescu 5 ☎0230/217 048, ☏520 250. Typical 1970s high-rise on the centre's southern fringe. A bit shabby, though all rooms have private bath, a/c, Internet connection and cable TV; the unrenovated rooms are remarkably affordable. Breakfast extra. ❸–❺

Burdujeni Str. Jean Bart 24 ☎0230/518 851. In an apartment block just a few hundred metres in front of Gara Suceava, this offers en-suite rooms with TV and is a small cut above the adjacent *Socim*. ❷

Classic Str. Universităţii 32 & 36 bis ☎&☏0230/510 000, ⊛www.classic.ro. Excellent new hotel in the university district, 700m southwest of the centre. The main wing has spotless modern rooms with a/c and Internet access, while the annexe, a few doors down, has smaller, good-value rooms that are just as well furnished. ❺–❼

Continental Arcaşul Str. Mihai Viteazul 4
☎0230/210 944, ✉arcasul@warpnet.ro. One of
the better central hotels, with restaurant, bar and
disco. Cheek by jowl with the fifteenth-century
church of St Nicolas. ❼
Gloria Str. V. Bumbac 4 ☎0230/521 209, ⓦwww
.hotelgloria.apps.ro. Thoroughly renovated (with a
new glass foyer stuck on front, but still no lift, alas)
and with Internet access in all rooms. ❺
🏃 High Class Hostel Str. Eminescu 19
☎0723/782 328, ⓦwww.classhostel.ro. On a
quiet street (fork left at B&B Restaurant), this is a
clean and friendly hostel, with bunk-bed dorms with
glassed-in balconies, one double room, bathrooms
upstairs and down, and a kitchen (plus barbecue in
the garden). Monika leads excellent trips to the
monasteries. A simple breakfast (8am–2pm!) of jam,
butter and bread, and unlimited coffee and tea all day
is included in the price; a full breakfast is extra. ❶
Pensiunea Omega Str. Traian Vuia 10C
☎0744/253 877, 0741/358 652. In an industrial

area 1.5km north of the centre, but on the bus
route to Suceava Nord station, this is a cheap but
adequate hostel with Internet café. ❶
Socim Str. Jean Bart 24 ☎0230/516 901, ⓕ257
133. Budget option in an apartment block just a
few hundred metres in front of Gara Suceava.
Clean and decent, but the showers are very
communal and hot water is only available for a
couple of hours from 6am and from 7pm. ❶
Villa Alice Str. Simion Florea Marian 1 bis
☎0230/522 254, ⓦwww.villaalice.ro. Reliable
centrally located pension with small but modern,
clean and very comfortable rooms, plus sauna, gym
and restaurant, and free Internet in the best rooms.
One of the best-value places in town. Breakfast
and laundry service extra. ❸–❺
Zamca Str. Zamca 28 ☎0230/520 985, ⓦwww
.hotelzamca.ro. Modern hotel with two- and three-
star rooms, overlooking the Zamca Monastery and
reached by maxitaxi #12. Comfortable, with a lively
outdoor bar and restaurant. ❹–❺

The Town

Most of Suceava's sights relate to its past as a princely capital; the Princely
Citadel and the Zamca Monastery are a good twenty minutes' walk east and
west from the centre respectively, but most other sights are close to the city's
main square, **Piaţa 22 Decembrie**.

The fourteenth-century **Princely Court** (Curtea Domnească), now little more
than ruins behind rusty hoardings, is just north of Piaţa 22 Decembrie. To its
northwest is the **Church of St Dumitru**; built by Petru Rareş from 1534–35, it
is typical of Moldavian churches of the period, with a double row of niche-bound
saints under its eaves, and coloured tiles ornamenting its drum. The interior
frescoes of gruesome martyrdoms date from the sixteenth to the nineteenth
centuries and have recently been restored. The freestanding belltower, added in
1561, bears the Moldavian crest (see box, p.298).

The **Church of St John the Baptist**, built as his court chapel by Basil the
Wolf in 1643, is just east of Piaţa 22 Decembrie, on the far side of the main
B-dul. Ana Ipătescu. It's simple yet attractive, with a tiny dark interior and a
small bell tower linked only by its roof to the church. At weekends, visitors may
witness funerals here, where the deceased is laid out in an open coffin, amid
candles and loaves of bread, while a horse-drawn hearse waits outside. Corteges
often parade around Piaţa 22 Decembrie, as do wedding parties – on spring
Saturdays one sometimes follows close behind another.

Five minutes' walk east from the Princely Court along Str. Mirăuţi is the
Mirăuţi Church of St George, the oldest in Suceava. Founded by Petru I
Muşat in about 1390, this was the Metropolitan cathedral, where the early
princes of Moldavia were crowned. Its facade is decorated with blind arches and
a sawtoothed cornice sandwiched between thick cable mouldings, while below
the eaves are frescoes of saints, added when it was heavily over-restored between
1898 and 1903 by Emperor Franz Jozef I. There's also a good view (if you can
call it that) over the industry of Burdujeni.

West from the Court, Str. Curtea Domnească will bring you to Suceava's
market, which is busiest on Thursdays, when cartloads of peasants roll into

town to sell their produce. Some wear traditional dress, such as leather or sheepskin waistcoats lined with polecat fur, wrap-around skirts or white woollen pantaloons. Fine embroideries and crafts are exhibited in the **Ethnographic Museum** at Str. Ciprian Porumbescu 5 (Tues–Sun 10am–6pm), one block west of Piaţa 22 Decembrie via Str. Bălcescu. The museum is housed in a half-timbered building, the oldest civil edifice in Suceava county, which served as the court guesthouse in the seventeenth century.

To the south from Piaţa 22 Decembrie, Str. Ştefan cel Mare runs parallel to B-dul. Ana Ipătescu; the drab **Natural History Museum** (Muzeul de Ştiinţele Naturii; Mon 8am–3pm, Tues–Sun 9am–5pm), at no. 23, is full of stuffed wildlife, and also houses the **tourist information centre** (Mon–Fri 8am–4pm). Alongside it, the Roman Catholic church, built in 1836, is a plain Neoclassical building now shared by Greco-Catholic and Armenian-Catholic congregations. The **Bucovina History Museum** (Tues–Sun 10am–6pm), at no. 33, begins with an array of Neolithic shards, and works stolidly on through medieval times and the independence struggles. There's better coverage of World War II here than in most Romanian museums, plus there are some portraits by local artists. The main attractions are the treasury, full of gold ornaments, and a life-size model of Stephen's throne room, occupied by richly costumed figures. Continuing west on Str. Ştefan cel Mare you'll come to the big half-built **Orthodox cathedral** (at the junction of Str. Mârăşeşti and Str. Enescu), to be the seat of the new archbishopric of Suceava and Rădăuţi, which was only created in 1991.

Midway between the two museums, Str. Mitropoliei heads east to the **Monastery of St John the New** (Mănăsteria Sf. Ioan cel Nou), easily identified by its colourful steeple striped with blue, black and yellow chevrons. Started by Bogdan the One-Eyed in 1514 and finished by his son Ştefăniţă in 1522, its monumental **Church of St George** was intended to replace the Mirăuţi Church as Suceava's Metropolitan cathedral, so no expense was spared. In 1534 it was painted inside and out with frescoes like those of the painted monasteries of Bucovina, but only the *Tree of Jesse* on the south wall (the far side) and a fragment of the *Last Judgement* on the west end remain, both in very poor condition. The interior frescoes are now being restored. The relics of St John the New rest here, to the right of the nave, and are taken on a grand procession through the city each year on June 24, the feast of St John the Baptist (the feast of Sânziene). St John the New's martyrdom is depicted inside a small chapel near the church, where the nuns now run a shop selling religious paraphernalia. Arrested for preaching in Turkish-occupied Moldavia in 1332, he was dragged through the streets of Cetăţii Alba behind a horse, and slashed to death by enraged Muslims. There's also a pavilion housing a 230-litre drum of holy water, for the faithful to take away in bottles.

Prince Dragoş and the aurochs

Throughout Moldavia churches display the emblem of the medieval principality, often over the main gateway: an aurochs' head and a sun, moon and star. This symbolizes the legend of **Prince Dragoş**, who is said to have hunted a giant **aurochs** (the *zimbru* or European bison) all the way across the mountains from Poland, until he cornered it by a river and slew the beast after a fight lasting from dawn to dusk – hence the inclusion of the Sun, Moon and Morning Star in the emblem. Dragoş's favourite hunting dog, **Molda**, was killed in the fight, and the prince named the River Moldova in her honour, adopting the aurochs, the mightiest animal in the Carpathians, as his totem. The last wild aurochs in Romania was killed in 1852 near Borşa, although captive breeding populations survive, notably at Vânători Neamţ, just west of Târgu Neamţ (see p.277).

The Princely Citadel and the Village Museum of Bucovina

Suceava's most impressive monument is the **Princely Citadel** (Tues–Sun 10am–6pm), which overlooks the city from a hill to its east. Also known as the Throne Citadel of Moldavia (Cetatea de Scaun a Moldovei), it was built by Petru I Muşat (reigned 1375–91), who moved the Moldavian capital from Siret to Suceava; it was subsequently strengthened in the fifteenth century by Alexander the Good. Stephen the Great added the moat, curtain walls and bastions that enabled it to defy the artillery of Mohammed II, conqueror of Constantinople, in 1476. Although blown up by Dumitrascu Cantacuzino (as ordered by the Turks) in 1675, much of the three-storey keep and the outlying chambers remain; from the ramparts, there's a fine view across the valley to the Mirăuţi Church and the city.

In a former pasture opposite the citadel, you'll find the **Village Museum of Bucovina** (Muzeul Satului Bucovinean; March 15–Oct 15 Tues–Fri 10am–6pm, Sat & Sun 10am–8pm), a work in progress currently displaying some two dozen wooden buildings, all removed from Bucovina villages and reassembled on the site, with informative trilingual signs in Romanian, English and French or German. A few, including a family house from Roşu (near Vatra Dornei) and a tavern from Şaru Dornei, both near the entrance (and toilets), have been furnished with colourful textiles, handmade furniture and housewares; there's also a wooden church from Vama and a watermill.

To reach the citadel and the museum, which are a fifteen-minute walk from the centre, head east from Piaţa 22 Decembrie through the park and across the bridge into the woods, where rather steep steps lead up to a giant equestrian **statue of Stephen the Great**, unveiled in 1977; the bas-reliefs on the pedestal depict his victory over the Turks at Vaslui in 1475. From here a road leads around the Village Museum to the car park and cafés between it and the citadel. It is also possible to take a taxi from town (€2).

Zamca Monastery

The neglected ruins of the Armenian **Zamca Monastery** straddle a plateau on the northwest edge of town, 25 minutes' walk from the centre along Str. Armenească or a short walk from Str. Mărăşeşti (maxitaxi #12). The Armenian diaspora had reached Moldavia by 1350, and Alexander the Good founded the Armenian bishopric of Suceava in 1401; in 1551, they fell foul of the Rareş family, leading to a pogrom, but in 1572 an Armenian actually became ruler of Moldavia. The buildings here, which combine Gothic and classical elements with oriental motifs, were founded in 1606 and later fortified with ramparts and a gate tower. A long and slow restoration project is under way. The three-storey gatetower and guesthouse, where dignitaries were once accommodated, is currently closed, while the plain white church is home to a few lovely **frescoes**. Though not much from a monumental standpoint, the site has a desolate grandeur, particularly at dusk, when you can walk around the earthworks. It's also worth mentioning the simple sixteenth-century **Armenian church of the Holy Cross** (Sfânta Cruce; open daily 9am–2pm), immediately south of the bus station, and the active **Hagigadar Monastery**, dating from 1513, 15km south of Suceava.

Eating, drinking and entertainment

Though there are a few good **restaurants** in town, the selection is limited – if you want to sample Bucovina's indigenous cuisine, you'll be much better off in village guesthouses near the monasteries. The restaurant in the *Balada* hotel offers decent Romanian food, with tasty *sarmale*; of the other hotel restaurants, the *Zamca* is the best. There are several fast-food outlets around the centre; just north of the bus station on Str. Petru Rareş, *Cina* and *Mirasco* (open to 10pm) are fast-food joints where teenagers hang out.

B&B Restaurant Str. Eminescu 18B. An adequate alternative to *Latino* (below), though don't be fooled by the "Pensiunea" sign, as this is only a pizzeria.

Chagall Str. Ştefan cel Mare 19 ☎0230/530 621. A pub serving Romanian food in the courtyard east of the pedestrian plaza and south of the church of Sf. Dumitru; there's also a branch in the student area at Str. Universităţii 19 (☎0230/523 264).

La Fitze Str. Vasile Bumbac 3 (☎0230/523061, 0721/701 886, ⓦwww.lafitze.com. A lively pub-pizzeria with a three-course lunch menu for €4 and an attractive terasa open until 1am.

Latino Str. Curtea Domnească 9 ☎0230/523 627.

A stylish and affordable Italian place opposite the bus station, with superb pasta and pizza, German beer, the best coffee in Suceava, and professional and friendly service (daily 10am–midnight).

Melibeea Piaţa 22 Decembrie ⓦwww.melibeea.ro. Pretty good pastries and coffee.

Sempre Pizza Str. A. Ipătescu. Near the Princely Court, this fast-food joint run by Romanian Pentecostals is a favourite with university students (open until 10/11pm daily).

Taco Loco Str. Vasile Bumbac 5 ☎0230/220 032, ⓦwww.tacolocosv.ro. A fair attempt at a Mexican *cantina*, with a lively *terasa* open until 1am.

Suceava's **nightlife** is scarce, though there are at least two somewhat atmospheric places to drink: *Underground Club*, beneath the Natural History Museum (entry at the rear of the museum), which has a subterranean bar and a pleasant summer terrace, and the *60's Club*, at the corner of Str. Ştefan cel Mare and Str.Republicii, where there are pool tables and comfortable couches. There are cinemas at Str. Ştefan cel Mare 25 and on the roundabout at the bottom of Str. Eminescu. The excellent **Ciprian Porumbescu Dance Ensemble** (Ansamblul Artistic Ciprian Porumbescu; ☎&🖷0230/531 280), a folk dance troupe named after the Romanian composer, performs in the Dom Polski, at B-dul. Ana Ipătescu 5, beside the Sfânta Înviere Church. The ensemble is often away on tour, but is sure to appear at the **folklore festival** at Ilişeşti, in July (see box opposite).

Listings

Air tickets The TAROM office, at Str. Bălcescu 2 (☎0230/214 686; Mon–Fri 9am–7pm), sells tickets for flights to Bucharest (six a week, via Bacău) and international connections. Carpatair, at Str. Ştefan cel Mare 74 (☎0230/529 559, Ⓔsuceava @carpatair.com), has flights to Timişoara, for international connections.

Books Librăria Alexandria, on the roundabout at the top of Str. Bălcescu, has an English section with a few paperback classics, as well as Alan Ogden's sumptuous Bucovina photo album, *Revelations of Byzantium*. General Cart, on the corner at Str. Ştefan cel Mare 28, is excellent, with lots of maps, and stays open until late.

Car rental Autonom, at Str. Bălcescu 8 (Mon–Fri 9am–6pm; ☎0230/521 101, ⓦwww.autonom.ro). Also Icar Rentacar, at Str. V. Alecsandri 10 (☎0230/523 553); Instant Travel, at Str. Ştefan cel Mare 28 (☎0722/778 778); Travis Rentacar, at Str. C.A. Rosetti (☎0230/521 603).

Consulates Ukrainian Consulate, Str. Mihai Viteazu 48 (☎0230/520 167, Ⓔgc_ro@mfa.gov.ua). Tourist visas for most nationalities can be purchased within one–two days.

Hospital B-dul. I Decembrie 1918 (☎0230/222 098).

Internet access Games Pit, at Str. Eminescu 13, is run by asocial teenagers, but adequate; at Str. Jean Bart 18 in Burdujeni, the noisy Jocuri also has a good connection.

Pharmacies Farmacia Centrală, at the bottom of Piaţa 22 Decembrie, is open daily 7am–9pm; nearby, Sensiblu is open Mon–Fri 8am–9pm, Sat & Sun 9am–6pm.

Post office On Str. Dimitrie Onciul, next to the synagogue (Mon–Fri 8am–7pm, Sat 8am–1pm).

Shopping and supermarkets There's a small, 24hr supermarket at the bottom of Str. Eminescu, next to the cinema, while the larger and much more modern Supermarket Premier is 300m up the street, at Str. Mărăşeşti 39A, opposite the new Orthodox Cathedral. The Metro hypermarket is southwest of the centre at B-dul. 1 Decembrie 1918, and Selgros is at Str. Cernăuţi 118, by the river on the way to the Suceava Nord station.

Train tickets Seats on trains out of Suceava can be reserved a day in advance at the CFR at Str. Bălcescu 8 (Mon–Fri 7.30am–8.30pm).

Festivals at Ilişeşti

Many villages in northern Moldavia, including Ilişeşti, 15km along the main road west from Suceava, still hold **winter festivities** that mingle pagan and Christian rites. Preparations for Christmas begin in earnest on St Nicholas's Day (December 6), when people butcher pigs for the feast beside the roads – not a sight for the squeamish. Women get to work baking pies and the special *turte* pastries, which symbolize Christ's swaddling clothes, while the men rehearse songs and dances. On Christmas Eve (Ajun), boys go from house to house, singing carols that combine felicitations with risqué innuendo, accompanied by an instrument that mimics the bellowing of a bull. After days of feasting and dancing, the climax comes on the day of New Year's Eve, when a dancer, garbed in black and red, dons a goat's-head mask with wooden jaws, which he clacks to the music of drums and flutes, and whips another dancer, dressed as a bear, through the streets. It's a rather bizarre twist on the new year driving out the old, apparently. Ilişeşti also hosts the **From the Rarău Mountain Folklore Festival** (De sub montele Rarău), on the second Sunday of July. Ensembles from three counties – Bacău, Neamţ and Maramureş – participate, and it's a chance to experience a round dance (horă) and shepherds' dances, fiddles, flutes and alpine horns, and a panoply of costumes. Ilişeşti is easily reached from Suceava by buses and maxitaxis towards Gura Humorului, which will also drop you at the Motel Han Ilişeşti (☎0788/404 290, 0722/345 221, ⊛www.hanulilisesti.ro) to the west at km232 (although this will be full at festival times).

Dragomirna Monastery and Pătrăuţi Church

The nearest of the Bucovina monasteries to Suceava is the (unpainted) Dragomirna Convent, 3km beyond the village of **Mitocul Dragomirnei**, which is 12km north of Suceava. As there is almost no public transport to the monastery, the best way to get there without taking a taxi is to get a ride, in a minibus or private car, from the Dragomirna turn-off on the outskirts of Suceava. Take bus #1 to Iţcani, get off under the road bridge by the railway, and walk across the tracks to the right-hand or east side of the main road, Str. G.A. Ghica. The turn-off is on the right, 50m ahead, from where it's 4km to the start of the village and 4.5km more to the monastery, which is hidden from view by rolling plains until the last moment. You may have to walk from the village, but you'll pass a couple of sheepfolds along the way.

Massively walled like a fortress, the **Dragomirna Monastery** was founded in 1602 by Metropolitan Anastasie Crimca, who designed its **church**, which is dramatically proportioned at 42m high but only 9.6m wide. There's a cable moulding around the exterior, and Renaissance windows. The octagonal tower, set on two star-shaped pedestals, is carved with meanders and rosettes, like the Church of the Three Hierarchs in Iaşi. Inside, it doesn't seem so high and thin, gradually rising by steps to the *pronaos* and *naos*, with an unusual star-vault and a very ornate Baroque iconostasis. Crimca himself is buried in the *pronaos*; his portrait is visible on the pillar to the left as you walk through.

The complex's solid walls and towers were added in 1627 owing to the threat of foreign invasions; these were so frequent that wooden village churches were sometimes mounted on wheels so that they could be towed away to safety. The complex is in excellent condition, with living quarters on two sides for the nuns who farm much of the surrounding land, and a **museum** harbouring five of the surviving 26 manuscripts of the school of illuminators founded here by Crimca, himself a talented artist. One 1602 manuscript features Crimca's self-portrait, the earliest known by a Romanian. Also on display is an enormous candle first lit for the monastery's consecration in 1609. The tiny original church is in the cemetery, to the left as you leave by the gateway, but it is usually locked.

Accommodation in the convent is for women only, and only up to four of them at a time. The lodgings are comfortable (but lacking hot water), and the ambience is tranquil. Opposite the convent, and open to both sexes, is a complex of cabins (❶) with a snackbar. A guesthouse is due to open in 2008 on Str. Pâtrăuţi, about 1km from the monastery on the edge of the state forest.

A few kilometres further north on the main DN2/E85 is the turning to **Pătrăuţi**, the first church founded by Stephen the Great, in 1487. After the turning it's 3km east through Pătrăuţi village to the church at the far end, facing a new museum about the church, where you should ask for entry if the church itself is locked. The prototype for subsequent Moldavian churches, it also contains the oldest paintings in Moldavia, and is on UNESCO's World Heritage list. Alas, only fragments of a *Last Judgement* are visible on the exterior.

From the church, signs show that it's just 6km to Dragomirna Monastery; the road is closed to cars, but it makes a lovely easy **hike**, once you're past the Gypsy area on the edge of the village and into the state forest. An easier option is to start from Dragomirna and then fork left to return via Lipoveni to Mitocul Dragomirnei, a loop of about 5km.

Southern Bucovina

The **painted monasteries of Southern Bucovina**, in the northwest corner of Moldavia, are rightfully acclaimed as masterpieces of art and architecture, steeped in history and perfectly in harmony with their surroundings. Founded in the fifteenth and sixteenth centuries, they were citadels of orthodoxy in an era overshadowed by the threat of infidel invaders. **Grigore Roşca**, Metropolitan of Moldavia in the mid-fifteenth century, is credited with the idea of covering the churches' outer walls with paintings of biblical events and apocrypha, for the benefit of the illiterate faithful. These **frescoes**, billboards from the late medieval world, are essentially Byzantine, but infused with the vitality of the local folk art and mythology. Though little is known about the artists, their skills were such that the paintings are still fresh after 450 years of exposure. Remarkably, the layer of colour is only 0.25mm thick, in contrast to Italian frescoes, where the paint is absorbed deep into the plaster.

Perhaps the best of these are to be found at **Voroneţ**, whose *Last Judgement* surpasses any of the other examples of this subject, and **Suceviţa**, with its unique *Ladder of Virtue* and splendid *Tree of Jesse*. **Moldoviţa** has a better all-round collection, though, and **Humor** has the most tranquil atmosphere of them all. Nearby **Putna Monastery**, though lacking the visual impact of the painted monasteries, is worth a visit for its rich historical associations.

The monasteries are scattered across a region divided by rolling hills – the *obcine* or "crests" which branch off the Carpathians – and by the legacy of history. Although settlers from Maramureş arrived here in the mid-fourteenth century, the area remained barely populated for two centuries until Huţul shepherds moved south from the Ukrainian mountains. They lived in scattered houses in the hills, and the region was a sort of free republic until the Habsburgs annexed northern Moldavia in 1774, calling it Bucovina, a Romanianized version of their description of this beech-covered land (Büchenwald). Soon the place was organized and the Huţuls moved into villages such as Argel, Raşca, Moldoviţa

and Ciocăneşti, where they could better be taxed and drafted into the army. Bucovina remained under Habsburg rule until the end of World War I, when it was returned to Romania, only to be split in half in 1940 – the northern half being occupied by the Soviet Union and incorporated into Ukraine, where it remains today. Thus, Romanians speak of **Southern Bucovina** to describe what is actually the far north of Moldavia – implying that Bucovina might be reunited one day. Names aside, the scenery is wonderful, with misty valleys and rivers spilling down from rocky shoulders heaving up beneath a cloak of beech and fir. The woods are at their loveliest in May and autumn.

Gura Humorului

The monasteries of Voroneţ and Humor lie a few kilometres either side of **GURA HUMORULUI**, a small logging town an hour west of Suceava by bus or train that has more than enough facilities to make a satisfactory base. In the nineteenth century its population was seventy to eighty percent Zipser German and twenty percent Jewish; the Germans left after 1945 and the last Jew died in 2006, so the population is now all ethnic Romanian.

Be sure to leave the train at Gura Humorului Oraş station, adjacent to the bus station ten minutes' walk west of the town centre, and not Gura Humorului station amid the fields to the east. Humor Monastery is serviced by maxitaxis that shuttle to and from Gura Humorului every twenty to thirty minutes, but

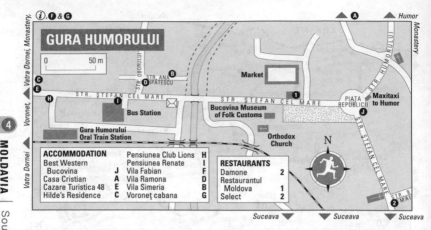

there's just one service a day to Voroneţ (at 11am, returning around 11.30am), which doesn't wait long. Both monasteries, however, are within walking distance of Gura Humorului; there are also plenty of taxis.

Near the edge of town on the road towards Voroneţ you'll find a welcoming *Dispecerat Cazare* (accommodation service) and **tourist information office** (℡0230/233 263, 0744/288 447), run by the same people as the *Vila Fabian* pension across the road (see opposite). Here you'll be able to find information on the region, arrange accommodation in Humor, Voroneţ and elsewhere, and organize monastery tours (see p.307). You can leave your baggage if you want to walk to Voroneţ, and may even be able to rent a bike at reasonable cost. The **post office** (Mon–Fri 8am–9pm, Sat 8am–noon) is across the bridge to the west of the town centre.

The new **Bucovina Museum of Folk Customs** (Muzeul Obiceiurilor Populare din Bucovina; Tues–Sun 8am–4pm), by the huge new Orthodox church at Piaţa Republicii 2, displays temporary shows of art, usually by émigré Romanians, on the ground floor, and ethnographic displays upstairs. These are built around tableaux of Christmas, New Year and Easter scenes, showing carol singers, masque costumes (such as the king and queen, bears, witches and gypsies), fish traps, beehives, a smithy and a sheepfold.

Accommodation

Best Western Bucovina Piaţa Republicii ℡0230/207 000, ⊛www.bestwesternbucovina.ro. A ten-storey block towering over the roundabout at the centre of town, this is the finest large hotel in this part of Romania. Facilities include room service, Internet access (with Wi-Fi in the lobby), sauna, Jacuzzi and conference rooms. ❼

Casa Cristian Str. Victoriei 22 ℡0230/230 864, 0744/621 094, ⊛www.cristianhouse .com. Just off the road to Humor, 1.5km north of the centre, this magnificent four-star pension is the best place to stay in town, with individually designed rooms and Austrian-style glassed-in balconies. Casa Cristian's top-class facilities are complemented by gracious hospitality, a manicured garden with over a hundred varieties each of roses and tulips, and Sun-morning concerts (not in summer) by Romania's finest classical musicians. Excellent organic meals can also be provided, with a few hours' notice, and a new Audi is available for rent (with or without driver/guide). ❻

Cazare Turistică 48 Str. Ştefan cel Mare 48 ℡0230/234 089, 0751/674 646. A self-styled hostel that vibrates alarmingly when lorries pass in the night; the very sociable owner is likely to meet you at the train station. Facilities are simple, with shared bathroom, but clean. ❷

Hilde's Residence Str Şipotului 2 ℡0230/233 484, ⊛www.lucy.ro. A nice newish guesthouse with a lovely garden and Internet access. ❺

Pensiunea Club Lions Str. Ştefan cel Mare 39 ☎0744/502 128, ⓦwww.motel-lions.ro. A new hotel at the turning to the train station with small but nice rooms with balcony and good bathroom; breakfast costs €3 extra. ❸

Pensiunea Renate Str. Ştefan cel Mare 43 bis ☎0230/235 039. The best budget option, with clean rooms with shared bath, good laundry service and a downstairs café-bar. ❷

Vila Fabian Str. Câmpului 30 ☎0230/232 387, 0744/153 724. Out on the road towards Voroneţ, this is a clean and friendly mid-range option,

offering good food, saunas and massages, plus billiards and other games. ❸

Vila Ramona Str. Oborului 6 ☎0230/232 996, ⓦwww.ramona.ro. A comfortable place but less than friendly. ❷

Vila Simeria Str. A. Ipătescu 19 ☎0230/230 746. Just west of the river, this is an adequate guest-house. ❷

Voroneţ cabana Near the bridge, 1.3km from Gura Humorului on the road to Voroneţ village ☎0230/231 024. Open over the summer, there's also camping space here. ❶–❷

▲ Hills of Southern Bucovina

Eating and drinking

The best **restaurant** in Gura Humorului, though you wouldn't know it from outside, is *Restaurantul Moldova* at Str. Ştefan cel Mare 16 (℡0230/230 992), but it does tend to close early. The menu, which is translated into English, features a variety of delicious and inexpensive local specialities. The *sarmale* are good, as are *pârjoale moldoveneşti* (lightly fried meatballs in a rich tomato sauce). The restaurant in the *Best Western* also offers a few Moldavian dishes, in addition to reliable international cuisine. A cheaper option is the *Damone cofetărie*-patisserie-fast-food joint on the corner of Str. 9 Mai, with the communist-era Select hanging on above. For self-catering, there are various minimarkets along Str. Ştefan cel Mare, all stocking more or less the same range of products, but it's better by far to head for the Aldona supermarket next to the station.

Voroneţ Monastery

Ion Neculce's chronicle records that Stephen the Great founded **Voroneţ Monastery** in 1488 to fulfil a pledge to his confessor, the hermit Daniil, who had previously assured the despondent *hospodar* that, should he undertake a campaign against the Turks, he would be successful. The Turks were duly forced back across the Danube, and Voroneţ was erected in three months; chronologically, it comes between Putna and Neamţ monasteries. Its superb **frescoes** – added at the behest of Metropolitan Roşca between 1547 and 1550 – have led to Voroneţ being dubbed the "Oriental Sistine Chapel", and put "Voroneţ blue" into the lexicon of art alongside Titian red and Veronese green. Obtained from lapis lazuli, this colour appears at its most intense on a rainy day, just before sunset.

The church was designed to be entered via a door in the southern wall, with a closed exonarthex replacing the usual open porch, thus creating an unbroken surface on the western wall (at the far end). Here is painted a magnificent *Last Judgement*, probably the finest single composition among the painted monasteries. Fish-tailed bulls, unicorns and other zodiacal symbols form a frieze below the eaves, beneath which Christ sits in majesty above a chair symbolizing the "Toll Gates of the Air", where the deceased are judged and prayers for their souls counted. On either side are those in limbo, the Turks and Tatars destined for perdition. Beneath them, devils and angels push sinners into the flaming river that sweeps them down to hell. In response, graves open, a sunken ship is returned from the deep, and wild animals come bearing the limbs of those they have devoured – all except the deer (a symbol of innocence) and the elephant (no threat in Romania). Amusingly, there's a crush of righteous souls at the gates of the Garden of Heaven.

The south wall, seen as you enter, is covered by three compositions: comic-strip scenes from the lives of St Nicholas and St John on the buttress; a *Tree of Jesse*; and a register of saints and philosophers where Plato is depicted with a coffin-load of bones. There are more saints and philosophers on the curved east end. Weather has damaged the frescoes along the north-facing wall, but you can still distinguish Adam and Eve (clothed in the Garden of Eden; semi-naked and ashamed thereafter), the first childbirth, the discovery of fire and the invention of ploughing and writing. Also notice *Adam's Deed*, illustrating the myth that Adam made a pact with Satan.

Inside, the walls and ceiling of the exonarthex are painted with martyrdoms and miracles. The second row from the bottom on the left depicts Elijah in his "chariot of fire" (like a standard Romanian *caruţa*), intent on zapping devils with his God-given powers. According to local folklore, God promptly had second thoughts and restricted Elijah's activities to his name day. On the right-hand

Tours

Given that almost everyone comes to Southern Bucovina to visit the **painted monasteries** but public transport to them is limited, it's not surprising that many visitors opt for organized **tours**, which can be arranged either in Suceava or (better) Gura Humorului. In **Suceava**, tourist agencies (see p.296) will provide a comfortable car with a driver for between €40 and €80, depending on the number of sights, and an additional €5 for an English-speaking guide. The fee is generally for the car (or minibus), not per person; however Gigi Turism offers a rate of €20–30 per person for those willing to share a car with others. Alternatively, contact either Sorin Fodor (℡0745/248 119, Ⓔfosso@iname.com) or Ciprian Slemcho (℡0744/292 588, Ⓔmonasterytour@yahoo.com), both of whom are knowledgeable, independent guides. Monica, at Suceava's *High Class Hostel* (see p.297), offers a good day tour of the main four monasteries for €27 per person (minimum three), and Claudiu at the Info Turism office (see p.296) may also be able to help. Another option, which may be a bit cheaper if you bargain well, is to hire a taxi driver for the day and rely on the nuns who can usually give tours in French (and sometimes German). You'll have more time to see the monasteries if you choose to stay in **Gura Humorului** (see p.303), where *Vila Fabian* (see p.305) run tours for between €50 and €80, and there are plenty of private taxis for hire. The higher prices for tours from both Suceava and Gura Humorului include Putna Monastery, which is out of the way and thus more expensive to visit (and also makes for a long, rushed day).

On your own

By making the trip independently, you'll be able to spend more time at each monastery and stay in Bucovina's charming **pensions**, many of which serve lavish home-cooked meals. There's not much choice at Moldoviţa, but plenty at and around the other monasteries. Most are modern pensions for affluent Bucureşteni at which the true meaning of agrotourism has been lost; this guide focuses on more authentic places (even if bathrooms are not always en suite), especially those where organic and home-grown food is a speciality. The route entails striking out from Suceava and following a circular course that requires some backtracking, although this can be avoided by hiking across the hills at certain points. It can be done in reverse, but it's most convenient to head first to **Gura Humorului**, the jumping-off point for Voroneţ and Humor. From Gura Humorului, it's relatively easy to reach Vatra Moldoviţei, site of Moldoviţa Monastery, but from here travel becomes more difficult; the road that leads from here to Suceviţa Monastery is traversed only by two buses a day, and light traffic makes hitching uncertain. The road continues from Suceviţa Monastery to Rădăuţi, where you're likely to have a long wait for a train to Putna; otherwise there are hourly maxitaxis back to Suceava. A good compromise is to make Gura Humorului your base, see Voroneţ and Humor on your own, and then either book a tour to the rest with *Vila Fabian* (see p.305) or commandeer a taxi for the day.

Though the monasteries have no set **visiting hours**, you can assume they'll be open daily from 9am to 5pm (8pm in summer). There is a modest **admission charge** (€1.20), which includes entrance to the **museums** (all closed Mon) attached to the monasteries, plus a surcharge (€3) for cameras or videos (which are not allowed inside the churches anyway). As working convents or monasteries, they prohibit smoking and ask that visitors dress appropriately; a few robes are kept on hand for those who arrive in shorts. The small markets set up outside the monastery entrances in summer are among the best places in the country to buy **traditional handicrafts**.

sides of the gloomy narthex and star-vaulted sanctuary are the **tomb of Daniil** the hermit, and, facing the altar, a fresco of Stephen, his wife Maria Voichiţa and their son Bogdan presenting the monastery to Christ. After 1786, the monastery was dissolved and the surrounding monks' cells disappeared, but are now being rebuilt; the **bell tower** also survives. More information about the iconography of the frescoes can be found in *The Sacred Monastery of Voroneţ*, a passionate and intelligent (though awkwardly translated) guide to the monastery by resident nun Elena Simionovici, on sale at the entrance for about €3.

Practicalities

A **taxi** from Gura Humorului to Voroneţ shouldn't cost more than €2, but on a fine day it's no hardship to walk the 4km; from the train station (where you can leave baggage), head left along the main road, Str. Ştefan cel Mare, for 750m to the clearly signposted turn-off. There's no chance of going astray on the valley road – fork right after 3.5km to the monastery, entered by a gate near the cemetery. Be warned, however, that the number of tour buses heading for the monastery is on the rise. Although you're unlikely to be run over, their warning horn blasts can seem offensive after a while. Of all the monasteries, Voroneţ is the busiest with tourists and, being the smallest, can feel very crowded if you come at the wrong moment. Larger groups, however, rarely stay long; wait a bit and you may have the place to yourself.

If you want to stay **overnight**, there are a couple of very good options: at the north end of the village, *Casa Elena* (☎0230/230 651, ⓦwww.casaelena.ro; ❻) includes some palatial villas, complete with WiFi, sauna and billiards, and an affordable but sophisticated **restaurant** that uses produce from its own farm. Across from *Casa Elena*, you'll find the simple and comfortable *Motel Căprioara* (☎0230/232 542; ❷), which also has a restaurant. At the junction to the monastery is another good choice, *Obcina Voroneţului* (☎0230/233 732, 0720/219 278; ❸), which has a rustic dining room and a wine *crama*, as well as cheaper rooms (❷) with communal facilities. A further 3km south (turn left at the fork then right), *Vila Maria* (☎0744/231 279; ❶) is basic but wonderfully peaceful. Turning left after the bridge (1.3km from the main road), you can stay at the Voroneţ cabana or camp nearby; there are some pleasant new guesthouses here too, as well as houses offering rooms (*cazare*) throughout the village.

Humor Monastery

In another valley 4km north of Gura Humorului, passing the Jewish cemetery, the tranquil village of **Mănăstirea Humor** straggles towards its namesake, the sixteenth-century **Humor Monastery**.

Unlike the other complexes, Humor is protected by a wooden stockade rather than a stone rampart (although the ruins of the stone wall can be seen), and lacks a spire over the *naos* – indicating that it was founded by a boyar, in this case Teodor Bubuiog, Chancellor of Petru Rareş, in 1530; he is now buried here

Moldavia's fortified monasteries

Moldavian **fortified monasteries** were usually sited at the head of a valley to form a defensive bottleneck against the Turks or Tatars. The exact spot was decided by shooting arrows from a nearby hill top; where the first one landed, a water source was dug and henceforth deemed holy; the second arrow determined the location of the altar; the third the belfry, and so on. After the monastery was finished, crosses were raised on the hill from where the arrows had been fired.

with his wife Anastasia. The **frescoes** were painted by Toma of Suceava; the prevailing hues are reddish brown (from oriental madder pigment), but rich blues and greens also appear.

The *Last Judgement* on the wall beneath the unusual open porch is similar to that at Voroneţ, with the significant difference that the Devil is portrayed as the Scarlet Woman, though this patch is now so faint that you can't actually tell. Such misogyny had its counterpart in the peasant conception of hell – said to be a cavern upheld by seven old women who had surpassed Satan in wickedness during their lifetimes. Since the women are mortal, the legend goes, the Devil (Dracul) must constantly search the world for replacements – and he never fails to find them. The *Tree of Jesse* along the northern wall has been virtually effaced by weathering, but restorers have touched up the *Hymn to the Virgin* on the south front (with a wonderful Adoration of the Virgin and Child in the middle). As at Voroneţ, this depicts her miraculous intervention at the siege of Constantinople by the Persians – although the enemy was changed into Turks for propaganda purposes. Morale may have been stiffened, but neither murals nor the stone watchtower added by Basil the Wolf could save Humor from marauding Turks, and the monastery was eventually declared derelict in the eighteenth century. The interior is also fully painted with the usual calendar of saints and martyrdoms, as well as St Luke painting the Virgin and Child. It is now a small convent – the villagers use another church, on a nearby hillock.

Twelve kilometres further up the Humor valley, three **trails to Suceviţa Monastery** have their starting point at the long strung-out, Slovak-populated village of **Poiana Micului**; the easiest (marked by blue stripes) follows a forestry track and takes about five hours.

Practicalities

Maxitaxis leave for Humor from Gura Humorului's Piaţa Republicii, next to the *Best Western*. Note that the number of schoolkids waiting for a seat often outstrips supply, and the ride can be very crowded and uncomfortable. By contrast, the walk is pleasant, and there's little danger here of a bus chasing you into a ditch; you can also walk on the west side of the stream. The monastery is 200m to the left of the cemetery.

Tiny Humor has some excellent **pensions** clustered near the monastery. The best of these are ⚶ *Casa Buburuzan*, opposite the monastery (℡0745/849 832, ℡&℻0230/572 861, ⓦwww.ruraltourism.ro/stela; ❸), which has five simple rooms with traditional rugs and TV, and two bathrooms; and *La Maison du Bucovine* (℡0744/373 931; ❸), around the left side of the stockade, which has rooms with private and shared bathrooms. The generous meals at *Casa Buburuzan*, which are prepared entirely from local products (largely their own), are especially recommended, and similar fare is available at *Colţ de Rai* (℡0230/572 800, 0745/978 140, ⒺLviorica.macovei@yahoo.com; ❸), in a peaceful location on the edge of the fields – follow the sign for the Schitul Buna Vestire near the bridge and fork right at once. *Vila Andreea*, 150m north of the monastery at Str. Ştefan cel Mare 157 (℡0745/558 629; ❸), is a cheaper option, with clean doubles, almost all en suite. Another choice, across the road, is *Casa Ancuţa* (℡0744/638 749; ❶), which has ten clean rooms with shared bath and serves delicious meals. *Casa Gheorgiţa*, another 100m north (℡0230/572 784, 0744/793 485; ❶), has upstairs rooms giving a lovely panorama of the valley. It's also possible to **camp** here. French is spoken at all of the above places (and by the nuns); owners' children are likely to speak English. There aren't any restaurants in the village, but the pensions can prepare meals if you call in advance. If you don't want to walk back, wait for a maxitaxi at the bench just below the fork in the road. If a local gives you a ride back to Gura Humorului, you should pay about €1, as for the maxitaxi.

Moldoviţa Monastery and Vatra Moldoviţei

Approaching from Gura Humorului, you'll find the **Moldoviţa Monastery**, a couple of hundred metres to the right shortly after entering the village of **Vatra Moldoviţei**. The monastery is a smaller complex than Suceviţa but equally well defended, its ivy-clad walls enclosing white stone buildings with lustrous black-shingled roofs. It was founded in 1532 by Stephen the Great's illegitimate son, Petru Rareş, during whose reign the Turks finally compelled Moldavia to pay tribute and acknowledge Ottoman suzerainty. The monastery was painted (inside and out) by Toma of Suceava in 1537, at a time when Petru Rareş still hoped to resist the Turks, despite the inexorability of their advance since the fall of Constantinople in 1453.

To raise morale, the Turkish siege was conflated with an earlier, failed attempt by the Persians in 626 AD. A delightfully revisionist *Siege of Constantinople* along the bottom of the south wall depicts Christians routing the infidel with arrows and cannons, and miraculous icons being paraded around the ramparts. Illustrated above this is the *Hymn to the Virgin*, composed by Metropolitan Sergius in thanksgiving for her intervention, while to the right is a lovely *Tree of Jesse*, with dozens of figures entwined in foliage. All the compositions are set on an intense blue background. There's a parade of saints and philosophers on the east end, but little remains on the north wall.

The open porch contains a fine *Last Judgement*, showing a crowd of dignitaries growing agitated as a demon drags one of their number, said to be Herod, by his beard towards the fires below, where Satan sits on a scaly creature – defaced with oddly formal German graffiti, left during the years 1786 to 1931 when the monastery was closed down by the Austrians. Within the church, saints and martyrs are decapitated en masse around the narthex, nave and the intervening tomb chamber, whose doorway bears an expressive *Virgin and Child*. Although built on a Byzantine plan, the church has Gothic windows and Renaissance internal doors. Note the charming mural of Petru Rareş with his wife and sons, dutifully presenting the monastery to Jesus, on the right as you enter the nave, and the superb Crucifixion and Pentecost in the conches (virtually side apses) of the nave.

Nuns' cells line the south side of the compound, while in the northwest corner rises an imposing two-storey *clisarniţa*, a guesthouse for passing dignitaries, with a circular tower. Built in 1612, this contains a **museum** of monastic treasures (Tues–Sun 10am–6pm) including a silver-chased Evangelistry presented by Catherine the Great and the wooden throne of Petru Rareş, a bust of whom stands outside.

There are no other important sights here, but of all the monastery villages Vatra Moldoviţei is the most isolated and picturesque. It's also the highest, and the air here feels cleaner than elsewhere in Bucovina. Shepherds' trails in the surrounding hills offer ample opportunities for **walking**, with the added incentive of a view of the monastery from above.

Practicalities

Vatra Moldoviţei can be reached by a limited number of bus and train services, only two of which continue to Suceviţa Monastery. Even hitching is likely to take a while, as there's not much traffic over the Ciumârna Pass, which separates the two monasteries. This is a very scenic route, built only in the

1950s by the army, with a viewpoint at the pass over the low, parallel Obcinele Bucoviniei ridges.

Trains to Vatra Moldoviței run from Câmpulung Moldovenesc via Vama (see below), heading up a branch line that runs through Vatra Moldoviței's main street, en route, confusingly, to Moldovița proper. Trains depart from Vama at 7.10am, 3.35pm and 11.24pm; the fourteen-kilometre trip takes 45 minutes. Returning, they pass through Vatra Moldoviței at 1pm and 7.15pm. A few buses and maxitaxis from Câmpulung Moldovenesc pass through Vama and Vatra Moldoviței on the way to Moldovița and the obscure Huțul hamlet of Argel. The two daily **buses** from Câmpulung to Rădăuți that cross the Ciumârna Pass leave Vatra Moldoviței at 7.45am and 3.30pm, reaching Sucevița Monastery at 8.30am and 4.30pm. In the other direction they leave Rădăuți at 6.30am and 3pm, passing Sucevița about half an hour later and Vatra Moldoviței about an hour after that.

There's not much **accommodation** in Vatra Moldoviței, and the best of it is the charming *Vila Crizantema* (T&F0230/336 116, 0745/922 447; ②) at Str. Mănăstirii 204, just off the main road on the way to the monastery. It's an attractive and comfortable pension with small and well-furnished en-suite doubles and simple, delicious meals. The friendly owners (they speak French; their children speak English) have information about fishing and trips to local handicraft studios. Another good choice is *Vila Lulu* (T0230/336 440; ②), a chalet-style pension/campground that's popular with Romanian families and has a bar, swimming pool, tennis court and trout pond, as well as the only restaurant in the area. It's 1.5km north of Moldovița Monastery on the road to Sucevița. Some villagers also rent rooms on request; ask the nuns at the monastery if you're interested. For self-catering, there are a few basic shops on the main street, as well as a Sunday market that stretches for 1km through the village.

VAMA, the next village west of Gura Humorului on the Suceava–Câmpulung highway and railway, is the jumping-off point for Vatra Moldoviței and offers more opportunities for staying overnight. It's pretty enough, but less remote and tranquil than Vatra Moldoviței. The best place to stay is *Casa Lucreția* at Str. Caragiale 18 (T0230/314 929, 0744/555 837, W www.casa-lucretia.ro; ④), a superb pension with huge rooms and fantastic food at affordable prices set on a hillside 400m west of the Moldovița road. It's a stylish modern building with a lovely patio and garden (with orchids on the lawn), and a very friendly dog. Other good guesthouses are well signed nearby, and in the centre you can stay at *Pensiunea Letiția* (T0230/239 212; ②), just south of the main road near the BRD minibank (with ATM), or *Casa Iasmina* (T0722/784 648; ②), just north to the west of the churches.

Sucevița Monastery

Sucevița Monastery – the last and grandest of the monastic complexes to be built in Bucovina – it is a monument to Ieremia Movilă, Prince of Moldavia, his brother and successor Simion, and his widow, Elisabeta, who poisoned Simion so that her own sons might inherit the throne. The family first founded the village church in 1581, followed by the monastery church in 1584, and its walls, towers and belfry in stages thereafter. The fortified church's massive, whitewashed walls and steep grey roofs radiate an air of grandeur; its **frescoes** – painted in 1596 by two brothers – offset brilliant reds and blues with an undercoat of emerald green.

Entering the monastery, you're confronted by a glorious *Ladder of Virtue* covering the northern wall, which has been largely protected from erosion by the building's colossal eaves. Flights of angels assist the righteous to paradise, while sinners fall through the rungs into the arms of a grinning demon. The message is reiterated in the *Last Judgement* inside the unusual fully closed porch – reputedly left unfinished because the artist fell to his death from the scaffolding – where angels sound the last trumpet and smite heathens with swords, Turks and Jews can be seen lamenting, and the Devil gloats in the bottom right-hand corner. Outside the south porch, you'll see the two-headed Beast of the Apocalypse, and angels pouring rivers of fire and treading the grapes of wrath. The iron ox-collar hanging by the north doorway is a *toacă*, beaten to summon the nuns to prayer.

The *Tree of Jesse* on the south wall symbolizes the continuity between the Old Testament and the New Testament, being a literal depiction of the prophecy in Isaiah that the Messiah will spring "from the stem of Jesse". This lush composition on a dark blue background amounts to a biblical Who's Who, with an ancestral tree of prophets culminating in the Holy Family. *The Veil* represents Mary as a Byzantine empress, beneath a red veil held by angels, while the *Hymn to the Virgin* is illustrated with Italianate buildings and people in oriental dress. Along the bottom is a frieze of ancient philosophers clad in Byzantine cloaks; Plato bears a coffin and a pile of bones on his head, in tribute to his meditations on life and death.

Inside the narthex, the lives of the saints end in burning, boiling, spit-roasting, dismemberment or decapitation – a gory catalogue relieved somewhat by paintings of rams, suns and other zodiacal symbols. Ieremia and Simion are buried in the small tomb chamber (*camera mormintelor*) between narthex and *naos*, in marble tombs carved with floral motifs. The frescoes in the tomb chamber are blackened by candle smoke, but those in the nave have mostly been restored and you can clearly see a votive picture of Elisabeta and her children on the wall to the right. Ironically, her ambitions for them came to naught as she died in a Sultan's harem – "by God's will", a chronicler noted sanctimoniously.

Sucevita's **museum**, to the east in what was once the council chamber, displays a collection of richly coloured tapestries, including sixteenth-century tomb covers featuring the portraits of founder Ieremia Movilă and his brother Simion, as well as icons, an ancient wooden lectern and illuminated manuscripts bound in silver. By climbing the **hill** behind the village church's graveyard, you can see the complex as a whole, and appreciate its magnificent setting at the foot of the surrounding hills, carpeted with firs and lush pastures. The **trail to Humor** starts next to the *Hotel Plai de Dor*. It's not well marked, but heading southeast from here it should take about five hours to reach **Poiana Marului**, 12km north of Humor along a logging road that's busy enough to make hitching feasible. Opposite the monastery a forestry road leads north, continuing over the watershed (as a trail marked with blue crosses) to Putna.

Practicalities

Sucevita lies midway between Moldovita Monastery, 30km to the west beyond the Ciumârna Pass, and Rădăuți, 17km to the east. The two daily **buses** from Rădăuți to Câmpulung that cross the Ciumârna Pass leave at 6.30am and 3pm, passing Sucevita about half an hour later and Vatra Moldoviței about an hour after that. In the other direction, they leave Vatra Moldoviței at 7.45am and 3.30pm, reaching Sucevita at 8.30am and 4.30pm. There are more to the east of Sucevita, with half a dozen a day heading for Rădăuți and three turning south at Marginea (known for its black pottery) for Solca, Gura Humorului and Câmpulung.

There are plenty of **places to stay** in Suceviţa, with most of the options to be found southwest of the monastery along the main road. The *Plai de Dor* (☎0230/417 400, 0744/609 494, ⓕ417 200, ⓦwww.plaidedor.ro; ➌), 3km from the monastery, is a new establishment with pool and sauna. Much more fun is the *Popas Turistic Bucovina* (☎&ⓕ0230/417 000, ⓦwww.popas.ro), 500m further southwest at km49, which has rooms in two charming wood-panelled houses (➌), and nine traditional cabins (➋), all rather overwhelmed by a range of modern villas (➍–➎). There's space for fifty camper vans (with electrical hook-ups) but not for tents, and facilities for tennis, archery and horse-riding, as well as a good restaurant.

Rooms are also available at the *Han Sucevita* (☎0230/563 824; ➋), a clean if dull motel at km53.5, 500m east of the monastery towards Rădăuţi; this also has a decent restaurant. Immediately beyond it is the *Reteaua Verde* ("Green Network") information centre (☎0745/333 402, ⓔinforeverde@yahoo.com), where you can enquire about local crafts, architecture and accommodation, as well as **walking trails**, for instance to Putna or Humor (you can arrange to have your baggage transferred). Also here is the excellent 🍴 *Pensiune Felicea* (☎0230/417 083, 0745/560 253, ⓔcazac_dama@yahoo.co.uk; ➋), with five bedrooms (with shared bathrooms) including two absolutely gorgeous ones in a traditional wooden house.

Putna Monastery

Putna Monastery lacks the external murals of the painted monasteries, but as the first of the great religious monuments of Southern Bucovina and the burial place of Stephen the Great, it is rich in historical associations and is as important to Romanian patriots as to the Orthodox faithful. The slow train ride past meandering rivers and fir-clad hills whets your appetite for **PUTNA** village, a wonderful jigsaw of wooden houses with carved gables and shingled roofs. Head west from the station to the main road and bear left for the monastery, which is at the end of a tree-lined drive, 1km further on, beyond a cemetery and a garish new church. Behind this church is the **wooden church** (Biserica de Lemn) of Dragoş-Vodă, supposed to be the oldest in Romania, built by Dragoş in 1346 and moved to its present location by Stephen in 1468. It's very picturesque, with no tower.

In 1466, Stephen chose the site of **Putna Monastery** (6am–10pm daily) by firing an arrow from the steep hill that now bears a white cross (see box, p.308). The monastery was burnt down and rebuilt in 1484, 1536 and 1691, ravaged by war three times in the seventeenth century, and repaired in the eighteenth (by Metropolitan Iacob Putneanu, who was born here and is buried in the porch), only to be damaged by an earthquake and restored again in 1902 and from 1955 to 1988. Its walls and bell tower were plainly intended for defence; in these less troubled times, they emphasize Putna's status as a patriotic reliquary. The bust of Eminescu inside the entrance identifies the national poet with Moldavia's national hero Stephen the Great, and commemorates the speech he gave here in August 1871, on the occasion of the monastery's quadricentennial: "Let us make Putna the Jerusalem of the Romanian people, and let us also make Stephen's grave the altar of our national conscience". The Pan-Romanian Festival he organized in 1871 was followed by others in 1904 and 2004.

The **church** itself is plain and strong, its facade defined by cable mouldings, blind arcades and trefoil windows, while the interior follows the usual configuration of three chambers: the sanctuary, containing the altar, at its eastern end, separated by the iconostasis from the nave, and the narthex, just inside the *pridvor* or porch – although at Putna this has also been enclosed to form an exonarthex. Prince Bogdan the One-Eyed, the wife of Petru Rareş, and Stephen's daughter and nephew are buried in the narthex, which is separated from the nave by two thick, cable-moulded columns. Here, a graceful arch and a hanging votive lamp distinguish the **tomb of Stephen the Great** from those of his two wives, both called Maria, and two sons. In the narthex lie voievodes Bogdan and Petru and their family members. The frescoes, illuminated by stained-glass windows, are now being repainted with gold leaf.

▲ Suceviţa Monastery

Outside, under the western eaves, stand three **bells**, the largest of which, cast in 1484, was only used to herald events such as royal deaths, and was last rung in 1918, when it was heard as far away as Suceava. Hidden from the communists for almost fifty years, it only reappeared after the 1989 revolution. The middle bell traditionally served for everyday use, while the end one was the gift of an archimandrite who repaired its sixteenth-century precursor. At the rear of the yard stands the **Treasury Tower**, the only building surviving intact from Stephen's time; it kept safe one of the world's most important collections of Byzantine embroidery, now in the Abbot's House to its north. The Abbot's House was converted in 1976 to a museum (daily 10am–5pm) and displays a wealth of icons, antique embroidery and illuminated manuscripts, as well as a fourteenth-century carved chest that once held the relics of St John the New. The monks' cells along the wall date from 1856 (the other Bucovina monasteries now house nuns, but Putna is still all male). Uphill and slightly to the east of the monastery, there's a curious hollowed-out rock with a door and window, reputedly once the **cell of Daniil the Hermit** – Stephen's confessor, whose prediction led to the foundation of Voroneţ Monastery (see p.306).

Practicalities

Putna is accessible by **train** from Suceava via Rădăuţi, but services on this route are few and very slow. There are four or five **maxitaxis** a day from Rădăuţi, where you need to change to a bus or maxitaxi to reach Suceviţa and the other monasteries. Alternatively, you could **hike to Suceviţa** in about five hours, a route now dubbed "the Prince Charles hike" after he walked it. Pick up the route (marked by blue crosses) from Putna station and follow the main valley for about an hour; ignore the turn-off to the left near a hut and a bridge, but take the next turning right, cross another bridge and carry on round to the left, which will bring you out at a forestry hut, called Canton Silvic 13. From here, stick to the track up to another forestry hut, Strulinoasa Sud, which deteriorates into a pony trail as it approaches the watershed, but improves once it descends into an open valley. You should reach the monastery about an hour and a half after crossing the watershed. If in doubt, take the major route at every junction, turning left at the only really ambiguous one.

The best **place to stay** is *Pensiunea Muşatini*, at Str. Mănăstirii 513A (☎0230/414 444, ⓦwww.pensiuneamusatini.ro; ❹), a big modern place on the main road near the station; all rooms have a balcony, minibar, a big TV and a good bathroom. Five cheaper rooms with a shared bathroom are being added in the attic, and there's also a restaurant, sauna and Jacuzzi. On the left just before the monastery, the friendly *Pensiunea Isidora* at Str. Mănăstirii 228A (☎0740/776 017, ⓦwww.pensiunea-isidora.ro; ❷–❸) has simple, clean rooms with shared/ private bathrooms and cable TV. Otherwise, try the good-value pensions *Carola* (☎0230/414 188, 0745/295 149; ❶), near the station, or *Aga* (☎0230/414 223; ❶) at. Str. Mănăstirii 165, on the right just before the monastery gates. The monastery itself has a guesthouse as well as a summer **campsite** with cabins, and various houses offer *cazare* (rooms). Other than the *Muşatini*, the *Bucovina* restaurant, halfway to the monastery, is the sole **place to eat**.

Rădăuţi

Going to and from Putna you're obliged to pass through the market town of **RĂDĂUŢI**, which plays a key role in the local transport network as the junction for roads to Suceava, Putna and the painted monasteries of Suceviţa and Moldoviţa (see p.311 & p.310). If you find yourself with a long wait between connections, there are a few sights of interest in the town centre, including the **Bogdana Church**, facing the roundabout just south of the centre of town, which makes a welcome refuge on a hot day. It's the oldest stone church in Moldavia, built between 1359 and 1365 and in its original state except for the addition of a closed porch in 1559 and a semi-fortified bell tower in 1781. Unlike the monasteries, it has aisles alongside the nave. A few blocks northwest at Piața Unirii 63, on the corner of Str. Republicii (the Sucevița road), the **Ethnographic Museum** (Muzeul Etnografic; Tues–Sun 9am–5pm) has a fine collection of local costumes and artefacts. It also displays **black pottery** made in Marginea and houses a studio which makes the painted ceramics of birds and flowers that are also typical of the region; items can be bought from their workshop. On the north side of the central plaza, Piața Unirii, the town's large synagogue faces down Str. Putnei. There's also a stud (*herghelia*), known for its Arabian horses, on Str. Bogdan Vodă, on the southern edge of town, where you can ride (ask at the stud for details; ℡0230/561 524 – Romanian only).

On Thursdays and Fridays, the town hosts a **bazaar** attended by peasants from the surrounding villages. To add to the mayhem, there's also a car spares market on Fridays that draws people from all over Moldavia, making this the worst time to try to change buses or get a room in town.

Practicalities

Rădăuți's **bus station** is 750m west of the centre of town on the Sucevița road. The **train station** is nearby, facing a modern private bus station used mainly by the hourly Suceava maxitaxis (which also pick up on Piața Unirii and a block east of the Bogdan church). To reach these from the main bus station, turn left on the side road and go a couple of hundred metres; in the other direction turn left out of the train station or right out of the new bus station. There's a good bike shop (which does repairs) opposite the train station. Local **maxitaxis** to Putna, Arbore, Ulma and Brodina wait on Piața Unirii.

If you need **accommodation**, the *Hotel Fast* (℡0230/560 060; ❹), within sight of the bus station at Str. Ștefan cel Mare 80, is the best in town, and has a decent bistro. The *Casa Albă* (℡0230/561 783; ❸), next to the train station at Str. Gării 9, is, despite its name, yellow, and is clean and comfortable. The restaurant here is a convenient place to while away a few hours, though the music can be loud. A slightly cheaper and more central alternative is *Hostel La Galan*, 200m north of the synagogue at Str. 1 Mai 9 (℡0230/561 987, ⓦwww.lagalan.ro; ❸), which has a restaurant but doesn't serve breakfast. A budget option, the gloomy *Hotel Azur*, can be found nearby at Calea Cernăuți 29 (℡&℻0230/564 718; ❶).

The best place to eat is *Orso Bruno*, opposite the synagogue at Str. Puteni 1, a cheery Italian restaurant and pizzeria. For supplies, the Merito supermarket is at Piața Unirii 5, on the south side of the plaza.

Arbore and Solca

Though **ARBORE** is often grouped together with the painted monasteries by virtue of its external frescoes, it is in fact merely a village church. This quibble aside, however, its kinship in form and spirit is undeniable. Arbore lies on a back road about 35km northwest of Suceava, and **public transport** from the city is intermittent, so that you'll be lucky to get any further than Sucevița or Gura Humorului the same day. **Buses** leave Suceava for Arbore on weekdays at 6.30am, noon and 6.30pm, and at 6.30am on Saturdays; alternatively, the church is 9km west from the village of Milisăuți (populated by Ukrainians who are known for making pickle barrels), served by maxitaxis from Rădăuți.

Opposite the cemetery, 1km east of Arbore's central crossroads, stands the **church** (daily 8am–8pm), built in 1503 by Luca Arbore, lord of the village and Marshal of Moldavia, who defended Suceava for forty years before he was treacherously killed in 1523. While its wooden stockade and stone bell tower are rustic enough, its frescoed walls and sweeping roof are as majestic as any monastic edifice. Like the painted monasteries, its **murals**, dating from 1541, follow iconic conventions inherited from Byzantium, which designated subjects for each wall, arranged in rows according to their hierarchical significance. This is obvious on the apses, where the angels and seraphim appear at the top; archangels and biblical saints below; then martyrs; and lastly a row of cultural propagators or military saints.

The best-preserved **frescoes** are found on the relatively sheltered south and west walls. The west wall has eight rows of scenes from Genesis and the lives of the saints, while the eaves and buttresses have protected half of the battered *Last Judgement* at the east end of the south wall, which consigns "heathens" awaiting hell to the top right-hand corner. In the courtyard lie two heavy, hollowed-out stone slabs used for mixing dyes to paint the walls, after they had been rendered with charcoal and lampblack. The founder now lies in the *pronaos*, under a Gothic baldachino with his wife and family members. The **iconostasis**, brought here in 1777 and blackened by centuries of smoke and incense, is at last being cleaned, together with the frescoes of the *naos*.

From Arbore, it's 7km west to a road junction 2km north of the centre of **SOLCA**, where a road leads 500m west to a **church** founded in 1614 by Ştefan Tomşa II. It's also possible to get here by occasional maxitaxis from Rădăuţi. The church was a monastery until 1785 and like other Bucovina monasteries was fortified and used as a garrison in times of crisis. It is tall and heavily buttressed, with the characteristically Moldavian octagonal belfry on a double star-shaped base. The exterior is plain except for its Renaissance doors and windows; the church is unpainted but there are strong cable mouldings inside and a score of processional crosses and banners, as well as a horse-drawn hearse and bier outside.

Just before the monastery you'll pass the *Han Solca* (☎0230/477 508; ❷), a local inn which has six three/four-bed rooms and one double, all en suite with a fridge and cable TV. Clean & friendly, it's been nicely renovated.

A less worthwhile detour is to **Părhăuţi**, midway between Suceava and Solca, where there is a small church built in 1503, notable for its frescoed, two-level porch.

Cacica

The old salt mine of **CACICA**, 12km south of Solca, was founded in the late eighteenth century by Austrian emperor Franz Joseph II. The first miners to be settled here were Polish, and they named the village after wild ducks (*kaczki* in Polish) found nesting in nearby swamps. Workers of other nationalities followed, and by the mid-nineteenth century Cacica was known for its ethnic mix and nicknamed "little Austria". The Czechs, Germans and Slovenes who once laboured here are long gone, but there is still a sizeable Polish community and there are lots of Polish visitors to the church (a Minor Basilica) and summer events.

The **old mine** (daily 10am–4pm) is in the centre of town, adjacent to the modern mine. Inside, a moderately treacherous staircase descends to a large chamber 25m below the surface, where there is a chapel featuring salt reliefs. Stairs from the chapel open into the next cavern, which is adorned with biblical sculptures, also carved from salt. From here, a long hallway leads to a swimming pool and a tennis court. The rest of the more than 50km of underground passages are off limits to the public.

The Cacica air is said to be beneficial for those suffering from respiratory diseases. However, the salt vein here is mixed with clay and needs to be heated to the point of evaporation to crystallize: for many years, fuel oil was used in this process, and today a strong odour of petroleum acts as a deterrent to would-be convalescents.

The easiest way to visit Cacica is as part of a monastery tour, but several slow **trains** run here each day from Suceava, stopping 2km east of the town centre and the mine; one leaves Suceava at 8.30am, arriving in Cacica around 45min later, while another in the opposite direction departs Cacica at noon.

Câmpulung Moldovenesc and Vatra Dornei

Câmpulung Moldovenesc and **Vatra Dornei**, to the west of the painted monasteries, are chiefly of interest as bases for **hiking** in the Rarău and Giumalău massifs, and as way-stations en route to Transylvania or Maramureş; Vatra Dornei also serves as a springboard for reaching several **festivals** just across the Carpathians. There's less reason to come out of season – particularly once the snow arrives, a month or two earlier than in the lowlands. Both towns are situated along the main train line and highway from Suceava to Cluj.

Câmpulung Moldovenesc

CÂMPULUNG MOLDOVENESC, 72km from Suceava and 37km from Vatra Dornei, is a logging town with a concrete centre and some old wooden houses in the backstreets. Being strung out along the valley, it has two **train stations** – alight at Câmpulung Est only if you want to hike straight off up Rarău (or to the *Hotel Eden*). To reach the centre from Câmpulung Moldovenesc station, go ahead then left along Calea Transilvaniei, the main street, which becomes Calea Bucovinei east off the town centre. Turning left from the train station and following Str. Viitorului for a couple of blocks parallel to the rail tracks brings you to the **bus station**, and the market (with a small Ukrainian bazaar), from where Str. Alexandru Bogza leads south to a pseudo-Byzantine church with a gaudy mosaic roof, on Calea Transilvanei just west of the centre. Another longish block east by the tracks brings you to memorials to the Red Army soldiers killed in 1944 and to political prisoners under communism (a telling conjunction) at Str. D. Cantemir. Left of here is a **riverside park** with embankment paths and decent footbridges east and west; right is the main pedestrianized plaza on Calea Bucovinei – don't miss the impressively kitsch bronze **statue of Prince Dragoş and the aurochs** (see box, p.298).

The **Museum of Wooden Art** (Muzeul Artei Lemnului; Tues–Sun 9am–5pm), beside the gaudy pseudo-Byzantine church at Calea Transilvaniei 10, demonstrates the absolute ubiquity of wooden products in traditional life here. The displays upstairs include fish traps, log beehives, a honey centrifuge, a butter churn and mould, wooden ploughs, hayforks, ceremonial hatchets, carved shepherds' staves, musical instruments, plates, spoons and mugs, and everything else from limebark sandals up to oil and fruit presses and carts and sleighs, with black-and-white photos of them in use. Many are intricately carved, but all have the beauty of functionality and some are very imaginative. There are also some sculptures inside the front door, as well as portrait plaques and modern abstract sculptures; in the yard at the rear are a few wooden houses and gateways. There are captions in English, French and German, but sadly no mention of which kinds of wood are used.

Câmpulung also boasts the late Professor Tugui's vast **collection of wooden spoons** (Colecţia de Linguri din Lemn), a bizarre delight that's said to be the only one of its kind in Europe, just west of the centre (and near the station) at Str. Gheorghe Popovici 1. Look for the numerous colourful plates affixed to the exterior.

Practicalities

Buses leave at 7am and 2.30pm for Rădăuţi via Vatra Moldoviţei (for Moldoviţa Monastery) and Suceviţa Monastery; there are also regular services to Iaşi and Piatra Neamţ. The best hotel in Câmpulung Moldovenesc is the new, three-star *Eden* (℡0230/314 733, Ⓦwww.hotel-eden.ro; ❻), with pool, sauna, fitness facilities and Internet access, at Calea Bucovinei 148, on the edge of town 1km west of the Câmpulung Est station. There's also a tightly packed row of bungalows here (❸). More conveniently located is the high-rise *Zimbrul*, a clean, warm hotel at Calea Bucovinei 1–3 (℡0230/314 356, Ⓕ314 358, Ⓦwww .rarau-turism.ro; ❹). Although it's in a communist apartment block, the *Restaurant-Pensiune Bucovina*, at Calea Transilvaniei 13 (℡&Ⓕ0230/311 883, Ⓦwww.pensiunebucovina.ro; ❹), is in fact pretty nicely presented, with clean tidy rooms. To reach the smaller *Hotel Minion* (℡&Ⓕ0230/314 694; ❸), walk past the *Zimbrul* and turn left at the plaza. It's 300m north of here, at Str. D. Cantemir 26B, and has boxy rooms with decent bathrooms and cable TV. The best budget bet is *Pensiunea Incom* (℡0230/307 074; ❷), an old-style workers' guesthouse with shared bathrooms, set back to the north at Calea Bucovinei 43.

Apart from the hotels, **restaurant** options are limited to the usual Italian imitations. Even so, *La Taverna*, opposite the *Zimbru* at Calea Bucovinei 2, is well above the Romanian average. The *Grand Pizzeria del Corso* at Calea Bucovinei 26 is also decent. There's an **Internet café** (Mon–Sat) hidden inside a photocopy shop at Calea Transilvanei 27 – look for the sign that says *Pro Vogue*.

The Rarău Turism agency (Mon–Fri 8am–4pm, ℡0230/314 358, Ⓔrarau -turism@sv.ro) inside *Hotel Zimbrul*, has information about hiking, caving and mountain accommodation, and offers a slightly pricey day tour of the monasteries. You can also contact Fundaţia Baltagul's Ecotourism Club at Calea Bucovinei 13 (℡0722/272 626, Ⓦecotourismclub@flash.ro), who are involved with marking hiking trails and developing equestrian tourism, especially around Moldoviţa. The CFR office (Mon–Fri 8.30am–3.30pm) is across the square from the *Zimbrul*, next to a disused synagogue, dating from 1873 and in good condition. A hundred metres further east, the post office is on the main pedestrianized plaza, and the Merito supermarket just north at Str. D. Cantemir 2.

The Rarău massif

The **Rarău massif** to the south of Câmpulung is a popular **hiking** spot, with its dense spruce forests harbouring lynx, bears, roebuck and other **wildlife**. Most visitors base themselves at the *Rarău* cabana (❷), 14km and three to four hours' walk up the road from Câmpulung Est station. Reservations can be made through the Rarău tourist agency in Câmpulung. From the cabana, a four-hour trail marked by red triangles leads past the **Pietrele Doamnei** ("Princess's Rocks"), three huge Mesozoic limestone towers, to reach the ancient **Slătioara Secular Forest** of fifty-metre-high firs and spruces. Another route (red-striped) runs southwest from *Rarău* to the *Giumalău* cabana (three to four hours), from where you can hike on to Vatra Dornei via the Obcina Mică peak (five to six hours). None of these trails is feasible in winter.

The road **to Vatra Dornei** crosses the Mestecăniş Pass (1096m), by way of two villages with Ukrainian-style **wooden churches**, to enter the Bistriţa valley. The *Mestecăniş* cabana (●) is here, 8km east of the large village of Iacobeni, the site of a murder by poison recounted in Gregor von Rezzori's *The Snows of Yesteryear* (see p.483), and where trains usually halt after emerging from a tunnel below the pass. Accommodation is available at the *Roşan* cabana in the village of Mestecăniş (℡0742/469 589, ✉eugene@go.ro; ●) and the good new *Pensiunea Braduţul* in Iacobeni (℡0745/357 891; ❸).

Vatra Dornei

Originally a logging town, **VATRA DORNEI** has been better known as a spa since Habsburg times, and has dabbled in skiing and other outdoor activities since the 1970s. The skiing facilities in particular have developed in recent years, and though the slopes themselves are not challenging, Vatra Dornei is an increasingly popular winter destination for Romanians and Ukrainians, and is rich in hotels and pensions, if not sights. Across the river by a footbridge from Vatra Dornei Băi train station (more useful than the Vatra Dornei station, east of the centre), you'll see the ochre and white Baroque casino, once the focal point for visitors but now derelict and awaiting investment for renovation. Behind this is the spa's **park**, home to a few red squirrels, a mineral spring piped through a mock-Gothic tower, a neo-Byzantine church and a small restaurant opposite an onion-domed bandstand. Turning left at the casino and following the river east, you'll come to a junction: to the right is Str. Unirii (the Piatra Neamţ road), with a small **Museum of Natural Science and Hunting** (Muzeul de Ştiinţe Naturale şi Cinegetica; Tues–Sun 10am–6pm) at no. 3. The **Ethnographic Museum** (same hours) is back in the town proper on the corner of Str. Eminescu and Str. Gării, in the Florentine-Renaissance town hall built in 1897.

Arrival

Vatra Dornei's **bus station** and **market** are both 200m east of the casino, although a few long-distance maxitaxis call at the train station instead. The excellent **tourist information office**, across from Vatra Dornei Băi station at Str Gării 2 (℡0230/372 767; Mon–Fri 9am–5pm), has town **maps** showing hotels and pensions, as well as a map of area **hiking trails.**

Accommodation

Most of Vatra Dornei's **hotels** are located on the spa side of the river. There are a dozen or more **pensions** (all ●), many located in the maze of side streets between the ski lifts. Alternatively, Antrec's county office (℡0230/371 306, ●www.biosan.ro), at Str. Runc 2 (at the western end of Str. Eminescu), can help you find **homestay accommodation**. At Str. Runc 6 is *Camping Autoturist* (℡0230/371 829), where cabins (●) are available in summer, and there's also tent space at the *Pensiunea Dornelor* (℡0230/374 973) at Str. Unirii 198, at the exit from town towards Piatra Neamţ. One excellent agrotourism pension, easily accessible only if you're travelling by car, is ⚜*Poiana* (℡0745/809 234; ❷), located in the mountain village of Poiana Negri, 15km southwest of Vatra Dornei.

Alpin Str. Tudor Vladimirescu 5A ℡0230/370 038, ●www.hotel-alpin.ro. By the Parc ski drag, this is the most luxurious place in town, with a spa (with indoor pool, dry and wet saunas, Jacuzzi, solarium and massage, all included in the room rates), lift, Internet access and a good restaurant. ❺–❽

Carol Str. Republicii 3 ℡0230/374 690, ●www .hotelcarol.ro. Over the footbridge from the train station and just to the right of the casino, this classy place has good rooms and obliging staff who can arrange spa treatments and other activities. ❹–❻

Maestro Str. Republicii 1 ☎&🅵 0230/375 288, ⓦ www.hotelmaestro.ro. Just to the left of the casino, this has smaller rooms, plus a sauna, Jacuzzi, gym, Internet access and a fine restaurant. ❺
Pensiunea Monica Str. Alunis 5 ☎ 0230/375 154. At the top of Str. Independenţei, 100m west of the park, this has garishly furnished doubles and triples, and a yard full of chickens. ❶

Silva Str. Dornelor 12 ☎ 0230/371 033, ⓔ chirutavelentina@yahoo.com. By the station, this is a modern hotel, with sauna and gym. ❺
Vila Musetti Str. Republicii 19 ☎&🅵 0230/375 379. West of the centre, this Italian-themed hotel is a friendly and comfortable mid-range option. ❸

Eating and drinking

Of the hotel **restaurants**, the one in the *Carol* is the grandest, while those in the *Alpin*, *Maestro* and *Silva* serve as decent alternatives. Another restaurant worth seeking out is *Camy Lact* on Str. Coşbuc, which also has a small shop where local cheeses are sold. *Les Amis*, at Str. Luceafărului 15 (on the pedestrianized street leading north from the footbridge by the station) has average fare and blaring music, though there is an English menu; next door is the adequate *Cofetărie-Patiserie Dolce Vita*. Around the corner, opposite the train station, is a 24hr supermarket.

Activities

There are fine hikes on all sides of Vatra Dornei, as shown on maps available at the tourist office and in hotels such as the *Silva*. One of these (which takes approximately 22hr), to the Rotunda Pass in the Rodna mountains (marked by blue stripes), begins at the Băi station. It then runs up Str. Luceafărului and west along Str. Eminescu, past an abandoned Moorish-style synagogue, and leaves town past a self-styled motel (actually a bar full of hunting trophies), and the **campsite**; you'll need your own camping gear for this hike as there are no cabanas along the route. A shorter trail (marked with blue then red stripes), with more dramatic scenery and a choice of mountain cabanas, heads east from the Băi station to Giumalău (5.5hr), Rarău (9–10hr from Băi station) and Câmpulung Moldovenesc (11–13hr from Băi station). The **chairlift** at the top of Str. Negreşti is open year-round (daily 10am–5pm but sometimes closed from 1–3pm; €1 each way); from Str. Republicii, walk up Str. G. Coşbuc or Str. Negreşti, following the *telescaun* signs. The lift takes 25min to ascend to the peak of Dealul Negrii (1300m), where ravens circle over alpine meadows. Bring provisions; the café at the top of the lift is frequently closed. There's also a shorter ski-drag, the Teleschi Parc, immediately west of the park, that operates only in winter, with ski rental shacks and a bar at its foot. An Olympic cross-country ski centre is near the campsite at the top of Str. Runc.

The headquarters of the Căliman National Park are at Str. 22 Decembrie 5 (☎ 0230/371 104, ⓦ www.calimani.ro). The local Salvamont mountain rescue group can arrange guided hiking, ice-climbing, cross-country skiing and mountain biking, and rafting is a particular speciality. Contact Petru Ariciuc at Str. Eminescu 17 (☎ 0230/372 767, ⓔ salvamontdorna@yahoo.com).

Routes to Maramureş and Transylvania

From Vatra Dornei, you can head southeast towards **Neamţ county**, northwest into **Maramureş**, or west into **Transylvania**. Seven buses a day follow the scenic Bistriţa valley down to Poiana Largului, at the northern end of Lake Bicaz and in the vicinity of the Ceahlău massif (see p.279); three of them carry on to Piatra or to Târgu Neamţ.

The route to Maramureş heads up the valley past such lovely villages as **Ciocăneşti**, where Huţul houses with decorated facades are perched on hillocks.

There are ski-drags here and newish hiking trails on both sides of the valley, and facilities for equestrian tours. The various guesthouses have a central booking system (☏07739/189 396, ✉accommodation@ciocanesti.com; ❷–❸). The village holds a Painted Egg Festival before Easter and a trout fishing festival in July or August. Just north, **Botos** has a new **wooden church** in the Ukrainian style: very broad and square, with one large and four small cupolas. The good *Hotel Mario & Ema* (☏0230/575 879, ⓦwww.hotelmario-ema.ro; ❷) with cabins (❶) is north of the centre of **Cârlibaba**, founded by Zipser German foresters in the late eighteenth century. Eight kilometres north of the village the road forks towards the Rotunda Pass into Transylvania, and the Prislop Pass into Maramureş, where the **Horă at Prislop Festival** occurs on the second Sunday in August. One bus daily (leaving Vatra Dornei at 1.30pm) crosses the mountains to Vişeu de Sus in Maramureş, while two others run as far as Cârlibaba, from where you could probably hitch over the pass. Heading north instead of west from Cârlibaba, a battered road that ends at the Ukrainian border passes through the tiny Huţul hamlet of Moldova Suliţa. From there it's 7km up a dirt path to the **Lucina Stud**, where the famous Hutzul horses, used for cavalry in Austrian times, are bred. It's possible to ride here for around €10 per hour, although the stud's hotel is semi-derelict.

Of the three routes into Transylvania, the most dramatic is via the **Tihuţa Pass** – otherwise known as the Bârgău Pass, where Bram Stoker located Dracula's castle. Along the way, you'll find accommodation in **Poiana Ştampei**, at the *Vila din Carpaţi* (☏0230/379 312; ❺), located high up beside the main road. There are also a few **pensions** here. Three buses a day from Vatra Dornei run through the pass en route to Bistriţa. Travelling **by train**, you'll take a more northerly route via Ilva Mică; the Leşu Ilvei halt, one stop before Ilva Mică, is within walking distance of Leşu (see p.255). The third route, only possible if you're driving, crosses the 1271-metre-high **Rotunda Pass**, which is prone to blizzards.

Travel details

Trains

Adjud to: Braşov (1 daily; 4hr 45min); Ghimeş (8 daily; 1hr 55min–2hr 45min); Iaşi (2 daily; 2hr 45min–4hr 45min); Siculeni (5 daily; 2hr 50min–3hr 55min); Suceava (8 daily; 2hr 35min–4hr 25min); Târgu Mureş (1 daily; 7hr 25min).

Bacău to: Bicaz (6 daily; 1hr 35min–2hr 45min); Iaşi (5 daily; 2hr 10min–3hr 25min); Piatra Neamţ (9 daily; 1hr–1hr 45min); Suceava (11 daily; 1hr 50min–3hr 10min).

Galaţi to: Braşov (1 daily; 5hr 25min); Bucharest (5 daily; 3hr 15min–3hr 50min); Cluj (1 daily; 13hr 30min); Constanţa (1 daily; 8hr 15min); Iaşi (1 daily; 3hr 45min); Mărăşeşti (5 daily; 2hr 10min–2hr 55min); Suceava (1 daily; 6hr 45min); Târgu Mureş (1 daily; 10hr); Timişoara (1 daily; 16hr 50min).

Ghimeş to: Adjud (8 daily; 1hr 55min–3hr 40min); Braşov (1 daily; 2hr 50min); Galaţi (1 daily;

4hr 45min); Miercurea Ciuc (4 daily; 1hr 15min–1hr 30min); Siculeni (6 daily; 50min–1hr 15min); Suceava (1 nightly; 5hr); Târgu Mureş (1 daily; 5hr 25min); Timişoara (1 daily; 12hr).

Gura Humorului to: Câmpulung Moldovenesc (10 daily; 40–55min); Suceava (9 daily; 50min–1hr 10min); Vama (10 daily; 20min); Vatra Dornei (8 daily; 1hr 40min–2hr 10min).

Iaşi to: Bucharest (6 daily; 5hr 30min–7hr); Cluj (1 daily; 8hr 35min); Constanţa (1 daily; 8hr 15min); Suceava (5 daily; 1hr 50min); Timişoara (3 daily; 14hr 30min–16hr).

Mărăşeşti to: Iaşi (1 daily; 5hr 20min); Panciu (1 daily; 30min); Suceava (5 daily; 3hr 10min–5hr).

Paşcani to: Bacău (19 daily; 1hr–1hr 45min); Iaşi (7 daily; 1hr–1hr 25min); Suceava (21 daily; 40min–1hr 10min); Târgu Neamţ (4 daily; 50min).

Piatra Neamţ to: Bacău (9 daily; 1hr 10min–1hr 35min); Bicaz (6 daily; 35–50min); Bucharest (1 daily; 5hr 30min).

Suceava to: Bucharest (6 daily; 6hr 15min–6hr 50min); Cacica (2 daily; 1hr); Câmpulung Moldovenesc (9 daily; 1hr 25min–2hr 25min); Cluj (6 daily; 6hr 30min–7hr 15min); Iaşi (8 daily; 1hr 55min–2hr 45min); Putna (3 daily; 2hr 35min–3hr); Rădăuţi (5 daily; 1hr 15min–1hr 40min); Timişoara (5 daily; 12hr 30min–14hr); Vama (9 daily; 1–2hr); Vatra Dornei (9 daily; 2hr 20min–3hr 30min).
Vama to: Moldoviţa (3 daily; 48min).
Vatra Dornei to: Cluj (6 daily; 3hr 50mni); Iaşi (4 daily; 4hr 40min–5hr); Ilva Mica (9 daily; 1hr 30min–2hr 15min); Suceava (5 daily; 2hr 35min–3hr 20min).

Buses and maxitaxis

Bacău to: Adjud (6 daily); Braşov (9 daily); Bucharest (24 daily); Comăneşti (17 daily); Constanţa (4 daily); Galaţi (1 daily); Ghimeş (4 daily); Gura Humorului (1 daily); Iaşi (20 daily); Oneşti (7 daily); Piatra Neamţ (hourly); Sfântu Gheorghe (1 daily); Slănic Moldova (3 daily); Suceava (2 daily); Târgu Neamţ (3 daily); Vatra Dornei (2 daily).
Brăila to: Bucharest (3 daily); Constanţa (1 daily); Focşani (2 daily); Galaţi (every 20min); Tulcea (2 daily).
Buzău to: Bacău (24 daily); Bucharest (every 45min); Braşov (2 daily); Iaşi (4 daily); Ploieşti (hourly).
Câmpulung Moldovenesc to: Cluj (2 daily); Gura Humorului (8 daily); Iaşi (3 daily); Moldoviţa (4 daily); Piatra Neamţ (1 daily); Rădăuţi (3 daily); Suceava (7 daily); Târgu Mureş (1 daily); Vatra Dornei (7 daily).
Galaţi to: Brăila (every 20min); Braşov (3 daily); Bucharest (15 daily); Constanţa (13 daily); Focşani (5 daily); Iaşi (4 daily); Piatra Neamţ (5 daily); Sibiu (2 daily); Soveja (1 daily).
Gura Humorului to: Arbore (1 daily); Bacău (1 daily); Câmpulung Moldovenesc (8 daily); Cluj (1 daily); Iaşi (3 daily); Moldoviţa (1 daily); Piatra Neamţ (2 daily); Rădăuţi (3 daily); Solca (1 daily); Suceava (12 daily); Târgu Mureş (1 daily); Vatra Dornei (5 daily); Voroneţ (1 daily).
Iaşi to: Bacău (20 daily); Bicaz (3 daily), Bistriţa (1 daily); Brăila (2 daily); Braşov (1 daily); Bucharest (15 daily); Câmpulung Moldovenesc (3 daily); Cluj (1 daily); Comăneşti (2 daily); Constanţa (2 daily); Durău (4 daily); Galaţi (4 daily); Gura Humorului (3 daily); Oneşti (1 daily); Otopeni airport (2 daily); Piatra Neamţ (15 daily); Rădăuţi (6 daily); Sibiu (2 daily); Slănic Moldova (2 daily); Suceava (12 daily); Târgu Mureş (2 daily); Târgu Neamţ (17 daily); Tulcea (2 daily); Vatra Dornei (1 daily).
Oneşti to: Bacău (33 daily); Braşov (11 daily); Bucharest (6 daily); Galaţi (1 daily); Iaşi (2 daily);

Piatra Neamţ (2 daily); Slănic Moldova (2 daily); Târgu Ocna (10 daily).
Piatra Neamţ to: Agapia (2 daily); Bacău (hourly); Bicaz (every 30min); Braşov (4 daily); Bucharest (10 daily); Câmpulung Moldovenesc (1 daily); Cluj (1 daily); Comăneşti (1 daily); Constanţa (1 daily); Durău (Mon–Sat 2 daily); Galaţi (5 daily); Gheorgheni (3 daily); Gura Humorului (2 daily); Iaşi (15 daily); Oneşti (2 daily); Rădăuţi (2 daily); Sibiu (1 daily); Suceava (3 daily); Târgu Mureş (1 daily); Târgu Neamţ (hourly); Topliţa (1 daily); Văratec (2 daily); Vatra Dornei (2 daily).
Rădăuţi to: Arbore (5 daily); Braşov (1 daily); Bucharest (4 daily); Câmpulung Moldovenesc (3 daily); Gheorgheni (1 daily); Iaşi (5 daily); Putna (4 daily); Solca (4 daily); Suceava (hourly); Sucevița (8 daily); Târgu Neamţ (1 daily); Vatra Dornei (1 daily).
Suceava to: Bistriţa (4 daily); Braşov (2 daily); Bucharest (5 daily); Câmpulung Moldovenesc (9 daily); Cluj (2 daily); Constanţa (2 daily); Gura Humorului (12 daily); Iaşi (12 daily); Moldoviţa (1 daily); Pătrăuţi (Mon–Fri 7 daily, Sat–Sun 5 daily); Piatra Neamţ (1 daily); Rădăuţi (hourly); Solca (Mon–Fri 3 daily, Sat 2 daily); Târgu Mureş (2 daily); Târgu Neamţ (5 daily); Văratec (Mon–Fri 6 daily, Sat–Sun 3 daily); Vatra Dornei (7 daily).
Târgu Neamţ to: Agapia (5 daily); Bacău (1 daily); Bicaz (1 daily); Braşov (1 daily); Câmpulung Moldovenesc (1 daily); Durău (6 daily); Gura Humorului (2 daily); Iaşi (6 daily); Neamţ Monastery (3 daily); Piatra Neamţ (13 daily); Rădăuţi (2 daily); Sihistria (1 daily); Suceava (4 daily); Târgu Mureş (1 daily); Văratec (3 daily); Vatra Dornei (2 daily).
Vatra Dornei to: Bacău (2 daily); Bistriţa (4 daily); Cârlibaba (3 daily); Cluj (2 daily); Gura Humorului (3 daily); Iaşi (1 daily); Piatra Neamţ (3 daily); Poiana Largului (4 daily); Rădăuţi (1 daily); Suceava (7 daily); Târgu Mureş (2 daily); Târgu Neamţ (3 daily); Timişoara (1 daily); Vişeu (1 daily).

Flights

Bacău to: Bucharest (TAROM; five flights a week); Suceava (TAROM; five flights a week); Timişoara (Carpatair; daily Mon–Sat).
Iaşi to: Bucharest (TAROM; Tues & Thurs 3 daily; Mon, Wed, Fri 2 daily); Timişoara (Carpatair; Mon–Sat daily).
Suceava to: Bucharest (TAROM; six flights a week); Timişoara (Carpatair; daily).

International trains

Iaşi (Nicolina) to: Chişinău, Moldova (1 daily; 5hr 10min).

Suceava Nord to: Cernăuţi, Ukraine (1 daily; 5hr 30min); Kiev, Ukraine (1 daily; 20hr); Moscow, Russia (1 daily; 32hr); Sofia, Bulgaria (1 daily; 18hr).

International buses

Bacău to: Chişinău, Moldova (2 daily).
Galaţi to: Varna, Bulgaria (2 daily).

Iaşi to: Bălţi, Moldova (2 daily); Chişinău, Moldova (2 daily); Istanbul, Turkey (1 daily).
Suceava to: Cernăuţi, Ukraine (5 daily); Chişinău, Moldova (1 daily); Balţi, Moldova (1 daily); Przemyşl, Poland (via Ukraine; 1 daily); Istanbul, Turkey (1 daily); Athens, Greece (4 weekly).

International flights

Iaşi to: Vienna (Sun–Fri daily).

Maramureş

HUNGARY
N
UKRAINE
⑤
MOLDOVA
③
④
⑥
UKRAINE
②
①
⑦
SERBIA
Black Sea
BULGARIA

MARAMUREŞ

325

CHAPTER 5 **Highlights**

❉ **Wooden churches** With their magnificent spires, wooden churches, such as the finely crafted structure at Şurdeşti, are an integral part of the Maramureş landscape. See p.335

❉ **Prison Museum, Sighet** Illuminating and moving tributes to the victims of communism in Sighet's notorious prison. See p.342

❉ **Winter Customs Festival, Sighet** Lively Christmas spectacle featuring folk music, wacky costumes and traditional customs. See p.344

❉ **Merry Cemetery, Săpânţa** Exuberantly coloured and beautifully crafted wooden headstones in one of Romania's most unusual attractions. See p.344

❉ **Logging train, Vişeu de Sus** Jump aboard the early-morning *mocăniţa* for a picturesque ride up the Vaser valley. See p.352

❉ **Rodna mountains** Beautifully unspoilt mountain range offering some of the country's most enjoyable and secluded hiking. See p.355

▲ Traditional weaving

5

Maramureş

Romania has been described as a country with one foot in the industrial future and the other in the Middle Ages – still an accurate enough characterization of **Maramureş**, crammed up against the borders with Hungary and Ukraine and little changed since Dacian times. Within 30km of the heavily industrialized town of Baia Mare, thickly forested mountains and rough roads maintain scores of villages in a state of almost medieval isolation, amid a landscape of rounded hills with clumps of oak and beech and scattered flocks of sheep.

The historic county of Maramureş lies to the north of the Gutâi Pass; in 1968, this was merged with parts of Someş and Satu Mare counties to form present-day Maramureş, though for convenience we also include in this chapter the town of Satu Mare and the Oaş region, both in Satu Mare county. Sitting roughly in the centre of the region, **Baia Mare**, the capital of Maramureş, makes a good base from which to explore the county's **villages**, which are the main reason for visiting the area: the majority of buildings are made of wood by skilled craftsmen, with carvings decorating the eaves, doorways and windows of the houses that line each main street. Every family shares a compound – fenced with timber, brush or latticework, and entered via a beamed gateway (*poarta*), the size of which indicates the family's status and prosperity – with its livestock, and produces virtually everything that they wear, use and eat. Nowhere else in Europe do **folk costumes** persist so strongly, the men wearing tiny *clop* straw hats and medieval rawhide galoshes (*opinchi*) or archaic felt boots bound with thongs, and the women weaving boldly striped *catriniţa* aprons with cloth from the water-powered fulling mills, and embroidering intricate designs on the wide-sleeved cotton blouses worn by both sexes – most conspicuously during markets and **festivals**, when the villages are ablaze with colour. On Sunday afternoons people promenade, and there may be a public dance, either in the street or on a purpose-built wooden platform. Just as folk costume endures, so villagers have retained their traditional **religion** (a mixture of pagan beliefs and the Uniate rite), myths and codes of behaviour.

Most interesting of all is the marvellous **woodwork** of Maramureş: the village compound gateways, many elaborately carved with symbols such as the Tree of Life, sun, rope and snake, continue to be produced today, and are only surpassed in their intricacy by the *biserici de lemn* or **wooden churches**, mostly built during the eighteenth century when this Gothic-inspired architecture reached its height. Originally founded upon huge blocks of wood rather than stone, they rear up into fairy-tale spires or crouch beneath humpbacked roofs, and are generally sited on the highest ground in the village to escape seasonal floods. While many wooden churches are in a poor state, around twenty of the most

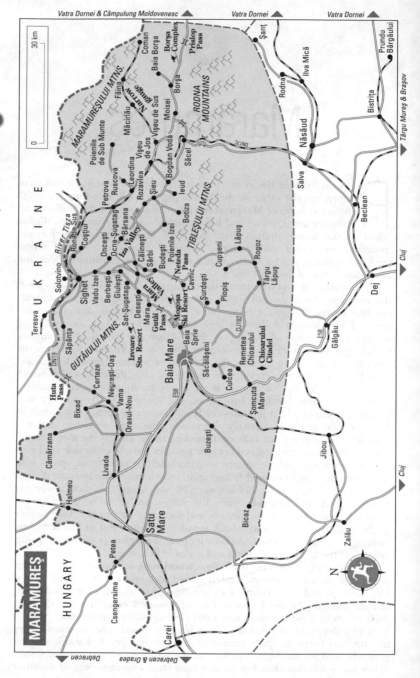

MARAMUREȘ

valuable have been restored in recent years, eight of which are on UNESCO's World Heritage list. In recent years many new monasteries have also been constructed, in a modern version of the traditional style. Wooden houses, on the other hand, are vanishing from Maramureș' villages, as modern homes are built and old timbers sold off to panel bars across western Europe.

It's particularly worth making the effort to see the towering wooden church at **Şurdeşti**, the beautiful church paintings at **Bârsana**, **Rogoz** and **Deseşti**, the frescoes and icons of **Călineşti** and **Budeşti**, the superb prison museum in **Sighet** and the quirky "Merry Cemetery" at **Săpânţa**. Further afield in the Iza Valley, the visions of hell painted inside the church at **Poienile Izei** are the most striking images you'll see in Maramureș, while the frescoes at **Ieud** are the most famous. Maramureș also offers hiking in the peaceful **Rodna mountains** on the borders with Moldavia and Ukraine.

Getting around is tricky, as side roads are rough and **public transport** is patchy, especially at weekends. The alternatives to renting a car are cycling – which is a great way to see the region, especially given the short distances between villages – or hitching, though be prepared for intermittent lifts or short rides in the back of carts or vans. **Hotel accommodation** is generally limited to towns, but there are **homestay schemes** in many villages; otherwise, come prepared to camp wild, and bring plenty of supplies. If you get really stuck in a village, ask the priest (*popă* or *preot*) for advice, and try to repay any hospitality with gifts (tea and coffee are ideal).

Baia Mare

Lying to the south of the Gutâi and Igniş mountains, **BAIA MARE**, the largest town in Maramureș, makes a good base for forays into the surrounding countryside. As a major non-ferrous metals centre, mining has waxed and waned here since the fourteenth century when, under its Magyar name of Nagybánya, it was the Hungarian monarchs' chief source of gold. The town has an attractive old core, now being restored, and a couple of worthwhile museums, the best of which is the **Village Museum**.

Arrival and information

The **train** and **bus stations** lie some 2km west of town on Str. Gării, with maxitaxis linking them to the centre. Your first stop for **information** should be MaramureşInfoTurism, in the Prefectura (County Hall) at Str. Şincai 46 (☎0262/216 674, ⓦwww.visitmaramures.ro); for dates of village **festivals** contact the Cultural Inspectorate at the same address (☎0262/212 042). **Information** is also available from the Mara Holiday agency (☎0262/226 656, ⓔagentie@hotelmara.ro) inside the *Mara* hotel, which can also organize horseback excursions and caving trips. Otherwise, there's the Mara agency (Mon–Fri 9am–5pm; ☎0262/411 043), hidden away on the north side of Str. Culturii 1, just off Piaţa Revoluţiei, which sells a good **map** of the region, essential for touring the villages. **Hiking maps** and gear can be bought at Mountain Experts, Str. Şincai 1.

The **CFR office** is at Str. Victoriei 57 (Mon–Fri 7am–8pm; ☎0262/221 613) and the **TAROM** office at B-dul. Bucureşti 5 (Mon–Fri 9am–6pm; ☎0262/221 624), with a flight to Bucharest early on weekday mornings. **Cars** can be rented from Rentamar, Str. Victoriei 47 (Mon–Fri 9am–5pm, Sat 9am–1pm; ☎0262/226 774). There's **Internet** access at Andernet, B–dul. Traian 12.

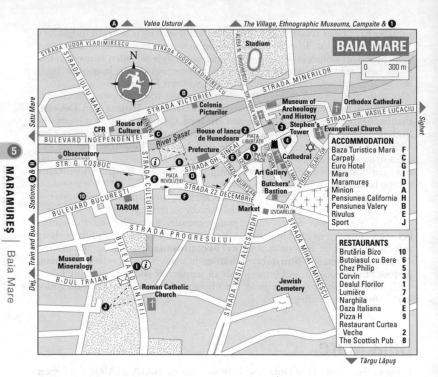

Map labels:

Valea Usturoi · The Village, Ethnographic Museums, Campsite & ❶

Stadium

BAIA MARE

0   300 m

STRADA TUDOR VLADIMIRESCU · STRADA TUDOR VLADIMIRESCU

STRADA IULIU MANIU

ALEEA N. GHEORGHIU

STRADA MINERILOR

STRADA VICTORIEI

N

Colonia Picturii

Museum of Archeology and History

Orthodox Cathedral

STRADA DR. VASILE LUCACIU

House of Culture

CFR

River Şasar

House of Iancu de Hunedoara

PIAŢA LIBERTĂŢII

Stephen's Tower

Evangelical Church

BULEVARD INDEPENDENŢEI

Observatory

Prefecture

PIAŢA PĂCII

Cathedral

STR. G. COŞBUC

PIAŢA REVOLUŢIEI

STRADA GH. ŞINCAI

Art Gallery

Butchers' Bastion

STRADA 22 DECEMBRIE

TAROM

Market

PIAŢA IZVOARELOR

STRADA CULTURII

BULEVARD BUCUREŞTI

STRADA PROGRESULUI

B-DUL BUCUREŞTI

Museum of Mineralogy

Roman Catholic Church

Jewish Cemetery

B-DUL TRAIAN

BULEVARDUL UNIRII

STRADA VASILE ALECSANDRI

STRADA MIHAI EMINESCU

Satu Mare · Sighet · Dej, Train and Bus Stations, ❾ & ❶

ACCOMMODATION

Baza Turistica Mara	F
Carpaţi	C
Euro Hotel	G
Mara	I
Maramureş	D
Minion	A
Pensiunea California	H
Pensiunea Valery	B
Rivulus	E
Sport	J

RESTAURANTS

Brutăria Bizo	10
Butoiasul cu Bere	6
Chez Philip	5
Corvin	3
Dealul Florilor	1
Lumière	7
Narghila	4
Oaza Italiana	E
Pizza H	9
Restaurant Curtea Veche	2
The Scottish Pub	8

Târgu Lăpuş

Accommodation

Baia Mare has a good selection of **hotels**, most of them affordable; in addition, if you contact the Mara Holiday agency (see p.329) or Antrec Maramureş, Str. Şincai 46 (☏0262/214 118, ⓦwww.antrec.ro), you can also arrange a **homestay** in a local village. There are also a couple of nearby **cabanas**: the *Apa Sărăta* (*Salty Water*), 7km west of town on the Satu Mare road, reached by city bus #7 (last at 10.30pm), and the *Firiza*, at Firiza dam, 10km north of town and served by bus #18 eight times a day (last at 8.30pm, or 10.20pm from the station). The nearest **campsite** is also here, attached to the *Capcioara* guesthouse (☏0262/222 099). Beyond Firiza, at a trout farm 18km from Baia Mare, the *Complex Listriţa*, Str. Blidari 13B (☏0262/270 216, ⓦwww.complexlostrita.ro; ❹) is a good modern **guesthouse**.

Baza Turistica Mara Str. Culturii 7a ☏0262/217 123, ⓦwww.e-tineretemm.ro. Down an alley on the south side of Piaţa Revoluţiei, between a pharmacy and Constructiv Grup, this is a youth hostel with large, clean, shared rooms with basin, toilet and TV but shared showers. ❶

Carpaţi Str. Minerva 16 ☏0262/214 812 or 3 or 4, ⓦwww.hotelcarpati.ro. A pricey little hotel with modestly sized rooms and small bathrooms – it's worth paying slightly more for the better rooms – but in a nice location by the river. ❽

Euro Hotel B-dul. Bucureşti 23 ☏0262/222 405, ⓦwww.eurohotel-bm.ro. A pretty decent modern

hotel towards the station, with Internet access, gym, sauna, bowling and the city's only indoor swimming pool. Some rooms are a/c. ❺–❻

Mara B-dul. Unirii 11 ☏&ⓕ0262/226 656, ⓦwww.hotelmara.ro. This big, white cumbersome building southwest of the centre conceals comfortable rooms. ❻

Maramureş Str. Şincai 37a ☏0262/216 555. Reasonable, if somewhat dull, the *Maramureş* is frequented in the main by tour groups. It has a gym. ❺

Minion Str. Malinului 22a ☏0262/276 056. A small private hotel with swimming pool and sauna, but it's all rather tacky in style. ❺

Pensiunea California Str. Lăpuş 5 ☎ 0262/250 005, Ⓦ www.pensiuneacalifornia.ro. Out towards the station, this chalet-style guesthouse has comfortable rooms with TV. ❸

Pensiunea Valery Str. Victoriei 38A ☎ 0741/291 979. Comfortable en-suite rooms with TV in a new building opposite the Colonia Picturilor; plenty of single rooms. ❸

Rivulus Str. Culturii 3 ☎ & Ⓕ 0262/216 302, Ⓦ www.hotelrivulus.ro. Newly refurbished, with stylish design, a lift, and a/c and Wi-Fi in all rooms; the *Rivulus* is not huge but it's right in the city centre. ❻

Sport B-dul. Unirii 14a, but actually one block west on Str. Transilvaniei ☎ 0262/226 869. A classic (that is very basic and very cheap) sport hotel intended for visiting teams but open to all. Plenty of space, unless there's a big tournament on. ❶

The Town

Baia Mare's main attraction is its open-air **Village Museum** (Muzeul Satului; Tues–Fri 9am–5pm, Sat & Sun 10am–2pm), ten minutes' walk north of the town on Florilor hill, and although not as well maintained as many of the country's other open-air venues, it has an eye-catching collection. There are over a hundred examples of peasant houses, wine presses, watermills and other structures from the surrounding region, but in particular look out for the wooden church – raised in 1630 in the village of Chechiş, just south of Baia Mare – and, close by, the homestead from Berbeşti, featuring a fine carved gate with the Tree of Life motif. The **Museum of Ethnography and Folk Art** (Muzeul de Etnografie şi Artă Populară; same hours), on nearby Str. Dealul Florilor, offers a neatly presented array of agricultural and viticultural implements, ceramics, textiles and garments.

The heart of Baia Mare's **old town** is **Piaţa Libertăţii**, a beautifully restored square lined with sixteenth- to eighteenth-century houses; its eastern half, and parts of the neighbouring streets, are pedestrianized. At no. 18, the thick-walled **Casa Elisabeta** was the **house of Iancu de Hunedoara**, fifteenth-century Regent of Hungary; next door is the house where the great Hungarian actor Lendvay Márton was born in 1807. To the south of the square rises the fifty-metre-high **Stephen's Tower**, built in 1442–6 and all that remains of a twin-naved cathedral that burnt down in 1769; the adjacent Baroque pile, built by the Jesuits in 1717–20, subsequently took over as the city's Roman Catholic cathedral. Behind the cathedral at Str. 1 Mai 8, the **Art Gallery** (Tues–Fri 9am–4pm, Sat & Sun 10am–2pm) contains eighteenth- and nineteenth-century paintings on wood and glass, and a number of canvases by artists of the **Nagybánya School** (see box, p.332). Much of the work is now in Budapest, however, and the stuff here is attributed to the "Baia Mare School" – a sly piece of Romanian revisionism. There's more art on show north of the river at the **Colonia Picturilor** at Str. Victoriei 21, where temporary exhibitions (Tues–Fri 9am–4pm, Sat & Sun 10am–2pm) are held in a villa that housed the Nagybánya School in 1910–12. Temporary shows (notably of photography) are also held in the **Galeria Millennium** (Tues–Sun 10am–4pm) on the east side of Piaţa Libertăţii, and the modern library next to the House of Culture.

The **Reformat church** of 1809 at the junction of Str. Monetăriei and Str. Podul Viilor, just north of Piaţa Libertăţii, is a landmark, topped by what seems to be a giant red diver's helmet, which appears in many works of the Nagybánya School. Nearby, in the old mint building (1738–42) at Str. Monetăriei 1, is the **Museum of Archeology and History** (Muzeul de Arheologie şi Istorie; Tues–Fri 9am–4pm, Sat & Sun 10am–2pm), whose exhibits include coverage of the local mining industry, with Bronze Age metalwork and coins produced in this very mint and elsewhere, as well as around 300 clocks, sixteenth- to

The Nagybánya School

The **Nagybánya (or Baia Mare) School** was responsible for transforming Hungarian art at the close of the nineteenth century. Its founder was **Simon Hollósy** (1857–1918), born of Armenian stock in Sighet and trained in Munich, where he was influenced by the refined naturalism of Jules Bastien-Lepage, and in 1886 set up his own school there. From 1896, he brought his students to a summer school in Baia Mare, where he painted *en plein air* for the first time. An exhibition in 1897 of the school's paintings was seen as marking the start of a new era in Hungarian art and the school became known as the "Hungarian Barbizon", although the area's motifs and colours were closer to those of Provence.

In 1902, Hollósy suffered a creative crisis, and the leadership of the school was taken over by **Károly Ferenczy**; tuition fees were abolished, and the embittered and jealous Hollósy left to set up a rival school in Técső, now the Ukrainian town of Tyachiv, just downstream of Sighet. Ferenczy suffered a similar crisis in 1910, and did little work thereafter. Of the second generation of artists, the most gifted was Cavnic-born Jenő Maticska (1885–1906). After his untimely death, Béla Czóbel, Csába Vilmos Perlrott, Sándor Ziffer and others revolted against creeping stagnation; their 1906 exhibition, influenced by German Expressionism and by Cézanne and Matisse, again marked the start of a new era in Hungarian art. After World War I the school was opened to both Hungarian and Romanian students – up to 150 a year – but interest in it faded away in the 1930s and the school closed its doors.

Other renowned artists associated with the school include Eugen Pascu (1895–1948), Tibor Boromisza (1880–1960), János Krizsán (1886–1948) and Krizsán's wife Antónia Csikos (1887–1987).

nineteenth-century religious books and an impressive collection of medieval ceramics. The **Museum of Mineralogy**, towards the stations at B-dul. Traian 8 (Muzeul de Mineralogie; Tues–Sun 9am–5pm), displays a myriad varieties of rocks, crystals and ore deposits extracted from the region's mines.

Running east from Piața Libertății, **Strada Dr Vasile Lucaciu** has some interesting old buildings whose cellars are entered from the street. At the early twentieth-century Orthodox Cathedral, head south along Str. Olarilor (which follows the line of the old city walls) to reach Piața Izvoarelor, where the fifteenth-century **Butchers' Bastion** (Bastionul Măcelarilor) overlooks the market place in which the Robin Hood-style outlaw Pintea Viteazul (Pintea the Brave) was shot in 1703.

Eating, drinking and entertainment

The choice of **restaurants** in Baia Mare is improving fast. In addition to the places reviewed below, the restaurant in the *Mara* hotel is also perfectly agreeable, serving very reasonably priced Romanian and international dishes. For **buying food supplies**, the best supermarket is the Artima by the bus station (Mon–Sat 8am–10pm, Sun 8am–6pm).

As for **drinking**, try the traditional *Butoiasul cu Bere* at Str. Șincai 13, or the *Café-Club Narghila*, just off Piața Libertății at Str. Vasile Lucaciu 4 (daily 5pm–3am). *Chez Philip*, Piața Libertății 4, on the south side of the square, is a fashionable café-bar specializing in Belgian beers; the *Scottish Pub*, on the northeast corner of Piața Revoluției, is, of course, totally Romanian. The city's best **nightclub** is the *Pasha Club*, on Piața Libertății at the corner of Str. Podul Viilor (℡0741/060 445; ⓦwww.pasha-club.ro).

The **Chestnut Festival** (Sărbătoarea Castenelor), held over the last weekend of September, celebrates – appropriately enough – the chestnut season, with exhibitions and a riotous beer festival. The **Zilele Culturale Maramoreşeni** (Maramureş Cultural Days) take place in the first week of May.

Restaurants

Brutăria Bizo B-dul. Bucureşti 8. A fine patisserie that also serves baguette sandwiches and cold soft drinks.

Corvin Piaţa Libertăţii 16. Medieval-style restaurant serving hearty Romanian dishes including game. Daily 11am–midnight.

Dealul Florilor Str. Bernard Shaw 14. In a semi-rural setting just east of the Village Museum with fine views over the city, this is an understandably popular spot for weddings at weekends.

Lumière Piaţa Libertăţii 3. Very stylish restaurant-café-gelateria appealing to the city's affluent youth.

Oaza Italiana Str. Culturii 3. In the *Hotel Rivulus*, this is less an Italian oasis than a pleasant Romanian restaurant that also serves pizza. Daily 10am–midnight.

Pizza H B-dul. Bucureşti 6. Bright and breezy, better-than-average pizzeria that also dabbles in pasta and chicken dishes.

Restaurant Curtea Veche Str. Lăcătuş 4. A slightly touristy place serving good Romanian food in a historic building. Daily 10am–10pm.

Southern Maramureş

The area to the south of Baia Mare was part of Someş county until it was dismembered in the 1968 reforms. The southwestern corner of the present Maramureş county, beyond the River Someş, is known as **Codrul**; the area immediately south of Baia Mare is **Chioarul**; and further east is **Lăpuş**. Whilst the landscape of southern Maramureş is not as dramatic as that in the north, it is unremittingly lovely, and you could easily spend a couple of days pottering around the region's fine wooden churches, at settlements such as **Baia Sprie**, **Şurdeşti** and **Plopiş**. Folk costumes here are similar to those of Maramureş proper, although the tall straw hats are unique to the region.

Codrul and Chioarul

The most accessible village in Codrul is **BUZEŞTI**, 30km west of Baia Mare. Its wooden church, built in 1739, has a bulbous steeple that bears witness to the penetration of Baroque influences into this area, while its four corner pinnacles echo the Gothic towers of both Transylvania and Hungary. Much more remote, in the far western extremity of the county (though served by two or three buses a day from Baia Mare), is **BICAZ**, whose Orthodox church and wall paintings both date from the early eighteenth century. As in Buzeşti, a new church has been built here and the old one, though recently repaired, is disused.

Many of the villages of Chioarul have old churches, but the most interesting is at **SĂCĂLĂŞENI**, just 10km south of Baia Mare. Rebuilt at the end of the seventeenth century, the church originally dates from 1442, with a carved doorway and paintings from 1865. There's a good **motel** here: the simple, but clean and modern, *Moara Veche* at no. 137 (☎0262/289 353; ❷), which has two-, three- and four-bed rooms and a swimming pool. Just 2km to the southwest, in **CULCEA**, is an early eighteenth-century wooden church with plastered walls – it's hidden away on a small elevation just beyond the ugly modern church. Continuing south for a further 5km, you'll come to the larger village of **REMETEA CHIOARULUI**, which also has a fine church, dating from 1800 – to gain entry, pop across to the neighbouring modern church, where the caretaker should have the key. The village is also the starting point for the three-hour return trip south through the gorge of the River Lăpuş to the ruins of the sixteenth- to eighteenth-century **Chioarului citadel**

There is a strong tradition of building **wooden churches** right across Eastern Europe, from northern Russia to the Adriatic, but in terms of both quality and quantity the richest examples are in Maramureş. From 1278, the Orthodox Romanians were forbidden by their Catholic Hungarian overlords to build churches in stone, and so used wood to ape Gothic developments. It's long been thought that most were rebuilt after the last Tatar raid in 1717, acquiring large porches and tall towers, often with four corner-pinnacles, clearly derived from the masonry architecture of the Transylvanian cities. However in 1996–7 a dendrochronological study showed that the wood used in many churches (notably those of Cormeşti, Breb and Onceşti) was far older, the oldest dating from 1367.

In general, the walls are built of blockwork (squared-off logs laid horizontally) with intricate joints, cantilevered out in places to form brackets or consoles, which support the eaves. However, in Maramureş, Western techniques such as raftering and timber framing have enabled the development of the high roofs and steeples that are characteristic of the area, rather than the tent roofs or stepped cupolas used further north. Following the **standard Orthodox ground plan**, the main roof covers the narthex and *naos* and a lower one the sanctuary; the *naos* usually has a barrel vault, while the narthex has a low-planked ceiling under the tower, its weight transmitted by rafters to the walls and thus avoiding the need for pillars. The main roof is always shingled and in many cases double, allowing clerestory windows high in the nave walls, while the lower roof is sometimes extended at the west end to form a porch (exonarthex or *pridvor*).

Inside, almost every Maramureş church has a choir gallery above the west part of the *naos*; always a later addition, as shown by the way it is superimposed on the **wall paintings**. These extraordinary works of art were produced by local artists in the eighteenth and early nineteenth centuries, combining the icon tradition with pagan motifs and topical propaganda. They broadly follow the standard Orthodox layout, with the *Incarnation* and *Eucharist* in the sanctuary (for the priest's edification), the *Last Judgement* and moralistic parables such as the *Wise and Foolish Virgins* in the narthex (where the women stand), and the *Passion* in the *naos*; the treatment of the last, however, changed in the nineteenth century as the Uniate Church gained in strength, with more emphasis on the *Ascension* and the *Evangelists*.

Sixteenth-century **icons** (such as those found in Budeşti) show a northern Moldavian influence; the seventeenth-century Moisei school was the first to show the imprint of the Renaissance, and from the late eighteenth century, Baroque influences were added. The first of the major painters was **Alexandru Ponehalski**, who worked from the 1750s to the 1770s in Călineşti and Budeşti, in a naïve post-Byzantine style with blocks of colour in black outlines. From 1767 to the 1780s, **Radu Munteanu** worked around his native Lăpuş and in Botiza, Glod and Deseşti, painting in a freer and more imaginative manner. A far more Baroque style developed in the first decade of the nineteenth century, with **Toader Hodor** and **Ion Plohod** working in Bârsana, Cormeşti, Văleni, Năneşti and Rozavlea.

Since 1989, there has been a **renaissance of the Uniate or Greco-Catholic faith**, repressed under communism and forcibly merged with the Romanian Orthodox Church: many parishes have reverted to Greco-Catholicism, reclaiming their churches; in others, one church is now Orthodox and the other Uniate, while in some villages the congregations have even agreed to share one building. Many villages have started to build large, new churches, making it more likely that you'll find the wooden churches locked up – even on a Sunday. Finding the key-holder can be problematic, but ask around long enough and someone is bound to help out. Remember that people **dress conservatively** here, and the wearing of shorts, particularly for visiting churches, is not appropriate.

(6km each way). Ten kilometres further south of Remetea, on the DN1C, is **ŞOMCUTA MARE**, where choirs and bands assemble for the **Stejarul festival** on the first or third Sunday of July – check with the Mara Holiday agency (see p.329) in Baia Mare. Five buses a day run from Baia Mare to Şomcuta Mare, via Săcălăşeni and Remetea.

Lăpuş

In the centre of the Lăpuş area, the small, nondescript town of **TÂRGU LĂPUŞ** has no hotel but various pensions and numerous houses offering **private rooms** should you wish to make the town your base. One good option is *Pensiunea Elena*, Str. Stadion 19 (℡0744/753 430, ✉pensiunea_elena@yahoo .com; ❷). Seven daily buses from the station (five minutes' walk east of the centre across the bridge) run to Baia Mare and the surrounding villages, many of which boast fine wooden churches. The best examples are the two in **ROGOZ**, 5km east of Târgu Lăpuş, which despite the arrival of a large modern church, remain well maintained: the Uniate church, built around 1695 in Suciu de Sus and moved here in 1893, stands within the grounds of the Orthodox church, built of elm some time between 1661 and 1701. The latter is unique thanks to its naturalistic horse-head consoles, which support the roof at the west end, and its asymmetric roof, which has a larger overhang to the north to shelter a table where paupers were fed by the parish. Some of the paintings by Radu Munteanu were painted over in the 1830s, but even so this remains one of the most beautifully decorated churches in Maramureş: look out for a *Last Judgement*, to the left inside the door, and the *Creation* and the *Good Samaritan*, on the *naos* ceiling. There are four buses a day from Baia Mare heading for Băiuţ or Grosii Tibleşului via Rogoz, as well as local services from Târgu Lăpuş. Buses to Băiuţ also pass through **LĂPUŞ**, 7km east of Rogoz, which boasts a village museum and a seventeenth-century wooden church with carved and painted walls. The oldest murals in the church date from the early eighteenth century, and its icons include the first works of Radu Munteanu (see box opposite). **CUPŞENI**, 11km north of Rogoz (just one bus a day from Târgu Lăpuş), is one of the most idyllic villages in the region and home to some of its best carpenters. Here, the upper church, built in 1600, has a fine tower, but badly damaged paintings, and the tiny lower church, moved here from Peteritea in 1847 by the Uniates, was beautifully painted in 1848 by Radu Munteanu.

Baia Sprie, Şurdeşti and Plopiş

The small town of **BAIA SPRIE** lies 10km east of Baie Mare along the Sighet road (served by city bus #21), and, like most Romanian mining towns, it is highly multiethnic, as reflected by its multiplicity of churches. On Piaţa Libertăţii, just north of the modern centre (at the Şurdeşti junction), you'll find the massive Neoclassical Roman Catholic church (1846–58) and Calvinist church; down a lane to the right is the wooden-roofed Orthodox church, built in 1793. From Baia Sprie, you can detour off the main road to reach some classic Maramureş villages, on the fringes of the Chioar district.

The magnificent Uniate wooden church at **ŞURDEŞTI**, 10km south of Baia Sprie, stands just beyond the village on a hill overlooking a stream. Built in the early eighteenth century, the church is clad in thousands of oak shingles, and boasts a forty-five-metre-high tower, three times the length of the church itself, which was the tallest wooden structure in Europe until the new monasteries at Bârsana and then Săpânţa (see p.348 and p.344) topped it; you can climb up into the tower and roof space from the porch for excellent views of the surrounding countryside. Inside the church, which someone from the painted house near the stream will unlock for you, there are remarkable wall paintings dating from 1810, and also some interesting late eighteenth-century icons. **Rooms** are available at *Pensiunea Amethyst* (☎0744/883 216; ❷).

PLOPIŞ, 1km or so south across the fields, has a similar, though slightly smaller, church, built between 1798 and 1805, which features four corner turrets on its spire, a characteristic of many wooden churches here and in the Erdehát region of Hungary. If you continue north along the minor road, it eventually leads through the former mining town of Cavnic (now reinventing itself as a ski resort), over the **Neteda Pass** (1039m) and down to **Budeşti** (see p.339); there are five buses a day from Baia Mare to Cavnic via Şurdeşti, of which one continues to Budeşti and Sighet; otherwise, you'll have to hitch.

Northern Maramureş

The historic county of Maramureş – and the heart of Maramureş proper – lies north of Baia Sprie, beyond the Gutâi Pass. Here, you'll find idyllic rolling countryside, still farmed in the traditional manner, together with some of the finest **churches** in the region, set in picturesque villages where customs have remained virtually unchanged for centuries. The main town is **Sighet**, worth stopping off at for a couple of splendid museums, and a good place to base yourself for visiting the villages.

The Mara valley

Four kilometres northeast of Baia Sprie, a road breaks off the main DN18 up to the **Mogoşa ski complex**, 3km east, where there's accommodation at the simple *Motel Mogoşa* (☎0262/260 800; ❷) and the very comfortable *Şuior Hotel* (☎0262/262 080; ❹), which also has sporting facilities. Back on the DN18, the road zigzags up to the 987-metre-high **Gutâi Pass**, at the top of which is the *Hanul lui Pintea*, a basic **restaurant with rooms**. Not far beyond, a paved road heads left to the **Izvoare ski resort** (☎0262/270 318, ⓦwww.statiuneaizvoare.ro), 27km from Baia Mare, where there's **accommodation** at the *Cabana Izvoare* and the three-star *Ignis* and *Merişor* hotels (both ☎0262/276 984). There follows a winding fifteen-kilometre-long descent into the Mara valley, past the splendidly carved houses and gateways of **Mara** village. One kilometre beyond Mara, the village of **DESEŞTI** conceals a lovely wooden church, hidden among some trees to the left, above the road and the trackbed of an old forestry rail line now used as a cycle path. Built in 1770, the church has a fine example of the "double roof" or clerestory style that enabled the builders to construct windows high up inside the nave to increase the illumination. Nevertheless, it's dark inside and even with candles you'll find it hard to pick out the marvellous **wall paintings**. Executed by Radu Munteanu in 1780, the paintings seem more primitive and less stylized than the frescoes in the Moldavian monasteries that were painted some two hundred years earlier. Boldly coloured in red, yellow and white, the figures of saints and martyrs are contrasted with shady-looking groups of Jews, Turks, Germans, Tatars and Franks. The frescoes also include folk-style geometric and floral motifs, while the inscriptions are in the Cyrillic alphabet – Old Church Slavonic remained the liturgical language of Romanian Orthodoxy until the nineteenth century. Deseşti's museum complex, made up of preserved and furnished wooden houses, also offers **accommodation** (❷).

Some 2km along the road, in the village of **HĂRNICEŞTI**, the next church dates from about 1679 and houses some fine icons; in 1942, the apse was widened, and in 1952 the porch was added, so that now the tower seems disproportionately short. The **Casa Iurca** at Str. Principală 8, by the exit to Sighet, is a museum house, built in 1792 and supposedly the only remaining eighteenth-century noble home in Maramureş; it's possible to **stay** here (☎0262/372 933; ❷). The church stands just north of the junction of a back road east towards Ocna Şugatag and Budeşti; two buses a day from Baia Mare to Ocna Şugatag take this road via **HOTENI**, 3km east of Hărniceşti. Hoteni has its day in the spotlight on the first or second Sunday of May. As in many of the villages of the Mara valley, this is a celebration of the **First Ploughman**, a fertility rite that dates back at least to Roman times. In the ritual, a dozen youths adorn bulls and lead them to the house of the chosen First Ploughman, the hardest-working farmer in the village, for him to plough the first field of the season, before dunking him into a stream or pool and commencing the feasting and dancing. Check with the Mara Holiday agency (see p.329) in Baia Mare or Etnic Tours in Sighet (see p.341) for details of the next event. Hoteni also has a wooden church, built in 1657 and brought here in 1788. If you can, stay at *Pensiunea Popicu*, no. 37A (☎0262/425 267 or 0742/979 048; ❷), run by famed local musician and cultural activist Ioan Pop.

Continuing a couple of kilometres further along the main road towards Sighet brings you to **SAT-ŞUGATAG**, site of another church, this one located, unusually, on a flat piece of land beside the road. Accessed via a finely carved wooden gate, this beautifully compact church was built in 1642 and painted internally in 1783, and features a twisted rope motif just below the eaves. The graveyard contains beautiful stout wooden crosses and the village itself has some quite picturesque cottages. A minor road heads off from here to Ocna Şugatag, Călineşti, Sârbi and Budeşti, with another right turn 2km north leading to **MĂNĂSTIREA GIULEŞTI**, a tiny village with a tiny church, founded in 1653 and now shared by Orthodox and Uniate congregations; it boasts fine paintings from 1653 and 1783, as well as late eighteenth-century icons by Alexandru Ponehalski.

The main road continues northwards to **GIULEŞTI**, one of the main villages in the Mara valley, which has a stone church and, like many of these villages, an ancient **watermill**: its two mill wheels grind wheat and corn, with the miller traditionally taking one cupful of each hopper-load. Everything is made of wood, right down to the little channels siphoning off water to lubricate the spindles of the wheels, and the whole setup doubles as a fulling mill, its large wooden mallets beating the cloth clean.

Further north, on the edge of **BERBEŞTI**, a 300-year-old carved wooden crucifix (*troiţa*), adorned with four mourning figures and symbols of the sun and moon, stands beside the road, a throwback to the time when travel was considered a hazardous undertaking; no journeys were made on a Tuesday, deemed an unlucky day, and it was believed that after sundown ghosts and vampires (*strigoi*) roamed the highways, seeking victims. From Berbeşti, the DN18 continues to Vadu Izei, the mouth of the Iza valley (see p.348), and beyond to Sighet (see p.340).

The Cosău valley

At **Fereşti** (2km southeast of Berbeşti), where the wooden church dates from the 1790s, a minor road turns off to the right and leads up the **Cosău valley** – the most interesting of all in Maramureş – to several picturesque villages where traditional costume is still worn. These villages can also be approached from the

Maramureş funerals

The **Cult of the Dead**, central to Romanian culture, is particularly well developed in Maramureş, where the rituals are fixed and elaborate; if anything is omitted, it's believed that the soul will return as a ghost or even a vampire. There are several phases that cover the separation from the world of the living, preparation for the journey, and entry into the other world. A dying person asks forgiveness of his family and neighbours, who must obey his last wishes. Black flags are hung outside the house where the deceased lies for three days, a period during which the church bells are rung thrice daily, neighbours pay their respects and women (but not men) lament the deceased in improvised rhyming couplets.

When the priest arrives at the house on the third day, the wailing and lamenting reach a climax before he blesses a bucketful of water, extinguishes a candle in it, and consecrates the house with a cross left etched on the wall for a year. The coffin is carried by six married male relatives or friends, stopping for prayers (the priest being paid for each stop) at crossroads, bridges and any other feature along the way, and then at the church for absolution. The funeral itself is relatively swift, with everyone present throwing soil into the grave and being given a small loaf with a candle and a red-painted egg, as at Easter; these must also be given to passers-by, including tourists (if you're ever offered one, be aware it would give great offence if you refused it). The knot-shaped loaves or *colaci* bear the inscription NI KA ("Jesus Christ is victorious"), which is stamped in the dough by a widow or some other "clean woman" using a special seal called a *pecetar*. The seal's handle, usually wooden, is often elaborately carved with motifs such as the Endless Column, the Tree of Life, wolf's teeth or a crucifix.

Three days later there is another *pomană* or memorial meal, when bread is again given to all present; after nine days, nine widows spend the day fasting and praying around the deceased's shirt; six weeks and then six months after the funeral, the absolution is repeated with another meal, as the dead must be given food and drink, and after a year a feast is given for all the family's dead. Mourning lasts for one year, during which time the close family may not attend weddings or dances and women wear black. As elsewhere in Romania, *Şergare* (embroidered napkins) are hung over icons in the church or over plates on house walls in memory of the dead. The Uniates also remember their dead on All Souls' Day.

Marriage is seen as essential in Maramureş, so much so that if a person of marriageable age (in fact from eight years old, the age of first confession) dies unmarried, a **Marriage of the Dead** (Nunta Mortului) is held. A black flag is carried, while the deceased and a bridesmaid or best man (and, in the case of a man, a stand-in bride) dress in wedding costume, although everyone else wears mourning garb.

south over the Neteda Pass (see p.336); from the west, using the road via Hoteni; or from Bârsana, to the east.

Across the river from Fereşti is small, tranquil **CORNEŞTI**, where the church (painted in 1775) dates in part from 1406, making it the second oldest in Maramureş; there's another **watermill** here, which also serves as a laundry. Here, women beat clothes with carved wooden laundry bats beside the river, often improvising songs and verses as they work, using a distinctive local technique called singing "with knots", in which the voice is modulated by tapping the glottis while the singer doesn't breathe for lengthy periods.

Continuing south, you come to three villages about 4km apart, with two **wooden churches** apiece. At sprawling **CĂLINEŞTI**, the beautiful Susani (Upper) or Băndreni church, high above the road just north of the junction, was built and painted in the 1780s. Its companion, the Josani (Lower) or Caieni church, built in 1628, is one of the loveliest in Maramureş, with its huge nineteenth-century porch and beautiful internal paintings by Ponehalski. It's best reached by taking a path across the fields next to house no. 385, on the road east to Bârsana. There are also wooden *vâltoare* or whirlpools (used for giving woollen blankets back their loft) and *horincă* stills at nos. 96 and 129. **SÂRBI** has two unassuming little wooden churches – the Susani to the north, built in 1638 and painted by Ponehalski in 1760, with icons by Radu Munteanu, and the Josani, to the south, built in 1703 – and some fine watermills, notably at no. 181, along with *vâltoare*, two fulling mills and a *horincă* still, as well as various craftsmen.

BUDEŞTI, 4km further south, is a large village but one of the least spoilt in Maramureş, with even its new houses largely built in the traditional style. The Josani church, in the centre of the village by a memorial to the dead of the 1989 revolution, was built in 1643 and contains a chain-mail coat that belonged to the outlaw Pintea the Brave (see p.332). Its frescoes are amongst Alexandru Ponehalski's finest works, especially the *Last Judgement*. The Susani church, dating from 1586, has particularly fine paintings from the 1760s, also by Ponehalski, and has been gradually extended westwards, so that the tower is now almost central. From here, there's a particularly fine ten-kilometre walk through idyllic countryside to **Hoteni** (see p.337) via **BREB**, a small village with a very lovely and tranquil wooden church dating from 1531 hidden away in the valley, and a couple of simple guesthouses.

Budeşti's **guesthouses** include *Pensiune Maria* at no. 449 (☎0262/373 634 or 0743/887 951); the village can be reached by four **buses** a day from Sighet, taking the high road via **OCNA ŞUGATAG** (also known as Ocna Maramureşului), a former salt-mining centre that is now a small spa. Ocna Şugatag itself has two smart and very good-value **hotels**, the *Salina* (☎0272/374 362, ⓦwww.hotelsalina.ro; ❸) and *Crăiasca* (☎0262/374 034, ⓦwww.craiasca.ro; ❸), with some adjoining two- and four-bed huts (❶) and, soon, a proper campsite. It's also one of the few villages hereabouts with any amenities, including a bank and some shops.

Standing at the junction of the roads along the Iza and Mara valleys, **VADU IZEI** has a well-developed rural **homestay scheme** (❷). The scheme also operates in Botiza (see p.349) and Ieud (see p.350), but you can book for all three villages at Vadu Izei's Agro-Tur-Art office (June–Aug daily 9am–9pm, Sept–May Mon, Tues & Thurs–Sat 9am–4pm; ☎0262/330 228, or 0742/749 608, ⓦwww.vaduizei.ovr.ro), in a fine wooden house set back between the post office and the library at Str. Principală 161, just north of the Săcel junction. They can also arrange local excursions – walking, cycling (there are also bikes for hire) and tours of the wooden churches – as well as visits to local *artisanat* (carpet-makers, basket-weavers, wood carvers and icon painters) workshops. The co-ordinator, Ioan Borlean, is himself a renowned glass icon painter. There are plenty of guesthouses here, making it an alternative base to Sighet; these include *Casa Teleptean*, 1km south of the centre at Str. Principală 320 (☎0262/330 341 or 0744/828 898), with a couple of other decent options nearby, as well as a similar group near the bridge at the northern end of the village, and the new *Pensiunea Dumbrava Minunata*, with good views across the river at Str. Dumbrava 534 (☎0262/330 038 or 0740/493 516; ❷). You could also stay 1.5km east of Vadu Izei on the Bârsana road at the excellent *Casa Muntean*, Str. Dumbrava 505 (☎0262/330 091 or 0744/664 955, ⓔcasamuntean @yahoo.com, ⓦwww.casamuntean.home.ro; ❶), which gives discounts for Hostelling International members (and only charges by the bed); there are seven twin rooms, plus meals, Internet access, *horincă*, and excursions. Right at the heart of the village, at the road junction, the *Restaurant La Petre* provides a simple alternative to **home cooking**. Vadu Izei is known as the workplace of

Gheorghe Borodi (1917–91), who carved monumental **gateways** erected by Maramureş families as symbols of nobility; as most people claimed to be *nemeşi* or nobles, there's no shortage of gateways. The village hosts two interesting **festivals**, the Festival Nunţilor or Wedding Festival on July 1 (including performers from Năsăud, as well as Ukrainians and Hungarians), and the Maramuzical **festival** of folk fiddle-playing in August.

Though in some ways it comes close to being a suburb of Sighet, the tiny hamlet of **VALEA STEJARULUI**, 5km east on a rough road (cart and sleigh rides available), remains remarkably unspoilt, with many fine wooden beam gates and a wooden church dating from 1620 and painted in 1809.

Sighet

Sighetu Marmaţiei, or **SIGHET** as it's generally known, is just 1km from the Ukrainian border and was a famous smuggling centre before World War I when the territory to the north was called Ruthenia. History is repeating itself today; the bridge to Solotvino, destroyed in World War II, reopened in 2006, is now clogged with traffic crossing into Ukraine to buy cigarettes and petrol for resale on Romania's black market. A peaceful modern town of around 42,000 inhabitants, it has always been highly multi-ethnic, with a plethora of churches and high

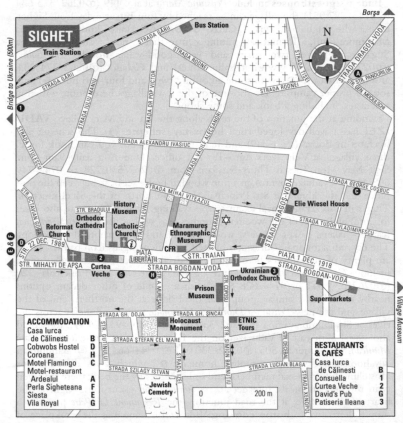

schools catering for Ukrainians, Hungarians and others. You can see residents of the surrounding villages in local costume, especially on the first Monday of the month, when a livestock market is held 1km out on the Baia Mare road. The key attractions are the superb **Prison Museum** – one of Romania's best museums – and the **memorial house** dedicated to holocaust survivor Elie Wiesel. The town is also famed for its **winter carnival** on December 27 (see box, p.344), when many of the participants wear extraordinary shamanistic costumes and masks.

Arrival and information

The **train and bus stations** are located north of town on Str. Gării, from where it's a fifteen-minute walk south along Str. Iuliu Maniu to the centre. The small Pangaea **tourist office** (Mon–Fri 9am–4pm; ☎0262/312 228, ⊛www .pangaeaturism.ro), on the corner of Str. Plevnei at Piaţa Libertăţii 15, can distribute basic **information** and **maps** and sells international bus tickets. Etnic Tours, Str. Şincai 20 (Mon–Fri 9am–5pm; ☎&℉0262/315 011, ⊛www .etnictours.ro), is also a great source of information on the region, especially festival dates; they can book you into village guesthouses (with bikes available in every village, as well as cart rides and music) and arrange accommodation and tours in Solotvino, across the river in Ukraine. Look out also for Teo Ivanciuc's excellent new guidebooks (in Romanian) to Maramureş and to Sighet, and his English/Romanian map of Maramureş, sold at major bookshops, the Memorial Museum and the Merry Cemetery in Sapânţa.

Internet access is available at *Milenium Internet Café*, in a basement off Str. Barnuţiu just south of Str. Şincai; *Bar Plimob* (Mon–Fri 7.30am–3.30pm), just north on Str. Coposu; at Str. Tudor Vladimirescu 5 (daily 8am–9pm); and *Naroma*, on the north side of the Curtea Veche. **Bike repairs** can be tackled at Str. Mihaly de Apşa 31 (Mon–Fri 9am–5pm, Sat 9am–3pm). Sighet's **hospital** is just west of the centre on the Sapânţa road (☎112).

Moving on, there are good, if sporadic, bus connections to the surrounding villages, although some are reached by a single departure at about 4pm. **Trains** depart regularly to Vişeu de Jos, most continuing to Salva and Beclean, the junctions for Suceava, Cluj and Braşov. There's also a train across the Ukrainian border to Teresva, just west of Sighet, leaving at 9am on Mondays, Wednesdays and Fridays and returning the same afternoon. Train tickets can be booked at the CFR office north of the Ethnographic Museum at Piaţa Libertăţii 25 (Mon–Fri 7am–2.30pm).

Accommodation

Sighet has a good selection of reasonably priced **hotels**, though none particularly excels; alternatively, **homestays** are available in nearby villages such as Vadu Izei or Rona de Jos, from where you can easily visit Sighet. Contact Maramureş Microregion Association (☎0262/312 552, ⊛www.mtmm.ro), Piaţa Libertăţii 21. To the west of town, Str. Eminescu leads in ten minutes to the Grădina Morii park and a footbridge over the river to Solovan hill, where it is perfectly possible to **camp** wild.

Casa Iurca de Călineşti Str. Dragoş-Vodă 14 ☎0262/318 882, ℮riurca@casaiurca.com. The best rooms in town, with a good restaurant, all in "new Maramureş style" and a bit pretentious. Rooms have a/c, Internet, hairdrier and minibar, but there's no lift. ❺
Cobwobs Hostel Str. 22 Decembrie 1989 42 ☎0745/615 173 or 0740/635 673,

℮cahul1@yahoo.com, ⊛http://cobwobs-hostel .freehostia.com. British-run, this is a genuine backpackers' hostel, in a modern house with very spacious dorms (with light pine furniture, proper duvets and big towels) and good showers, as well as a kitchen. If in doubt, ask at The Loom shop in front. They also organize tours to Bârsana, Călineşti, Sârbi, Budeşti and Breb, Ieud and Poienile Izei. ❶

Coroana Piaţa Libertăţii 21 ☎0262/312 645 or 315 484, ⊛www.hotelcoroana.ro. The most central of Sighet's hotels, now partially renovated; some rooms are big, and there are lots of small ones with single beds. ❸

Motel Flamingo Str. George Coşbuc 36 ☎0262/317 265, ⊛www.sighetumarmatiei .alphanet.ro. Despite the unprepossessing exterior, this has comfortable rooms, though it can get quite loud with the downstairs bar. ❸

Motel-restaurant Ardealul Str. Gen. Mociulschi 7 ☎0262/318 450. Above a bar-restaurant with video games, just north of the Frontier Police barracks, this has en-suite rooms with TV and hot

water, but if you're bothered by the noise from the bar it should not be your first choice. ❸

Perla Sigheteană Str. Avram Iancu 65 ☎0262/310 613, ⊛www.perlasigheteana.ro. A little way out of town, on the road to Săpânţa, this motel has a pool, sauna and gym, plus a pretty decent restaurant. ❹

Siesta Str. Avram Iancu 42 ☎0262/311 468, ⒺÂ motelsiesta@yahoo.com. To the west, 300m beyond the Perla Sigheteană, this is marginally more enticing, with slightly better facilities. ❹

Vila Royal Str. Mihaly de Apşa 1 ☎0262/311004, ⊛www.vilaroyal.ro. Although little more than rooms above a bar (with entry from the side alley), Vila Royal is nicely designed, with parking at the rear. ❹

The Town

From the train and bus stations, it's a ten-minute walk south down Str. Iuliu Maniu to the **Reformat church**, a fourteenth-century structure rebuilt just before World War I on an unusual ground plan. The town centre extends to the east of here and comprises two one-way streets, both of which change their names and are linked by several squares, so it can be hard to make sense of addresses.

Immediately east of the Reformat church is the **Curtea Veche**, the Baroque county hall of 1691, now housing a restaurant and shops. Beyond here is Piaţa Libertăţii, with the Baroque **Roman Catholic church**, built by the Piarist order in 1730–34, on its northern side. On the east side of the church at Piaţa Libertăţii 22, the **Ukrainian high school** is a splendid piece of Art Noodle, as some jokingly refer to the Hungarian version of Art Nouveau. The **Museum of History, Archeology and Natural Sciences** (Muzeul de Istorie, Arheologie şi Ştiinţele Naturii; Mon–Fri 9.30am–3.30pm), on the west side of the church at Piaţa Libertăţii 16, is relatively dull, with its displays of Stone Age axes and hunting trophies. To the east of the square is the far more enticing **Maramureş Ethnographic Museum** (Muzeul Etnografic Maramureşului; Tues–Sun 9am–5pm), featuring a better-than-average collection of local pottery and woodwork – including some beautifully carved gates and gateposts typical of the region – as well as a selection of costumes and masks worn by participants during the town's Winter Carnival (see box, p.344). A little further east, between the two carriageways, is a tiny **Ukrainian Orthodox church**, built in 1803–4 and thoroughly rebuilt in the 1990s.

At Str. Coposu 4, to the south of the Ethnographic Museum, stands the town's former **prison** (see box opposite), which opened in 1997 as the **Memorial Museum of the Victims of Communism and of the Resistance** (Memorial Victimelor Comunismului şi Rezistenţei; mid-April to mid–Oct daily 9.30am–6.30pm; mid–Oct to mid–April Tues–Sun 10am–4pm; ⊛www .memorialsighet.ro). The prison cells have been converted into exhibition spaces, with themes pertaining to the oppression of the communist era; little is in English but the general outlines are clear enough. In addition to memorials to Iuliu Maniu and Gheorghe Brătianu, the prison's two most famous inmates, there are displays on collectivization, forced labour on the Danube–Black Sea Canal, the deportations to the Bărăgan, and the demolition of the heart of Bucharest during the 1980s. There's also fascinating coverage of the feared Securitate, and another cell-full of Ceauşescu-oriented memorabilia (amusingly entitled "Communist Kitsch"), including paintings, busts, lists of the Romanian leader's honorary doctorates, and photos of him lording it with world dignitaries such as Castro and Nixon. In the courtyard to the rear of the

The prison of the ministers

Sighet prison operated from 1898 until 1977, and in that time achieved a notoriety gained by few others. Its nadir was between 1950 and 1955, when political prisoners (former government ministers, generals, academics and bishops) were held here so that they could be "protected" by the Red Army or rapidly spirited away into the Soviet Union if the communist regime was threatened. The prison's 72 cells held 180 members of the pre-war establishment, at least two-thirds of them aged over sixty; they were appallingly treated and, not surprisingly, many died. The most important figure to perish in Sighet prison was **Iuliu Maniu**, regarded as the greatest living Romanian when he was arrested in 1947 (at the age of 73) and now seen as a secular martyr – the only uncorrupt politician of the pre-war period, organizer of the 1944 coup, and notably reluctant to pursue revenge against Transylvania's Hungarians after the war.

The leading Hungarian victim was **Arón Márton**, Roman Catholic bishop of Alba Iulia, who opposed the persecution of the Jews in 1944 and of the Uniates in 1949, and was imprisoned from 1950 to 1955, surviving until 1980. Others who died in Sighet included two of the three members of the Brătianu family imprisoned here – Dinu, president of the National Liberal Party and Finance Minister 1933–34, and Gheorghe, historian and second-division politician – as well as Mihail Manoilescu, theoretician of Romanian fascism, and Foreign Minister in 1940. Their graves can be seen at the rear of the Cimitrul Săracilor or Paupers' Cemetery, just off the main road to the west of town, by a new Pentecostal chapel.

museum is an underground memorial hall, its walls inscribed with the names of some 8000 people detained in Romanian prisons during the communist period, and a dozen or so uninspiring bronze statues.

Heading one block west of the museum along Str. Şincai brings you to a **monument** to the 38,000 Maramureş Jews rounded up by Hungarian gendarmes and deported in 1944. The community's synagogue, dating from 1904, survives at Str. Basarabia 10, on the far side of Piaţa Libertăţii. One block east at Str. Tudor Vladimirescu 1, at the corner of Str. Dragoş Vodă, is a plain house that was the childhood home of **Elie Wiesel**, Auschwitz survivor and winner of the 1986 Nobel Peace Prize for his work in helping to understand and remember the Holocaust. It's now an impressive **memorial house** (Tues–Sun 9am–5pm), complete with books, furniture and religious items donated by local Jewish families; there are documents on the Jewish and other communities in Sighet before World War II, along with photos of the deportation of the Jews, of Wiesel in a group liberated at Buchenwald, and of his many visits to Sighet, including his most recent visit in 2002 to open the house. The photo captions are in English and French, but otherwise the texts, including quotations from Wiesel, are in Romanian only.

Situated on Dobăieş hill on the town's eastern outskirts, the **Village Museum** (Muzeul Satului; Tues–Sun 10am–6pm) presents dozens of houses, farm buildings and churches collected from the Iza valley – worth viewing if you're intending to give the real thing (see p.348) a miss. If you don't fancy the half-hour walk, take bus #1 to the bridge and School no. 5, then walk northeast for five minutes up Str. Muzeului.

Eating and drinking

There are precious few options for **eating out** in Sighet. The best restaurant, with excellent service, is at the *Casa Iurca de Călineşti*, although it's a bit pricey and rather touristy in feel, serving Western dishes like chateaubriand, schnitzel and "roast beef anglaise". *Consuella*, at the corner of Stradas Titulescu and Gării,

Winter Customs Festival

Held in Sighet on December 27, the annual **Winter Customs Festival** (Festivalul Datinilor de Iarna) is a vibrant display of music, and winter costumes and customs, all combined to depict the dual influences of ancient pagan and Christian beliefs. The festival is heralded by brightly decorated horses galloping down the main street. Upon the arrival of the official party, the parade begins with up to fifty groups from villages all over Maramureș, Bucovina, Transylvania and Ukraine slowly making their way down the street to present their song or skit to the mayor.

Thereafter, the rather mishmash play is enacted thus: soldiers arrive to tell King Herod about the rumour of a saviour, while bears roll around the ground to raise the earth spirits. Meanwhile, horsemen are called to find the infant child and men bearing heavy iron cowbells arrive to drive away the evil spirits – represented by multi-coloured, animist-style *dracus*. Present throughout is the clapping wooden goat (*capra*), warding off evil spirits to ensure that spring will return. In the afternoon, a full-length concert takes place both on the streets and in a nearby theatre, which lasts until early evening when more impromptu celebrations take over.

is also excellent, and rather cheaper; the soups are particularly good. You could also try your luck at *Curtea Veche*, Str. Mihalyi de Apșa 2, which serves solid Romanian food, or *David's Pub* across the road at Str. Mihalyi de Apșa 1 (next to the painter Simon Hollósy's birthplace), which offers Romanian/international food and has one smoke-free room. *Patiseria Ileana* on Str. Bogdan Vodă serves fine French-style pastries. For **picnic food**, head for the Artima or (less good) Unicarm supermarkets, on Str. Bogdan Vodă just east of the centre.

Săpânța and the Oaș depression

Eighteen kilometres northwest of Sighet (via the Hungarian village of Câmpulung la Tisa, known for its cabbages), and served by six buses a day, **SĂPÂNȚA** has achieved widespread fame thanks to the work of the woodcarver Stan Ion Pătraș (1908–77). Its **Merry Cemetery** (Cimitir Vesel), 1km south of the main road, features an absolute forest of beautifully worked, colourfully painted wooden headstones carved with portraits of the deceased or scenes from their lives, chosen by relatives and inscribed with witty doggerel (in Romanian) composed by Pătraș as he saw fit. Some are terse – "who sought money to amass, could not Death escape, alas!" – while a surprising number recall violent deaths, like that of the villager killed by a "bloody Hungarian" during World War II, or a mother's final message to her son: "Griga, may you pardoned be, even though you did stab me." Pătraș himself is buried right in front of the church door, his headstone marked by two white doves either side of his carved portrait ("Ever since I was a lad, I have been Stan Ion Pătraș…"). His funerary masterwork was continued by his two apprentices, Turda Toader and Vasile Stan, but the headstones are now carved and painted by Dumitru ("Tincu") Pop, whom you may be lucky enough to see going about his work in the cemetery. Nowadays the rhymes are less inspired, all beginning Aici Eu Ma Odihnesc/Pop Maria ma Numesc … ("Here I now take my rest, Pop Maria was I blessed …"). You can find more of Pătraș' artistry in his old house, a modest wooden cottage located some 250m along the dusty road behind the cemetery (it's signposted). The barn where he worked is adorned with some spectacularly colourful fixtures and fittings, as well as highly unusual wood-carved portraits of Nicolae and Elena Ceaușescu. The village, also known for its traditional *cergi* or woollen blankets, is lined with handicraft stalls and has become rather too accustomed to busloads of tourists making a stop for thirty minutes and then rushing on.

Săpânța's most recent claim to fame, the world's highest wooden tower, is at the **Peri monastery**, which has been under construction since 1995; follow the main road east from the Merry Cemetery road for 200m across the Râul Sapânța bridge then (at an ATM) turn left/north for 500m (if you're on foot, take the path diagonally through the Pădurea Parc Livada forest reserve). The church, though wooden, is not at all traditional in detail, set on a very high concrete base and with a 38-metre tree trunk inside its tower, which soars to a height of 75m.

Săpânța practicalities
There's plenty of simple **accommodation** in Săpânța, including four basic rooms in Ileana Ştețca's pension (℡0262/372 137 or 0745/491 756; ❹) directly opposite the cemetery at no. 656; the nearby *Pensiunea Maryuka* (℡0262/372591 or 0745/469480; ❸); *Pensiunea Miuța* (℡0262/372 355; ❸), on the road to the Peri monastery, and, just off the main road to the east, *Pensiunea Anca* (℡0262/372 148; ❸). OVR **homestays** are available through Traian Telaptean (℡0262/318 498, ℻330 171). There's also the simple Poieni **campsite** (℡0262/372 228 or 0794/398 047, ℮camping@camping.poieni .ro), with a handful of two-bed **cabins** (❶), at a trout farm 2.5km south of the cemetery. The only **places to eat** are the guesthouses.

The Oaş depression
Beyond Săpânța, the road turns south towards Satu Mare, winding up to the **Huta Pass** (587m) to enter the **Oaş depression**. Oaş is sometimes billed as "undiscovered Maramureş", but so many local men now work or trade abroad that the roads are lined with new bungalows and imported Mercedes, and traditional costume is little worn except at festivals and in the remotest villages such as Cămârzana, where you'll find just about the only wooden houses left in Oaş. The shepherds of this region assemble on the first or second Sunday of May for the **festival of Sâmbra Oilor**, when the milk yield of each family's sheep is measured. Whether this process – known as Ruptul Sterpelor – occurs in May (as here) or early July (as it does further south), the participants dress for the occasion in waist-length sheepskin jackets (*cojoc*) covered in embroidery and tassels, or fluffy woollen overcoats called *guba*, and heartily consume fiery *horincă* (double-distilled plum brandy) and sweet whey cheese.

NEGREŞTI-OAŞ, some 35km southwest of Săpânța, is the largest settlement in the region. Here, the **Oaş Museum** has a display of local landscapes (Tues–Fri 9am–4pm, Sat & Sun 10am–4pm), at Str. Victoriei 17, just north of the systematized centre, and a far more worthwhile open-air **ethnographic display** (Tues–Fri 9am–5pm, Sat & Sun 9am–2pm) on Str. Livezilor, to the south beyond the bridge. Here there are half a dozen blue-painted houses, most dating from the nineteenth century, and a wooden church, built in 1600, from Lechința; its interior was painted in 2006. Negreşti's **festival** is on September 1.

In addition to local **buses** and hourly **maxitaxis** from Satu Mare, Negreşti can be reached by **trains** on the Satu Mare–Bixad line: get off at the Negreşti halt, rather than at the station, which is a couple of kilometres west of town. **Accommodation** is available at the dated *Oşanul Hotel*, 400m south of the museum at Str. Victoriei 89 (℡0261/854 162, ℻851 163; ❸). The adequate *Regal* and *Orizont* **restaurants** are on the square just north of the hotel, and there are plenty of **ATMs**.

Other **places to stay** in Oaş include the *Valea-Măriei* (☎0261/850 750; ❷), 4km north of Vama, the *Călineşti* (☎0261/851 400; ❷) in Călineşti-Oaş, by a reservoir 15km west of Negreşti, and the *Motel Muideni*, just north of the pass into Satu Mare county.

Satu Mare

When the diplomats at Versailles signed the Trianon Treaty, they cut Hungary's Szabolcs-Szatmár county in half, leaving its capital Szatmárnémeti in Romanian hands, since when its Hungarian population has fallen to about 30 percent of the total. Renamed **SATU MARE** (meaning "Big Village" in Romanian) and shorn of its traditional links with the Great Plain, the town lost its original function as a trading post along the River Someş, shipping salt from Ocna Dejului downstream to Vásárosnamény on the River Tisza; today, it's a relatively prosperous place, largely due to its position near the border. Although there's really very little of interest to detain you here, it's a useful spot to break up a journey en route to or from Oradea or Hungary.

Arrival and information

The **bus and train stations** are 1km east of the centre on Str. Griviţei (a continuation of B-dul. Traian, which runs east from Piaţa Libertăţii), and are connected to town by **maxitaxis**. Bus #9 links the **airport** (10km south on the Zalău road; €3 by taxi) with Piaţa Libertăţii. The *Aurora*, *Astoria* or *Dacia* hotels (see opposite) can provide limited **tourist information**. **Internet access** is available at Str. Corvinilor 22, just south of B-dul. Traian (Mon–Sat 10am–11pm, Sun 6–11pm).

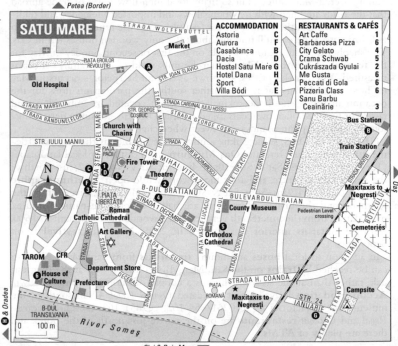

Hourly **maxitaxis to Negreşti** leave from Piaţa Romană and head north on Str. Botizului. Tickets for **flights** to Bucharest can be bought at the **TAROM** office (Mon–Fri 9am–6pm; ☎0261/712 033), next door to the **CFR** office (Mon–Fri 7am–8pm; ☎0261/721 202) at Piaţa 25 Octombrie 9. Carpatair's office (☎0261/706 806, ✉satu-mare@carpatair.com) is at the airport, from where they have daily flights to Budapest.

Accommodation

There's plenty of **accommodation** in Satu Mare, whether you want to stay in the heart of things around Piaţa Libertăţii or out by the bus station. Satu Mare's **campsite** is fifteen minutes' walk southeast of the centre by the River Someş on Str. Ştrandului. Next to it, in the Centrul de Vacanţa Ştrand at Str. 24 Ianuarie 17, the HI-affiliated *Hostel Satu Mare* (☎0261/750 472 or 0741/190 544, ✉djtsatumare@gmail.com; ❶) has comfortable rooms with hot water and large TVs, as well as cheaper *căsuţe*.

Astoria Str. Kogălniceanu 1 ☎0261/806 185, ⓦwww.hotel-astoria.ro. Across an alley to the north of Piaţa Libertăţii, this new hotel has large stylish rooms, good bathrooms and Internet access – but no lift. ❻

Aurora Piaţa Libertăţii 11 ☎0261/714 946, ⓦwww.aurora-sm.ro. The ugliest of the hotels on the main square, although the rooms are modern and decent enough. ❺

Casablanca At the bus station ☎0261/768 188, ⓕ768 204. The rooms (including triples) are perfectly fine, though the downstairs bar is very noisy. ❸

Dacia Piaţa Libertăţii 8 ☎0261/714 276, ⓕ715 774, ⓦwww.hoteldacia.ro. A Secession-era gem

built in 1902, with good facilities including a/c, cable TV and modern bathrooms. ❹–❻

Hotel Dana Drum Carei 128 ☎0261/768 465, ⓦwww.dana-hotel.ro. Peaceful, newish hotel, 2km west of town out on the road to Oradea. ❺

Sport Str. Mileniului 25 ☎0261/712 959, ⓕ711 604. A reasonable, if predictably unspectacular place, north of the centre. ❸

Villa Bódi Piaţa Libertăţii 5 ☎0261/710 861, ⓦwww.villabodi.ro. By far the best of the cluster of hotels on Piaţa Libertăţii, this Hungarian-run place has a lovely foyer and beautifully furnished rooms with wooden floors, plus Jacuzzi, sauna, and Internet ports in all rooms. ❼–❽

The Town

The centre of town, **Piaţa Libertăţii**, dominated by the neoclassical **Roman Catholic cathedral** (1785–93) on its east side, provides a pleasant green space and a minor haven from the grinding traffic. Just north of the square, off the alley alongside the *Dacia*, you'll see the **fire tower**, a slender 45-metre-high red-brick structure raised in 1904 and resembling a Turkish minaret. Just north is the Reformat **"Church with Chains"**, a long and relatively low Baroque church built at the turn of the nineteenth century in the middle of Piaţa Păcii; from here you can return to the square along Str. Ştefan cel Mare, lined with some interesting if tatty turn-of-the-century buildings. On the south side of Piaţa Libertăţii, in a neo-Gothic mansion at no. 21, the town's **Art Gallery** (Sun & Tues–Fri 10am–6pm, Sat 10am–2pm) features the work of local artist Aurel Popp (1879–1960), who produced sun-dappled post-Impressionist views of Baie Sprie, and much darker images depicting World War I and the death of capitalism. Strada Decebal leads south from the square, past the twin synagogues that served the city's 13,000 Jews, to the river, where you'll find the ghastly 1980s **Centru Civic**, a smelly, run-down plaza incorporating the moribund Casa de Cultură, a department store and the striking tower of the prefecture. Some 500m east of Piaţa Libertăţii along B-dul. Brătianu, at Piaţa Vasile Lucaciu 21, the **County Museum** (Muzeul Judeţean; Tues–Sat 10am–6pm, Sun 10am–2pm) has both ethnographic and archeological exhibitions. The former contains the standard rural implements and folk costumes, as well as brightly coloured ceramics from Hollóháza in Hungary and Vama in Oaş, while the beautifully presented archeological exhibitions feature fine Daco-Roman remains, clay vessels and grave goods, including some intricate jewellery kept in the treasury (Tues–Sun 11am–2pm).

Eating and drinking

There are few decent **places to eat** in Satu Mare other than in the hotels, of which the *Astoria* and *Villa Bódi* are the best. Just west of the Centru Civic is a cluster of **Italian restaurants**, of which *Peccati di Gola* and, below it, *Pizzeria Class* (open daily until midnight) are acceptable; *Me Gusta* and *Barbarossa Pizza*, just to the west, are both more like bars. For **coffee and cakes**, try the stylish *Art Caffe* on Ştefan Ruha (the alley west of the fire tower); *Sanu Barbu Ceainărie* at Str. Tibleşului 2 (on the west side of Piaţa Libertăţii), a dark teahouse and café, also serving cocktails with and without alcohol; and *Cukrászada Gyulai*, a café (closed Sun) at the corner of Str. Doja, facing *City Gelato* at Str. Brătianu 3. For a **drink**, try the *Crama Schwab bierkeller*, courtesy of the town's Swabian (German) minority, at Piaţa Lucaciu 9 (Mon–Fri 9am–5pm, Sun 9am–2pm), which also puts on German films and choir recitals.

The Iza valley

Some of the loveliest villages and wooden churches in Maramureş are situated in the **Iza valley**, which extends for roughly 60km from Sighet to the Rodna mountains, which form the frontier with Moldavia. There are regular buses to Vişeu de Sus and Borşa – most following the DJ186 along the Iza valley, although some follow the DN18 along the Rona and Vişeu valleys – and a daily bus to most of the villages in the Iza's side valleys.

Onceşti

Despite being on a main road, **ONCEŞTI**, 11km from Sighet, is perhaps the village that has best preserved its folk customs, with many people wearing traditional dress on Sundays. It still boasts two fine groups of wooden houses, one by Str. Principală 241 (just east of the school), but the old wooden church is now in Sighet's Village Museum. There are some fine **guesthouses** here, including *Pensiunea Anamaria* (T&F 0262/348 468; ②) and the slightly larger ♞ *Pensiunea Sub Cetate la Matei* (T 0262/348 498 or 0742/342 328, W www.oncesti.rdsor.ro; ②), which share a yard at Str. Principală 480, at the west end of the village; the latter has rooms with TV and a small museum including tools saved from a blacksmith's forge.

Bârsana and Rozavlea

The wooden church of **BÂRSANA**, 19km southeast of Sighet on the DJ186, is small and neat and perfectly positioned atop a hillock to the west of the village centre. Built in 1711, its florid **paintings**, among the best in Maramureş, date from 1720 and 1806. Hodor Toador and Ion Plohod were responsible for the later set of paintings, with icons on wood by the former artist – the narthex is adorned with saints and processional images, while the *naos* is painted with Old and New Testament scenes, each in its own decorative medallion. Look in particular for the images of angels covered in eyes. At the east end of the village, 4km from the centre, stands the new **Bârsana Monastery**, a large complex comprising several wooden buildings, all constructed in the local style, including the wooden church which, unusually, has a pentagonal *privdor* and two apses, as well as a 57-metre steeple, which was briefly the highest in the world but now overtaken by the one at Sapânţa (see p.345). The original sixteenth-century church was confiscated by the Austrians in 1791 and handed over to the

Greek–Catholic Cernoc monastery (now in Ukraine) before being returned to the Orthodox church in 1993, the year construction of Bârsana monastery began. The monastery attracts many visitors, some staying in its **guesthouse** (☎0262/331 101; ❶); however, non-pilgrims may be happier in a **homestay** such as *Pensiunea Paşcă*, Uliţa Pietriş (☎0262/331 165; ❷), or *Pensiunea Dumbrava*, Str. Principală 332 (☎0262/331 187; ❷).

As a border region, Maramureş remained vulnerable to attacks by nomadic tribes until the eighteenth century, and the wooden church at **ROZAVLEA**, 20km further along the valley, was one of many rebuilt after the last Tatar invasion in 1717 and painted by Ion Plohod. Its magnificent double roof, recently restored, is now weathering nicely. There are **homestays** (❷) here – including *Casa Tomşa* at no. 961 (☎0262/333 155 or 0740/826 484) and *Pensiunea Caia* at no. 763 (☎0262/333 099) – and in **ŞIEU**, 2km east, which has another wooden church built after 1717.

Botiza, Poienile Izei and Glod

BOTIZA, 10km south of Şieu, is one of the most comprehensive centres for **agrotourism** in the area, with a few competing networks. The best is the Asociaţia Agroturistică Botiza (AAB), based near the church at no. 742 (☎&☎0262/334 233), while rooms can also be booked through Agro-Tur (see p.339) in Vadu Izei, the Mara Holiday agency (see p.329) in Baia Mare,

▲ Worshippers attending Mass, Bârsana

or Etnic Tours (see p.341) in Sighet. There are also comfortable **private rooms** at no. 743 (℡0262/334 207; ❷), whose owner, Victoria Berbecaru, is renowned locally for her craftwork, notably carpet-making using natural dyes. The **wooden church**, beautifully located on a hillside, with a view down the valley to the peaks of Ukraine, was built in 1699 in Vişeu de Jos and moved here two hundred years later. Beyond a handful of blackened frescoes of the Apostles and some floral motifs, there's little to see inside, but if you want a look, ask for the key at no. 743. Several **mineral springs** are located along the road to Poienile Izei, notably a sulphurous well at a ruined spa by the bridge about 1km from the village centre. A **folk festival** takes place in Botiza over the last weekend of August.

From the northern edge of Botiza, a rough sidetrack leads 6km into the hills to the village of **POIENILE IZEI** (The Meadows of the Iza), famous for its old wooden church (1604–32) filled with nightmarish **paintings of hell**. The red walls depict dozens of sinners being tortured by demons (*draci*) with goat-like heads and clawed feet, while beneath them, processions of more sinners are driven into the mouth of hell – an enormous bird's head with fiery nostrils. These pictures constitute an illustrated rulebook too terrifying to disobey, and whose message is still understood by the villagers. Within the paintings, a huge pair of bellows is used to inflict punishment for farting in church, while a woman guilty of burning the priest's robes while ironing them is herself pressed with a hot iron. Women violating traditional morality face torments in the afterlife: adultresses are courted by loathsome demons and a woman who aborted children is forced to eat them. These hell scenes presumably formed the nasty part of a huge *Day of Judgement* in the narthex, the other half of which has, ironically, not been saved. Opposite are paintings of gardens and distant cityscapes in a sort of Gothic Book of Hours style, executed around 1793–4. Murals in the nave are badly damaged and soot-blackened, but from the balcony you can recognize *Adam and Eve*, *The Fall*, and episodes from the lives of Christ and John the Baptist. If the church is locked, anyone in the house above the new church will unlock it for you. Local **homestays** include *Pensiunea Domniţa* at Str. Dubului 135 (℡0262/334 383 or 0724/764 036, Ⓔ domnitailies@yahoo.com; ❷).

An even worse road leads on to the tiny and unspoilt village of **GLOD**, which is known for its folk beliefs (for instance in wolfmen and spirits of the night) and associations with the outlaw Pintea Viteazul; local tales tell of his treasure buried under a spring and protected by a curse. The excellent *In Poiana* guest-house (℡0262/332 367 or 0720/071 787; ❷) provides **accommodation**.

Ieud and beyond

Back in the Iza valley, a turn-off at Gura Ieudului, about 6km east along the valley road, leads upstream to the village of **IEUD**, 3km south. Lanes fenced with lattices run between the houses, clustered within their courtyards, and during summer the air is full of the scent of lady's mantle, a plant mixed with elder and wormwood to make "face water" for the complexion; it was once used for baths to invigorate weak children. Divorce is virtually unknown in this religious and traditional village; about fifty of Ieud's women are "heroine mothers", having borne at least ten children each, and almost half the population of 5000 is of school age. It was Ieud artisans, supervised by the master carpenter Ion Ţâplea, who restored Manuc's Inn in Bucharest (see p.82), and master carpenter Gavrilă Hotico is currently building new wooden churches all over Maramureş and beyond; the tradition of woodworking has been maintained since the superb Orthodox **Church on the Hill** was first raised here in 1364.

Long thought to be the oldest church in Maramureş (though largely rebuilt in the eighteenth century), with a double roof and tiny windows, it once housed the Ieud Codex (now in the Romanian Academy in Bucharest), the earliest-known document in the Romanian language. It has perhaps the best-known paintings of any Maramureş church, executed by Alexandru Ponehalski in 1782; look out for Abraham, Isaac and Jacob welcoming people in their arms, in the *pronaos*. Ask opposite at the Textile-Incaltimente shop for the church key, and don't miss the ingenious removable ratchet used to open the bolt in the main door. No less splendid than the Orthodox church is the Uniate **lower church** (the Val or Şes church), built by 1718 and featuring an immensely high and quite magnificent roofline, though, unusually, no porch; there are few wall paintings left, but the icons on glass and the iconostasis are of great artistic worth. A nunnery with a 58-metre-high tower (1m higher than that at Bârsana) is under construction. **Homestay** accommodation (❷) is available in the village: if you haven't already booked it in Vadu Izei, contact Dumitru Chindriş at no. 233 (☎0262/336 100).

BOGDAN VODĂ, stretching east along the valley road from Gura Ieudului, is one of the valley's main villages, located on the road leading to Moldavia and with long-standing ties to that region. The village was known as Cuhea until the late 1960s, when it was renamed in honour of the local voivode, Bogdan, who left in 1359 supposedly to hunt bison (see p.433), but ended up founding the Moldavian state. The influence of Stephen and other Moldavian rulers has imparted a semi-Byzantine style to the frescoes inside Bogdan Vodă's wooden church, though the building materials used in 1718 were typical of eastern Maramureş – thick fir beams rather than the stone used at Putna and other Moldavian monasteries, or the oak of western Maramureş. Unfortunately, the church is now dwarfed by a huge modern successor erected far too close to it.

From Bogdan Vodă's churches, a rough road leads 14km north to Vişeu de Jos in the Vişeu valley (see below), while the main road continues east to **DRAGOMIREŞTI**, whose original village church stands in Bucharest's Village Museum (see p.86); a new Uniate wooden church (on a concrete base) was completed in 2000 just west of the village centre. The **Muzeul Tarancii** (daily 9am–7pm) displays a wide range of domestic and agricultural implements, almost all made of wood. There's an ATM here, and half a dozen houses offering **homestays**; look out for the signs. The next village you come to is **SĂLIŞTEA DE SUS**, 4km east, which boasts two old wooden churches, one built in 1680 and the other in 1724 – the latter painted by Radu Munteanu in 1775. There are also two new churches, and various guesthouses. The road passes the *Iza cabana* at the Iza rail halt and ends, 53km from Vadu Izei, at **SĂCEL**, known for its unglazed red ceramics, from where the DN17C heads for Moisei (11km north) or Salva and Bistriţa (44km and 71km south, in Transylvania). You can **stay** at *Pensiunea Maria*, just east of the centre at Str. Centru 235 (☎0262/339 064, ⓦwww.pensiuneamaria.ro; ❷).

The Vişeu valley and the Rodna mountains

The railway east from Sighet follows the River Tisza for 25km before heading up the beautiful **Vişeu valley**; the DN18 runs just to the south of the railway, and local buses from Sighet pass through the villages of Rona de Jos and Rona de Sus before terminating at the tiny spa of **COŞTIUI**, 22km from Sighet, which has a motel and *căsuţe*. **RONA DE JOS** has few obvious sights, beyond a cave and mineral springs, and a wooden church built in 1720, which was taken over by the Uniates in 2001 and restored, but the proactive guesthouse-owners' association organizes cart rides and bike hire, and there's a new festival, Fii Satului (Sons of the Village) on the last Sunday of August or the first of September. At the west end of the village, 11km from Sighet, the excellent *Pensiunea Rusucu* (☎0262/361 148 or 0724/063 143; ⓦwww.rusucu.com; ➋) has a minibus for tours and transfers, while *Pensiunea Marin* (☎0262/361 048; ➋) can sleep up to five people in one of its five rooms. Beyond the Ukrainian village of Rona de Sus (and the turning to Coştiui) the road climbs to a pass in lovely beech forest before finally meeting the railway again at **PETROVA**, 16km further on. About 7km southeast of Petrova, at **Leordina** (once home to Harvey Keitel's parents), a rough side road follows the River Ruscova north into an enclave of Huţul or Ruthenian people, the archetypal inhabitants of the Carpathians, who speak a dialect of Ukrainian incorporating many Romanian words. There's still a synagogue in **RUSCOVA**, once home to the British politician Michael Howard's father. The centre of the area is the village of **POIENILE DE SUB MUNTE**, where there's a Ukrainian-style wooden church dating from 1788 and a couple of guesthouses. Back in the Vişeu valley, trains continue 10km east from Leordina to **VIŞEU DE JOS**, where most turn south, passing through Săcel and Salva en route to Beclean; passenger trains no longer run up the branch line from Vişeu de Jos to the alpine resort of Borşa, but there's a good bus connection as far as Vişeu de Sus, and less frequent buses on to Borşa.

Vişeu de Sus and the logging train

The next settlement along from Vişeu de Jos is **VIŞEU DE SUS**, a fair-sized town with several useful services, and the starting point for the logging train up the steep Vaser valley. A **Museum of History and Ethnography** (Muzeul de Istorie şi Etnografie) opened in 2003 at Str. Libertăţii 7; it's far from finished, but there's a display on the ethnography of the Romanian, Ruthenian, Jewish and Zipser communities. The Zipsers (Ţipţerai in Romanian) were German foresters who until World War II lived here in some numbers, trading mainly with Jewish timber merchants. On the far side of Str. 22 Decembrie is a wooden church built for the Uniate congregation in 1993–5 by Gavrilă Hotico of Ieud, and the very attractive town hall lies just to the east. Across the river, by Str. Republicii, the market stands on the edge of the Ţipţerai Quarter.

The **mocăniţa**, or narrow-gauge logging train, usually hauled by a small diesel engine, leaves early (Mon–Sat around 6.30am/7am; €5 return) from the yard about 1.5km north of the centre on Str. A.I. Cuza (head up Str. Carpaţi, opposite Str. I. Maniu) and chugs up the picturesque Vaser valley. It carries lumberjacks (*butinarii*) the 41km up to their camps at Coman, near the Ukrainian border (5–6hr), and at about 3pm begins the journey back down again. Call in advance (☎0262/353 535 or 0744/986 242) to check whether the train is leaving at all, and make sure you get there in plenty of time. In addition, in July and August a **steam locomotive**, preserved by Swiss enthusiasts, runs to Făina (3–4hr), returning in theory at about 5pm (Mon–Sat 8.30am; €6 return; ☎0744/231 671 or 0262/986 242, ⓔinfo@ecotours.ro, ⓦwww.cffviseu.ro). At Făina there's a cabana with *căsuţe*; beyond this the valley is far wilder.

Along the route, you may see bears and deer drinking from the river, unperturbed by the trains and loggers, while in the mountain forests live stags, elusive lynxes, and wolves. The River Vaser, rich in trout and umber, descends rapidly through the fifty-kilometre-long valley; its whirling waters have begun to attract kayaking enthusiasts to logging settlements like **MĂCIRLĂU**, the start of a very rugged trail over the Jupania ridge of the Maramureş mountains to the former mining centre of Baia Borşa, just north of Borşa.

Vasertour, on a corner with the main road, Str. 22 Decembrie, at Str. Libertăţii 1 (Mon–Sat 9am–5pm; ☎0262/352 285), can organize private **rooms** here and in the surrounding area; at the same address is Fundaţia ProVişeu (🌐www .turismviseu.ro), and the Andra Internet café in the basement.

The *Hotel Brad* (☎0262/352 999; ❸), at Str. 22 Decembrie 50 (at the junction of Str. Iuliu Maniu), is perfectly decent but often full; *Hotel Gabriela* (☎0262/354 380, 🌐www.hotel-gabriela.ro; ❸), about 1km east of town on the road to Moisei at Str. Rândunelelor 1, is a better bet. There are various cheap guesthouses near the *mocăniţa* station, such as *Pensiunea Jurj*, Str. A.I. Cuza 26 (☎0262/3550 054; ❶), and *Pensiunea Sanda* (☎0262/352 032; ❶); as well as the better *Pensiunea Casa Alba* (☎0745/297 457; ❷) 100m down Str. I. Maniu; *Pensiunea Nagy*, Str. Prislop 82 (☎0262/354 681, 🌐www.pensiunea-nagy.ro; ❷), which has a sauna and Jacuzzi; and *Pensiunea Casa Chira* (☎0740/123 497 or 0727/730 791; ❷) at Str. Teilor 60, north of the river in the Ţipţerai Quarter.

For **eating**, *Caffe Danielli* and *Pizzeria Andra*, both on Str. 22 Decembrie are nothing special but decent enough, and convenient for the *Hotel Brad*, across the road; ; there are **ATMs** nearby. **Buses** depart from the dusty yard about 300m south of the tourist office at the bottom of Str. Libertăţii, but local maxitaxis for Moisei and Borşa start from km125, on the main road just east of the centre.

Beyond Vişeu de Sus

Back in the main Vişeu valley, 12km beyond Vişeu de Sus, the straggling village of **MOISEI** lies beneath the foothills of the Rodna massif, whose peaks are often still snowy while fruit is ripening in the village's orchards. Though today it seems tranquil, within living memory Moisei suffered a tragedy that's become a symbol of atrocity and martyred innocence throughout Romania: in October 1944, retreating Hungarian troops machine-gunned 29 villagers and set Moisei ablaze – a massacre commemorated by a circle of twelve stone figures by Vida Geza, with faces modelled on two of the victims and on the masks that are worn during festivals in Maramureş. The memorial is 5km east of the centre, opposite a small museum at km141. A couple of kilometres along a side valley south of the village (off the Săcel road) stands a **monastery** that on August 15, the Feast of the Assumption, is the scene of a major pilgrimage. **Accommodation** in Moisei is limited to the pleasant *Motel Lido* (☎0262/347 622; ❷) at Str. Principală 410, just east of the village centre on the road to Borşa; and the *Pensiunea Călina* (☎0262/347 602; ❶) at no. 380, at the west end of the village, half a kilometre east of the Săcel turning.

Most of the valley's amenities, including several cheap **hotels**, lie in **BORŞA**, a grubby little town 5km east of Moisei – and naturally, there's also a wooden church here, hidden away north of Str. Libertăţii, west of the centre; it was rebuilt in 1718 and painted internally by Zaharia Zugrav in 1765. At km143, 3km west of the centre, is the clean and tidy *Pension Rominvest* (☎0745/275 910; ❷), while the *Motel Rodna* (☎0262/344 122, 🌐www.borsa.ro /motelrodna; ❷–❸), down an alley opposite Str. Libertăţii 197, just 300m west of the centre, has small but neat and good-value rooms. Right in the centre, the dilapidated *Hotel Iezer* (☎0262/343 430 or 0740/141 156; ❷) offers very cheap rooms without breakfast. Otherwise, there's the excessively rustic *Perla Maramureşului*, opposite the hospital at Str. Victoriei 37 (☎0262/342 539; ❷), and the bright but surprisingly modest *Hotel Fraţii Mihaly*, some 300m beyond the *Perla* at Str. Victoriei 65 (☎0262/343 103 or 0742/797 599; ❷). For **food**, the *Motel Rodna* houses an autoservire restaurant and pizzeria, and there's the *Spaghetteria Nicol* by the hospital, east of the centre. You'll find a big Unicarm supermarket just west of the *Perla Maramureşului*, and **Internet** and video games just beyond. **Hiking maps** (in French and Hungarian) are available in shops and tourist agencies. **Maxitaxis** to the west (to Vişeu de Sus during the week, but only as far as Moisei at weekends) turn around at the west end of the bridge (just west of the centre); those to the east leave from the hospital, opposite the *Perla Maramureşului*.

It's 10km (maxitaxis leave every 40min) to the fast-growing **Borşa Complex ski resort** (beginners and intermediates only), where there's also a plentiful supply of **accommodation**, most of which is open year-round: the best is the modern *Hotel AS* (☎0262/342 333, ⓦ www.hotel.as.borsa.ro; ❹) at the bottom of the complex, right by the main road, but it's more convenient to stay near the chairlift (daily 9am–5pm), just above the maxitaxi terminal. Here you'll find the *Cerbul* (☎0262/344 199; ❸) and the slightly more attractive *Focus* (☎0262/344 038; ❸), which also houses a ski school (☎0744/154 933). There are also several friendly little **pensions** (❷) in the resort, with two- to five-bed

▲ Borşa village and Rodna mountains

rooms, such as *Pensiunea Calin* (☎0262/344 263), 300m beyond the *Cerbul*, *Pensiunea Favorit* (☎0722/621 649) and *Pensiunea Mihali* (☎0740/490 397), both just below the maxitaxi terminal, and *Pensiunea Hantig-Lucian* (☎0262/343 663; ❶), at Str. Cascada 6. The last is 1km up the track to the Cascada Cailor (Horses' Waterfall), the highest in Romania. There's also a **camping** spot at the start of Str. Cascada. A new wooden church has been built in the resort, in traditional style except for its massive stone plinth. From Borşa Complex, a hairpin road heads up to the **Prislop Pass** – 2km away as the crow flies, but a dozen kilometres by this tightly twisting road.

There are four buses a day to Borsa from Baia Mare via the Iza valley, one each from Bistriţa and Vatra Dornei, and three daily Sighet–Cluj services at Săcel. **Buses** from Borşa to Baia Mare and elsewhere usually set off from either Borşa Complex or Baia Borşa (and vice versa).

Hiking in the Rodna mountains

The **Rodnas** are one of Romania's best **hiking** areas, largely because you're sure to have them virtually to yourself. The easiest way into the mountains is either by the chairlift from Borşa Complex (you may have to wait until a dozen or so people have gathered) or from the 1416-metre **Prislop Pass**; from the pass you can head either north into the Maramureş mountains, wild and largely unvisited, although scarred by mining and forestry, or south into the Rodnas. Following red triangles, then blue stripes, it should take you two hours at most to reach the main crest at the Gărgălău saddle, from where you can follow red stripes east to the Rotunda Pass and ultimately to Vatra Dornei (see p.320), or west into the highest part of the massif. The route west will get you to La Cruce in four-and-a-half hours, from where you can turn right to follow blue stripes up to the weather station on the summit of **Mount Pietrosul** (2303m), ninety minutes away. There are great views in all directions, particularly deep into Ukraine to the north. Borşa is 1600m below, and it takes another two-and-a-half hours to get back there. Alternatively, you can just follow red stripes from the Complex to the Cascada Cailor (see above), which takes ninety minutes.

The new **Rodna National Park** is based on the south side of the mountains (☎0263/377 175; ✉parcrodna@email.ro), but there's an office in Borşa at Str. Zorilor 2B (☎0740/002 125, ✉pnmrborsa@ddcnet.ro). Apart from camping, the only place to **stay** in the mountains is the *Puzdrele cabana* – two to three hours' trek from the hamlet of Poiana Borşa (east of Borşa), following the route marked by blue triangles, which continues to the main ridge in another couple of hours. With a map, you can hike on south and down towards the Someş Mare valley and Năsăud (see p.254) in two days, camping wild en route.

Routes on to Moldavia and Transylvania

Just before the Prislop Pass, at the border of Maramureş with **Moldavia**, you'll see a monument marking the site where the last Tatar raid was finally driven off in 1717. At the pass, close to the Hanul Prislop bar, the *Cabana Alpina*, and a new (stone) monastery, the **Horă at Prislop festival** takes place every year on the nearest Sunday to August 1, attracting thousands of participants and spectators. On the far side of the pass, the road runs down the lovely Bistriţa Aurie Valley to Câmpulung Moldovenesc (see p.318), from where you can reach Suceava and several of the painted monasteries by rail. A daily bus runs from Vişeu (at 7am) to Vatra Dornei; you can change either there or at Iacobeni for trains to Câmpulung Moldovenesc. Travelling to **Transylvania**, four trains a day link Vişeu de Jos with Salva, 61km to the south and a junction on the busier line from Cluj to Vatra Dornei and Suceava; there's also a daily bus from Borşa to Bistriţa, and three from Sighet to Cluj via the Iza Valley and Săcel.

Travel details

Trains

Baia Mare to: Beclean (2 daily; 3hr); Braşov (3–4 daily; 7hr 45min–9hr 35min); Bucharest (3 daily; 10hr 30min–12hr 10min); Cluj (4 daily; 2hr 45min–5hr 20min); Dej (8 daily; 1hr 55min–3hr 50min); Satu Mare (10 daily; 1hr 10min–2hr); Timişoara (1 daily; 6hr).

Satu Mare to: Baia Mare (10 daily; 1hr 10min–1hr 50min); Braşov (2–3 daily; 9hr–11hr 10min); Bucharest (2 daily; 12hr–13hr 30min); Cluj (2 daily; 4–5hr); Negreşti-Oaş (5 daily; 1hr 35min–2hr); Oradea (6 daily; 1hr 55min–3hr 10min); Timişoara (1 daily; 4hr 45min).

Sighet to: Beclean (3 daily; 4hr 15min); Braşov (1 daily; 10hr 20min); Bucharest (1 daily; 13hr 30min); Cluj (2 daily; 5hr 40min–6hr); Salva (4 daily; 3hr 35min–4hr); Timişoara (1 daily; 12hr 35min); Vişeu de Jos (6 daily; 1hr 50min).

Buses and maxitaxis

Baia Mare to: Bicaz (3 daily); Bistriţa (3 daily); Borşa (4 daily); Bucharest (2 daily); Cavnic (4–5 daily); Cluj (7 daily); Hoteni (1 daily); Negreşti-Oaş (3 daily); Oradea (2 daily); Satu Mare (8 daily); Sighet (7 daily); Târgu Lăpuş (7–9 daily); Vişeu (4–5 daily); Zalău (2 daily).

Borşa to: Baia Mare (4 daily); Bistriţa (1 daily); Sighet (3 daily); Vatra Dornei (1 daily).

Satu Mare to: Baia Mare (8 daily); Bistriţa (3 daily); Cluj (2 daily); Negreşti-Oaş (4 daily); Oradea (7 daily); Sighet (3 daily Mon–Fri, 1 daily Sat & Sun); Timişoara (1 daily).

Sighet to: Baia Mare (7 daily); Borşa (4 daily); Botiza (2 daily Mon–Fri); Budeşti (5 daily Mon–Fri); Cluj (3 daily); Coştiui (7 daily); Ieud (1 daily); Mara (10 daily); Satu Mare (3 daily Mon–Fri, 1 daily Sat & Sun); Săpânţa (10 daily); Târgu Lăpuş (1 daily); Oradea/Timişoara (2 daily); Poienile de sub Munte (2 daily Mon–Fri, 1 daily Sat & Sun); Poienile Izei (1 daily Mon–Fri); Vişeu (2 daily).

Târgu Lăpuş to: Baia Mare (7 daily); Băiuţ (2 daily); Cluj (1 daily); Cupşeni (1 daily); Sighet (1 daily).

Viseu to: Baia Mare (2–3 daily); Borşa (4 daily Mon–Fri); Botiza (1 daily); Sighet (2 daily).

Planes

Baia Mare to: Bucharest (5 weekly).
Satu Mare to: Bucharest (7 weekly).

International buses

Baia Mare to: Budapest, Hungary (Tues & Fri).
Satu Mare to: Budapest (1 daily Mon–Sat).

The Banat

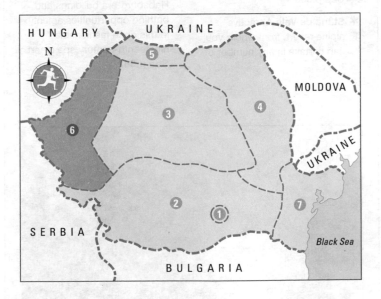

CHAPTER 6 # Highlights

✳ **Oradea** Charming town, rampant with Secessionist architecture and located close to a couple of small spa resorts. See p.359

✳ **Chişcău and Meziad Caves** Take a tour through these atmospheric caves, featuring stunning stalactite and stalagmite formations. See p.366

✳ **Stâna de Vale** Attractive alpine resort, from where you can partake in any number of hikes along the western spur of the Apuseni mountains. See p.367

✳ **Timişoara** Birthplace of the 1989 revolution, this vibrant, engaging city is characterized by colourful squares, green parks and a lively nightlife scene. See p.374

✳ **Băile Herculane** Elegant Habsburg-era buildings and bathing opportunities aplenty in this once fashionable nineteenth-century spa resort. See p.382

▲ Piaţa Victoriei, Timişoara

The Banat

T he **Banat** (Bánság) is the historical term for the western marches of Romania between the Timiş and Mureş rivers, but it has also come to include the Crişana, which encompasses the northwesternmost part of the region between the Apuseni massif and the Hungarian border. With its largely featureless scenery, great rivers, historical sites and an intermingling of different ethnic groups, the Banat has much in common with its neighbours, Hungary's Great Plain and Serbia's Vojvodina region. The frontiers were finally settled according to the principle of national self-determination at the Versailles conference of 1918–20, to which each country's delegates brought reams of demographic maps and statistics to support their claims. During the communist era, policies towards ethnic minorities were comparatively fair until the 1960s, when an increasingly hard line began to cause a haemorrhaging of the population in the Banat region, particularly of ethnic Magyars. In both 1988 and 1989, around 80,000 left, as liberalization gained apace in Hungary but things went downhill fast in Romania. The Schwab Germans, who originally settled in this area when the marshes were drained and colonized after the expulsion of the Turks, have now almost all emigrated to Germany. Nevertheless, many villages of Slovaks, Serbs, Magyars and other minority groups remain.

Key attractions are the cities of **Oradea**, **Arad** and **Timişoara**, partly on their own merits, but also because each town dominates a route between Transylvania and Hungary or Serbia, and provides access to most other places of interest in the region. Timişoara, in particular, is hugely enjoyable, and the city not to miss should you make a beeline for just one in the region. Away from the cities, there are rural temptations aplenty, such as the western ranges of the **Apuseni mountains**, with their stalactite caves and wooden churches, and the spas at **Băile Herculane** and **Băile Felix**; moreover, there are some terrific **festivals** to be experienced in the smaller villages.

Transport links with major towns in Transylvania, such as Cluj and Sibiu, as well as major cities across the border in Hungary (Debrecen and Szeged) and Serbia (Belgrade), are excellent.

Oradea and around

Situated on the banks of the River Crişul Repede, the congenial city of **ORADEA** is the capital of Crişana. The city is located close to the site of Biharea – the capital of the Vlach voivode, Menumorut, who resisted Hungarian claims on the region during the tenth century. Founded around a monastery,

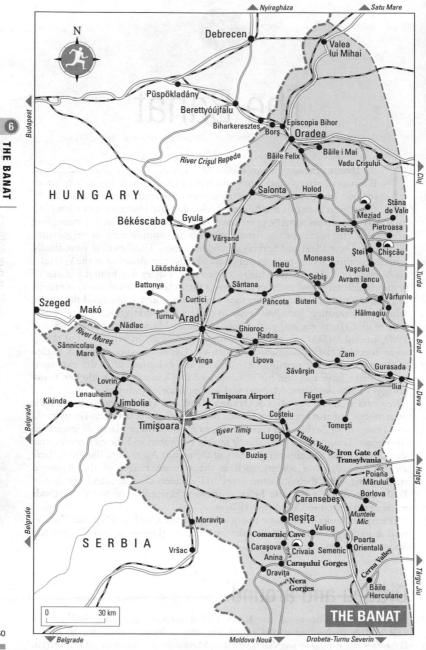

THE BANAT

the medieval town of Nagyvarad (as the Magyars still call it) prospered during the reign of **Mátyás Corvinus**, who was raised at the Bishop's Palace here, and later acquired a mammoth Vauban-style citadel and the wealth of stately Neoclassical, Baroque and Secession piles which constitute Oradea's most characteristic feature today. Aside from serving as a useful place to break a journey en route to or from Hungary, Oradea is just a short bus ride away from the spas at **Băile Felix** and **Băile 1 Mai**.

Arrival and information

From the **train station** on Piaţa Bucureşti, trams #1 and #3 run south along Calea Republicii towards the town centre (those with black numbers run from the station and those with red numbers run to it), past the Crişul department store and southeast along Str. Gen. Magheru. To reach the town centre proper, get off the tram at the department store stop and continue on foot along Str. Republicii. The **bus station**, southeast of the centre at Str. Războieni 81, is immediately adjacent to the Oradea Est train halt, from where it's a thirty-minute walk into town (or take bus #12). The **airport** is on the southern edge of Oradea, on the Arad road; buses for the airport leave from the TAROM office (see below) seventy minutes before each flight. A taxi to or from the airport should cost no more than €5.

In the absence of a tourist office, the best place to obtain information is from Apuseni Experience, at Piaţa 1 Decembrie 4–6 (☎0259/472 434, ⓦwww .apuseniexperience.ro); members of the Association of Eco-tourism in Romania, they can arrange visits to the Chişcău and Meziad caves (see p.366), as well as organize a range of hiking and biking trips in the Apuseni, and various cultural tours.

The **post office** is at Str. Ciorogariu 12 (Mon–Fri 7am–1.30pm & 2–8pm, Sat 8am–1pm); the **CFR office** at Str. Republicii 2 (Mon–Fri 7am–8pm); and **TAROM** at Piaţa Regele Ferdinand 2 (Mon–Fri 8am–6pm, Sat 10am–1pm; ☎0259/231 918). There's **Internet access** at the Internet Club, Str. A. Edy 2 (daily 10am–2am) and the Computer House, Str. Iuliu Maniu 6 (daily 8am–9pm).

Accommodation

Oradea's **hotels** tend to be either budget or high-end, with little in between. There's **hostel**-type accommodation at the Posticum cultural and youth centre at Str. Teiului 26 (☎0259/431 398; ⓔkim@posticum.ro), while you could also try chasing up a **dorm bed** from the County Youth and Sport Office at Str. Vulcan 11 (☎0259/414 254). Otherwise, there are possibilities in **Băile Felix** and **Băile 1 Mai**, two resorts located a short distance southeast of town (see p.365). The latter also has a **campsite**.

Astoria Str. Teatrului 1 ☎&ⓕ0259/430 508. A pleasant Secession building with a range of rather antique looking, but clean and cheap one- to three-bed rooms, with or without baths or showers. ❷–❸

Atrium Str. Republicii 38 ☎0259/414 421, ⓦwww.hotelatrium.ro. Exceptional, very good-value hotel designed within a large atrium, with windows facing towards an airy, indoor courtyard. The rooms, all with Wi-Fi, are very stylish, while the bathrooms come with fabulous little corner

tubs. Home to a quality restaurant, too (see p.365). ❻

Continental Aleea Ştrandului 1 ☎0259/418 655, ⓦwww.continentalhotels.ro. Part of the Romanian *Continental* group, this thoroughly modern and efficient hotel is frequented almost exclusively by businessmen and tour groups. ❾

Elite Parcul I.C. Bratianu 26 ☎0259/414 924, ⓦwww.hotelelite.ro. A far classier, and less expensive, option than the nearby *Continental*, this small hotel has sumptuous rooms with bags of

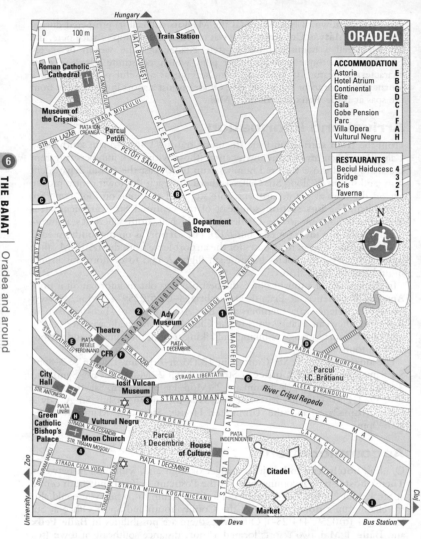

Map labels:

ORADEA

Scale: 0 — 100 m

Hungary ▲

Train Station

Roman Catholic Cathedral

Museum of the Crișana

PIATA ION CREANGĂ

Parcul Petöfi

STR. GH. LAZĂR

STRADA MUZEULUI

STR. SF. CANONICILOR

PIAȚA BUCUREȘTI

CALEA REPUBLICII

PETÖFI SÁNDOR

STRADA CASTANILOR

STRADA M. EMINESCU

STRADA H. COSBARGIU

STR. ADY ENDRE

STR. TEATRULUI

STR. MOSCOVEI

Theatre

PIAȚA REGELE FERDINAND

CFR

City Hall

STR. ANTONESCU

PIAȚA UNIRII

Green Catholic Bishop's Palace

STRADA V. ALECSANDRI

Vulturul Negru

STR. TRAIAN MOȘOIU

Moon Church

STRADA CUZA VODĂ

STR. AVRAM IANCU

STRADA MIHAI VITEAZU

STRADA MIHAIL KOGĂLNICEANU

PIAȚA 1 DECEMBER

Parcul 1 Decembrie

House of Culture

Iosif Vulcan Museum

STRADA ROMANA

STRADA INDEPENDENTEI

STRADA LIBERTĂȚII

Ady Museum

STRADA REPUBLICII

STR. A. LAZĂR

PIAȚA 1 DECEMBRIE

STRADA GEORGE

STRADA GENERAL MAGHERU

STRADA ENESCU

Department Store

STRADA SPITALULUI

STRADA GHEORGHE DOJA

N

Parcul I.C. Brătianu

STRADA ANDREI MUREȘAN

ALEEA ȘTRANDULUI

River Crișul Repede

STRADA D. CANTEMIR

PIAȚA INDEPENDENTEI

Citadel

CALEA 1 MAI

CALEA CLUJULUI

STRADA D. GHEREA

Market

ACCOMMODATION
Astoria E
Hotel Atrium B
Continental G
Elite D
Gala C
Gobe Pension I
Parc F
Villa Opera A
Vulturul Negru H

RESTAURANTS
Beciul Haiducesc 4
Bridge 3
Cris 2
Taverna 1

University ◀ Zoo ◀   Deva ▼   Bus Station ▼   ▶ Cluj

character; facilities include private parking, sauna and Jacuzzi, not to mention an enchanting little restaurant (see p.365). ❽

Gala Str. Bogdan Petriceicu Hașdeu 20 ☎0259/467 177. ⓦwww.hotelgala.ro. Reasonable-value hotel with comfortable and stylish, if slightly colourless, rooms; facilities include sauna, massage, private parking and an inviting cellar bar. ❼

Gobe Pension Str. D. Gherea 26 ☎0259/413 513, ⓦwww.gobe.ro. Located a short way south of the citadel, this is a little gem of a guesthouse, with fittings in the style of a Hungarian *csarda*, such as brightly coloured

hand-woven duvets and wooden furniture painted with Hungarian peasant motifs. Friendly owners and very reasonably priced, too. ❺

Parc Str. Republicii 5 ☎0259/411 699, ⓕ418 410. Another pleasant, if slightly shabby, Secession building on the city's main pedestrianized street. The rooms – singles, doubles and triples with and without shower – are perfectly clean and spacious. ❸–❹

Vulturul Negru Str. Independenței 1 ☎0259/450 000, ⓦwww.vulturalnegro.ro. Housed in an extraordinary Secessionist building, the "Black Eagle" has been spectacularly reincarnated and remains the city's most characterful hotel. From

6 **THE BANAT** | Oradea and around

the mosaic-floored lobby and glittering chandeliers, to the beautifully refined rooms with their wrought-iron beds, thick soft carpets and colourfully tiled bathrooms, the place oozes class. ⑤

The City

Oradea's sights are broadly concentrated in two main areas north and south of the **Crişul Repede river**. To the north lies a triumvirate of museums, while across the river are the city's most interesting buildings and the large citadel.

North of the river

In the large leafy park just west of the train station on Str. Şirul Canonicilor stands the **Roman Catholic Cathedral**, built by countless serfs between 1752 and 1780, and reputedly the largest Baroque building in Romania. Unattractive from the outside, its interior is decorated with gold leaf and marble and accommodates a huge organ – posters give details of regular concerts held here. The serfs' labour was also doubtless exploited to construct the vast U-shaped **Bishop's Palace** adjacent to the cathedral; built by Franz Anton Hillebrandt in 1762–77, the vast three-floored building was modelled on Lucas von Hildebrandt's Belvedere Palace in Vienna. It's currently home to the **Museum of the Crişana** (Tues, Thurs & Sat 10am–3pm, Wed, Fri & Sun 10am–6pm), which contains fairly standard history, natural history and ethnographic displays, as well as a good selection of nineteenth- and twentieth-century art. There are plans to move the museum by 2010.

Heading south towards the river, **Calea Republicii** becomes a pedestrianized promenade, lined with shops, cafés, fast-food joints and many ostentatious Secession buildings in various states of decay. Of particular interest are the buildings at the intersection of Calea Republicii and Str. Eminescu; despite being stripped of much of their original plasterwork, the buildings at no. 10 and no. 12 (the former Apollo Palace) have retained some outstanding features, notably heavily stuccoed facades and corner turrets.

Calea Republicii eventually opens onto **Piaţa Regele Ferdinand**, dominated by the 1900 State Theatre, a typically pompous design by the Viennese duo Helmer and Fellner. Just behind the theatre stand a couple more fine Secessionist buildings; at Str. Patrioţilor 6, the pink-brick Adorjan house, built in 1903, sports a flurry of rosettes, as does the rough grey stone facade of the second Adorjan house at no. 4.

Just to the east of Str. Republicii are two small memorial houses: the lovely, custard-coloured **Muller building** (Wed, Fri & Sat 10am–2pm & 4–6pm, Tues, Thurs & Sun 10am–3pm) in the centre of the tiny Traian Park commemorates the celebrated Magyar poet **Endre Ady** (1877–1919) who lived in Oradea for four years and, unusually for his era, opposed Hungarian chauvinism towards the Romanians. Formerly a society café where Ady and his pals would gather for evenings of drinks and bonhomie, it now keeps a handful of personal effects and Ady-era furnishings, including a neatly arranged editorial suite complete with beautiful oak bureau – to the rear is a cool, shaded terrace café and basement bar (see p.365).

The other memorial house, at Str. Vulcan 16 (same times), remembers the poet and novelist **Iosif Vulcan** (1841–1907), who lived here between 1880 and 1906. Vulcan was instrumental in gathering the works of key literary players of his day, resulting in the foundation of the literary journal *Familia*, which is still going strong – it was in this magazine that Mihai Eminescu made his debut in 1866 with the poem "De-aş avea" ("If I Had"), a copy of which is on display. The house contains a few items of furniture, including Vulcan's Biedermeier desk, though it largely seeks to recreate the atmosphere of a late nineteenth-century literary salon.

South of the river

Crossing the Crişul Repede from Piaţa Regele Ferdinand brings you to **Piaţa Unirii**, a vast open space which, aside from the nondescript Catholic church half-blocking the square's north side, is replete with fanciful Secessionist buildings. The former **City Hall** in the northwestern corner is a monumental restatement of well-worn classical themes to which the architects added a fun touch: chimes that play the March of Avram Iancu every hour. Given that the Austro-Hungarians were still in control when the building was raised in 1902–03, it seems odd that they allowed this commemoration of Iancu, a Romanian revolutionary whose agitation inspired the protest on the "Field of Liberty" at Blaj in 1848 (see p.204), and who then took to the hills with a guerrilla band, harassing Magyar troops and landlords and urging the serfs to revolt. Standing just south of City Hall is the **Greek Catholic Episcopal Palace** (1905), a more spectacular piece of architecture spotted with all manner of protrusions and jutting towers.

Facing these across Piaţa Unirii is the splendidly named **Vulturul Negru** (Black Eagle), an ornate Secession-style edifice dating from 1908. Running through it is an arcade, notable for its beautiful stained-glass roof connecting three neighbouring streets; recently renovated, the arcade is now lined with cafés and bars, now making it one of the most enjoyable places in town for a drink. Part of the complex is occupied by a hotel of the same name (see p.362); formerly an ill-lit labyrinth of rooms and corridors inhabited by brooding staff and a furtive clientele, it's now the city's most luxurious hotel.

To the south of the hotel, on the corner of Piaţa Unirii and Str. Alecsandri, the **Moskovits Palace** is another enduring Secessionist edifice – cut into the brickwork on the upper half of the green-and-yellow checked facade are several fine carvings illustrating men and women going about their daily chores. Beyond here, Oradea's main Orthodox church, built in 1792, marks the stylistic transition from Baroque to Neoclassical; it is better known as the **Moon Church** after the large sphere mounted beneath its clock, which rotates to indicate the lunar phases over a period of 28 days.

A short walk east of here, along Str. Traian Moşoiu, is the city's small Jewish quarter. There are no fewer than three imposing **synagogues** nearby (there were once eleven in the city), testament to Oradea's role as a major Jewish settlement prior to World War II: on Str. Independenţei near the Vulturul Negru; on Piaţa Rahovei; and just east of Piaţa Unirii, at Str. Mihai Viteazul 2, which is the only one still functioning. In December 1927, Codreanu's League of the Archangel Michael, soon to become the Iron Guard (see box, p.282), held a congress here – they wrecked four synagogues before leaving.

To the east of Piaţa Unirii rises the imposing bulk of Oradea's **citadel**, a Renaissance stronghold enlarged during the eighteenth century by Italian disciples of the Swiss military architect Vauban. Pentagonal in shape, with bastions guarding each corner, the citadel used to be additionally protected by a moat filled with warm water from the River Peţea, which runs around the southern edge of the town. A major reconstruction project is finally under way, as many of the external walls are very dilapidated, though several buildings remain standing, including the bakery and officers' barracks, both dating from 1692, and the food warehouse and administration block, built in 1775. Housed in a section of the old Princely Palace is the university's art faculty – head through into the courtyard and you can view some interesting bits of sculpture.

Heading south from Piaţa Unirii, Str. Avram Iancu becomes Calea Armatei Romăne, with a **Military Museum** (Mon–Fri 10am–4pm) on the left at no. 24 – containing a dusty collection of costumes, weaponry and medals through the ages – and the university on the right. Opposite the museum is a **wooden church**, built in Letca in 1760 and moved here in 1991 to serve as the theological faculty's chapel; with its new porch and radiators, its spick-and-span pine pews, it no longer has the authentic atmosphere of a village church, but it is usually open and you can climb up into the tower.

Eating, drinking and entertainment

There's rather scant choice when it comes to **eating in Oradea**; the most impressive restaurant is *Beciul Haiducesc*, Str. Traian Moşoiu 5, which, with its pine bench seating and sheepskin rugs draped over wooden partitions, makes for a cosy venue to tuck into the above-average Romanian food. Also pretty good is *Taverna*, Str. Eminescu 2, with more traditional Romanian fare and waitresses dressed in local costume; it also has a no-smoking section. There's pizza and pasta at the convivial *Bridge* restaurant, at the southern end of the bridge linking Str. Libertăţii and Str. Independenţiei. Oradea also possesses one of Romania's few vegetarian restaurants, the delightful *Cris*, secreted away at Str. G. Enescu 30 (Sun–Thurs 9am–9pm, Fri 9am–5pm). Beyond here, you could try the smart, and not too expensive, restaurants in the *Atrium* and *Elite* hotels, both of which have accomplished international menus. The Unic **supermarket** on Str. Eminescu (Mon–Fri 7am–7pm, Sat 8am–2pm) is a good place to stock up before moving on.

The town has a smattering of fairly lively **drinking** venues; the most popular spots are the *Bridge*, a large, atmospheric riverside pizzeria/pub (see above); and the cool *Chanson Café* in the basement of the Endre Ady memorial house (see p.363) – it also has live music on selected weekdays. *Kelly's*, at the corner of Str. Republicii and Str. Moscovei, is a poor imitation of an Irish pub, but it has a pleasant enough terrace and also serves a limited bar menu. Otherwise, there is a cluster of cafés and bars inside the revamped Vultural Negru acrcade.

Theatrical and **operatic** performances (in both Romanian and Hungarian) at the State Theatre on Piaţa Regele Ferdinand are well regarded, as are concerts by the town's **Philharmonic Orchestra**, housed at Piaţa 1 Decembrie 10 (tickets from Str. Republicii 6). Children are sure to enjoy performances at the Arcadia **Puppet Theatre**, inside the Vulturul Negru arcade on Piaţa Unirii – the entrance is on Str. Alecsandri.

Băile Felix and Băile 1 Mai

Located within easy reach of Oradea are the **spa towns** of Băile Felix and Băile 1 Mai. Neither is especially attractive, but they're enjoyable places to spend an afternoon relaxing; treatments (available at hotels) include healing mud baths, either in sapropelic fossil gunge or the local peat bog, and dips in pools fed by the warm and slightly radioactive River Peţea, in which the **thermal lotus**, otherwise found only in the Nile Delta, has survived since the Tertiary Period.

Just 8km southeast of Oradea along the DN76, **BĂILE FELIX** is a small, compact town whose atmospheric residential core has been almost totally subsumed by an ugly jumble of concrete high-rise hotels. Its central attractions are a large **thermal pool** (daily 8am–7pm; €3) surrounded by mock-rustic buildings, and a park containing a **wooden church**. Most of the resort's dozen or so **hotels** are bland and not particularly good value, though there are one or two reasonable choices: the best of the upper-end places are the *Termal*

(☎0259/318 214, ✉hotel.termal@turismfelix.ro; ❼), which has pool, sauna and solarium, and *Nufărul* (☎0259/318 142, 📠319 172; ❼). Decent-value two-stars include the *Lotus* (☎0259/318 361, 📠318 399; ❺) and the very basic *Felix* (☎0259/318 421, 📠318 422; ❸). Much more homely is the bright little *Pension Sebastian* (☎0745/048 367; ❸), near the market stalls, and, nearby, the *Bungalow Monaco complex* (☎0722/318 180; ⓦwww.hotelmonacofelix.com; ❹), with hotel rooms and bungalows in its own little compound – and **bikes** for rent.

You'll also find many houses in the residential area advertising private rooms (*cazare* or *camera*), not to mention proprietors hanging about the streets with signs – expect to pay around €30 for a double with bathroom. As for **restaurants**, take your pick from any number of identical places. The resort is served by tram #4 from Oradea's train station or bus #12 from the Moon Church to the Nufarul terminal on the outskirts of Oradea, and then bus #14; alternatively, six trains a day head for Felix.

The much smaller and less developed spa of **BĂILE 1 MAI** (Ântâi Mai) is reached by bus #15 from Nufarul, turning off the DN76 just before Băile Felix. There's some great-value accommodation here, mostly in the form of excellent **pensions**; two of the best are *Catalin* at no. 15a (☎0259/319 848; ❸), and, a few paces along at no. 87, *Chrisland* (☎0259/319 048; ❸). Opposite here, the small *Apollo* **campsite** has some two-bed huts (May to mid-Oct; ❶).

The western Apuseni mountains

The **Apuseni mountains** lie predominantly in Transylvania (see p.243), but a few attractions along its **western approaches** are within easy reach of Oradea. Most are close to the DN76, but trains to Beiuş and Vaşcău now take a very roundabout route, following the main Arad line through **SALONTA**, birthplace of the Hungarian poet Arany Janos (1817–82). Housed in the seventeenth-century tower on the main square, Str. Libertaţii, a small **museum** (April–Oct Tues–Fri & Sun 10am–2pm & 4–6pm; Nov–March daily 10am–4pm) dedicated to Janos exhibits a few of his personal effects.

Beiuş and the caves

The small town of **BEIUŞ**, 55km southeast of Oradea, is the main jumping-off point for the impressive stalactite **caves of Meziad and Chişcău**, excursions to which are organized by Apuseni Experience in Oradea (see p.361).

Travelling independently from Oradea, take the bus to Beiuş, then one of four daily buses from the station on the southern edge of town to the village of **MEZIAD**, some 10km northeast. The famous Meziad cave, with its huge entrance arch, is a further 3km beyond the village. The cave was first explored in 1859, and after the construction of a road in the 1960s it was visited by some 25,000 people a year until its popularity was usurped by the opening of the even more spectacular cave at Chişcău in 1980. Hour-long **tours** (daily 9am–5pm; €2) start as soon as there are enough people; guides shepherd parties around the caves, commenting on the stalactites and other features of this warren, whose total length is almost 5km.

There are also bus services (Mon–Sat 2 daily) between Beiuş and **CHIŞCĂU**, some 25km to the southwest, where in 1975 local quarry workers discovered a cave containing dozens of Neolithic bear skeletons – hence its name, "**Bears' Cave**" (Peştera Urşilor). Unlike other caves in Romania, this one is atmos-pherically lit, making the one-hour guided tour (Tues–Sun 9am–5pm; €2) an experience not to be missed. The rock formations of the 488-metre-long upper gallery – shaped like castles, wraiths and beasts – are accompanied by the sound of water crashing into subterranean pools.

Some 38km east of Beiuş is **STÂNA DE VALE**, a modest alpine resort, where an excellent three-star **hotel**, the *Iadolina* (☎0259/322 583; ●), **cabins** and a **campsite** serve the hiking fraternity in summer and skiers in winter. There's a long **ski** season here, with the resort's three **pistes** usually open from November to April, and lessons available for beginners. From the resort, it's about six hours' walk to the *Padiş cabana* (see p.249), taking a path marked with red stripes that runs via the Poieni peak, the Cumpănăţelu saddle and the Vărăşoaia clearing. Experienced hikers might prefer the more challenging trail to Meziad (6–8hr, marked by blue triangles; not recommended in winter or bad weather); with many twists and turns around karstic features, this follows the ridge above the Iad valley, surmounting the Piatra Tisei peak.

East into the mountains

Buses run from Beiuş to **PIETROASA**, a picturesque village on the upper reaches of the River Crişul Pietros, where water-powered sawmills remain operational and the older residents still wear traditional Bihor costume. Each year, on a Sunday in August, the villagers troop 8km north up the Aleu valley for the **festival** of Bulciugul de Valea Aleu. The forest road, which leads up to the Padiş plateau near the Citadels of Ponor (see p.249), can be covered on foot or by car – there are no bus services beyond Pietroasa – and the hiking trail to the *Padiş cabana*, marked with blue crosses, follows the road for the most part, with a path diverging south after about 5km (marked by yellow triangles) to the Focul Viu cave, near Ponor. If you do plan to do any extensive hiking in the mountains, arm yourself with the 1:200,000 *Munţii Apuşeni* **map**.

About 3km south of the turning to Pietroasa is **RIENI**, worth a look for its **wooden church**, just west of the village, by the train halt. Built in 1753, the church is now slightly run-down, with lots of woodpecker damage, but interesting for its doorway and its spire, typical of this area. However, the best part of the journey to Scarişoara comes once you leave the DN76 and the rail line beyond the grimy industrial town of **Ştei** – known as Dr Petru Groza under communism (see box below) – and head eastwards along the sinuous DN75, where the scenery becomes more dramatic. The village of **BĂIŢA**, 10km east along the DN75, has several caves nearby and holds a lively **fair** on the last Sunday in September. On the far side of the Vârtop Pass (1160m) lie **Arieşeni** and **Gârda de Sus**, southern entry points to Padiş (see p.249).

Dr Petru Groza

A delegate at the Assembly of Alba Iulia in 1918, **Dr Petru Groza** (1884–1958) was an important politician before and after World War II. With the Communist Party banned since 1924, it was he who, in 1933, founded the agrarian party known as the Ploughmen's Front, which was actually a cover for the communists; as a prosperous lawyer and landowner, Groza was well camouflaged. He was imposed as prime minister of the coalition government in 1945 – after communist *agents-provocateurs* had gunned down communist demonstrators to discredit the democratic parties then leading the government – and organized elections in 1946 to establish the communists in power. The people voted overwhelmingly against them but to no avail: the result was falsified, and in mid-1947 the remaining leaders of the democratic parties were arrested.

Groza tried to moderate the nationalism of the Communist Party leader Gheorghiu-Dej; however, on December 30, 1947, he visited King Mihai with Gheorghiu-Dej to force the king's abdication. As an internationalist Groza sought reconciliation with Hungary, and his dismissal in 1952, along with Ana Pauker's Hungarian acolyte Vasile Luka, was a harbinger of the regime's crackdown on Romania's Magyar minority.

The branch line from Oradea terminates at **Vaşcău**, but the DN76 continues through the mountains for 32km until it joins the Arad–Brad road and rail line at the village of **Vârfurile**. En route, just south of Criştioru de Jos, a rough track leaves the main road and leads 30km east into Transylvania to the village of **Avram Iancu** below **Mount Găina**, where the famous Girl Fair occurs every year (see p.248). There are several more festivals in the villages around Vârfurile, but these are easier to approach from Arad (see below).

Arad and around

One of the oldest towns in the Banat, **ARAD** is neither as vibrant, nor does it possess nearly the same number of sights, as either Oradea or Timişoara. However, it can showcase an impressive number of Habsburg-era buildings as well as an eighteenth-century citadel, while its position on the main road and rail routes between these two cities, and its status as a major rail junction for international connections, makes it a convenient place to stop off for an afternoon's discovery. It also makes a good base from which to strike out towards many of the nearby **villages** in the foothills of the Apuseni mountains.

Arrival and information

The **train and bus stations** lie 500m apart in the north of the city on Piaţa Gării and Calea Aurel Vlaicu respectively; take tram #1, #2 or #3 for the city centre. All trains from Timişoara halt in the southern suburb of Arad Nou, from where trams #3 and #5 head into the centre. Arad's tiny **airport** (☎0257/254 440) is about 3km west of town, though you'll have to rely on taxis (around €5), as there's no public transport – check with the tourist office (see below) for taxi companies.

The town's **tourist office** is located opposite the *Continental* hotel at B-dul. Revoluţiei 84–86 (April–Sept Mon–Fri 10am–5pm, Sat 10am–2pm; Oct–March Mon–Fri 10am–3pm; ☎0257/270 277, ⓔturism@primariaarad.ro). Another good source of **information** is the Sirius travel agency at B-dul. Revoluţiei 55 (Mon–Fri 8am–8pm, Sat 9.30am–1.30pm; ☎0257/255 545, ⓦwww.siriustravel .ro), a friendly little office that can also arrange **homestays** in villages such as Moneasa (see p.372). The **CFR office** is at Str. Metianu 16 (Mon–Fri 8am–8pm); the main **post office** at B-dul. Revoluţiei 46–48 (Mon–Fri 7am–8pm, Sat 8am–1pm), and there's **Internet access** at the Call Net Café (daily 8am–midnight), located behind the Lutheran church just off B-dul. Revoluţiei.

Accommodation

There's plenty of accommodation in town, with a good stock of **hotels** and **pensions** both in the centre and the suburbs. There are also two reasonable **motels** within reach of the city: the *Hanul de la Răscruce* (☎0257/237 963; ❷), 7km west of town along the Nădlac road, and the *Vinga* (☎0257/460 630; ❷), located in the village of the same name some 20km south of Arad on the road to Timişoara. If you're looking for something a bit more rural, call in at the Sirius agency (see above), who can help arrange **homestays** outside Arad.

Arad B-dul. Decebal 9 ☎0257/280 894, ⓔhotel_arad@yahoo.com. This decent place, in a fairly quiet, excellent central location, has large, high-ceilinged rooms – with and without bathroom. Good value. ❸–❹

Ardealul B-dul. Revoluţiei 98 ☎0257/280 840, ⓦwww.hotelardealul.ro. Arad's most characterful hotel is a former coaching inn where Brahms, Liszt, Johann Strauss and Casals all once performed. The grand, spiralling staircase rather belies the faded,

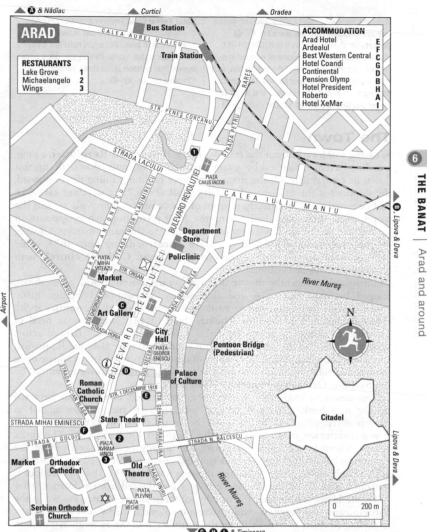

ARAD

▲ Ⓐ & Nădlac   ▲ Curtici   ▲ Oradea

RESTAURANTS

Lake Grove	1
Michaelangelo	2
Wings	3

ACCOMMODATION

Arad Hotel	E
Ardealul	F
Best Western Central	C
Hotel Coandi	G
Continental	D
Pension Olymp	B
Hotel President	H
Roberto	A
Hotel XeMar	I

Bus Station

Train Station

CALEA AUREL VLAICU

STR PENEŞ CORCANUL

STRADA LACULUI

PIAŢA CAIUS IACOB

STRADA PETRU RAREŞ

BULEVARD REVOLUŢIEI

CALEA IULIU MANIU

STRADA D A ANTONESCU

STRADA TUDOR VLADIMIRESCU

Department Store

Policlinic

STR CRIŞAN

STRADA CALU MILEA

PIAŢA MIHAI VITEAZU

STR GHEORGHE POPA

Market

STRADA GEORGE COŞBUC

Art Gallery

STRADA HORIA

River Mureş

City Hall

PIAŢA GEORGE ENESCU

Pontoon Bridge (Pedestrian)

N

Palace of Culture

Roman Catholic Church

STRADA LUCIAN BLAGA

B-DUL DECEBAL

STR 1 DECEMBRIE 1918

STRADA GENERAL DRAGALINA

State Theatre

STRADA MIHAI EMINESCU

STRADA V. GOLDIŞ

PIAŢA AVRAM IANCU

Market

Orthodox Cathedral

Old Theatre

STRADA N. BĂLCESCU

STRADA UNIRII

Citadel

River Mureş

PIAŢA PLEVNEI

PIAŢA VECHE

Serbian Orthodox Church

0   200 m

▲ Airport

► Ⓑ Lipova & Deva

► Lipova & Deva

▼ Ⓖ, Ⓗ, Ⓘ & Timişoara

soulless rooms (triples and quads available, too), but it's reasonably cheap and there's a hearty breakfast included. ④–⑤

Best Western Central Str. Horia 8 ℡0257/256 636, ⓦwww.bestwesternarad.ro. This modern, central hotel has a range of well-furnished rooms, some of which have been freshly renovated and are only a fraction pricier than the older ones; the welcoming staff also makes this one of the better places to stay. ⑥–⑦

Continental B-dul. Revoluţiei 79–81 ℡0257/281 700, ⓦwww.continentalhotels.ro. The town's most

expensive hotel is much like all the others in the *Continental* chain, a slick but ultimately charmless place predominantly aimed at foreign businessmen. ⑧

Pension Olymp Str. Vrancei 36 ℡0257/279 443. A sweet little pension out in the eastern suburbs with fifteen clean and inviting rooms (including three-bed rooms), all with TV and bath; laundry facilities, too. Bus #5 or #7. ⑤

President Calea Timişorii 164 ℡0257/278 804, ⓦwww.hotel-president.ro. This classy place, 2km south of town, across the river and out on the road to

Timişoara, has neat, colourful and airy rooms; there's a decent restaurant here, too. Bus #3 or #5. **6**
Roberto Str. C. Brâncoveanu 5 ☎0257/289 014, Ⓦwww.hotelroberto.ro. Reasonable pension in a dull but safe area 1km west of the bus station, with large rooms with and without shower. Take any bus heading north from the train station and alight at the second stop; it's just off Str. Cocorilor. **2–3**

Hotel XeMar Calea Timişorii 1 ☎0257/287 485, Ⓔoffice@xemar.ro. Located just across the bridge 1.5km south of town, this smart hotel has lovely, warmly decorated rooms; they've also got a simple, homely little pension 200m down the road at no. 13 (same tel. no). **3–5**

The Town

Spearing southwards from the train station is **Bulevardul Revoluţiei**, a long, tree-lined avenue, bisected by a continual stream of trams that rattle up and down its central strip. Of the many impressive buildings lining the boulevard, the standout is the brilliant white **City Hall** at no. 75, a wedding-cake-like edifice raised in 1876. Directly in front of it a commemorative plaque lists the names of all those who died during the 1989 revolution, while opposite, in the middle of the road, is a simple monument to the same martyrs. Closing off the street's southern end is the **State Theatre**, dating from 1874, while close by is the massive turn-of-the-century **Roman Catholic church**, with an impressive domed entrance hall.

Immediately behind the theatre is **Piaţa Avram Iancu**, a large green square fringed by numerous two- and three-storey Secessionist buildings, many adorned with interesting stucco work and motifs. East of the square, at Str. Gheorghe Lazăr 2, is the **Old Theatre**, built in 1817 and now in need of extensive renovation – it was here that Eminescu and many famous actors worked – while, to the west, is the main **market** and the Baroque Romanian Orthodox cathedral (1865). The jumble of dusty streets south of the square once comprised Old Arad, and was also home to a large Serb minority, as evinced by the **Serbian Orthodox church** on Piaţa Sărbească.

Commanding a loop of the River Mureş, Arad's huge **citadel** faces the town on the west bank. A six-pointed star with ramparts and bastions angled to provide overlapping fields of fire, it was the state of the art in fortifications when it was constructed, in the style of Vauban, between 1762 and 1783. The Turks, against whom it was ostensibly raised, had already been pushed out of the Pannonian basin in 1718, but its underground casements provided the Habsburgs with a ready-made prison following the suppression of the 1848 revolution. It remains a barracks to this day, and can only be admired from a distance. After 1718, the Habsburgs drained the marshy southern Banat, an area known as the Partium, and colonized it with Swabians, Slovaks, Serbs and Romanians, excluding Magyars so as to facilitate the assimilation of this strategic region into their empire. But despite this, Arad's population rose up against Habsburg rule several times in 1848–49; the revolt was finally crushed with the help of Tsarist Russia, and the Habsburgs made an example of the ringleaders by executing thirteen generals, mostly Hungarian, outside the fortress walls.

The executions feature prominently in the **County History Museum** (Tues–Sun 9am–5pm) housed within the eclectic **Palace of Culture** (1913) behind the City Hall on Piaţa George Enescu; there are also decent archeological and ethnographical displays here, though the absence of English captions will leave you none the wiser as to what you're looking at. Far more engrossing is an exhibition on the **1989 revolution**, housed in another wing of the palace – the entrance is on the river side. Documenting the events of December 21 and 22, there are some moving exhibits, including possessions of those killed – such as a blood-soaked jacket and a trainer with a bullet hole through it (and the offending bullet) – in addition to some superb photos. Officially, nineteen people died in Arad, a relatively small number compared to other cities.

On the opposite side of B–dul. Revoluţiei, in the library building at Str. Gheorghe Popa 2, the **Art Gallery** (Tues–Sun 10am–5.30pm) features furniture from the seventeenth century on, as well as the odd painting by the likes of Grigorescu and Aman.

Eating and drinking

The best of what few **restaurants** Arad possesses is *Michaelangelo*, a cosy little pizza and pasta house just off Piaţa Avram Iancu at Str. Unirii 12 (Mon–Sat noon–midnight, Sun 6pm–midnight) – though with just half a dozen tables, you'd do well to get in early. Two places worth investigating on Piaţa Avram Iancu are *Wings*, on the south side, whose varied menu (in the style of a newspaper) features such delights as goose in barbecue sauce and baked mushrooms stuffed with cheese and spinach; and *Manhattan* on the eastern side, which offers less fanciful food such as beef and goulash (daily 11am–midnight). North of town, opposite the new church on Piaţa Caius Iacob, there's the *Lake Grove* restaurant, which has a large terrace overlooking an artificial lake. *Libelula*, at B–dul. Revoluţiei 51, is the place to indulge in cakes and ices, while the fabulous little *La Creperie*, on the corner of Str. Bălcescu and Str. Dragalina, offers a terrific selection of sweet and savoury pancakes to eat in or take away (Mon–Fri 10am–8pm, Sat & Sun 4–10pm). The **markets** in Piaţa Catedralei and Piaţa Mihai Viteazu sell bread, cheese and seasonal fruit and veg.

During the summer, most townsfolk head to the Neptun Strand Park, across the bridge by the citadel, which is rammed with **cafés**, **bars** and open-air **discos**. Otherwise, in town itself, the liveliest **drinking** spot is *Wings*, an energetic cellar pub next to the restaurant of the same name (see above).

West of Arad

The area to the west of the Arad–Timişoara route is the quintessence of the Banat – originally marshy plains drained after the expulsion of the Turks and settled with a patchwork of diverse ethnic groups, some of whom still remain. One of the largest towns here is **SÂNNICOLAU MARE** (Nagyszentmiklós), known for the Nagyszentmiklós Hoard, the largest known find of ancient gold; 23 ten-kilogram vessels, believed to be made in the late eighth or ninth century and buried at the time of the Magyar invasion of 896, were found here in 1799 and removed to Vienna, where they still reside in the Imperial collection. The town is also famed as the birthplace of the Hungarian composer **Béla Bartók** (1881–1945), some of whose personal effects can be see inside the House of Culture, located at the beginning of the main pedestrianized street (Tues–Sun 9am–5pm). The house in which he was born, a simple dwelling marked by a plaque denoting his birth date, is a long walk north of town at Str. Cerbului 3.

Arriving at the **train station**, it's a long trudge into town – exit right, turn left past the petrol station and continue for about 2km along the main road, whereupon a church marks the centre. If you need to stay here, there's the modern and very pleasant *Malvina* **hotel** (☎0256/370 867; ❹), a short walk south of the church at Str. Republicii 18.

Moving on into Hungary and Germany
Arad, like Oradea, 117km to the north, lies just inside the border from Hungary. The crossing at Nădlac on the E68, some 50km away, is now mainly frequented

by trucks; **cars** and buses are encouraged to use a new, quieter route off the DN7 (E68) to Turnu, 17km from Arad, to Battonya in Hungary. Travelling **by train**, you'll cross over from Curtici, 12km to the north of Arad, to Lőkösháza just inside Hungary. All international **bus services** to Budapest and most of those to Germany run from the train station forecourt in Arad. Tickets for Budapest can usually be bought on the bus, but you may need to buy your ticket to Germany in advance from Atlassib Reisen, B-dul. Revoluţiei 35 (☎0257/252 727), or Andronic, Calea Victoriei 104 (☎0257/222 105).

Northeast of Arad

From Arad, it's possible to reach a number of villages noted for their **festivals**, either by road, or by branch rail lines. The formerly Schwab village of **SÂNTANA**, 7km east of the Arad–Oradea highway (a 35min journey by train from Arad towards Oradea or Brad, then a 15min walk to the centre), hosts the Sărbătoarea Iorgovanului festival in late May. Although nowadays little more than an excuse for dancing, music and dressing up in traditional costumes, the festival originated as a parish fair, like the one on February 1 at **PÂNCOTA**, 15km east and another thirty minutes by train towards Brad. Twenty kilometres northeast of Pâncota is **INEU**, where there's nothing except an abandoned castle, which once held one of Romania's notorious orphanages, but a further 18km to the east lies the village of **BÂRSA**, noted for its pottery and its fete, Sărbătoarea Druştelor, held on the first Sunday in April.

Continuing southeast towards Brad, you'll come to **Vârfurile** at the junction with the DN76 from Oradea. Just west, a minor road runs 6km north to the small village of **AVRAM IANCU** (not to be confused with the other village of the same name just over the mountains), where people from thirty mountain villages gather for the mountain **festival Tăcaşele**, on the second Sunday of June. Besides being an occasion for trading and socializing, this large fair provides a chance for musicians to play together, and is an excellent time to hear *cetera* (fiddles), *nai* (pan-pipes) and *buciume* or *tulnic* (alpine horns). The connection between new life and stirring lust probably underlies a good many spring festivals, and it is one that the delightfully named **Kiss Fair** (Târgul Sărutului) at **HĂLMAGIU**, 10km and two stops by train to the south of Vârfurile, acknowledges. Traditionally, the event enabled young men and women to cast around for a spouse while their elders discuss the fecundity of livestock and crops; the festival takes place in March, but the exact date varies from year to year so check with the tourist office in Arad (see p.368) first. Continuing towards Transylvania, trains terminate at **Brad**, but around a dozen buses a day plug the 32-kilometre gap to Deva; there are also daily services to Cluj, Oradea and Timişoara.

From Bârsa, another road branches off to the east, through the villages of Sebiş and Dezna, and up to **MONEASA**, a small spa resort in the Codru-Moma mountains. There's a fair amount of **accommodation** here, including the very average *Hotel Moneasa* (☎0257/313 151, ✉office@hotelmoneasa .ro; ❸–❹), which has a thermal pool and various treatments; the similarly unspectacular *Hotel Parc* (☎0257/313 231; ❸); and, opposite the *Parc*, the colourful *Vila Ana* pension (☎0257/499 737; ❻), which has four sumptuous rooms, a pool, sauna and Jacuzzi. Cheaper alternatives include the *Dallas* cabana (☎0257/313 202; ❶), serenely located beneath the wooded slopes to the north of the village, and the many private rooms advertised all around. Just two buses a day make the journey from here to Arad, and there are also local buses to Sebiş train station.

East of Arad

In 1934, the travel writer Patrick Leigh Fermor walked from Arad into Transylvania, staying with Magyar aristocrats whose dusty mansions and diminished bands of retainers spoke eloquently of the decline in their fortunes since the Trianon Treaty. Nowadays, you're more likely to make the journey by road or train, but be warned that rapid services stop at few places of interest. Passing through **SÂMBĂTENI**, 17km east of Arad, you'll see huge Gypsy palaces with colonnaded and pedimented fronts, built with the proceeds of sanction-busting trade with former Yugoslavia. **GHIOROC**, just off the DN7, 22km from Arad but reached by trams as well as local trains from the city, serves as a jumping-off point for the **Zărand mountains**; there's a chalet 500m away, from which you can make the three-hour hike (marked with blue stripes) to the *Căsoia* cabana (❶).

Radna and Lipova

RADNA, 35km from Arad, is the first major stop on the DN7 towards Transylvania. Here, Leigh Fermor played skittles with a Franciscan monk, until "we were both in a muck-sweat when the bell for vespers put an end to play". The great Abbey of Maria-Radna is now a hospital, but the echoing church is open, and the corridor to its left, lined with sacred hearts and images of bloody crashes in which Mary supposedly helped make things less bloody, opens onto the abbey's courtyard. The Abbey is an old pilgrimage site, where many churches were built, only to be destroyed by the Turks. The Baroque edifice of the current church was begun in 1756, but only consecrated in 1820; behind it, steps lead up to shrines and the Stations of the Cross in the oak woods.

Radna station, served by slow trains from both Arad and Timişoara, is actually nearer to **LIPOVA**, a dusty but quaint little town on the south bank of the Mureş. Its main sight is the lovely fifteenth-century **Orthodox Church of the Annunciation**, with its classical facade and a rather eccentric spire; these features belie the interior, which dates from 1338 and contains the most important **murals** in the Banat – in a pure Byzantine style, though painted in the early fifteenth century. Fragments of old murals are also visible on the exterior of the north wall. The church served as a mosque from 1552 to 1718, and was then rebuilt in 1732 in the Baroque style. Ask at the parish house, immediately north, for access. The town **museum** (Tues–Sun 9am–5pm), on the main street at Str. Bălcescu 21 and identified by casts of Trajan's Column over the door and two cast-iron lanterns either side, holds a painting apiece by Grigorescu and Aman, as well as bits of sculpture and furniture. Unlikely as it is that you'll need to stay here, the *Faleza* pension at Str. P Maior 13 (☎0257/561 702) is a perfectly respectable place northeast of town on the banks of the Mureş. Four kilometres south of town, and reached by eight buses a day from Radna station, is the spa of **Lipova Băile**; the pool aside, there's little here save for some two-bed huts (☎0257/563 139; ❷) and a campsite, a restaurant and terrace bar. There's also the *Bistro* **campsite**, west of Radna on the DN7, just beyond the service station.

The Mureş defile

Just a couple of kilometres beyond Lipova lies the ruined castle of **Şoimoş**. Built in the thirteenth century, and beefed up by Iancu de Hunedoara and his son Mátyás Corvinus in the fifteenth century, it guards the entry to the **Mureş defile** between the Zărand and Poiana Ruscă mountains. At the narrowest point of the defile is **SĂVÂRŞIN**, which hosts fairs on January 30 and November 27; the *Săvârşin* hotel (☎0257/557 322; ❷) offers simple rooms. Slow trains make half a dozen more stops, notably at **ZAM**, which marks the frontier with Transylvania, before they reach **ILIA**, scene of fairs on July 1 and March 25. If you want to break the journey, there's a hotel (●) on the main road to the east of the centre, and in **LESNIC**, 10km east, there are several homestays (contact Dorinel Ilea, no. 174; phone ahead on ☎0254/623 160). From here, the railway and the DN7 continue eastward towards Deva, Cluj and Sibiu, a route described more or less in reverse order in the Transylvania chapter of this book. Alternatively, you can head southwest across the Poiana Ruscă range towards Lugoj (see p.380), on the DN68A or the secondary railway (three fast and five slow trains daily).

Timişoara

An engaging and, in parts, enchanting city, **TIMIŞOARA** has long been the most prosperous and advanced of the cities of the Banat, claiming to be the first place in Romania to have a public water supply, the first in Europe to have

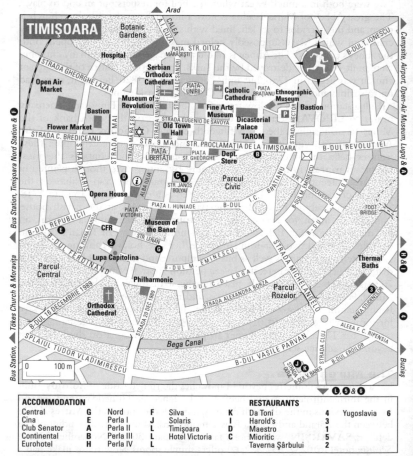

ACCOMMODATION				RESTAURANTS	
Central	**G**	Nord	**F**	Silva	**K**	Da Toni	**4**	Yugoslavia	**6**
Cina	**E**	Perla I	**J**	Solaris	**I**	Harold's	**3**
Club Senator	**A**	Perla II	**L**	Timişoara	**D**	Maestro	**1**
Continental	**B**	Perla III	**L**	Hotel Victoria	**C**	Mioritic	**5**
Eurohotel	**H**	Perla IV	**L**			Taverna Şârbului	**2**

electric street lighting, and one of the first in the world to have horse-drawn trams. It still boasts Romania's premier technical university.

From the fourteenth century onwards, Timişoara functioned as the capital of the Banat, playing a crucial role during the 1514 uprising and Hunyadi's campaigns against the Turks, who in 1552 conquered the town, from where they ruled the surrounding area until 1716. The Habsburgs who ejected them proved to be relatively benign masters over the next two centuries, the period when Temeschwar, as they called it, acquired many of its current features. These days, Timişoara is best known as the **birthplace of the 1989 revolution**, and still sees itself as the only true guardian of the revolution's spirit, swiftly hijacked by the neo-communists of Bucharest.

Close to the borders with Serbia and Hungary, and with an airport operating regular scheduled international flights, Timişoara is also a major hub for travel.

Arrival and information

From the city's main **train station**, Timişoara Nord, it's a thirty-minute walk east to the centre along B-dul. Republicii (or trolley buses #11, #14 and #18). The hectic and grubby **bus station** is across the canal from the train station and one block west, at Str. Reşiţa 54, next to the largest of Timişoara's markets. Timişoara **airport** (T0256/493 123) is 12km east of the city; bus #26 runs hourly to and from the airport, while a taxi should cost no more than €8 (call T940, T942, T945 or T949).

The very helpful **tourist office** is at Str. Alba Iulia 2 (Apri–Sept Mon–Fri 9am–8pm, Sat 9am–5pm; Oct–March Mon–Fri 9am–6pm, Sat 10am–3pm; T0256/437 973, @infoturism@primariatm.ro); as well as a basic city-centre **map**, they should also have copies of the useful English-language listings magazine, *Timişoara What, Where, When*.

Accommodation

Timişoara has a staggering number of **hotels**, the vast majority of which are optimistically aimed at the business traveller. The only **budget** accommodation is in two student-type residences, both of which are pleasantly modern and clean. The *Casa Politehnica*, at B-dul. Ferdinand I 2 (T0256/496 850) – it's the one with the black door – has double rooms with breakfast included (③); the National Authority for Youth, on the corner of Str. 20 Decembrie 1989 and Str. Eminescu (T0256/490 469; ②), is cheaper (breakfast not included).

There's a very good year-round **campsite** (T0256/208 925, Wwww .campinginternational.ro), with well-equipped cabins (③–⑤) sleeping one to four people, on Aleea Pădurea Verde, 4km east of the city in the Green Forest. Take trolley bus #11, which terminates just beyond the 24-hour PECO filling station on Calea Dorobanţilor (the DN6), opposite the campsite.

Central Str. Lenau 6 T0256/490 091, Wwww .hotel-central.ro. Simple but clean, modern and a/c rooms, a great central location and extremely welcoming staff. ⑤

Cina B-dul. Republicii 7 T&F0256/490 130. One of the cheapest city-centre options, this completely renovated hotel has rather gloomy rooms and small bathrooms, but it's perfectly acceptable. Breakfast is extra. ④

Club Senator Calea Lugojului 7 T0256/225 463, Wwww.hotelclubsenator.ro. This bright and breezy

three-star hotel, 6km east of town on the road towards the airport, has a swimming pool, sauna and smart restaurant. ⑤

Continental B-dul. Revoluţiei 3 T0256/494 144, Wwww.hotelcontinental.ro. Used predominantly by businessmen and tour groups, this ugly white high-rise is as charmless and expensive as all the others in this Romanian chain. ⑧

Eurohotel Str. Mehadia 5 T0256/201 251, Wwww .eurohotelsite.com. High-standard hotel with plush, a/c rooms, although its location is somewhat out of

sync amongst a jumble of apartment blocks; it's a 15min walk east of the centre across the canal. **⑥**
Nord B-dul. Gen. Dragalina 47 ☏ 0256/497 504, ℱ 491 621. Cheerless, but better than average, station hotel – the cheapest place going. **④**
Perla I Str. Oltul 11 ☏ 0256/195 202; **Perla II** (and **IV**) Str. Turgheniev 9 (☏ 0256/195 203); **Perla III** Str. Paltinis 14 (☏ 0256/197 858); all ⍟www .hotelperla.ro. Four uniformly excellent hotels; modern, chic and supremely comfortable. **④–⑤**
Silva B-dul. V. Babeş 25 ☏&ℱ 0256/201 406. One of the city's best small hotels, just around the corner from *Perla I*, with comfortable, bright, and very spacious rooms. **⑤**

Solaris Str. Daliei 7 ☏ 0256/294 619, ⍟www .hotelsolaris.ro. Very pleasant ten-room hotel near the *Eurohotel*, with big square rooms, huge beds and ultra-modern furniture. No twins. **⑥**
Timişoara Str. 1 Mai 2 ☏ 0256/198 856, ⍟www .hoteltimisoara.ro. In a plum location overlooking Piaţa Victoriei, this decent hotel offers three- and-four-star rooms, the latter being far superior and well worth paying that little bit extra. **⑥**
Victoria Str. Lucian Blaga 3 ☏ 0256/431 602, ℮receptie@victoria-hotel.ro. Renovated hotel in a lovely old building with large, albeit spartanly furnished rooms. There's no lift, so it's a bit of a trek up the stairs. **⑦**

The City

Timişoara originally grew up around a Magyar fortress in the marshes between the Timiş and Bega rivers, the draining of which created the **Bega Canal**, which now separates the old town, to the north, from the newer quarters. The city's sights are largely concentrated around the two large main squares, **Piaţa Victoriei** and **Piaţa Unirii**.

Piaţa Victoriei and around

A wide, pedestrianized boulevard flanked on either side by shops and cafés and sliced down the middle by an attractive strip of greenery, **Piaţa Victoriei** was where, in December 1989, the **revolution** in Romania first took hold; demonstrators came out in force and the tanks rolled in for what turned out to be a series of bloody and tragic battles. There's now little sign of those events, save for the odd memorial or pockmarked building, such as the one above *McDonald's* at the square's northern end. At the square's southern end, near the Bega Canal, is the monumental **Romanian Orthodox Cathedral**, constructed between 1936 and 1946 after the signing of the Treaty of Trianon. The cathedral, whose architectural style blends neo-Byzantine and Moldavian elements, houses a fine collection of eighteenth-century Banat icons in its basement, but is best known as the site where many of the protesters were gunned down in the 1989 uprising; there are memorials and candles to the victims outside. With its 83-metre-high middle dome (Pantocrator), it's quite a startling sight, especially when lit up at night.

Beyond the cathedral, across the canal, **Tökes Reformed Church** is where Lászlo Tökes ignited the 1989 revolution (see box opposite). There is now a plaque on the plain apartment building at Str. Timotei Ciprariu 1 (left off B-dul. 16 Decembrie 1989), where his eviction took place – Tökes's church was on the first floor and its stained-glass windows can just about be seen from the street.

A few paces to the west of the square, the **Museum of the Banat** (Tues–Sun 10am–5pm) occupies the fourteenth-century castle raised for the Hungarian monarch Charles Robert, extended by Hunyadi in the fifteenth century. Alas, no effort has been spared to make the voluminous display of historical exhibits as dull as could possibly be, and you're best off giving this a miss. Outside, two street lamps proudly attest to the fact that Timişoara was the first city in Europe to have electric street lighting, in 1884.

Leaving the square to the north, you'll pass the charmless-looking **Opera House**, another effort from the Viennese duo Helmer and Fellner, before heading towards **Piaţa Libertăţii**, which boasts a substantial Baroque pile on

Despite doubts about the authenticity of the events of **December 1989** in Bucharest, Timişoara's popular uprising is still regarded as the catalyst of the revolution. The spark was lit to the southwest of the centre, when crowds gathered to prevent the internal exile of the Reformat pastor **László Tökes**.

Pastor László Tökes came from a distinguished dynasty of Reformed (Calvinist) churchmen. Born in 1952, he followed his father into the priesthood, but was soon in trouble for teaching Hungarian culture and history to his parishioners in Dej; after two years without a job, he was posted to Timişoara in 1986. Here, he became increasingly outspoken in his criticism of the government and the church authorities, while stressing that he spoke not only for Hungarians but also for the equally oppressed Romanians. In particular, he protested against the systematization programme, denouncing it on Hungarian television in July 1989. This led to an increasingly vicious campaign against him by the local Securitate, who spread slanderous rumours about him, smashed his windows and harassed his family and friends, culminating in the murder in September 1989 of one of the church elders.

László Papp, Bishop of Oradea, a government placeman, agreed that he should be transferred to the tiny village of Mineu, north of Zalău, but he refused to leave his parish and resisted legal moves to evict him. Being officially deemed unemployed, he lost his ration book, but his parishioners brought him food despite continuing harassment. Eventually, he was removed to Mineu on December 17, and stayed there until the 22nd; the fact that it took so long for a police state to shift him, and that the eviction was so clearly signalled and then delayed for a day or two, is cited as evidence that plotters against Ceauşescu were deliberately trying to incite an uprising. After the removal of Tökes, **riots** erupted on the streets of Timişoara, culminating in Ceauşescu's order for the army to open fire on protesters.

The new National Salvation Front (FSN) tried to co-opt Tökes onto its council, along with other dissidents, but he soon asserted his independence; appropriately, in March 1990 he took over the job of Bishop Papp, who fled to France. Romanian nationalists have always accused him of being an agent of the Hungarian government and of the CIA, and he continues to be a hardliner, pushing for autonomy for the Magyar-dominated areas.

its north side; originally built as the **Town Hall** in 1734 and now used as the university's music faculty, it stands on the site of the Turkish baths. The square was the setting for the particularly gruesome execution of György Dózsa (Gheorghe Doja), leader of the peasant uprising that swept across Hungary and Transylvania in 1514; an iron throne and crown for the "King of the Serfs" were both heated until red-hot, then Dózsa was seated and "crowned" before his body was torn asunder by pincers. Some of his followers were starved, compelled to watch his torture and then force-fed parts of the charred corpse, before themselves being executed, while others were hanged above the gates of Oradea, Alba Iulia and Buda as a deterrent.

Piaţa Unirii and around

Two blocks north and east of Piaţa Libertăţii is the vast **Piaţa Unirii**, a splendid traffic-free showpiece of Baroque urban design lined with delightful yellow, green and red buildings, though quite a few could now do with a spruce-up. At the heart of the square is the Holy Trinity, or **Plague Column**, a stone-carved column depicting a number of plague-ridden victims, which was raised in 1740 following a particularly virulent attack of the Black Death in 1738–39. On opposing sides of the square are two monumental cathedrals: the **Roman Catholic Cathedral**, which stands along the eastern side, was built between

1736 and 1754 to the design of the younger Fischer von Erlach and is a fine example of the Viennese Baroque style; the **Serbian Orthodox Cathedral** was built, ironically enough, at the same time (1744–48), with its beautiful religious paintings completed by the local artist Constantin Daniel.

The **Museum of Fine Arts** (Tues–Sun 10am–6pm; €2), on the southeast corner of the square at no. 1, features work by several eminent Romanian artists, such as Cornelia Baba – whose most notable pieces are three portraits of George Enescu – as well as work by rather lesser-known Italian, German and Flemish masters. There's some decorative art here, too, but of more interest are the rotating temporary exhibitions – often photographic. To the east of Piaţa Unirii, the huge but dull **Dicasterial Palace** (1754), a complex of 450 rooms built for the Habsburg bureaucracy of the nineteenth century, is worth a look for its sheer bulk. One block west, on the corner of Str. Eugeniu de Savoya and Str. Augustin Pacha, a plaque marks the house in which Cuza apparently spent his last two nights in Romania on his way to exile (see p.436) – as the Banat was not part of Romania until 1918, he was presumably under the impression that he was already in exile.

To the west of Piaţa Unirii, at Str. Ungureanu 8, is the marvellous **Museum of the Revolution** (Tues–Sun 10am–5pm), which is actually part of the National Centre of Research into the 1989 Romanian Revolution. A small memorial chapel remembers the one hundred or so (the official number is unknown) martyrs gunned down in the city, while photos, newspaper cuttings and a moving set of paintings by local school children illustrate vividly those extraordinary few days. Equally as gripping is a twenty-five-minute documentary film (subtitled in English) containing some remarkable footage, such as Ceauşescu's final, fatal, speech on the balcony of the Communist Party Headquarters building, and the moment when he and Elena Ceauşescu were being informed of their impending execution.

In 1868, the municipality purchased the redundant citadel from the Habsburg government, and demolished all but two sections, loosely known as the **Bastions**, to the west and east of Piaţa Unirii. Today, the western section contains a flower and fruit and veg market – both called Timişoara 700, in honour of the city's 700th anniversary in 1969 – and to the east, the entrance at Str. Hector 2 admits you to a beer and wine bar. Just to the west of here, at Str. Popa Şapcă 4, is the **Ethnographic Museum** (Tues–Sun 10am–4.30pm), with some nicely presented displays of textiles and folk costumes, icons on glass, and beautifully carved staffs and musical instruments. Disappointingly, though, there's little mention of the region's ethnic diversity, or of the 40,000 Serbs exiled to the Dobrogea in 1951, which radically altered the Banat's ethnic make-up. The museum also has an **open-air section** about 5km east of town, where old Banat homesteads and workshops have been reassembled in the **Pădurea Verde** (Green Forest) – take trolley bus #11.

Eating, drinking and entertainment

For such a large and cosmopolitan city, Timişoara has a disappointingly meagre selection of **restaurants**. Conversely, there's no shortage of **drinking** venues, particularly down by the canal in the summer, and, during term-time, around the lively student area – principally Aleea Studenţilor.

Restaurants

Da Toni Str. Daliei 14. Genuinely excellent, and extremely popular, pizzeria near the student quarter, just behind the Petrom station off B-dul. Eroilor.

Harold's Aleea Studenților 17. A touch of class amid the fast-food joints dominating the student quarter, this neat place offers Chinese, Mexican and Romanian food and is also one of the best restaurants in town for vegetarians.

Maestro Str. Janos Bolyai 3. Stylish establishment with a prodigious international menu. Choose between the cosy interior or the small but convivial outdoor terrace. Live music some nights.

Mioritic Str. Cluj 26. Characterful litte restaurant decked out with traditional Romanian ornaments and textiles, and serving some of the best (and most inexpensive) Romanian food in town – try the tochitură haiducească (outlaw's stew). Located ten minutes' walk south of the canal.

Taverna Sârbului Piața Victoriei 4. Good Serbian restaurant; though it's less authentic than Yugoslavia (below), it offers a hearty choice of standard meat-heavy Serb specialities.

Yugoslavia Str. G. Dragomir 10. Hugely enjoyable, and typically hospitable, Serbian restaurant in the south of town, opposite the Perla II/IV hotel, serving specialities such as Čevapi (minced spiced meat rolls) and sarma (cabbage leaves wrapped around rice and meat). Vegetarians need not bother.

Cafés and bars

In summer, outdoor **drinking** principally takes place at two locations; along the canal-side behind the Orthodox cathedral, and on Piața Unirii, where numerous – albeit identical – terraced cafés vie for custom. The best of the city's **cafés** is Timis Ice Café, Str. Alecsandri 7, a fresh and funky place with waiting staff buzzing around in luminous orange outfits – they've got a delectable range of coffees, iced drinks, sandwiches, cakes and desserts. The hectic student quarter also offers some good possibilities, such as Café Olli, next door to Da Toni's restaurant at Str. Daliei 14, which is worth venturing to for its fabulous **ice cream**.

The pick of the **bars** are Café Colt, at Str. Ungureanu 9, a vibrant, two-floored café-cum-bar open round the clock; Komodo, Str. Gheorghe Lazar 5, a cool lounge-bar with big leather sofas and large windows that open onto the street; and The Note, a loud and banging bar with DJ nights at Str. Mehadia 10. The town's only serious **live music** venue is Jazz Club Pod 16, a small but excellent club hidden under the B-dul. 16 Decembrie 1989 bridge (W www.jazzclubpod16 .ro), with a classy line-up of acts. Otherwise, there's Club 30, at Piața Victoriei 7 (the southern end), which throws '70s and '80s retro-style gigs and parties. If you're looking for somewhere to **dance**, then head for Discoland on Piața I. Huniade, by the Opera House.

Entertainment

The city's main concert venue is the **Opera House** on Piața Victoriei, which also houses two theatres that stage plays in German and Hungarian; the box office is at Str. Mărășești 2 (daily 10am–1pm & 5–7pm; €6–10 for theatre and €4–6 for opera; ☎0256/433 020). The Banat **Philharmonic** gives occasional concerts at B-dul. C.D. Loga 2 (box office 9am–1pm and 1hr before perform-ances; ☎0256/492 521).

The city stages several terrific **festivals**, and there's plenty going on over the summer; in early May there's the **Timișoara Muzicală Festival**, a series of classical concerts and opera at the Opera House, and during the first week of July, the lovely Rozelor Park (Park of Roses) by the Bega Canal is the setting for the **International Folklore Festival**, featuring a host of high-calibre artists. **Little Venice** is a continual run of concerts and plays on Piața Unirii every weekend (weather permitting) between May and September.

Listings

Airlines British Airways, Calea Victoriei 15 (☎0256/303 222); Carpatair, Timișoara airport (☎0256/202 701); TAROM, B-dul. Revoluției 3–5

(Mon–Fri 8am–8pm, Sat 9am–2pm; ☎0256/490 150).

Car rental All the following have offices at the airport: Avis (☎0256/203 234); Europcar

(☎0256/194 074); Hertz (☎0256/220 552).
Hospital Str. Gheorghe Dima.
International buses Services to Germany are run by Atlassib, B-dul. Republicii 1 (☎&🖂0256/226 485) and at Gară Est (☎&🖂0256/226 486), and Priamus, B-dul. 16 Decembrie 1989 (☎&🖂0256/190 202). There are also services running to Istanbul (Oz Murat; ☎0256/497 868) and Athens (Bocheris Express Travel; ☎&🖂0256/436 283).
Internet access Argus, Str. Mercy 4 (Mon–Thurs 9am–11pm, Fri & Sat 9am–midnight, Sun 2–11pm); Java Coffee House, Str. A. Pacha 6 (daily 10am–midnight); Online Center, Str. Eminescu 5 (daily 7am–1am).
Pharmacy Both the following are open 24hr: Vlad, B-dul. 16 Decembrie no. 53; Vladarmed, Str. Brăncusi 13.

Post office B-dul. Revoluţiei 2 (Mon–Fri 7am–8pm, Sat 8am–1pm) and Str. P. Craiului (Mon–Fri 8am–7pm).
Shopping The Bega Shopping Complex (Mon–Fri 9am–8pm, Sat 9am–7pm, Sun 10am–4pm) next to the *Continental* hotel has a good supermarket (Mon–Fri 8am–9pm, Sat 8am–8pm, Sun 10am–4pm). For Romanian books in English, try Humanitas, Str. Lucian Blaga 2 (Mon–Sat 10am–7pm, Sun 1–7pm); Cartureşti, Str. Mercy 7 (Mon–Fri 10am–9pm, Sat 11am–8pm); and Librărie Noi, Str. Hector 2–4 (Mon–Fri 9am–8pm, Sat 10am–6pm, Sun 11am–5pm), which has a particularly good arts section.
Train tickets The CFR office is just off Piaţa Victoriei at Str. Măcicsilor 3 (☎0256/220 534; Mon–Fri 7am–8pm).

The Timiş valley

The main rail line and the DN6 follow the River Timiş southeast from Timişoara towards Băile Herculane and Wallachia, passing through the small Habsburg towns of **Lugoj** and **Caransebeş**. From Caransebeş, there is easy access into the mountains, either west into the Semenic massif, or east to Muntele Mic, Ţarcu, Godeanu and, ultimately, to the Retezat range.

Lugoj

LUGOJ, 63km east of Timişoara, is notable as the birthplace of several Romanian musicians, including the operatic tenor Traian Grozăvescu (1895–1927), and the composers Tiberiu Brediceanu (1877–1968) and Ion Vidu (1836–1931). Its non-Romanian sons are less likely to be remembered by plaques, but Béla Ferenc Blasko (1882–1956) immortalized his birthplace's Hungarian name when he became Béla Lugosi, Hollywood's most famous Dracula and its nearest thing yet to a genuinely Transylvanian Count.

From the **train station** on Splaiul Gării, exit left and head up Str. Al. Mocioni – which becomes pedestrianized beyond the Hotel *Timiş* – towards the junction of Str. Bălcescu and the River Timiş. Here, you'll find the dusty old **town museum** (Tues–Sun 9am–5pm), which has displays of weapons, ceramics and local costumes. Continue east across the Iron Bridge to the **Uniate Cathedral** on Piaţa Republicii, which has some fine neo-Byzantine paintings. Nearby, on Piaţa Victoriei, is the **Orthodox Church of the Assumption**, a hall-church built between 1759 and 1766 by the younger Fischer von Erlach, which is one of the most important Baroque buildings of the Banat. The fifteenth-century tower of the church of St Nicholas stands next door.

There are three **hotels** in Lugoj, two of which are on Str. Al. Mocioni. The *Timiş*, at no. 20 (☎0256/355 045, 🖂350 671; ❹), is a quiet, dull place with large clean rooms – breakfast costs extra – while the rather expensive *Dacia*, 300m further up at no. 7 (☎0256/352 740, 🖂350 671; ❼) and a hotel of sorts since 1835, has individually (and tastefully) designed rooms. The third, and best, is the sleek *Tivoli*, across the bridge at Str. A. Popovici 3 (☎0256/359 567, 🖰www .hoteltivoli.ro; ❺), which has seven air-conditioned, designer-furnished rooms. Its classy restaurant is also the best **place to eat** in town. In addition to these places, there's the very cheap but perfectly acceptable *Tirol*, 3km out along the road to Făget and Deva (the DN68A) at Str. Salcâmului 15 (ⓣ0256/353 832, ⓕ354 183; ❷), and reached by bus #7. The **CFR office** (Mon–Fri 9am–4pm) is just down from the *Dacia* hotel.

Caransebeş and the Muntele Mic

CARANSEBEŞ lies beneath the mountains at the confluence of the Timiş and Sebeş rivers, around which Gypsies of the Zlatari tribe used to pan for gold. Having served as the Banat's judicial centre during the Middle Ages and commanding communications through the Eastern Gate, Caransebeş inevitably became a Habsburg garrison town – hence, the outcrops of *belle époque* buildings among the prefabricated structures of the socialist era. There's little to occupy you here today, other than the **County Museum of Ethnography and the Border Regiment** (Mon–Sat 10am–4pm), housed in the eighteenth-century barracks on Piaţa Dragolina, and featuring some impressive local artefacts from central and south Banat, but you may well be passing through or need to stay the night if you're heading for the mountains.

The main **train station** is located well north of town, from where maxitaxis will take you into the centre; otherwise, it's a good thirty-minute walk. Some local services also stop 2km further south at the Caransebeş halt, west of the centre. Most trains from Caransebeş run north to Timişoara, or south to Orşova and Turnu Severin on the Danube (see p.134), but there are also branch services west to Reşiţa (see p.383). The **bus terminal** is on Splaiul Sebeşului, south of the River Sebeş; for the town centre, cross the bridge and turn right at the spiky neo-Gothic synagogue.

There are several **hotels** in Caransebeş, all of which are located on or just off the main road leading from the main train station to the centre of town: exiting right at the station, walk 300m and cross the road for the cheap, though not particularly cheerful, *Vila Natalia* (ⓣ0255/517 645; ❸). Over the bridge, the modern *Gea* at Str. Crişan 1a (ⓣ0255/511 637; ❹) also has a superior sister hotel across the road (same phone; ❺). Easily the best of the bunch, though, is the *Armando*, in town at Str. Libertăţii 35 (ⓣ0255/517 308, ⓔoffice@hotelarmando .ro; ❹), whose beautifully furnished rooms are tremendous value – the hotel's **restaurant** is pretty fine, too.

Borlova and the Muntele Mic

BORLOVA, 13km from Caransebeş, is noted for its embroideries and peasant weddings, and holds a **Measurement of the Milk festival** around April 23 every year. Most visitors, however, pass straight through en route to the **Muntele Mic** (Little Mountain) resort. You can hitch a ride to the resort on the staff bus or make the ten-kilometre walk from Borlova, followed by a chairlift ride. Thanks to the heavy snowfalls in the area, you can **ski** here from late autumn until late spring; there are also good **hiking** trails for the summer months. The resort's one hotel is the *Sebeş* (❸), but there's also a selection of less expensive villas and chalets. You can walk north to the Muntele Mic itself in an hour, or south to the weather station (2190m) atop Mount Ţarcu in three hours. Outside the winter months, suitably equipped hikers can take trails heading eastwards towards Lake Gura Apei and the Retezat mountains in four hours (following red stripes), or southwards to Godeanu and the Cerna valley in six hours (red dots) – be prepared for an overnight expedition (a tent is essential). From Muntele Mic, there's also a route (following blue stripes) to Poiana Mărului, to the east, from where three buses a day head back to Caransebeş via Oţelu Roşu.

The Cerna valley

Continuing south by road or rail from Caransebeş, you pass through the **Poarta Orientalis** or Eastern Gate of Transylvania before reaching **Băile Herculane** and its spa at the bottom of the **Cerna valley**. The middle and upper reaches of the valley itself are still much as Patrick Leigh Fermor described them when he travelled through the region in the 1930s: "a wilderness of green moss and grey creepers with ivy-clad water-mills rotting along the banks and streams tumbling through the shadows [illuminated by] shafts of lemon-coloured light". Among the butterflies and birds that proliferate here are bright blue rollers, which the Romanians call *dumbrăveancă*, "one who loves oakwoods".

Băile Herculane and around

BĂILE HERCULANE gets its name from the Roman legend that Hercules cured the wounds inflicted by the Hydra by bathing here, and the nine springs, with their varied mineral content and temperature (38–60°C), are used to treat a wide range of disorders. During the nineteenth century, royal patronage made Herkulesbad, as it was then known, one of Europe's most fashionable watering holes. Today, Băile Herculane is split between the old spa area, centred around elegant Piaţa Hercules, and the ugly modern satellite spa of **PECINIŞCA**, 2km towards the train station and dominated by half a dozen or so grim high-rise hotels.

Other than to wallow in the renowned **Apollo Baths**, Băile Herculane's chief attraction is its surroundings – statuesque limestone peaks clothed in lush vegetation and riddled with caves. You can bathe in the **Seven Hot Springs** (Şapte Izvoare Calde) about 35 minutes' walk upstream, just beyond the Cerna rapids, while another two hours' hiking will bring you to the white **Gisella's Cross**, from where there are magnificent views. From here, an unmarked path leads you in thirty minutes to a forest of black pines, dotted with boulders, and a spectacular 300-metre precipice. Other paths provide access to the vaporous

▲ Filling bottles at a mineral spring, Băile Herculane

Steam Cave on Ciorci Hill (1hr 30min), the **Outlaws' Cave** where Stone Age tribes once sheltered (30min), and the **Mount Domogled nature reserve**, which has trees and flowers of Mediterranean origin and more than 1300 varieties of butterfly (4hr).

It's roughly 40km from Băile Herculane to the watershed of the River Cerna, on a forestry road that continues to Câmpuşel and the Jiu valley. A path marked with red stripes runs parallel along the ridge to the north to Piatra lui Iorgovan in the **Retezat mountains** (see p.211) – allow one or two days.

Practicalities

From Băile Herculane's lovely turn-of-the-century **train station**, 5km from the spa, maxitaxis run every thirty minutes to Piaţa Hercules. A stack of **hotels** offers a good range of accommodation both here and in Pecinişca: the best-value place in the old spa area is the recently renovated *Cerna* (℡0255/560 436, ℻560 440; ❹). Beyond the currently defunct *Apollo* hotel, where the road narrows, is the *Hotel Roman* (℡0255/560 390, ℻560 454; ❺), location of the **Imperial Roman Baths** (daily 8am–6pm).

None of the big and unsightly hotels in Pecinişca differs much from each other, but they're all pretty cheap, and there should be plenty of availability. The one exception is the pleasantly isolated *Pension El Plazza* (℡0255/560 768, ℮elplazza@baile-herculane.ro; ❸), located about 1km from the train station, just off the main road across the bridge; this terrific-value place has large, homely rooms, a swimming pool and play area for kids.

There are also numerous houses along Pecinişca's main street advertising **private rooms**. There are a couple of **campsites** here, the best of which is *Camping Hercules* (℡0255 523 458), about 800m north of the train station along the DN6 to Timişoara: this excellent little site also has a handful of rooms available, as well as a good **restaurant**. The other site is the *Flora* (℡0255/560 929), just north of the new part of the resort, which also has some very basic huts (❶).

Reşiţa and the Semenic range

People have been beating iron into shape around **REŞIŢA**, 40km southwest of Caransebeş, since Dacian times. The foundry can trace its history back to 1771, and steam locomotives were manufactured here from 1872 until 1964; if you're entering from Timişoara on B-dul. Revoluţiei din Decembrie, you'll pass a rusting collection of **locomotives** outside the Reşiţa Nouă train halt. The iron works, and the ropeway across town, are still active, but the town has a depressed feel about it: the county **History Museum** resides at Str. Republicii 10, but has yet to open due to lack of funds, while the bus service to Văliug, starting point for excursions into the Semenic mountains, has ceased to operate. A private bus may run on summer weekends, but otherwise you'll have to hitch or take a taxi. However, the town does stage a couple of festivals: local steelworkers take pride of place in the **Spring Parade** (Alaiul Primăverii), normally held during the first week in April, while there's also the **Bârzava Song Festival** in August. At other times you may as well continue straight on to the mountains.

Arriving at the town's grubby **bus station** on Str. Traian Lalescu, walk west past the post office and theatre, over the footbridge and under the ropeway, and you'll come to the town's horrible concrete central square, Piaţa 1 Decembrie

1918. Arriving by **train**, get off at Reşiţa Sud station, just across from Piaţa 1 Decembrie 1918, as opposed to the Nord stop.

The town's chief **hotel** is the *Rogge*, Str. I. Caragiale 12 (℡0355/411 111, ⓦwww.hotelrogge.ro; ❼), whose fabulous rooms are equipped with comfortable, wood-framed beds and large plasma TV screens. The alternative is the *Semenic*, an ugly, squat **hotel** on Piaţa 1 Decembrie 1918 (℡0355/213 481; ❺–❻), whose rooms are actually quite smart. You could also stay more cheaply outside town at Semenic or Crivaia (see below) or at one of the three **cabanas**, the *Constructorul*, *Splendid* or *Turist* (all ❶), 13km east on Lake Secu. If you're planning to do some hiking, Reşiţa is the last chance before the Semenic mountains to stock up on food; just east of the Sud train station there's a good covered **market** selling fruit, veg and dairy products.

Into the Semenic mountains

From Văliug, 12km southeast of Reşiţa, one road leads 3km south to **CRIVAIA**, a good base for hikes, where there are bungalows and a **campsite**, while another leads up to **SEMENIC**, also accessible by chairlift from Văliug, which has chalet-style **accommodation** and two hotels, the *Central* (℡0255/214 450; ❸) and *Gozna* (℡0255/223 599; ❸). **Skiing** is possible here from November to April – pistes are graded from very easy to difficult.

Although the massif is lower and less rugged than others in the Carpathians, it still offers the chance of good **hiking**. One of the most popular treks heads west from Semenic through Crivaia to the Comarnic Cave and on to the **Caraşului Gorges** (10–11hr; blue stripe markings). Situated just before the eastern entrance to the gorges, the **Comarnic Cave** is the Banat's largest grotto, with a spectacular array of rock "veils" and calcite crystals distributed around its four hundred metres of galleries on two levels (guided tours daily until 3pm). The gorges themselves are extremely wild and muddy and harbour several more caves, of which Popovăţ (also open for tours) to the south is the most impressive. If you don't fancy hiking here from Semenic or Crivaia, the gorges can also be entered near **CARAŞOVA**, a village 16km south of Reşiţa on the main road. However, they may be impassable in part thanks to occasional flooding, in which case you should follow the blue stripes onwards from Comarnic to the hamlet of **PROLAZ**, and pick up the route through the gorges there.

Travel details

Trains

Arad to: Brad (3 daily; 4hr 30min–5hr); Braşov (6 daily; 6hr–7hr 45min); Bucharest (6 daily; 8hr 30min–10hr 15min); Deva (14 daily; 2hr–3hr 15min); Hălmagiu (3 daily; 4hr); Oradea (8 daily; 1hr 30min–2hr 30min); Radna (11 daily; 30–45min); Sânnicolau Mare (5 daily; 2hr); Sântana (12 daily; 25–40min); Satu Mare (1 daily; 4hr 30min); Sebiş (3 daily; 2hr 30min); Sibiu (1 daily; 5hr); Sighişoara (3 daily; 4hr); Timişoara (16 daily; 50min–1hr 15min); Vârfurile (3 daily; 3hr 30min).

Caransebeş to: Băile Herculane (14 daily; 1hr 15min–2hr); Bucharest (7 daily; 7hr–9hr 30min);

Drobeta-Turnu Severin (10 daily; 2–3hr); Lugoj (16 daily; 30min–1hr); Orşova (10 daily; 1hr 30min–2hr 15min); Reşiţa (9 daily; 50min–1hr 15min); Timişoara (16 daily; 1hr 15min–2hr 30min).

Oradea to: Arad (8 daily; 1hr 45min–3hr); Baia Mare (2 daily; 3hr 30min); Bucharest (3 daily; 10–11hr); Ciucea (8 daily; 1hr 15min–2hr 45min); Cluj (12 daily; 2hr 30min–4hr 30min); Iaşi (2 daily; 11hr 45min); Satu Mare (5 daily; 2–3hr); Suceava (1 daily; 9hr 30min); Târgu Mureş (1 daily; 4hr 45min); Timişoara (2 daily; 3hr–4hr 15min).

Timişoara to: Arad (15 daily; 50min–1hr 15min); Bucharest (7 daily; 7hr 30min–10hr 30min); Buziaş

(9 daily; 40min–1hr); Caransebeş (14 daily; 1hr 15min–2hr 30min); Lugoj (13 daily; 45min–1hr 30min); Oradea (6 daily; 2hr 45min–3hr 30min); Reşiţa (5 daily; 2hr 30min); Sânnicolau Mare (4 daily; 2hr).

Buses and maxitaxis

Arad to: Abrud (1 daily); Câmpeni (1 daily); Deva (2 daily); Lipova (5 daily); Moneasa (2 daily); Oradea (9 daily); Satu Mare (3 daily); Timişoara (10 daily).
Băile Herculane to: Orşova (Mon–Fri 1 daily).
Caransebeş to: Borlova (7 daily).
Oradea to: Alba Iulia (1 daily); Arad (10 daily); Cluj (4 daily); Deva (2 daily); Sighet (1 daily); Târgu Lăpuş (1 daily); Timişoara (10 daily).
Reşiţa to: Băile Herculane (1 daily); Caransebeş (1 daily); Deva (Mon–Sat 1 daily); Drobeta (4 daily); Lugoj (Mon–Fri 1 daily); Târgu Jiu (Mon–Fri 1 daily); Timişoara (3 daily).
Timişoara to: Anina (1 daily); Arad (10 daily); Băile Herculane (1 daily); Caransebeş (1 daily); Câmpeni (1 daily); Lipova (3 daily); Lugoj (1 daily); Moneasa (1 daily); Oradea (10 daily); Reşiţa (2 daily); Sibiu (2 daily).

Planes

Arad to: Bucharest (10 weekly).
Oradea to: Bucharest (12 weekly).
Timişoara to: Bucharest (24 weekly); Cluj (3 weekly); Iaşi (2 weekly).

International trains

Arad to: Budapest, Hungary (7 daily; 4hr 30min–5hr 15min); Prague, Czech Republic (1 daily; 15hr); Vienna, Austria (1 daily; 10hr).
Oradea to: Budapest (2 daily; 4hr 30min), Szeged, Hungary (1 daily; 3hr 30min).
Timişoara to: Belgrade, Serbia (1 daily; 3hr 15min); Budapest (2 daily; 6hr 15min).

International buses

Arad to: Békéscaba & Szeged, both Hungary (2 weekly).
Oradea to: Budapest (1 daily); Debrecen, Hungary (1 daily); Kecskemet, Hungary (1 daily).

7

The Delta and the coast

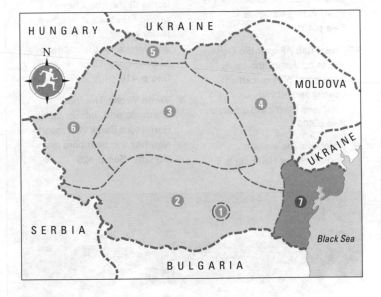

CHAPTER 7

Highlights

* **Birdlife in the Delta** Even visitors without a special interest in winged fauna will be taken aback by the abundance and diversity of bird life on view in the Danube Delta. See p.391

* **Sfântu Gheorghe** This cluster of brightly painted houses of mud and reed, a short walk from the Black Sea, is one of the prettiest of the Delta's fishing villages and a perfect base for exploring the surrounding wetlands. See p.401

* **Fresh fish** All over the Delta, meals consist of the day's haul: carp, pike or catfish, usually served with juicy tomatoes from local gardens. See p.403

* **Halmyris** The ancient Roman city of Halmyris is an archeological work in progress that recently saw the discovery of the remains of legendary martyrs Epictet and Astion. See p.404

* **Constanţa** Romania's principal port is rich in historical associations, and offers an attractive mix of places to stay and eat. See p.409

* **Mamaia** The epicentre of Black Sea tourism and home to the finest hotels outside Bucharest, Mamaia is, for better or for worse, a showpiece for the aspirations of post-communist Romania. See p.416

* **Vama Veche** The most charming and untouched of Romania's Black Sea resorts also has the best bars and nightlife. See p.426

▲ Pelicans on Uzlina Lake

7

The Delta and the coast

N early three thousand kilometres downstream from the Black Forest, the **Danube Delta** is a vast network of reeds and shifting land clinging to the far eastern side of Romania. Rich in **wildlife**, the Delta provides a unique habitat for 325 species of bird, many of which are found nowhere else in Europe. Most visitors head for the main arm (*braţ*) of the Danube that flows from the Delta capital of **Tulcea** down to **Crişan** and **Sulina**, and it can feel very crowded in July and August; the southern arm, which terminates at the fishing village of **Sfântu Gheorghe**, is an attractive alternative. To really appreciate the diversity of bird life, however, you'll have to take a tour or pay one of the local fishermen to row or motor you into the backwaters and lakes; travel in the Delta can be time-consuming, so if you're seriously bent on birdwatching, be prepared to spend at least a week here.

To the south, Romania's **Black Sea coast** is blessed with abundant sunshine, warm water and sandy beaches, and numerous Roman remains, but due to the popularity of summer resorts such as **Mamaia**, **Neptun** and **Venus** it's best to book a package holiday from home (see Basics), or head to one of the prettier former fishing villages near the Bulgarian border: **Doi Mai** is quiet and family-oriented, while **Vama Veche** grows more fashionable by the year. There are fewer tourists in the port city of **Constanţa**, but better restaurants, and lots of sights in the old quarter.

Transport to the region is fairly simple. **Trains** to Constanţa are reasonably fast and frequent, but very overcrowded in season, when many services continue to Mangalia. In addition, quick (but cramped) **maxitaxis** regularly run between Bucharest and Constanţa, and between Constanţa's train station and the various resorts. **Driving** from Bucharest will be made easier by a new toll motorway (the Autostrada Soarelui or Sun Highway); work proceeds slowly, but much of the new road was open by 2007, with the rest due in 2010.

The Danube Delta

Every year, the River Danube dumps forty million tonnes of alluvium into the **Danube Delta** (Delta Dunării), the youngest, least stable landscape in Europe, abutting the oldest, the heavily eroded Hercynian hills immediately south. Near **Tulcea**, the river splits into three branches (named after their respective ports, Chilia, Sulina and Sfântu Gheorghe), dividing the Delta into more than 4000 square kilometres of reeds and marsh, half of which is flooded in spring and autumn. The **grinduri**, tongues of accumulated silt supporting oak trees, willows and poplars, account for the five percent of the Delta that remains permanently above the water. Over time, the distinction between these and the **plauri** (floating reed islands) is a fine one, since flooding continually splits, merges and often destroys these patches of land, making any detailed map of the delta outdated almost as soon as it's drawn. Although fishing communities have lived here for centuries, it's an inhospitable environment for humans: a Siberian wind howls all winter long, while in summer the area is inundated with mosquitoes.

Yet it's a paradise for wildlife, and after years of environmental neglect culminating in Ceauşescu's plan to drain the Delta for agricultural use, it was declared a **Biosphere Reserve** in 1990, with over 500 square kilometres strictly protected, and a UNESCO World Heritage Site the following year. Today it is under threat once again, this time from the new Bystroye Canal, dug by Ukraine despite international protests, which is expected to cut the water to Letea and Rosca-Buhaiova lakes. The area is particularly important for **birds**, which pass through during the spring and autumn migrations, or come from Siberia to winter here or from Africa to breed in summer. Besides herons, glossy ibis, golden eagles, avocets, shelduck and other Mediterranean breeds, the Delta is visited by reed buntings, white-tailed eagles and various European songbirds; whooper swans, arctic grebes and half-snipes from Siberia; saker falcons from Mongolia, and egrets, mute swans and mandarin ducks from China. Its lakes support Europe's largest pelican colonies, which come from Africa to breed. The best time to see birds is from April to early June, the latter being the wettest month of the year. The Delta is also home to otters, mink, boars, wolves and other **animals**. At night, streets in the Delta villages are alive with frogs, beetles and hawk moths. There are ninety species of fish here; while stocks of carp and pike have gradually improved since intensive fertilizer use seriously diminished their numbers in the mid-1980s, sturgeon, the most lucrative of all, has largely vanished.

Tulcea

Clustered around the south bank of a bend in the Danube, **TULCEA** has been tagged the "Threshold of the Delta" ever since ancient Greek traders established a **port** here. Its maritime significance was slight until the closing stages of the period of Ottoman domination (1420–1878), when other powers suddenly perceived it as commercially and strategically important. Nowadays, the outskirts of the town are heavily industrialized, and the port is too shallow for large modern freighters, but it's still the chief access point for passenger vessels entering the Delta – though without the decent restaurants and transport links you might expect. The uninspiring town centre has enough attractions to fill a day, but your time will be better spent in the Delta; it's worth arriving early enough to catch one of the ferries that depart at 1.30pm. Tulcea is busiest in August and December, when its regular **festivals** take place: the International Folk Festival of the Danubian Countries, held in odd-numbered years, and an annual winter carnival.

Arrival and information

Tulcea's futuristic **train station** is on the western edge of town, from where it's an easy walk along the waterfront to Piaţa Republicii, passing the new NAVROM-*Delta* **ferry terminal** (Gara Fluviala; tickets daily 11am–1.30pm) and office and the **bus station** on the way. Since the closure of the hydrofoil from Galaţi in Moldavia (see p.266), you're now forced to take a ferry from Galaţi across the Danube to I.C. Brătianu (also known as Bac Galaţi) and then a maxitaxi or a (slower and bumpier) local bus to Tulcea. There are fifteen buses and **maxitaxis** a day from Bac Galaţi and six from Brăila, all of which arrive at

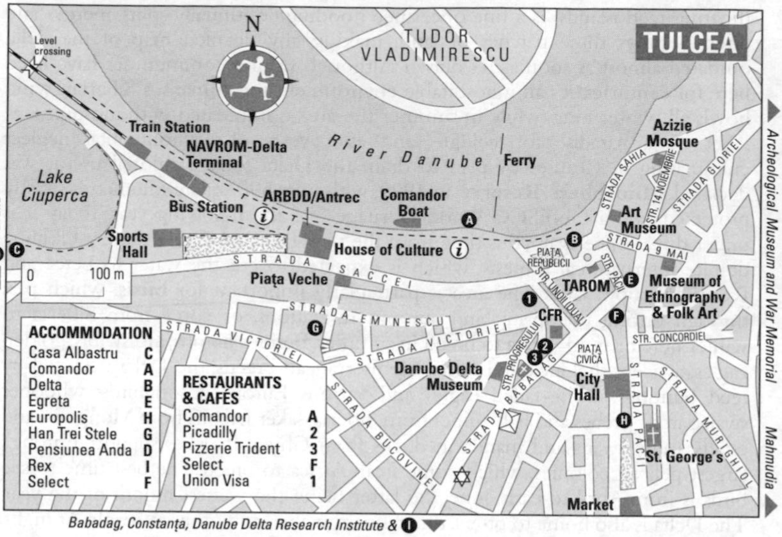
TULCEA
N
TUDOR VLADIMIRESCU
Level crossing
Train Station
NAVROM-Delta Terminal
River Danube
Ferry
Azizie Mosque
Lake Ciuperca
Bus Station
ARBDD/Antrec
Comandor Boat
STRADA SAHIA
STR. 14 NOIEMBRIE
STRADA GLORIEI
Art Museum
Sports Hall
House of Culture
PIAŢA REPUBLICII
STRADA 9 MAI
D & Brăila
0 100 m
STRADA ISACCEI
Piaţa Veche
TAROM
STR. PĂCII
STR. UNIRII (DUAL)
Museum of Ethnography & Folk Art
STRADA EMINESCU
CFR
STR. CONCORDIEI
STRADA VICTORIEI
STR. PROGRESULUI
PIAŢA CIVICĂ
Danube Delta Museum
STRADA BABADAG
City Hall
STRADA PĂCII
STRADA MURIGHIOL
STRADA BUCOVINEI
St. George's
Market
Archeological Museum and War Memorial
Mahmudia
Babadag, Constanţa, Danube Delta Research Institute & I
ACCOMMODATION
Casa Albastru C
Comandor A
Delta B
Egreta E
Europolis H
Han Trei Stele G
Pensiunea Anda D
Rex I
Select F
RESTAURANTS & CAFÉS
Comandor A
Picadilly 2
Pizzerie Trident 3
Select F
Union Visa 1

the bus station; however, the daily Istanbul service calls in front of the sports hall on Str. Isaccei.

Tourist information is available at the EuroDelta information centre at Str. Garii 3, on the waterfront to the west of the Port Captain's headquarters (Mon–Fri 8am–5pm; ⓣ0240/516 180, ⓔeurodelta@tim.ro), although the signs appear to lead you to the Centrul de Informare şi Documentare Ecologică of the Universitatea Ecologică din Bucureşti, nearby at Str. Portului 36, which only has dry ecological data.

The **Danube Delta Biosphere Reserve Administration** (ARBDD; Mon–Fri 8am–4pm; ⓣ0240/518 945, ⓦwww.ddbra.ro), on the waterfront just east of the bus station, can provide information on accommodation and trips in the Delta, as well as issuing entry permits and fishing licences. For **permits** you need to enter at the east end of the building, and for information at the south side, where you'll also find the Antrec office (ⓣ0240/519 214 or 0721/092 150 evenings and weekends, ⓦwww.deltaturism.ro), where you can make reservations for **homestay** and **pension accommodation** in the Delta. Most **travel agencies** are concerned with Delta trips (see box opposite); some also sell international bus and plane tickets. The all-night **pharmacy** is Farmacia 29, at Str. Babadag 4. **Internet access** can be had at Future Games at Str. Isaccei 12.

Moving on, Tulcea is linked to Bucharest and Constanţa by train, but it's a slow journey down to the junction at Medgidia. Regular **maxitaxis** serve both cities between 7am and 7pm. **TAROM**, at Str. Isaccei 1 Bloc M1 (ⓣ0240/510 493), sells tickets for flights, mostly from Constanţa's Mihail Kogălniceanu airport, but also summer flights from Bucharest to Tulcea. For rail tickets, **CFR** is at Str. Babadag 4 (Mon 11am–5pm, Tues–Thurs 9am–5pm, Fri 9am–4pm), where you can also book international air and bus tickets. **Car rental** is available at the *Hotel Egreta.*

Accommodation

Tulcea has several decent **hotels** spread across town. You might also find a **floating hotel** moored alongside the promenade; look for the one owned by

Travel agencies in Tulcea mostly offer packages to **floating hotels** (*hotel plutitoare*) in the heart of the Delta; note that their tours generally stick to the main axes, from which most of the wildlife has been scared off. ATBAD, Str. Babadag 11 (℡0240/514 114, ⊠atbad@tlx.ssitl.ro, ⓦwww.atbad.ro), offers two nights full board in its three-star floating hotel for €150 per person, including transfers, while Sincron Delta, Str. Isaccei 29 (℡0240/517 769, ⓦwww.sincrondelta.ro) has a four-star vessel with nine a/c rooms costing from €65 per night plus tax. Other companies with floating hotels include Amatour, on the waterfront near the *Hotel Delta* (℡0240/518 894, ⓦwww.amatour.ro), Ibis Tours (who specialize in birdwatching) at Str. D. Sturza 6 (℡0240/512 787, ⊠ibistours@gmail.com, ⓦhttp://ibis-tours.ro) and Europolis SA, in the *Hotel Europolis*, Str. Păcii 20 (℡0240/512 443, ⓦwww.europolis.ro). Most of these companies also have tourist complexes on dry land – ATBAD's holiday village at Lake Roşu, south of Sulina, is reached by boat from its pontoon near the Art Museum (May–Oct every 5 days; €25 return), and three-star accommodation costs €50 per person per day. Simpa Tourism at the *Hotel Delta*, Str. Isaccei 2 (℡040/515 753, ⓦwww.simpaturism.ro), charges €32 to €72 per night for two people at its *Complex Cormoran* in Uzlina. Europolis has the *Europolis Tourist Complex* on Lake Casla, just 2km west of Tulcea. Both these options offer high standards of accommodation, but are isolated from the Delta's fascinating village life. Most travel agencies in Constanţa (see p.415) can also organize Delta tours, but only for groups of five or more.

ATBAD, Amatour and Europolis (see above) offer day-trips to Crişan, Mila 23 and the other canals from €30 per person, as do Danubius, in the *Hotel Europolis*, Str. Păcii 20 (℡0240/517 836, ⊠danubius@clicknet.ro); Escape Travel, also in the *Hotel Europolis* (℡0240/516 649 or 0743/609 626); Icar, Str. Isaccei 6 (℡0240/515 965, ⊠icartulcea@xnet.ro, ⓦwww.icar.ro), and Liscom Tour, Str. Viitorului 13 (℡0240, 536 726, ⓦwww.turismdelta.ro). Smaller and less formal outfits along the Tulcea waterfront charge from €10 to €50 per group per hour, depending on the size of the boat. Pensions in Murighiol can also arrange various excursions.

You'll need a **permit** to **travel independently** around the Delta, but you can make all the necessary arrangements in Tulcea (see box, p.398) or, for the southern arm, Murighiol.

Amatour (℡0240/518 894, ⓦwww.amatour.ro; ❸) opposite the *Hotel Delta* – facilities are basic but the atmosphere compensates.

Casa Albastru Lake Ciuperca ℡0240/535 662, ⊠dtsj@x3m.ro. A basic youth hotel with 20 twin rooms with bathrooms and TV. ❷
Delta Str. Isaccei 2 ℡0240/514 720, ℻516 260. Functional but pricey three-star on Piaţa Republicii. Crisp service and a lively, stylish lobby provide an air of sophistication, but the rooms themselves aren't much better than those at the *Europolis*. ❻
Egreta Str. Păcii 3 ℡0240/506 250, ⓦwww.unita-turism.ro. A communist-era tower decently refurbished to three-star standard. ❺
Europolis Str. Păcii 20 ℡0240/512 443, ⓦwww.europolis.ro. A respectable but bland and slightly run-down two-star just south of the Piaţa Civică. ❹
Han Trei Stele Str. Carpaţi 16 ℡0240/516 764 or 0724/774 064. On the right as you start up

the steps behind the Piaţa Veche, this pleasantly chaotic budget option has communal bathrooms. ❷
Pensiunea Anda Str. Livezilor 13 ℡0240/537 774, ⓦwww.andaturism.ro. By Lake Cazla, 2km west of the city, this five-room guesthouse is run by a tour company that also operates Delta tours. ❷
Rex Str. Toamnei 1 ℡0240/511 351, ⓦwww.hotelrex.ro. A four-star hotel, just beyond the synagogue on Str. Babadag, with a/c, conference rooms and pleasant staff. ❻
Select Str. Păcii 6, with entrance on Str. Babadag ℡0240/506 180, ⓦwww.calypsosrl.ro. A new three-star, nice enough and not at all flashy; sauna, Jacuzzi, gym and massage are all available. ❺

The Town

Tulcea is centred around Piaţa Republicii, northeast of which, on the corner of Str. 9 Mai at Str. G. Antipa 2, is the town's main attraction, the **Art Museum** (Muzeul de Artă; Tues–Sun: May–Oct 10am–6pm; Nov–April 8am–4pm), built by Ismail Pasha in 1870; its fine collection of paintings includes Impressionistic female nudes by Pallady, Delta landscapes by Sirbu and Stavrov, and a selection of avant-garde works, including the country's best collection of works by the Romanian Surrealist Victor Brauner (1903–66). You'll also see Igolesco's *Balchik*, a depiction of the thriving artistic community in southern Dobrogea, a village so loved by Queen Marie that she asked for her heart to be buried there. When the area was handed over to Bulgaria, the queen's heart was brought back in a casket that now rests in the National History Museum in Bucharest (see p.76). From Str. 9 Mai, Str. 14 Noiembrie heads north to the nondescript nineteenth-century **Azizie Mosque**; having been fairly inconspicuous under communism, the local Turkish women are now much more visible, dressed in bright colours and baggy trousers. Beyond the mosque, Str. Gloriei runs through a pretty area of small white houses with gardens, ending at the **Parcul Monumentului Independenţei**, where you'll find an **obelisk** to the dead of the 1877–78 war, some **Roman remains**, and the **Museum of History and Archeology** (Muzeul de Istorie şi Arheologie; Tues–Sun: May–Oct 10am–6pm; Nov–April 8am–4pm), noted for its collection of Roman, Greek, Byzantine and medieval coins. A newer building houses prehistoric remains and temporary exhibitions.

Back in the centre, the **Museum of Ethnography and Folk Art** at Str. 9 Mai 2 (Muzeul de Etnografie şi Artă Populară; Tues–Sun: May–Oct 10am–6pm; Nov–April 8am–4pm) has displays on the varied groups inhabiting the region. On the far side of the systematized Piaţa Civică is the **Danube Delta Museum of Natural Sciences**, Str. Progresului 32 (Muzeul de Ştiintele Naturii Delta Dunării; Tues–Sun 9am–5pm); equipped with multilingual guides and captions, it has a fascinating geological display showing the formation of the Delta, and on its lower level a modest aquarium featuring local aquatic species. It's one of several attractive but very tatty houses in the area dating from the late nineteenth century. A few blocks east, on Str. Păcii, **St George's** is one of the town's several barn-like churches built under Turkish occupation, with its separate bell tower added later.

Back on the waterfront near Piaţa Republicii, **ferries** (every 15min from dawn to dusk) shuttle across the river to the largely Russian suburb of **Tudor Vladimirescu**, where there's a sandy bank for sunbathing.

Eating and drinking

The main **market**, good for buying snacks and provisions for trips into the Delta, is just south of the centre down Str. Păcii, beyond St George's. The smaller Piaţa Veche, off Str. Isaccei, is handier for the stations and NAVROM terminal. The **supermarket** at Str. Unirii 2 (between the Piaţa Civică and Piaţa Republicii) has Tulcea's best selection of imported foods, as well as decent bread and fruit; there's also a small supermarket on the south side of the *Hotel Europolis*.

The finest **restaurant** in town is in the *Hotel Select,* at Str. Păcii 6; take your pick from a varied menu, presented in six languages. The restaurant in the *Comandor Boat* has a basic menu and a good wine list, although the cabin tends to fill up with smoke; the open upper deck is preferable in summer. A more conventional choice is the reasonably priced *Picadilly*, at Str. Babadag 3, with the *Pizzerie Trident* a little further up the street. The classiest **place for a drink** is the bar in the *Hotel Delta*; the floor-to-ceiling windows looking out on the

Danube are perfect for watching passing bird life. *Union Visa*, a snack bar on Str. Unirii, brews surprisingly rich and aromatic coffee. During the summer, **outdoor cafés** on the waterfront serve Danubian staples such as beer and grilled sausages; there are also two floating *bar-terasas* just east of the *Comandor*.

Upstream from Tulcea

West of Tulcea, the Danube is up to 1km wide, with a **floodplain** of almost 100 square kilometres that is inundated every spring as nature intended. The area near **Rotundu**, 25km west of Tulcea, is especially rich in plankton and fish, and although it's a closed reserve there are plenty of birds, such as swans, little bittern and white-tailed eagles (Romania's largest raptor), to be seen in the vicinity. The *Delta Nature Resort*, 3km north of the DN22 on the road to Parcheş (℡0725/408 000 or 021/311 4532, Ⓦwww.deltaresort.com; ❽), is a luxury villa complex with friendly, relaxed service and great food, in a superb location overlooking the wetlands; there's an environmentally conscious philosophy and a range of excursions including a sunset cruise (€37 including drinks), a fishing/nature safari in the Delta (€100/boat) or a visit to Saon monastery (see below; €50), as well as rental of rowing boats and kayaks (€10/hr) and motor boats (€22/hr).

Three kilometres south of the main road, the village of **NICULIŢEL** boasts a church dating from around 1300, which, according to legend, was found, by a shepherd, buried underground – clearly influenced by the Turkish restrictions on the height of churches, which led to them being built half-underground in places. There are also the remains of a paleo–Christian church, dating from the fourth century, with a triple nave and a crypt built to house the relics of four martyrs. The village is also known for its wine flavoured with wormwood. There are two simple **pensions** here, *Nichy* (℡0722/522 955; ❷) and *Dascalu Stere* (℡0240/542 308; ❷). Inland is a beautiful **open forest**, more typical of the Dobrogean steppes than the Delta, which was established as a nature reserve in 1927 by the botanist King Ferdinand, thanks to its rare species of peonies; bird life includes buzzards, nightingales, ortolan buntings, tawny pipits and woodpeckers. Three famous **monasteries** are nearby, at Cocos, 7km south of Niculiţel (founded in 1833, although the present church dates from 1916, and much visited due to the relics of four martyrs held there); Chilic-Dere (1840, where there's a wooden windmill), 8km south of the main road; and Saon (1846), 3km north of the main road. It's possible to sleep at these monasteries, and the monks (or, at Saon, nuns) may even feed you.

ISACCEA, on the main road 36km west of Tulcea, is a wine-making centre where you can see a sixteenth-century mosque (next to the bus yard) and, 2.5km north, the remains of the Roman fortress of Noviodunum, founded in 369. In addition to ruined walls and towers there are stone sarcophagi to be seen.

Into the Delta

The following sections cover each arm of the Delta in turn, starting from Tulcea, and then the Lake Razim region. If you just want to take a trip down to the sea and back, **Sfântu Gheorghe** is probably the best choice; it's prettier than Sulina, has a more tranquil beach, and is within easy reach of several good birdwatching spots. **Sulina** is more crowded and built up, but richer in historical associations. Of the numerous ancient ruins in the vicinity of the Delta, the Roman city of **Halmyris**, near Murighiol, is rewarding and easily accessible.

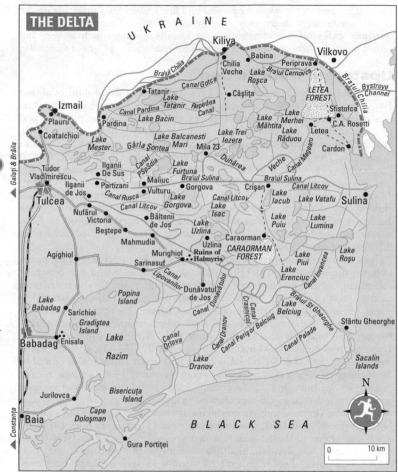

THE DELTA

Bratul Chilia

The **Chilia arm** of the river (Braţul Chilia), which branches off upstream from Tulcea and marks the border with Ukraine, carries more than half of the Danube's water, but very little tourist traffic, mainly because boats will only carry you as far as the largely Lipovani village of **PERIPRAVA** (100km from Tulcea but still 30km from the Black Sea), where there's a total lack of tourist facilities. In the days when the entire Delta was part of Moldavia, **CHILIA VECHE**, 35km from Periprava, was merely a suburb of Chilia (now Ukrainian Kiliya) across the river. When the town repelled a Turkish invasion in 1476, Chilia was just 5km from the coast – today, it's 40km away. There are three **pensions** in Chilia Veche: *Mariuţa* (☎0744/556 671; ❷); *Bata* (book through Antrec ☎0240/519 214; ❷); and the cheaper but better connected *Vital* (☎0240/533 575 or 0744/276 435, ✉vital_delta@yahoo.com; ❷). There's also the 40-site *Camping Chilia* (☎0240/519 090 or 0744/336 685).

The Lipovani

Descendants of the Old Believers who left Russia around 1772 to avoid religious persecution, the **Lipovani** (identifiable by their blond hair, blue eyes and, among the men, beards) were once dispersed all over the Delta but are now found only at Periprava, Mila 23, Mahmudia and Letea, as well as Jurilovca and Sarichioi on Lake Razim.

Adapting to their environment, the Lipovani became skilled **fishermen** and gardeners, speaking a Russian dialect among themselves but equally fluent in Romanian. Since you're likely to rely on Lipovani boatmen to guide you through the confusing side channels (*gârla*), smokers should be prepared for their fundamentalist abhorrence of the "Devil's weed", tobacco; their consumption of vodka, however, is legendary.

Lake Roşca, roughly 10km south of Babina on the Cernovca tributary between Chilia Veche and Periprava, is one of the larger strictly protected reserves, harbouring geese, egrets, storks and Europe's largest **white pelican colony**. Immediately to the east is **Periprava**, south of which lies the **Pădurea Letea**, a forest of oaks tangled with lianas, now a haven for falcons, white-tailed eagles, boar and wildcats. Surrounding the forest are **sand dunes** inhabited by tortoises, lizards and the horned viper.

One way of seeing a little of the Braţul Chilia route is to travel as far as **Ceatalchioi**, 20km north of Tulcea, where the reeds (*stuf*) that are used to build Delta houses are gathered in winter, when it's possible to drive tractors on the ice. Not far beyond Ceatalchioi (due north as the river flows), boats pass **Izmail**, the main Ukrainian city in the Delta, whose bloody recapture from the Turks in 1790 is described in Byron's *Don Juan*.

Braţul Sulina

Between 1862 and 1902, the **Sulina arm** (Braţul Sulina) was shortened from 84km to 63km by the digging of long straight sections, now paralleled by a communist-era power line. Distances from the sea were marked in **nautical miles**, as opposed to the kilometres later used on the other arms. Constant dredging and groynes running 10km out to sea still enable 7000-tonne freighters to take this route from Tulcea; with the additional tourist traffic, this is the busiest and least serene of the Danube's branches. However, it does have a tourist infrastructure and several settlements that offer a fair chance of renting boats to visit a variety of wildlife habitats. **Sulina** itself has seen something of a revitalization in recent years and is now the Delta's most popular tourist destination. It's also the most built up, and the only one with streets and cars. There are a few interesting sights in Sulina, but the fishing villages along the way make much better bases for seeing wildlife and exploring the wetlands. The journey from Tulcea to Sulina takes ninety minutes by hydrofoil, two hours by fast catamaran, or four-and-a-half by ferry.

Travellers attempting to explore the Delta **by canoe** will face turbulence from the wakes of passing ships on the main waterway, but **beyond Ilganii de Sus** you can escape into calmer backwaters leading to the inland lakes. Just east of Ilgani, on the north bank where the Sulina and Sfântu Gheorghe arms split (and just 6km from Tulcea), the *Complex Mila 35* (☎0240/515 004 or 0745/082 221, ⓦwww.mila35.ro; ⑤) is a reed-thatched three-star resort that's less grandiose than most of the Delta's new resorts.

Delta practicalities

To enter the **Danube Delta Biosphere Reserve** (**RBDD**), you need a **permit**, which gains you access to everywhere except the strictly protected reserves. If you're taking a tour, this will be handled by the tour company; independent travellers can get permits from the ARBDD, the Gara Fluviala, the prefecture and travel agencies and hotels in Tulcea for a basic price of L10 per day, with supplementary charges for boating and fishing. The ARBDD recommends the use of electric boats and a 10km/hr speed limit, but both are generally ignored by tourboats. Organized tours, which cost about twenty times as much as travelling independently, are limited to seven fixed routes. If you're planning to explore beyond these, take a compass and a detailed **map** – the green Olimp map (available in Tulcea at bookstores and at the *Europolis* hotel), which has English text and shows the eighteen strictly protected zones, and the Amco Delta map (available in Bucharest) are the best. The boat rental kiosk in Murighiol also sells good maps.

Camping is prohibited except in Murighiol, Crișan, Partizani and on the shore of Lake Roșu, but the regulations are laxly enforced. There are **hotels** only in Sulina and Murighiol, in addition to a number of **resort complexes**, but good **pensions** can be found virtually everywhere, at least between May and September, after which most of them close for the season. If these are full – and in July and August they might be – you should be able to find **bed and breakfast** accommodation in a **private home**, though this will likely be without hot water. The Antrec agency in Tulcea (see p.392) will help you find a pension. Alternatively, try one of the agencies in Tulcea, particularly Simpa Turism, Sincron and ATBAD (see box, p.393), which have their own hotels in the Delta. Wherever you end up staying, expect generous fish dinners and lovely tomato salads. Most pensions routinely offer full board, but our price codes reflect the bed-and-breakfast equivalent. The shops in Sulina sell a respectable variety of **food** supplies; elsewhere, the selection can be very limited – finding still water can be especially difficult. Before you set off, it's worth buying **essential supplies** like canned food, fruit and cheese in Tulcea; candles and plenty of mosquito repellent are also vital. Most Delta villages have a bakery, but fresh bread sells quickly – locals tend to start queuing when there's a batch in the oven.

Maliuc

Fishermen in **MALIUC**, on the left bank of the river 27km from Tulcea, can row you to see the pelicans and marsh terns nesting on **Lake Furtuna**. The reeds in this area provide a home for pike, great-crested grebes, the solitary red-necked grebes, bearded reedlings – which nest in piles of cut reeds – and herons and little egrets, which favour nesting in overhanging willow trees. Maliuc has a **campsite** (①) and the *Salcia* **hotel** (④). From Lake Meşter or the Păpădia channel, **canoeists** can try following the Gârla Şontea to reach the original Dunărea Veche course of the river near Mila 23 (see p.400); be warned, though, that submerged roots and aquatic plants may block the way. Nearby **Lake Gorgova** hosts a large colony of glossy ibis, and has a small cabana (①).

Crișan

CRIŞAN, a fishing settlement that consists of a single dirt path, lined with houses and straggling along the south bank of the shoreline for 7km, is the main tourist centre in this part of the Delta, and a good place to see the region's most common bird species; the ditch that runs behind the houses shelters herons, egrets and other waders, and you're likely to find hoopoes, rollers and goldfinches in the brushland at the west end of the village. Pelicans glide high

There are currently three weekly **ferries** operated by NAVROM-Delta (Ⓦwww
.navrom.x3m.ro) to Sulina (from Tulcea Mon, Wed & Fri; returning Tues, Thurs & Sat),
two to Sfântu Gheorghe (from Tulcea Wed & Fri, returning Thurs & Sun) and two to
Periprava (from Tulcea Tues & Fri; returning Wed & Sun). They leave Tulcea at 1.30pm
(a little later if there's a crowd) and take four-and-a-half hours to Sulina or Sf.
Gheorghe and five-and-a-half to Periprava. Ferries return early: from Sulina and Sf.
Gheorghe at 7am and from Periprava at 6am. The ferries are lumbering vessels
crammed with people and piled high with dinghies, rods and camping gear; it's worth
avoiding the cabins, where the air is poisonous. Note that projecting empty beer cans
and cigarette ends from the deck into the Danube is a holiday ritual here.

NAVROM-Delta also operates a pair of *rapid* **fast catamarans**, Delta Expres 1 and
2, which traverse all three branches of the Delta (to Sulina Tues, Thurs & Sat,
returning Mon, Wed & Fri; to Sf. Gheorghe Mon & Thurs, returning Tues & Fri; to
Periprava Mon & Wed, returning Tues & Thurs). These also leave Tulcea at 1.30pm
and take two hours to Sulina and three to Sf. Gheorghe or Periprava; returns are at
7am from Sulina and Sf. Gheorghe and 6am from Periprava. Tickets cost relatively
little more than for the *clasica* slow boats and sell out early; however, there's a 30kg
baggage limit.

On the **winter schedule**, from October to June, Sulina is reached by ferries (Mon,
Wed & Fri) and *rapids* (Tues & Thurs); Sfântu Gheorghe by a ferry (Wed) and *rapids*
(Mon & Fri); and Periprava by a ferry (Fri) and *rapids* (Mon & Wed).

The Sageaţa (Arrow) **hydrofoils**, once state-owned, are now operated by private
companies and operate from Tulcea's Gara Fluviala to Sulina only, leaving daily at
7am and noon and returning at noon and 6pm. Don't expect a view: these
are swift, businesslike craft with opaque windows, taking just ninety minutes for
the journey.

In Tulcea the **ticket office** for all the services outlined above (open sailing days only
11am–1.30pm) is in the Gara Fluviala on the waterfront; **tickets** (€6.50 by ferry to
Sulina, or €8 by fast cat, around €10 by hydrofoil) can only be bought on the day
you're travelling, up to two hours before departure.

overhead in long formations throughout the day, making their way from Lake
Merhei to Lake Iacob. Across the river at Mila 13, there is a **monument**
unveiled by Carol I in 1894 to inaugurate the new short-cut sections. Also on
the north bank, before Mila 14, is the ARBDD's **Centru de Informare şi
Documentare** (May–Oct Tues–Fri 10am–4pm, Sat & Sun 10am–2pm;
Nov–April Mon–Fri 8am–4pm), a good source of **information** on all areas of
the Biosphere Reserve, with an excellent viewing tower.

Ferries stop on the south bank, in the centre of Crişan; both the best shop
and the bakery are by the ferry pier. **Accommodation** is available at a couple
of moderately luxurious **hotels**, the *Lebăda* (☎0240/543 778; ❼), on the north
bank, and the *Sunrise* (☎0240/547 191, Ⓦwww.hotelsunrise.ro; ❻), with four-
star rooms plus villas. There are also several good **pensions**, the best of which
is the *Pensiunea Nufărul* (☎0721/092 150, Ⓔgolo@tim.ro; ❷), a professionally
run establishment a few hundred metres east of the ferry landing, which can
arrange day-trips to remoter parts of the Delta. In the other direction, 500m
west of the landing, *Pensiunea Delia* (☎0240/547 018 or 0745/116 186,
Ⓦwww.deltadelia.ro; ❸) is larger, with comfortable rooms, permanent hot
water and a good laundry service, as well as camping space. *Pensiunea Oprişan
Andrei* (☎0240/547 034 or 0744/912 651; ❷), 200m east of the ferry landing,
is also recommended. Private homestays are cheaper (usually ❶) and often serve

more generous fish dinners, but facilities can be basic. Crişan's **campsite** (℡0745/832 293; ❶) is at the far west end of the village.

Around Crişan

Boats meet the ferry (but not the hydrofoil or fast catamaran) at Crişan to take you across to the north bank, and continue on to **MILA 23**, 10km northwest on the "old" branch of the Danube; this is the starting point for excursions to most of the surrounding lakes. Mila 23 is a large Lipovani village of thatched cottages (rebuilt after a flood in the 1960s), where the men fish and the women tend to gardens of vegetables, plums, pears, grapes and quinces, and look after the poultry, pigs and beehives. Golden orioles – which nest high in deciduous trees – and bladder frogs are widespread around here. **Pensions** include *Marcov 2* (℡0240/546 411; ❷) and the better-value *Cris* (℡0240/546 446; ⓦwww.deltacris.ro; ❷).

South of Crişan, the forest of **Pădurea Caraorman**, now a strict reserve, is the best area of dunes in the Delta, striped with unusual linear forests of ancient oaks, poplar, ash and willow and protecting wildlife such as Ural owls, white-tailed eagles, wildcats, boars and wolves. The dyke that runs south from Crişan leads to a dead end; to get to the forest, catch the boat that meets ferries at Crişan to take passengers to the predominantly Ukrainian village of **CARAORMAN**, where there are a couple of **pensions**: *Grindul Verde* (℡0722/732 076, ⓦwww.caraorman.ro; ❷), which has English-speaking staff, and the small but slightly more upmarket *Purda Nicoara* (℡0744/381 528; ❷). Half-a-dozen unfinished skeletal apartment blocks are testament to plans, under Ceauşescu, to remove the dunes en masse; the 1989 revolution intervened.

Three remote and very different settlements lie to the north of Crişan, on the south side of the Letea forest: **LETEA**, a village of Lipovani/Ukrainian fisherfolk, where there's a rangers' house and birdwatching tower; neighbouring **C.A. ROSETTI**, home to Romanian cattle breeders and the Delta's last windmill; and **SFISTOFCA**, an even smaller Lipovani village. You may get a room in these places on the spot, but it's best to check with the ARBDD in Tulcea (see p.392) before setting out. The **Letea forest**, just north of Rosetti and Letea, is strictly off-limits, but the **Sfistofca forest**, to the south, is almost as good, a maze of trees up to two hundred years old, tangled with lianas and orchids.

Sulina

Ever since it was recorded as a port by a Byzantine scribe in 950, **SULINA** has depended on shipping. Genoese vessels used to call here during the fourteenth century, while throughout the Ottoman period it was not so much a trading port as a nest of pirates who preyed on traffic in the Black Sea. Devastated during the Crimean War – only the church and lighthouse survived after the British, driving out the Russians, burnt the place down – Sulina was rebuilt and went on to prosper as the headquarters of the European Commission of the Danube, established in 1856 to regulate free passage along the waterway. In 1900 it became a free port, and its freewheeling multinational life was captured in the novel *Europolis* by Jean Bart (pseudonym of the Romanian sea captain Eugeniu Botez, 1874–1933). Within a decade, however, larger vessels and worldwide recession had emptied Sulina, so that by 1940 the writer John Lehmann found "a hopeless, sinking feeling" in a place where "people get stranded, feel themselves abandoned by civilization, take to drink, and waste into a half-animal existence". Today, expensive annual dredging is required to enable even small-capacity ships to enter, while larger freighters can now bypass the Delta altogether by taking the Danube–Black Sea Canal. Tourism is succeeding where trade failed, and, drawn by the long sandy beach 2km from the port, a small but growing contingent of Romanians has chosen Sulina as an alternative to the more established resorts further south.

A taste of the ambience of Sulina's golden days survives in the nineteenth-century houses along the waterfront, and at the **Old Lighthouse** (Farul Vechi; Tues–Sun: summer 8am–noon & 4–8pm; winter 8am–4pm); built in 1870, it is now a history museum, with a room dedicated to Jean Bart and another to the European Commission of the Danube. The lighthouse is two blocks south of the ferry landing at Str II no. 15; 500m further to the southeast, between the town and the sea, is the **cemetery**, which provides an evocative record of all the nationalities who lived and died here in the town's days as a free port. Greeks dominated business, but there was also a large British contingent, some now resting beneath dignified Victorian tombstones in the Anglican plot, directly behind the chapel. Like so much of the Delta, the cemetery is full of birds; this is one of the best places to see hoopoes, and possibly cuckoos and orioles. From the cemetery, it's a one-kilometre walk to the **beach** (maxitaxis also run this route). Also look for two **churches** from the nineteenth century: the Greek Church of Saint Nicholas on the waterfront, and the Russian church near the west end of town.

Practicalities

The useful **Visitor Centre** (May–Oct Tues–Sat 9am–noon & 4–7pm, Sun 9am–1pm; Nov–April Mon–Fri 10am–6pm) is near the dock in the centre of town on Str. I. There are a number of **pensions** in Sulina, many of which send touts to meet the ferries. The most exclusive is the waterfront *Casa Coral* (☎0240/543 777 or 0745/228 788; ❹), a new three-daisy establishment with smart rooms (with cable TV) and a restaurant. Shabbier, but much more atmospheric, is the *Pensiunea Jean Bart*, Str. I (or Str. Botez) 190 (☎0240/543 128; ❸); the fish **restaurant** here is the best place to eat in Sulina. Around the corner from the *Jean Bart* is *Pensiunea Vâlcu* (☎0240/543 403; ❷), and a few blocks further in, at Str. IV no. 144, the modest but friendly *Pensiunea Ana* (☎0230/543 252; ❷). You'll find a youth hostel, *Hostel Danube Delta*, also known as *Cazare Camping Sulina*, at Str. II no. 1 (☎0742/920 431, ✉holidays.danubedelta@yahoo .com, ⓦhttp://holiday-danube-delta.ro; ❶); it has six-bed rooms and camping space. At the beach, there's a **campsite** with cabanas (❶) and rooms (❷). There are a few **bars** in Sulina, but the principal evening activity is strolling on the promenade, where the shops do a brisk trade in ice cream.

Bra**ț**ul Sf**â**ntu Gheorghe

The Delta's oldest, most winding arm, **Bra**ț**ul Sf**â**ntu Gheorghe**, is the least used by freighters and fishing boats; it's wider but shallower than the Sulina arm. It carries a fair amount of tourist traffic and, unlike other parts of the Delta, some of its settlements can be reached by bus from Tulcea. If you plan to visit these, it's easiest to go direct to **Sf**â**ntu Gheorghe**, then head by boat head to **Murighiol**, from where you can make a boat trip to the fishing village of **Uzlina** or visit the ruins of **Halmyris**. There's plenty of parking in Murighiol; if you've come by car, it's better to leave it there rather than in Tulcea.

Sf**â**ntu Gheorghe

SFÂ**NTU GHEORGHE**, 75km downriver from Murighiol, is a small village of brightly painted Lipovani and Ukrainian cottages that has subsisted on fishing since the fourteenth century. Most prized is the **sturgeon**, whose eggs, *icre negre* or black caviar, once drew thousands of Romanian tourists here on

▲ Sfântu Gheorghe

shopping trips. The catch is not what it used to be, though you still might find some caviar if you come in late August or early September. The **reed and mud houses**, most of which support colonies of swallows, are the main attraction of the village itself, but most tourists come for the relatively untouched **beach** (stretching 38km north to Sulina) or to make trips into the surrounding **marshes**. A large tractor, one of the two or three motorized land vehicles in the village, carries tourists the 2km to and from the beach in a trailer, departing every hour or so from the centre – the schedule should be posted on one of the information boards near the main square.

Practicalities

The best **place to stay** in Sfântu Gheorghe is the *Delfinul Tourist Village* (☎021/230 0507 or 0508, or 0749/187 551, ⑩www.delta-resort.ro; ❺), 700m east on the road to the beach; it includes villas (some actually in the village) and cabins. The best of the dozen or so pensions in town is the *Mareea* (☎0744/306 384, ⑩www.mareea.go.ro; ❺), which has ten attractively furnished air-conditioned rooms and superb meals – if not caviar, there's at least a chance of finding sturgeon on the menu. The owner, who speaks English well, can arrange fishing and birdwatching excursions. Less exclusive, and without air-conditioning but with hot water, is the ten-room *Pensiunea Sperante*, at Str. I no. 30 (☎0744/197 042; ❸), which funds a charity in Bucharest. Locals know it as *casa galben*, the yellow house. Dora Dumitru has a summer home (☎0240/540 219; ❷) one block north of the *Sperante*, with four bedrooms and an enclosed, mosquito-free dining room. She makes excellent salads, and prepares fish in a mouthwatering variety of ways. She speaks French; her daughters, who are sometimes around, speak English. *Casa Ichim* (☎0745/600 650, ⓔadriana.ichim@gmail.com; ❷) has three rooms and an open porch for dining, plus a boat that is available for excursions. There are half a dozen simple guesthouses rated with one daisy (all ❷); their owners and other villagers with private rooms (❶) will meet your ferry. You can camp, either wild (officially forbidden) or at the *Delfinul*, which has tent space and cabins. Sfântu Gheorghe's **shops**, sparsely stocked and with relatively high prices, are in the centre near the dock, as is the bakery. There's also a **bar** – where occasionally a band of local fishermen play a mix of Beatles covers and traditional songs – and, on Friday and Saturday nights, a **disco**.

The *Delfinul Tourist Village* has three cinemas used for the **Anonimul Film Festival** in mid-August, a celebration of independent films from around the world (⑩www.festival-anonimul.ro).

Around Sfântu Gheorghe

During July and August, the Sfântu Gheorghe tractor makes occasional day excursions to **Sulina** (1hr 30min) – look for a sign in the town centre or ask around if you're interested. Otherwise you can take **boat trips** north to **Lake Roşu**, or south down the Gârla de Mijloc canal to **Lesser Sacalin Island** (Insula Sacalinu Mic) at the river's mouth, which is inhabited by all three species of marsh tern, stilts, ibis and other waders, as well as goosanders, red-breasted geese, and goldeneyes. This is one of the oldest parts of the Delta and a strictly protected reserve, so boats are not allowed to moor: to get to the beach on the island, you'll have to wade through the ankle-deep mud at the canal's end. Depending on the wind, the trip takes an hour or more; the motorboat is faster but, at €10 per hour, at least twice as expensive. Look for kingfishers along the way. Further south still is **Greater Sacalin Island** (Insula Sacalinu Mare), while to the west, on Lake Lejai and near the Crasnicol sand bank, is the remote area where the Delta's three hundred or so Dalmatian pelicans breed. The trip to **Lacul Roşu** (Pink Lake) is longer than that to Lesser Sacalin Island, but you're likely to see white pelicans. There's an isolated **campsite** on the canal between Roşu and Puiu lakes. Also here is ATBAD's *Complex Roşu*, with a three-star **hotel** (❾) and two-star **bungalows** (❼), a **restaurant**, **disco** and **water-skiing**. To see the most birds, boat trips should be taken as early as possible; note that fishermen can be unreliable on the mornings after the disco.

Murighiol

Returning towards Tulcea, the main settlement en route is **MURIGHIOL**, which, though connected to the outside world by road as well as water, still has some of the isolated feeling of an interior Delta village. Murighiol has its natural attractions – namely black-winged stilts, red- and black-necked grebe, Kentish plover, avocets, and red-crested pochards, and Romania's only colony of Mediterranean gulls, all nesting around the late-freezing **salt lakes** (Sărături Murighiol) nearby, but the principal reason to come here is to visit the ruin at **Halmyris** or the fishing village of **Uzlina**. Seven buses and maxitaxis a day run to and from Tulcea, on a circular route via either Mahmudia or Sarinasuf. Be warned that the buses don't go anywhere near the ferry landing, which is 5km northeast from the centre of town – if you're on your way to or from Sfântu Gheorghe, you'll have to walk or hitch. Arriving by bus from Tulcea, you'll be dropped off in the centre of Murighiol, next to the shell of an abandoned Centru Civic; from here, walk downhill past the two or three main shops, beyond which you will see **pensions** on either side of the street, including, on your left, *Pensiunea Riviera* (℡0240/545 910; ❶), open year-round, where you can arrange four-hour Delta trips from €45 for up to six people. For more **accommodation**, continue down the main road, turning left just before Murighiol's last house, and follow the dirt path to the excellent *Motel Halmyris* (℡0742/197 177; ❹), one of the cheapest three-star **hotels** in Romania, although it has only ten rooms. Nearby is the larger *Complex Turistic Pelican* (℡0240/545 877), which has a hotel (❸), villas (❷) and a **campsite** with cabins (❷). Between the *Halmyris* and the *Pelican* is a boat-rental kiosk affiliated with Simpa Turism; staff here can arrange day-trips or transportation (€11 per person) to their *Complex Cormoran* at Lake Uzlina (see box opposite). For **ferries** to Sfântu Gheorghe, follow the forested road that begins next to the *Halmyris*; it's 1.5km on to the ferry landing, where there's also a large car park.

Halmyris

Several hundred metres east of the *Motel Halmyris* lies its namesake, the ruined Roman city of **HALMYRIS**. One of the most important ancient sites in Romania, Halmyris was continuously inhabited from the sixth century BC to the seventh century AD, when a combination of marauding barbarians, climatic changes and dwindling imperial support led to its demise. Originally a small seafront fort – in ancient times, a Danube channel met the Black Sea only a few hundred metres to the east – it grew in size and importance until it became the permanent home to vexilations of Roman legions and a station for the Danube fleet *Classis Flavia Moesica*, serving as a stopping point on the road that connected the major Roman settlements of the Delta.

Today, Halmyris is best known for the **tomb of Epictet and Astion**, two Christians from Asia Minor who were tortured and executed here on July 8, 290, after refusing to renounce Christianity, thus becoming the earliest Romanian martyrs (and earning a place on the Romanian Orthodox calendar). One of their judges was said to have been converted by the resolve with which Epictet and Astion met their fates, and to have secretly buried their remains, which were then kept hidden until the conversion of Constantine, when they were interred in Halmyris's **basilica**. The story seemed to be the stuff of legend until 2001, when a **crypt** containing two skeletons was discovered beneath the basilica's altar, along with a **fresco** (currently under restoration) bearing the name "Astion".

In addition to the basilica and the crypt, the two-hectare site also features extensive remains of an L-shaped private **bathhouse**. The Western Gate, which dates from the sixth century AD, was constructed largely of stones carved with honorary inscriptions that had in earlier times adorned the homes of the town's more prominent citizens. Much of Halmyris, as well as the surrounding cornfields that cover its harbour, remains unexcavated (digging only began here in 1981), and its greatest attraction is not the ruins themselves, or the tombs of Epictet and Astion, but the chance to see an ancient city still in the process of being uncovered.

Uzlina, Dunavatu de Jos and Mahmudia

Murighiol is also the jumping-off point for the tiny fishing village of **UZLINA**, the site of the scientific centre of the Biosphere Reserve and the Cousteau Foundation, and an **EcoInfoCenter** in what was Ceaușescu's lodge. North of Uzlina, the Isac and Uzlina lakes are home to a protected **pelican colony**, which you can see from a respectful distance. Heading downstream, the new channel is edged by high levees, but the meanders of the old channel are tree-lined and populated by deer, boar, foxes, water snakes, black ibis and egrets. **Lake Belciug**, roughly halfway back towards Sfântu Gheorghe, is one of those least affected by algal blooms and deoxygenation, and retains the submerged vegetation once typical of the Delta, as well as a colony of glossy ibis.

To the southeast, 8km beyond Murighiol, the road ends at **DUNAVATU DE JOS**, on a channel between the Sfântu Gheorghe arm and Lake Razim, where you can stay at the three-star *Hotel Egreta* (☏0742/828 831, ⌨www.hotelegreta.ro; ❻), with 34 a/c rooms; *Complex Holbina* (☏0240/514 114; ❺); or half a dozen pensions including the three-daisy *Pelicanul* (☏0744/568 878; ❸), which has rooms with private and shared bathrooms. Ferries also call at **MAHMUDIA**, on the Tulcea road 7km west of Murighiol; there's accommodation at the *Hotel Teo* (☏0240/545 550, ✉office@hotelteo.ro; ❹), another amazingly cheap three-star, with a/c rooms, cable TV, boat rental, restaurant and what they call their "new-fangled bar", and at three pensions including the *Hornoiu* (☏0240/545 378; ❷).

Around Lake Razim

South of the Delta proper, **Lake Razim** is separated from the Black Sea by two long, tongue-like *grinds*. Like other parts of the Delta, Razim has been adversely affected by development: the western shores were empoldered in 1969 for fish farming, and in 1974 a sluice at Gura Portiței cut the lake off from the sea, causing it to fill with fresh water, which has led to frequent algal blooms, deoxygenation, and a steady decline in fish yields and biodiversity. It's still a good spot for birdwatchers, however, particularly in November and December, when the western shoreline is invaded by a million white-fronted and red-breasted geese from arctic Russia, which stay here and on Lake Sinoe just south until the reed beds freeze. In the north of the lake, Popina island is now a closed reserve.

Babadag and Enisala

From Tulcea, the DN22 and the rail line head south to **BABADAG**, home to the **Ali Ghazi Mosque**, Romania's oldest, dating from 1522. There's a visible Turkish minority here, present since 1263, but the mosque is little used. Just down the street, though, the **Museum of Oriental Art** (Muzeul de Artă Orientală; Tues–Sun 10am–6pm) has a small but engaging display of the folk art of the Dobrogean Turks, including embroidered robes and copper vessels. Maxitaxis between Tulcea and Constanța, as well as the less frequent services to Enisala and Jurilovca, call at the **bus station** across the street from the mosque. The only **accommodation** in Babadag itself is the basic *Motel Dumbrava*

(☎0240/561 302; ❷), five minutes north of the bus station at Str. Republicii 81; the *Popas Doi Iepuraşi* (☎0240/562 035; ❷) offers a peaceful night in the oak forest a couple of kilometres south of Babadag. Babadag is the base for Romania's élite Marine Battalion, forcibly disbanded after World War II but then re-established in 1971 as Ceauşescu increasingly defied Moscow; since 2007 US Marines have also been stationed here and at Constanţa's Mihail Kogălniceanu airport.

A quiet village of reed-thatched cottages, **ENISALA** lies 8km east of Babadag. In the centre of town, a traditional peasant home has been preserved as a **museum** (Punct Muzeal Gospodăria Ţărănească; Wed–Mon 10am–6pm) displaying colourful tapestries, painted carts and a wealth of implements. About 1km north, overlooking the lake, is the **ruined citadel of Heracleia**, built by Genoese merchants late in the thirteenth century at the behest of the Byzantine emperor, on the site of a seventh-century Byzantine fort. Taken by Sultan Mehmet I in 1417, it was held by the Ottomans until they abandoned it around the sixteenth century. This area is one of Europe's prime bird-watching sites, thanks to a mix of habitats: a vast area of reedbeds along the shoreline, stretching back to open land and the Babadag forest. You're likely to spot white-fronted and red-breasted geese, terns, waders, pelicans, herons and warblers. If you're coming from Tulcea, watch the left side of the road: shortly before passing the citadel, you'll see an apiary that supports a sizeable colony of bee-eaters. Nine daily maxitaxis from Tulcea take the rough backroad through Enisala en route to Babadag.

Jurilovca and Gura Portiţei

The tiny fishing village of **JURILOVCA**, 17km further down the coast and served by three daily buses from Tulcea, is of interest mainly for its access to Lake Razim's outer rim. It also has a small **Ethnographic Museum**, which bears witness to the village's population of Romanians, Lipovani and a few Muslim Turks and Tatars: unlike Transylvania, the Delta has never really been noted for ethnic rivalry, since all groups are relatively recent colonists. Around 5km east of Jurilovca, on Cape Doloşman, lie the remains of the second- to sixth-century Greek citadel of **Arganum**, which faces **Isla Bisericuţa (Chapel Island)**, itself the site of some medieval ruins. The only **place to stay** in Jurilovca is *Pensiunea Milica* (book through Antrec ☎0240/519 214; ❷).

From Jurilovca (where there's guarded parking), three boats (departing 9am, 2pm & 6pm; €6) sail daily to **GURA PORTIŢEI**, on a spit of land between Lake Razim and the sea. Before 1989, this was one of the few remote corners of Romania where it was possible to escape the Securitate for a week or two; today, it consists of a few Lipovani huts and the new *Complex Turistic Eden* (April–Oct; ☎0724/214 224, ⓦwww.guraportitei.ro) with a three-star **hotel** (❺), **bungalows** (❷) and cabins (❶). The hotel rooms are air-conditioned and have private baths; bungalows have shared showers with hot water. Activities include volleyball, tennis, and fishing, as well as birdwatching excursions to the **Periteaşca-Leahova reserve**, just north, where 20,000 red-breasted geese (half the world population) spend the winter. Continuing towards Constanţa, you'll rejoin the main DN22 at the north end of **BAIA**, better known as **Hamangia**, site of Romania's most famous Neolithic finds.

Istria

Heading south from Babadag and Baia and turning left at Mihai Viteazul, you'll pass through **ISTRIA**. Eight kilometres east of the village (and 35km north of Constanţa), on the shores of Lake Sinoe, is the **ruined city of Histria** with its shattered Greek temples to diverse deities, as well as Roman baths and other Romano-Byzantine edifices. The **ruins** (Wed–Sun: June–Sept 8am–8pm; Oct–May 9am–5pm) cover a fairly small area, despite the fact that this was long the most important of the ancient Greek settlements along the coast. It was founded in 657 BC, though none of the remains dates from before 300 BC. Istria's decline began soon after that, but it was inhabited until early in the seventh century AD, when the port was smothered in silt and the town abandoned after attacks by Avar-Slavic tribes. There's a **museum** (Tues–Sun 9am–8pm) near the entrance to the site, with coins, ceramics and other relics. Today, this strictly protected zone is one of Europe's best areas for birdwatching, with more than 200 species making an appearance in the winter months. Near the ruins is a **campsite** with chalets (❶); there's another site just south along the road to Năvodari at **NUNTAŞI** (5km east of the main Constanţa-Tulcea road). Four **maxitaxis** a day run from Constanţa to Istria village; the Istria train stop is on the DN22, too far west to be of use.

The coast

Romania's **Black Sea coast** (the *litoral*) holds the promise of white beaches, dazzling water and an average of ten to twelve hours of sunshine a day between May and October. Under communism, over a million people flocked to the resorts during the season; visitor numbers then halved but have since recovered to close to a million again, with far better conditions than previously. Travelling from the Delta, your first stop on the coast will almost certainly be **Constanţa**, a relaxed seaport-cum-riviera town, dotted with Turkish, Byzantine and Roman remains, which has always seemed to keep a discreet distance from the surrounding resorts.

Unless you're planning on staying in one of the five-star hotels in **Mamaia**, the region's hotspot, the best option is to take a **package tour** (see Basics, p.31), which guarantees you a room, minimizes extraneous hassles, and tends to work out cheaper than doing it independently. Otherwise, travel agencies in most towns on the coast offer rooms in bungalows or basic hotels. Though not as isolated as they once were, **Doi Mai** and the stylish **Vama Veche**, just a few kilometres from the Bulgarian border, offer an escape from the crowds.

The Dobrogea and the Danube–Black Sea Canal

The overland approaches to Constanţa cross one part or another of the bleak northern **Dobrogea**, a poor area where donkeys still haul metal-wheeled carts. While there's no reason to break your journey here, the changes wrought over

7

The Canal of Death

Work on the **Danube–Black Sea Canal** started in 1949 when the Communist Party launched its "hero project", and soon writers like Petru Dumitriu (who made his name with a book on the canal, *Dustless Highway*) were waxing lyrical about the transformation of humble peasants into class-conscious proletarians through the camaraderie of the construction site. But, as Dumitriu acknowledged after his defection in 1960, the Canalul Mortii (Canal of Death), as it came to be known, claimed the lives of around 50,000 workers, the bulk of whom were there under duress – **forced labour** was permitted from 1950, with six-month sentences doled out without trial by the Ministry of the Interior. Those "convicted" included Uniate priests, peasants who resisted collectivization, and people caught trying to flee abroad.

In 1953, after years of untold suffering, it was realized that the chosen route through the Canara Hills towards Năvodari, north of Constanța, was impossible and the project was abandoned. Work on a new route resumed in 1973, this time with better conditions, and the canal was successfully pushed eastwards to reach the sea at Agigea, south of Constanța, with a branch to the Năvodari petrochemical works following.

the last forty years certainly merit some explanation. Driving on the DN2A, you'll cross the Danube at **Giurgeni** and see orchards and fields planted on what used to be pestilential marshland; this transformation is nothing compared to the great works further to the south, starting at **Cernavodă**, where the Danube is spanned by what was, when it opened in 1895, Europe's longest bridge (4037m, with a main span of 1662m); trains now run alongside on a bridge built in 1987. A road bridge was added in the same year, linking the DN3A and the DN22C to provide the most direct road route to Constanța, parallel to the rail line and the **Danube–Black Sea Canal**. The motorway bridge, opened in 2006, passes diagonally under the 1895 rail bridge, with its carriageways continuing on either side of the railway.

Cernavodă and the canal

CERNAVODĂ, whose name rather ominously translates as "Black Water", was chosen in the late 1970s to be the site of Romania's first nuclear power station (problems with welding have meant that only two of the five reactors have so far come into service) but it's better known as the western entrance to the **Danube–Black Sea Canal**. Opened to shipping in 1984, the canal put Cernavodă a mere 60km from the Black Sea, offering obvious savings in time and fuel. However, realizing a profit on such a huge investment remains dependent on European economic revival and on the success of the Rhein–Main and Nürnberg–Regensburg canals. Charlemagne's vision of a 3000-kilometre-long waterway linking Rotterdam with the Black Sea finally came to fruition in 1993, although environmental protests in Bavaria and soaring costs had stalled the final stage of the project for ten years.

Along the canal

Most trains through the Dobrogea stop at the town of **MEDGIDIA** (the junction for Tulcea and Negru Vodă, the crossing point to Bulgaria) on the canal, 24km east of Cernavodă, while slow trains also halt at the canal-side town of **BASARABI** and its eastern suburb of **MURFATLAR**, which gives its name to the surrounding wine-growing region. Three million bottles a year are produced here, seventy percent white, although the full fruity reds are more distinctive. You can only visit on **tours** organized by travel agencies in the beach

The great outdoors

Romania's abundant mountains, forests, hills, rivers and lakes offer unlimited potential to indulge in a wide range of outdoor pursuits, from hiking the dramatic peaks of the Carpathian mountains, hitting the pistes in Poiana Braşov, or tracking an astonishing range of birds in the extraordinary Danube Delta. Moreover, and although still in their infancy, adventure sports such as kayaking and canoeing are beginning to make their mark.

Hiking in the Bucegi mountains, Transylvania ▲

Scaling the peaks

Crisscrossed by an intricate nexus of forestry tracks and waymarked paths, the beautiful and unspoilt Romanian countryside offers some of the most enjoyable hiking anywhere in Europe, with trails to suit all abilities. Moreover, you're more likely to encounter local shepherds and foresters, or, if you're lucky, brown bear, than you are other hikers. Cutting across the country are the sinuous Carpathian mountains – a continuation of the Alps – whose best-known range is the Făgăraş (see p.171), between Braşov and Sibiu in the south of Transylvania, harbouring more than seventy lakes and Romania's highest peaks, the highest of which is Moldoveanu (2544m). However, it's the Retezat and Piatra Craiului mountains (see p.211 & p.169) which present Romania's most challenging and scenically rewarding hikes, the former spotted with dozens of glacial lakes, and the latter a small but stunning limestone ridge. Nearby, just south of Braşov, the Bucegi massif (see p.148) offers shorter and easier walks among dramatic crags, caves and waterfalls. Less well known, and consequently less visited, options include the remote and lovely Rodna mountains (see p.355), near the Ukrainian border in Maramureş; the more modest Bucovina hills (see p.302) – studded with glorious painted monasteries – immediately east; and, closing off the western end of the Transylvanian plateau, the Apuseni mountains (see p.243), which offer comparatively undemanding hikes and great karstic phenomena such as limestone caves, potholes and gorges. Scattered around all these ranges are cabanas, convivial places offering basic accommodation and sometimes meals. Many Romanians, meanwhile, simply pitch camp by rivers, and provided you're not in a nature reserve, you can do the same.

Useful hiking terms

aven	doline
cabana	mountain hut
cascada	waterfall
colţ	cliff
cota	altitude
hartă	map
izvor	spring
nerecomandabil iarna	unsafe during winter
poiana	glade
potecă/traseu	path/route
refugiu (salvamont)	refuge (with first aid)
şau	col (saddle)
stăna	sheepfold
stânca	rock
telecabina	cable car
telescaun	chairlift
teleschi	ski-drag
vârf	peak

Hitting the slopes

Although the skiing is nowhere near as advanced or challenging as it is in many other European countries, Romania's ten or so small but rapidly developing ski resorts are well equipped, efficient and safe – and inexpensive. By far the most popular ski centre is Poiana Braşov (see p.166), thanks to its superior slopes and facilities; it also has the longest season (Nov–March/April). Elsewhere, there's good skiing at Predeal, Buşteni and Sinaia, a chain of resorts along the lovely Prahova Valley (see p.148); Borşa in Maramureş (for beginners); Păltiniş south of Sibiu; Semenic in southwestern Transylvania; and Durău/Ceahlău on the edge of Moldavia. The majority of Romania's pistes are rated "medium" (red) or "easy" (blue), but each of the major resorts has at least one difficult (black) run.

▲ Poiana Braşov
▼ Hiking in the Făgăraş mountains

Birdwatching

As Europe's most extensive wetland, and the world's largest continuous reedbed, the Danube Delta (see p.390) is heaven for birdwatchers. Millions of birds winter here, or stop over during the spring (March–May) and autumn (Aug–Oct) migrations – a unique, and often wonderfully colourful, concentration of different species, including herons, little egrets, red-breasted geese, the endangered pygmy cormorant, and Europe's largest pelican colonies. Although the best times for viewing are late March to early June and late July to early October, visit at any time of year and you'll be rewarded with a fantastic birding experience. Agencies can arrange boat tours down the main Sulina channel of the Delta, and their Tulcea or Crişan offices may sometimes

▼ Rodna mountains at sunset, Maramureş

rent small boats, which are the only means to penetrate the backwaters, where most of the birds nest. Canoes, kayaks or rowing boats are best for **exploration**, since motors scare the wildlife and get caught up in vegetation. Also fun is to negotiate with a local fisherman for a boat (*Pot s'închiriez o barcă?*), bearing in mind that he'll probably act as rower and guide.

Caving

Romania possesses some marvellous **large caves** (*peşteri*), replete with magnificent stalactites and stalagmites, and many **mountain caves** known only to a dedicated band of potholers. Indeed, the science and practice of caving owes much to a Romanian, Emil Racoviţa, who founded the world's first speleological institute at Cluj University, near the karst zone of the Apuseni mountains (see p.243). This region offers the most possibilities, from easy strolling passages to vertical shafts and flooded tunnels: the most renowned **tourist caves** are Meziad and the even more spectacular "Bear's Cave" at Chişcău (see p.366); in addition, there are big **river caves** such as Humpleu, Magura and Cetăţile Ponorului; and any number of crevices that should only be attempted by experts. The other main areas are the Mehedinţi massif in the southern Banat, which has river caves such as Topolniţa, Cloşani and Comarnic, and the Piatra Craiului, where you'll find the Dâmbovicioara cave. If you're interested in potholing, contact the Racoviţa Institute (Str. Clinicilor 5, 3400 Cluj, ☎0264/595 954, or Str. Frumoasă 11, 78114 Bucharest, ☎021/211 3874). Offering to contribute gear and a share of the costs should increase your chances of acceptance by a local club.

Pelican, Uzlina Lake, Danube Delta ▲
Dâmbovicioara cave, Piatra Craiului ▼

resorts; these take in the wine cellars at Calea Bucureşti 10, and the nearby **Vine and Wine Museum** (Muzeul Viei şi Vinului), displaying Greek and Roman amphorae and more recent presses.

Adamclisi and crossing into Bulgaria

Just north of the DN3 and the village of **ADAMCLISI** stands an arresting marble structure, a reconstruction of the **Tropaeum Traiani** (Wed–Sun: June–Sept 8am–8pm; Oct–May 9am–5pm). An armoured, faceless warrior gazing over the plateau from a height of 30m, the trophy-statue was erected here in 109 AD to celebrate Trajan's conquest of the Dacians, every facet reflecting unabashed militarism, not least the dedication to Mars Ultor. Carved around the side of its 32-metre base are 49 bas-reliefs or **metopes** portraying the Roman campaign. Each of the six groups of **metopes** comprises a marching scene, a battle, and a tableau representing victory over the enemy, an arrangement identical to the one that underlies scenes XXXVI–XLII of Trajan's Column in Rome, a copy of which is in Bucharest's National History Museum (see p.76). Around the statue are **ruins** of buildings once inhabited by the legionary garrison or serving religious or funerary purposes. **Buses** run from Cernavodă and Medgidia (heading for Băneasa and Ostrov), and three daily maxitaxis from Constanţa via Băneasa stop here on their way to Oltina; it may also be possible to take a private tour from Constanţa or Mamaia (see p.416).

Into Bulgaria

Sixty kilometres west of Adamclisi along the DN3 is the small border town of **OSTROV**, where you can cross over to the Bulgarian town of **Silistra** (also accessible on a ferry across the Danube from Călăraşi). Although the **Vama Veche** crossing (see p.426) is more suitable if you're driving down the coast to Varna, it's also possible to enter Bulgaria from **NEGRU VODĂ** at the south end of the DN38 (57km southwest of Constanţa), a crossing that's also used by three local trains a day from Medgidia. All three crossings are open 24 hours a day; if you need a visa, make sure you get it either before leaving home or in Bucharest (see Listings, p.96). The duty-free shops at the borders accept dollars and euros only.

Constanţa

Most visitors first encounter the Black Sea coast at **CONSTANŢA**, a busy riviera town and Romania's principal port. Its ancient precursor, Tomis, was supposedly founded by survivors of a battle with the Argonauts, following the capture of the Golden Fleece; centuries later, the great Roman poet Ovid was exiled here for nine years until his death in 17 AD. These days, the town is an attractive mix of Greco-Roman remains, Turkish mosques and crisp modern boulevards, home to several interesting **museums** and a lively restaurant scene. Pilot cutters mounted by the road at its northern and southern entries attest to its status as a maritime town, as does its biggest festival, **Navy Day** on August 15, when up to 10,000 people watch the parade.

Arrival and information

Constanţa is served by **Mihail Kogălniceanu airport** (℡0241/258 378), 25km northwest of town, from where it's a half-hour journey into the centre; a taxi

ACCOMMODATION
Capri	C
Casa Harghita	A
Class	H
Dali	D
Ferdinand	G
Florentina	M
Guci	E
Ibis	I
New Safari	J
Royal	B
Sport	F
Tineretului	L
Voila	K

RESTAURANTS & CAFÉS
Can	15
Chinese Garden	9
El Greco	3
Guci	E
Irish Pub	8
La Pizza	10
Marco Polo	6
Nur Kaptan Baba	12
On Plonge	14
Terasa Colonadelor	13

BARS & CLUBS
Amsters	11
Bourbon House	1
Cazino	16
Club Deep	5
Club Phoenix	2
Davia Brau	7
New Orleans	4

should cost about €8. There are also hourly maxitaxis (6am–8pm) on the main road outside the airport, heading for Constanţa's **Autogară Sud**, the main **bus station**. The **train station** and *Autogară Sud* are 2km west of the centre; the train station has a 24-hour left-luggage service. **Maxitaxis** and **buses** for the resorts (*staţiuni*) south of Constanţa leave from just south of the train station.

From the train station, **trolley buses** #40 and (in summer) #41 run along B-dul. Ferdinand to the centre and then swing north. Buses run from 5am (5.45am at weekends) to 11pm and tickets, each good for two rides within Constanţa or one if you're going all the way to Mamaia (see p.416), are available from most kiosks. There are also tickets valid for three hours (€5), six hours (€8) and twelve hours (€12). Note that inspectors are especially vigilant here, with a stiff fine for riding without a ticket. Remember to cancel your ticket on the bus (both ends if you're going to Mamaia). General Taxi (☎0241/617 844) and Romaris (☎0241/690 000) are trustworthy **taxi** companies.

Constanţa's **tourist information office**, Info Litoral, is at B-dul. A. Lapusneanu 185A (Mon–Fri 9am–4pm; ☎0241/555 000, ⓦwww.infolitoral .ro); taking bus #100 from the Gara, it's the tenth stop (Str. Suceava) north of the centre. Its friendly, English-speaking staff have good, free maps and can provide useful information on the Black Sea coast, book hotel accommodation and arrange excursions. For trips outside the region, it's best to book through Mamaia's tourist information office (see p.416).

Trolley bus #40 runs from the train station to the southern edge of **Mamaia**; in summer #41 runs all the way through the resort. Buses #32 and #100 run frequently to the **Sat de Vacanţă** (holiday village) just south of Mamaia, passing the **Autogară Nord** (Str. Soveja 35), from which maxitaxis head north to destinations along the coast, including **Tulcea** and **Galaţi**; maxitaxi #23 takes the same route from just north of the train station to Mamaia. Özlem Tur (☎0241/662 626) runs the overnight **bus to Istanbul**, departing daily at 3pm; its office is in the bus station. The **CFR office** is at Str. Vasile Canarache 4 (Mon–Fri 7.30am–7.30pm, Sat 8am–2pm; ☎0241/614 950), overlooking the docks. The international counter is open from 9am to 4pm Monday to Friday; you need to book several days in advance in summer. The RO-RO (roll-on/roll-off) **ferry terminal**, 11km south of Constanţa at Agigea Sud, specializes in sending trucks to Turkey, Georgia and Ukraine, but some of the ferries do carry passengers – enquire at Danubius or SimpaTurism (see p.415) or Tourism and Transaction, B-dul. Tomis 20–26 (☎0241/616 624). For information on crossings to **Batumi** (Georgia) you can contact CFR-Marfa on (☎&ⓕ0241/741 424). In addition, there's a **fast ferry to Istanbul** on Tuesday and Friday nights, arriving just twelve hours later; it's operated by Med Lines (Calea Dorobantiler 184, Bucharest; ☎021/230 5832; ⓦwww.medlines.ro) and tickets cost from €35, although you can pay considerably more for a good cabin.

For **travel agents**, see p.415.

Accommodation

The number of **hotels** in Constanţa has grown as the port has flourished in recent years, though there are still few budget options. If you're looking for something less expensive, take bus #32 or #100 from the station to the far end of **Lake Tăbăcărie**, or #40 to **Pescărie**, where you'll find the **Sat de Vacanţă** (holiday village); its eastern half is all funfair rides and fast food, but across a stream to the west is an area of restaurants named after *judeţs* (counties), some of which have remarkably cheap rooms too (see *Casa Harghita*, below). Be warned that it can be very noisy and crowded during the summer. Otherwise, locals with **private rooms** sometimes wait by the train station, holding signs reading *cazare*.

Capri Str. Mircea cel Bătrân 109 ☎0241/553 090, ⓦwww.capri.ro. Competent establishment with indoor swimming pool, sauna and Jacuzzi, Internet access, a/c rooms, a lift and underground parking. ❼

Casa Harghita Sat de Vacanţă ☎0241/513 738, ⓦwww.casaharghita.ro. The best of the pensions in the holiday village, with en-suite a/c rooms with cable TV. There's also a good restaurant, open – alas – until 1am. ❸

Class Str. Răscoalei 1907 1 ☎&ⓕ0241/660 909, ⓦwww.hotelclass.ro. Near the Art Museum, this stylish new three-star hotel has a/c rooms, a lift, a restaurant and both Wi-Fi and dial-up Internet access. ❼

Dali Str. Smărdan 6A ☎0241/619 717, ⓦwww.hotel-dali.ro. Modern four-star hotel with pastel facade and spacious, comfortable rooms, including some with a sea view. Well run and often full; free Internet access in every room and Wi-Fi in the lobby. ❽

Ferdinand B-dul. Ferdinand 12 ☎/ⓕ0241/407 761, ⓦwww.hotelferdinand.ro. A classic mid-twentieth-century Deco building, newly converted to a three-star hotel, with a/c rooms, all with TV, good bathrooms and showers, free cable Internet access, and tiny balconies (though those in the apartments are larger). ❻

Florentina Str. I. C. Brătianu 24 ☎0241/512 535, ⓕ510 202. Excellent-value hotel 250m north of the railway station (turn left, go past the bus terminal and it's just to the left on the main road); spacious, clean rooms, all with bath, cable TV and refrigerator and hot water until midnight; there's Wi-Fi on the lower floors and a restaurant. ❹

Guci Str. Răscoalei din 1907 23 ☎&ⓕ0241/695 500, ⓦwww.hotel-guci.ro. Classy central hotel with first-rate facilities – a/c rooms, sauna, Jacuzzi, and a rooftop Mexican restaurant. ❼

Ibis Str. Mircea cel Bătrân 39 ☎021/300 2722, ⓦwww.ibishotel.com. Reliably the same as any other *Ibis*, although this one has its own museum of archeological finds. There's bowling and billiards, and free Internet access in every room; breakfast costs an extra €9. ❼

New Safari Str. Karatzali 1 ☎0241/555 571, ⓦwww.newsafari.ro. The best-value place in the centre, this new, seven-room pension overlooking the harbour has comfortable, Mediterranean-style rooms and a lovely *terasa*. ❻

Royal B-dul. Mamaia 191 ☎0241/542 690, ⓦwww.hotelroyal.ro. North of town, on the road to Mamaia (at the Dorobanți bus stop), this is one of the best hotels in Constanța; attractively furnished, with gym and sauna, and international papers on sale in the lobby. ❽

Sport Str. Cuza Vodă 2 ☎0241/617 558. All rooms in this clean and busy hotel have bathroom and cable TV. There's also a restaurant and bar; the terrace has a pleasant sea view but suffers from stultifying disco music. ❹

Tineretului B-dul. Tomis 20–26 ☎0241/613 590, ⓕ611 290. Constanța's youth hotel, with basic rooms all with bath and TV. ❸

Voila Str. Callatis 22 ☎0241/508 002/3/45 or 0744/385 359, ⓦwww.voilahotel.ro. A relatively small new four-star hotel, idiosyncratically decorated with pseudo-Roman mosaics, big cast-iron beds and an amazing array of trinkets. Prices include breakfast, parking, Wi-Fi, sauna, gym and massage, as well as lots of toiletries. There's a small restaurant on top with great views. ❼

The Town

The oldest area of Constanța, centred on **Piața Ovidiu**, stands on a headland between what is now the tourist port and the huge area of the modern docks to the south and west, and is home to the excellent **Archeological and National History Museum**. Walking up the shore from the tourist port, you'll find Constanța's passable **beach**, and inland, beyond the remains of the walls of ancient Tomis, the modern **commercial area**, along boulevards Ferdinand and Tomis. Further north, nearing the resort of **Mamaia**, are various sights designed to appeal to children (but perhaps more likely to frighten them), including a **funfair** and **planetarium**.

Around boulevards Ferdinand and Tomis

The focal point of the new town is the junction of **Bulevardul Ferdinand and Bulevardul Tomis**. Here, you'll find an archeological park displaying sections of ancient walls, serried amphorae and other **ruins of Tomis**. Tomis was settled by Greeks from Miletus in the sixth century BC as an annex to Histria, which it later superseded before being incorporated within the Roman empire at the beginning of the Christian era. The most prominent remains are those of the defensive wall created in the third and fourth centuries and the Butchers' Tower, raised in the sixth century by Byzantine colonists who revived the city and renamed it to honour the emperor's sister Constantia.

South of the archeological park, Str. Traian overlooks the north end of the commercial *port maritim*, and provides an appropriate setting for the **Museum of the Romanian Navy** at no. 53 (Muzeul Marinei Române; Tues–Sun: May–Sept 10am–6pm; Oct–April 9am–5pm). Despite its name, the museum includes models of Greek triremes that sailed long before Romania existed, and photographs recording the unexpected visit of the battleship *Potemkin*, whose mutinous sailors disembarked at Constanța in July 1905 and scattered. Little is said about the role of Romania's own navy during World War II, when it supported the occupation of Odessa and aided the Nazi fleet.

Back on B-dul. Tomis, north of B-dul. Ferdinand, the **Art Museum** at no. 82 (Muzeul de Artă; Wed–Sun: June–Sept 9am–8pm; Oct–May 9am–5pm) has some interesting canvases by Iosif Iser, Ştefan Dumitrescu and other painters of the Dobrogean landscape. Much of the top floor is devoted to the abstract artist Ion Gheorgiu; his paintings are less engaging than the collections of seashells, beetles and primitive icons decorating his *atelier*, which is preserved intact. South of here, at no. 32, the **Ethnographic Museum** (Muzeul de Artă Populară; Wed–Sun: June–Sept 9am–7pm; Oct–May 9am–5pm) has a fine display of colourful Dobrogean rugs, pewter vessels and eighteenth- and nineteenth-century Lipovani and Greek icons. Immediately south of the museum fast-food joints and coffee houses sprawl across a pedestrianized section of the road, with the **Geamia Hunchiar**, a small mosque built in 1869, overlooking them to the south. Watch out for **thieves** here, typically idle teens who will ask you for the time – just keep walking, and you shouldn't have any problems. A couple of blocks east, at Str. Mircea cel Bătrân 36, is the **Church of the Transfiguration**, dating from 1865, when the Greek community finally got permission from the Ottoman rulers to build the city's first church in modern times.

Piaţa Ovidiu

At the southern end of B-dul. Tomis, **Piaţa Ovidiu**, the central square of the old quarter, is dominated by a mournful statue of Ovid, exiled here from Rome by Emperor Augustus in 8 AD. Marooned in backwater Tomis, the poet spent his last years unsuccessfully petitioning emperors for his return, and composing his melancholy *Tristia*:

Rain cannot pit it, sunlight fails in burning
this snow. One drift succeeds another here.
The north wind hardens it, making it eternal;
it spreads in drifts through all the bitter year.

On the southern side of the square, Constanţa's **Archeological and National History Museum** (Muzeul de Istorie Naţională şi Arheologie; Wed–Sun: June–Sept 9am–8pm; Oct–May 9am–5pm) has an excellent collection of statues of deities, including – in the first room on the left – the extraordinary **Glykon Serpent**, a unique creation about the size of a squatting toddler, with an antelope's head, human hair and eyes, and a gracefully coiled serpentine body ending in a lion's tail, which dates from the second or third century BC. Upstairs are mammoth tusks and menhirs, while the top floor is devoted to more recent history. Outside, on the south side of the museum, is an array of funerary steles from the second to fourth centuries AD, their touching inscriptions translated into Romanian and English.

To the west of the museum, a modern structure encloses extensive remains of the fine **Roman mosaic** (Edificiul Roman cu Mozaic; Tues–Sun 10am–6pm), close to 700 square metres in area, that was discovered 5m below street level in 1959; it may have once graced the upper hall of the Roman baths, whose outer walls can be seen from Aleea Canarache. Built in the late fourth century AD, this was part of a three-storey structure linking the upper town to the port, which also incorporated warehouses and shops.

South of Piaţa Ovidiu

From **Piaţa Ovidiu**, it's a short walk south to the **Mahmudiye Mosque** (daily except Fri 9.30am–9.30pm), whose fifty-metre-high minaret spikes the skyline and offers a great **view** of the town and harbour. Built in 1910, it's the seat of the Mufti, the spiritual head of Romania's 55,000 Muslims (Turks and Tatars by origin), who live along the coast of the Dobrogea. South from the mosque along Str. Arhiepiscopei (look for the fine Art Nouveau ironwork gates) is the fancy **Orthodox Cathedral of St Peter and St Paul**, an early (1884) neo-Byzantine design by Ion Mincu, and, at the street's end, opposite more ruins of ancient Tomis, the **Ion Jalea collection** (Muzeul Ion Jalea; Wed–Sun: May–Sept 10am–6pm; Oct–April 9am–5pm), an assortment of conventional and academic sculptures in a nice neo-Brâncovenesc villa.

On the pedestrianized **waterfront**, the former **casino** stands on a jutting promenade. Originally erected as an Art Nouveau pavilion for Queen Elisabeta (Carmen Sylva) in 1904–10, it is now a summer-only restaurant/bar. During a visit in 1914 by the Russian Imperial family, it was the venue for a disastrous gala performance that ended in smashed scenery and broken limbs; the Russians sailed away the next day, Grand Duchess Olga having refused a proposed marriage to Prince Carol and thus sealed her fate at the hands of the Bolsheviks three years later. Opposite it is a small **aquarium** (daily 9am–6pm). Just beyond, you can see the so-called **Genoese Lighthouse**, erected in 1860 in memory of the thirteenth- and fourteenth-century mariners who tried to revive the port.

The beach and Lake Tăbăcăriei

Visitors with children or a low tolerance for provincial museums head straight for the **beach** north of the *port turistic*, spread beneath a terraced cliff behind the art museum, or the park at **Lake Tăbăcăriei**, between Constanţa and Mamaia, where there's a huge wooden church, built by carpenters from Maramureş. Bus #32 heads up B-dul. Alexandru Lapuşneanu on the west side of the lake, while buses #40 and #41 (from the train station) run along B-dul. Mamaia, to the east of the park, passing a more than usually depressing **dolphinarium** (daily: July & Aug 8am–9pm; Sept–June 9am–5pm; shows on the hour) at the southeastern corner of the park, at B-dul. Mamaia 255. There's also a **planetarium here** (same hours, with shows at 40 minutes past the hour) and a collection of **exotic birds** (daily 9am–8pm). From the nearby **Tăbăcăriei Wharf**, a **miniature train** carries children around the lake, which due to algal bloom may be a toxic-looking hue of green. On the other side is the **Sat de Vacanţă**, and just to the north, at the entrance to Mamaia, the noisy **Luna Park** (Parc Distracţii), with various decrepit rides and games. There's a **bowling alley** here, and an **ice-skating rink** on the edge of the Pioneers' Park.

Eating, drinking and entertainment

The number of worthwhile **restaurants** in Constanţa continues to grow; you'll find variety enough to rival any Romanian city outside of Bucharest. The city's main **theatre** is at B-dul. Ferdinand 11, and the Teatrul Liric (putting on opera, ballet and symphonic concerts) at Str. Mircea cel Bătrân 97; buy tickets at the agency at B-dul. Tomis 97. The city's **International Festival of Music and Dance** takes place in late May and early June.

Restaurants

Can At the bus station. Turkish restaurant favoured by the Istanbul bus drivers. Good *pide, lahmacun* and kebabs; open 24hr.

Chinese Garden B-dul. Caragiale 4. The best of Constanţa's Asian restaurants.

El Greco Str. Decebal 18. Fine Greek cuisine, if a bit pricey. Daily noon–1am.

Guci On the top floor of the *Guci* hotel, Str. Răscoalei din 1907 no. 23 ☏ 0241/695 500. This little-known Romanian/Mexican restaurant is a delight, offering exemplary food and service. Daily 10am–1am.

Irish Pub Str. Ştefan cel Mare 1. Not so much a pub as an upscale restaurant, serving Irish beers and

expertly prepared but pricey meals. Its fine terrace with lovely views across the port makes it an ideal venue for early-evening drinks. Open 11am–1am.

La Pizza Str. Răscoalei din 1907 no. 15. Central branch of popular local chain. Decent pizza, pasta and espresso; excellent *gelato*. Daily 9am–11pm.

Marco Polo Str. Sarmisegetuza 2 ☏ 0241/617 357 or 0722/230 976. Constanţa's best Italian restaurant, for fine pasta, pizzas and salads; good service, but no smoke-free area. Daily 11.30am–midnight.

New Safari Str. Karatzali 1. Seafood restaurant perched on a cliff over the beach. The view from the terrace is the best in Constanţa, and the food is almost as good. Daily 10am–midnight.

Nur Kaptan Baba B-dul. Tomis 55. A Turkish restaurant serving oriental salads, soups, *lahmacun* and *shaworma* (kebab) as well as baklava and coffee; next door is a Lebanese place serving similar food.

On Plonge Portul Turistic Tomis ☎0241/601 905. Lovely harbourside restaurant primarily serving fish dishes. It's usually crowded, but the atmospheric terrace makes this an enjoyable place to dine. Daily 10am–1am.

Terasa Colonadelor Str. Traian 57. Beer garden serving up grilled sausages, pizza and pasta, as well as more adventurous dishes such as brain and testicles. Daily 9am–midnight.

Bars, pubs and clubs

Amsters B-dul. Tomis 55. A Dutch-themed café-restaurant with pub-style dark wood decor. It also serves Romanian food (chicken, pork, soups, salads and *clatițe*).

Bourbon House Str. Pușchin 36 ⓦ www.bourbon.ro. Not far from the intersection of boulevards Tomis and Mamaia. Sophisticated bar with a long list of cocktails; music is a mix of house and R&B. The garden out back is ideal for an afternoon drink. Daily 10am–2am.

Cazino in the old casino, B-dul. Elisabeta 2. Old-style communist set-up with a great sea view from the terrace and a pool table in the bar. Summer only.

Club Deep B-dul. Tomis 125. A dark, very popular cellar bar.

Club Phoenix 2 B-dul. Mamaia 67 at Tomis ⓦ www.club-phoenix.ro. A café that often hosts live jazz and blues.

Davia Brau Str. Smârdan 18. A real pub, with live acoustic music on Sat nights. Daily to 1am.

New Orleans B-dul. Mamaia at Str. Siretului. Massive, four-level disco with lots of fluorescent lights.

Listings

Air tickets TAROM is at Str. Ștefan cel Mare 15 (Mon–Fri 8am–7pm, Sat 9am–1pm; ☎&℻0241/662 632). In summer they operate flights from Constanța to Cluj, Iași and Timișoara. Carpatair (at the airport; ☎0241/255 422, ⓔconstanta@carpatair.com) flies to Timișoara via Craiova; Malev (at the airport, ☎0241/252 999, ⓔconstanta@malev.hu) flies twice a week to Budapest. The travel agents listed below sell tickets for most major airlines.

Car rental Autonom (☎0788/903 369, ⓔconstanta@autonom.ro); Avis c/o TAROM (☎0241/616 733); Budget c/o Latina, B-dul. Ferdinand 71 (☎0241/639 713, ⓔlatina@latina.ro); Cronos Car (☎0730/111/004); Europcar at the airport (☎0722/211 518) and in the *Hotel Dobrogea*, B-dul. A. Lapușneanu 194 (☎0241/543 311); Hertz c/o Paradis, B-dul. Tomis 65 (☎0241/661 100 or 0744/338 776, ⓔparadis@rdsct.ro); Icar, B-dul. Tomis 130 (☎0241/521 728, ⓦwww.icar.ro).

Consulates Turkey, B-dul. Ferdinand 82 (Mon–Fri 9am–noon; ☎0241/611 135).

Hospital B-dul. Tomis 145 (☎0241/516 800 or 961).

Internet *Planet Games*, at the intersection of Str. Ștefan cel Mare and Str. Răscoalei din 1907, is open 24hr, as is *Café-bar R9* at B-dul. Tomis 31 (south of the mosque). There's also an Internet café upstairs in the green building by the Autogară Sud. Wi-Fi is available in most hotels and at *Café Mosaic*, opposite the Archeological Museum on the corner of Str. Arhiepiscopei, and at *BT Café*, B-dul. Tomis 57 (at B-dul. Ferdinand).

Pharmacy Euro, at Str. Ecaterina Varga 55 (at B-dul. Ferdinand), is open 24hr, as is Dumifarm, in the Tomis Mall at Str. Ștefan cel Mare 49 (at Str. Mihai Viteazul).

Post office B-dul. Tomis 79 (Mon–Fri 7am–8pm, Sat 8am–1pm).

Shopping Str. Ștefan cel Mare is the main shopping street – especially the pedestrianized stretch from Str. Răscoalei din 1907 to Str. Duca – with the Tomis Mall (Mon–Sat 9am–9pm, Sun 9am–6pm; ⓦwww.tomis.ro) opposite the Eminescu bookshop. The supermarket in the basement (same hours as the mall) is the best in the centre. Supermarket Grand, below B-dul. Tomis 57 (at B-dul. Ferdinand; open 24hr), is not huge but adequate. There are much bigger places to the south of the centre on Șos. Mangaliei, with Billa at no. 74 (by bus #56, one stop south of the Far, a modernistic lighthouse in a plaza), Metro and Real at no. 211, and Selgros at km9; Carrefour is just out of town to the northwest on the DN2A. Anticvariat, at Str. Mircea cel Bătrân 4, has used books in English and French. There is a Kodak photographic shop on Str. Ștefan cel Mare.

Travel agents Danubius, Piața Ovidiu 11A (☎0240/619 032, ⓦwww.danubius.ro); Gamma, Str. Unirii 80 (☎0241/540 604); Latina, B-dul. Ferdinand 71 (☎0241/639 713, ⓔlatina@latina.ro); Litoral, B-dul. Tomis 133 (☎0241/831 152); Simpa Turism, Str. Răscoalei din 1907 no. 9 (☎0241/660 468, ⓦwww.simpaturism.ro).

Mamaia

MAMAIA, 6km north of Constanţa, is Romania's best-known coastal resort, and the place where the majority of package tourists end up. Legend has it that the gods created the **beach** to reunite a kidnapped princess with her daughter, who was abandoned on the seashore wailing "Mamaia, Mamaia!"; its fine, almost white sand, fringed with wild pear trees, is the resort's greatest asset, especially since its gentle gradient and the absence of currents and strong tides make it particularly safe for children.

Arrival and information

In summer, **buses** #32 and #41 run from **Constanţa's train station** to the far end of Mamaia; out of season, you'll have to take the #40, which claims to go to Mamaia but in fact terminates at Pescărie, one stop south of the beginning of the resort, where you'll have to change to the #47 or the frequent yellow midibuses heading north to Năvodari. Alternatively, you could walk the short distance to the **telegondola** (see p.418), a cable car that can carry you the 2km to the heart of Mamaia, near the casino. Arriving by car in high summer, you'll find tollbooths operating immediately north of Pescărie.

If you arrive without a **room reservation**, look for a Dispecerat de Cazare (room allocation) office, such as at **Litoral SA** (May–Sept daily 8am–9pm, Oct–April Mon–Fri 9am–5pm; ⓉⓍ⑤0241/831 517), in the middle of the resort; **Agenţia de Turism Mamaia**, just west of the *Hotel Condor* (Ⓣ0241/831 517, ⑥travelagency@sc-mamaia-sa.ro) and in front of the *Hotel Hefaistos* (Ⓣ0241/831 936 or 831 000). The agencies may also be able to arrange day-trips to the Danube Delta or Transylvania, and half-day **excursions** to Histria, Adamclisi or the Murfatlar vineyards.

The Bazar, Mamaia's main **shopping centre**, where you'll find a small supermarket and a **pharmacy** (daily 9am–9pm), is just south of the *Best Western Savoy*; in the **Cassa Verde** shopping centre, near the casino, shops sell sunscreen, beachballs and clothing, and there's a small Aliment Murfatlar supermarket and lots of exchange offices. There are **post offices** in the Bazar and just south of the casino and a summer-only **Internet café** in the *Hotel Unirea*.

For rail tickets, try the **CFR office** (Ⓣ0241/831 062) in the Zona Tic-Tac, across the main road west of the Hotel Condor.

Accommodation

Most of Mamaia's seventy-odd **hotels** (all but a handful of which are ageing concrete-block structures) lie within 100m of the beach. With the exception of the *Best Western Savoy* and a couple of others, all of the four- and five-star hotels listed below are clustered together, several hundred metres north of the casino. At the far end of the resort is a very basic little **campsite**, with several larger ones (with *casuţe* cabins) just a few hundred metres further north, such as *Camping GPM* (Ⓣ0241/831 002, ⓦwww.gpm.ro), *Camping Pescăresc* (Ⓣ0241/831 170), and *Camping Marina Surf* (Ⓣ0241/831 208, ⓦwww.marinasurf.ro), which is open all year but is focused more on chalets than tents.

Albatros By the northern terminal of the telegondola Ⓣ0241/831 381. Reliable, smallish three-star hotel, open all year, in a nice mid-twentieth-century modernist building. ❼
Best Western Savoy Northern end of Mamaia Ⓣ0241/831 426, ⓦwww.savoyhotel.ro. A

refurbished communist-era block with competent staff and a long list of amenities. ❾
Club Scandinavia Northern end of Mamaia Ⓣ0241/607 000, ⓦwww.clubscandinavia.ro. Built in 2002 and refurbished in 2007, the sleek and modern *Club Scandinavia* is once again the pride of

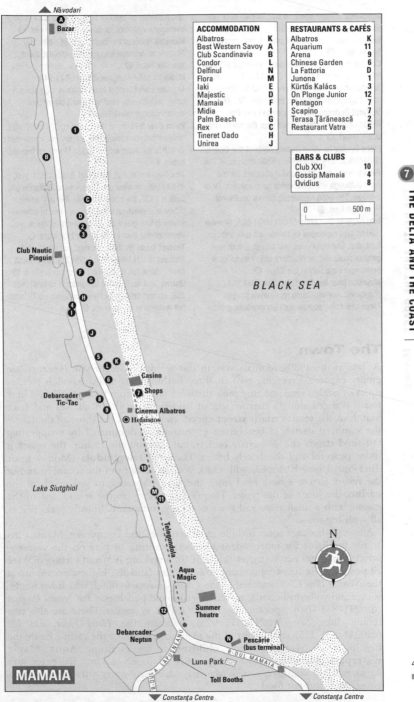

Nǎvodari

A Bazar

ACCOMMODATION	
Albatros	K
Best Western Savoy	A
Club Scandinavia	B
Condor	L
Delfinul	N
Flora	M
Iaki	E
Majestic	D
Mamaia	F
Midia	I
Palm Beach	G
Rex	C
Tineret Oado	H
Unirea	J

RESTAURANTS & CAFÉS	
Albatros	K
Aquarium	11
Arena	9
Chinese Garden	6
La Fattoria	D
Junona	1
Kürtős Kalács	3
On Plonge Junior	12
Pentagon	7
Scapino	7
Terasa Tǎrǎneascǎ	2
Restaurant Vatra	5

BARS & CLUBS	
Club XXI	10
Gossip Mamaia	4
Ovidius	8

0   500 m

BLACK SEA

Club Nautic Pinguin

Casino
Shops
Debarcader Tic-Tac
Cinema Albatros
Hefaistos

Lake Siutghiol

Telegondola

Aqua Magic

Summer Theatre

Debarcader Neptun

Pescǎrie (bus terminal)

Luna Park

Toll Booths

MAMAIA

N

Constanța Centre   Constanța Centre

Romania's tourism scene; it has its own dock on Lake Siutghiol and a west-facing beach. First-class facilities include an outdoor pool, tennis court and fitness suite. **⑨**

Condor Just north of the casino and west of the telegondola ☎0241/831 142, ⓕ831 758, ⓦwww .hotelcondormamaia.ro. Four-star hotel, offering a/c rooms with Internet access and cable TV. **⑦**

Delfinul Opposite the entrance to Luna Park ☎0241/831 640. Basic place near the south end of the resort. **④**

Flora Several hundred metres north of the *Delfinul* ☎0241/831 059, ⓔhotelflora98@yahoo.com. The *Flora* is well refurbished and a standout for the price (although you'll pay extra for breakfast, TV or a fridge). The good restaurant serves traditional Romanian food. **⑤**

Iaki North of the centre ☎0241/831 025, ⓦwww .iaki.ro. Well renovated by Romania's greatest footballer, Gheorghe Hagi, this boasts indoor and outdoor pools and an excellent spa. International newspapers are sold in the lobby. **⑨**

Majestic Near the *Rex* ☎&ⓕ0241/831 981, ⓔmajestic.mamaia@pmg.ro, ⓦwww.pmg.ro. Three-star hotel, popular with German tour groups

and featuring an outdoor pool and, out back, a small menagerie with rabbits, doves and peacocks. **⑧**

Mamaia North of the casino ☎0241/831 100, ⓦwww.sc-mamaia-sa.ro. Small, sophisticated five-star hotel. **⑨**

Midia By Lake Siutghiol ☎0241/831 940. Mamaia's best budget hotel (open in high season only), with friendly staff and small but decent rooms without television. **③**

Palm Beach North of the casino ☎0241/607 900, ⓦwww.palmbeachhotel.ro. The seventy-room *Palm Beach* is the most welcoming of Mamaia's five-star hotels. **⑨**

Rex Northern end of the resort ☎0241/831 520, ⓕ831 690, ⓦwww.grandhotelrex.ro. A stately pile built in 1936, the hacienda-style *Rex* is Mamaia's oldest and swishest hotel, the only one to achieve anything like grandeur, although prices are less stratospheric than at the newer four-stars. **⑨**

Tineret Oado By the main road just south of the *Mamaia* ☎0241/609 958. A typically basic youth hotel – good fun if you don't need much sleep. **③**

Unirea Just north of the telegondola ☎0241/488 259. Budget hotel, with flimsy curtains, no TV, and hot water only *cu program*. **③**

The Town

As late as the 1930s, Mamaia was, in the words of Gregor von Rezzori, "an empty expanse, excepting two or three bathing huts and a wooden pier, of miles of golden sand and tiny pink shells"; a far cry from what you'll find here today. Ranged along a narrow spit of land between the Black Sea and Lake Siutghiol, the resort's **main street** curves away around the shore of the lake – the southern stretch of beachfront promenade is dominated by unappealing fast-food stands and *autoservire* buffets, but, beyond the casino, the resort is more peaceful and the hotels better. The new **telegondola** (Mon 4–6pm, Tues–Sun 10am–10pm; €3) will whisk you the 2km from the southern end of the resort (across a busy road from the Sat de Vacanţă; to just north of the **casino**, the heart of the resort. There's a big plaza on the inland side of the casino, with a small stage and rows of family restaurants (mostly pizza places, all with big *terasas*).

Although package tours include most activities and equipment, Mamaia has ample **facilities** for independent travellers wanting to play on the **water** – waterskiing (€60 per hour), jet-skiing (€40), kayaking (€3) and surfing (€3) are all possible. The finest equipment and facilities (and the highest prices) are at the *Nautica Blue Club*, attached to the *Club Scandinavia* hotel, which has tennis, soccer and volleyball courts, as well as jetskis and pedaloes. *Club Nautic Pinguin* (☎0241/831 050), opposite the *Hotel Majestic*, is similar. There are also two tennis clubs, *Sen* (☎0241/831 025), opposite the *Hotel Flora*, and *Idu* (☎0241/831 225), to the west of the main road south of the casino. Easily the best place in Mamaia to take **children** is the gleaming **Aqua Magic waterpark** (May–Sept daily 8am–8pm; €10 adults, €5 children, half price after 4pm), near the southern end of Mamaia, which has water attractions, a disco, a restaurant and fast food.

Day trips from Mamaia

From Mamaia, regular **motorboat trips** (every 30min 10am–2pm; €3) run from the Tic-Tac dock opposite the casino to **Ovid's Island** – where there's a suitably rustic restaurant, the *Insula Ovidiu* (☎0241/252 494) – at the northern end of **Lake Siutghiol**. Also known as Lake Mamaia, **Lake Siutghiol** was formed when a river's outlet silted up, and for many centuries it was a watering hole for herds of sheep and cows brought down from the Carpathians – hence the name, meaning "Lake of Milk" in Turkish.

Maxitaxi #23 and yellow midibuses run frequently from the northern suburbs of Constanța, just south of Mamaia, to Năvodari, an anonymous concrete town beyond which a minor road heads north past a reeking petrochemical complex and **Lake Nuntaşi** (and its **campsite**) to the Greek ruins at **Histria** (see p.407).

Eating and drinking

Though not at the level of Constanța's cuisine, there are some good **restaurants** in Mamaia, although dining is inevitably accompanied by blaring pop music. The restaurants in the *Rex, Mamaia, Junona* and *Palm Beach* **hotels** are excellent, as is the *Aquarium* (☎0241/831 868), an upscale **seafood** place near the *Flora* hotel whose menu features swordfish, sturgeon and Portuguese carp. The best **Italian food** is at *La Fattoria* (☎0241/831 010; daily 10am–midnight), next to the *Majestic*, north of the centre. Nearby is the *Albatros*, a jolly family restaurant and terrace, serving pizza, steak and fish, opposite the Romanian *Terasa Țărănească* and the Hungarian *Kürtős Kalács* by the beach. For **Romanian food**, you can also try the *Restaurant Vatra*, or the *Pentagon*, just north of the casino. *Scapino*, on the promenade just south of the casino, is also good for pizza and pasta, while the *Chinese Garden*, on the plaza by the casino, is the best of Mamaia's three **Chinese** establishments. *On Plonge Junior* (☎0724/036 633), at the Debarcader Neptun dock at the south end of Mamaia, has little in common with *On Plonge* in Constanța, but serves Romanian and Italian food and has a lovely lakeside *terasa*. There's also a **Serb** restaurant, the *Arena*, at the *Tennis Club Idu*.

Nightlife

The best places to go for **dancing** and house music are the pricey *Gossip Mamaia* at B-dul. Mamaia 218, next to the *Hotel Midia*, and *Club XXI*, south of the casino; both are open late. The open-air *Amnesia*, held on the beach near the casino, hosts international DJs such as Fatboy Slim. The *Ibiza Summer Club* disco is opposite the *Hanul Piratilor* campsite, 5km beyond Mamaia's northern end. Otherwise, there are downmarket outdoor **discos** at hotels such as the *Perla, Select* and *Delta*. Alternatives consist of glitzy **cabaret** most nights at the *Melody* near the casino, or the *Nunta la Romani* (Wedding in Romania) **folklore show** at the *Majestic*. The *Ovidius* **floating restaurant-bar** is just west of the casino, and there's an open-air *Cinema Albatros* just north of the *Hotel Hefaistos*. The kitschy **Mamaia Pop Music Festival** is held over the last weekend of August, in the open-air Summer Theatre.

Agigea to Vama Veche

Just south of Constanța, the road and rail line cross the Danube–Black Sea Canal where it meets the coast at the **Agigea** port complex. Beyond this, the array of **resorts** extending to **Mangalia** is another facet of Romania's development over the last quarter century – modern complexes created where only scrubland or run-down villages existed before. Except for the fact that most are situated along a cliff top overlooking the beach, they are fairly similar to their prototype, Mamaia, to the north, although they have a shorter season. The exceptions are Mangalia, which is not dependent on tourism and is thus more alive off season, and **Doi Mai** and **Vama Veche**, neither of which saw any development until after the fall of communism.

From Constanţa, the resorts down to Mangalia are best reached by **maxitaxis** and **private buses**; these leave several times per hour, from early morning to around 8pm, from a spot 100m to the right of the railway station as you exit. For Doi Mai and Vama Veche, you'll have to change at Mangalia.

⑦ Eforie Nord, Eforie Sud and Lake Techirghiol

Trains, buses and maxitaxis run 14km south along a decent dual carriageway from Constanţa to **EFORIE NORD**. Founded in 1899 by Bucharest's Eforia hospital as a spa for convalescent patients, Eforie Nord extends along a cliff top above the rather narrow beach. The resort is, however, best known for the therapeutic **black mud** scooped from the shores of **Lake Techirghiol**, whose mineral-saturated waters gave the lake its name, derived from *tekir*, Turkish for "salt" or "bitter". **Baths** by the lake (a few minutes' walk south of the train station) specialize in treating rheumatic disorders and the after-effects of polio, while on the lake's single-sex nudist beaches, people plaster themselves with mud, wait until it cracks (happily exposing themselves to passing trains), and then jostle good humouredly beneath the showers.

The resort itself comprises two parallel streets, B-dul. Tudor Vladimirescu, along the cliff top, and B-dul. Republicii, where you'll find the bus stops, shops and offices. As a spa, Eforie Nord has some fine **hotels** that are more likely to be open out of season than elsewhere: the *Europa*, for example, at B-dul. Republicii 13 (☏0241/702 801, ⓦwww.hotel-europa.ro; ⓪), a towering, steel-blue four-star designed by two of Romania's best-known architects. More than half of its rooms are non-smoking, and amenities include a swimming pool and one of the top spas in the country, the *Ana Aslan Health Spa* (ⓦwww.anaspa.ro). Closer to the beach at B-dul. Tudor Vladimirescu 9 is the *Astoria* (☏0241/742 475, ⓦwww.anahotels.ro; ⓧ), a smaller and more compact facility under the same management as the *Europa*. Guests at both hotels have access to tennis and bowling facilities and to a private section of the beach. Just south of the central bus stop, the *Hotel Vera* (☏0241/742 200, ⓦwww.hotelvera.ro; ⓥ) is a modern three-star with air-conditioned rooms and a lift. The *Villa Ad-Ella*, an attractive Brâncovenesc villa at Str. Mureşanu 11 (☏0241/743 473, ⓦwww.ad-ella.ro; ⓥ), has pleasant rooms available all year and also houses an art gallery/tea shop/tea garden. The *Hotel Decebal* (☏0241/742 977; ③), adjacent to the train station and run by Romanian Railways, is unfriendly but good value and open year-round, and offers twin rooms with hot water and TV. A popular budget choice (open June–Sept only) is the *Cristal* (☏0241/742 828; ②), behind the bus stop. If you can't find a place to stay, the **Dispecerat de Cazare** at the northern entry to town (☏0241/742 012) may be able to find you a vacancy.

The nicer of the resort's two **campsites** is the *Meduza*, just inland at the northern end of B-dul. Tudor Vladimirescu. Food choices come down to pizzerias near the bus stop and self-service *autoservires* near the beach, all adequate but unexciting. For a **drink**, walk a couple of blocks north from the bus stop to *333*, a friendly Guinness-themed pub that also serves good espresso.

From Eforie Nord, it's a pleasant two-kilometre trip around the lake to **TECHIRGHIOL** (terminus of bus #11), where you can stay at the *Baze de Tratament* at Str. Ovidiu 4 (℡0241/735 614; Ⓦwww.sbtghiol.ro; ❷), a clean and friendly spa run by the Romanian Orthodox Church. Bizarrely, in this historically Muslim area, there's a wooden village **church** (moved here from Transylvania in 1951) in front of the spa.

Compared to its northern neighbour, **EFORIE SUD**, 4km south at the end of a narrow isthmus, can seem like a ghost town – most of the hotels are run-down or closed, and the quiet, tree-lined streets of the residential quarter are pleasantly dilapidated, but the beach itself is better than that in Eforie Nord. The best **hotel** here is the three-star *Edmond* (℡0241/748 522, Ⓔcosy012003 @yahoo.com; ❼), a modern establishment with swimming pool, sauna and Jacuzzi 50m from the beach and just south of the centre of town at Str. Dezrobirii 26. There's also the HI-affiliated *Hostel Eforie Sud* (℡0241/660 754, Ⓦwww.tineret-constanta.ro; ❷) at the northern entry to the resort, and the huge *Cosmos* **campsite**.

South to Mangalia

A fast four-lane highway runs a few kilometres inland from Eforie Sud to **Mangalia**; buses loop through the resorts, but the more frequent maxitaxis from Constanţa to Mangalia will only drop you off at the junctions to the resorts – it's usually best to go to Mangalia and return on the local maxitaxi from there. Express trains slow to a crawl between Constanţa and Mangalia, taking an hour to cover 43km; from mid-June to mid-September extra services run, providing a fairly frequent service along the coast, with reservations required only west of Constanţa.

Costineşti

The 8km of beach immediately north of Mangalia is lined with the modern hotels that have grown up in the last three decades. The stretch of cliffs to their north is broken only by the former fishing village of **COSTINEŞTI**, now the site of Romania's principal International Youth Camp, with a lake and a fine sandy **beach** sheltered to the north by Cape Tuzla. There are several **hotels** here, including the *Amiral Nord* (℡0241/734 944; ❺), next to the train station at Str. Tineretului 1, the *Criş* on Aleea Studenteasca (℡0241/734 738; ❻), and the *Meridian*, Str. Crizantemelor 30 (℡0241/734 040; ❻). Additionally, most of the villagers let their spare **rooms** during the summer; quality and prices (❶–❸) vary. Costineşti's premier **restaurant** is *Albert*, an excellent pizzeria at the north end of the lake; there's Romanian food at the *Livian*, Str. Radarului 42. An **independent film festival** is held in Costineşti at the end of August – films are shown in Romanian with English subtitles.

Neptun and Olimp

Eight kilometres further south is **NEPTUN**, the most desirable of the Black Sea resorts. It was built in 1960 between the Comorova forest and the sea, ensuring a lush setting for the artificial lakes and dispersed villas, and the shopping centres, discos, sports facilities and hotels here are a cut above the Romanian average. Originally enclaves for the communist *nomenklatura*, today Neptun and its classier satellite of **OLIMP**, just north, are patronized by relatively affluent Romanian families and some Western tourists. There are lots of well-designed new developments in Olimp in particular.

Fast trains stop only at the *halta* by the *Hotel Albert*; if travelling to or from Constanţa by road, note that it's a walk of nearly 3km from Neptun to the

▲ Beach at Neptun

highway. From the Complex Comercial, in the centre of Neptun, opposite a post office and ATM, a road leads down between a couple of lakes to the **beach**, with waterslides, beach bars and restaurants, and paths leading around the lakes; to the north are government-owned and private villas – from the path you can see albino peacocks in one garden.

Most rooms are still assigned to those on **package tours**, however, so if you're hoping to find **accommodation** in high season it may be best to go through

Rainbow Travel (daily 10am–10pm May–June & Sept, 24hr July & Aug; ☎0241/701 300, ✉anatravel@xnet.ro), which has links with many of the hotels; it's opposite Neptun's *Hotel Decebal*. There's also a Dispecerat de Cazare office by the *halta* (☎0744/130 588), offering accommodation in villas (❺) and hotels (from ❹). The best hotels in Neptun-Olimp are the *Majestic*, in the centre of Olimp (☎0241/701 130; ⊕www.pmg.ro; ❼); the *Cocor*, in a secluded spot at the southern edge of Olimp (☎0241/701 042, ⊕www.hotelcocor.ro; ❽), with two cool clamshell bars by the swimming pool; and, on the northern fringe of Neptun, the *Albert* (☎0241/731 514, ⊕www.hotelalbertneptun.ro; ❼), which has a terrific restaurant, and the *Doina* (☎0241/701 012, Ⓕ701 112, ⊕www .complexdoina.ro; ❻), which is open from March to November thanks to its sea-water pool and treatment centre. The **campsites** at the north and south ends of the resort, *Camping Olimp* and *Holiday Club Neptun*, are well above average. **Eating out**, try the chic but reasonably priced *Mediterraneo* **restaurant** (open year-round) in the centre of Neptun (just north of the post office), the *Rosemarie* for Romanian food and pizza, or in Olimp the classy *Ambasador*. For Romanian cuisine *Hanul Calul Bălan*, at the southern end of Neptun, is excellent, as is *Insula*, on a lake island behind the *Hotel Neptun*, for fish. It's also worth checking out the *Café-Bar Efendi*, also north of the post office, possibly the only Tatar hostelry you'll ever experience. The swinging **discos** are *Why Not*, just north of the centre of Neptun, and *Paparazzi* in Olimp. For family entertainment, try the nightly **folklore** show at the *Rustic* restaurant at the southern end of Neptun.

SC Neptun/Olimp has a tour agency and **tourist information office** at the road junction north of the Hotel Doina, with an **Internet** café in the bazaar alongside; for rail tickets, there's a **CFR office** in the *Hotel Apollo*.

Jupiter, Aurora, Venus and Saturn

The four resorts to the south of Neptun are more uniform, less lively and likely to have fewer hotels open outside July and August. The first, immediately abutting Neptun, is **JUPITER**, between the forest and the artificial Lake Tismana, beyond which is a gently sloping beach with fine sand. Jupiter draws a younger crowd than most of the others, many staying at the *Popas Zodiac Vest* **campsite** (May–Sept; ☎&Ⓕ0241/731 404, ⊕www.campingzodiac.ro; ❶), at the north end of the resort. Easily the best place to stay is *Sat Vacanţă Liliacul*, a comfortable new three-star villa complex in Jupiter's centre (☎0241/731 169, Ⓕ732 022; ❻). The cheaper *Violeta* (☎0241/731 115; ❹) is lively and well run. On the southern edge of the resort, the budget *Trandafirul* (☎0241/731 007 or 0721/700 089; ❸) has a tiny shower and toilet in every room. *The Four Seasons* pizza and grill is the standout **restaurant**; from here a road leads to the stylish new *Hercules* ship-shaped restaurant at the southern end of the beach. **Nightlife** focuses on *Captain Mondy's*, opposite the Liliacul, which has some extremely slick mixologists. The post office has closed, but there's an **ATM**, and an **Internet café** in the *Hotel Delta*, towards the south of the resort.

Imagine Maya architects called upon to redesign Palm Beach and you'll get some idea of the pyramidal multi-hotel complexes that characterize **AURORA**, the most recent resort, set on the cape of the same name immediately southeast of Jupiter. Small and elegantly designed compared to the other resorts, Aurora has ten **hotels**, all two stars, save the three-star (but slightly tatty) *California* (☎0241/731 293, ⊕www.californiahotel.panda.ro; ❺). The *Cristal* (☎0241/731 353; ❹) and *Topaz* (☎0241/731 292; ❹) both have a few cheaper rooms (❸), all with private bathrooms.

There's a minimal gap before you hit **VENUS** – broadly similar to Jupiter, but quieter and more family-oriented. There are several fine four-star **hotels** here, notably the excellent 🍴 *Dana* (☎0241/731 638, 🌐www.hotel-dana.ro; ❽), with air-conditioned rooms and villas set in gorgeous gardens, a poolside disco, terrace bar with Romanian restaurant, gyms, bikes and Wi-Fi Internet access. Other four-stars include the *Carmen* (☎0241/731 608, 🌐www.hotelcarmen.ro; ❾), which has an indoor pool and is open all year; *Afrodita* (☎0241/706 271, 🌐www.hotelafrodita.ro; ❽), with open and indoor swimming pools and free Internet access; and the new *Palace* (☎0241/732 065, 🌐www.palacehotel.ro; ❽) to the south of the resort. The *Euro Orlando* (May–Sept; ☎0241/731 605, 🌐www.yourhotels.ro/orlando.html; ❼), is a decent three-star. Good two-star places include the lively *Silvia* (☎0241/731 188; ❹), which attracts a young crowd. The *Popas Turistic Brateş* (☎0241/731 702), in the centre of Venus, has adequate one-star rooms (❷) and three-star villas (❸) with communal washblocks. *Calipso* is the best of the resort's four **discos**. **CFR** shares its premises with the **post office** at the southern end of the resort; to the south are a sulphurous **spa** and, just inland, the Herghelia Mangalia **stables** (☎0241/751 325) where you can **hire horses** to explore the forest, inhabited by roe deer, grouse and pheasants.

A reed-fringed lake lies between Venus and **SATURN**, a small resort with half a dozen low-rent, high-rise **hotels** – bookable through the accommodation office (☎0241/752 452). Water from mineral springs is piped through showers on the beach, and there's a small waterpark, **Aqua Park Balada** (summer daily 8am–7pm), with three pools, slides, snack bars and a stage for entertainment.

Mangalia

The modern suburbs of **MANGALIA** are close to swallowing up Saturn, and in fact Mangalia's train station is nearer to Saturn than to the centre of town. As with Constanţa, Mangalia's appearance of modernity belies its ancient origin – the Greeks founded their city of **Callatis** here during the sixth century BC, when population pressure impelled them to colonize the Black Sea coast. In Byzantine times it was renamed **Pangalia**, meaning "most beautiful". The **ruins of Callatis**, which include sarcophagi and the vestiges of a Christian basilica, are in Parc Stadionului, with the revitalized **Archeological Museum** (Muzeul de Arheologie Callatis; May–Sept daily 9am–8pm; Oct–April Tues–Sun 9am–6pm) on the main road to its west side at Şoseaua Constanţei 23. Other sights of note include the **Sultan Esmahan Mosque** just south of the small town centre at Str. Oituz 1. Founded in 1525 (and now air-conditioned), the mosque is surrounded by a Muslim graveyard.

Practicalities

Heading south from the **train station** (where maxitaxis wait in a layby) and left at the roundabout, you'll reach the *Hotel Paradiso*, Str. Matei Basarab 3 (☎0241/752 052, 🌐www.hotelparadiso.ro; ❺), a newly renovated spa **hotel** with an outdoor swimming pool and treatment centre. At Str. Teilor 6, just south by the town centre, rises the *Hotel President* (☎&🖷0241/755 861, 🌐www.hpresident.com; ❽), which relies more on business conferences than bikinis and is easily the best **place to stay**, with all the facilities you'd expect of a four-star, including Wi-Fi, gym, sauna and beauty centre. The *President* was built atop the southern boundary of ancient Callatis, and the extensive ruins that were uncovered during the hotel's construction in 1993–94 have been elegantly preserved. Along Str. Teilor on the seafront just north of the President are three near-identical hotels: the two-star *Zenit* (☎0241/751 645; ❹) and

Astra (☏0241/751 673; ❹), and the three-star *Corsa* (☏0241/757 422, ⓦwww
.hotelcorsa.com; ❻), which is open all year, with Internet ports in every room.
Other than the *Callatis* (☏0241/751 215; ❷), a busy one-star sanatorium
immediately south of the *President*, the one budget option is the modest
Pensiunea Oituz (☏0241/753 980; ❷), which has a basic restaurant, west of the
mosque at Str. Oituz 11. Mangalia's **campsite** is north of town – from
the train station, turn left, then right after five minutes at the *Saturn* sign. The
Constanţa County Antrec representative, Str. George Murnu 13 bl. D sc. B ap.
21 (☏0241/759 473, ⓔconstanta@antrec.ro), can help you find **homestay
accommodation** in Mangalia, Agigia and Eforie Sud.

The best **restaurants** are in the *President* hotel (overlooking the archeological
site) and, immediately across the street, the *Café del Mar*, which has an ambitious
menu and is open 24 hours in the summer. *Casa Rosemarie*, at Şos. Constanţei
23, is a cheery pizza place. The *Peach-Pit Patisserie*, at the top of the pedestrianized section of Şos. Constanţei, is a cracking little place for a quick bite or to
stock up on pastries; just north, *Dreams* is a good *terasa* **bar** (daily 7am–10pm).
You'll find *Captain Mondy's Irish Pub* on B-dul. 1 Dec 1918, a couple of blocks
south of the mosque.

For **car rental**, contact Icar at Şos. Constanţei, bl. P4ab (☏0241/753 232); for
rail tickets, **CFR** is at Str. Ştefan cel Mare 16 (Mon–Fri 8am–7pm). There's
Internet access (8am–midnight) at the *Lavrion* restaurant, immediately south of
the Archeological Museum.

Doi Mai and Vama Veche

The laid-back villages of **Doi Mai** and **Vama Veche**, traditionally the haunts
of artists, intellectuals and nonconformists, lie between Mangalia and the
Bulgarian border, 10km south along the coast. Though neither had a hotel until
just a few years ago, tourist facilities in both villages have grown rapidly since.
Fortunately, the new developments have been planned with consideration for
their surroundings and are on a reasonably modest scale. Doi Mai (2 May),
despite lying in the shadow of the massive yellow cranes of Mangalia's shipyard,
is peaceful and relaxed, and popular with families; Vama Veche (Old Customs
Post) has a better beach and, since its discovery by Bucharest cognoscenti, has
acquired an air of bohemian sophistication not found elsewhere on the coast.
The pace of change, however, is steady, and traditional donkey carts are now
outnumbered by imported cars – the sooner you come, the better.

Maxitaxis (6am–9pm) shuttle from Mangalia to the Bulgarian border every
twenty minutes or so during the summer and hourly out of season, with
additional services every fifteen minutes to Doi Mai. There are no **ATMs** in
either village, so bring what money you'll need with you.

Doi Mai

Coming from Mangalia, you'll be dropped off at the intersection of Şoseaua
Principală and Str. Scolii, **DOI MAI**'s two main streets. *Casa Margo* (☏0241/732
939; ❸), just south on Şoseaua Principală, is a clean **pension** offering thirteen
air-conditioned rooms with bath, cable TV and refrigerator. *Casa Vizante*, closer
to the beach at Str. Falezei 8 (☏0722/805 125; ❸), is smaller and quieter but
equally comfortable. The pleasantly bohemian ⚑ *Hellios Inn*, a Greek-owned
establishment 300m inland on Str. Scolii (May–Sept; ☏&🖷0241/732 929,
ⓦwww.hellios-inn.ro; ❹), has simple, attractive en-suite rooms with TV,
including some triples; the best, with bare stone floors, are on the ground floor
of the pension, but there's also a cheaper youth hotel wing. There's an outdoor
swimming pool, as well as a pleasant courtyard and a rustic seafood **restaurant**

(the best in the village) and *terasa*-**bar**. It's also possible to find **private rooms** in Doi Mai (①—②); look for signs reading *cazare*. Just north of the crossroads, the *Flamingo* **disco** has **Internet** access.

The **Doi Mai–Vama Veche Marine Reserve** begins just south of the Mangalia port and extends to the border. Loggerhead turtles can be seen here, as well as sea horses, two species of dolphin, and corals. **Diving** trips can be arranged through the *Hellios Inn*.

Vama Veche

Under communism, **VAMA VECHE**, just short of the border with Bulgaria, was closed to all but staff of Cluj University or those who could claim some vague affiliation with it; it became a haven for nonconformists looking for an escape from the surveillance of the Securitate. In recent years, locals and investors have begun to capitalize on Vama Veche's countercultural reputation, and there's now an attractive assortment of **accommodation** on offer, ranging from three-star hotels and pensions to wild camping on the beach. There are still, however, plenty of chickens and sheep wandering about, and the **Save Vama Veche** organization (Ⓦwww.savevamaveche.home.ro) has thus far succeeded in keeping the ravages of mass tourism at arm's length.

Heading towards the beach from the crossroads in the centre of the village, you'll pass *Bibi Vama Veche* (May–Sept 8am–10pm; ☏0241/743 870 or 0722/889 087, Ⓦwww.vama-veche.com), a private **tourist office** which can help you find a place to stay; it also acts as the reception for the *Bazart* youth hotel (☏0241/858 009; ❸). Immediately beyond are Bibi Market – the village's general store – and *Bibi Bistro*. On the beach is Vama Veche's finest **hotel**, *La John* (☏0722/270 878; ❺), with two storeys of wooden galleries and 54 rooms with bathroom and TV. Also by the beach, just to the south, *Ca'Bianca* (☏0721/820 122, Ⓦwww.cabianca.rdsct.ro; ❺) is almost as good; turning right just before reaching the beach brings you to the *Vila Dini* (☏0744/553 672; ❹) and the cheaper *Vila Madi* (☏0723/452 091; ❸), which has clean rooms with and without bath. Further south, just out of the village, the new *Hotel Laguna* (☏0241/407 782, Ⓔcomplex_laguna@yahoo.com, Ⓦwww.corsarul.net; ❺), with Daliesque mosaics on its exterior and an Arabian-style interior, has 48 rooms around a swimming pool, all with good bathrooms and cable TV. At the north end of the village, *Elga's Punk Rock Hotel* (☏0241/858 070 or 0722/366 711, Ⓦwww.punkrockhotel.com; ❸), housed in a small wooden chalet, doesn't seem at all punk but is certainly fun, with a youthful party scene.

Camping Vama Veche (☏0745/629 157) has a ten-room motel, with rooms with (❸) and without bathroom (❷), bungalows (❷) and pitches, at the north end of the village. **Camping** wild is easiest south of the main part of the beach, although it's also possible to the north; in either case there's a cleaning charge of €3 per tent per day.

Most of the hotels and pensions have **restaurants**. *Ca'Bianca*'s is best, while the *Pensiunea Lyana*, behind *La John*, is recommended for its fish. *La John* has a large self-service restaurant and a bar with a great view, while *Bibi Bistro* is cheaper, with a multilingual menu of standard dishes. There are *shaworma* (kebab) and burrito stands on the road down to the beach, as well as a pizzeria. Bibi Market stocks just enough provisions for a beachfront **picnic**.

There are some great little **bars** on the beach, wooden-walled and thatch-roofed, including *Stuf* and *Gulag* near the centre of the beach and *Corsarul* to the south. Vama Veche's **nightlife** is without equal on the coast, with open-air dancing till dawn and live music in some of the restaurants, notably the *Bibi Bistro*. Annual **events** include the **BB Jazz and Blues Festival**, held in the last week in August and featuring mostly Romanian jazz bands; and (usually a week earlier) **Stufstock** (ⓦ www.stufstock.ro), a music festival put on by Save Vama Veche. Once a free event protesting against environmental threats to the area, it's now a more sophsticated event. Four-day passes cost €80.

Travel details

Trains

Constanța to: Bucharest (7–9 daily; 3hr 25min–5hr 15min); Galați (1 daily; 5hr); Iași (1 daily; 8hr 40min); Mangalia (7 daily; 1hr–1hr 25min); Medgidia (12 daily; 33–57min); Suceava (1 daily; 9hr 40min).
Medgidia to: Babadag (3 daily; 1hr 55min–2hr 20min); Bucharest (6–8 daily; 2hr 50min–4hr 20min); Mangalia (7 daily; 2hr 10min–2hr 50min, summer 1hr 50min); Negru Vodă (3 daily; 1hr 20min); Tulcea (3 daily; 2hr 45min–3hr 20min).
Tulcea to: Bucharest (1 daily; 6hr 5min); Medgidia (3 daily; 2hr 50min–3hr 20min).

Buses and maxitaxis

Constanța to: Bacău (1 daily); Brăila (4 daily); Brașov (1 daily); Bucharest (every 45min); Cernavodă (every 30min); Costinești (every 30min); Galați (13 daily); Hârșova (4 daily); Iași (2 daily); Istria (4 daily); Jurilovca (5 daily); Mangalia (every 20min); Medgidia (every 15min); Oltina (for Adamclisi, 3 daily); Piata Neamț/Târgu Neamț (1 daily); Ploiești (2 daily); Suceava (2 daily); Techirghiol (every 20min); Tulcea (every 30min).
Mangalia to: Doi Mai and Vama Veche (May–Aug every 20min, Sept–April every 90min); Saturn-Olimp (frequent).
Tulcea to: Brăila (6 daily); Bucharest (hourly); Cocoș monastery (4 daily); Constanța (every 30min); Enisala (9 daily); Focșani (1 daily); Galați (15 daily); Iași (2 daily); Jurilovca (2 daily); Mahmudia (5 daily); Murighiol (7 daily); Niculițel (6 daily); Parcheș (9 daily).

Ferries

Tulcea to: Periprava (2 weekly in summer, 1 weekly in winter; 5hr 30min); Sf. Gheorghe (2 weekly in summer, 1 weekly in winter; 4hr 30min); Sulina (3 weekly; 4hr 30min).

Hydrofoils

Tulcea to: Sulina (3 daily; 1hr 30min).

Fast catamarans

Tulcea to: Sulina (3 weekly in summer, 2 weekly in winter; 2hr); Sf. Gheorghe (2 weekly; 3hr); Periprava (2 weekly; 3hr).

Planes

Constanța to: Cluj (TAROM, weekly in summer only); Craiova (Carpatair, 3 weekly); Iași (TAROM, weekly in summer only); Timișoara (Carpatair 3 weekly, & TAROM weekly in summer only).
Tulcea to: Bucharest (TAROM, weekly in summer only).

International trains

Constanța to: Budapest, Hungary (1 daily; 16hr).

International buses

Constanța to: Athens, Greece (Tues, Thurs & Sat, 1 daily); Chișinău, Moldova (2 daily); Istanbul, Turkey (2 daily); Varna, Bulgaria (1 daily).
Tulcea to: Istanbul (1 daily).

Contexts

Contexts

The historical framework

Although inhabited since prehistoric times, Romania only achieved statehood in the nineteenth century, and Transylvania, one third of its present territory, was acquired as recently as 1920. Hence, much of Romania's history is that of its disparate parts – Dobrogea, the Banat, Bessarabia, Maramureş and, above all, the principalities of Moldavia, Wallachia and Transylvania.

Greeks, Dacians and Romans

Despite the discovery of bones, weapons and implements within Carpathian caves, very little is known about the nomadic hunter-gatherers of the early **Stone Age**. With the retreat of the glaciers, humans seem to have established their first settlements in Dobrogea, where evidence suggests that a people known to archeologists as the **Hamangia Culture** probably had a matriarchal society, worshipping fertility goddesses.

Other societies developed in the Bronze and Iron Ages, followed by Celts who arrived from Asia in the last millennium BC; meanwhile, during the sixth and seventh centuries BC, **Greek traders** established ports along the Black Sea coast, the ruins of which can still be seen at Istria (Histria), Constanţa (Tomis), Mangalia (Callatis) and other sites, but the interior remained virtually unknown to the Greeks until 512 BC, when the Persian emperor Darius attempted to expel the Scythians, another Asiatic people newly settled along the Danube. In 335 BC, Alexander the Great occupied Dobrogea and crossed the Danube, defeating the Getae but failing to subdue them.

The chronicler Herodotus had reported in the sixth century BC that of the numerous and disunited tribes of **Thracians** who inhabited the mountains on both sides of the Danube, the "bravest and most righteous" were those subsequently known as the "Geto-Dacians". The word "Thracians" is now taken as an umbrella term for the mix of original East Balkan and incoming central European tribes then occupying this area, including the Getae on the Danube, the Dacians to their north, the Thracians proper to the south, and the Illyrians in present-day Albania. Over time these related tribes gradually coalesced until a single leader, Burebista (82–44 BC), ruled a short-lived **Dacian empire**, occupying the territory of modern-day Romania and beyond, the religious and political capital of which was **Sarmizegetusa**, in the Orǎştie mountains. Archeological digs have revealed Dacian settlements from the Black Sea to Slovakia, and the sheer size of the kingdom contributed to its fragmentation after Burebista's demise.

A Roman colony

Before **Decebal** (87–106 AD) managed to reunite this kingdom, the lower reaches of the Danube had already been conquered by the **Romans**, who then began to expand northwards. Decebal immediately defeated a Roman army but was then driven back; a stalemate followed until two campaigns (in 101–102 and 105–106 AD) by the Emperor Trajan (98–117 AD) led to the conquest of Dacia. Although the Apuseni mountains, Maramureş and Moldavia were never subdued, most regions fell under Roman rule, maintained by the building of roads linking the garrison posts and trading towns. For the **colonization of Dacia** (so rich and important that it was known as Dacia Felix or Happy Dacia), settlers were brought from imperial territories as far afield as Greece, Egypt and Persia. Later, the adoption of Christianity as the official religion led to its acceptance in Dacia, at least superficially; and under Hadrian, the region was divided into two provinces for easier administration. With increasing incursions by nomadic Asian tribes such as the Goths in the third century, however, the defence of Dacia became too costly, and in 271 AD, Emperor Aurelian withdrew Rome's presence from the region.

The Age of Migrations and Daco-Romanian Continuity

The Romans' departure was followed by the arrival of nomadic peoples sweeping out of Asia and into Western Europe during the **Age of Migrations**, including the Huns (4th and 5th centuries), Avars (6th century), Slavs (7th century) and Bulgars (7th century, along the coast en route to Bulgaria). The low-lying regions were greatly exposed to these invasions, whereas high mountains protected the area later to be called Transylvania, where coins have been found whose dates show that there continued to be trade with the empire despite Roman withdrawal; the Daco-Romanian Continuity theory holds that the Romanians are descendants of the Roman settlers and the indigenous Dacians, forming a hybrid culture, and Romanian philologists point to numerous words in their language derived from Latin. Yet while some Romanians boast loudly about their Roman heritage, many of the imperial settlers would have been not free Romans but former slaves and soldiers, many of them Greeks and Arabs.

The theory would be of academic interest only were it not entwined with the dispute, now centuries old, between the Magyars and Romanians over the **occupation of Transylvania**. By claiming this uninterrupted residence, Romanians assert their rightful ownership of Transylvania. Conversely, the Magyars (who had first passed through around 896 as just another Asiatic horde before settling Hungary) claim that their occupation, from about 997 to the thirteenth century, met little resistance, and that the indigenous people were of Slavic stock. According to some Magyar historians, **Vlachs** (Romanians) are first mentioned in Transylvania around 1222 as groups of nomadic pastoralists crossing the Carpathians, having wandered over the course of centuries from their original "homeland" in Macedonia and Illyria.

The medieval principalities

Whatever the indigenous population's identity, István I (Saint Stephen) and later monarchs of the Árpád dynasty gradually extended Hungarian rule over **Transylvania**, using foreigners to bolster their own settlements. Besides subduing local Cumans, Bulgars and Vlachs, the colonists had to withstand frequent invasions by the **Tatars** (or Mongols), nomadic warriors who devastated much of Eastern Europe in 1241–42 and continued to wreak havoc over the next five centuries.

While the Teutonic Knights colonized the Bârsa Land (around Braşov) in 1211 but were evicted in 1225, other groups of Germans – subsequently known as **Saxons** – built up powerful market towns like Hermannstadt (Sibiu) and Kronstadt (Braşov), which were granted self-government as "seats" (Sedes, or Stühle). Another ethnic group, the **Székely**, acted as the vanguard of colonization in the eastern marches, where they too were allowed relative autonomy.

Hungarians, however, were either classed as plebs liable to all manner of taxes, or as nobles and thus tax-exempt. This group dominated **the feudal system**, being represented alongside the Saxon and Székely "nations" on the Diet that advised the principality's military and civil governor, the **Voivode**, who acted for the Hungarian king. Under the Árpád dynasty, Diets included Romanian-speaking Vlachs who even then may have constituted the majority of Transylvania's population. From the mid-fourteenth century onwards, however, Vlachs faced increasing **discrimination**, both social and political. Besides the mistrust sown by Bogdan Vodă's revolt in Maramureş (see p.351), **religion** played an important part in this process. Whereas the Vlachs were Orthodox (barring a few apostate nobles), the other communities adhered to the Catholic Church.

Wallachia and Dobrogea

On the far side of the Carpathians, fully fledged principalities emerged somewhat later. Chronicles attribute the foundation of **Wallachia** (Vlahia or the Ţara Românească) to Negru Vodă (the Black Prince), who made Câmpulung its first capital in 1290, though they may instead refer to his son Radu Negru (1310–52), usually credited as the first of the Basarab dynasty. The shift in Wallachia's capitals over the centuries – from Câmpulung in the highlands down to Curtea de Argeş and Târgovişte in the foothills and then Bucharest on the plain – expressed a cautious move from the safety of the mountains to the financial opportunities of the trade routes with Turkey. Oppression, anarchy and piety were commonplace: the tithes and labour squeezed from the enserfed masses allowed the landowning **boyars** to endow Orthodox churches and engineer coups against the ruling voivodes. Yet commerce was entirely in the hands of Germans, Poles, Greeks and Jews; and though lavishly bestowed, the Orthodox Church was subordinated to the Bulgarian and Byzantine patriarchates, in part a legacy of Bulgar rule during the eighth and ninth centuries, but also reflecting the tendency of Wallachia's rulers to look south for allies (soon to be wiped from the map for centuries) against Hungary.

Moldavia and Bessarabia

Attempts to enforce Hungarian rule in Maramureş provoked some of the indigenous population to follow **Bogdan Vodă** over the Carpathians in 1359 to the cradle of a new principality, **Moldavia**; but the process of occupying the hills and steppes beyond the Carpathians had begun centuries earlier. Groups of Romanian-speaking pastoralists and farmers gradually moved to the Dnestr where they encountered Ukrainians who named them Volokhi. The Moldavian capital shifted southeastwards from Rădăuţi to Suceava and then to Iaşi. **Alexander the Good** (Alexandru cel Bun) may have gained his honorary title by ousting Turks from the eastern marches, though it could well have been bestowed by the Basarab family, whom he made feudal lords of the region, subsequently known as **Bessarabia**; or retrospectively by Moldavia's peasantry who suffered during the prolonged, violent anarchy that followed his death. Besides Tatar invasions and rebellious boyars, Moldavia faced threats from Hungary, Poland and the Turks.

Ottomans, Nationes and Phanariots

From the mid-fourteenth century, the fate of the Balkan countries was determined by the **Ottoman empire** of the Seljuk Turks, which spread inexorably northwards, finally subjugating Bulgaria in 1393. The Turks were briefly halted by **Mircea the Old** (Mircea cel Bătrân; 1386–1418) at the battle of Rovine in 1394, but subsequent defeats compelled Mircea to acknowledge Ottoman suzerainty in 1417. By surrendering the fertile **Dobrogea** region and paying tribute, outright occupation was avoided and Wallachia's ruling class retained their positions; but henceforth, both rulers and ruled were confronted with the alternatives of submission or resistance to an overwhelming force.

Even before the fall of Constantinople in 1453, Wallachia, Moldavia and Transylvania had become Christendom's front line of resistance to the Turks – and indeed, with Russia, the only Orthodox Christian land remaining free. Throughout the fifteenth century, the principalities' history is overshadowed by this struggle and the names of four remarkable military leaders. First was Transylvanian voivode **Iancu de Hunedoara** (Hunyadi János), who defeated the Turks near Alba Iulia and Sibiu in 1441–43 and lead multinational armies to victory at Niş and Belgrade. Iancu's son **Mátyás Corvinus** (1440–90, also known as Hunyadi Mátyás or Matei Corvin), Hungary's great Renaissance king, continued to resist the Turks, who were dislodged from southern Bessarabia by **Stephen the Great** (Ştefan cel Mare) of Moldavia and temporarily checked by the fortresses of Chilia and Cetatea Alba (now in Ukraine). However, their resurgence under Bajazid II, and peace treaties signed by the Turks with Poland, Hungary and Venice in the 1470s and 1480s, presaged the demise of Moldavian independence, as was apparent to Stephen by the end of his embattled reign (1457–1504). Meanwhile, due to Wallachia's greater vulnerablity, its rulers generally preferred to pay off the Turks rather than resist them – **Vlad Ţepeş** (Vlad the Impaler – see p.471) being a notable exception from 1456 to 1476.

In **Transylvania**, the least exposed region, the **Bobâlna peasant uprising** of 1437–38 rocked the feudal order. To safeguard their privileges, the Magyar nobility concluded a pact known as the **Union of Three Nations** with the Saxon and Székely leaders, whereby each of these three ethnic groups (Nationes) agreed to recognize and defend the rights of the others. As a consequence, the Vlachs were relegated to the position of "those who do not possess the right of citizenship…but are merely tolerated by grace", and they were effectively prohibited from holding public office or residing in Saxon and Magyar towns. The increasing exploitation of the Magyar peasantry led in 1514 to an uprising under György Dózsa (Gheorghe Doja), savagely repressed by governor **János Zápolyai** (Johann Zapolya, 1510–40), who imposed the onerous Werbőczy Code, or Tripartium, a feudal version of apartheid, in 1517.

The crushing defeat of Hungary by Suleyman the Magnificent at **Mohács** (1526) and the Turkish occupation of Buda (1541) exacerbated the isolation of the principalities. Although the Habsburg dynasty of Austria laid claim to what was left of Hungary after Mohács, Zápolyai won Ottoman support to maintain a precarious autonomy for Transylvania, even gaining control of Hungary east of the River Tisza (the Partium) in 1538. Successors such as István Báthori (1571–81, who was elected King of Poland from 1575 and drove back Ivan the Terrible) and Zsigmond Báthori (1581–97) were able to maintain this independence; in Moldavia, however, **Petru Rareş** could only hold his throne (1527–38 and 1541–56) by breathtaking duplicity and improvisations, while his successors plumbed even further depths.

Short-lived unification

Understandably, Romanian historiography has scant regard for such figures, and prefers to highlight the achievements of more successful leaders such as **Michael the Brave** (Mihai Viteazul, often known in Wallachia as Mihai Bravul). Crowned ruler of Wallachia in 1593, his triumph against the Turks in 1595 was followed by the overthrow of Andrew Báthori in Transylvania in 1599 and a lightning campaign across the Carpathians in 1600 to secure him the Moldavian throne. This opportunist and short-lived **union of the principalities** under one crown – which fragmented immediately following his murder in 1601 – has subsequently been presented as a triumph of Romanian nationalism, but it was only between 1604 and 1657 that Transylvania attained genuine independence from both Habsburgs and Ottomans.

From the 1630s onwards, Moldavia and Wallachia avoided direct occupation as Turkish *pashaliks* by accepting Ottoman "advisers", known as **Phanariots**. In Moldavia, they encouraged the Orthodox Church to abandon Old Slavonic as the language of the scriptures and ritual in favour of Greek, but this had the unintended result of stimulating a move towards the Romanian language. This presaged a minor cultural renaissance – particularly in the field of architecture – during a period of relative stability from 1633 to 1711 in Moldavia and to 1714 in Wallachia. Thereafter, the Turks dispensed with native rulers and instead appointed Phanariot princes, who were purely concerned with plundering the principalities; their rapaciousness, combined with more than seventy changes of ruler in Moldavia and Wallachia until 1821, crippled both regions.

The struggle for independence and unification

The end of the siege of Vienna in 1683 precipitated **Habsburg** control of Transylvania. As Catholics and imperialists, the Habsburg monarchy persuaded some Orthodox clergy to accept papal authority, promising that Vlachs who joined the **Uniate Church** (see p.203) would be granted equality with the Nationes. Although this promise was retracted in 1701, Bishop Inocenţiu Micu and the intellectuals of the Transylvanian School agitated for equal rights and articulated the Vlachs' growing consciousness of being **Romanians**. Thus Joseph II's edict of religious toleration in 1781, his dissolution of the monasteries and embarkation upon the abolition of serfdom all came too late to prevent the great peasant rebellion led by **Horea**, **Crişan** and **Cloşca** in 1784–85. Its crushing only stimulated efforts to attain liberation by constitutional means, however.

The gradual development of liberal and nationalist factions in **Moldavia and Wallachia** stemmed from a variety of causes, including the ideals of the Romantic movement and the French Revolution, the success of Serbian and Greek independence movements, and the emergence of capitalism in the principalities, showing that Turkish dominance and feudalism were in decline. The upshot was a major uprising against Phanariot rule in Wallachia in 1821, led by **Tudor Vladimirescu**. Although defeated, it persuaded the Turks that it was time to end Phanariot rule, and power was restored to native boyars in 1822.

The rise of Russia and World War I

As the power of the Ottomans declined, that of **Tsarist Russia** grew. Fired by imperialist and Pan-Slavist ideals and a fear of Habsburg encroachment (manifest in 1774, when Austria annexed the region henceforth known as **Bucovina**), Russia presented itself in 1779 as the guardian of the Ottomans' Christian subjects, and expanded its territories towards the Balkans as well as into the Caucasus and Central Asia. In 1792, Russian forces reached the River Dnestr; one Russo–Turkish war led to the annexation of Bessarabia in 1812, and another to the Treaty of Adrianople (1829), by which Moldavia and Wallachia became Russian protectorates, allowing Western European trade and ideas free access at last. The Tsarist governor **General Paul Kiseleff** was in no sense a revolutionary, but he introduced liberal reforms and assemblies in both principalities, which remained in force after the Russians withdrew in 1834, having selected two rulers. Of these, Michael Sturdza in Moldavia was the more despotic but also the more energetic, levying heavy taxes to construct roads, dykes, hospitals and schools.

Given the boyars' dominance of the assemblies, economic development took precedence over the political and social reforms demanded by bourgeois liberals such as Nicolae Golescu, Ion Brătianu, Nicolae Bălcescu and Mihail Kogălniceanu. The **democratic movement** they led campaigned for the unification of Moldavia and Wallachia and briefly came to power in 1848, the **Year of Revolutions** (see below).

Russia, now claiming to be "the gendarme of Europe", intervened militarily to restore the status quo, while the build-up to the Crimean War saw Russia also occupying Moldavia and Wallachia and fighting the Turks along the Danube. The Congress of Paris, ending the war in 1856, reaffirmed Turkish rule (although with increased autonomy for the boyars), and the nationalist cause was thwarted until January 1859, when the assemblies of Moldavia and Wallachia circumvented the restrictions imposed to prevent their **unification** under a single ruler, **Alexander Ioan Cuza**, who embarked on a series of reforms, the most important of which were the **abolition of serfdom** and agrarian reform, including the expropriation of the huge monastic estates, enraging the landowning classes and other conservative elements. Under Cuza's replacement, the German **Prince Carol I**, Rumania declared its **independence** on May 9, 1877.

Events in **Transylvania** followed a different course during the nineteenth century with popular support for the 1848 revolution split along nationalist lines. Whereas the abolition of serfdom was universally welcomed by the peasantry, the Romanian population opposed the unification of Transylvania with Hungary, which Magyars of all classes greeted with enthusiasm; the Saxons were lukewarm on both issues. Following protest meetings at Blaj, **Avram Iancu** formed Romanian guerrilla bands to oppose the Hungarians;

belated attempts by Kossuth and Bălcescu to compromise on the issue of Romanian rights came too late to create a united front against the Tsarist armies which invaded Transylvania on behalf of the Habsburgs. As in Hungary, the Habsburgs introduced martial law and widespread repression in the aftermath of the revolution.

In 1867, the Ausgleich, or Compromise, established the Dual Monarchy of the Austro-Hungarian Empire and the region became part of Greater Hungary, ruled directly from Budapest, with a policy of **Magyarization** in Transylvania making Hungarian the official language; a barrage of laws was passed to further undermine Romanian culture (Bucovina and Maramureş remained under Austrian rule and avoided the worst of this). The cultural association **ASTRA**, founded in 1861, acted in its defence until the establishment of the **National Party** in 1881, which maintained close links with kindred groups across the Carpathians.

The influence of foreign capital increased enormously around the turn of the century, as Rumania's mineral wealth – particularly its oil – inspired competition among the great powers. While the Liberal and Conservative parties squabbled ritualistically and alternated in power, nothing was done about the worsening impoverishment of the people. Peasant grievances exploded in the **răscoala** of 1907 – a nationwide uprising that was savagely crushed (with around 11,000 deaths) and then followed by a series of ineffectual agrarian reforms.

Rumania's acquisition of territory south of the Danube in 1878 was one of the many bones of contention underlying the **Balkan Wars** that embroiled Rumania, Bulgaria, Serbia, Macedonia and Greece. Rumania sat out the first Balkan War (1912–13), but joined the alliance against Bulgaria in 1913, gaining the southern part of Dobrogea in the process. King Ferdinand, who succeeded Carol in 1914, was married to Marie, granddaughter of both Queen Victoria and Tsar Alexander II; thus, when Rumania entered **World War I** in August 1916, it joined Great Britain, France and Russia and attacked the Austro-Hungarian forces in Transylvania. This disastrous campaign left it with an onerous peace treaty in May 1918, but by October the disintegration of the Central Powers reversed this situation entirely, and Rumanian armies advanced into Transylvania, and then on into Hungary to overthrow the short-lived communist régime of Béla Kun in August 1919. On December 1, 1918, the Romanian assembly of Alba Iulia declared **Transylvania's union with Rumania** to scenes of wild acclaim. The Romanian population of Bessarabia, set free by the Russian Revolution, had already declared their union with Rumania in March 1918, followed in November by Bucovina. The **Treaty of Trianon** in 1920 upheld Rumania's gains and as a nation it doubled both in population and territory, while Hungary lost half of its populace and two-thirds of its land – the source of great resentment ever since.

Greater Romania

The country's enlarged territory was dignified by the adoption of the name **Greater Romania**, but the lives of the masses hardly improved. Hungarian estates and farms in Transylvania were expropriated, but the many peasants who expected to benefit from agrarian reform were rapidly disillusioned when speculators and boyars appropriated much of the land. Similarly, Hungarian employees were dismissed on a huge scale and Romanian immigrants were brought in to replace them.

Romania was governed from 1920 by the **National Liberal Party**, favoured by the king but soon damaging the economy by pursuing nationalist and populist policies. On Ferdinand's death in 1927, it was dismissed and replaced by the **National Peasants Party**, led by **Iuliu Maniu**, which in 1928 won the only remotely fair election of this period. Despite a parliamentary majority and genuinely reforming policies, Maniu took a conservative line, constrained by the world economic crisis of 1929, vested interests and entrenched corruption.

However, it was a bizarre moral issue that led to the government's eventual fall: in 1930, after a three-year regency, **Carol II** took the throne on condition he put aside his divorced Jewish mistress, Magda Lupescu. He broke the promise, the puritan Maniu resigned and the government fell apart. Carol then exploited the constitution of 1923, which gave the king the right to dissolve parliament and call elections at will; a corrupt system soon developed whereby the government would fix elections by every means possible, only to be dismissed and replaced by the opposition when the king had tired of them. Between 1930 and 1940, there were no less than 25 separate governments, leading ultimately to the collapse of the political parties themselves. Strikes in the oil and rail industries in 1933 were put down by armed force; Carol set up his own "youth movement", and soon began routine phone-tapping by the **Siguranţa**, the Securitate's predecessor, enabling him to blackmail the entire political establishment, except for Maniu.

The Iron Guard and World War II

A **fascist movement** also established itself, particularly in Bessarabia, which had a long tradition of anti-Semitism. The main fascist party, taking much of the National Peasant Party's rural support, was the Legion of the Archangel Michael, founded in 1927; its green-shirted paramilitary wing, the **Iron Guard** (see box, p.282), extolled the soil, death, and a mystical form of Orthodoxy; it also fought street battles against Jews and followers of other political parties, and murdered four current and former prime ministers. In 1937, the anti-Semitic National League of Christian Defence and National Christian Party were installed in power by the king, but the prime minister, the poet Octavian Goga, immediately insulted Lupescu and was dismissed in February 1938, after just six weeks in power. This at last provoked Carol to ban all political parties (other than his own National Rebirth Front) and set up a royal dictatorship.

In February 1939, Germany demanded a monopoly of Romanian exports in return for a guarantee of its borders, and in March agreed an oil-for-arms deal. In April, Carol obtained feeble guarantees from Britain and France, but in August the equilibrium was shattered by the Nazi–Soviet Non-Aggression Pact. In June 1940, a Soviet ultimatum led to the annexation of Bessarabia and northern Bucovina, and, two months later, Hitler forced Carol to cede Northern Transylvania to Germany's ally Hungary, and southern Dobrogea to Bulgaria. Unable to maintain his position after giving away such huge portions of Romanian territory, Carol fled with Lupescu and his spoils in September, leaving his son **Mihai**, then nineteen years old, to take over the throne.

Mihai accepted the formation of a government led by **Marshal Ion Antonescu**, who styled himself Conducator ("leader", equivalent to Führer) but had little influence over local legionary groups who unleashed an orgy of violence against Jews and liberals. To ensure himself a stable and productive ally, Hitler forced Antonescu to disarm the Iron Guard; this provoked an armed uprising (and the savage butchery of 124 Jews in Bucharest) in January 1941, only suppressed by the army after a fierce struggle.

Romania entered **World War II** in June 1941, joining the Nazi invasion of Russia with the objective of regaining Bessarabia and northern Bucovina. Romanian troops took Odessa and participated in the battles of Sevastopol and Stalingrad, taking heavy casualties. Jews and Gypsies in Bessarabia, Bucovina and the Hungarian-controlled area of Transylvania were rounded up and deported

The Holocaust in Romania

In 1939, Romania had the third-largest **Jewish population** in Europe after Poland and the Soviet Union. Most lived in Bessarabia, Bucovina and parts of northern Moldavia, notably around Dorohoi. In June 1940, Bessarabia and northern Bucovina were ceded to the Soviet Union, as demanded by Hitler, and at least fifty Jews were killed in Dorohoi by retreating Romanian troops. A year later troops carried out an awful pogrom in Iaşi, killing about 8000 Jews, leading the Germans to comment, "we always act scientifically... we use surgeons, not butchers." As the army advanced (with units of the German Einsatzgruppe D following), there were many more massacres; at least 33,000 Jews died in Bessarabia and Bucovina between June 22 and September 1, 1941, and, in fact, the worst single massacre of the Holocaust was committed by Romanians whilst they took Odessa.

Deportations to Transnistria, the conquered territory beyond the River Dnestr, began in earnest on September 16; around 150,000 Jews were taken, of whom 18,000 to 22,000 died in transit. Up to 90,000 more died from starvation, disease and general mistreatment. Between November 21 and 29, 1941, all 48,000 Jews held in the Bogdanovka camp in southern Transnistria were killed; another 18,000 were killed in the Dumanovka camp.

In July 1942, the Germans began to press hard for the Jews of Wallachia, Moldavia and southern Transylvania to be deported to the camps, following the 120,000 already taken to Auschwitz from Hungarian-controlled Northern Transylvania. This was agreed but then refused after lobbying by neutral diplomats and the Papal Nuncio, although it was probably more due to the fact that the Jews were still vital to the functioning of the economy. In November 1942, it was decided that Romanian Jews in Germany should be sent to the German death camps.

When Romania was thinking of changing sides, the **World Jewish Congress** in Geneva proposed a plan to save 70,000 Romanian Jews, and possibly 1.3 million more in Eastern Europe, by paying the Romanian government twelve shillings per head to allow them to leave by ship for Palestine. This plan was blocked by opposition from anti-Semites in the US State Department and Britain, worried about the reaction of Arabs to further Jewish immigration to Palestine, as well as by the practical implications of sending money to a Nazi ally. Thirteen ships did leave, with 13,000 refugees, but two sank (with 1163 on board) and others were stopped by Turkey, under pressure from both Britain and Germany.

In 1944, Antonescu began a **limited repatriation** from the camps of Transnistria, bringing back 1500 in December 1943 and 1846 orphans by March 1944. He warned the Germans not to kill Jews as they retreated; nevertheless, a final thousand were killed in Tiraspol jail. On March 20, 1944, the Red Army reached the Dnestr, and the worst of the nightmare ended. In Antonescu's trial in 1946 it was said, "if the Jews of Romania are still alive, they owe it to Marshal Antonescu", who claimed to have saved about 275,000 Jews by his policy of keeping them for extermination at home; however, this did not save him from execution. Overall, between 264,900 and 470,000 Romanian Jews, and 36,000 Gypsies, died in the war; 428,000 Jews survived or returned alive. In 2003, a major row blew up with Israel when Iliescu appeared to claim that the Holocaust hadn't occurred in Romania and hadn't just affected the Jews, and comparing it to the suffering of prewar communists. Since 2004, **Holocaust Day** in October has been officially marked in Romania.

for slave labour and then on to extermination camps. By 1943, however, the Red Army was advancing fast, and Antonescu began to look for a way to abandon Hitler and change sides. Opposition to the war mounted as the Russians drew nearer, and, as they crossed the border, a **royal/military coup** on August 23, 1944 overthrew the Antonescu regime – a date commemorated until 1989 as **Liberation Day**, although it took a further two months to clear the Germans from the country.

The People's Republic

While the Romanian army subordinated itself to Soviet command, the first government formed by King Mihai was a broad coalition, with **communists** only playing a minor role. Gradually, however, they increased their influence, and, in March 1945, the Soviets forced the king to accept a new coalition under the premiership of **Dr Petru Groza** (leader of the Ploughmen's Front); again, this included politicians from the prewar parties, but the key posts were occupied by communists. Land reform in 1945 benefited millions of peasants at the expense of the Saxons and Swabians of Transylvania and the Banat, who had become the biggest landowners since the dispossession of the Magyars, while women voted for the first time in 1946, supposedly contributing to the election of another ostensibly balanced government. In fact, virtually every device ever used to rig an election was brought into play and the takeover steamed ahead.

Like Groza's first administration, this included leading capitalists and former Guardists, whom the communists initially wooed, since their first aim was to eliminate the left and centre parties, who were often forcibly merged with the communists. On December 30, 1947, King Mihai was forced to abdicate and Romania was declared a **People's Republic**. Antonescu and up to 60,000 were executed after highly irregular trials in 1946 and 1947. Eighty thousand arrests followed in an effort to overcome peasant resistance to **collectivization** (a reversal of the earlier agrarian reform), with around 180,000 more from 1948 in the campaign to "liquidate" the Uniate Church. Also in 1948, the **nationalization** of industries, banks and utilities placed the main economic levers in the hands of the Communist Party, which openly declared its intention to reshape society on Stalinist lines. **Police terror** was used against real or potential opponents, with victims incarcerated in prisons or conscripted for reed-cutting in the Delta or work on the Danube–Black Sea Canal, the "Canal Mortii" (see p.408) that claimed over 100,000 lives.

The Communist Party itself was split by bitter conflicts between the Muscovites (those who had spent the war in Moscow, led by Ana Pauker and Vasile Luca) and the nationalists, themselves divided between the prison-communists and the secretariat-communists who had remained free and in hiding. In 1952, the prison-communists emerged victorious, under **Gheorghe Gheorghiu-Dej**, General Secretary of the party's Central Committee since 1945, who had retained Stalin's confidence largely because the secretariat group was too ideologically flexible, while Pauker and her group were simply too Jewish. She and 192,000 other members were purged from the Party, and Lucreţiu Pătrăşcanu (Minister of Justice 1944–48) was executed in 1954. Stalin had died in 1953, but Gheorghiu-Dej took great exception to reformist trends in the USSR, and stuck grimly to the Stalinist true faith, developing heavy industry and claiming the impossible growth rate of 13 percent per year.

The USSR, having annexed Bessarabia once more, had given some of it to Ukraine and created the puppet **Republic of Moldova** from the rest. Therefore, Gheorghiu-Dej's increasing refusal to follow the Moscow line was a great success domestically, tapping into a vein of popular nationalism; and by arresting the leadership of the left-wing Hungarian People's Alliance and establishing an "Autonomous Hungarian Region" in the Székely Land in 1952, he simultaneously decapitated the Magyar political organization in Transylvania while erecting a facade of minority rights.

Gheorghiu-Dej died in 1965 and was succeeded by a collective leadership, but by 1969 **Nicolae Ceauşescu**, until then a little-known party hack, had outmanoeuvred his rivals and established undisputed power.

The Ceauşescu era

There seems little doubt that for the first few years of his rule, **Ceauşescu** was genuinely popular: he encouraged a cultural thaw, put food and consumer goods into the shops, denounced security police excesses (blaming them on Gheorghiu-Dej), and above all condemned the Warsaw Pact invasion of Czechoslovakia in 1968. His independent **foreign policy** gained Romania the reputation of being the "maverick" state of the Eastern bloc, building links with the West and maintaining ties with countries with which the USSR had severed contact.

However, he soon reverted to tried and tested methods of control as his **economic failure** became obvious. Ceauşescu stuck throughout to a Stalinist belief in heavy industry, and during the 1970s the country's **industrialization programme** absorbed thirty percent of GNP and $10.2 billion in foreign loans. Living standards plummeted as all but a minimal amount of food was exported, and the population was obliged to work harder and harder for less and less. Amazingly, all the foreign debt was repaid by 1989, although there was no prospect of any improvement in living standards thereafter.

Ceauşescu was convinced that the key to industrial growth lay in building a larger workforce, and in 1966 banned abortions and contraception for any married woman under 40 with fewer than four children (in 1972, the limits were raised to 45 and five); by 1989 11,000 women had died due to illegal abortions. In 1984, when his developing paranoia and personality cult were putting him increasingly out of touch, he introduced the **Baby Police** and compulsory monthly gynaecological examinations; unmarried people and married couples without children were penalized by higher taxes. Ceauşescu also **discriminated against the minorities**: it became increasingly hard to get an education or to buy books in Hungarian or German, or to communicate with relatives abroad; and families were persuaded to give their children Romanian names.

The two million-plus **Magyars** (including the Székely and Csángós) bore the brunt of this chauvinism, causing a notable worsening of diplomatic relations with Hungary. Neither this, nor criticism of the treatment of the **Gypsy** population, worried Ceauşescu, but he tried to keep on the right side of the German and Israeli governments, who purchased exit visas for ethnic Germans and Jews in Romania for substantial sums.

Abuses of human rights got worse through the 1980s, including the **systematization** programme for rural redevelopment (see p.98) and constant repression by the **Securitate** (secret police), which produced an atmosphere of fear and distrust even between family members, as up to one in four of the population was rumoured to be an informer. Increasingly, key posts were

Ceauşescu's orphans

The result of Ceauşescu's scheme to increase the workforce was that many women had children that they could not possibly afford to bring up and these were abandoned in dire **state orphanages**, grossly under-staffed and underfunded. With desensitized staff and with no mental stimulation, it's not surprising that many orphans were diagnosed (at three years old) as mentally handicapped and left without education in "Institutes for the Irrecuperable".

After the 1989 revolution, the Western media was saturated with distressing images of these orphanages, and emergency aid and volunteers flooded into Romania. Today, relief agencies focus on long-term strategies with emphasis on training and helping the Romanians to help themselves. Increasingly, orphanages are being replaced by family-home-type units, and family support centres have opened in some towns. In 2001, the EU published a shocking report linking adoptions to the organ trade and child pornography, and a two-year moratorium was imposed on adoption, during which time some improvements were made. The moratorium continues, to the approval of the EU; however, there's pressure from the US for adoptable children to be made available.

The problem of unwanted children remains, and will do so until there is comprehensive family planning, now the object of a huge programme, but official funds for charities have dried up and donations are welcome. Some Romanian families are now adopting, but most orphans are Gypsies and therefore not wanted. However, social security money is now reaching the Roma, so the numbers of children being abandoned has fallen greatly.

Charity contacts

Everychild UK ☎020/7749 2468, ⓦwww.everychild.org.uk

Cleaford Christian Trust UK ☎0845/124 9402, ⓦwww.cleafordchristiantrust.org.uk, ⓦwww.riac.org.uk

FARA UK ☎01328/821 444, ⓦwww.faracharity.org

Medical Support for Romania UK ☎01223/276 504, ⓦwww.msr.org.uk

Peace Corps US ☎1800/424 8580, ⓦwww.peacecorps.org

Regional Environmental Centre Romania ☎021/314 0433, ⓔrec@recromania.ro

Relief Fund for Romania UK ☎020/7733 7018, ⓦwww.relieffundforromania.co.uk

Romanian Angel Appeal Romania ☎021/323 6868, ⓦwww.raa.ro

allocated to relatives of the Ceauşescus, while all other senior figures were rotated every few years between jobs to prevent anyone building up an independent power base.

In the **1980s**, everything went downhill rapidly, as the truth about the country's economic collapse was hidden from Ceauşescu by his wife and subordinates. Absolutely everything was in short supply, but Nicolae and Elena pushed on with megalomaniac projects such as the Palace of the People in Bucharest, the Danube–Black Sea Canal (again) and the village systematization programme. Ceauşescu also made plain his opposition to *glasnost*.

The Revolution

By **1989**, the situation in Romania was so desperate that it seemed impossible for Ceauşescu not to bow to the wave of change that had swept over the whole of Eastern Europe. In December that year, events snowballed dramatically, with a series of strikes and riots culminating on December 20 with a mass demonstration of 100,000 people in Timișoara demanding Ceaușescu's resignation; despite his orders to fire, the army withdrew rather than launch into a massacre. The very next day, another crowd of 100,000, this time coralled into appearing by Ceaușescu's security forces as an intended show of support, gathered in Piața Republicii (now Piața Revoluției) in Bucharest to hear him speak, but he was soon interrupted by heckling. The police and Securitate opened fire but were unable to clear the crowds from the city centre, partly because the Minister of Defence, **General Vasile Milea**, ordered the army not to shoot. On the morning of December 22, Ceaușescu had Milea shot, but this merely precipitated the defection of many army units to the side of the protestors. By noon, the crowds had broken into the Party's Central Committee building, and the Ceaușescus fled by helicopter from the roof. After going to their villa at Snagov and then on to a military airfield near Titu, they hijacked a car before being arrested in Târgoviște. When the news of their capture proved insufficient to stop loyal Securitate units firing on the crowds, they were summarily tried and **executed** on Christmas Day.

Meanwhile, there was street fighting in many cities, with army and police units changing sides; it's unclear at what point their leadership had decided to abandon Ceaușescu, but evidence suggests that it was earlier rather than later. Nor is it clear at what stage the **National Salvation Front** (Frontul Salvării Naționale or FSN), which emerged to take power from December 22, had been formed; supposedly shaped in the Central Committee building on the afternoon of December 22 by people who had gathered there independently, it was clear many of them were already in contact. The key figures were Party members who had been sidelined by Ceaușescu, and **Ion Iliescu** was soon named president; his prime minister was **Petre Roman**, an up-and-coming member of the younger generation of communists.

Around a thousand people died in the revolution and the "terrorist" phase that lasted until January 18, although, initially, both the new government and the Hungarian media published inflated death tolls of 10,000 or more.

Free Romania

It didn't take long after the Ceaușescus' execution for the FSN to consolidate its power; within a month it had reversed its pledge not to run as a party in May's elections, and it was evident that the former governing élite had no intention of losing power. **Protests** in Bucharest even saw the government shipping in around 10,000 miners to deal (violently) with the crowds, leaving seven dead and 296 injured. The reaction abroad was dismay, with the US and EU suspending non-humanitarian aid and boycotting Iliescu's inauguration as president. At home, the nation went into shock, and it remained cowed for the next year while the economy collapsed.

In the meantime, the FSN easily won Romania's **first free election**, while Iliescu won the vote for president. The whole process was deemed fair enough by international observers, even though a million more votes were cast than were on the register, supposedly "due to the enthusiasm of the people for democracy". Most intellectuals soon took to referring to December 1989 as the "so-called revolution", and it was increasingly taken for granted that nothing much had changed.

Economic reform got under way slowly, but hardship was unavoidable as the country was rocked by its opening up to Western imports and by world recession. Food rationing had ended as soon as the FSN took power, along with a raft of prohibitions, and the government took care to empty the warehouses and fill the shops with groceries. However, food subsidies were cut in November 1990, and prices increased steadily from then on. Imports rose by 48 percent in 1990, and exports fell by 42 percent (due in part to food being kept for home consumers), while inflation climbed from 65 percent in 1990 to almost 300 percent in 1993. In 1991 the miners were brought back to force Roman to resign; he was replaced by Teodor Stolojan, and the FSN soon split.

A second general election was held in 1992, after the adoption of a new constitution making the country a presidential democracy, in which the prime minister has little autonomy and the two chambers of parliament have overlapping powers. Iliescu won the presidency, and a coalition government under the PSD's Nicolae Văcăroiu, with support from the ultra-nationalists, was installed. The administration survived a succession of parliamentary votes of confidence and strikes by key groups of workers, managing for the most part to avoid inflationary wage rises. The need for aid and a fear of international isolation kept the government on a seemingly reformist course. In 1992 Romania was granted Most Favoured Nation status by the US and Associate status by the EU; in 1993 it became the last Eastern Bloc state to join the Council of Europe, and in January 1994, it was the first to sign the Partnership for Peace.

Particularly welcome (and rewarded by substantial loans from the World Bank and IMF) was Iliescu's support for the tight fiscal policies of the National Bank's governor Mugur Isărescu, which halved inflation to 6 percent per month and allowed the leu to actually rise slightly against the dollar. The official exchange rate matched the black-market rate, and in 1995 taxes were cut to the lowest levels in Central or Eastern Europe.

The economy continued to improve, with unemployment falling and real wages rising 16 percent in 1995, but it wasn't enough to win Iliescu the 1996 general elections as a series of scandals alienated voters.

Constantinescu and the return of Iliescu

The 1996 election was won by the Democratic Convention of Romania (CDR), a coalition of four main parties and a dozen smaller ones. Emil Constantinescu, a professor of geology and former rector of Bucharest University, became president and appointed the youthful mayor of Bucharest, Victor Ciorbea, as prime minister. Their government was genuinely liberal-democratic and Western-oriented; its priorities were accelerated privatization, the slashing of the budget deficit and elimination of almost all price controls, introduction of a transparent tax system, and an attack on corruption, all with increased social protection. They soon found the coffers were empty due to Iliescu's attempts to buy re-election, and the result was the most radical "shock therapy" campaign anywhere in East Central Europe. In January 1997 alone, fuel and phone prices doubled, the cost of electricity rose five times, and rail fares rose by eighty percent, as subsidies were removed, so that real wages fell by twenty percent in that month; fuel prices rose by half again in February.

The King of Romania

In the early and mid-1990s, many people looked to **the King** for an escape from the intrigues of the politicians. **Mihai** was born in 1921 and reigned from 1940 to 1947; he earned his people's respect by his role in the coup of August 23, 1944, when he dismissed Antonescu, and by his attempts to resist communism thereafter. When forced to abdicate by the communists, he and his wife went into exile in England and then Switzerland. He was refused re-entry to his country, being expelled after twelve hours in 1990, until a brief visit in 1992, which drew large crowds. The situation changed totally with the election of Constantinescu; Mihai began to visit Romania frequently and in 2001 returned to live. From 1997 he was an active ambassador for Romanian entry to NATO and gained in stature, with even Iliescu calling him "Majesty" for the first time. Nevertheless, royalism has faded as a political force, although his daughter Princess Margarita is popular.

A castle at **Săvârşin** and the **Elisabeta Palace** in Bucharest have been restored to Mihai; the issue of Peleş has been more difficult, but in 2005 parliament voted to pay him €30m for the main castle while handing him Pelişor (which will remain open as a museum).

Ciorbea was unable to control the coalition members, notably the Liberals (PNL), soon corrupted by power, and the Democrats (PD), ruthlessly scheming for their own interests; he was forced to resign early in 1998 and was replaced first by **Radu Vasile**, who was better at politicking but less good at pushing ahead with reform, and then by the central bank governor **Mugur Isărescu**, who was keen to present an image of a stable country fit for NATO and EU membership. However, in 1999 an attempt by striking miners to march on Bucharest and overthrow the government only narrowly failed, and Constantinescu was widely seen to be in office but not in power. Increasingly, the government was perceived as failing to deliver, in particular in the war against corruption and in reforming and reviving the economy, and became particularly unpopular.

In the **general elections of 2000**, an angry electorate returned to power Iliescu and his Social Democratic Party (PSD; the latest incarnation of the FSN), with a huge vote for the ultra-nationalist Greater Romania Party (PRM); compared to their candidate, the rabid Corneliu Vadim Tudor, Iliescu suddenly seemed relatively benign to the West. **Adrian Năstase**, who had been successful as foreign minister, became prime minister of another coalition government, also supposedly committed to continuing the move towards a market economy and integration with the West; although various scandals led to resignations the government proved remarkably stable, and in 2002 the **EU** announced that Romania could join in 2007. By 2003 it was obvious that this was being pushed through, mainly due to Romania's strategic position close to the Middle East, but also for reasons of business (including the surprisingly favourable sales of the Sidex-Galaţi steelworks – accounting for 5 percent of GDP – to the Anglo/Indian Mittal company and of the car-maker Dacia to Renault). Romania also joined **NATO** in 2004. The PSD took the clear message that it only had to make a show of fighting corruption, and did all it could to entrench its position by patronage and abuse of power. By 2004 around 300 people closely tied to the PSD controlled approximately a quarter of Romania's economy; nevertheless, the EU decided the country had a functioning market economy, even as evidence to the contrary mounted.

Băsescu vs. Tariceanu – and the future

A new opposition alliance, **Justice and Truth** (DA), was formed in 2003 by the PNL and PD, and in November's general election won 31 percent of the vote, while the PSD and allies won 37 percent; however, there was widespread outrage at blatant vote-rigging and the run-off for the presidency was relatively clean. It was narrowly won by PD leader and mayor of Bucharest **Traian Băsescu**, who insisted the PSD had lost and asked PNL leader **Calin Popescu-Tariceanu** to become prime minister. He was able to form a coalition government, but not before the smaller parties had allowed the PSD to install its former prime ministers Adrian Năstase and Nicolae Văcăroiu as speakers of the House of Deputies and the Senate respectively. A lower flat rate of tax was swiftly introduced and many PSD figures were indicted on corruption charges; however, judicial reform (urgently required by the EU) was blocked by the Constitutional Court (which was stuffed with Iliescu's cronies).

In 2005 Dinu Patriciu, one of the richest men in Romania, was indicted for **corruption** in the privatization of the oil industry; his close friend the prime minister (himself very wealthy) was alleged to have phoned the Prosecutor-General to have the case dropped, causing a considerable scandal. In 2006 Năstase himself was charged with taking bribes, followed in early 2007 by Dan Voiculescu, leader of the Conservative Party, and several current and former ministers. The oligarchs, entrenched in all the major parties (and controlling the previously fairly free media), realized that Băsescu was the first Romanian leader to be serious about tackling corruption; once the country was safely in the European Union (which was promising up to €1.2 billion per year in badly supervised aid, perhaps €32 billion in all), on 1 January 2007, they forced the removal of Justice Minister Monica Macovei (widely praised as the only reason the EU finally decided to admit Romania) and then went for the president himself.

With president and prime minister now openly at war, the Liberal/Democratic alliance dead, and accusations of corruption flying on all sides, the PSD applied to the Constitutional Court for Băsescu's impeachment on grounds of abusing his office by interfering with cabinet government and criticizing the judiciary. The court ruled that he was guilty of minor infringements but nothing worthy of impeachment, to which PSD leader Mircea Geoana responded by accusing Băsescu of blackmailing the judges. In any case parliament voted by 322 to 108 the next day (just three and a half months after Romania joined the EU) to **suspend Băsescu** pending a referendum on his impeachment. **Nicolae Văcăroiu**, speaker of the Senate, became interim president, but it was generally assumed that Iliescu was still pulling the strings and this was his "second putsch" or his fourth term in office.

Efforts by Băsescu's opponents to fix the referendum rules failed, meaning that the president, by far the most popular politician in Romania, was always going to win, despite being largely banished from television. After a vicious campaign, on 19 May 2007 75 percent of those who voted (on a 44 percent turnout) voted **against impeachment**. Tariceanu and his government of course refused to resign, meaning that a very uncomfortable stand-off continued. The EU, meanwhile, was appalled by how thoroughly it had been hoodwinked, but despite talk of safeguard clauses there was little it could do – as Tariceanu plainly stated.

In June 2007 the European Commission decided merely to extend the monitoring period for legal reform and the anti-corruption campaign. Meanwhile, the justice minister was trying to sack the National Anti-Corruption Agency's deputy chief prosecutor for doing his job. There's no doubt that Băsescu, a bluff former sea captain, has often been tactless and impulsive, while the Eurocrats relate better to his suaver opponents, but he has widespread popular support. Parliament has very little credibility, with deputies jumping from party to party on a purely opportunistic basis and buying their place on a party's list with a view to profit. The constant infighting and fragmentation of Romania's political parties continues, with defectors from the PNL forming a **Liberal Democrat party**, and the Berlusconi-esque owner of the Steaua football club, **Gigi Becali**, forming the New Generation Party and at once becoming the country's second most popular politician. Until the EU makes a serious effort to convince the élite that it's in their best interests to comply with European standards, it's hard to see how things will improve. Even then, the tens of billions of euros already looted from the national economy are likely to persuade them to carry on as they are.

Romania's **economy** remains buoyant, helped by billions in Foreign Direct Investment and in earnings remitted by the million or so Romanians working in Western Europe. There's no doubt, however, that ongoing **extreme weather** – and the long-term effects of the country's recent disastrous floods (see p.451) – will take their economic toll.

Minorities and religions

While Wallachia and Moldavia are largely monocultural, Transylvania has always been pluralistic and multiethnic. Although there is a specifically Transylvanian culture and sensibility common to all the races living there, there are still those who seek to make political capital by setting one race against another. For visitors, meanwhile, this multi-ethnic mix is at the heart of Transylvania's charm. Since the end of communism the Magyar population has fallen by 15 percent and the Saxon population by 90 percent, due to emigration to Hungary and Germany, and around two million Romanians are working abroad, mainly in Italy and Spain.

For an overview of the history of the **Magyars** (Hungarians) and **Germans** in Romania, refer to the "History" section on p.431.

The Jews

Jews have been in Romania since Roman times, with more arriving in the eighth and ninth centuries after the collapse of the Jewish Khazar empire, and also in 1367 and in 1648 when they were expelled from Hungary and Poland. Most settled in Bessarabia and Bucovina, and prospered there; the community peaked around 1924, when it numbered 800,000. Romania was one of the few parts of the world where Jews were allowed to own land and form self-sufficient rural communities.

Although the Turks had treated Jews fairly, independent Romania increasingly regarded them as foreigners, and they began to emigrate, mostly to North America. In 1878, equal citizenship was forced on Romania by the great powers at the Congress of Berlin. The 1907 revolt was strongly anti-Semitic, and was followed by the rise of the Iron Guard and other nationalist parties; during **World War II**, the Jewish population was devastated (see box, p.439), leaving only 428,000 Jews in Romania by 1947.

In the new world of communism, the people were to be without ethnic distinction, and all national minorities' organizations were disbanded in 1953. However, Stalin was anti-Semitic and after the purging in 1952 of Romania's Jewish Foreign Minister, **Ana Pauker**, the climate turned against Romania's Jews again. Ceaușescu was happy to sell Jews to Israel for up to $3000 for each exit visa; at least 300,000 had left by 1989, and there remain fewer than 10,000 now.

The Gypsies

Gypsies, or Roma, left northern India in the tenth and eleventh centuries and arrived in Europe around 1407. Almost at once, many were enslaved, and in the sixteenth century came the first great period of **persecution**, a time of cruelty matched only by the Nazi Holocaust. In Wallachia and Moldavia, Gypsies were divided into two main groups, the nomadic **lăieţi** and the enslaved **vătraşi**. In 1837, the politician Mihail Kogălniceanu, who campaigned on their behalf, wrote: "On the streets of the Iaşi of my youth, I saw human beings wearing chains on their arms and legs, others with iron clamps around their foreheads, and still others with metal collars about their necks. Cruel beatings and other punishments such as starvation, being hung in the snow or the frozen river, such was the fate of the wretched Gypsy."

Wallachia and Moldavia **freed their Gypsies** between 1837 and 1856. Many stayed on with their owners as paid employees, while others emigrated, reaching Germany in the early 1860s, France in 1867, Britain and the Netherlands in 1868, and North America by 1881. At least 20,000 were deported to Transnistria by Antonescu's regime during World War II, and a higher proportion died then than in any other European country. The communist regime forced them to settle on the edges of villages, jailing them if they refused.

Today, Romania's Gypsies number between 550,000 and 2 million (of 8 million in Europe) – between 2 and 9 percent of the population – forming one of Europe's largest minorities. Economically speaking, more than sixty percent of those living in poverty in Romania are Roma. About 10 percent of them are still nomadic, spending the winter at permanent encampments. Meanwhile, around forty percent no longer speak Romany and barely consider themselves to be Roma – at the same time, there has been a rise in ethnic consciousness among those who do, and there are now five Romany newspapers.

Discrimination against Gypsies, seen as universal scapegoats, continues, although they still earn respect as **musicians**. They receive very little international aid, and bigotry, particularly in employment, has inevitably pushed many into crime. Perhaps more alarming is the great rise in **crime against Gypsies**, often condoned at a local level by authorities; indeed, police sometimes mount raids to beat up Gypsies at random for general intimidation.

Other minorities

Around 70,000 **Ukrainians** live in Maramureş and Bucovina, and 45,000 **Russians** (mostly Lipovani) in the Danube Delta, Dobrogea and Moldavia. Almost as many **Serbs** reside at the other end of the country, in the Banat, having fled from Turkish domination in the eighteenth and nineteenth centuries, and there are about 18,000 **Slovaks** in the same area, descendants of colonists brought into the region after the Turks had gone. Muslim descendants of the Turks and Tatars themselves still live on the Black Sea coast, around 23,000 of them, with 10,000 Bulgarians in the same area. In the thirteenth century, the **Armenian** diaspora reached Moldavia, and later moved on into Transylvania, settling in isolated but prosperous communities in towns such as Suceava, Brăila, Constanţa, Dumbrăveni, Gheorgheni and Gherla; they now number around 5000, almost totally assimilated, although their churches survive.

The **Aroumanians** are a group of ethnic Romanians who lived in Bulgaria and near Thessaloniki for many centuries as prosperous merchants with their own Romanian-language schools and culture; almost all returned to Romania between the World Wars, and they have virtually vanished as a recognizable culture, although their weaving (dark red geometrical patterns on a black background) can still be seen in museums.

Religion

The country's ethnic differences are reflected in its religions. The Romanian majority follows the **Romanian Orthodox** creed, which like the other Orthodox Churches is a hierarchical body not given to free thought or questioning dogma or authority. Under Ceauşescu, the Church did everything it was asked to, and positively discouraged dissidence. In Transylvania, and particularly in Maramureş, many Romanians follow the **Uniate** creed (see p.238), which was regarded by the communists as untrustworthy. Both churches are now resurgent.

The Hungarian population is divided more or less equally between the **Roman Catholic and Calvinist** (Reformat) faiths; the Calvinist Church was pretty much under the communist thumb, but the Catholic Church had the strength to resist and to keep its integrity. The Schwab and Landler Germans are also Roman Catholics, while the Saxons, Catholics when they arrived in Romania, later embraced the **Lutheran** faith, although a few are Seventh Day Adventists. In addition, about 75,000 Hungarians, mainly around Cluj, Turda and Odorheiu Secuiesc, are **Unitarian** (see p.238), and since 1989, the Baptists and newer evangelical churches have been making great gains, mostly among people who are disoriented by change and the loss of certainty and stability in society.

Wildlife and environmental issues

Thanks to its antiquated agriculture and extensive areas of untouched native forest and wetland, Romania is uniquely important for **wildlife** in Europe. While outside its borders the image of the country is of industrial pollution, the reality is that its landscapes are considerably less polluted than much of present-day Western Europe. As you climb up into the hills, you enter a world where pesticides and fertilizers have never been used and where meadows are full of an amazing variety of birds and wild flowers – a landscape representative of Europe two or three centuries ago.

That said, the country has suffered, and there are numerous **industrial plants** that cause immense damage in their immediate neighbourhood. While the bulk of the damage was inflicted during the communist period, some of the worst offenders, such as Copşa Mică's carbon-black plant and the Valea Călugărească fertilizer plant (east of Ploieşti), were built in the capitalist period, while the Reşiţa and Hunedoara steelworks and the Zlatna copper smelter date back to the eighteenth century.

With the end of communism, new problems have appeared, due mainly to the return of woodland to the families of the pre-communist owners and the subsequent felling of more than half a million hectares of forest. Coupled with extreme weather, this has led to disastrous **flooding and landslides**, made worse by the collapse of dams and dykes built on the cheap after corrupt deals. In 2005 floods caused more than a billion euros of damage, with at least seventy deaths. In January 2006 temperatures fell to -30°C, causing 45 deaths, while heatwaves killed 56 in 2005 and at least 35 in 2007, when temperatures were over 40°C nationwide, and up to 45°C in Bucharest.

Habitat

One third of Romania is mountain, largely forested, and this is where most of the more interesting flora and fauna are to be found. One third of the country is hill and plateau, with a fair quantity of woodland remaining, and one third is plain, mostly intensively farmed.

The **Carpathian mountains** form an arc sweeping south from Ukraine and around Transylvania to end on the Danube at the Iron Gates. At lower levels (up to around 800m) the natural vegetation is forest oak and hornbeam, lime (especially lower down) and ash. Romania still has impressive stretches of this kind of forest that has largely disappeared in other parts of Europe. This altitude is still too low for the large carnivores, though wolves may have started to repopulate some areas. Even the hill farmland at this height – largely grazing and hay meadows with small-scale plots of crops – is comparatively rich in wildlife, however, with an abundance of butterflies, and birds such as red-backed shrike. Above 800m, beech becomes increasingly common, and at around 1400m it forms an association with common silver fir and sycamore known as Carpathian Beech Forest (*Fagetum carpaticum*). Spruce is dominant above this, and above 1700m comes the lower alpine zone, characterized by dwarf pine, juniper and low-growing goat willow, and then, from 1900m upwards, the higher alpine zone of grass, creeping shrubs, lichen, moss and ultimately bare rock.

Elsewhere, particularly on the **Transylvanian plateau**, there is much more oak and beech forest, although large areas have been cleared for grazing and small-scale arable farming. Until the twentieth century, large areas of eastern Romania – particularly southern Moldavia and Dobrogea – were covered by grassy steppes, the western end of the immensely fertile Chernozem or "black earth" belt that stretches east for 4000km to Novosibirsk in Russia. The majority of this steppe went under the plough after World War II, though remnant areas can still be found, some (such as Cheia Dobrogea, 38km northwest of Constanța) protected as nature reserves.

In the **southwest** of the country, near the Iron Gates of the Danube, the spectacular Cerna Valley is notable for its more Mediterranean climate, with Turkey and downy oaks, Banat pine and sun-loving plant species on the limestone rocks of the Mehedinți, Cerna and Little Retezat massifs.

The **Danube Delta** is a unique habitat. Formed from the massive quantity of sediments brought down the river, it is Europe's most extensive wetland and the world's largest continuous reedbed. It is a uniquely important breeding area for birds, as well as a wintering area and a key stepping stone on one of the most important migration routes from northern Europe via the eastern Mediterranean to Africa.

Nature reserves have existed in Romania since the 1930s, and some 6.6 percent of the country is now protected. These reserves range from vast uninhabited areas to relatively modest, but still valuable, sites, including caves, rocks and even individual trees. The first National Park was created in 1935 in the Retezat mountains (for a few years treated by Ceaușescu as a private hunting reserve). The core area of the Danube Delta received similar protection at much the same time. The Retezat and Rodna mountains and the Danube Delta have been named as part of UNESCO's worldwide network of Biosphere Reserves, and at least ten other national parks are yet to be designated. These include the Bicaz and Nera gorges, the Cerna valley, and the Apuseni, Piatra Craiului and Căliman mountains.

Flora

The Romanian landscape has generally been less affected by man than that of Western Europe, and the richness of wild flowers is one result. In springtime, the **mountain meadows** of Romania are a riot of wild flowers, 12 percent of which are endemic to the Carpathians. The timing of this varies with the altitude, so that any time from April to July you should be able to find spectacular scenes of clover, hawkweed, burdock, fritillary and ox-eye daisy covered in butterflies and, at higher levels, gentians, white false helleborine, globeflower and crocus. **Alpine plants** include campanulas, saxifrage, orchids, alpine buttercup, pinks and, in a few places, edelweiss. The **hay meadows** lying below the areas of mountain forest are also extremely rich in flowers.

In the warmer **southwest** of the country, the Cerna and Nera gorges are especial suntraps, with rarities such as *Allium obliquum*, *Aconitum fissurae*, *Hieracium tordanum* and various species of *Dianthus*, while there are other rare varieties of *Hieracium* in the Retezat Scientific Reservation, and orchids, lilies and *Carduus* varieties on the limestone of the Little Retezat, as well as a number of rarities in Turda Gorge in the Apuseni. One of the most accessible flower-rich sites is the wonderful Zănoaga Gorge in the Bucegi mountains.

The **Danube Delta** is home to more than 1600 plant species, which fall into three main categories. The floating islets (*plaur*) that occupy much of the Delta's area are largely composed of reeds (80 percent *Phragmites australis*), with mace reed, sedge, Dutch rush, yellow water-flag, water fern, water dock, water forget-me-not, water hemlock and brook mint. In the still backwaters, wholly submerged waterweeds include water-milfoil, hornwort and water-thyme; while floating on the surface you'll find water plantain, arrowhead, duckweed, water soldier, white and yellow waterlily, frog bit, marsh thistle and épi d'eau. The river banks are home to white willow and poplar, with isolated strands of alder and ash, while the more mature forests of Letea and Caraorman also contain oaks, elm, aspen and shrubs such as blackthorn, hawthorn and dog rose. The Romanian peony can be found in woodlands such as Babadag Forest, just to the south.

Birds

Europe's most important wetland, the **Danube Delta**, serves as a breeding area for summer visitors, a stopping-off point for migrants and a wintering ground for wildfowl; permanent residents are relatively few. Dedicated birders time their visit to the area for two seasons – from the end of March to early June, and from late July to October – but the Delta and especially the more accessible lakes and reedbeds near the coast to the south are worth a visit with binoculars at any season. The Delta lies on the major migration route from east Africa via the Nile Delta, the eastern Mediterranean and the Bosphorus, northwards along the great river systems of Russia all the way to the Arctic.

The **spring period**, especially May, is an excellent time to visit, with the rare breeding species – black-winged pratincole, pygmy cormorant, glossy ibis, white and Dalmatian pelicans, and warblers including paddyfield warbler – all arriving. The reedbeds are alive with the returned songbirds, of which audibly the most obvious is the very noisy great reed warbler. These are accompanied by large numbers of waders still on passage to wetlands far to the north, such as the curlew sandpiper, broad-billed and marsh sandpipers and little stints, as well as more common species such as green, curlew and wood sandpipers and vast teeming flocks of ruff. By this time, the great colonies – of herons (night, grey and squacco herons, great white and little egrets), and of both species of cormorant – are at a peak of activity; the lower Danube holds most of the world population of the endangered pygmy cormorant, which is common in and near the Delta. The wader breeding colonies are also very active, and you will find yourself being scolded loudly when near the nests of avocets and black-winged stilts.

High summer is no less rich in birds, this being a good time to see the first of the returning waders and the population of summer visitors is at a peak in the period immediately after breeding. This is an excellent time to see formation-flying white pelicans (and the rare Dalmatian pelican), as well as birds of prey such as the colonial red-footed falcon, lesser spotted eagle, marsh harrier and long-legged buzzard.

In **winter**, the number of visiting birds in the Delta area is reduced but still impressive. Main visitors include most of the European population of great white herons (or egrets), at times the entire world population of red-breasted geese (around 70,000 birds) and hundreds of thousands (**rising** to a peak of around a third of a million) white-fronted geese; there are significant populations of other wildfowl including the exotic-looking red-crested pochard, as well as pintail, goldeneye, wigeon, teal, smew and red- and black-throated divers; just offshore the sea can teem with wintering black-necked grebes, and rough-legged buzzards are a common sight on roadside wires in open country.

On the **inland plains**, some species indicative of steppe country still persist, such as short-toed and calandra larks (the largest European lark), while summer visitors include the exotic-looking hoopoe, lesser-spotted and booted eagles, red-footed falcons, European rollers, bee-eaters and lesser grey shrikes – the last three often seen on roadside wires in Dobrogea and the lowlands.

Away from the Delta, the most worthwhile nature reserves are inevitably in the **mountains**; golden eagles are now rare, but ravens are common. On the tree line, black and three-toed woodpeckers can be found, together with ring ouzels in summer, while on the highest crags there are alpine accentors and wallcreepers, together with the common black redstart, water pipits and alpine swifts and, in some lower crags, crag martins and rock buntings. There are also birds usually associated with more northerly regions, such as shore larks and the rare dotterel (breeding only in the Cindrel mountains).

Mountain forests are home to the very shy capercaillie, as well as the (slightly easier to see) hazel grouse and (in the north, around dwarf pine areas) black grouse. Restricted to the vast forests, mainly of spruce, is the shy nutcracker, as well as the crested tit, willow tit and coal tit, and the crossbill. The forests are also home to raptors, including buzzards, honey buzzards, sparrowhawks and goshawks, as well as a number of owl species, including the Ural owl, eagle owl, pygmy owl and Tengmalm's owl. The relatively healthy state of Romania's conifer forests favours some birds that have declined elsewhere (for example in Scandinavia) due to mismanagement and a paucity of rotting wood – a prime example is the white-backed woodpecker.

The extensive **lowland deciduous forests** of Romania harbour huge numbers of common European woodland birds – chaffinches, hawfinches, nuthatches, song thrushes, treecreepers and great, marsh and blue tits. Oak woods in this area are the domain of the middle-spotted woodpecker, joined in summer by nightingales, wood warblers, chiffchaffs and common redstarts.

Romania is also a refuge for the white stork, whose large nests are characteristically built in the heart of human habitations, on telephone poles and chimneys. The much rarer black stork also occurs, breeding in extensive areas of forest near water, for example along the Olt in southern Transylvania.

Animals

Romania has the most important national populations of **large carnivore species** – bear, wolf and lynx – in Europe. Having been protected under Ceauşescu for his own personal hunting, there are now five or six thousand **brown bear** in Romania, particularly in the eastern Carpathians. Although they do raid garbage bins on the outskirts of Braşov and in Poiana Braşov – as well as almost all mountain huts that are near or below the tree line – they are generally afraid of humans and will keep well clear unless you come between a female and her cubs in April or May. Whilst they will take prey as large as red deer (not to mention sheep, cattle and horses), they are by diet omnivorous, famously raiding wild bees' nests not only for honey but also for the larvae. In addition to this they will eat carrion, especially wolf-kill, large amounts of wild fruit (occasionally raiding apple orchards in hill villages), wasps' nests, and beech mast in autumn. Bears are hunted, but in a strictly controlled way, and the population is at a healthy level.

There is currently a population of around two thousand **wolves** in Romania, generally restricted to forests. Although they do regularly take sheep in grazing areas, wolves represent no danger at all to mankind. Their prey consists almost entirely of red deer, roe deer, occasionally boar and chamois, and the odd sheep. They are hunted, especially in winter, when their tracks can be followed in the snow. **Lynx** are fairly widespread (but very hard to spot) in hill forests and are the most specialized large predator of all (bear and wolf are both happy to scavenge); they take roe deer in forest areas and chamois above the tree line.

Red deer can be found in some lowland forests but the species is most widespread in spruce forest in hill areas. The mating cries of the stags can be heard echoing through the valleys in September and October, and it's sometimes possible to observe their ritual conflicts from a distance. Above the tree line in the Transylvanian Alps and the Rodna, the most visible mammal is the **chamois**, which can be seen grazing in flocks with a lone male perched on the skyline to keep watch. **Wild boar** are also very widespread, being found in the lower forests (including the Delta), and all the way up to and beyond the tree line in the mountains. They appear mostly at night, and can leave a clearing looking as if it has been badly ploughed when they have finished digging for roots. Weighing up to 200kg, almost as much as a red deer stag, they have a reputation for aggression when protecting their young in the springtime.

Other mammals include the European bison, which is kept in a semi-wild state in several different areas; the golden jackal, which is spreading from its stronghold in the south, especially in Dobrogea; the wild cat, which occurs commonly in lowland forests as well as up to the highest forests in the mountains; the red fox, which is even more widespread, from the forests of the Delta to the very highest mountain summits; and the badger, which is widespread but very uncommon. There are three species of polecat, all of them very shy, and in the mountain forests pine martens are common, as are beech martens in woods at a lower altitude.

The Danube Delta is one of the last refuges of the European mink (which continues to thrive there), and also home to enot (or raccoon dog), coypu and muskrat, all North American species that have escaped from fur farms in the former Soviet Union. European beaver (a native mammal) has recently been reintroduced in Transylvania. Most of the predator species (in which Romania is so rich) depend to a large extent on various rodent species for their prey; in steppe areas it is impossible to miss the charming European souslik, Romania's very own gopher, found especially in Dobrogea. Three kinds of hamster occur, including the endemic Romanian hamster, and hikers in the Făgăraș, Retezat, Rodna and a few other areas will encounter the enchanting alpine marmot, living in colonies in the alpine zone, well above the tree line. In forest areas there are no fewer than four kinds of dormouse. Stoats and weasels are also widespread, as are bats.

The most frequently seen **amphibians** are the abundant little bombina toads: yellow-bellied toads in the hills and fire-bellied toads in the lowlands. More unusual amphibians include two species of spadefoot toad, the moor frog and the agile frog. The quite amazingly loud frog chorus of the Danube Delta and other lakes and reedbeds is formed by massed choirs of male marsh frogs. Newt fanciers find heaven in Romania's myriad ponds and watercourses; as well as the familiar warty, smooth and alpine newts there is the endemic Montandon's newt, restricted to the Eastern Carpathians. Fire salamanders with their vivid black and orange colouring are easily seen when wandering in the woods during or just after rain, while the exotic-looking green toad (with its trilling call) is frequently seen under village street lights in all areas as it hunts for bugs that are attracted by the light.

There is a healthy population of **snakes** – the commonest being the grass snake, found in the Danube Delta and up to some altitude in the mountains. In coastal areas is the more aquatic, fish-hunting dice snake; other non-venomous species include the smooth snake, four-lined snake and the impressively large whip snake. Europe's most venomous and fastest-moving snake, the horned viper, occurs near Băile Herculane, and the common viper (or adder) is more widespread, tending to be found in hill areas. The steppe viper (or Orsini's viper) survives in the Delta, for example in the woods north of Sfântu Gheorghe.

The warmer climate of the southern Banat and Dobrogea is especially suitable for **other reptiles** – not just snakes but also some fairly exotic-looking lizards, such as the Balkan green lizard, the green lizard and the Balkan wall lizard. More everyday lizard species, such as the sand lizard and viviparous lizard, are widespread. The aquatic European pond terrapin is common around the edge of lowland lakes and in the Danube Delta, and there are two species of tortoise: the rare Hermann's tortoise, found only in areas of the southwest such as the Cerna valley, and the more widespread spur-thighed tortoise, fairly common in woods in Dobrogea.

With little in the way of industry and an absence of fertilizers and pesticides in almost all hill areas, the river systems have impressive populations of **fish**. Grayling, for example, is much less rare in Carpathian hill streams than it has become in other areas of Europe. Six species of sturgeon occur in the Danube, and the picture for these is less rosy, the Iron Gates dam preventing the migration upstream of several species, with resulting hybridization. Rainbow trout have been less widely introduced than in western Europe, meaning that the native brown trout is much more common; the endemic Danube salmon or huchen is now very rare.

It is scarcely possible to avoid fish when in the Danube Delta; the common species caught are common carp, crucian carp, pike (especially in autumn), pike-perch or zander, and catfish or wels. In fact, the Delta is a remarkable place for fish, with catfish around 2m long being regularly caught and confirmed accounts of even larger specimens showing some interest in taking village women fetching water from channel banks. Sturgeon migrate through the Delta, as do Danube mackerel. Several fairly rare goby species also occur, especially in lakes and lagoons south of the Delta. Most of these species have declined to some extent due to pollution, over-fishing and eutrophication of the water due to algal blooms. For this reason, several areas of the Delta that are free from these problems have become strictly protected reserves, with great efforts made to preserve the water quality.

James Roberts, a true friend of Romania, who died far too young in 2002

The environment

Communist Romania's mammoth increase in industrial output – particularly of steel and fertilizer – was achieved by a total disregard for any considerations other than maximizing production. Thus, industrial injuries are commonplace, while **energy consumption** is shockingly wasteful; **pollution** is calculated to affect 10 percent of the population (5 percent severely), and 20 percent of the country's territory. **Rubbish**, too, is a developing problem, as Western-style packaging takes over.

The most polluted sites are Copşa Mică, Zlatna and Baia Mare, where smelters produced acid rain and a cocktail of heavy metals that ran straight into the water system; life expectancy remains up to ten years below average in all three places. In **Baia Mare**, for example, the industrial zone was built upwind of the residential area, and in a valley subject to thermal inversions that trap the pollution. Almost as bad were the artificial fibre factories of **Brăila** and **Suceava**, rivalled by fertilizer and petrochemical plants in Arad, Dej, Făgăraş, Piteşti, Ploieşti and Târgu Mureş. Emissions fell by half after 1989, due to industrial recession; nowadays, while both air and water are far cleaner than they were, emissions are rising again, due to increasing prosperity. It will cost between €20 billion and €30 billion over the next two decades to bring Romania upto EU standards.

Additionally, the use of **fertilizers**, **pesticides** and **insecticides** has caused problems, damaging 900,000 hectares of agricultural land and leaving 200,000 hectares totally unproductive; agricultural nitrates, too, entered the drinking water supply, putting millions of people at risk, and many of the country's rivers are now dead. Although fertilizer use has halved since 1989, this is due to cost rather than environmental awareness, and ecological disasters continue to occur. In January 2000, a dam at the Aurul goldmine near Baia Mare gave way, releasing water containing a hundred tonnes of cyanide, which made its way into Hungary, killing everything in the Someş and Tisa rivers – the situation wasn't helped when the chairman of Aurul's Australian owners claimed the fish had died of cold. In March that year, there was also a spill of of sludge contaminated with heavy metals from a mine at Baia Borşa, which also made its way into the Tisa, precipitating demands for international efforts to clean up Romania's mines.

Furthermore, the damming of the Iron Gates and the dyking of the Danube flood plain has led to the **Danube's flow** through the Delta being reduced dramatically, leading to algal blooms and lower fish yields; unless water flows can be sped up, the Delta may die. The Black Sea is one of the most polluted areas in the world – toxic wastes, over-fishing, and a one-fifth fall in freshwater inputs combining to disastrous effect. Surfeits of nutrients cause plankton blooms (red tides), leading to loss of light and dissolved oxygen, and thus decimating fish stocks.

For a brief period, Ceauşescu did take an interest in pollution problems, passing several environmental protection laws, but as he became more obsessed with expanding industrial capacity, environmental data became increasingly secret. After the revolution, a new **ministry** was created, with the aim of reducing pollution; two ecological parties were set up, and there's now an Environmental Protection Agency in each county.

Ceauşescu was also determined to have his own **nuclear power station** at Cernavodă, on the Danube. However, construction standards were so appalling that it had to be almost totally rebuilt. The second reactor entered service in 2007, and the complex now produces eighteen percent of Romania's power. Thirty percent of power comes from hydroelectric dams, a wind power project is to be developed in Constanţa harbour, and the Austrian government is sponsoring a scheme in Călimăneşti to provide domestic hot water from geothermal energy.

The protection of **historical monuments** was upheld until 1977, when the Historical Monuments Administration was disbanded for daring to oppose Ceauşescu's plans for Bucharest's Civic Centre. There was no effective protection from then until 1989, and many towns have simply been gutted. In 1990, the bureau was re-established but without financial support, and the required legislation got stuck in parliament. In 2001, a law was at last passed to end the demolition of listed buildings, but most conservation to date has been achieved with funding from the Church, or, in the case of Saxon monuments, from Germany. **Biertan**, the **Bucovina** and **Horez monasteries**, and a group of wooden **Maramureş churches** have all become UNESCO World Heritage sites.

Music

T
he Carpathian mountains trace a cultural fault line across Romania that separates Central Europe from the Balkans, sharply dividing the musical styles on either side. Of course such borders are rarely impermeable; the same language is spoken on either side and there is plenty of cultural and musical cross-fertilization. The many strands of Romanian music are extraordinarily varied and archaic, preserving almost archeological layers of development, from the "medieval" music at the extremities in Ghimeş and Maramureş, to the "Renaissance" sounds of Mezőség and the more sophisticated music of Kalotaszeg.

Tours to study Romanian folk dance are organized by the Doina Foundation, Aarhuispad 22, 3067 PR Rotterdam, Netherlands (☎10/421 8622, 📧 stichting .doina@hetnet.nl), which also helps organize an annual Balkan festival in Zetten and sells flutes, boots, costumes and icons.

Transylvania

With its age-old ethnic mix, Transylvania's music is extraordinary, with wild melodies and dances that are played all night. While it is recognizably part of a

---

Classical music

Classical music was lavishly funded by the communist state and still has far less elitist connotations than in the West. Main cities have a philharmonic orchestra and/ or an opera house, and tickets (available through the local Agenţia Teatrale) are very cheap. Additionally, the Saxon communities have maintained a Germanic tradition of singing chorales by Bach and his contemporaries.

Romanian classical music remains virtually synonymous with **George Enescu**, born near Dorohoi in 1881. His *Romanian Rhapsodies* were first performed in 1903 and remain his most popular works; his *Third Violin Sonata* is his best chamber work and also has a Romanian flavour. Later works also showed experimental features, such as the use of a musical saw in his masterpiece, the opera *Oedipe*, the most comprehensive treatment of the myth, covering Oedipus's entire life from birth to death. There is a good modern recording (1989) featuring José van Dam. Romania's greatest pianist was **Dinu Lipatti** (Enescu's godson), who died aged just 33 from leukaemia in 1950. In his lifetime he was referred to as "God's chosen instrument". His recordings (just five CDs) have never been deleted; one of them, made in Besançon just months before his death, is particularly highly regarded. **Sergiu Ceili-bidache** (1912–96) studied in Berlin and conducted the Berlin Philharmonic, the Swedish Radio Symphony Orchestra, the Stuttgart Radio Orchestra, and from 1980 the Munich Philharmonic, making his US debut only in 1984. Described as "transcendentally endowed", although not very interested in music outside the mainstream Germanic repertoire, he was also a perfectionist, demanding up to eighteen rehearsals for some concerts.

The most prominent **contemporary Romanian musicians** are soprano **Angela Gheorghiu** (born in 1965) – a true diva and regular performer at the world's greatest opera houses – and violinist Alex Bălanescu, founder of the **Bălanescu Quartet**, who has worked with David Byrne, Kraftwerk, Spiritualized, Gavin Bryars and Michael Nyman amongst others.

Central European tradition, it also springs from a distinctly Transylvanian culture – the composers Bartók and Kodály found this the most fertile area for their folk-song collecting trips in the early twentieth century. Music serves a social function, and in some areas there are still regular weekly dances, but everywhere, music is played around Christmas, at weddings, sometimes at funerals and at other occasions, including when conscripts go off to the army.

The **Romanians** and **Hungarians** share many melodies and dances and it takes a very experienced ear to tell the difference (and even then, a tune may be described as Hungarian in one village and Romanian in another just over the hill). Romanian dances may have a slightly less regular rhythm than the Hungarian, but often the only difference between one tune and another is the language in which it is sung. There's even a unique recording of an old man from the village of Dimbău (Küküllődombó) singing a song with the first half of each line in Hungarian and the second half in Romanian.

The music of Transylvania sounds much less Balkan than that from over the Carpathians. The traditional ensemble is a **string trio** – a violin, viola (*contra*) and a double bass, plus in certain parts of Transylvania, a cimbalom. The *primás*, the first violinist, plays the melody and leads the musicians from one tune into another, while the *contra* and bass are the accompaniment and rhythm sections of the band. The *contra* has just three strings and a flat bridge so it only plays chords, and it's the deep sawing of the bass and the rhythmic spring of the *contra* that gives Transylvanian music its particular sound. Often an extra violin or *contra* is added to give more volume.

Wedding parties

Wedding parties last a couple of days and often take place in a specially constructed wedding "tent" built from wooden beams and tree fronds. The place is strung with ribbons and fir branches, tables are piled high with garish cakes and bottles of *ţuică*, and fresh courses are brought around at regular intervals. There's a space for dancing and a platform where the band of

▲ Wedding band

musicians saw and scrape away at battered old fiddles, with a bass making the most mesmerizing sound.

Wedding **customs** vary slightly from region to region but generally the band starts things off at the bride's or groom's house, accompanying the processions to the church and possibly playing for one of the real emotional high spots – the bride's farewell song (*cântecul miresei*) to her family and friends, and to her maiden life. While the marriage takes place within the church, the band plays for the young people, or those not invited to the feast, to dance in the street outside. Once the couple come out of the church there's another procession to the wedding feast – either in the village hall or the wedding "tent" – where the musicians will play all night, alternating songs to accompany the feast with dances; there are even particular pieces for certain courses of the banquet.

Late in the evening comes the bride's dance (*jocul miresei*) when, in some villages, the guests dance with the bride in turn and offer money. Things usually wind down by dawn on Sunday; people wander off home or collapse in a field somewhere, and then around lunchtime the music starts up again for another session until late in the evening.

With the trend towards larger and larger weddings, all sorts of **instruments** have started to find their way into bands. Most common is the piano-accordion, which, like the *contra*, plays chords, though it lacks its rhythmic spring. Very often you can hear a clarinet or the slightly deeper and reedier *taragot*, which sounds wonderful in the open air. Unfortunately, with the increasing move of young people to work in towns, they often demand the guitars, drums and electric keyboards of urban groups – along with appalling amplification, which is increasingly brought in, too, by traditional acoustic bands. Groups that stick unswervingly to the traditional line-up include the marvellous **Pălatca** band, recognized as one of the finest in Transylvania.

Gypsy bands

The band from Pălatca (Magyarpalatka), like most of the village musicians in Romania, are **Gypsies**. In the villages, Gypsy communities all tend to live along one particular street in the outskirts, often called Strada Muzicanţilor or Strada Lăutari – both meaning "Musicians' Street". Gypsy musicians will play for Romanian, Hungarian and Gypsy weddings alike and they know almost instinctively the repertoire required. Children often play alongside their parents from an early age and grow up with the music in their blood.

Playing music can earn good money; the best bands command handsome fees, plus the odd chicken and bottles of *ţuică*. It's also an indication of the value of music in this society that the musicians are not only well rewarded but also well respected. When the old *primás* of the Pălatca band died, all the people he had played for in the village came to pay their respects at his funeral.

It's difficult to highlight the **best bands** – there are dozens of them – but in addition to the Pălatca band, those of the following villages of central Transylvania are excellent (the names are given in their Romanian form with the Hungarian in brackets): Vaida-Cămăraş (Vajdakamarás), Suatu (Magyarszovát), Sopuru de Câmpie (Mezőszopor), Sângeorz-Băi (Oláhszentgyőrgy) and Sic (Szék), an almost totally Hungarian village and one of the great treasure houses of Hungarian music.

For many, however, at least those outside Romania, Gypsy music is synonymous with two bands in particular, both of which have gone on to achieve world acclaim. The **Taraf de Haidouks**, from the village of Clejani near Bucharest, were formed in 1989 just prior to the demise of Ceauşescu. The line-up is fairly fluid, though it usually comprises at least seven or eight members at any one time, incorporating violins, flutes, double bass and cimbalom. Their recordings are extraordinary, packed full of truly virtuoso performances, while their live shows – they tour relentlessly throughout Europe – are fantastically entertaining. **Fanfare Ciocărlia**, from the tiny village of Zece Prăjini in Moldavia, is one of the finest Gypsy brass bands in the Balkans; a twelve-piece ensemble, featuring tenor and baritone horns, trumpet, tubas, clarinets, saxophones and bass drum; their extremely fast, high-energy sound is thrilling live.

The Hungarians

The music of the Hungarian minority has made most impact outside of Transylvania, as the Hungarians consciously promoted the culture of their brethren in the region to highlight their suffering under Ceauşescu. Hungaroton, the state label, produced a large number of excellent recordings, while Budapest-based groups such as **Muzsikás** and the **Ardealul Ensemble** have toured extensively and acted as ambassadors for the music.

Transylvania has always held a very special place in Hungarian culture as it preserves archaic traditions and medieval settlement patterns that have disappeared in Hungary itself. Under Ceauşescu's rule, the Hungarians were threatened, and there was a deliberate effort to wear their traditional costumes, sing their songs and play their music as a statement of identity, even protest. These days, national costume and dances are much more visible among the Hungarian minority than the majority Romanians (other than in Maramureş).

Regional styles

Within the overall Transylvanian musical language, there are hundreds of local dialects: the style of playing a particular dance can vary literally from village to village. But there are some broad musical regions where the styles are distinct and recognizable.

Bartók gathered much of his Romanian material in the area around **Hunedoara**. The area is still musically very rich, though, strangely enough, a recent musical survey found that virtually the entire repertoire had changed. Further north is the area the Hungarians call **Kalotaszeg**, home to some of the most beautiful music in the region. This area lies along the main route from Cluj (Kolozsvár) to Hungary and Central Europe, and the influence of Western-style harmony shows itself in the sophisticated minor-key accompaniment – a development of the last twenty years. Kalotaszeg is famous for its men's dance, the *legényes*, and the slow *hajnali* songs performed in the early morning as a wedding feast dies down, which have a sad and melancholy character all their own. One of the best of all recordings of Transylvanian music includes both these forms, featuring the Gypsy *primás* **Sándor Fodor** from the village of Baciu (Kisbács), just west of Cluj. There is also some fine Romanian music in **Sălaj county**, in the north of this area, which can be heard in the villages or on a very fine Romanian recording of dances from Sălaj (*Jocuri Sălajene*) by a small ensemble from Zalău.

Probably the richest area for music is known to the Romanians as **Câmpia Transilvanei** and to the Hungarians as **Mezőség**. This is the Transylvanian Heath, north and east of Cluj – a poor, isolated region whose music preserves a much more primitive feel with strong major chords moving in idiosyncratic harmony.

Further east is the most densely populated Hungarian region, the **Székelyföld** (Székely Land). The Székelys, who speak a distinctive dialect of Hungarian, were the defenders of the eastern flanks of the Hungarian kingdom in the Middle Ages, when the Romanians, as landless peasants, counted for little.

Rising up towards the Carpathians, their land becomes increasingly wild and mountainous, and the dance music is different once again, with eccentric ornamentation and very often a cimbalom in the band.

For Hungarian-speakers, the songs are fascinating as they preserve old-style elements that survive nowhere else. One village ballad about a terrible massacre of the Székelys by the Habsburgs in 1764 (see p.215), often sung as if it had happened yesterday, recounts their flight over the Carpathians into Moldavia, where they preserved music and customs that are no longer found in the Székelyföld itself. During World War II, 14,000 Székelys were resettled in the south of Hungary. In those outer reaches, the string bands of Transylvania have given way to a solo violin or flute accompanying the dances.

Moldavia and Maramureş

The music of Moldavia – with its archaic pipe and drum style – sounds wild and otherworldly, split across the divide between Transylvania and the Balkans. Hungarian records of the Csángós (the Hungarian occupants of this area) often feature music from the Ghimeş (Gyimes) valley, where you find peculiar duos of violin and *gardon* – a sort of double bass played by hitting its strings with a stick. The fiddle playing is highly ornamented and the rhythms complex and irregular, showing Oriental influence. The extraordinary Csángó singer **Ilona Nyisztor** from Oneşti (in Bacău county) has a growing reputation.

On the other side of Transylvania, sandwiched between Hungary, Ukraine and the Carpathians, are the regions of **Maramureş** and **Oaş**, both areas of distinctive regional character. Village costumes are worn for everyday life and the music includes magic songs and spells of incantation against sickness and the evil eye. You can still find Sunday-afternoon village dances, and a *băută* or musical party can be arranged on the slightest pretext. From birth, through courtship and marriage to death, life has a musical accompaniment.

The music of Maramureş, while recognizably Transylvanian, sounds closer to that of Romanians beyond the Carpathians. As often happens in the highland regions of Romania, here the music is played predominantly by Romanians, not Gypsies. With an instrumental group of violin (*ceteră*), guitar (*zongoră*) and drum (*dobă*), it has a fairly primitive sound, lacking beguiling harmonies and with a repeated chord on the *zongoră* (often played vertically and back to front) as a drone. Hundreds of years ago, much of the music of Europe probably sounded something like this. A *zăcală de băut* or drinking song is an instrumental piece during which people call out improvised couplets, usually men teasing women and vice versa; a *zăcală de jucat* is a dance, of which the most popular are the *bărbătesc* (men's dance), a circle dance for men with similar improvised lyrics, and the *învârtita*, a quick couple dance.

Wallachia

Most village bands in **Wallachia** comprise **Gypsies**: the group is generally named **Taraf** followed by their village name. These musicians (*lăutari*) are professionals who play a vital function in village life, yet their music sounds altogether different from that of their Transylvanian counterparts. The word *taraf* comes from the Arabic and suggests the more Oriental flavour of this music. Songs are often preceded by an instrumental improvisation called *taksim*, another name borrowed from the Middle East.

The lead instrument is the fiddle, played in a highly ornamented style. The middle parts are taken by the *ţambal* (cimbalom), which fills out the harmony and adds a rippling to the texture. At the bottom is the double bass, ferociously plucked rather than bowed Transylvanian style. In the old days, you'd always find a *cobză* (lute) in such bands, but it has given way to the *ţambal*, guitar and accordion. The staple dances are the *horă*, *sârbă* and *brâu* – all of which are danced in a circle.

In Romanian, the word *cânta* means both "to sing" and "to play an instrument", and the *lăutari* of Wallachia usually do both. Whereas in Transylvania the bands play exclusively dance music, the musicians in the south of the country have an impressive repertoire of **epic songs and ballads** that they are called on to perform. These might be specific marriage songs or legendary tales like *Şarpele* (*The Snake*) or exploits of brigands. One of the tunes you hear played by *lăutari* all over Romania is *Ciocârlia* (*The Lark*), which has also become a concert piece for the stage ensembles.

The region's most renowned Gypsy music comes from **Clejani**, a ramshackle village a short way southwest of Bucharest (see p.101); many of its five hundred or so Gypsies are professional musicians, much in demand throughout the area, and it's also where the Taraf de Haidouks hail from.

The doină

The **doină** is a free-form, semi-improvised ancient song tradition. With poetic texts of grief, bitterness, separation and longing, it might be called the Romanian blues. Very often, different texts are sung to the same melody, which may then take on a contrasting character. It is essentially private music, sung to oneself at moments of grief or reflection, although nowadays the songs are often performed by professional singers or in instrumental versions by Gypsy bands. Old *doinăs* of the traditional kind can still be found in Oltenia, between the Olt and Danube rivers in the south of the country.

Flutes and pipes

The pastoral way of life is fast disappearing in Romania, and with it the traditional instrumental repertoire of the *fluier* (shepherd's flute). But there is one form – a sort of folk tone poem – that is still regularly played all over the

Easy Listening?

For many, unfortunately, Romanian pop is exemplified by The Cheeky Girls – twins from Cluj who became famous (or rather, infamous) thanks to their performance on a UK reality show and subsequent release of a string of terribly naff records. Indeed, Romania's **pop** speciality is **musică uşoră** or easy music, dreadful stuff out of a 1970s' timewarp, but immensely popular, celebrated at big summer **festivals** in Mamaia (July–Aug) and Braşov (Aug/Sept). It's a mystery that Romania didn't regularly sweep the board at the Eurovision Song Contest. You can also hear slightly more interesting music, influenced by **hip-hop**, **reggae** and **Latin rhythms**, but still with utterly banal feelgood lyrics. Although **jazz** doesn't have a great following in Romania, there are an increasing number of clubs in the bigger cities, in addition to a handful of jazz festivals, by far the best of which is in Sibiu.

country: the **shepherd who lost his sheep**. Referred to as early as the sixteenth century by the Hungarian poet Bálint Balassi, it begins with a sad, *doină*-like tune as the shepherd laments his lost flock. Then he sees his sheep in the distance and a merry dance tune takes over, only to return to the sad lament when he realizes it's just a group of stones. Finally the sheep are found and the whole thing ends with a lively dance in celebration.

For years, Romania's best-known musician on the international stage was **Gheorghe Zamfir**, composer of the movie soundtrack for *Picnic at Hanging Rock*. He plays *nai*, or **pan-pipes**, which have existed in Romania since ancient times. In the eighteenth century "Wallachian" musicians were renowned abroad and the typical ensemble consisted of violin, *nai* and *cobză*. But by the end of the next century, the *nai* had begun to disappear and after World War I only a handful of players were left. One of these was the legendary **Fanica Luca** (1894–1968), who taught Zamfir his traditional repertoire. Nowadays, Zamfir plays material from all over the place, often accompanied by the organ of Marcel Cellier; **Radu Simion** is another fine player.

The Banat

The **Banat**, Romania's western corner, is ethnically very mixed, with communities of Hungarians, Serbs, Slovaks, Germans and Gypsies living alongside the Romanians. Its music is fast, furious and relatively new, having absorbed a lot from the *novokomponovana* music of neighbouring Serbia. It's extremely popular, played all the time on the national radio and by Gypsy bands everywhere. Probably its attraction is its fast, modern, urban sound, with saxophones and frequently erotic lyrics. The Silex recording of the Taraf de Carancebeş (sic) is a great introduction to this virtuoso style.

The Ceauşescu legacy

Nicolae Ceauşescu's legacy even extends to some of the country's folk music, which was manipulated into a sort of "fakelore" to glorify the dictator and present the rich past of the Romanian peasantry. Huge sanitized displays called **Cântarea Romaniei** (Song of Romania) were held in regional centres around the country with thousands of peasants dressed up in costume bussed out to picturesque hillsides to sing and dance. This was shown on television every Sunday (indeed, programmes of this kind are still used to fill the odd half-hour gap in the TV schedule). The words of songs were often changed – removing anything deemed to be religious or that questioned the peasants' love of their labours, and replacing it with bland patriotic sentiments or hymns to peace.

This gave folklore a pretty bad name among the educated classes, though the peasants were hardly bothered by it. They just did what they were told for Cântarea Romaniei and got on with their real music in the villages. The fact is that traditional music still flourishes throughout Romania – probably more than anywhere else in Europe – not thanks to Ceauşescu, but despite him.

Discography

Many of these recordings can be bought from Passion Music in the UK (☎01256/770 747; Ⓦwww.passiondiscs.co.uk); see also Ⓦwww.hungaroton.hu, Ⓦwww.fono.hu, Ⓦwww.etnofon.hu, Ⓦwww.crammed.be and Ⓦwww.cdroots .com. You can hear selections of Romanian music at Ⓦwww.bbc.co.uk/radio3 /world/guideromania.shtml.

General compilations

Romania: Musical Travelogue (Auvidis/Silex, France). An excellent disc with music from the Banat, Maramureş and Wallachia, including good music by ethnic minorities and beautiful *cobză* playing by Dan Voinicu.

Romania: Wild Sounds from Transylvania, Wallachia & Moldavia (World Network,

Germany). The best overall anthology of Romanian music, with great ensembles including the Taraf de Haidouks and the Moldavian Fanfare Ciocărlia.

Village Music from Romania (AIMP/VDE-Gallo, Switzerland). A three-disc box of archival recordings of specialized interest made by the musicologist Constantin Brailoiu.

Transylvanian music

Romanian, Hungarian and Gypsy village bands, as well as *táncház* groups from Budapest.

Ardealul Ensemble *Gypsy Music From Transylvania* (Ethnophonie, Romania). Instrumental music led by Emil Mihaiu, currently considered the best fiddler in Transylvania, with two Hungarian-speaking Roma. Excellent notes. Also Emil Mihaiu Ensemble, *Romanian and Hungarian Music from Transylvania* (Ethnophonie).

Budatelke Band *Budatelke/ Szászszentgyörgy* (Fonó, Hungary). The village band of Budatelke in northern Mezoség, playing mainly Romanian repertoire plus Hungarian, Gypsy and Saxon tracks.

Sándor Fodor *Hungarian Folk Music from Transylvania* (Hungaroton, Hungary). From the most respected Gypsy fiddler of the Kalotaszeg region, the energy and bite of this compelling disc of both Hungarian and Romanian music are fantastic. One of the essential Transylvanian

records. Also *The Blues at Dawn* (Fonó, Hungary), a beautifully produced CD of the slow, melancholy *hajnali* (morning songs).

Béla Halmos *Aza szép piros hajnal* (Hungaroton, Hungary). One of the leading musicians of the Budapest *táncház* scene with a selection of music from various regions of Transylvania.

The Mácsingó Family *Báré – Magyarpalatka* (Fonó, Hungary). One of the important musical Gypsy families from the villages of Báré and Déva in central Transylvania. This may be too raw for some tastes – the bass saws, grates and often slides onto its notes and the lead fiddle is heavily ornamented, drawing energy and emotion out of every note – but it is the real thing.

Sandor Mate and band *Most jöttem Gyuláról, Gyulafehérvárról* (Periferic, Hungary). Some of the best Kolozsvár (Cluj) musicians playing instrumental tunes from the Szamos-Maros region.

Muzsikás *Máramaros* (Hannibal/Ryko, UK). A fascinating CD from the top Hungarian *táncház* group joined by two veteran Gypsy musicians on fiddle and cimbalom to explore the lost Jewish repertory of Transylvania, distinguishable by the Oriental-sounding augmented intervals in the melody. Also *Blues for Transylvania* and *Morning Star*, fine selections of Hungarian music from Transylvania, and *The Bartók Album*, re-creating the music collected by Bartók (all Hannibal/Ryko, UK).

Ökrös Ensemble *Transylvanian Portraits* (Koch, US). Comprehensive guide to the various styles of Transylvania by one of the best Budapest *táncház* groups. The fiddle-playing of Csaba Ökrös on the last track is stunning.

Palatca Band *Magyarpalatka – Hungarian Folk Music from the Transylvanian Heath* (Hungaroton, Hungary). Probably the most celebrated band of central Transylvania, led by members of the Codoba family in the village of Magyarpalatka and typically comprising two fiddles, two contras and bass. A beautiful selection of traditional dance sets – one CD from the archives, the other by currently active musicians.

Katalin Szvorák, Márton Balogh, Márta Sebestyén and the Hegedos Ensemble *Tündérkert (Fairyland) – Hungarian and Romanian Folk Music from Transylvania* (Hungaroton, Hungary). Released in 1988 and something of a classic, a cross-section of the music to be heard in the various regions of Transylvania.

Szászcsávás Band *Folk Music from Transylvania* (Quintana/Harmonia Mundi, France). Szászcsávás (Ceuaş in Romanian) is a predominantly Hungarian village in the Kis-Küküllő region with one of the best Gypsy bands in the area. This is a great recording of a real village band with a wide dance repertoire, including Hungarian, Romanian, Saxon and Gypsy tunes.

Taraful Soporu de Cîmpie (Buda/ Musique du Monde, France). Another fine Gypsy band from Soporu in the Câmpia Transilvaniei. Several sets of dance tunes and songs sung by Vasile Soporan.

Váralmási Band *Váralmási Pici Aladárés Bandája* (Fonó, Budapest). One of the last old-time groups of the Kalotaszeg region, whose *primás* (leader) died shortly after the recording in 1997. Includes a bizarre Jewish tango.

Various *Magyarszovát – Búza* (Fonó, Hungary). A double CD of Hungarian music performed by musicians and singers from two villages in Mezőség; dance sets and many unaccompanied songs which are, perhaps, more of an acquired taste.

Various *Musiques de Transylvanie* (Fonti Musicale, Belgium). One of the best introductions to Transylvanian music, featuring a mainly Hungarian repertoire from Kalotaszeg, Mezőség and Ghimeş plus Romanian dances from Bihor and Moldavia.

Various *Romania – Music for Strings from Transylvania* (Chant du Monde, France). A great collection of dance music played by village bands from the Câmpia Transilvaniei, Maramureş and Oaş. Excellent notes and photos, too.

Various *Visa – Traditional Hungarian Music from the Transylvanian Heath* (Fonó, Hungary). From the Zoltán Kallós Archive, recordings from 1964–65 and 1987, made in the Mezőség village of Visa.

Various *La Vraie Tradition de Transylvanie* (Ocora, France). A pioneering disc from the 1970s that highlighted real peasant music from Maramureş and Transylvania when sanitized folklore was prevalent. It features some excellent ensembles, bagpipes and a violin with a horn, and from Maramureş there's a track from Gheorghe Covaci, son of a fiddler recorded by Bartók in 1913.

Hungarian music from Ghimeş and Moldavia

Mihály Halmágyi *Hungarian Music from Gyimes* (Hungaroton, Hungary). Halmágyi is a veteran Csángó violin player from Ghimeş who plays a five-stringed fiddle, producing strange and wild music. A great performance of "the shepherd and his lost sheep", with running commentary.

Ilona Nyisztor *To The Fat Of The Earth, To The Sun's Little Sister* (Fonó, Hungary), *The Little Bird Has Gone Away* and *Pusztinai Nagy Hegy Alatt – Csángó Hungarian Songs from Moldavia* (both Etnofon, Hungary). Ilona Nyisztor sings Csángó songs handed down from her mother, grandparents and great-grandparents.

Various *Giving You Golden Rod – Traditional Ballads from Moldova* (Fonó, Hungary). A two-CD set from the extensive folk music collection of Zoltán Kallós.

Various *Moldavia Csángómagyar "Síposok" – Csango-Hungarian Bagpipers of Moldavia* (Fonó, Hungary). Field recordings (1973–2001) of the unearthly Csángó bagpipe music.

Zerkula Janos *Zerkula Janos keservesei – Zerkula Janos's Laments* (Fonó, Hungary). Janos Zerkula and his wife Regina Fiko are renowned Csángó musicians from Ghimeş; this disc is packaged as a small book with full notes and bilingual lyrics.

Maramureş

Iza *Craciun in Maramureş (Christmas in Maramureş)* (Buda/Musique du Monde, France). This Maramureş-based group, led by *zongorǎ*-player Ioan Pop, with various fiddlers and drummer Ioan Petreuş, is trying to keep the traditional style intact. Excellent notes and translations.

Pitigoi Ensemble *Musiques de Mariage et de Fêtes Roumaines* (Arion, France). The best selection of the extraordinary music of Oaş, played by the Pitigoi brothers. Also a good selection of music from Maramureş and Bihor.

Popeluc *Blue Door* (Steel Carpet, UK). Maramureş dancing and drinking music (some recorded live at village bashes), with the odd Irish reel and English song too.

Ioan "Popicu" Pop and Ensemble *Romanian, Ukrainian and Jewish Music from Maramureş* (Ethnophonie, Romania). Maramureş party music: the *hori* are occasional, widely accessible lyrical songs sung individually or in groups, with or without instrument accompaniment; the *zicali* (instrumental pieces) are performed on fiddles, guitars and drums.

Various *The Edge of the Forest: Romanian Music from Transylvania* (Music of the World, US). A collection of dances from Codru and Chioar (southern Maramureş), part of the central Transylvanian tradition, and a few tracks from Maramureş proper and Oaş.

Various *Fiddle Music from Maramureş* (Steel Carpet, UK). Real peasant fiddlers, recorded in their own homes in the Mara Valley.

Various *Musiques de Mariage de Maramureş* (Ocora, France). Maramureş wedding music, performed by three village bands.

Lowland music compilations

Romania: Wedding Music from Wallachia (Auvidis/Ethnic, France). A selection of songs and dance tunes from various bands including members of the Taraf de Haidouks and more urban repertoire from Ion Albeşteanu. The Music of the World disc covers similar repertoire and is more attractive.

Taraf: Romanian Gypsy Music (Music of the World, US). A very good selection of tracks from various Wallachian *tarafuri* including members of the Taraf de Haidouks. Mostly small ensembles of a brace of violins, *ţambal* and bass, with *cobză* lute on a couple of tracks.

Specific artists

Ion Albeşteanu *The Districts of Yesteryears* (Buda/Musique du Monde, France). Albeşteanu, who died in 1998, was known as an expressive violinist and singer. Here he is accompanied by a good band with beautifully textured *ţambal*, accordion and fine *cobză* playing. "At the Reed House", sung in an intimate "head voice", is quite beautiful. Good notes.

Alexander Bălanescu *Possessed* (Mute), a fusion of classical, pop and jazz; *Luminitza* and *Angels and Insects* (Mute), scores to the films of the same name; and *Lume Lume* (Mute), a live festival soundtrack, all serve to demonstrate Bălanescu's diverse range. His most recent recording, *Maria T* (Mute), is a gorgeous reworking of the songs of the legendary Romanian singer.

Fanfare Ciocărlia *Radio Paşcani* and *Iag Bari* (Piranha, Germany). Frenetic romps, punchily recorded, with some fearsomely fast dance numbers, the pace occasionally breaks for a *doină*. Their most recent release, *Queens and Kings* (Asphalt Tango, Germany), is superb, featuring collaborations with other Gypsy legends such as Šaban Bajramovič, Esma Redzepova and Ljiljana Butler. There's also a terrifically entertaining DVD, *Gypsy Brass Legends* (Asphalt Tango, Germany), which features live concert footage.

Panseluţa Feraru *Lăutar Songs from Bucharest* (Long Distance, France). A live recording by the veteran "restaurant singer" (indicating that she's a cut above other Gypsy singers), with great backing from a band led by husband Gheorghe Stephane.

Nicolae Gutsa *The Greatest Living Gypsy Voice* (Auvidis/Silex, France). Nicolae Gutsa is a very popular singer, performing traditional music in a contemporary style. Despite the absurd title, this is a great disc.

Trio Pandelescu *Trio Pandelescu* (Auvidis/Silex, France). Vasile Pandelescu is a virtuoso accordionist who played for many years with Gheorghe Zamfir. Recorded live with high-quality, intimate playing, delicate moments of real poetry, and all the requisite fire; including a couple of beautiful *ţambal* solos by his son Costel.

Maria Tanase *Volumes 1, 2 & 3* (Electrecord, Romania). A versatile talent, Tanase distinguished herself as a stage and film actress, as an operetta singer, a music-hall star, but mainly as the finest interpreter of Romanian folk-songs.

Taraf de Carancebes *Musiciens du Banat* (Silex, France). A five-piece band of saxophone, trumpet, clarinet, accordion and bass. Some stunning virtuoso playing, explaining the popularity of the Banat style.

🏃 **Taraf de Haidouks** *Honourable Brigands, Magic Horses and Evil Eye, Dumbala Dumbala* (Crammed, Belgium). Romania's most recorded Gypsy band allows you to trace the dynamic development of Gypsy music in Wallachia as new styles are absorbed without diluting the distinctive flavour of the *taraf*. *Honourable Brigands* is the best starting point, while 2001's live set, *Band of Gypsies*, is probably their best-known recording in the West. 2007's *Maşkaradă* is a different work altogether, featuring classical interpretations. In addition, there's a marvellous DVD, *The Continuing Adventures of the Taraf de Haidouks*, comprising an entire UK concert, documentaries, interviews and rare archive footage of the band.

Other recordings

Dumitru Fărcaş & Marcel Cellier *The Art of the Romanian Taragot* (ARC Music Production, UK) and *Taragot et Orgue* (Pierre Verany Records, France). One of the leading players of the clarinet-like *taragot*, here with Zamfir's accompanist on church organ.

Toni Iordache *A Virtuoso of the Cimbalom 2* (Electrecord, Romania). One of the great virtuosi of the cimbalom (dulcimer), accompanied by small folk orchestras.

🏃 **Nightlosers** *Sitting on Top of the World, Plum Brandy Blues* (Genius Enterprise Ltd, Bucharest). Romanian "ethnoblues" – listen to the leaf solo on "Stormy Monday". 2007's *Rhythm and Bulz* (Macondo) is the superb follow-up.

Luca Novac accompanied by the Orchestras of Radu Simon and Paraschiv Oprea *A Virtuoso of the Taragot* and **Petrica Pasca accompanied by the Rapsozii Zarandului Band** *Un Virtuose du Taragote* (both Electrecord, Romania). Luca Novac and Petrica Pasca are among the numerous *taragot* virtuosi from the Banat.

The Rough Guide to Music of the Gypsies and **The Rough Guide to Music of the Balkan Gypsies** Romania is represented on both these CDs by the Taraf de Haidouks and Fanfare Ciocărlia; a fantastic introduction to the irrepressible sounds of Gypsy music.

Radu Simion *Pan pipe concert* (Electrecord, Romania). Radu Simion is one of the most gifted interpreters of the *nai* (pan pipe), here accompanied by various folk orchestras.

Gheorghe Zamfir *The Heart of Romania* (Pierre Verany, France). Born in Bucharest in 1941, *nai* player Zamfir must be Romania's most recorded musician, with albums of easy-listening arrangements of anything from Vivaldi to Andrew Lloyd-Webber. Zamfir's music has little to do with the traditional music of Romania, but his arrangements of *doinas* and folktunes have an ethereal beauty.

Various *Roumanie: polyphonie vocale des Aroumains* (Le Chant du Monde, France). CNRS/Musée de l'Homme recordings of the Romanians living in Dobrogea, Bulgaria and elsewhere in the Balkans. Hard-core ethnic stuff.

Various *YIKHES: Klezmer recordings from 1907–1939* (Trikont, Germany). Remastered 78s, including a couple of 1910 tracks by Belf's Romanian Orchestra, virtually the only European Klezmer band of the period to have been recorded.

Simon Broughton

Dracula and vampires

T ruth, legends and fiction swirl around the figure of **Dracula** like a cloak, and perceptions of him differ sharply. In Romania today, schoolbooks and historians extol him as a patriot and a champion of order in lawless times, while the outside world knows him as the vampire count of a thousand cinematic fantasies derived from Bram Stoker's novel of 1897 – a spoof-figure or a ghoul.

The disparity in images is easily explained, for while vampires feature in native folklore, Romanians make no associations between them and the historical figure of Dracula, the Wallachian prince Vlad III, known in his homeland as Vlad Ţepeş – **Vlad the Impaler**. During his lifetime (*c.*1431–76) Vlad achieved renown beyond Wallachia's borders as a successful fighter against the Turks and a ruthless ruler; his reputation for cruelty spread throughout Europe via the newly invented printing presses and the word of his political enemies – notably the Transylvanian Saxons. At this time, Vlad was not known as a vampire, although some charged that he was in league with the Devil – or (almost as bad) that he had converted to Catholicism.

The historical Dracula

He was not very tall, but very stocky and strong, with a cold and terrible appearance, a strong and aquiline nose, swollen nostrils, a thin reddish face in which very long eyelashes framed large wide-open green eyes; the bushy black eyebrows made them appear threatening. His face and chin were shaven, but for a moustache. The swollen temples increased the bulk of his head. A bull's neck connected his head to his body from which black curly locks hung on his wide-shouldered person.

Such was the papal legate's impression of **Vlad Ţepeş** – then in his thirties and a prisoner at the court of Visegrád in Hungary. He had been born in Sighişoara and raised at Târgovişte after his father, Vlad Dracul, became Voivode of Wallachia in 1436. Young Vlad's privileged childhood effectively ended in 1442, when he and his brother Radu were sent by their father as hostages to Anatolia, to curry favour with the Turkish Sultan. Vlad Dracul incurred the enmity of Iancu de Hunedoara, prince of Transylvania, who arranged his murder in 1447; his sons were released by the Turks to be pawns in the struggle between their expanding empire, Iancu and the new ruler of Wallachia. The experience of five years of Turkish captivity and years of exile in Moldavia and Transylvania shaped Vlad's personality irrevocably, and educated him in guile and terrorism.

Seeking a vassal, Iancu helped Vlad to become **ruler of Wallachia** in 1456 but promptly died, leaving him dangerously exposed. Signing a defence pact and free trade agreement with the Saxons of Braşov, Vlad quickly decided that it was also prudent to pay an annual tribute of 10,000 gold ducats to the Sultan while he consolidated his power in Wallachia. For generations the boyar families had defied and frequently deposed their own rulers, including Vlad's father and his elder brother Mircea, whom they buried alive.

His method of law enforcement was simple: practically all crimes and individuals offending him were punished by death; and Vlad's customary means of execution was **impaling people**. Victims were bound spread-eagled while a stake was hammered up their rectum, and then were raised aloft and left to die in agony, for all to see. To test his subjects' honesty, Vlad disguised himself and moved among them; left coins in shops and over-compensated merchants who had been robbed; and slew all that failed the test. Foreigners reported the demise of theft, and Vlad symbolically placed a golden cup beside a lonely fountain for anyone to drink from and no one dared to take it away. On Easter Day in 1459, Vlad eliminated the potentially rebellious boyars en masse by inviting them and their families to dine at his palace; guards then entered and seized them, impaling many forthwith, while the remainder were marched off to labour at Poienari. In a similar vein, he invited Wallachia's disabled, unemployed and work-shy to feast with him at Târgovişte, and asked if they wished to be free of life's sufferings. Receiving an affirmative reply Vlad had them all burnt, justifying his action as a measure to ensure that none of his subjects should ever suffer from poverty or disability.

All this was but a ramp for Vlad's ambition to be the acknowledged ruler of a mighty power, which caused much feuding with the Saxons of Braşov, Sibiu and the Bârsa Land. It began in 1457, when he accused them of supporting claimants to his throne, and decided to end the Saxon merchants' practice of trading freely throughout Wallachia. When they persisted, Vlad led his army through the Red Tower Pass to burn Saxon villages, and had any of their people found inside Wallachia impaled. In 1460, Vlad annihilated the forces of his rival, Dan III, who invaded with the support of Braşov; and on this occasion dined in a garden among the impaled bodies of his enemies, using a holy icon as a dish, according to the *Chronicon Mellicense*. A month later, he attacked the Bârsa Land, and impaled hundreds of townsfolk on Sprenghi Hill within sight of Braşov's defenders before marching off to ravage the Făgăraş region.

At the same time, Vlad plotted to turn **against the Turks** and form alliances with his cousin Stephen of Moldavia, and the Hungarian monarchy. Having defaulted on payments of tribute for two years, and nailed the turbans of two emissaries to their heads when they refused to doff them, Vlad **declared war** by raiding Turkish garrisons from Vidin to Giurgiu. A massive army led by Sultan Mehmet II crossed the Danube into Wallachia in 1462, but found itself advancing through countryside denuded of inhabitants, food and water, "with the sun burning so that the armour of the ghazzis could well be used to cook kebabs". On the night of June 17, Vlad's army raided the Turkish camp, inflicting heavy casualties, and a few days later the demoralized invaders approached Târgovişte only to recoil in horror. En route to the capital, Vlad had prepared a forest of stakes 1km by 3km wide, upon which 20,000 Turkish and Bulgarian captives were impaled. Shattered by their losses and these terror tactics, the Turks retreated in disorder.

Vlad's downfall has been attributed in part to the Saxons, who used every opportunity to support his enemies and defame him throughout Europe, after he had raised customs duties to pay for his army. Most likely, they forged the implausible "treason note" (in which Vlad purportedly offered to help the Sultan capture Transylvania) – the pretext for Mátyás Corvinus to order Vlad's arrest in 1462, after a fresh Turkish attack had forced him to flee over the Făgăraş mountains from Poienari. Until 1475 he was a "guest" at Visegrád, where Mátyás would introduce him to Turkish ambassadors to disconcert them; Wallachia's throne was occupied by Vlad's pliable brother Radu "The Handsome", who had once served as the Sultan's catamite. Having married a relative of Mátyás, Vlad was released to continue the anti-Turkish struggle, spending a year in Sibiu (the townsfolk deeming it politic to be hospitable) and regaining his throne in 1476. His triumph was short-lived, however, for Radu offered the boyars an alternative to "rule by the stake" and a chance to placate the Turks, which they seized gratefully. In circumstances that remain unclear (some say that a servant was bribed to slay him), Vlad was betrayed by the boyars and killed. His head disappeared – supposedly sent to the Sultan as a present – while the Impaler's decapitated body was reputedly buried inside the church at Snagov Monastery, where it's said to remain today.

The lack of any inscription on Vlad's tomb and of any portraits of him in medieval church frescoes suggests that attempts were made for some time to erase the memory of Dracula in Romania, although he was remembered in the nineteenth century, and also in the Ceauşescu epoch, as a fighter for national independence and a wise lawmaker.

Vampires

Horrible though his deeds were, Vlad was not accused of **vampirism** during his lifetime. However, vampires were an integral part of folklore in Eastern and Southeastern Europe, known as *vámpír* in Hungarian and *strigoi* in Romanian. Details of their habits and characteristics vary from place to place, but in their essentials are fairly similar. A vampire is an **undead corpse**, animated by its spirit and with a body that fails to decay, no matter how long in the grave. Vampirism can be contagious, or people might occasionally be born as vampires, bearing stigmata such as a dark-coloured spot on the head or a rudimentary tail. However, a vampire is usually created when a person dies and the soul is unable to enter heaven or hell. The reason may be that the person has died in a "state of sin" – by suicide, for example, or holding heretical beliefs – or because the soul has been prevented from leaving the body. Hanging was a form of death dreaded by Romanians, who believed that tying the neck "forces the soul down outward"; while the Orthodox custom of shrouding mirrors in the home of the deceased was intended to prevent the spirit from being "trapped" by seeing its reflection. As Catholicism and Orthodoxy competed for adherents in the wake of the Ottoman withdrawal from the Balkans, priests also claimed that the cemetery of the opposing church was unconsecrated land, thereby raising the fear of vampires rising from the grave.

Once created, a vampire is almost immortal, and becomes a menace to the living. In Romanian folklore, vampires frequently return to their former homes at night, where they must be propitiated with offerings of food and drink, and excluded by smearing garlic around the doors and windows. Should a newborn baby lie within, it must be guarded until it is christened, lest a vampire sneak in and transform it into another vampire. Two nights of the year are especially perilous: **April 23**, St George's Day (when, as Jonathan Harker was warned in Bram Stoker's novel, "all the evil things in the world will have full sway"), and **November 29**, the eve of St Andrew's Day. On that night, vampires rise with their coffins on their heads, lurk about their former homes, and then gather to fight each other with hempen whips at crossroads. Such places were considered to be unlucky, being infested by spirits called *Iele* (Man's enemies). In Gypsy folklore, vampires (*mulè*) also live at the exact moment of midday, when the sun casts no shadow. Gypsies must cease travelling at that time, for it is then that *mulè* control the roads, trees and everything else. Interestingly, Gypsies only fear their own *mulè* – the ghosts and vampires of *gadjé* (non-Gypsies) are of no account.

The greatest danger was presented by **vampire epidemics**, which began in the seventeenth century, perhaps due to the influence of Gypsy folklore.

Although in horror films and Bram Stoker's novel, vampires must bite their victims and suck blood to cause contagion, in Eastern European folklore, the vampire's look or touch can suffice. A classic account refers to the Austro-Hungarian village of Haidam in the 1720s. There, before witnesses, a man dead ten years returned as a vampire to his son's cottage, touched him on the shoulder and then departed. The man died the next morning. Alarmed by this report and others relating how long-dead villagers were returning to suck their children's blood, the local military commander ordered several graves to be exhumed, within which were found corpses showing no signs of decay. All were incinerated to ashes – one of the classic methods of exterminating vampires. Another epidemic occurred in the village of Medvegia near Belgrade, starting in 1727. A soldier claimed to have been attacked by a vampire while in Greece (where vampire legends also abound), and died upon his return home. Thereafter, many villagers swore they had seen him at night, or had dreamt about him, and ten weeks later complained of inexplicable weakness. The body was exhumed, was found to have blood in its mouth, and so had a stake driven through its heart. Despite this precaution, there was an outbreak of vampirism a few years later, and of the fourteen corpses examined by a medical commission in 1732, twelve were found to be "unmistakably in the vampire condition" (undecayed).

This was the catalyst for an explosion of interest across Europe, until Pope Benedict XIV and the Austrian and Prussian governments declared vampirism a fraud and made it a crime to dig up dead bodies. But in 1899 Romanian peasants in Caraşova dug up thirty corpses and tore them to pieces to stop a diphtheria epidemic, and in 1909 a Transylvanian castle was burned down by locals who believed that a vampire emanating from it was causing the deaths of their children. Only recently, in 1988, outside Niş in southern Serbia, a thirteen-year-old girl was killed by her family, who believed her to be a vampire.

Sceptics may dismiss vampires and vampirism entirely, but some of the related phenomena have rational or scientific explanations. The "return of the dead" can be explained by premature burial, which happened frequently in the past. Nor is the drinking of blood confined to legendary, supernatural creatures. Aside from the Maasai tribe of Kenya – whose diet contains cattle blood mixed with milk – numerous examples can be found in the annals of criminology and psychopathology.

Bram Stoker's Dracula

During the eighteenth century, numerous well-publicized incidents of vampirism sparked a **vampire craze in Europe**, with both lurid accounts and learned essays produced in quantity. The first respectable **literary work** on a vampire theme was Goethe's *The Bride of Corinth* (1797), soon followed by Polidori's *The Vampyre*, which arose out of the same blood-curdling holiday on Lake Geneva in 1816 that produced Mary Shelley's *Frankenstein*. Other variations followed, by Kleist, E.T.A. Hoffmann, Mérimée, Gogol, Dumas, Baudelaire, Arminius Vambery, and Sheridan Le Fanu, whose *Carmilla* features a lesbian vampire in Styria.

These fired the imagination of **Bram Stoker** (1847–1912), an Anglo-Irish civil servant who became manager to the great actor Sir Henry Irving in 1878 and wrote a few other novels, now being rediscovered. In 1890 he conceived the suitably *fin-de-siècle* idea of a vampire novel; initially it, too, was to be set in Styria, with an antihero called "Count Wampyr", but after detailed research in

Whitby Public Library and the Reading Room of the British Museum, the setting moved east to Transylvania, and **Count Dracula** was born. Stoker's fictional Count was possibly influenced by the "Jack the Ripper" murders which happened a decade earlier in Whitechapel, where Stoker lived for a time while writing his book. Stoker delved deep into Romanian folklore, history and geography, and the book is a masterpiece in its mixture of fantasy and precise settings.

Other books on the same theme followed, but it was the advent of cinema and the horror **film** that has ensured the fame of Dracula. The silent *Nosferatu* (1922) is perhaps the greatest vampire film, followed by Béla Lugosi's 1931 *Dracula*, while Hammer's 1958 classic *Dracula* boasted the dream coupling of Christopher Lee as the Count and Peter Cushing as Van Helsing. The BBC's *Count Dracula* (1978) is the most faithful to Stoker's novel, while Coppola's camped-up *Bram Stoker's Dracula* (1992) confuses things by including the historic Vlad Țepeș in a prelude. There is also a fine tradition of **spoofs** such as *Love at First Bite* (1979), which opens with the communists expelling Dracula from his castle, not to mention *Count Duckula* (1988–93), the vegetarian vampire duck.

Books

T he surge in interest in Eastern Europe since 1989, and the particularly dramatic nature of Romania's revolution and its problems since then, have led to several excellent writers visiting in quick succession. In addition, there is a wealth of nineteenth-century and early twentieth-century travellers' accounts, although many are out of print. Romanian literature is still under-represented in translation.

The **Center for Romanian Studies**, based in Iaşi, publishes many books on Romanian history and literature – for details contact their distributors, ISBS (920 NE 58th Ave, Portland, OR 97213, USA; ☎1800/944 6190, Ⓦwww .isbs.com). Note that out-of-print titles are indicated as (o/p).

Specialized guides

John Akeroyd *The Historic Country-side of the Saxon Villages of Southeast Transylvania*. A detailed account of the human and natural ecology of a wonderfully unspoilt medieval landscape.

Dave Gosney *Finding Birds in Romania*. This covers the Danube Delta only. Informative, but strangely it does not include a checklist of possible species.

Teofil Ivanciuc *Ghidul Turistic al Ţării Maramureşului*. Only in Romanian at present, but the definitive guide to the historic land of Maramureş.

James Roberts *Romania – a Birdwatching and Wildlife Guide*; and *The Mountains of Romania*. Detailed guides to the fauna and habitats of Romania, and information for hiking.

Travellers' tales

Many of the out-of-print accounts listed below may be found online, in secondhand bookshops or at Marijana Dworski Books, 21 Broad St, Hay-on-Wye HR3 5DB, UK (☎&🖶01497/820 200, Ⓦwww.dworskibooks.com).

Recent accounts

Nick Crane *Clear Waters Rising*. A walk along the mountain spine of Europe, from Finisterre to Istanbul, including the entire length of the Carpathians – interesting contrasts between life in the mountains of Eastern and Western Europe.

Helena Drysdale *Looking for Gheorghe*. A search for a lost friend leads to unsavoury insights into life with the Securitate and finally to a hellish "mental hospital". The picture

of Romanian life both before and after the revolution is spot-on.

Jason Goodwin *On Foot to the Golden Horn*. An engaging and well-informed writer walking from Gdansk to Istanbul in 1990 – almost half the book is, in fact, set in Transylvania. Very thoughtful, but it's annoyingly hard to work out which are the author's opinions and which those of the characters he meets.

Brian Hall *Stealing from a Deep Place*. Hall cycled through Hungary, Romania and Bulgaria in 1982 and produced a beautifully defined picture of the nonsense that communism had become.

Georgina Harding *In Another Europe*. Another cycle tour, this one in 1988. Slimmer than Hall's book but concentrating far more on Romania, with a more emotional response to Ceauşescu's follies.

Eva Hoffman *Exit into History*. Not a patch on *Lost in Translation*, her superb account of being uprooted from Jewish Kraków to North America, but this tour of East-Central Europe in 1990 still yields seventy insightful pages on Romania.

Caroline Juler *Searching for Sarmizegetusa*. A captivating glimpse of traditional life and the pressures that are undermining it.

Andrew MacKenzie *Romanian Journey* and *Dracula Country* (both o/p). *Romanian Journey*'s dollops of history, architectural description and bland travelese wouldn't be so bad if MacKenzie didn't also whitewash the Ceauşescu regime. *Dracula Country* is preferable, and assembles interesting facts about folklore and Vlad the Impaler.

Rory MacLean *Stalin's Nose*. With its wonderfully surreal humour, this is not exactly a factual account, but it is fundamentally serious about the effects of World War II and communism all over Eastern Europe.

Claudio Magris *Danube*. Full of scholarly anecdotes and subtle insights as Magris follows the Danube from source to sea.

Dervla Murphy *Transylvania and Beyond*. A serious, analytical book that tussles with the problems that Transylvania faced immediately post-revolution, and its ethnic tensions in particular. Tellingly, she uses the Hungarian spelling "Rumania" throughout.

Peter O'Conner *Walking Good: Travels to Music in Hungary and Romania* (o/p). Another Irish fiddler in search of Gypsy music, forty years after Starkie (see p.478). O'Conner's quest took him to Slobozia, Cojocna and Făgăraş, staying with local people a few years before this became illegal. Entertaining.

Alan Ogden *Romania Revisited*. An anthology and bibliography of English travellers to Romania between 1602 and 1941, interwoven with the author's own journeys in 1998.

Bronwen Riley *Transylvania*. Evocative account of the vanishing rural lifestyle of Transylvania and Maramureş, with superb photos.

Julian Ross *Travels in an Unknown Country*. A summer-long horse-ride across Transylvania and Moldavia, witnessing a fast-disappearing rural world.

Sophie Thurnham *Sophie's Journey*. Heart-warming story of work in the orphanages.

Giles Whittell *Lambada Country*. Another trip to Istanbul, at the same time as Jason Goodwin's. Less than a quarter of the book is on Romania, but it's interesting and informative, particularly on Magyar attitudes.

Older classics

Henry Baerlein (ed). *Romanian Scene* and *Romanian Oasis* (o/p). Two fine anthologies of travellers' tales in which most of the prewar authors listed below are featured.

Emily Gerard *The Land Beyond the Forest* (o/p). One of the classic nineteenth-century accounts of Transylvania – rambling, but highly informative on folk customs, superstitions, proverbs and the like.

Donald Hall *Romanian Furrow*. Newly republished, the definitive account of 1930s Romanian rural life, clearly threatened by the modern world even then.

Patrick Leigh Fermor *Between the Woods and the Water*. Transylvania provides the setting for the second volume in this unfolding trilogy, based on Leigh Fermor's diaries for 1933–34, when he walked from Holland to Constantinople. His precocious zest for history and cultural diversity rose to the challenge of Transylvania's striking contrasts and obscurely turbulent past; the richness of his jewelled prose is impressive.

Lion Phillimore *In the Carpathians* (o/p). A fascinating account of a journey by horsecart through the Maramureş and Székelyföld just before World War I, by a proto-hippy who wants only to commune with the mountains and the trees.

Sacheverell Sitwell *Romanian Journey*. Motoring around, the Sitwells were both politely appalled, and vaguely charmed, by Romania; but most of all seem to have been relieved that their gastronomic fortunes didn't suffer unduly.

Walter Starkie *Raggle Taggle* (o/p). After his exploits in Hungary, Starkie tramped down through Transylvania to Bucharest, where his encounters with Gypsies and lowlife are recounted in a florid but quite amusing style.

Teresa Stratilesco *From Carpathians to Pindus* (o/p). Covers the same ground as Gerard, with an equally sharp eye for quirky details.

Rosa G Waldeck *Athene Palace* (o/p). Eyewitness account of demimondaines and spies of all sides in wartime Bucharest.

History and politics

Mark Almond *The Rise and Fall of Nicolae and Elena Ceauşescu* (o/p). Very readable account by one of the best academics writing on Romania, though too kind to the sinister Silviu Brucan. Rather wayward footnotes and accents.

Dan Antal *Out of Romania*. An insider's version of the dreadful oppression under Ceauşescu and even worse disillusion after the revolution. Well enough told by a sympathetic character.

Ed Behr *Kiss the Hand You Cannot Bite*. A good, populist account of the Ceauşescus' rise and fall.

Burton Y Berry *Romanian Diaries 1944–47*; and Donald Dunham *Assignment: Bucharest*. The communist takeover of Romania, as seen by senior US diplomats.

Dennis Deletant *Communist Terror in Romania: Gheorghiu-Dej and the Police State, 1948–65*; *Ceauşescu and the Securitate: Coercion and Dissent in Romania 1965–89*; *Romania under Communist Rule*. Fascinating coverage of many hidden aspects of communist Romania.

Terence Elsberry *Marie of Romania*. A colourful biography of Queen Marie.

Mary Ellen Fischer *Nicolae Ceauşescu: A Study in Political Leadership*. Academic, detailed and readable description of the system created by

Ceaușescu that was soon to drag him down.

Stephen Fischer-Galați *Twentieth Century Rumania.* An easy read with good illustrations, basically sympathetic to many changes that happened under communism.

Tom Gallagher *Theft of a Nation: Romania since Communism.* A fine analysis of the continuing crisis of Romanian politics, including its historical roots and the IMF and EU's blindness; also *Romania After Ceaușescu*, focusing on the cynical exploitation of nationalism.

Vlad Georgescu *The Romanians: A History.* The best modern history in translation, although the importance of dissidents under Ceaușescu seems overstated. Georgescu, head of the Romanian Service of Radio Free Europe, died in 1988, but an epilogue covers the events of 1989.

Keith Hitchins *Rumania 1866–1947.* An academic history, showing how attempts to establish an independent modern state are paralleled today.

Nicolae Klepper *Romania: an Illustrated History.* Paperback history giving the standard view of the progress of the Romanian people towards nationhood.

Alan Ogden *Fortresses of Faith.* A history of the Saxon churches with fine black-and-white photos; also *Revelations of Byzantium*, on the painted churches of Bucovina; *Winds of Sorrow*; and *Moons and Aurochs*, two historical tours.

Ion Pacepa *Red Horizons.* A lurid, rambling "exposé" of the Ceaușescu regime, written by its former intelligence chief (who defected in 1978), describing disinformation and espionage abroad, corruption and perversions among the élite, and much else. Pacepa was deeply

involved but reveals little about himself.

Prince Paul of Hohenzollern-Roumania *King Carol II: A Life of my Grandfather* (o/p). The nephew of King Mihai, Paul doesn't deny his grandfather's dreadful personal life, but attempts to rehabilitate him as a statesman placed in an impossible position.

Ioan Aurel Pop *Romanians and Romania – A Brief History.* Romanian history and civilization from the first century BC to the present.

Ivor Porter *Michael of Romania – the King and the Country.* A careful account of Mihai's life and of his role in the country's history.

Martyn Rady *Romania in Turmoil.* Wonderfully clear account of Ceaușescu's rise and fall, continuing to the end of 1991.

Nestor Ratesh *Romania: The Entangled Revolution.* A careful account of the revolution, laying out all the confusion that still surrounds it.

Ion Rațiu *Contemporary Romania.* A generally negative portrayal of the communist system by an émigré who made a million in Britain and was to return after Ceaușescu's downfall to lead an opposition party.

George Schöpflin *The Hungarians of Romania.* A careful presentation of the evidence on communist discrimination against the Magyars.

R.W. Seton-Watson *A History of the Roumanians.* Although it largely ignores social history and eschews atmospherics, and even the author admits his despair at the welter of dynastic details, this is still the classic work in English on Romanian history before 1920. Seton-Watson's *Roumania and the Great War* (1915) and *The Rise of Nationality in the Balkans* (1917) somewhat influenced

British policy in favour of the Successor States, and for this reason he attracted great hostility in Hungary.

Christine Sutherland *Enchantress: Marthe Bibesco and her World.* A brilliant snapshot of both Romanian and French society and politics in the first half of the twentieth century, and of one of its most charismatic figures, Queen Marie's rival.

László Tökes *With God, for the People.* The autobiography of the man who lit the spark of the revolution and continues to be a thorn in the establishment's side, even as a bishop.

Kurt Treptow (ed) *A History of Romania.* From ancient times to the 1996 elections; with accompanying CD-ROM.

Richard Wurmbrand *In God's Underground.* The memoirs of a Lutheran priest who spent many years incarcerated at Jilava, Piteşti and other notorious prisons.

Folklore

David Buxton *Wooden Churches of Eastern Europe* (o/p). A learned and thorough tome.

Nicolae Klepper *Taste of Romania; its Cookery and Glimpses of its History, Folklore, Art and Poetry.* Cookery and cultural asides.

Gail Kligman *The Wedding of the Dead; Căluş: Symbolic Transformation in Romanian Ritual; The Politics of Duplicity – Controlling Reproduction in Ceauşescu's Romania.* The first is a wonderful book if you want to know everything about the anthropology and rituals of one Maramureş village, Ieud; the second is a slim but interesting anthropological study of the

Whitsun Căluş rite, which still lingers in parts of southern Romania; and the third is a similar study of Ceauşescu's efforts to boost the birth rate.

Karsten D McNulty *Romanian Folk Art: a Guide to Living Traditions.* A paperback overview of Romania's many types of crafts, with colour photos.

Katherine Verdery *Transylvanian Villagers: Three Centuries of Political, Economic and Ethnic change.* Based on field work west of Sebeş – a duller area than Maramureş, but therefore more broadly applicable than Kligman's book, though not as readable.

Dracula

Paul Barber *Vampires, Burial and Death: Folklore and Reality.* Proclaims itself as "a scholarly work on human decomposition and historical attitudes to it", which says it all.

Barbara Belford *Bram Stoker: A Biography of the Author of Dracula.* A more rigorous biography than Farson's, though marred by cod psychology.

Daniel Farson *The Man who wrote Dracula: A Biography of Bram Stoker.* Entertaining account of the life of the fictional Dracula's creator.

Radu Florescu and Raymond McNally *In Search of Dracula; Dracula: A Biography; Dracula, Prince of Many Faces, His Life and Times.* Founts of knowledge on the Impaler but overstating his connection with Dracula.

Christopher Frayling
Vampyres. Primarily a study of the vampire theme in literature and broader culture, but also a near-definitive review of the phenomenon itself.

Clive Leatherdale *Dracula: The Novel and the Legend*. More concerned with the novel than with its Romanian background.

Elizabeth Miller *Reflections on Dracula; Sense & Nonsense*. Essays on Stoker's novel, an entertaining debunking of many of the myths surrounding Stoker and his most famous book.

Nicolae Stoicescu *Vlad Țepeș: Prince of Wallachia*. The standard Romanian biography of the Impaler, whom Stoicescu practically attempts to sanctify.

Bram Stoker *Dracula*. The Gothic horror original that launched a thousand movies. From a promising start with undertones of fetishism and menace in Dracula's Transylvanian castle, the tale degenerates into pathos before returning to Romania, and ending in a not too effective chase.

Kurt Treptow *Vlad III Dracula*. A balanced biography of the historical Vlad.

Romanian prose

Miklós Bánffy *They Were Counted, They Were Found Wanting* and *They Were Divided*. The *Transylvanian Trilogy*, written in the 1930s, is a tale of two Transylvanian cousins that has been compared to Proust, Dostoevsky and Trollope. Also *The Phoenix Land*, a memoir of Hungary after the Trianon Treaty dismembered it.

Emil Cioran *On the Heights of Despair*. A key early work (1934, reissued in 1992) by this nihilist anti-philosopher.

Petru Dumitriu *The Family Jewels, The Prodigals* and *Incognito*. All (o/p). A literary prodigy lauded by the Party for his book *Dustless Highway*, Dumitriu fled Romania in 1960 and subsequently published two tales of dynastic ambition, followed by his masterpiece of moral and psychological exploration, *Incognito*, set against the backdrop of the war and the communist takeover.

Mircea Eliade *Shamanism; Youth without Youth; Fantastic Tales*. The first is the most interesting and informative example of the academic work for which he is internationally

known. The latter two are fiction, which don't quite match his reputation as a magical realist in the South American tradition, although this is partly due to the translation.

Norman Manea *On Clowns: The Dictator and the Artist*. Deported to the camps of Transnistria at the age of five, after the war Manea became an engineer and then an increasingly dissident writer, fleeing to the US in 1986. This collection consists largely of over-intellectual musings on the nature of dictatorship and the subjected populace's complicity. See also his memoir *The Hooligan's Return* of 2003, which hinges on his anti-climactic first return to Romania in 1997.

Herta Müller *The Passport; The Land of Green Plums*. Müller is a Schwab who left Romania in 1987. *The Passport* is a tale, in a distinctive staccato style, of the quest for permission to leave for Germany; *The Land of Green Plums* deals more with repression under Ceaușescu and is in a more accessible style.

Dumitru Popescu *The Royal Hunt*. One of seven volumes, this novel describes the way in which terror can overwhelm a community. Popescu is perhaps Romania's best-known contemporary novelist.

Liviu Rebreanu *Uprising; Ion; The Forest of the Hanged.* This trilogy comprises a panoramic picture of Romanian social life from the late nineteenth century to World War I. *Uprising*, which deals with the 1907 peasant rebellion, shocked Romanian readers with its violent descriptions when it first appeared in 1933.

Elie Wiesel *Night.* Wiesel was born in Sighet in 1928 and was deported to Auschwitz, where his family died, in 1944. After the war, he pursued an academic career in the US and was awarded the Nobel Peace Prize in 1986. This slim book opens in the ghetto of Sighet, but soon moves to the death camps.

Romanian poetry

George Bacovia *Plumb/Lead.* Along with Arghezi (none of whose work is available in translation), Bacovia is the leading prewar Romanian poet. Exquisitely melancholy.

Maria Banuş *Demon in Brackets.* Born in 1914, Banuş was a left-wing activist through the 1930s and 1940s, but her intimate lyricism remains popular today.

Lucian Blaga *Complete Poetical Works.* At last, one of Romania's finest and most popular poets available in English translation.

Ion Caraion *The Error of Being.* A leading poet of the older generation, who composed many of his poems in the camps of World War II.

Petru Cârdu *The Trapped Strawberry.* A Romanian-Yugoslav, Cârdu writes ironic poems in both Romanian and Serbo-Croat.

Nina Cassian *Call Yourself Alive? Cheerleader for a Funeral.* Savagely sensual and wickedly funny work from one of Romania's best poets.

Paul Celan *Selected Poems.* Romania's greatest poet – although all his work is in German – and one of the best of the twentieth century. Born in Bucovina in 1920, Celan survived the camps of Transnistria and emigrated to Paris, killing himself in 1970.

Mihai Eminescu *In Celebration of Mihai Eminescu; Selected Works of Ion Creangă and Mihai Eminescu; Poems and Prose of Mihai Eminescu.* The national poet – it's a scandal that there isn't a paperback in English of his greatest hits.

John Farleigh (ed) *When the Tunnels Meet.* A great idea – contemporary Romanian poems in versions by contemporary Irish poets, with a corresponding volume published in Romania: Dinescu, Sorescu and, most notably, Blandiana interpreted by Seamus Heaney.

Ioana Ieronim *The Triumph of the Water Witch.* Prose poems about the destruction of a Saxon community by Ceauşescu, written before 1989 and only published (and shortlisted for the Weidenfeld Prize) ten years later.

Jon Miloş *Through the Needle's Eye.* A Yugoslav-Romanian now living in Sweden, Miloş writes about universal social and environmental problems.

David Morley and Leonard-Daniel Aldea (eds) *No Longer Poetry: New Romanian poetry.* Striking work by eleven young poets, in Romanian and English.

Oskar Pastior *Many Glove Compartments: Selected Poems.* A Saxon, Pastior spent five years in a Soviet labour camp after World War II, and has since been obsessed by themes of freedom and determinism.

Marin Sorescu *Let's Talk About the Weather; Selected Poems 1965–73; The Biggest Egg in the World; Censored Poems; The Bridge.* Hugely popular and respected both before 1989 (when his readings had to be held in football stadiums) and after (when he was briefly Minister of Culture), Sorescu died in 1996. His style is more ironic and accessible than that of many of his contemporaries.

Adam Sorkin (trans & ed) *Transylvanian Voices; City of Dreams and Whispers.* Anthologies of contemporary poets from Cluj and Iaşi respectively. Sorkin has also translated Magda Carneci, Ioan Flora, Saviana Stănescu and Daniela Crasnaru.

Nichita Stănescu *Bas-Relief with Heroes.* Stănescu died aged fifty in 1982, but his prolific work is still very influential.

Ion Stoica *As I Came to London one Midsummer's Day; Gates of the Moment.* A poet of the older generation, blending old and new influences.

Grete Tartler *Orient Express.* An excellent Schwab writer, translated by Fleur Adcock.

Liliana Ursu *The Sky Behind the Forest.* "Carnivorous and tender, majestic and human", a clear insight into her country and its people.

Brenda Walker (ed) *Anthology of Contemporary Romanian Poetry.* Features the work of Romania's two best living poets, Nina Cassian and Ana Blandiana.

Foreign prose

Paul Bailey *Kitty and Virgil.* A fine novel of survival in Ceauşescu's Romania and love found and lost in Britain.

Saul Bellow *The Dean's December.* The repression and poverty of Ceauşescu's Romania is contrasted with the hypocrisy and decadence of 1980s America.

Garth Cartwright *Princes Among Men – Journeys with Gypsy Musicians.* An exhilarating tour of Southeastern Europe, with 68 pages on Romanian gypsy music.

Olivia Manning *The Balkan Trilogy.* This epic story of thoroughly exasperating characters renders the atmosphere of wartime Bucharest well, but as an extended study of human relationships it's weakly constructed.

Bel Mooney *Cascades: The Voices of Silence.* A 13-year-old's experience of Ceauşescu's overthrow; written for the same age group, studying themes such as the individual and society.

Gregor von Rezzori *Memoirs of an Anti-Semite; The Snows of Yesteryear.* Two evocative accounts of growing up in the largely Romanian city of Czernowitz (Cernăuţi, now in Ukraine).

Jules Verne *The Castle of the Carpathians.* A Gothic adventure tale, long loved by French children and now in English too.

Barbara Wilson *Trouble in Transylvania.* Inveterate traveller Cassandra Reilly goes to Sovata to investigate a murder, and gets the hots for most of the women she meets. Pretty strong on local colour in other respects.

Language

485

Language

Language

omanian is basically a **Romance language** with a grammar similar to
Latin. This familial resemblance makes it easy for anyone who speaks
French, Italian or (to a lesser extent) Spanish to recognize words and
phrases in Romanian, even though its vocabulary also contains words of
Dacian, Slav, Greek and Turkish origin, with more recent additions from French,
German and English.

German may be understood – if not spoken – in the areas of Transylvania
and the Banat traditionally inhabited by Saxons and Swabians; and many
educated Romanians have learned the language for professional reasons,
although the tendency among students nowadays is increasingly towards
English. Foreigners who can muster any scrap of **Hungarian** will find it
appreciated in the Magyar enclaves of Transylvania, but its use elsewhere
invites hassle rather than sympathy, which is even more the case with **Russian**
– a language greeted with derision by almost everyone except the Lipovani
communities of the Delta.

Romanian **nouns** have three genders – masculine, feminine and neuter.
Adjectives (usually placed after the word they describe) and **pronouns** always
"agree" with the gender of the noun. *Mai* and *cel mai* are generally used to
make comparatives and superlatives: eg. *ieftin* (cheap); *mai ieftin* (cheaper); *cel
mai ieftin* (the cheapest). In Romanian, **articles** are not always needed: the
indefinite article "a" comes before the noun and is *un* for masculine and neuter
words, *o* for feminine ones; the definite article "the" is added to the end of the
noun: *-a* for feminine words, *-ul* or *-le* for masculine or neuter ones. The plural
forms of nouns are slightly more complicated, but tend to end in *-i or -le*.
Verbs are conjugated, so do not require pronouns such as "I" or "you",
although these may be added for emphasis.

Pronunciation is likewise fairly straightforward. Words are usually, but not
always, stressed on the syllable before last, and all letters are pronounced

Elementary Hungarian

Yes	**Igen**	Cheap	**Olcsó**
No	**Nem**	Expensive	**Drága**
Please	**Kárem**	Good	**Jó**
Thanks	**Köszönöm**	Bad	**Rossz**
Hello	**Jó napot, servus, csokolom**	Open	**Nyitva**
		Closed	**Zárva**
Goodbye	**Viszontlá tósra**	Station	**Palyaudvar, vasú, allomas**
Cheers!	**Egeszegedre!**		
I don't understand	**Nem értem**	Hotel	**Szálloda**
Where is...?	**Hol van...?**	Restaurant	**Étterem**
When?	**Mikor?**	Bar	**Pince**
Today	**Ma**	Bread	**Kenyér**
Tomorrow	**Holnap**	(No) meat	**(Nem) hús**
How much is it?	**Mennyibe kerül?**		

Elementary German

Yes	**Ja**	How much is it?	**Wieviel kostet es?**
No	**Nein**	Cheap	**Billig**
Please	**Bitte**	Expensive	**Teuer**
Thanks	**Danke**	Good	**Gut**
Hello	**Guten Tag, Grüss Gott**	Bad	**Schlecht**
		Open	**Offen**
Goodbye	**Auf Wiedersehen**	Closed	**Geschlossen**
Cheers!	**Prost!**	Station	**Bahnhof**
I don't understand	**Ich verstehe nicht**	Hotel	**Gasthaus**
Where is...?	**Wo ist...?**	Restaurant	**Restaurant**
When?	**Wann?**	Bread	**Brot**
Today	**Heute**	(No) meat	**(Kein) Fleisch**
Tomorrow	**Morgen**		

except for the terminal "–i". However, certain letters change their sounds when combined with other ones. When speaking, Romanians tend to slur words together.

A "o" sound as in done.

Â (or **Î**) is pronounced "uh", midway between the O in lesson and the O in sort.

Ă "er" sound as in mother; the combinations AU and ĂU resemble the sounds in how and go.

C and **Ch** are hard, like "k" or as in country, except when C precedes E or I when it sounds like "ch".

E sounds as in ten; but at the start of a word it's pronounced as in year; while the combined **EI** sounds like bay or ray.

G is hard as in gust, except in the diphthong EG (like sledge), or preceding E or I when it is soft as in gesture; GHI is hard (as in gear).

I is as in feet; except for the vowel combinations IU as in you; IA as in yap; and IE as in yes.

J is like the "s" in pleasure.

K only occurs in imported words like kilometre.

O is as in soft; except for OI, which is like boy, and OA as in quark.

R is always rolled.

Ş is slurred as in shop.

Ţ is a "ts" sound as in bits.

U sounds like book or good; but UA is pronounced as in quark.

W occurs in such foreign words as whisky and western.

Linguistic politics

The letter î replaced â when **Stalin** forced Romania to change the rules to make the language seem more Slavic in form, although a few exceptions such as România and Brâncuşi were allowed to survive. In 1994 the Romanian Academy decreed that î should revert to â, so that Tîrgu Mureş is now Târgu Mureş, and Cîmpulung is Câmpulung. As a rule, this does not apply where a word begins with Î.

The rules (to do with whether words have a Latin root, where in the word the letter falls, and whether it follows a prefix) are too complex for most Romanians to follow, and many old maps and signs are still in use; therefore you should be aware of the potential for confusion, for instance in words such as *vânători* (hunters).

See also the specialist vocabularies for eating and drinking (pp.492–493) and hiking (in the *Great Outdoors* colour insert), and the glossary on the following pages.

Words and phrases

Basics and greetings

Da, nu, şi	Yes, no, and	Bună dimineaţă	Good morning
Vă rog, mulţumesc	Please, thank you	Bună ziua (or Servus)	Good day
Îmi pare rău, permiteţi-mi	Sorry, excuse me	Bună seară	Good evening
		Noapte bună	Good night
Bun, rău	Good, bad	Ce mai faceţi?	How are you?
Vorbiţi englezeste?	Do you speak English?	Cum vă numiţ?	What's your name?
Nu ânţeleg	I don't understand	Noroc!	Cheers! (literally Good Luck!)
Vă rog să vorbiţi mai rar	Please speak slowly	Bun, minunat (De acord = it's agreed)	Good, that's fine
Scrieţi, vă rog	Please write it down		
Vreţi să repetaţi, vă rog	Say that again, please	La revedere (or ciao, pa)	Goodbye
Eu, noi, dumneaĉa (tu is informal)	I, we, you	Drum bun	Bon voyage (literally "Good road")
Salut	Hello	Lăsaţi-ma ân pace!	Leave me alone!

Directions and accommodation

Unde?/Când?	Where?/When?	Două paturi	Twin beds
Cel mai aproape	The nearest	Un pat dublu	Double bed
Un hotel (ieftin)	A (cheap) hotel	Pentru o persoană (singura)	For one person (alone)
Loc de campare, popas	Campsite		
Toaletă, WC (pronounced vay-say-oo)	Toilet	Duş, baie	Shower, bathroom
		Nu curge apă	There's no water
Este departe?	Is it far?	Cald/fierbinte, frig/rece	Hot, cold
Ce autobuz trebuie sa iau?	What bus must I take?	Cât costa pentru o noapte?	How much per night?
Există potecă spre...?	Is there a footpath to...?	Micul dejun este inclus în preţ?	Is breakfast included?
Dreapta, stânga, dreapt ânainte	Right, left, straight on	Nu aveţi altceva mai ieftin?	Have you nothing cheaper?
Nord, sud, est, vest	North, south, east, west	Puteţi să-mi recomandaţi un alt hotel (un hotel mai ieftin)?	Can you suggest another (a cheaper) hotel?
Aveţi o cameră?	Have you a room?		
Cu, fără	With, without		

Signs

Sosire, plecare	Arrival, departure	WC femei (bărbaţi)	Ladies' (Gents') WC
Intrare, ieşire	Entrance, exit	Sală de aşteptare	Waiting room
Liber, ocupat	Vacant, occupied	Circulă, anulat	Operating, cancelled
Nu mai sânt locuri	No vacancies	Fumatul oprit	No smoking
Deschis, închis	Open, closed	(Nefumatori)	
Intrare gratuită	Admission free	Intrare interzisa, pericol	No entry, danger

Requests and buying

(Aş) vreau...	I want (should like)...	Încă un rând, vă rog	Same again, please
Nu vreau...	I don't want...	Ce este acesta?	What's that?
Cât costă?	How much?	Merita?	Is it any good?
(Mai) puţin	A little (less)	Poftă bună	Bon appétit
Există...?	Is there...?	Notă, chitanţă	Bill, receipt
Aveţi...?	Have you/do you sell...?	Când este gata?	When will it be ready?
Unde pot să cumpăr...?	Where can I buy...?	Imediat, noi grăbim	At once, we're in a hurry
Prea scump	Too expensive		
Ce îmi recomandaţi?	What do you recommend?	Care este cursul lirei sterling/ dolaruli?	What's the rate for the pound/dollar?
Chelner, Chelneriţa	Waiter, waitress	Vă rog sa-mi daţi banii ânapoi?	Will you refund my money?
S-a terminat	It's finished		
Două pahare (sticle) de bere	Two glasses (bottles) of beer	Aveţi vreo scrisoare pentru mine?	Any letters for me?

Getting around

Autobuzul acesta merge la gară?	Does this bus go to the train station?	Le ce ora pleacă trenul?	When does the train leave?
La autogară	Bus terminal	Două locuri pentru... (mâine)	Two seats for... (tomorrow)
La plajă	Beach		
În centru	Into the centre	Vreau sa rezerva loc de vagon de dormit (cu cuşete)	I want to reserve a sleeper (couchette)
Opreşte la?	Does it stop at?		
A trecut ultimul autobuz?	Has the last bus gone?	Aş vreau să schimba rezervă pentru...	I want to change my reservation to...
(Vreau să) merg la...	I (want to) go to...	Acesta este trenul de...?	Is this the train for...?
Unde mergeţi?	Where are you going?		
Opriţi aici (la...)	Stop here (at...)	Unde schimb trenul?	Where do I change?
Drumul este bun?	Is it a good road?	sosire (sos.)	arrival time
Nu este departe	It isn't far	plecare (pl.)	departure times
Intersecţie	Crossroads	Există curse de vapor de aici la...?	Is there a boat from here to...?
Rascruce, pod	Bridge		
De la ce peron pleacă trenul către...?	Which platform does the train to... leave from?	Când pleacă vaporul următor?	When does the next boat leave?

Pot să închiriez o barcă (cu vâsle)?	Can I rent a (rowing) boat?		Cât costa ora/ziua?	How much do you charge by the hour/ for the day?

Time and dates

Ce oră este?	What's the time?		În fiecare zi	Everyday
Este devreme/târziu	It's early/late		Ianuarie	January
Azi dimineaţă	This morning		Februarie	February
Zi, după masă	Day, afternoon		Martie	March
Amiază, miezul nopţii	Midday, midnight		Aprilie	April
Seară, noapte	Evening, night		Mai	May
Săptămână, lună	Week, month		Iunie	June
Azi/astăzi, ieri, (poi) mâine	Today, yesterday (day after) tomorrow		Iulie	July
			August	August
Curând, niciodată	Soon, never		Septembrie	September
Duminică	Sunday		Octombrie	October
Luni	Monday		Noiembrie	November
Marţi	Tuesday		Decembrie	December
Miercuri	Wednesday		Anul Nou	New Year
Joi	Thursday		Paşte	Easter
Vineri	Friday		Crăciun	Christmas
Sâmbătă	Saturday			

Numbers

zero	0		douăzece	20
un, una	1		douăzeci şi un(a)	21
doi, doua	2		treizeci	30
trei	3		patruzeci	40
patru	4		cincizeci	50
cinci	5		şaizeci	60
şase	6		şaptzeci	70
şapte	7		optzeci	80
opt	8		nouăzeci	90
nouă	9		o sută	100
zece	10		cinci sute	500
unsprezece	11		o mie	1000
doisprezece	12		întâi	first
treisprezece	13		al doilea	second
paisprezece	14		un kilo	1 kilo
cincisprezece	15		jumatăte	a half
şaisprezece	16		o treime	a third
şaptsprezece	17		un sfert	a quarter
optsprezece	18		trei sferturi	three-quarters
nouăsprezece	19			

Food and drink glossary

Basic foods

brânză	cheese
iaurt	yoghurt
lapte	milk
omletă	omelette
orez	rice
oţet	vinegar
ouă	eggs
pâine or pîine	bread
piper	pepper
sandvici or tartină	sandwiches
sare	salt
smântână	sour cream
ulei	oil
unt	butter
zahăr	sugar

Soups (supe)

ciorbă	mixed soup, with sour cream
ciorbă de burtă	tripe soup
ciorbă de cartofi	potato soup
ciorbă de fasole	dried or green bean soup
ciorbă de miel	lamb broth
ciorbă de perişoare	soup with meatballs
ciorbă de peşte	fish soup
ciorbă ţărănească	soup with meat and mixed vegetables
supă	soup with one main component
supă de carne	consommé
supă de găină	chicken soup
supă de găluşti	dumpling soup
supă de roşii	tomato soup
supă cu tăiţei	noodle soup
supă de zarzavat	vegetable soup

Salads (salate)

salată de cartofi cu ceapă	potato and onion salad
salată de fasole verde	green bean salad
salată de icre de crap	carp roe salad
salată de roşii şi castraveti	tomato and cucumber salad
salată de sfeclă roşie	beetroot salad
salată verde	lettuce salad

Meat and poultry (carne şi pasăre)

babic (ghiudem)	smoked (goat's meat) sausage
berbec/oaie	mutton
biftec	steak
chiftele	fried meatballs
crenwurst	hot dog
curcan	turkey
ficat	liver
gâscă	goose
ghiveci cu carne	meat and vegetable hotpot
miel	lamb
mititei	spicy sausages
parizer	mortadella-type sausage
(pastramă de) porc	(salted and smoked) pork
patricieni	sausages (skinless)
pui	chicken
raţă (pe varză)	duck (with sauerkraut)
rinichi	kidneys
salam	salami
slănină	bacon fat
şniţel pane	wiener schnitzel
şuncă	ham
tocană de carne/de purcel	meat/pork stew
vacă	beef
varză acră cu costiţă afumată	sauerkraut with smoked pork chops

Vegetables (legume)

ardei (gras/iute)	(green/chilli) pepper
cartofi	potatoes
ceapă (verde)	(spring) onion
ciuperci	mushrooms
conopidă	cauliflower
dovlecei	courgettes/zucchini
dovleci	marrows
fasole (albă grasă/ verde)	(broad/string) beans
ghiveci	mixed fried vegetables, sometimes eaten cold
gogoşari	red peppers
lăptucă	lettuce
mazăre verde	peas

morcovi	carrots
roşii	tomatoes
salată verde	green salad
sfeclă roşie	beetroot
spanac	spinach
usturoi	garlic
varză	cabbage
vinete	aubergine/eggplant

Fish and seafood (peste)

cegă	sterlet
chiftele de peşte	fish cakes
crap	carp
icre negre	caviar
midii	mussels
nisetru	sturgeon
păstrăv	trout
scrumbie	herring
şalău	pike-perch
ton	tuna

Fruit (fructe)

caise	apricots
căpşune	strawberries
cireşe	cherries
fragă	wild strawberries
mere	apples
pepene galben	melon
pepene verde	watermelon
pere	pears
piersici	peaches
prune (uscate)	plums (prunes)
struguri	grapes
zmeură	raspberries

Desserts and sweets (dulciuri)

bomboane	sweets (candy)
clătită (cu rom)	pancake (with rum)
cozonac	brioche
dulceaţă	jam (served in a glass)
ecler	éclair
gogoşi or langoş	doughnut
halva	halva
ânghetată	ice cream
măr in foietaj	baked apple in pastry
mascotă	chocolate fudge cake
miere	honey
papanasi	cheese doughnut
pască	Easter cake

plăcintă cu brânză	cheese pie
plăcintă cu mere	apple pie
plăcintă cu vişine	cherry pie
prăjitură	cake
rahat	turkish delight
ruladă	sponge and jam roll
strudel cu mere	apple strudel

Drinks (băuturi)

apă minerală	mineral water
suc de fructe	fruit juice
cafea filtru	filter coffee
cafea mare cu lapte	large white coffee
cafea neagră	sweet black coffee
cafea naturală	plain black coffee
cafea turcească	turkish coffee
o ceaşcă de ceai	a cup of tea
bere	beer
vin roşu (alb)	red wine (white)
şampanie	sparkling wine
sticlă	bottle (of beer)
ţuică	plum brandy
vodca	vodka
rom	rum

Common terms

aveţiâ...	do you have a...
Aş/am vrea	I/we would like
cină	dinner
cu maioneză	with a mayonnaise sauce
cu mujdei de usturoi	in a garlic sauce
dejun	lunch
fiert	boiled
friptură	roast
la grătar	grilled
meniu or listă	menu
micul dejun	breakfast
murăti	pickled
noroc!	cheers!
pahar	a glass
piure de	mashed
poftă bună	enjoy your meal
prăjit	fried
prânz	lunch
proaspăt	fresh
pulpă de... la tavă	roast leg of ...
rasol	poached
tare/moale	hard/soft boiled
umplut	stuffed

Glossary

Alimentară food store.

Ardeal "forested land", the Romanian name for Transylvania.

Baie bath, spa (plural Băile; not to be confused with Baia or mine).

Biserică church.

Biseri de lemn wooden churches.

Bivol buffalo, introduced from India by the Gypsies.

Boyar or **Boier** feudal lord.

Bucium alpine horn used by shepherds, also known as a Tulnic.

Bulevardul (B-dul. or Blvd.) boulevard.

Calea avenue.

Căluş traditional Whitsun fertility rite performed by Căluşari in rural Wallachia and southwestern Transylvania.

Câmpulung or **Cîmpulung** meadow or long field, for which settlements like Câmpulung Moldovenesc are named.

Capră masked "goat dance" to celebrate the New Year.

Casă house.

Cetate fortress or citadel.

CFR Romanian Railways.

Chei gorge.

Csángó Hungarian "Wanderers" from Transylvania.

Dacians earliest established inhabitants of Romania.

Deal hill.

Drum road.

Erdély the Magyar name for Transylvania.

FSN Frontul Salvării Naţional, the National Salvation Front set up as an umbrella front during the revolution and soon transformed into a new government.

Gadjé Roma (Gypsy) term for non-Gypsies.

Gradiniţa garden.

Grind raised area of accumulated silt in the Danube Delta.

Gură mouth.

Horă traditional village round dance.

Iconostasis literally "icon-bearer", decorated screen in an Orthodox (or Uniate) church containing tiers of icons that separates sanctuary from nave and priest from congregation during the Eucharist.

Judeţ county.

Lac lake.

Legion or Iron Guard, Romanian fascist movement, 1927–41.

Lipovani ethnic group living by fishing and gardening in the Danube Delta, descended from Russian "Old Believers".

Litoral the coast.

Magazin large store.

Magyars Hungarians, roughly two million of whom live in Romania, mainly in Transylvania.

Mănăstirea monastery or convent.

Maxitaxi minibus.

Moară mill.

Muntenia the eastern half of Wallachia, paradoxically not at all mountainous.

Nai panpipes.

Naos nave or central part of an Orthodox church, lying below the central cupola and in front of the iconostasis.

Narthex entrance hall of an Orthodox church, often decorated with frescoes.

Nations or **Nationes** historically, the privileged groups in Transylvania.

Nedeia village fair or festival characteristic of the mountain regions.

Oltenia the western half of Wallachia, flanking the River Olt.

Pădure woods.

Pas a mountain pass.

PCR Partidul Communist Roman – until 1989, the Romanian Communist Party. Since reconstituted as the Socialist Party of Labour (PSM).

Peştera cave.

Piaţa square; also a market.

Piatra stone or crag.

Plajă beach.

Plaur floating reed islands, characteristic of the Delta.

Pod bridge.

Poiana glade, meadow.

Popă or **Preot** Orthodox priest.

Poteca path.

Pronaos see Narthex.

Răscoala peasant rebellion; usually refers to the great uprising of 1907.

Râu river.

Regat the "Old Kingdom", as Moldavia and Wallachia were known after they united in 1859.

Rom or **Roma** Gypsies.

Sanctuar sanctuary or altar area of a church, behind the iconostasis.

Sat village.

Saxons name given to Germans who settled in Transylvania from the twelfth century onwards.

Schwaben (Swabians) name given to Germans who settled in Banat in the eighteenth century; others who moved to Transylvania at this time are known as Landler.

Securitate Communist security police, now reborn as the SRI or Romanian Information Service.

Siebenburgen Saxon name for Transylvania (literally, "seven towns").

Șoseaua (Șos.) long tree-lined avenue.

Stâna sheepfold.

Strada (Str.) street.

Székely Hungarian-speaking ethnic group inhabiting parts of eastern Transylvania known as the Székelyföld.

Țara land, country (Romanian); Gypsy encampment.

Târg or **Tîrg** market, fair or festival.

Vad ford.

Vale valley.

Varf peak, mount.

Vătaf leader of Călușari dancers (Romanian); tribal chieftain (Gypsy).

Vlachs or **Wallachs** foreign name for the Romanians of Wallachia, Moldavia and Transylvania before the nineteenth century.

Voevod or **Voivode** Ruling prince of Transylvania or Wallachia.

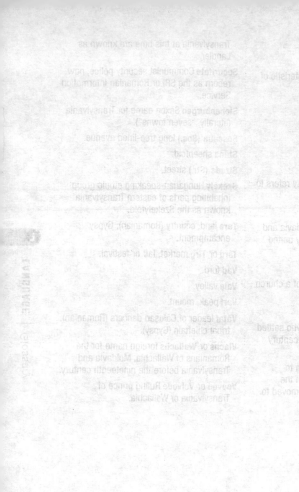

Travel store

Avoid Guilt Trips

Buy fair trade coffee + bananas ✓

Save energy - use low energy bulbs ✓
- don't leave tv on standby ✓

Offset carbon emissions from flight to Madrid ✓

Send goat to Africa ✓

Join Tourism Concern today ✓

Slowly, the world is changing.
Together we can, and will, make a difference.

Tourism Concern is the only UK registered charity fighting
exploitation in one of the largest industries on earth: people forced
from their homes in order that holiday resorts can be built,
sweatshop labour conditions in hotels and destruction of the
environment are just some of the issues that we tackle.

Sending people on a guilt trip is not something we do. We know as
well as anyone that holidays are precious. But you can help us to
ensure that tourism always benefits the local communities involved.

Call 020 7133 3330
or visit **tourismconcern.org.uk** to find out how.

*A year's membership of Tourism Concern costs just £20 (£12 unwaged)
- that's 38 pence a week, less than the cost of a pint of milk, organic of course.*

Available from all good bookstores

D: Rough Guide
DIRECTIONS for
short breaks

Visit us online

www.roughguides.com

Information on over 25,000 destinations around the world

- **Read** Rough Guides' trusted travel info
- **Access** exclusive articles from Rough Guides authors
- **Update** yourself on new books, maps, CDs and other products
- **Enter** our competitions and win travel prizes
- **Share** ideas, journals, photos & travel advice with other users
- **Earn** points every time you contribute to the Rough Guide community and get rewards

BROADEN YOUR HORIZONS

NOTES

NOTES

NOTES

NOTES

NOTES

Small print and

Index

A Rough Guide to Rough Guides

Published in 1982, the first Rough Guide – to Greece – was a student scheme that became a publishing phenomenon. Mark Ellingham, a recent graduate in English from Bristol University, had been travelling in Greece the previous summer and couldn't find the right guidebook. With a small group of friends he wrote his own guide, combining a highly contemporary, journalistic style with a thoroughly practical approach to travellers' needs.

The immediate success of the book spawned a series that rapidly covered dozens of destinations. And, in addition to impecunious backpackers, Rough Guides soon acquired a much broader and older readership that relished the guides' wit and inquisitiveness as much as their enthusiastic, critical approach and value-for-money ethos.

These days, Rough Guides include recommendations from shoestring to luxury and cover more than 200 destinations around the globe, including almost every country in the Americas and Europe, more than half of Africa and most of Asia and Australasia. Our ever-growing team of authors and photographers is spread all over the world, particularly in Europe, the USA and Australia.

ROUGH
GUIDES

In the early 1990s, Rough Guides branched out of travel, with the publication of Rough Guides to World Music, Classical Music and the Internet. All three have become benchmark titles in their fields, spearheading the publication of a wide range of books under the Rough Guide name.

Including the travel series, Rough Guides now number more than 350 titles, covering: phrasebooks, waterproof maps, music guides from Opera to Heavy Metal, reference works as diverse as Conspiracy Theories and Shakespeare, and popular culture books from iPods to Poker. Rough Guides also produce a series of more than 120 World Music CDs in partnership with World Music Network.

Visit www.roughguides.com to see our latest publications.

Rough Guide travel images are available for commercial licensing at www.roughguidespictures.com

Rough Guide credits

Text editor: Samantha Cook and James Rice
Layout: Jessica Subramanian
Cartography: Alakananda Bhattacharya and Animesh Pathak
Picture editor: Sarah Cummins
Production: Rebecca Short
Proofreader: Jan McCann
Cover design: Chloë Roberts
Photographer: Gregory Wrona
Editorial: **London** Ruth Blackmore, Alison Murchie, Karoline Thomas, Andy Turner, Keith Drew, Edward Aves, Alice Park, Lucy White, Jo Kirby, James Smart, Natasha Foges, Róisín Cameron, Emma Traynor, Emma Gibbs, Kathryn Lane, Christina Valhouli, Monica Woods, Mani Ramaswamy, Joe Staines, Peter Buckley, Matthew Milton, Tracy Hopkins, Ruth Tidball; **New York** Andrew Rosenberg, Steven Horak, AnneLise Sorensen, April Isaacs, Ella Steim, Anna Owens, Sean Mahoney, Courtney Miller, Paula Neudorf; **Delhi** Madhavi Singh, Karen D'Souza
Design & Pictures: **London** Scott Stickland, Dan May, Diana Jarvis, Mark Thomas, Nicole Newman, Emily Taylor; **Delhi** Umesh Aggarwal, Ajay Verma, Ankur Guha, Pradeep Thapliyal, Sachin Tanwar, Anita Singh, Nikhil Agarwal
Production: Vicky Baldwin
Cartography: **London** Maxine Repath, Ed Wright, Katie Lloyd-Jones; **Delhi** Jai Prakash Mishra, Rajesh Chhibber, Ashutosh Bharti, Rajesh Mishra, Jasbir Sandhu, Karobi Gogoi, Amod Singh, Swati Handoo
Online: Narender Kumar, Rakesh Kumar, Amit Verma, Rahul Kumar, Ganesh Sharma, Debojit Borah, Saurabh Sati
Marketing & Publicity: **London** Liz Statham, Niki Hanmer, Louise Maher, Jess Carter, Vanessa Godden, Vivienne Watton, Anna Paynton, Rachel Sprackett, Libby Jellie; **New York** Geoff Colquitt, Katy Ball; **Delhi** Ragini Govind
Manager India: Punita Singh
Reference Director: Andrew Lockett
Operations Manager: Helen Phillips
PA to Publishing Director: Nicola Henderson
Publishing Director: Martin Dunford
Commercial Manager: Gino Magnotta
Managing Director: John Duhigg

Publishing information

This fifth edition published June 2008 by
Rough Guides Ltd,
80 Strand, London WC2R 0RL
345 Hudson St, 4th Floor,
New York, NY 10014, USA
14 Local Shopping Centre, Panchsheel Park,
New Delhi 110017, India
Distributed by the Penguin Group
Penguin Books Ltd,
80 Strand, London WC2R 0RL
Penguin Group (USA)
375 Hudson Street, NY 10014, USA
Penguin Group (Australia)
250 Camberwell Road, Camberwell,
Victoria 3124, Australia
Penguin Books Canada Ltd,
10 Alcorn Avenue, Toronto, Ontario,
Canada M4V 1E4
Penguin Group (NZ)
67 Apollo Drive, Mairangi Bay, Auckland 1310,
New Zealand

Cover concept by Peter Dyer.
Typeset in Bembo and Helvetica to an original design by Henry Iles.
Printed and bound in China
© Tim Burford and Norm Longley
No part of this book may be reproduced in any form without permission from the publisher except for the quotation of brief passages in reviews.
520pp includes index
A catalogue record for this book is available from the British Library
ISBN: 978-1-85828-366-1

Help us update

We've gone to a lot of effort to ensure that the fifth edition of **The Rough Guide to Romania** is accurate and up to date. However, things change – places get "discovered", opening hours are notoriously fickle, restaurants and rooms raise prices or lower standards. If you feel we've got it wrong or left something out, we'd like to know, and if you can remember the address, the price, the hours, the phone number, so much the better.

Please send your comments with the subject line "**Rough Guide Romania Update**" to mail@roughguides.com. We'll credit all contributions and send a copy of the next edition (or any other Rough Guide if you prefer) for the very best emails.

Have your questions answered and tell others about your trip at community.roughguides.com

Acknowledgements

Tim: Mike and Angie Morton, Colin Shaw, Julian Ross, Gavin Bell, Kristen Soper, Alex Popescu, Maria Iordache, Ramona Mitrica, Alan Ogden, Tom Gallagher, Lucreţia Lucuţar, Florin Lazarean, Monica Leitner, Adrian Adam and Virgil Munteanu, Irina Amariuţei, Rob Larcombe and Lia, Timea Homei, Teofil Ivanciuc and, at Rough Guides, Norm Lomgley, Sam Cook, James Rice, Richard Lim, Alison Murchie and Reem Khokhar.

Norm: To my editors, Sam and James, for their fantastic support and patience during the writing up of this edition; likewise, to my colleague and dear friend, Tim – they all know why; and Richard Lim for getting the project up and running. Very special thanks to: Andrei Mahalnischi and the team at Pan Travel in Cluj for their help and assistance; Colin Shaw in Braşov, for outstanding help and wonderful company; John Matthews in Bran; Claudia Câmpeanu in

Sighişoara; Paul Iacobas in Oradea. Thanks are also due to Maria Iordache in London; Mike and Angie Morton; Radu and Ina Vadeanu in Cluj; Andrea and Gavin Bell in Braşov; the team at Fundatia Adept in Saschiz; Andreea Sighinas and the girls at the *Villa Butterfly* in Bucharest; Craig Turp, Monica Nilca and Frederik Deman in Bucharest; Julian Ross in Lunca Ilvei; Doru Munteanu in Bistriţa; Robert Roth in Odorheiu Secuiesc; Mihaela Vacariu in Sibiu; Nicoleta Turc in Deva. Also to Jon Bousfield for the beers and providing me with somewhere to stay. But most of all, to Ürün, for keeping me going.

Sam and James: Thanks to Tim and Norm, Sarah Cummins for great picture research, Jessica Subramanian for the layout, and cartographers Alakananda Bhattacharya and Animesh Pathak for the maps.

Readers' letters

Thank you to all those readers who took the trouble to write in with their comments and suggestions (apologies for any misspellings or omissions):

Sandra Agius, Duncan Aldred, Johan Bel, Vicky Bullard, Ben Cijffers, Ann Clark, Daniel Cobarzan, Martin Grimwood, Raoul Gunning, Christian Herzmann, Iain Kearsley, Jacob Levy, Kristin

Luna, Marco & Emanuela, Fab Marsani, Catrinus Nouta, Alan Robertson, Chris Shaw, Jan Thiré, Geert Vanhoovels & Annemie Van Linthoudt, Winnie Wong.

Photo credits

All photos © Rough Guides except the following:

Things not to miss

01 Piaţa Sfatului, Braşov © Pictures Colour Library
02 European Grey Wolf © Corbis
04 Cetăţile Ponorului © Blickwinkel/Alamy
15 Pageant of the Juni © Florin Andreescu
19 Measurement of the Milk festival © Florin Andreescu
21 View from Mount Postăvaru © Travel Ink /Alamy
23 Girl Fair of Muntele Găina © Florin Andreescu
25 Folk violinist © Charles & Josette Lenars /Corbis
26 Rozavlea wooden church, Maramureş © Romanian National Tourist Office

Black and whites

p.101 Lenin statue, Mogoşoaia palace, Bucharest © allOver photography/Alamy
p.144 View over Braşov © Pictures Colour Library

colour insert: The great outdoors

Poiana Braşov © Richard Wareham/Fotografie /Alamy
Lake Uzlina, Danube Delta © PCL/Alamy
Limestone cave at Dâmbovicioara © Gary Cook /Alamy

colour insert: Romania's religious architecture

Interior painting of Christ being nailed to the cross, The Church of the Holy Paraskeva, Desesti, Maramureş © Kristen Soper/Alamy
UNESCO-protected fortified church, Harman, Transylvania © Kristen Soper/Alamy

SMALL PRINT

Selected images from our guidebooks are available for licensing from:

ROUGH GUIDES PICTURES .COM

Index

Map entries are in colour.

H

I

J

K

L

M

N

INDEX

I

INDEX

517

Map symbols

maps are listed in the full index using coloured text

▬▬▬·	International boundary	👁	Waterfall
▬ ▬ ▬	Chapter division boundary	✡	Synagogue
▭▭▭	Motorway	⚓	Lighthouse
══	Major road	🏛	Monument
──	Minor road	⌂	Refuge hut
▭▭▭	Pedestrianized road	∴	Ruin
·········	Road under construction	🏛	Monastery
▥▥▥	Steps	♛	Castle
─ ─ ─	Path	▮	Tower
▬▬▬	Railway	✈	Airport
●--●	Cable car	∩	Arch
──	River	ⓘ	Tourist office
▭▭▭	Canal	◉	Accommodation
──	Wall	✉	Post office
Ⓜ	Metro station	★	Bus stop
▲	Peak	⬭	Stadium
◆	Place of interest	▮	Building
⚠	Campsite	⊞	Church (town maps)
♦	Museum (village)	⊹	Christian cemetery
⌒	Cave	⊡	Jewish cemetery
⋀⋀	Mountain range	▦	Park
⌇	Gorge	⋮	Beach
∥	Mountain pass	▨	Marsh land

We're covered. Are you?

ROUGH GUIDES Travel Insurance

Visit our website at www.roughguides.com/website/shop or call:

COLUMBUS
Travel Insurance

ROUGH GUIDES

- Ⓣ UK: 0800 083 9507
- Ⓣ Spain: 900 997 149
- Ⓣ Australia: 1300 669 999
- Ⓣ New Zealand: 0800 55 99 11
- Ⓣ Worldwide: +44 870 890 2843
- Ⓣ USA, call toll free on: 1 800 749 4922

Please quote our ref: *Rough Guides books*

Cover for over 46 different nationalities and available in 4 different languages.